LEE'S TIGERS
REVISITED

LEE'S TIGERS

-REVISITED-

The Louisiana Infantry in the
Army of Northern Virginia

TERRY L. JONES

Louisiana State University Press
Baton Rouge

Published by Louisiana State University Press
Copyright © 2017 by Louisiana State University Press
This volume is a revised and expanded edition of *Lee's Tigers: The Louisiana Infantry in the Army of Northern Virginia*, copyright © 1987 by Louisiana State University Press.
All rights reserved
Manufactured in the United States of America
First printing

DESIGNER: *Mandy McDonald Scallan*
TYPEFACE: *Whitman*
PRINTER AND BINDER: *Sheridan Books Inc.*

Library of Congress Cataloging-in-Publication Data

Names: Jones, Terry L., 1952– author.
Title: Lee's Tigers revisited : the Louisiana Infantry in the Army of
    Northern Virginia / Terry L. Jones.
Other titles: Lee's Tigers
Description: Baton Rouge : Louisiana State University Press, [2017] |
    Includes bibliographical references and index.
Identifiers: LCCN 2017019256| ISBN 978-0-8071-6851-6 (cloth : alk. paper) | ISBN
    978-0-8071-6852-3 (pdf) | ISBN 978-0-8071-6853-0 (epub)
Subjects: LCSH: Louisiana—History—Civil War, 1861–1865—Regimental
    histories. | United States—History—Civil War, 1861–1865—Regimental
    histories. | Confederate States of America. Army of Northern
    Virginia—History. | Virginia—History—Civil War, 1861–1865—Campaigns. |
    United States—History—Civil War, 1861–1865—Campaigns.
Classification: LCC E565.4 .J65 2017 | DDC 973.7/3—dc23
LC record available at https://lccn.loc.gov/2017019256

To my wife, Carol

CONTENTS

ILLUSTRATIONS

PHOTOGRAPHS

following page 142

An early war photograph of the 8th Louisiana's Thomas Taylor
Coppens' Battalion at Pensacola, Florida, with vivandière Amelia Riliseh
Postwar photograph of Gen. Richard Taylor
Col. Eugene Waggaman
Edwin Jemison of the 2nd Louisiana, killed at Malvern Hill
George L. P. Wren
Gen. Harry T. Hays
Gen. Francis T. Nicholls
Louisiana Tigers holding the line at Second Manassas
Louisiana dead of Starke's Brigade at Antietam
Postwar photograph of Capt. William J. Seymour
Alfred Waud's sketch of the Louisiana Tigers' twilight
  attack on Cemetery Hill
Gen. Leroy A. Stafford
Gen. Zebulon York
Postwar photograph of Gen. William Raine "Big" Peck

MAPS

ILLUSTRATIONS

PREFACE

As the sun slowly set, Gens. Robert E. Lee and Jubal A. Early anxiously watched Early's division advance across a rugged, open plain toward the Union positions. The ragged gray line suffered occasional casualties as federal gunners found the range and pounded it with solid shot and canister. Steep hills and deep gullies further broke up the Confederate charge as the rebels closed in on the Union breastworks. Watching from his vantage point, Early became dismayed when it appeared that his division would be repulsed before even closing with the enemy, but his spirits lifted when he saw Gen. Harry T. Hays' Louisiana Brigade rush in and penetrate the enemy line. The blue defenders could be seen scampering back to a secondary position, only to be swept away again by the surging gray tide closing in behind them. As the victorious rebel yell rose over the field, Early momentarily forgot Lee beside him and jubilantly threw his hat on the ground and cried out, "Those damned Louisiana fellows may steal as much as they please now!"[1]

Jubal Early was one of many Confederate officers who struggled with the paradox known as the Louisiana Tigers. He tended to agree with those who called the Tigers "wharf rats from New Orleans" and the "lowest scrapings of the Mississippi," and accused them of plundering and foraging on nearby farms wherever they camped. However, the Tigers were reliable in combat, and the general readily forgave the Louisianians for their past transgressions as he watched them swarm over two Union lines near Fredericksburg, Virginia, on May 4, 1863. Even though the federals finally stopped and then repulsed the attack, the Louisiana Tigers had once again proven themselves to be the premier shock troops of the Army of Northern Virginia.[2]

The Tigers' fierce reputation was well earned, for Louisiana probably had a higher percentage of criminals, drunkards, and deserters in its commands than any other Confederate state. This fact might be attributable to the large number of poor immigrants who filled their ranks. The Irish and Germans made excellent fighters, but many were newcomers to America and had little enthusiasm for the war. As a result, hundreds deserted when a chance arose to escape the rigors and dangers of campaigning. Other foreigners who enlisted off the rough New Orleans waterfront, where drinking, fighting, and thievery were a way of life, naturally brought their vices with them to the army. However, this is not to imply that all of Louisiana's foreign-born soldiers became deserters and thieves. The majority did not. Most of them were dedicated soldiers who behaved as well as the native-born Americans. Nevertheless, the Tiger units that were dominated by foreign-born men were the units most often mentioned in connection with such deviant behavior.

Several Louisiana units were responsible for creating the Tigers' infamous reputation. Most prominent were the 1st Battalion, Louisiana Zouaves (Coppens' Battalion), and the 14th Louisiana Volunteers. Those units' wholesale rioting, looting, and robbery did more to tarnish the image of Louisiana's soldiers during the first few months of the war than any other. However, it was Maj. Roberdeau Wheat's 1st Special Battalion that gave birth to the nickname "Louisiana Tigers." The Tiger Rifles, a Zouave company in Wheat's Battalion, proved to be as lawless as Coppens' Battalion and the 14th Louisiana, and its well-publicized mayhem eventually led to all Louisiana soldiers in Virginia being dubbed "Tigers."[3]

In an effort to glorify the Louisiana troops, some early historians only touched on the Tigers' seamier side, or else portrayed their misdeeds as more childlike mischief than criminal behavior. Such apologies are unnecessary. Despite the Tigers' dark reputation, Confederate commanders time and again called on them in the most desperate situations. From First Manassas to Appomattox they consistently played key roles in the most important campaigns. It was the Louisianians who held back the initial federal onslaught at First Manassas, made possible Gen. Thomas J. "Stonewall" Jackson's famous Valley Campaign, used rocks to defend their position at Second Manassas, broke the Union lines at Gettysburg, contained the Union breakthrough at Spotsylvania's Bloody Angle, and led Lee's attempted breakout from the Petersburg siege at Fort Stedman. For all their vices, Lee's Louisiana infantry emerged from the Civil War with one of the most respected military records, and the name "Louisiana Tigers" was recognized across the North and South.

The first person to write a history of the Louisiana Tigers apparently was W. Albertus Koch, an editor for the New Orleans *Daily Item*. Koch spent forty-two years compiling his "History of the Louisiana Tigers," only to lose it in 1915 when the satchel it was in disappeared while he was traveling by train to a veterans' reunion. Infuriated, Koch rushed to a group of Tiger veterans and interrupted their singing of "We're Burying the Yankees in the Big Bayou" to inform them of the theft. "Comrades," he cried, "some tarnation rapscallion has sloped with my gripsack." They quickly organized a search party, but nothing was found, and Koch was inconsolable. Vowing to continue the hunt, he promised, "When I lay these hands of mine upon him I promise you I will twist the rascal around his own neck until there is nothing left of him but the ends of his shirt collar sticking out of his thievish eyes." As it turned out, a Virginia veteran had mistaken the satchel for his own and taken it from the train. When he realized his error, he contacted Koch and returned his property. Unfortunately, Koch never published his "History of the Louisiana Tigers," and its location today is not known.[4]

Surprisingly, no history of the Louisiana Tigers was published until Alison Moore released his book *The Louisiana Tigers; or, The Two Louisiana Brigades in the Army of Northern Virginia, 1861–1865* in 1961. Moore, however, based his work on the *Official Records* and did not take advantage of the many extant letters and diaries that were held in various repositories. Thus, when I was a doctoral student at Texas A&M University, I decided to write my dissertation on the Louisiana Tigers using the letters, diaries, memoirs, muster rolls, and other primary material that were literally scattered across the country. When Louisiana State University Press published *Lee's Tigers: The Louisiana Infantry in the Army of Northern Virginia* in 1987, the History Book Club chose it as an alternate monthly selection, and it was awarded the Louisiana Historical Association's General L. Kemper Williams Prize as the best book on Louisiana history that year. I am proud to say that it retained its popularity and has remained in print for thirty years. Since the initial release, more primary sources have come to light and several important new works have been published on some of the Tiger units and personalities. The rise of the Internet, in particular, made it possible to access contemporary newspapers and other digitized primary material. These sources have provided a plethora of new information on the Tigers, particularly concerning their activities during the last year of war, and have made it possible to produce this new edition of *Lee's Tigers* to commemorate its thirtieth anniversary of publication.

ACKNOWLEDGMENTS

Locating primary material requires luck, patience, and the help of persons familiar with the sources. I was most fortunate because the various library and archival personnel consulted during this project invariably proved extremely helpful in turning up useful material. A special thanks is extended to the staff of the interlibrary loan departments of Texas A&M University, College Station, and Northwestern State University, Natchitoches, Louisiana, for making available elusive printed sources. Thanks are also in order to the archival staffs of the following institutions for their indispensable aid in locating important manuscript collections: Louisiana State Archives and Louisiana State University, Baton Rouge; Tulane University and the Historic New Orleans Collection; Virginia Historical Society, Richmond; Duke University, Durham, North Carolina; the University of North Carolina, Chapel Hill; the National Archives and Library of Congress, Washington, D.C.; Centenary College and Louisiana State University at Shreveport; New York City Public Library; University of Michigan, Ann Arbor; Northwestern State University, Natchitoches; East Carolina University, Greenville, North Carolina; University of Texas, Austin; the Huntington Library, San Marino, California; the U.S. Army Education and Research Center, Carlisle, Pennsylvania; and the Mansfield State Commemorative Area, Mansfield, Louisiana. I would also like to thank the Texas A&M University Graduate College's minigrant program and Ruth Smith of the University of Louisiana at Monroe's School of Humanities and Dean Sandra Lemoine of the College of Arts, Education, and Sciences for providing travel funds that helped pay for a portion of my research.

A number of people deserve special recognition for going the extra mile in providing information and helping me put together the story of the Louisiana Tigers. They include Hal Jesperson for his cartography skills; Ken Legendre for sharing his encyclopedic knowledge of Civil War flags; Wayne Cosby for sharing information gathered by the Camp Moore Museum and Cemetery; Stuart Salling and his *Louisiana in the Civil War* Web site; Matt Atkinson and John Heiser of the Gettysburg National Military Park; E. Kathleen Shoemaker of Emory University's Rose Library; Pati Threatt of the Frazar Memorial Library at McNeese State University; John Coski, Ruth Ann Coski, and Cliff Dickinson of the Museum of the Confederacy; John Hennessy of the Fredericksburg and Spotsylvania National Military Park; Robert Krick of the Richmond National Battlefield Park; Ted Alexander and Stephanie Gray of the Antietam National Military Park; Diane B. Jacob of the Preston Library at the Virginia Military Institute; Lisa McCown of Washington and Lee University; Jerry Holsworth of the Handley Library in Winchester, Virginia; George Martin for sharing his information on the Louisiana vivandières; James D. Watkinson of the Virginia Commonwealth University for sharing information on Frederick Ober and the 1888 Gettysburg reunion; Warren B. Randall for providing information on Zebulon York; Brandon Beck of Shenandoah University for bringing the W. B. Tull memoir to my attention; Scott C. Patchan for sharing information from one of Hays' brigade's inspection reports; Benjamin Calvin Duke for providing information on his Galvanized Rebel ancestor Victor Braud; H. Eric Hartman for providing the memoir and information on his ancestor John H. Charlton; Gordon Berl for sharing information on his ancestor Eugene Waggaman; Earl Sundmaker for providing a copy of his ancestor William P. Snakenberg's diary; George W. Gervais for providing a photograph of his ancestor William J. Seymour; and Charles Hunter Coates Jr. for supplying information on the history of the LSU mascot's name.

Researching a historical topic is only half the task. One must then sift through thousands of pages of notes and present the narrative in a comprehensible form. This process requires advice, criticism, and editing. Robert Calvert, Don Hamilton, Larry Hill, and Betty Unterberger of Texas A&M University receive my sincere appreciation for their valuable input. Rand Dotson of Louisiana State University Press was patient in guiding me through the publishing process, and Stan Ivester made the manuscript better with his judicious editing. I would especially like to thank Allan Ashcraft, without whom this study might never have been completed. Professor Ashcraft's kindly patience and constructive criticism helped immensely in guiding me through this project with a minimum of trauma.

And finally, I would like to thank my wife, Carol, who has patiently tolerated my frequent absences on research trips and listened to countless Tiger stories for forty years.

LEE'S TIGERS
REVISITED

CHAPTER 1

On to Richmond!

RICHMOND! The threatened Confederate capital and symbol of the South was the goal of thousands of Louisiana recruits when the Civil War began. By May 1861 it was apparent that Virginia would be the focal point of the coming clash, and Louisiana's young men were eager to be there. From Pensacola, Florida, a soldier in the Shreveport Greys wrote that his comrades "had become tired of living like flounders and crabs in the deep sands of Pensacola, and the cry was 'on to Richmond.'" Andrew Newell of the Cheneyville Rifles exuberantly wrote his family on the eve of departure that the company was in good health and spirits and "eager to get into the fight." Newell made it to Virginia but, along with scores of others, died less than four months after writing his letter.[1]

After the bombardment of Fort Sumter, Louisiana hastily recruited thousands of men for military service and ultimately sent ten regiments and five battalions of infantry to Virginia. They were the 1st, 2nd, 5th, 6th, 7th, 8th, 9th, 10th, 14th, and 15th Louisiana Volunteers; the 1st Special Battalion, Louisiana Infantry (Wheat's Battalion); 1st Battalion, Louisiana Volunteers (Dreux's Battalion); 1st Battalion, Louisiana Zouaves (Coppens' Battalion); 3rd Battalion, Louisiana Infantry (Bradford's or Pendleton's Battalion); and St. Paul's Foot Rifles (Washington Infantry Battalion). The 4th Louisiana Battalion (Waddell's Battalion) also went to Virginia but is outside the scope of this study because it served there only briefly before being assigned to other areas.

Forming individual companies was the first step in creating these units. A community leader usually took it upon himself to raise a company of about one hundred men who adopted colorful or patriotic names such as the Tiger Bayou Rifles, Louisiana Swamp Rangers, and Jeff Davis Guards. Great excitement ensued when residents learned that a local company was being formed, and parades, parties, and ceremonies were often held to honor the volunteers.

Years after the war, William E. Trahern recalled the excitement in St. Joseph when its volunteer company was organized. "The one long street, and the main one in old St. Joseph was one day, a few weeks after [the firing on Fort Sumter] . . . filled to over flowing by surging humanity. The motive was the organization of a military Company. Patriotism was rampant, and the scattered humanity was converted speedily into what was known as the 'Tensas Rifles.'"[2]

Local ladies often ridiculed any man who was of military age and in good health but did not join his neighbors in volunteering. William B. Tull, who served in the 9th Louisiana's Washington Rifles, wrote, "It was interesting in those days to see the attitude which our young women assumed toward any young man who would not go to war and fight with their brothers in a common cause." When one man in the neighborhood did not enlist, some of the women decided to take action. "They made him a little baby suit of corn sacks and in one of the pockets to this suit they placed a nursing bottle and a sugar tit, then appointed a committee of six to wait on him." After receiving the items, the unnamed man slipped out of the area and remained in a safe place until the war was over. Tull claimed that he "lived a batchelor many years after the surrender."[3]

The festive mood of 1861, however, belied the dark days that lay ahead. William "Wolf" Lichenstein, a member of the 2nd Louisiana's Lecompte Guards, would experience some of the war's worst fighting and suffer five wounds and captivity. One comrade described Lichenstein as being "among the most gallant of those gallant ten regiments that Louisiana sent to Virginia! He was, as a young man, full of quaint humor and his practical jokes were without number."[4] With the benefit of hindsight in his old age, Lichenstein wrote, "Who could at this moment have the least premonition that a monster lies hidden behind this scene, like a masked battery in its fearful aim, that must bring distruction and mutilation in its wake. Who at that moment could believe that this monster is about to rise in its fury and tear this country asunder [and] bring war and sorrow to every stretch of this wide land and lay a million souls on the altar of a sacrificial name, "My Country!"[5]

Once a volunteer company was formed, its members elected all of the officers and noncommissioned officers, with the man who played the greatest role in organizing the company usually being elected the commanding captain. This democratic process was in keeping with America's military tradition, but it often weakened a unit's efficiency because it only ensured that the most popular men got elected, not necessarily the most qualified. A year later, however, the Confederate army was reorganized under the Conscription Act, and the soldiers were given the opportunity to replace the companies' original officers with better qualified men.

Recruiting a company from one neighborhood had a significant impact on both the soldiers and their families. On the positive side, it helped maintain *esprit de corps*. A half-dozen or so soldiers would form a "mess," which was an informal group that lived and ate together. A soldier's messmates were usually his closest friends and relatives, and they looked out for each other during sickness and battle. Forming companies from local populations also helped thwart cowardice. Soldiers were more willing to stand toe-to-toe with the enemy and exchange volleys of musketry at close range or charge an artillery battery because the men who stood in line with them were neighbors and relatives. If a soldier showed cowardice, word of it inevitably reached home and ruined his reputation.[6]

On the other hand, raising companies from the same area caused some families to suffer grievous losses. The Pelican Rifles, a company in the 2nd Louisiana, is an extreme example of the high casualties a community could suffer. Of the 151 men who served in the unit, 119 died in the war. Of the 32 who survived, 31 were wounded. Another example is the 3 brothers who served together in the 10th Louisiana. In a sixty-day period, 2 were killed and the other permanently blinded.[7]

Many activities surrounded the formation of a volunteer company, but none was more important than the presentation of the company's flag. This ceremony was often held just before the unit left home, and it was usually well attended. When the Cheneyville Rifles company received its flag, which was made from Mrs. T. B. Helm's donated wedding dress, one witness claimed the presentation had "more the resemblance of a festive gathering than one to [say] 'good-by' to loved ones on their departure for the seat of war."[8]

The New Orleans *Daily Picayune* covered the flag ceremony for a company in Coppens' Battalion. The men marched in formation to City Hall, where a delegation of women awaited them, and listened to several patriotic speeches. Afterward, each of the officers ascended the steps, solemnly drew his sword, and presented it to the women to be kissed. The reporter was impressed with the presentation and claimed the ceremony was much like the officers "being dubbed a knight."[9]

One of the most detailed descriptions of a flag ceremony involved the 5th Louisiana's DeSoto Rifles. Handing the flag to the color guard, the spokeswoman for the seamstresses declared: "Receive then, from your mothers and sisters, from those whose affections greet you, these colors woven by our feeble but reliant hands; and when this bright flag shall float before you on the battlefield, let it not only inspire you with the brave and patriotic ambitions of a soldier aspiring to his own and his country's honor and glory, but also may it be a sign that cherished ones appeal to you to save them from a fanatical and heartless foe." The company's color sergeant and corporals then stepped forward to receive the flag, and the sergeant replied:

> Ladies, with high-beating hearts and pulses throbbing with emotions, we receive from your hands this beautiful flag, the proud emblem of our young republic. . . . To those who may return from the field of battle bearing this flag in triumph, though perhaps tattered and torn, this incident will always prove a cheering recollection and to him whose fate may be to die a soldier's death, this moment brought before his fading view will recall your kind and sympathetic words, he will . . . bless you as his spirit takes its aerial flight. . . . May the God of battles look down upon us as we register a soldier's vow that no stain shall ever be found upon thy sacred folds, save the blood of those who attack thee or those who fall in thy defence. Comrades you have heard the pledge, may it ever guide and guard you on the tented field . . . or in the smoke, glare, and din of battle, amidst carnage and death, there let its bright folds inspire you with new strength, nerve your arms and steel your hearts to deeds of strength and valor.[10]

In the rush to recruit volunteers, some prominent Louisianians bypassed state officials and appealed directly to Confederate authorities for permission to raise units for the army. Governor Thomas O. Moore bitterly complained of this practice to Secretary of War Leroy P. Walker because he wanted the units to be mustered into Louisiana service first so that the state could appoint the field-grade officers and have the prestige of naming the commands. Governor Moore was particularly incensed when George Auguste Gaston Coppens successfully lobbied Jefferson Davis in March for permission to raise and equip a battalion of Zouaves.

A graduate of the French Marine School, Coppens was highly regarded in New Orleans social circles. One woman claimed that he was "a fine example of grace and beauty," but Coppens was also a duelist who had been involved in an infamous fight just two years earlier. Emile Bozonier, an opera aficionado, accused Coppens of hissing at his favorite singer during a performance. When Bozonier confronted Coppens in the street afterward, tempers flared, and Coppens dared Bozonier to challenge him. Bozonier complied, but rather than simply slapping Coppens as was the custom, he knocked Coppens to the ground. Armed with swords, the men soon met on the dueling ground, and in the ensuing fight Bozonier deeply slashed Coppens' face and chest. Coppens then cut Bozonier's upper arm to the bone and stabbed the helpless man twice in the side. Incredibly, both men survived their wounds.[11]

Like many Louisianians, Coppens was impressed with the French Zouaves, a colorful set of soldiers who had received a great deal of publicity during the Crimean War. The Zouaves were considered to be elite troops because they were specially trained in small-unit tactics to roam away from the main battle line and engage in skirmishing and swift hit-and-run raids. Shortly before the Civil War began, tour groups wearing gaudy Zouave uniforms and performing intricate drills to French commands and bugle calls made the soldiers popular in America. Elmer Ellsworth led one such group, and during the Civil War he organized the Union army's 11th New York, more popularly known as Ellsworth's Zouaves. Inkerman's Zouaves, whose members claimed to be French army veterans, was a New Orleans theater group that toured several Louisiana towns before the war. In announcing an upcoming performance, one Baton Rouge newspaper reported, "The Zouaves Are Coming! . . . There is something about the name of 'Zouave' that is highly pleasing to Southern ears in these 'piping times'—of war." Inkerman's tour group was so popular that a number of Louisiana units adopted the Zouave name and uniform. In addition to Coppens' Battalion and the Tiger Rifles (discussed below), individual companies in the 5th, 7th, 10th, and 14th Louisiana may also have worn Zouave uniforms. While it is possible that Coppens' Battalion was trained in the special French Zouave tactics, the other companies drilled in traditional linear maneuvers like regular infantry units.[12]

Coppens quickly organized six companies and in late March left New Orleans for Pensacola, Florida. There his six hundred men were mustered into service as the 1st Battalion, Louisiana Zouaves. Among the officers were Maj.

Waldemar Hylested, a Swiss national who had sixteen years' service in various armies, and Capt. Fulgence de Bordenave, a French veteran of the Algerian and Crimean wars who spoke no English. Many of the men were Louisianians of French extraction, and a large number had immigrated from Switzerland, the Germanic states, Italy, Spain, Ireland, and England. Some of these foreign-born men later deserted and told their Union captors that they had been forcibly impressed into the unit. It was also claimed that the mayor of New Orleans gave Coppens permission to set up recruiting stations within city jails to give criminals a choice between prison or military service. This story has not been verified, but the battalion's subsequent record of lawlessness lends credence to the claim.[13]

There were various styles of Zouave uniforms, but Coppens' men wore a red fez or skull cap with a blue tassel, a blue shirt, a dark blue jacket with gold trim, a blue vest with red trim, a sky blue sash, baggy red trousers, white gaiters, and black shoes. Eventually, the men had to give up their Zouave outfits for traditional Confederate uniforms, but sources do not agree as to when that occurred.[14]

Competition for Louisiana's recruits became fierce as the war crisis deepened. By the end of April 1861 the state was offering ten dollars to anyone who joined a state regiment and an additional two dollars for each friend induced to sign up. Some parishes offered additional bounties, so many potential recruits traveled from parish to parish looking for the best offer. Local planters and businessmen also competed against one another by offering to supply weapons and uniforms to volunteers, sometimes with the understanding that they would be elected captain of the company, or the company would be named in their honor.

The 8th Louisiana's Violet Guards, for example, was named for prominent New Orleans businessman W. A. Violett, who probably supported the company financially. The men were mostly firemen from one of the city's fire companies and wore violet-colored pants to honor their sponsor. Other volunteer companies wore blue pants, and some had yellowish home-made uniforms. Such individualized uniforms and weapons caused regimental commanders much grief when trying to standardize their units' equipment.[15]

The Perret Guards, which became part of the 5th Louisiana, had one of the more unusual origins. Most of the men were gamblers, and membership in the company was said to be reserved for those able to "cut, shuffle, and deal on the point of a bayonet." The English writer Sir William Howard Russell encountered the 116 men during a visit to Camp Moore and claimed the company was formed at the spur of the moment. Mr. Perret was a leading member of a New Orleans gambling fraternity, and one night while in the St. Charles Hotel he heard that a man not particularly known for his philanthropy had donated one thousand dollars to a local company that was to take his name. Perret scoffed at the idea and declared that "he would give $1,000 to any one who should be fool enough to form a company and call it after him." In less than an hour, fifty-six professional gamblers signed up for the Perret Guards, and Perret dutifully donated the money. Russell described the men's uniforms as being made of Mazarin blue flannel with red facings. Captain Arthur Connor, a veteran of Mexico and Nicaragua, claimed "there is not a pair of shoes in the company that cost less than $6, and that no money has been spared to perfect other appointments." Russell saw firsthand the company's lavish style when he visited the captain's quarters and enjoyed iced drinks in silver goblets that were served by an "African in uniform."[16]

Another noted philanthropist was Kentucky native and Louisiana plantation owner Alexander Keene Richards. Richards was said to be Kentucky's wealthiest man, and he was appointed a captain on Gen. John C. Breckinridge's staff after helping the former vice-president avoid arrest in the Bluegrass State for his secessionist sympathies. While in New Orleans, Richards became fond of one volunteer company called the Tiger Rifles. Recruited from the back alleys, steamboats, levees, and jails of New Orleans, the Tiger Rifles became notorious for thievery and brawling. Eighteen-year-old John F. Charlton's company was stationed with the Tiger Rifles at New Orleans' Camp Walker and noted in his diary, "Our excitement in camp with the Tiger Rifles was our first experience being often aroused during the night by cries of 'fall in fall in' expecting to be attacked by the 'Tigers.' They never liked us because we often accused them of Stealing."[17]

The mysterious Capt. Alex White organized and commanded the company. About the only thing that is definitely known about him is that he was born in Kentucky around 1825 and that he worked on a steamboat. White was said to have been the son of a Kentucky governor and was imprisoned once for murdering a boat passenger, but that has never been proven. There is also no evidence to support the claim that he fought in the Mexican War and then served in the navy.[18]

When White first organized the Tiger Rifles, the men were issued regular uniforms and wore wide-brimmed hats with hatbands bearing such slogans as

"Lincoln's Life or a Tiger's Death," "Tiger in Search of a Black Republican," and "Tiger in Search of Abe." Soon, however, Richards provided the company with Zouave uniforms. Each man wore a red fez with tassel, a red shirt of the style known as "Garibaldi" or "battle" shirts, a blue jacket trimmed in red, baggy blue trousers with white stripes, and white gaiters. Company members were also armed with a .54 caliber Mississippi Rifle and a bowie knife because the Mississippi Rifle had no bayonet lug. The company's flag was just as notable as the uniforms, with its gamboling lamb and the motto "As Gentle As."[19]

White's Tiger Rifles became part of Maj. Roberdeau Wheat's 1st Special Battalion, Louisiana Volunteers. Born in Virginia to an Episcopal minister, Wheat studied under Rev. William Nelson Pendleton, a West Point graduate and future commander of Robert E. Lee's artillery. When Wheat served as an officer under Gen. Zachary Taylor in the Mexican War, Taylor called him the best natural soldier he had ever seen. After the war, Wheat fought in Cuba, Mexico, and Nicaragua with various private filibustering expeditions, which led to his being indicted, but not convicted, for violating the nation's neutrality laws, and with Garibaldi in Italy. By 1861, "Rob" Wheat had probably experienced more combat than any other living American.[20]

Wheat became major of the 1st Special Battalion and won a lasting place in history as commander of the famous Louisiana Tiger Battalion. A huge man who stood six feet, four inches, in height and weighed 275 pounds, he proved to be the only officer capable of handling the rowdy Tiger Rifles. One man recalled hearing Wheat yell at his men, "If you don't get to your places, and behave as soldiers should, I will cut your hands off with this sword!" "His men loved him—and they feared him," wrote another soldier, "the power or spell he had over his men was truly wonderful." To help rein in the men, Wheat had the able assistance of Capt. Robert Harris, who commanded the Walker Guards and served as the battalion's executive officer. Harris and many of the men in his company had served with Wheat in Nicaragua.[21]

Wheat's Battalion originally included five New Orleans companies that reflected the city's diverse population. The soldiers were said to have been everything from laborers, steamboat crewmen, stevedores, pickpockets, and pimps to lawyers and merchants. Many were Irish immigrants; all seemed to have a penchant for drunkenness and thievery. General Richard Taylor wrote years later that "so villainous was the reputation of this battalion that every commander desired to be rid of it." In June 1861, the Catahoula Guerrillas was added to Wheat's Battalion as a sixth company. Historians often cite this collection of planters' sons, yeomen farmers, clerks, and laborers as being the tamest company in the battalion. Although they were not usually associated with the villainous acts committed by the rest of the unit, one officer referred to the Catahoula Guerrillas as "Free Booters and Robbers" when they left Catahoula Parish, which suggests that they may not have been as innocent as previously believed.[22]

Like many Louisiana units, Wheat's Battalion contained a large number of foreign-born men. Between 1850 and 1855, more than 240,000 immigrants flooded into New Orleans. Thousands fled Ireland after the Potato Famine ravaged that land, but large numbers of Germans and English also arrived. By 1860, 11.44 percent of Louisiana's population was foreign-born, the most of any southern state, and 38 percent of the people in New Orleans had been born outside of the United States, which was the most of any southern city. State officials recognized the importance of this immigrant population and made a special effort to incorporate it into the war effort. To promote foreign enlistments, newspaper advertisements frequently called for recruits for such companies as the Scotch Rifle Guards, British Guards, and Irish Brigade.[23]

Most immigrants lived in poverty and were desperate to find any kind of work. Irish immigrants competed with free blacks and slave labor in digging canals, building levees, and working on steamboats and wharves. Because the Irish were considered expendable, unlike valuable slaves, and were willing to work for less money than free blacks, they were often used to perform the most exhausting or dangerous jobs. One steamboat captain declared, "If the Paddies are knocked overboard or get their backs broke nobody loses anything." Another boatman explained that Irishmen were used as stokers because "every time a boiler bursts [the owners] would lose so many dollars' worth of slaves; whereas by getting Irishmen at a dollar-a-day they pay for the article as they get it, and if it's blown up, they get another."[24]

The outbreak of war provided immigrants like the Irish an opportunity to prove themselves loyal Louisiana citizens. John Francis Maguire, an Irish native and member of the British Parliament, shed some light on the Irishmen's motivation to enlist after studying Irish immigrants in America shortly after the Civil War ended. Maguire interviewed a number of Union and Confederate Irish veterans, and most told him that they had enlisted in the army because they were loyal to their friends and community. "[T]hey acted, as they felt, with the community amid whom they lived, and with whom their fortunes were identified. The feeling was the same on both sides of the line. The Irish in the South stood with the state to which, as they believed, they owed their first allegiance, and, as was the case in the North, they caught the spirit of the community of whom they formed part." Maguire also reported that Irishmen living in the South were sympathetic with the secessionists because they believed the northern states were oppressing the South just as England was oppressing Ireland.[25]

Whatever their reasons for enlisting, most Irishmen made excellent soldiers, and Louisiana produced more Irish rebels than any other southern state. One former Confederate general who claimed that Irishmen comprised half of his brigade told Maguire, "[I]f I had to take from one to 10,000 men to make a reputation with, I'd take the same men as I had in the war—Irishmen from the city, the levees, the river, the railroads, the canals, or from ditching and fencing on the plantations. They make the finest soldiers that ever shouldered a musket."[26]

When thousands of Irishmen began to enlist in 1861, the New Orleans *Daily Delta* reported, "As for our Irish citizens—whew!—they are 'spiling' for a fight." State officials attempted to take advantage of this enthusiasm and raise an Irish Brigade from among the immigrants. The attempt failed, but numerous Irish-dominated companies became part of the regiments and battalions heading to Virginia. Twenty-one percent of the 1st Louisiana hailed from Ireland, with the Emmet Guards and Montgomery Guards having the largest numbers. Almost one-half of the men in the 7th Louisiana were born in Ireland, including 96 percent of its Irish Volunteers company. Half of the companies in the 10th Louisiana were mostly Irish, and anecdotal evidence suggests that large numbers of Irishmen also served in the 14th Louisiana, Wheat's Battalion, and Coppens' Zouaves.[27]

Colonel Isaac Seymour's 6th Louisiana was the state's most famous Irish-dominated regiment. The fifty-six-year-old Seymour was a Georgia native who had graduated with honors from Yale University. After practicing law for a while, he became a successful newspaper editor and served as the first mayor of Macon, Georgia. Under Winfield Scott, Seymour led a company of volunteers against the Seminole Indians in 1836 and a battalion of cavalry in the Mexican War. In 1848, he moved to New Orleans and became editor of the city's leading financial newspaper, the *Commercial Bulletin*. About one-half of the 6th Louisiana hailed from Ireland, and Gen. Richard Taylor described the men as being "turbulent in camp and requiring a strong hand."[28]

Irishmen were so common in the Louisiana units that one soldier felt compelled to mention them missing in his regiment. Reuben Alan "Al" Pierson served in the 9th Louisiana's Bienville Blues, a regiment and company made up mostly of North Louisiana Protestants. He wrote his brother, "We have not a single French or Irish company in our whole regiment. They are all whole souled country boys and will do as hard fighting as any regiment that ever left La. or any other state."[29]

As part of the effort to enlist Louisiana's foreign born, officials also attempted to create a brigade out of the state's Polish population. In the spring of 1861, Maj. Gaspard Tochman, a native of Poland, arrived in New Orleans to encourage foreign enlistments. Tochman came to the United States after Russia exiled him for participating in the 1830 Polish Revolution. Once here, he became a popular lecturer on Poland and cultivated the friendship of prominent government officials. In May 1861, Tochman's friend Jefferson Davis gave him permission to raise two regiments of Poles. Unfortunately, there were only a couple of hundred Polish men, women, and children residing in Louisiana at the time, making it impossible to raise an entire brigade from the immigrants. The attempt, however, did induce other foreign groups to enlist. Tochman succeeded in raising two units that were referred to as "Polish regiments" even though they mainly consisted of other nationalities. These two regiments were separated instead of being consolidated into one brigade, with the 1st Polish Regiment being designated the 14th Louisiana Volunteers and the 2nd Polish Regiment the 3rd Battalion, Louisiana Infantry.[30]

Colonel Valery Sulakowski was made commander of the 14th Louisiana. Born in Poland to a noble family, he received his military training during the 1848 Hungarian uprising against Austria. When the revolution failed, Sulakowski fled to the United States and settled in New Orleans as a civil engineer. He enthusiastically supported Tochman's efforts to raise a Polish brigade and was rewarded with the command of the 1st Polish Regiment. Like Wheat, Sulakowski was a strict disciplinarian and perhaps the only officer capable of controlling the wild soldiers in his unit. The regiment resembled Wheat's Battalion in makeup because it contained many foreign-born members who spoke a variety of languages and had worked along the violent Mississippi waterfront. Regimental member William P. Snakenberg declared that three of the companies "could claim anywhere they were at as home, men who worked on the levee, loading and unloading boats all day and spend their wages at night for drink, sleep off their carousal under a canvas or tarpaulin until morning, then go to work again." Sulakowski ruled with an iron fist and was described by one soldier as being "a most exacting military commander, disciplinarian, and organizer" and as the "incarnation of military law—despotic, cruel and absolutely merciless." Once while putting the men through drill, Sulakowski's horse became unmanageable and the colonel lost his temper. Dismounting, he drew his sword and stabbed the animal to death on the parade ground while his shocked men watched. Sulakowski's soldiers never became fond of him, but they did admire his talents. He was, one Louisianian claimed, "without doubt the best colonel in the service."[31]

The men of the 14th Louisiana quickly earned a reputation for being violent troublemakers, and on June 4, 1861, the *Daily True Delta* reported on a deadly brawl that erupted within the regiment. Becoming impatient for marching orders while in New Orleans' Camp Walker, the soldiers in two companies that were camped near one another "concluded to get up a local quarrel and a domestic fight. . . . [S]ome were evidently under the influence of liquor, and with the weapons intended for their enemies they turned upon each other. The result was two killed and eight or ten seriously wounded." The two who died killed each other. "One received a bullet or bayonet thrust through the head, and the other a ball in his neck." It required another company with loaded muskets to restore order and arrest the instigators of the fight. The newspaper lamented such behavior among the soldiers but added "when 'valor's fever' is at its height men cannot be easily restrained."[32]

While thousands of immigrants eagerly volunteered for military service, others were forced to join. Shortages in state levee funds threw many Irishmen out of work before the war, and the army was a way to obtain a steady paycheck and food. Other foreigners were literally shanghaied into service. One English correspondent in New Orleans wrote, "British subjects have been seized, knocked down, carried off from their labor at the wharf and forced . . . to serve." Other foreign nationals were dragged into barracks and hogtied until they agreed to enlist. The British consulate in New Orleans was so swamped by pathetic pleas from its subjects that it finally pressured Governor Moore to discharge all English citizens so impressed. One company in the 1st Louisiana Volunteers had eight members discharged for this reason.[33]

The forced enlistment of these unwilling soldiers and the reluctant enlistment of immigrants who were just trying to survive caused serious problems for commands with large numbers of foreign members. Some of these reluctant rebels quickly deserted, committed crimes, and generally failed to assimilate into army life. Invariably, the Louisiana commands most complained about for committing depredations were those with the greatest number of foreign-born members. The vast majority of immigrants made excellent soldiers and brought much deserved praise upon their commands, but there were enough of the criminal and dissatisfied elements in the units to earn a bad reputation for all. (See the appendix for information on desertion rates.)

Besides trying to fill its quota of men, Louisiana was also faced with the problem of providing a central training camp for its regiments. A site eighty miles north of New Orleans in the piney woods of St. Helena Parish was finally chosen. Named Camp Moore, it was a dry area with a good water supply and isolated from corrupting bars and taverns. Although several smaller camps were also used, the vast majority of the troops sent to Virginia received their initiation into army life at Camp Moore.

Al Pierson, the eldest of four Bienville Parish brothers who would serve in the war, was one of the first soldiers to arrive. The twenty-seven-year-old teacher began his military career as a private, but he would be elected company captain a year later. Pierson informed his sister that all of the soldiers were sworn into the army upon their arrival at Camp Moore. The oath, as he remembered it, was "You and each of you do solemnly swear true and faithful allegiance to the state of La., that you will defend her, that you will obey all orders in camp and will be subject to the orders of the Confederates States when formed into a regiment and having elected officers for the same so help you God."[34] During the official induction, the men signed up for either one year's service or for the duration of the war. It is unclear why this was allowed because it only led to confusion and anger later when individual companies within a regiment, and apparently individual soldiers within a company, were permitted to leave the service at different times.

The soldiers' impressions of Camp Moore varied greatly. Pierson declared, "The camp is one of the filthiest places I have ever been permitted to see. There are more flies in and around Camp Moore than there are in all Bienville Parish. . . . It would turn the stomach of any other being except a soldier to go into one of the eating houses kept on this encampment. The flies are so thick until you have to be careful in carrying a mouthful from your plate to your mouth lest a fly should alight upon it before it is received. This is no exaggerated statement. . . . [Y]ou will seldom hear anyone mention the flies after he has been in camp three days."[35]

William E. Trahern, on the other hand, was quite pleased with the facilities. "It seemed to me to be too beautiful a spot to make use of, for the purpose of training men to kill their fellow-man. It was a pure Magnolia Vale, abounding in Magnolia trees from fifty to one hundred feet high, all loaded with large white fragrant flowers. Many sparkling limped streams gurgled and splashed as they fought their way through this tropical section. The banks were clothed in a vast number of all kinds of colored flowers."[36]

The first few days at Camp Moore were exciting for the new recruits as company officers wheeled and dealed to get their men assigned to a "fighting unit" destined for Virginia. Company officers also fiercely competed with one another for field commissions in the newly formed regiments. Because regimental field offices were filled through elections, Camp Moore's atmosphere was much like that of a political convention. Bribery and payoffs were common among the campaigning officers, and some commissions were bought and sold openly.[37]

One of the best documented elections involved Capt. Jonathan W. Buhoup, a thirty-five-year-old Pennsylvania native and merchant. When his Catahoula Guerrillas company was assigned to the 8th Louisiana Volunteers, Buhoup tried to get St. John R. Liddell, a prominent Catahoula Parish planter, elected colonel of the regiment. When that failed, Buhoup complained to Liddell that the "Head Quarters Clique" tried to bring in field officers from outside the regiment—ignoring his own attempt to do the same. After much bickering, Buhoup was nominated for lieutenant colonel, along with Capt. Francis T. Nicholls of the Phoenix Guards, but Buhoup wrote, "They have only nominated me I think to stop my mouth."

Buhoup claimed that all nominees for the regimental offices agreed to support one another against outside influences. At the last moment, however, three urban companies replaced three of the regiment's rural companies, and the tickets were redrawn with the rival Nicholls being nominated for colonel rather than lieutenant colonel. Nicholls supposedly told Buhoup that he was not interested in the position and asked Buhoup to support retired U.S. Army officer Capt. Henry B. Kelly instead. Buhoup agreed, but shortly before the election the camp was swamped with circulars promoting Kelly for colonel and Nicholls for lieutenant colonel as originally nominated. When the election was held, Nicholls beat Buhoup for the position of second-in-command.[38]

Buhoup claimed, "I publicly denounced Nichols . . . as a coward and a puppy" for his deceitfulness and then followed the wishes of the Catahoula Guerrillas to transfer to Wheat's Battalion. Earlier there had been talk of adding more companies to Wheat's Battalion and reorganizing it as the 8th Louisiana regiment with Wheat as its colonel. However, this plan was derailed when the 8th Louisiana was formed with Kelly as the commander. Buhoup must have believed that Wheat still had a chance to get his own regiment and transferred his company to Wheat's Battalion in hope of receiving a future field commission. When informed of Kelly's election, Liddell wrote his son in the Catahoula Guerrillas that Buhoup "sold the co. for a field office for himself. . . . Buhoup has never succeeded in anything but diciving those who were foolish enough to rely upon him—God help you if you have such men for field officers."[39]

Captain Nicholls explained the episode differently. As the election approached, some of his men accused him of intending to use the company as a stepping stone to a higher command. Nicholls, a twenty-seven-year-old West Point graduate, was certain to be tapped for early promotion because he came from a military family and had served one year in the army before resigning to study law. However, he had earlier promised his men that he would stay with the Phoenix Guards for the duration of the war. Thus, when Nicholls was nominated for colonel, he refused to campaign and threw his support to Kelly. Then, at election time, the company released Nicholls from his promise and opened the way for his unsolicited election to lieutenant colonel.[40]

Buhoup never received the field commission he so coveted. After serving bravely at the First Battle of Manassas, he died in January 1862 while on recruiting duty in New Orleans. Colonel Henry Kelly ably led the 8th Louisiana until April 1863, when he was transferred to the military court system. One of Kelly's soldiers claimed he was "one of the best commanders in the Confederate army—always at home when in the scene of action." Nicholls lost his left arm and foot in the war but rose to the rank of brigadier general.[41]

Not all commands resorted to subterfuge and intrigue to elect their field-grade officers. Some, like the 9th Louisiana, were more pragmatic in choosing a commanding officer who could best serve them. The regiment's North Louisiana farmers asked Richard Taylor, son of President Zachary Taylor, to leave his position on Gen. Braxton Bragg's staff in Pensacola and come serve as their colonel. Although Taylor had no prior military experience, the men of the 9th Louisiana knew the former state senator carried considerable political weight by being the son of a former president, former brother-in-law of Jefferson Davis, and one of the most prominent planters in Louisiana. If anyone could get the regiment to Virginia, it was Taylor.

When Taylor was elected colonel, the men of the 9th Louisiana seemed pleased. Al Pierson wrote home, "Our officers were elected yesterday evening and I think we have as good ones as the world could afford us." Another soldier declared, "With such officers this regiment will certainly make a name in history." Taylor proved a good choice and quickly whipped the regiment into shape. Henry Handerson, an Ohio native who came to Louisiana to tutor planters' families and then enlisted with his friends when war came, wrote, "Col. Taylor is a regular martinet in the line of discipline, and aspires to have the most orderly regiment in the service." Ezra Denson agreed and claimed, "Our colonel seems to have a great deal of sympathy for his men. True, he is quite rigid in his discipline as all military commanders should be, but he is a gentleman in every sense." As it turned out, it was not so much Taylor's leadership that turned the 9th Louisiana into one of the camp's best trained regiments, but rather his executive officer, Lt. Col. Edward G. Randolph. Randolph was a veteran of the Mexican War and was described by Taylor as being "a well-instructed officer for the time." The 9th Louisiana would prove to be one of the best Louisiana regiments in Virginia, suffering the highest fatality rate (40 percent) and producing three generals. (See the appendix for more information on the 9th Louisiana.)[42]

After electing their officers, the men got down to the business of becoming soldiers. The Yankee-born Handerson claimed Camp Moore was "where we were fairly initiated into the mysteries and miseries of a soldier's life." Company and battalion drill consumed much of the men's time because they had to learn the intricacies required in maneuvering large bodies of troops. Lieutenant Edward A. Seton of the 10th Louisiana found the drill to be rather impressive and wrote his mother, "I wish you could see all the regiment a drilling to gether at a support arms; you can not look at the bayonets when reflecting in the sun. All the officers have to wear read caps it is very absured you would think so if you would only see me with mine on and my large striped pants and long tailed coat."[43]

Unfortunately, the recruits discovered that performing degrading manual labor was also part of a soldier's life. Handerson's Stafford Guards company found it difficult to adjust to hauling garbage, digging ditches, and clearing brush, but Colonel Taylor admired his men for being determined to become soldiers despite the menial labor. It was, he claimed, "'niddering' in gentlemen to assume voluntarily the discharge of duties and then shirk." This determination was characteristic of most soldiers, but W. G. Ogden of the 7th Louisiana wrote his father that he felt like "the Rich Man in the Bible and biseach the officers to let me warn my brothers against the folly which has brought me here. . . . I do implore you to think well before telling any more of the family [to] enter [the] ranks."[44]

Some of the men did not adjust to military life as well as others. John McGrath recalled how his company was once called out to suppress a mutiny in Wheat's Battalion. It was, he claimed, "the first time ball cartridges were served and inserted into our guns." Wheat's men had refused orders to perform some unspecified duty and dared their superiors "to do their worst." McGrath's company, the Delta Rifles, accompanied the camp's adjutant general to confront the "Tigers." When the adjutant ordered them to fall in, they refused and began cursing the Delta Rifles and daring them to open fire. McGrath described what happened next: "We were then ordered to load and come to a ready and the Adjutant General taking out his watch notified the malcontents that he would give them just two minutes to form ranks and unless they obeyed in that time he would order us to fire up on them. At first they laughed and guyed him but noticing the firmness of the Deltas and believing they would fire at the command they were in ranks before the expiration of the two minute limit. Strange to say these toughs had a more friendly feeling for us than for any other troops in camp and many of them honored us as visitors and when we entrained to leave the Tigers turned out in full force to bid us a farewell."[45]

This was not the only time Wheat's Battalion caused problems at Camp Moore. Whit Martin reported, "We are encamped next to Maj. Bob Wheat's Battalion and a rough set of neighbors they are. One company is composed of levee rats of New Orleans and they have a row among themselves nearly every day. The whole camp has been under arms twice since we have been here to put down their rows but we have not been obliged to whip them in."[46]

It so happened that the first man to be buried at Camp Moore was one of Wheat's Tigers. On May 16, the day after Wheat's Battalion arrived in camp, a train struck and killed Pvt. William Douglas while he was on guard duty. The *Daily Delta* reported on the incident in a rather tongue-in-cheek manner. It claimed that Douglas was on guard duty on the railroad under orders from Wheat to not allow anything to pass. "By and by the locomotive came up. Bill called out 'halt!' The locomotive did not heed the order; then Bill fired his musket at the infernal, obstinate old 'bullgine,' and seeing it wouldn't halt, charged bayonets on it, and was run over and mashed into a 'regular jelly.'"[47]

Camp Moore's constant drill and drudgery quickly erased the initial excitement of army life and encouraged the men to find ways to make the monotony bearable. Drinking became a favorite pastime, but acquiring liquor posed a problem because the regimental sutlers controlled all of the camp's alcohol, and no taverns were located close by. Officers could purchase liquor directly from the sutlers, but enlisted men had to secure the written permission of a company officer. For a brief time this regulation kept liquor a privileged item. Andrew Newell wrote home that "Tom Furlong is in good health; quit drinking per necessity can't get it." The Louisiana privates, however, quickly learned to circumvent the rules. One wrote, "The enlisted men secured the signature of captains when they could do so, but to save time and chances of being met by a refusal, most frequently forged the name of their officers."[48]

The rigors and boredom of camp life, plus the availability of liquor, corrupted many innocent boys. One of Francis T. Nicholls' men wrote, "I was told today that men even to Captains & Lieutenants had been drunk and had played cards that were never known to have touched them before coming to this place."[49] This taste for the spirits had a devastating effect on the Louisiana troops in the next few months because most of the incidents of lawlessness attributed to them were directly related to too much liquor.

Some of the Louisiana troops were sent to Pensacola, instead of Camp Moore, to strengthen General Bragg's forces there. Among them was the 1st Battalion, Louisiana Volunteers, under the dashing twenty-nine-year-old New Orleans socialite Lt. Col. Charles D. Dreux. Dreux was educated in France, at Amherst College, and at two military institutes in Kentucky. After college he studied law and became one of Kentucky's Whig delegates at the 1850 national convention, where he delivered an inspiring speech supporting Winfield Scott for president. Returning to New Orleans, Dreux was elected district attorney and state legislator and organized the Orleans Cadets when war loomed closer. This company consisted of New Orleans' most prominent young bachelors and claimed to have thirty-four men under eighteen years of age, with Dreux being the only married member. With four other companies, Dreux's men were dispatched to Pensacola and mustered into Confederate service as the 1st Battalion, Louisiana Volunteers—the first Louisiana unit to be accepted into the Confederate army. Dreux was elected the battalion's commander and won his men's admiration by mixing strict military discipline while on duty with friendly familiarity while off.[50]

Coppens' Zouaves joined Dreux's Battalion to help protect Pensacola from the Union forces still occupying Fort Pickens on Santa Rosa Island. With their colorful uniforms and French aura, the Zouaves became the center of attention. William Howard Russell dined with them and noted that many of Coppens' officers were veterans of various European wars and that they were the only unit at Pensacola "with a military exactness." Mornings on the sandy beach were uniquely French, the Englishman wrote, as "the well known *reveille* of the Zouaves, and then French clangors, rolls, ruffles and calls ran along the line."[51]

As at Camp Moore, the Louisianians at Pensacola quickly became bored with their duty station. The monotony of camp life was relieved only by persistent rumors of an impending attack by the Union fleet, but after weeks in the burning sun even this threat of combat failed to arouse the men. As William E. Moore put it, "I dread the mosquitoes and sand flies more than the black republicans." He reported that the insects and heat combined to make conditions miserable and tempers to flare. In a fit of anger, a Shreveport Grey once used his musket to crack the head of a New Orleans soldier who called him a liar, and a nearby saloon was placed off limits when the Louisiana soldiers engaged in a barroom brawl with civilians. Some of the men found this punishment unbearable—"kill me," they cried, "but don't take my whiskey." The soldiers apparently found ways to circumvent the saloon closures, however, because four Louisiana soldiers were discharged at Pensacola in early June for excessive drinking.[52]

Swimming in Pensacola Bay offered some distraction and relaxation to the bored men, but even that held its own risks. A reporter for the *Mobile Advertiser* filed a story titled "A Floating Arsenal" in which he wrote, "A shark was caught this morning with a pair of red breeches and a whole parcel of bowie-knives in his belly, supposed to be the remains of a Zouave."[53]

By late spring most of the commands destined for Virginia were organized and ready to ship out, and they reflected the state's cosmopolitan population.

At least twenty-four nationalities were represented among the approximately 12,000 soldiers, but the muster rolls give the birth places of only about 7,000. Of these, only 2,303 were native Louisianians, while 2,485 were born in other states. Most of the latter were poor farmers who migrated to the piney woods of North Louisiana from other southern states, but quite a few were from the North. One Yankee from Maine explained why he had enlisted when someone asked him, "Well, how in the blazes to you happen to belong to this crowd?" The soldier replied that he was a sailor and had been paid off in New Orleans after his latest voyage ended about a month before the war began. "I frolicked around until my money was all gone, and when I came to myself the trouble had commenced. Well, I wanted to see some fun, and as the boys were good fellows I joined them."[54]

There were almost as many foreign-born soldiers in the Virginia-bound units as native Louisianians. Of the men whose place of birth is known, approximately 3,000 were born outside the United States, with most of them serving in the New Orleans companies. Their places of origin were as follows:[55]

Ireland	1,743	Denmark	6
Germanic states	611	Poland	6
England	184	Cuba	5
France	124	Gibraltar	5
Canada	59	Holland	4
Italy	33	Portugal	4
Scotland	32	Brazil	3
Spain	21	Russia	3
Switzerland	17	Sicily	3
Mexico	14	Martinique	2
Norway	8	Corsica	1
Austria	7	Hungary	1
Greece	7	Malta	1
Sweden	7	Sardinia	1
Belgium	6	West Indies	1

In addition to the 12,000 men who made up these units, quite a few women went along, as well. After visiting Col. Isaac Seymour's 6th Louisiana's camp at Fairfax, Virginia, a Charleston *Mercury* reporter wrote:

Many of the officers have their wives with them. Their tents gave unmistakable evidences of care and taste. The grounds of the encampment are arranged with a more decided reference to appearances. The men all gave evidence of a consciousness that women were about; all were as nearly in full dress as their wardrobes permitted; all who came upon the parade have their hair combed; and I am very sure that in that case there was more of physical comfort and convenience than in any others of the army. . . . It might be supposed that in case of a fight their sympathies and fears would occasion trouble, but this was not the case, in one instance at least. One of the lieutenants mentioned, that upon the occasion of an alarm the night before, his wife declined to get up, as he was being armed for the encounter, upon the ground that if she should, she did not know what better place to go to, and an hour afterward, when the alarm proved to be false, and he went back, she was sound asleep.[56]

In addition to soldiers' wives, the Louisianians also brought vivandières, or "daughters of the regiment," with them to Virginia. A French army custom, vivandières were not camp followers but rather members of the unit who performed myriad duties for the soldiers and often wore uniforms. When the 14th Louisiana passed through Augusta, Georgia, on its way to Virginia, a reporter wrote, "A really beautiful and exquisitely formed lady, a vivandiere, of the 14th Louisiana regiment, was in the city this morning and created considerable curiosity on the streets. She is in company with several officers of the regiment. She is dressed in full costume—short dress, &c.,—and is very beautiful."[57]

Vivandières were mentioned most often in association with Coppens' Battalion. One New Orleans correspondent observed that the Zouaves "had the good taste" to bring women with them to Pensacola to wash, cook, and clean their quarters. Earlier, a "good looking vivandière" had accompanied the Zouaves when they assembled at the New Orleans City Hall for a flag ceremony. She reportedly marched behind the band and drew much attention from the crowd of onlookers.[58]

Coppens' Battalion had three vivandières, but the identity of only two are known: Mrs. William Clark, whose husband was a veteran of the Crimean War and served as the battalion's orderly sergeant, and Miss Amelia Riliseh, who carried the unit's First National Flag to Pensacola. Riliseh appears in a famous photograph taken of the Zouaves standing in formation at Pensacola. The photograph shows her wearing a distinctive uniform, but it is not known if the other two vivandières were similarly dressed. A newspaper reporter described Riliseh's uniform as being "unique and pretty—pair of high heel shoes, over the top of which shine white gaitor tops, above these are tight fitting pieces of leather extending to the knee; there they unite with red, white drawers; they have a blue skirt with red border from waist to their knee and a blue jacket from waist to neck. On the head is a little hat with a feather in it." Riliseh can also be seen wearing a sword.[59]

Wheat's Battalion is also known to have had vivandières. Just before the First Battle of Manassas, a Virginia officer wrote, "A wagon passed by with four women in it, belonging to Col. Wheat's 'Louisiana Tigers,' all dressed up as men. I presume they are vivandieres from New Orleans. They are disgusting looking creatures that have followed the camp. They are being moved back to a safer place in anticipation of an attack."[60]

One of Wheat's vivandières was Lavinia Williams, who appeared at charity benefits after the First Battle of Manassas to help raise money to care for the battalion's wounded men. In reporting on one of Williams' appearances, a South Carolina newspaper informed its readers that she demonstrated the Louisianians' knife-fighting techniques. "She is a very strong looking woman and tells with perfect nonchalance of killing Yankees and the like. You may depend on it, the children crowded to see her, dressed as she was in the gay costume of her vocation."[61]

Rose Rooney was also identified as a Louisiana vivandière who served as a cook and nurse with the Crescent (City) Blues. Her company was assigned to the 49th Virginia Infantry just a few days before the First Battle of Manassas, and during the fight she was credited for tearing down a rail fence while under heavy fire to allow an artillery battery to enter the battle. The Crescent (City) Blues eventually became part of the 15th Louisiana, and Rooney remained on duty throughout the war.[62]

Catherine Hodges, a vivandière in the 5th Louisiana's Monroe Guards, had the distinction of being the first woman buried among the 12,000 Confederate dead in Richmond's Hollywood Cemetery. She died in Richmond on April 7, 1862, while nursing the wounded. In 1903, the Richmond *Times Dispatch* wrote of her, "She made the camp and march merry for the men when alive, and dying, chose to be buried with her comrades. We dare say there is material there for a good story." Another good story would be the circumstances of a vivandière who served as a laundress for the 15th Louisiana. In late 1862 or early 1863, Drury Gibson reported that the unidentified woman gave birth to a baby boy. "I officiated on the occasion. It seemed rather strange in a military camp."[63]

Wives and vivandières helped care for the men's physical well-being while chaplains tended to their spiritual needs. The Confederate Congress authorized the president to appoint regimental chaplains on May 3, 1861, and to pay them eighty-five dollars per month. However, when a senator complained that the only duty a chaplain had was to preach once a week, the pay was reduced to fifty dollars. The truth is that chaplains performed many valuable services other than preaching. They served as nurses and counselors, wrote and read letters for illiterate soldiers, and helped men send money back to their families. While Protestant chaplains concentrated on preaching to the men and winning converts, their Catholic counterparts spent more time hearing confessions and holding communion, although they also preached at Protestant services if there was no other chaplain available. Sometimes the priests held communion before a battle. Father James Sheeran of the 14th Louisiana claimed that "no men fight more bravely than Catholics who approach the sacraments before battle." Louisiana's known Catholic chaplains were Egidius "Giles" Smulders, a Belgian Redemptorist who attended to the victims of ten military executions during his service with the 8th Louisiana and the 1st Louisiana Brigade; Hypolite Gache, a French Jesuit who served the 10th Louisiana; the Irish-born Redemptorist James B. Sheeran of the 14th Louisiana; and Darius Hubert, a Jesuit who served the 1st Louisiana and was wounded at Gettysburg. Smulders, Gache, and Sheeran wrote interesting accounts of their service with the Louisiana troops. Protestant chaplains included Robert Hardee Jr., G. W. Roberts, and S. B. Suratt of the 2nd Louisiana; L. H. Baldwin (who was captured at Antietam), Dr. R. H. Read, and Dr. William M. Strickler (who was wounded and captured at Gettysburg) of the 5th Louisiana; F. McCarthy of the 9th Louisiana; and George W. Stickney of the 14th Louisiana. Alfred Flournoy Jr. declared that Dr. Read was "a magnificent Preacher. . . . I never saw such profound attention in all my life by a very large crowd indeed . . . and many a soldiers eye was wet with tears when he closed."[64]

Anecdotal evidence indicates that a large number of African Americans also accompanied the men to Virginia, but there is no way even to estimate how many. Virtually all of them were slaves who accompanied officers as servants and sometimes even wealthy enlisted men. Their tasks ranged from cooking, nursing, and entertaining to chopping wood and driving wagons. In a biographical sketch of her father, the daughter of the 6th Louisiana's Pvt. Theodore Woodard wrote that her wealthy grandparents pampered Woodard and sent him off to war with "Champ," one of the family's slaves. However, "at the sound of the first big gun, Champ melted into the night making his way back home on foot." Slaves like Champ are a shadowy presence about which little is known other than an occasional mentioning in soldiers' diaries, memoirs, and letters. Typical of these comments is Charles Batchelor's remarks in a letter home in which he wrote, "Tell [the slaves] that Mad. and Albert are very anxious to see them as well as the white folks" and that they would bring them lots of presents.[65]

Two of the best documented slaves who went to Virginia are Levy S. Carnine and Ed Merritt. Carnine was born around 1810 and belonged to the Hogan family of Alabama. He accompanied his master to fight the Seminoles in 1837, and when Hogan was killed, Carnine buried him and then served one of Hogan's cousins until the war ended. The Hogans eventually moved to Mansfield, Louisiana, and Carnine again went off to war with Dr. W. R. K. Hogan, who had enlisted in the 2nd Louisiana's Pelican Rifles. Reportedly, 119 members of this company died during the war, and Carnine's obituary claimed "old Levy helped to bury about 100 of them." When Dr. Hogan was killed at the Wilderness, Carnine remained with the company until late in the war and then returned to Louisiana to serve another family member who had come of military age. When the war ended, Carnine remained in the Mansfield area and supported the Democrats during Reconstruction. His Pelican Rifles comrades considered him to be a member of the company and when Carnine died in 1886, the few surviving members conducted his military funeral and laid him to rest in the Confederate cemetery. His tombstone reads "Levy S. Carnine, CSA, Co. D, 2 La Cav, Pelican Rifles."[66]

Ed Merritt was a slave who served Perry Murrell and R. A. Smith, friends from Claiborne Parish who joined the 8th Louisiana's Minden Blues. In 1922, Smith discussed Merritt in a letter to his cousin and explained that the men's fathers were going to provide personal servants for their sons but then came to a financial agreement whereby Merritt would serve both soldiers. According to Smith, Merritt "was closer to us than a brother. He carried our money, cooked, washed our clothes and counseled us as to health and conduct to the end of the War." Merritt and Smith were the only survivors out of eight close friends who served together.

While in Virginia, Merritt once fell ill and was left behind with the enemy. When he recovered, he hired himself out to cook for a Union officer even though he still had one hundred dollars in gold that he was holding for his rebel messmates. Merritt eventually deserted his Union employer and made his way back to his friends. Smith wrote, "I shall never forget the day when Perry and I were cooking apple dumplings and Ed came up dressed in a linen citizen's suit, how I hugged and kissed him."

When Smith and Murrell were wounded in 1862, Merritt searched in vain for them and then collected their belongings and returned to Louisiana. Eventually, the two soldiers came home on wounded furlough, and the trio reunited and returned to Virginia. Merritt accompanied the regiment on its march to Gettysburg, where Murrell was killed and Smith was wounded and captured. Smith did not explain what happened to Merritt afterward but noted that Merritt and Murrell's father searched northern cemeteries after the war looking for the young man's grave. Merritt and Smith remained friends after the war and sometimes visited one another. "The last time I saw Ed," recalled Smith, "he showed me the belt that he carried the money in when he was in the War."[67]

Levy S. Carnine, Ed Merritt, and slaves like them accompanied the Army of Northern Virginia and performed important tasks for its soldiers. Despite claims to the contrary, however, there is no evidence to support the notion that thousands of African Americans served in the Confederate army as enlisted men. It is possible, however, that some of the black servants may have fought on occasion. Such was said of Carnine, and Wolf Lichenstein made a cryptic comment on the subject when writing about his Lecompte Guards company in the 2nd Louisiana. In reference to Lt. Ross E. Burke, a wealthy Natchitoches Parish resident who later commanded the regiment, Lichenstein wrote that Burke "was a man of iron & blood [and his] negroes of Steel stood him well in hand later when wading through fields of blood."[68]

Noted historian Arthur W. Bergeron Jr., who worked with the Louisiana State Archives for many years, conducted an exhaustive study of blacks serving in Louisiana's units. He was able to document only twelve, although he believed that there could have been a few more who were light skinned enough to pass for being white. The only African American known to have served officially in the units bound for Virginia was Charles F. Lutz of St. Landry

Parish who joined the 8th Louisiana's Opelousas Guards. He was captured at the Second Battle of Fredericksburg and after being exchanged was badly wounded and captured again at Gettysburg.[69]

The white soldiers, female vivandières, and black slaves who made up the Louisiana regiments finally departed for Richmond in late spring 1861. One of the first to go was Coppens' Battalion, which left Pensacola on June 1 on a wild train ride that would help create the image of the notorious Louisiana Tiger. A journalist who was on hand when they boarded the train left a vivid description of the Zouaves:

> One gray dawn, six hundred Zouaves filed out of the pines and got aboard our train. They were a splendid set of animals; medium sized, sunburnt, muscular and wiry as Arabs; and a long, swingy gait told of drill and endurance. But the faces were dull and brutish, generally; and some of them would vie, for cunning villainy, with the features of the prettiest Turcos that Algeria could produce.
>
> The uniform was very picturesque and very dirty. Full, baggy, scarlet trowsers, confined round the waist by the broad, blue band or sash, bearing the bowie-knife and meeting, at mid-leg, the white gaiter; blue shirt cut very low and exhibiting the brawny, sunburnt throat; jacket heavily braided and embroidered, flying loosely off the shoulders, and the jaunty *fez*, surmounting the whole, made a bright *ensemble* that contrasted prettily with the gray and silver of the South Carolinians, or the rusty brown of the Georgians, who came in crowds to see them off. . . .
>
> Nor were they purer morally. Graduates of the slums of New Orleans, their education in villainy was naturally perfect. They had the vaguest ideas of *meum* and *tuum*; and small personal difficulties were usually settled by the convincing argument of a bowie-knife, or brass knuckle.
>
> Yet they had been brought to a very perfect state of drill and efficiency. All commands were given in *French*—the native tongue of nearly all the officers and most of the men; and, in cases of insubordination, the former had no hesitancy in a free use of the revolver. . . . Their officers we found of a class entirely above them; active, bright, enthusiastic Frenchmen, with a frank courtesy and soldierly bearing that were very taking.[70]

The Zouaves' officers precipitated trouble when they chose to leave their men unattended and ride in a special car at the end of the train. When they stopped at Garland, Alabama, the officers left their car to enjoy a quiet breakfast at the station, but they were quickly interrupted by a shrill whistle and the low rumble of a moving train. Rushing to the windows, the startled Creoles saw their special car sitting beside the station while their men and train slowly disappeared down the tracks. The Zouaves had hijacked the train. The cursing officers quickly wired for another locomotive and were soon in hot pursuit of their runaway men.[71]

The Zouaves arrived in Montgomery, Alabama, long before their enraged officers. The tension and frustration built up at Pensacola were unleashed as the men embarked upon a drunken spree of looting, robbery, and harassment. After an hour of lawlessness, city officials called out the 1st Georgia Volunteers to restore order. With loaded muskets and fixed bayonets, the Georgians were forcing the Zouaves out of the stores when the abandoned officers finally pulled into town.

The fuming officers sprang from the moving train with their pistols drawn and ran toward the drunken mob as a bugler led the way blowing the call for "rally." One witness claimed, "The charge of the Light Brigade was surpassed by these irate Creoles." Into the midst of the mob they ran, cursing some, pistol whipping others. One young lieutenant spotted a huge sergeant emerging from a store with an armload of shoes. The startled soldier hesitated when the young officer yelled for him to drop his loot, so the lieutenant ran up, grabbed him by the throat, and cracked his head with the pistol barrel. The sergeant collapsed as if pole-axed, but the officer simply roared, "Roll that carrion into the streets!" and hurried off to seek more of his men.[72]

After a half hour of cursings and beatings, the Zouaves finally dropped their plunder, fell into line, and reluctantly boarded the train to continue the trip to Richmond. Bloodied and sullen, Coppens' men were in an ugly mood. Along the way one officer shot and killed a Zouave for leaving ranks to buy tobacco, and another was accidentally killed under unknown circumstances. The train crew was horrified when others began riding on top of the train and on the couplings between the cars. When warned of the danger, the Zouaves only cursed the crew, laughed, and clung tighter. One was killed when the train passed under a low bridge, and three others were crushed to death on the couplings when the train lurched suddenly.[73]

News of the wild train ride spread to Atlanta, and citizens there dreaded the Zouaves' arrival. The Atlanta *Constitution* reported: "For hours before their arrival telegrams kept the wires hot advising our citizens to keep out of the way. Rumors reached here of the murderous assaults made by Zouaves upon people en route, and just before the train was due in the afternoon the women, children and timid citizens were in a state bordering on hysterics." When the train rolled in, the Tigers began jumping off before it stopped under the car shed, and they at once scattered in every direction, looking for liquor. The sight of their bronzed, foreign-looking faces and their bizarre uniforms scared the spectators into fits, and most of the noncombatants made a rush for their homes, where they bolted their doors and did not again venture out until the next day.

The Zouaves had a few fights among themselves, but they did not bother the inhabitants as much as had been expected. They were so noisy and threatening, however, that the provost guard rounded them up at night and penned them up in the old courthouse yard, where Dr. d'Alvigney made a speech to them in French, which had the effect of putting them in a good humor.[74]

At Columbia, South Carolina, the Zouaves again ran amuck. "Sich a shooting of cattle and poultry, sich a yelling and singing of their darned french stuff—sich a rolling of drums and a damning of officers, I arn't hear yit," declared one railroad agent. Reflecting on the trip so far, he added, "and I'm jest a-thinkin' . . . ef this yere reegement don't stop a-fightin' together, being shot by the Georgians and beat by their officers—not to mention a jammin' upon railroads—they're gwine to do darned leetle sarvice a-fightin' of Yanks!"[75]

Despite their riotous reputation, Coppens' Zouaves continued to impress civilians with their colorful uniforms and military bearing. After watching them pass through Petersburg, Virginia, one onlooker wrote a friend:

> The greatest sight I have yet seen in the way of military was a body of about 600 Louisiana Zouaves, uniformed and drilled it was said in the true French Zouaves style. Most of them were of foreign extraction—the French predominant—but there were Irish, Italians, Swiss, etc., etc. Their uniforms consisted of loose red flannel pants tied above the ankles, blue flannel jackets, and for headgear a kind of red flannel bag large enough at one end to fit the head and tapering to a point at the other where it was generally decorated with a piece of ribbon. This end fell behind. In this cap which, you see, did not protect

their faces from the sun in the least, they had been wasting for a month or two in the burning sun of Pensacola, and of course were as brown as they could well get—browner than I ever saw a white man. Add to their costume and complexion that they were hard specimens before they left the "crescent city" as their manner indicated and you may perhaps imagine what sort of men they were. In fact they were the most savage-looking crowd I ever saw.[76]

When the Zouaves stormed Richmond a few days later, a local newspaper reported that the city was "thrown into a paroxysm of excitement." One man who witnessed their entry wrote home that the battalion was "composed of 'Wharf Rats' of New Orleans. . . . & look wilder, & are usually drunker than any Indians. They are the lions of the town now & cut out all the other uniforms."[77]

The citizens of Richmond were curious about the much publicized Zouaves, but their curiosity was soon satisfied. "From the time of their appearance in Richmond," remembered one resident, "robberies became frequent. Whenever a Zouave was seen something was sure to be missed." Housed at first on the second floor of the tobacco warehouse that later became Libby Prison, the Zouaves eluded guards posted at doorways by using their sashes as ropes and scampering out the windows. They then "roamed about the city like a pack of untamed wildcats." Stalking into saloons, the men ordered "what they wished to eat and drink, and then directed the dismayed proprietor to charge their bill to the government." It was claimed that "thieving, burglary, and garroting in the streets at night" were common as long as the Zouaves were in town. Understandably, "the whole community, both military and civil, drew a long breath of relief" when they were dispatched to Yorktown on June 10.[78]

The 14th Louisiana rivaled Coppens' Battalion for riotous behavior. While making its way to Virginia, the regiment turned a routine stop at Grand Junction, Tennessee, into a bloody fratricidal battle. During the layover, the regiment debarked from the train to stay overnight at a nearby camp. As a precaution, Colonel Sulakowski ordered the closure of all the liquor stores in town and posted guards to prevent the men from entering them. It is not known if he was aware that many of the soldiers were already inebriated. The men had smuggled aboard the train two barrels of whiskey, and some had jumped off the cars at previous stops to procure more.

At Grand Junction, a few soldiers lagged behind at the depot when the reg-

iment marched to the overnight camp and then circumvented Sulakowski's orders by slipping into bars through the back windows and getting drunk. When
they straggled into camp later, a fight erupted between members of two companies, which soon escalated into a general brawl involving more than one hundred men. Lieutenant Harry Myatt commanded the camp guard and arrested
some of the drunken instigators, but as he was escorting them to the town's jail
to sober up, other inebriated soldiers attacked the column with bowie knives
and tried to seize the guards' weapons. The outnumbered guards carried unloaded guns but fought back with bayonets and clubbed muskets. According
to Private Snakenberg, "Many of both guard and prisoners were clubbed
and cut with the bayonet and large knives which many soldiers carried."[79]

As the mob became uncontrollable, a pistol shot rang out from a lieutenant's revolver, followed in quick succession by others. Several mutineers
fell, but the surviving horde of screaming, cursing men chased the guards
into a nearby hotel and set fire to the building even though several hundred
civilians were also inside. Loyal soldiers and civilians were able to extinguish
the fire, but the rioters succeeded in breaking down the door. They "rushed in
like a mob of infuriated devils," one newspaper reported. "Drawers were torn
open, the contents were destroyed, the furniture was broken and pitched out,
the dining room table was thrown over and all the table furniture broken, the
chairs smashed to pieces, and such a general wreck you have never witnessed
in a civilized community."[80]

Snakenberg recalled that at that moment Colonel Sulakowski arrived "with
a revolver in each hand, and going into the crowd ordered first one, then another, to go back to the camp, and if the man spoken to did not turn immediately at the command and go, he shot him down." The outraged Sulakowski
screamed at the mutineers, "Go to your quarters!" When one man hesitated,
the colonel dropped him with a pistol ball. Another was shot in the face but
jumped back to his feet, spit out a tooth, and continued on his way. A sergeant
trying to help the officers control the men failed to move quickly enough for
Sulakowski and was mistaken for a rioter. The colonel killed the sergeant in
front of his wife, who had traveled to Grand Junction to visit him. According
to Snakenberg, a couple of officers were also shot, probably by Sulakoswki.[81]

The pistol-wielding Sulakowski soon cleared the hotel of rioters with the
help of other officers who followed his example. The battle then continued in
the streets for another hour, but finally, after seven men lay dead and nineteen

wounded, the mutineers were subdued. Surveying the carnage, one correspondent wrote, "The hotel looks like a hospital after a hard fought battle. The dead and wounded are strewn all over the second floor."[82]

The wounded men were left behind in Grand Junction to recover while the rest of the regiment continued on to Virginia. To prevent future disturbances, Sulakowski slapped a number of men in chains, but friends freed them. The colonel apparently decided not to press the issue, but he did telegraph the stations along the way to make sure the saloons were closed when they arrived, and he refused to allow the men to leave the train until it reached Knoxville, Tennessee. Once there, he shut them up inside a walled foundry and posted guards around the perimeter. Undeterred, some of the men still managed to slip out and get drunk. Snakenberg claimed they "tore one man's house partly down, got him out and rode him on a rail, because he refused to let them have more liquor. At that place the 14th La. were given the name of WILD CATS."[83]

And so it continued all the way to Richmond. At Bristol, Tennessee, the Wildcats were unable to find any liquor but did discover a container addressed to Gen. P. G. T. Beauregard and relieved it of some hams which they boiled and ate on the way to Lynchburg. There some of the men again hid out at the depot and got drunk, one to the point "so as to have fits." When he discovered this breach of discipline, Sulakowski whacked the drunks with the flat of his sword and sent them to the fairgrounds where the rest of the regiment was camped.[84]

Sulakowski was enraged over the various incidents, particularly the Grand Junction riot, and bitterly denounced several of his officers for allowing the situation to get out of hand. Once in Richmond, however, he had to face a court of inquiry, himself, to answer for his stern style of discipline. The army not only cleared Sulakowski of any wrongdoing but convicted several of his men of various misdeeds, shaved half their heads, and drummed them out of the service. Snakenberg said of these miscreants, "They went to Richmond, carried on as before, and we understand that they were soon killed by the citizens of Richmond." The Franco Rifle Guards (a company that was also involved in the Camp Walker, New Orleans, incident) was disbanded for being the major instigator of the Grand Junction riot. The secretary of war forced the company's officers to resign, and the enlisted men were distributed among the regiment's other companies.[85]

Wheat's Battalion left Camp Moore in mid-June and had its own violent escapade on the way to Virginia. After the war, while addressing a crowd, Col. William C. Oates recounted how some of Wheat's men seized control of a hotel and its saloon when their train stopped at Opelika, Alabama. When local authorities were unable to clear the building, they appealed to Major Wheat, who was asleep on the train. Wheat rushed over with his pistol drawn and ordered the men back on the train. All obeyed except a few who were led by two desperadoes. "Wheat shot both of them dead," Oates recalled. The colonel had known Major Wheat well during the war and explained, "He told me the only way to control his men was to shoot down those who disobeyed or defied him, yet they loved him with the fidelity of dogs."[86]

There apparently were other violent incidents involving Wheat's Battalion, but the details are not known. When the train pulled into Richmond, a member of the 18th Virginia claimed that "one freight car was pretty nearly full of [so-called] Louisiana 'Tigers' under arrest for disorderly conduct, drunkenness, etc., most of which were bucked and gag."[87]

The violent nature of the 14th Louisiana and Coppens' and Wheat's battalions convinced many people that all Louisiana soldiers were from the same mold. As word of their exploits spread, and as they continued their depredations in Virginia, civilians and soldiers, alike, began to fear and dread the Louisianians. Of course, the belief that all Louisianians were thieves, drunkards, and brawlers was wrong, for other units made the trip to Virginia without incident. Drinking was just as prevalent among the men, but it did not cause the trouble it did for Coppens, Sulakowski, and Wheat. Lieutenant Colonel Charles de Choiseul of the 7th Louisiana wrote that his regiment "rattled quietly along, for a couple of days, nothing more exciting happening than the contest between the officers, & a portion of the men. The latter seemingly bent on trying the experiment of how much whiskey they could consume, while the former were endeavoring to make them members of the total abstinence society."[88]

Even when the men behaved themselves, traveling by train during the Civil War posed enough risks in itself. The multinational 10th Louisiana lost five men on the trip to Virginia. Three foreign-born men were killed after falling off the train in separate incidents: a German fell underneath the train and lost his arm, and a native Louisianian broke his leg and suffered an amputation.[89]

Despite the dangers, for most Louisianians the journey to Virginia was a pleasant experience, with civilians jubilantly welcoming them to their towns and hailing them as heroes. An anonymous member of the 1st Louisiana wrote: "The enthusiasm manifested all along the road, and the attentions and hospitalities showered upon us amount to a perfect ovation. The ladies threw up bouquets and presented us with flags, and the men cheered us most lustily. The bewitching ladies of Amite City, particularly, will ever be remembered by every man of our corps. Hundreds of bouquets were handed in the cars, and pinned to each was a note written by fair and delicate hands, in such eloquent words as cheered the hearts of all and showed us that if we aspired to their smiles, we must first show that we are men, if not heroes."[90]

B. C. Cushman, also of the 1st Louisiana, claimed that, when they passed through Tennessee, "At every little town and village, the inhabitants (especially the ladies) greeted us with cheers and welcomed us to their soil, opened their doors to us all and treated us to the best fare they had without charging any one a single cent." After crossing into Virginia, the regiment was treated "more in the manner of the Prince of Wales than as common soldiers." Sometimes the officers wired ahead to the next station to alert the citizens of their impending arrival, and by the time the train arrived "we would find [the town] thronged with ladies moving their hand-kerchiefs, tossing us flowers, and bidding us to be of good cheer, and fight like brave fellows." Similar receptions greeted other Louisiana commands all the way to Virginia.[91]

For soldiers like Private Cushman, the spring of 1861 was an exciting time when war was still glorious—and bloodless. Within a few months, it was believed, the Yankees would be vanquished and the gray-clad warriors of the Pelican State would be returning to Louisiana in victory. The only concern for most of the men was to reach the contested field before peace broke out.

CHAPTER 2

The Louisiana Tigers

W HEN THE LOUISIANA SOLDIERS arrived in Virginia, they were quickly dispatched to the two critical military theaters—to the northern Potomac District around Manassas and Centreville to help block any Union advance from Washington and to the southeast on the Virginia Peninsula formed by the James and York rivers to check the enemy at Fort Monroe. By summer's end the 6th, 7th, 8th, and 9th Louisiana, Wheat's Battalion, and the independent companies of Maj. Henry St. Paul (1st Company of Foot Rifles) and Capt. McGavock Goodwyn (Crescent City Blues, Company B) were assigned to the Potomac District eighty miles north of Richmond. These commands were placed in several different brigades, with St. Paul's and Goodwyn's companies being temporarily attached to the New Orleans Washington Artillery and the 49th Virginia Infantry, respectively. In August, however, the four regiments and Wheat's Battalion were designated the 8th Brigade under Gen. William H. T. Walker of Georgia, and in October, St. Paul's and Goodwyn's companies were formed into a battalion known as St. Paul's Foot Rifles and transferred to the Peninsula to serve in Col. Micah Jenkins' brigade. Meanwhile, on the Peninsula, the 1st, 2nd, 5th, 10th, and 14th Louisiana and Coppens' and Dreux's battalions were put in Gen. John Bankhead Magruder's command. They were placed in several small brigades and were often shifted from point to point and reassigned to various commanders.[1]

The 2nd Louisiana was stationed at Yorktown, and the men often acted more like tourists than soldiers in the historic town. In describing his duty station to his mother, Thomas Phifer wrote: " It is distinguished in the history of our country as the place where the last battle of the revolution was fought—where Cornwallis surrendered his sword. . . . Many houses have the holes still in them made by Washington's cannon. We have built upon the

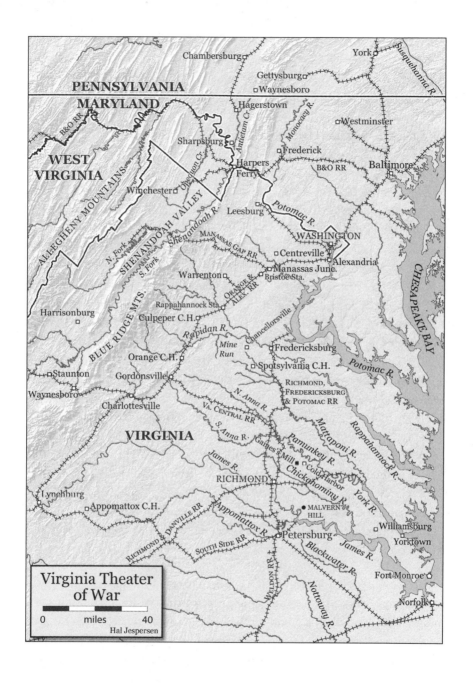

Virginia Theater
of War

0   miles   40

Hal Jespersen

same breastworks that Cornwallis threw up, and rendered them much more effectual, and we have Southern Soldiers to stand behind them—therefore, we may hope for something better than his fate. . . . There are many interesting relics to be found. We dig up human bones in throwing up breastworks. We find pieces of bomb shells and swords."[2]

Unfortunately, the sightseeing soldiers also absconded with numerous historical documents. One newspaper printed a letter from an anonymous Louisianian who reported: "The old brick building, occupied by General Washington, as head quarters, still stands, strong and substantial, and is in many places, deeply marked by cannon balls. Many old papers—more than an hundred and ten years old—have been picked by our soldiers, found in it, and some with the old General's own signature to them. They are greatly prized.—I was fortunate enough to find one written by General Washington to General La Fayette, dated Nov. 17, 1775; and were I to offer it to the highest bidder, there is no telling what it would bring, yet strange to say, there were hundreds of old letters, dating quite as far back, and several written by General Washington himself. The soldiers now have them all."[3]

The Louisianians came to Virginia expecting quickly to engage the enemy, rout them in a great battle, and return home to a victory parade and a heroes' welcome. Since no forethought was given to the more mundane aspects of army life, the monotony of soldiering came as a complete shock. "Dull, dull, dull," is the way William E. Moore of Dreux's Battalion described the realities of campaigning.[4] Leon Jastremski, an eighteen-year-old native of France who served in the 10th Louisiana, complained to a friend of his daily routine:

Reveille at 5 o'clock a.m. Roll call. Then we cook our breakfast which of course we are supposed to eat. Half past eight, guard mounting, which is equal to a small parade as it each day consists of 40 men, 1 Lieut., 1 sergt. & 3 corporals. At 9 o'clock company drill until 10 o'clock, after which we are free until 12 o'clock when we have dinner call, after which comes what is called fatigue duty which means Spades and [*illegible*] and when there is no digging to be done, we have to clean up Quarters. After which we are again free until 6 o'clock. Then dress parade & dismiss [to] cook our supper, eat, loaf & spin yarns until 9 o'clock when tattoo beats & are all sent to bed like a parcel of schoolboys. . . . This occurring every day makes it very tiresome.[5]

Although the men complained about the seemingly constant drill and lack of free time, for some the worst part of military life was preparing for each day's routine. The 9th Louisiana's Sgt. Edmond Stephens described a typical morning to a friend:

About one hour before the brake of day you are interrupted by a loud beating of a base drum which they call revile. You then at once rise & on double quick time drag on your old dust wallowed coat, & as for your pants it [is] contrary to the rules of camp to take them off during the hours of rest. You then lay an old wool hat on your head which [you] have picked up in the road while traveling up on some wild march & it having been refused to be owned by some layboring Negro. You then lay your feet into a pair of Shoe soles without any uper leather being attached to them. You start with said clothing around you with the speed of some wild flying fowl for the parade ground to answer your name at Roll call. You then proceed to kindle you a fire with a few sticks of wood which was hauld [to] you [a] number of miles, & that [is] nearly imposible with me because there [is] not the first splinter of lightwood here. . . . By chance you get you a little smothered fire to burning, then aply your cooking utensils which are near nothing, iron mashed to geather. . . . You take from the pan some burnt biscuit without either salt, flour or water in them & from said kettle you take a little beefs ncck boil[ed] without any water. You then seat yourself with four or five of your filthy handed, snot nosed, frisele headed mess mates which would seem to white men not only to be wild but naturally breathed filth & after this is finished about one third are detailed to guard the others & keep them all to wollern in one hole as if they were a parcel of hogs.[6]

Al Pierson's experiences in the 9th Louisiana led him to attempt to talk his younger brother out of enlisting because he did not think the teenager could tolerate the daily grind. "[Y]ou are put on guard once at least every 2 weeks and have to be up all night and day and out in the weather rain or shine. You have your own cooking to do, your gun to keep as bright as silver and your quarters swept out perfectly clean. You have to sleep on the ground or some leaves or grass which you may pick up, and lastly if sick you have nothing except fat meat and baked bread to eat unless you should meet with a very kind mess mate to care for you which is hard to find. Such is a true soldier['s] life—pause and think before you go farther."[7]

Although the army had obviously lost its appeal for Stephens and Pierson, they were proud of some of their newly found talents. Before coming to Virginia, most of the men had little experience in cooking and housekeeping— two tasks that were now required daily. Stephens proudly boasted, "I can just stack the world a cooking. I can bake a plate of bisquit without any water, fire or flour." Apparently, the men did not worry about the usual drudgery of washing up after meals because one of Stephens' messmates remarked that "the general rule in camp is not to wash the dishes as long as you can recollect what was in them last."[8]

Cooking was a duty the Louisianians accepted because it was an accomplishment in which they could take pride. More demanding, and insulting, was the constant digging of earthworks. Charles I. Batchelor, an eighteen-year-old member of the 2nd Louisiana's Atchafalaya Guards, declared, "The sound of spade and axe handled by individuals who never before dreamed of becoming experienced in an art so extremely fatiguing and unprofitable would remind a visitor of the Sable Sons of Africa felling timbers for their masters . . . . Among those becoming experienced in the use of the spade you might find your humble sevt." Henry C. Monier of the 10th Louisiana wrote in his diary that "spades and pickaxes [were] so disgustingly plentiful that the mere sight of them was enough to send men to the hospital." Such exhausting work caused some of the more affluent soldiers to reflect upon times past. Lieutenant Alfred Flournoy, another weary member of the 2nd Louisiana, promised his wife, "If I ever get home I will give the negroes a heap more Saturday evenings than I ever did before. Bless the name of Saturday."[9]

The worst problem in the Virginia camps was not the drilling or manual labor but the threat of disease. During their first year of military service, disease struck down more Louisianians than Yankee bullets. On Christmas Day, a depressed George Wren noted in his diary that he had been in the army with the 8th Louisiana since the war began but had not seen any combat. "[Y]et many of my *best* friends have been snatched away by the *cold hand of death*." Exposure and crowded, unsanitary living conditions were the major causes of sickness. When performing picket duty, men were often required to live for days at a time without any shelter, and even in permanent camps they had only flimsy tents that offered little protection against the elements. Once near Manassas the men of the 7th Louisiana were drenched and battered when a violent wind destroyed their camp. The soldiers were on the parade ground when the storm hit and rushed back to camp in a futile attempt to save their quarters. When the weather system passed, many of the tents lay collapsed, and clothes, equipment, and other personal items were strewn in every direction. Despite their predicament, W. G. Ogden recalled that it was amusing to see "officers' heads every now and then popping up from admist the ruin."[10]

More substantial housing was finally constructed when the harsh Virginia winter set in. Most of the Louisianians were unused to such cold weather but proved quite adept at building winter quarters of logs and mud. Ogden wrote his father, "The extreme cold here brought out all the house building knowledge our Regiment possessed. With astonishing rapidity the La. Regiments have felled almost all the trees for miles around."[11] An anonymous reporter for the Richmond *Daily Dispatch* visited the winter camp of St. Paul's Foot Rifles near Norfolk in January 1862 and wrote a descriptive account of the cabins:

> The cabins, about forty in number, were built in the form of a square, leaving a large and level compass or parade ground in the centre. They were uniform in size and appearance, 30 by 20 feet, having capacious fire places, fine brick chimneys, and, in a majority of cases, glass windows and half glass doors. The roofs were covered with shingles made by the men, the battalion having drawn from the Government brick for their chimneys, instead of shingles. Inside there was some similarity in the arrangement of furniture, although that was left entirely to the taste and desire of the men. It was optional with them to sleep in double or single beds, to have the bunks, arranged like steamboat berths, as double beds, as in ordinary houses, or like the single cots of a hospital ward. . . . The beds were neatly made up and had a plenty of warm and cleanly looking blankets, furnished, I was told, by the State of Louisiana in every house there was a table, several constructed cupboards, board chairs, rocking chairs, sofas, ottomans, and in one instance I saw a charming tete-a-tete setting before a blazing pine-knot fire. All had racks upon one side for the arms, and a cleaner, brighter set of muskets I have never seen in the Army since I commenced writ-

ing about it, more than 12 months age [sic]. . . . In one was a miniature steamboat, which had been carved by some skillful volunteer.[12]

The building of so many cabins had a serious impact on the area's ecology. Ogden reported that the countryside took on "the appearance . . . of one immense plantation." Sergeant Pierson, whose regiment was camped nearby, also wrote of the adverse effect that thousands of men cutting wood for campfires and huts had on the neighborhood. "Wood is quite scarce," he informed his father, "and in a few days there will not be a single oak tree in sight of camps; we will have to haul wood a mile or more." After returning from a short furlough home, Lt. Edward Seton was surprised at how much the landscape had changed on the Peninsula during his absence. He wrote his mother in early 1862, "Aperences are quite changed here all the brest works have been removed & all the timber cut down."[13]

The winter quarters may have been comfortable, but they were also crowded—a sixteen-by-twelve-foot structure often lodging as many as eight soldiers. Although protecting the men from the elements, the cabins also helped spread disease because the soldiers were often confined in their small huts for long periods of time during bad weather. Lice were another constant torment because they inevitably took up permanent residence with the men. George Zeller of the 6th Louisiana's Violet Guards informed his mother that "them under Clothes will do me for some time for my others I had to burn my Clothes up on the acount of those horrible things they call lise."[14]

The stale air and cramped living space made the soldiers particularly susceptible to such contagious diseases as mumps and measles, and the unsanitary practices of waste disposal spawned outbreaks of typhoid and dysentery. The soldiers' latrines, or "sinks," were dug two hundred yards from the camps but only consisted of an open ditch with a fresh layer of dirt thrown over the contents each morning. At best, such accommodations were a health hazard, and many of the undisciplined men refused to use even these rudimentary facilities. The regiments camped around Manassas also had to contend with unburied horses and poorly buried soldiers from the July battle. The 7th Louisiana camped along Bull Run after the fight, but dead horses polluted the water and the men complained of the foul odor. When two-thirds of the soldiers were placed on the sick list in August suffering from fever and diarrhea, the regimental surgeon blamed it on the "decomposition of dead Yankees."[15]

Typhoid, pneumonia, and measles were the primary killers of Louisiana's soldiers, but numerous ailments can be found on the sick lists. The 7th Louisiana's hospital ledger shows that 645 men out of a total regimental strength of 920 were taken ill during August 1861. By month's end most of the sick had returned to duty, but 62 soldiers were forwarded to a general hospital, 15 were discharged from the service, and 3 died. Acute diarrhea was the most common complaint, but medical discharges were also given for hernias, epilepsy, lead poisoning, syphilis, opium addiction, old age (sixty-two years old), under age (sixteen years old), and idiocy. In addition to medical discharges, some soldiers were also dismissed on suspicion of being disloyal. Lieutenant Seton reported that 5 men in the 10th Louisiana were so discharged.[16]

All of the Louisiana commands suffered heavily from disease in the summer of 1861. During August, 239 of 421 men in Wheat's Battalion and 276 out of 623 in Dreux's Battalion were on the sick list. Of the 600 men in Coppens' Battalion, fewer than 100 were fit for duty that September. No other unit, however, matched the farm boys of Richard Taylor's 9th Louisiana in falling victim to epidemics. By August, nearly 100 soldiers had died or been medically discharged, and so many others were sick that the regiment could barely muster 300 men for duty. Pierson wrote his brother that "the boys have suffered almost incredibly from disease. [My company] had as many as 50 cases either on the sick roll or left behind on the road for more than a week in succession and . . . we have only 16 or 18 men to drill after deducting those for guard service." Immediately after writing this letter, Pierson was stricken with typhoid fever and laid up for nearly two months.[17]

Everyone hoped cooler weather would slow the raging epidemics, but it only brought severe cases of pneumonia. That winter, six men in Sergeant Pierson's Bienville Blues contracted the dreaded illness and died within a three-week period. Company member Richard Colbert claimed that death had become so commonplace that "the death of one of our poor soldiers is hardly noticed. One of the Bossier [Parish] boys died day before yesterday and one of ours yesterday and it seemed to me that it was not noticed no more than if a dog had died." The high rate of sickness and death in the 9th Louisiana illustrates how supposedly hardy farm boys usually fell victim to disease at a higher rate than city dwellers. Living in sparsely populated rural areas, the country lads had not been exposed to infectious diseases as much as their city brethren. For many, the crowded Virginia camps provided their first contact with smallpox, mumps, and measles while most urban soldiers had survived some of these diseases and were now immune. Both regiments served in the same brigade, but during the war 349 men (23.6 percent) in the 9th Louisiana died from disease while the urban 6th Louisiana lost only 104 men (9 percent). This loss ratio holds true for other rural and urban regiments. (See the appendix for details.)[18]

Regimental surgeons desperately tried to alleviate the suffering, but their primitive cures did little good, and crowded, unsanitary hospitals often made patients worse. Suffering from typhoid fever, Sergeant Stephens complained from his hospital bed that "we get nothing to eat but bread and coffee, [and] in addition to that it is very filthy and nasty." The 5th Louisiana's Theodore Mandeville echoed Stephens' sentiments when he wrote of his liver ailment, "I believe these damn quacks we have got for Drs. in this regt. are doing me more harm than good. They know nothing but Calomel & Quinine. . . . Yesterday they dosed me with Elixor of Vitriol and today, intend giving me Iodine of Potash & paint me in the region of the liver with Iodine which burns like the devil." Soldiers serving on the Peninsula fared little better. The 14th Louisiana's Lt. Field F. Montgomery informed President Jefferson Davis in February 1862 that typhoid had ravaged his company to the point that only four men were still healthy. "The Regimental Surgeon," Montgomery declared, "seems unable to treat the disease successfully. . . . The men have become alarmed and very much dispirited. The disease advances steadily on & every man seems doomed to fall before its fatal stroke."[19]

Like the soldiers in Montgomery's company, Sergeant Pierson also became disillusioned because of the ever-present disease. He wrote his father in November:

> I have heard and as often read the famous stories of the Revolutionary days, the pleasures & the miseries of camp life depicted by the ablest pens of that day & the stories rehearsed by every mother to her prattling boy of the great deeds performed by his ancestors in the great struggle for independence. To all of these have I listened while my imagination was conjuring up a thousand horrid pictures of fields strewn with dead and groaning wounded—with blood standing upon the ground in puddles or trickling down the hillside in small streams. All these have I fancied to be the scenes of a soldier[']s life. But now I

have experienced the true life of a soldier. I find them quite different from what I had always believed them to be. Go to the hospitals and there see every kind of disease that preys upon the human system, devouring men as fast as coffins can be made by a large factory or shrouds by a large clothing establishment, to inter them. See men with some contagious disease lying upon the cold wet ground an[d] in the rain till life cannot be their lot but a few short hours. I shall never, no never forget the scenes of 1861.[20]

Accidental shootings and brawls were another danger the new recruits faced in the crowded camps. On the Peninsula, the 14th Louisiana's Pvt. John Zimmerman was accidentally shot and killed on the picket line. According to William Snakenberg, the picket shot Zimmerman "because he ran across his guard line in the night and did not halt when challenged." After one man in the 2nd Louisiana accidentally shot his sleeping messmate, orders were issued that soldiers on duty had to keep their muskets on half-cock for safety purposes and then uncap them when off duty.[21]

Such violent incidents seemed to have been more prevalent around Manassas than on the Peninsula. Four men in the Tiger Rifles company were killed between July 16 and October 4, and an officer accidentally shot himself in the camp of the 6th Louisiana on the night of October 3. According to William Trahern, "Four or five drinking Irishmen were in the habit of coming into camp late at night, and in a drunken condition, making life hideous. One night they broke the record for bacchanalian revelry, and it took nearly the whole Company D to stop them." Captain Charles B. Tenney of the Calhoun Guards felt threatened by the drunks and grabbed his pistol by the barrel to use as a club. Unfortunately, the pistol went off and shot Tenney in the stomach. He died two hours later. Two weeks later, another killing occurred when Tiger Rifles Pvt. John Travers stabbed to death Pvt. James McCormack of the 6th Louisiana in a brawl. Travers was held for murder but released several months later when the stabbing was ruled accidental. He eventually was discharged from the service with $226.50 in back pay.[22]

Later in the war, after having survived a number of major battles, Al Pierson made reference to the accidental shootings in a letter home. After discussing the hard fighting that had occurred in the Chancellorsville Campaign, he claimed that his 9th Louisiana company had been in the thickest of all the regiment's battles but had suffered the fewest casualties. Pierson attributed it to the prayers of family members and the fact that the company was made up of country boys who knew firearm safety. "Our men are all accustomed to the use of fire arms and do not shoot each other, while other companies (at least some of them) have foreigners mixed up with them, who are as awkward with a gun as a ten year old boy and consequently are greater to be feared than our enemies."[23]

As the military hospitals began to fill with sick and wounded soldiers, many Louisianians were sent to the homes of civilians who volunteered to care for them. Sanitary conditions were better there, and those men fortunate enough to be taken in had a much better chance for survival than those in the army hospitals. A welcomed result of this civilian care was the many friendships and romances that blossomed between the Louisianians and the Virginia girls who nursed them. Correspondence throughout the war mentions girlfriends, many of whom were met during times of illness. Sergeant Stephens wrote in early 1864, "There is hardly a young man in our company but what has a Virginia sweetheart—at any rate a friend correspondent in Va." He added, "We get a great many articles of clothing in that way." Apparently clothing was not all the Louisianians received. In the back of his diary, Boling Williams listed three prescriptions for gonorrhea—one paste and two injections.[24]

Some of the men were not completely honorable in their relationships with the Virginia girls. The Richmond *Daily Dispatch* warned its readers in 1863 that soldiers with wives back home were marrying unsuspecting local women. As an example, it cited an anonymous Louisiana officer who wrote two long, affectionate letters to his wives in Louisiana and Virginia and then put them into the wrong envelopes.[25]

As time passed, the disease, monotony, and for some men, the shock and horror of combat at Manassas, caused the soldiers to lose their youthful enthusiasm for war and long to return home. On the Peninsula, Benjamin Smith told of changing attitudes in the 5th Louisiana:

> We all take things rather easy now. . . . Not so much gas about exterminating unfortunate yankees, and a great deal more solicitude about our bodies wants and comforts. Once we waked up in the dead of night to repel an expected attack. We were assigned to a certain post and instead of waiting with breathless expectations for the ruthless invader,

as the newspapers would express it, all the men just rolled themselves in their blankets and went to sleep with many an expression of pity for the poor devils, who should have to be tramping toward us that time of night. . . . I loaded my musket once or twice with the expectation of hurting somebody, but was disappointed. . . . As for my bayonet it had only been stained by the blood of a unfortunate pig, who was foolish enough to tempt a hungry soldier. I devoutly hope, that, he was a Yankee pig.[26]

How well the soldiers adjusted to military life in Virginia greatly depended on their mental condition and physical comfort. When things back home were going badly or when food and clothing ran short, they naturally longed to return to Louisiana. The spring of 1862, in particular, was a time of depressing homesickness when news of New Orleans' capture reached the soldiers. Lt. Robert H. Miller spoke for many when he wrote that his physical suffering "is nothing to the mental anxiety I have undergone since the whole state of Louisiana has been abandoned to the enemy." General Lafayette McLaws noted that his Louisianians openly displayed their feelings of grief and that several officers begged him for permission to go home "as the enemy were in New Orleans and their 'wives and children would be homeless wandering on the face of the earth.'" The soldiers apparently vented their anger more on Gen. Mansfield Lovell, who lost the city, than on Union Gen. Benjamin Butler, who ruthlessly ruled over it. Edward Randolph wrote a friend that "it does seem to me that there was a screw loose somewhere" in the city's defense, and another soldier declared that "curses 'not loud but deep,' are freely bestowed upon Gen'l Lovell." Some men, like Col. Isaac Seymour, even believed treasonous activity might have caused the city's loss. He wrote, "[In camp] there is no mincing of words in giving expression to those opinions and feelings."[27]

During their first year in Virginia, the Louisianians could attribute little homesickness to shortages in food and clothing. Unlike later times when the Confederate soldier was usually ill-clothed and poorly fed, the men enjoyed a fairly comfortable first year. In July 1861, Caddo Parish sent $1,500 each to its four companies to buy supplies, and that autumn the 9th Louisiana received several large shipments of goods from home. One delivery contained twelve cases of blankets, 872 pairs of drawers, four hundred flannel shirts, four hundred jackets, four hundred pairs of pants, and twenty-two dozen pairs of socks.

Along with these regimental supplies were numerous bundles addressed to individual soldiers. Typical of these was the one received by Robert L. Tanner containing three towels, two blankets, one pillow, a pair of pants, a pocket-knife, a necktie, a cake of soap, a comb, and a bottle of medicine.[28]

Food was usually plentiful, and few complaints were made about its quality or quantity. The 2nd Louisiana's B. C. Cushman wrote from Norfolk, "We fare finely here, get more vegetables, and strawberries and cream than we know what to do with. I think this is the greatest vegetable market in the world. And besides we get any quantity of fish of every description. I am living and growing fat on oysters and soft shell crabs." Near Centreville, Sergeant Pierson informed his father that the commissary provided "plenty of fat beef, and enough bacon for about 2 days in every week—we also draw a small ration of sugar & coffee enough for to make a cupful per day to each man. As for breadstuffs we have more than we use a portion of which is cornmeal."[29]

Sometimes the men were sent into the surrounding area to collect food for the commissary department. In November, the 10th Louisiana participated in what the men called the "corn campaign," a two-week period in which they marched eight miles to and from a cornfield near Bethel each day to collect corn. The regiment and several other units loaded as many as two hundred wagons with corn each day, but the work was hard. Phifer wrote his mother, "For thirteen days and nights we slept without tents and only a blanket when the ponds presented a sheet of ice every morning. But so well have we become inured to such exposure that we slept sound every night and without any inconvenient sensation of cold."[30]

The 1861 holiday season seems to have been an especially bountiful time. At Centreville, Richard Taylor hosted a Christmas dinner for his officers while the enlisted men enjoyed a smorgasbord of delights. The 7th Louisiana's Henry Caldwell wrote in his diary, "[W]e had a baked turkey stuffed with oysters a cold cabbage slaw. Boiled cabbage and corn beef rice boiled oyster stewed and coffee after dinner all enjoyed ourselves very well." New Year's Day saw another feast, and Caldwell "baked the turkey stuffed with oyster and I made oyster stewe we had plenty of cabbage and fresh pork nicely fried."[31]

Alcohol also flowed freely around Centreville during the 1861 Christmas season thanks to the 7th Louisiana's Thomas Kennedy. He went to Gordonsville on Christmas Eve and bought eleven gallons of whiskey for three dollars a gallon and sold it at camp for eight dollars a gallon. The next day Charlton claimed, "Most every one had head ache from the effects of last night." Sergeant Pierson and his comrades in the 9th Louisiana also had easy access to spirits. He wrote his brother, "On the night before Christmas my mess had a nice little nogg and on the next our kind Lieut gave a nogg to the company which the boys appreciated highly indeed. Some of them got as funny as you please and the whole day was a scene of merriment seldom witnessed in camp." George Zeller and his messmates in the 6th Louisiana moved into their newly finished cabin on New Year's Day and celebrated by making two buckets of egg nog from a gallon of whiskey. "[W]e stayed up most all night drinking and A sining [singing?] then we went to bed." Such drinking apparently was just as prevalent among the Louisianians on the Peninsula because the 2nd Louisiana's Thomas Phifer wrote his mother, "We had a very dull Christmas here, at least the sober list did. Some of the boys who were inebriated seemed to enjoy themselves very much for awhile but many of them were quartered in the guard house before the close of the day."[32]

An exception to the general rule of bountiful supplies can be found in some of the units stationed on the Peninsula. Hiram Sample, a member of St. Paul's Foot Rifles, reported tough times from the very beginning. "When we arrived in Richmond, for a hat, I had a pants leg cut off and sewed together at the top for a hat; a red undershirt, no top shirt, a pair of pants that needed repairs badly and an apology for shoes. And the balance of the army were about the same condition." While at Yorktown in June, Phifer claimed he had so little to eat that he sometimes slipped past the sentinels to hunt hogs with his pistol, and the men in the 5th Louisiana were so destitute in early 1862 that they began referring to their bivouac area as Camp Starvation.[33]

Because of the abundance of food around Manassas, enlisted men and officers alike often held large, elaborate dinners. Major Roberdeau Wheat became famous for his gourmet meals, and he and Col. Frederick A. Skinner of the 1st Virginia engaged in a friendly contest to see who was the better cook. Skinner found it difficult to top Wheat's "cabeza de buey al ranchero"—an ox head, with skin and horns intact, covered in a pit of coals and baked like a potato. To prepare the meal, Wheat decapitated an ox, sewed the loose skin over the neck cut, and buried the head in the coals at tattoo. At next morning's reveille, Skinner returned to watch the unearthing: "The head, when dug up and brought into the tent covered with ashes and dirt, was, I think, about as repulsive an object as my eyes ever beheld, but giving out a most appetizing odor. The dirt and ashes were brushed off and the skin and horns speedily and skillfully removed, and lo! a metamorphosis occurred . . . . We had before us a dish as grateful to the eye as it was to the nostrils." After stuffing themselves, Wheat's guests declared that the unusual breakfast was a "gastronomic triumph" and proclaimed the major to be a culinary genius. Wheat's hospitality did not end there. In the autumn of 1861 he hosted a "Tiger Dinner" for Gens. Joseph E. Johnston, Jubal Early, Gustavus Smith, and Earl Van Dorn. While the generals wined and dined inside, Wheat's men got roaring drunk outside and spent the night racing around the banquet tent on the generals' horses.[34]

In February 1862, the Louisianians in northern Virginia again entertained their comrades by sponsoring a Grand Military Ball at their Camp Carondelet. Tickets cost ten dollars (privates earned just thirteen dollars a month), but admission apparently was free to women. Elaborate handbills promoted the event, and the officers listed as "managers" constituted a veritable who's who. It included Gens. E. Kirby Smith, Arnold Elzey, Isaac R. Trimble, and Richard Taylor and Major Wheat.[35]

From the time of their arrival in Virginia, the Louisiana soldiers were the objects of bemused curiosity. Citizens and soldiers alike were fascinated by their colorful uniforms, multinational makeup, and use of the French language. After watching Wheat's Battalion drill one day, an Alabama soldier wrote that "they went at double quick charge Bayonets. They yell like a pack of hounds making the most frightful noise I ever heard." A Georgian who saw a Louisiana officer put his men through battalion drill did not understand French and declared, "That-thur furriner *he* calls out er lot er gibberish, an them-thur Dagoes jes maneuver-up like Hell-beatin' tanbark! Jes' like he was talkin' sense!" The 15th Alabama's William Oates, who enjoyed watching Sulakowski drill the 14th Louisiana, agreed. Oates recalled, "The foreign accent of Sooli Koski and the alacrity and precision with which his men obeyed his commands, not a word of which we could understand, presented a good entertainment for the edification of our officers and men." To integrate the Louisianians more fully into the command structure, Confederate authorities eventually ordered them to abandon the use of French and to adopt English commands, but it is not known exactly how it was done. When one regiment in Louisiana was ordered to do so, an Irish soldier declared to his commander, "Leftenant, I don't know what oi'll do. You want us to drill in English, and the divil a wurd I know but French."[36]

General McLaws, under whom the 10th Louisiana was placed, found it difficult even to communicate with that regiment's officers. The unit was led by forty-nine-year-old Col. Mandeville Marigny, the son-inlaw of Louisiana's first governor, William C. C. Claiborne, and the son of one of the Crescent City's wealthiest men. The French had invited the New Orleans native to study at the Saumur Military College as a young man, and he had served in the French cavalry until his involvement in a duel caused him to resign his commission. Marigny then returned to Louisiana to manage his father's plantations. He was said to have been the epitome of the suave French Creole in both looks and behavior.[37]

When war erupted, Marigny organized the 10th Louisiana and adopted the French drill manual for the regiment. His men hailed from twenty-two nations and eighteen states. Native Louisianians were a majority in only two of the ten companies, and most of them spoke French. In Virginia, the 10th Louisiana was sometimes incorrectly referred to as a Zouave unit. Only one company may have worn the Zouave uniform, but at least some of the officers did wear red caps and striped pants that may have led to the confusion. Consisting of soldiers from so many nations, the 10th Louisiana seemed to be a regiment from Babel with the strange, bewildering jabbering of its members. When Marigny and his adjutant first reported to McLaws, the resultant interview was difficult because of this language barrier. Immediately afterward, the general wrote his wife, "Indeed, the Colonel & Adjutant who have just left my tent speak English but indifferently well. The Adjutant did not say much. I think but two words & I do not believe he can talk English."[38]

For the most part, the Virginia people welcomed these strange soldiers from the Deep South and appreciated their service. The women of Williamsburg even made and presented a flag to the 5th Louisiana, and the appreciative regiment turned out and drilled for them. Because it was the first time the ladies had presented a flag to a non-Virginia unit, Charles Moore declared, "We should prize it only the more." The 5th Louisiana seems to have been particularly popular with the locals because another flag was presented to the regiment's Perret Guards. Some Baltimore women made this flag, and Mrs. John James smuggled it to Jamestown and presented it to the company in a ceremony attended by First Lady Varina Davis and Vice-President Alexander Stephens. The Williamsburg ladies also made a First National Flag for Company B in Coppens' Battalion that was later donated to the Museum of the Confederacy in Richmond.[39]

In appreciation of the support they had received, the Louisianians entertained the people of Williamsburg on several occasions. In early 1862, Dreux's Battalion put on a "burlesque circus" for the locals, and during the carnival season about two hundred of the battalion's men held a Mardi Gras parade for the town. Materials for costumes were gathered from all over Williamsburg, and on Mardi Gras day a long, wild procession wound through the streets and halted at General Magruder's headquarters. As a practical joke, Billy Campbell, one of Dreux's men, dressed as a girl and strode gracefully into Magruder's office on the arm of Ned Phelps, another battalion member. Phelps very properly introduced his escort to the unsuspecting general and claimed that the baby-faced Campbell was the sister of one of the battalion's soldiers. The gallant Magruder quickly took the "lady's" hand and began entertaining Campbell with food, drink, and lively conversation. During this interlude, other battalion members entered the room above Magruder, ripped apart a feather mattress and shoveled the feathers through cracks in the floor. Magruder was covered with feathers, and the men laughed and yelled that it was a "Louisiana snowstorm!" While the confused Magruder tried to make sense of it all, Campbell and Phelps quietly slipped away, leaving the puzzled general standing alone amid his Louisiana "snow."[40]

Ned Phelps, the ringleader of the Mardi Gras caper, had another encounter with Magruder on the Peninsula. During a night march, Phelps slipped away from the battalion to forage and at daybreak came upon a farmhouse where Magruder and his staff were sitting down to breakfast. Seeing a vacant chair, the private plopped down as well and hungrily eyed the meal. Amazed at the soldier's gall, Magruder leaned back in his chair and asked, "Young man, are you aware whom you are breakfasting with?" "Well," mused Phelps, "before I came soldiering I used to be particular whom I ate with, but now I don't care a damn—so [long as] the victuals are clean." Magruder appreciated this honest retort and declared, "Young man, stay where you are and have what you want." Despite his begrudging admiration of Phelps' style, Magruder must have had his fill of the impetuous soldier because in June 1862 he approved a transfer for Phelps to the Washington Artillery.[41]

According to Sgt. John F. Charlton of the 5th Louisiana, practical jokes like the one Ned Phelps pulled on Magruder were common. "The boys alive to everything seized every opportunity to perpetrate jokes upon one another, to relieve the monotonous life we were then leading." Charlton told how Pvt. Robert E. Lott once spent all of his money buying treats for the men in an attempt to get elected lieutenant. When told that he had won, Lott added a lieutenant's bar to his uniform and took his new charges out to drill. However, when he ordered the men to form a skirmish line, they surprised him by running back to camp. It then dawned on Lott that he had not been elected after all. "Poor fellow," Charlton wrote, "although not possessed of sound sense he was a good soldier. brave to a fault." Lott survived being shot through the body and legs at Second Fredericksburg but died from smallpox in Point Lookout prison after being captured at Spotsylvania.[42]

Charlton also recalled a mock duel that was fought between John "Big Feet" Trust and William "Nosey" Bunce. Bunce often bragged about his connection to duelists, and Charlton admitted that there "was pluck in him." When Trust challenged Bunce over some insult, Bunce accepted and wrote some farewell letters just in case he was killed. Unknown to Bunce, the duel was a joke and the guns were loaded with blanks. When the command was given, both men fired, Trust fell to the ground, and Bunce immediately ran away. "After a great deal of search," Charlton wrote, "he was found hid away in the loft of his house, not a little overjoyed at finding it all a joke."[43]

Numerous sources indicate that the Louisianians had a well-developed sense of humor and that they made many friends in Virginia. However, there were enough criminals and poorly disciplined soldiers in the units to taint everyone's reputation. Some of the Louisiana commands on the Peninsula openly killed livestock and created havoc in any town unlucky enough to be located near one of their camps. Members of Dreux's Battalion and the 5th Louisiana publicly bayoneted hogs, and McLaws once claimed that, in the twelve hours the 10th Louisiana was camped on Jamestown Island, its members "eat up every living thing on the Island but two horses and their own species." The Richmond provost marshal's record of arrests for this time also shows numerous Louisiana soldiers being arrested for robbery, desertion, forgery, and drawing double pay through fraudulent means. Louisianians were even accused of destroying Gunston Hall, the historic Mount Vernon home of Founding Father George Mason.[44]

The 14th Louisiana, in particular, continued its violent ways despite Colonel Sulakowski's harsh discipline. While camped on the Peninsula, some of the men made their way to Richmond and indulged in a spree of drunkenness and robbery. Private Snakenberg claimed civilians killed several of the soldiers, and that the others were convicted of various crimes, had their heads shaved, and were drummed out of the service.[45]

While traveling to North Carolina for a brief tour of duty, the 14th Louisiana even engaged in another bloody riot. As on their earlier train ride to Grand Junction, some of the men prepared for the journey by freely indulging in whiskey and began brawling aboard the train. Upon reaching Petersburg, the soldiers had to disembark and march through town because the tracks did not run through the city. It was not long before they took their squabble into the streets, using what one witness described as "paving stones, clubs, bowie knives, and every available weapon that was at hand." The regiment's officers tried to quell the rioters but were attacked immediately. One lieutenant was stabbed three times and seriously wounded, and knife-wielding soldiers chased a store owner's wife when she protested the looting of her business. The officers and loyal soldiers finally restored order but not before the Louisianians' reputation for violent behavior was further enhanced.[46]

While Sulakowsi's 14th Louisiana received a great deal of bad press, Coppens' Battalion had the most lawless reputation of all the Louisiana commands on the Peninsula. One Virginian camped near them conceded that the Zouaves were excellent soldiers but wrote, "The pirates are from the dregs of all nations and the ten days they were here, they killed some eighteen or twenty head of cattle." A Louisianian, upon hearing that his company was to be transferred to Coppens' Battalion, exclaimed, "The men swear they will be shot first." So blatantly did Coppens' men raid neighboring farms and pastures that General Magruder was forced to denounce them publicly one hot, sultry day in June during an inspection of his troops. After a short speech thanking certain regiments for their bravery during the Battle of Big Bethel, Magruder cautiously approached Coppens' Battalion. The Zouaves stood rigidly at attention in their fezzes and blue flannel jackets while their commanding officer berated them for the rash of cattle killings. One witness wrote that Magruder "informed the Zouaves that he had heard of their depredations and that they must be stopped, or every man who was guilty of [such] conduct . . . should be shot immediately." A North Carolina soldier claimed that the Zouaves' reputation was so fierce that officers feared they might mutiny if pressed too hard on the issue, and that many soldiers believed Magruder chose this particular time to deliver his harangue because he had six thousand men to support him.[47]

The tension that developed between the Louisianians and their generals gradually diminished as McLaws and Magruder learned to enjoy the lighter side of their feisty soldiers. In October, McLaws wrote his wife that the 10th Louisiana had "warmly invited" him several times to Williamsburg, where the soldiers were "giving parties and picnics, singing and serenading." He also told her some amusing anecdotes that were circulating around camp. One Frenchman who was hiding in tall grass and waiting for a nearby pig to wander within reach was beaten to his prey by a North Carolina soldier who suddenly appeared and boldly shot the hog. Rising up on his hands, the Louisianian surprised the Tar Heel by shouting, "A, Ha! De Zouave is not the only one who stole de pig, some body else is the damned rascal besides." When two other Louisianians were caught red-handed pulling boards off a house, the owner demanded to know their units. With a straight face, one of them replied in a heavy French accent, "Ve belongs to the first Georgiy." Nonsense, the civilian shot back, Georgians did not have that accent. "Vera well," shrugged the soldier, "Bonjour," and off the two went, still clutching the boards.[48]

In his attempt to win the Louisianians' confidence, General Magruder sometimes overplayed his hand. He once issued a general order for the Louisianians immediately to engage any enemy they encountered—even if they faced fifty-to-one odds. The men were pleased that Magruder held such confidence in them, but one of Dreux's soldiers later recalled, "Crazy as we were at that period regarding our ability to eat up such and such a number of live Yankees before breakfast, it began to dawn upon the intellects of most of us that fifty to one was slightly in excess of what we had calculated upon."[49]

The tumultuous activity of Coppens', Sulakowski's, and Marigny's Louisianians created a tarnished image of the Pelican soldiers that never faded. From the Peninsula, the 10th Louisiana's Father Louis Hippolyte Gache wrote, "The Louisiana soldiers have gained a reputation for pilfering and general loutishness that as soon as anyone sees them coming they bolt the doors and windows. Usually any affiliation at all with the Louisiana boys is enough to assure one a cold welcome no matter where he shows his face."[50]

Although the Peninsula was where the Louisianians' reputation was largely made, it was near Manassas and Centreville that the term "Louisiana Tiger" came into being. Wheat's Battalion became known as the "Tiger Battalion" because of its fierce fighting at First Manassas and subsequent career of unbridled lawlessness. The name was taken from the Zouave company, Tiger Rifles, because its members were the most conspicuous and proved to be the wildest of Wheat's men. The term was widely used by the autumn of 1861, and because the deeds of the Peninsula Louisianians received so much publicity it was soon applied to all of the state's soldiers in Virginia. During and after the Civil War, the term "Louisiana Tigers" became a household word in both the North and the South.[51]

Wheat's Battalion earned its reputation for lawlessness as soon as it arrived in Virginia. The Richmond *Enquirer* claimed the battalion "let loose upon Richmond the most desperate cutthroats and scoundrels that ever a city was cursed with." The battalion quickly became feared by civilians and soldiers alike. In recalling his first view of these original Louisiana Tigers, Alabaman William Oates recalled that they were dressed in "half-savage uniforms" and were "adventurers, wharf-rats, cutthroats, and bad characters generally." James Cooper Nisbet of Georgia remembered years later, "I was actually afraid of them, afraid I would meet them somewhere and that they would do me like they did Tom Lane of my company; knock me down and stamp me half to death." Even other Louisianians were leery of Wheat's men. Henry Handerson and the 9th Louisiana's Stafford Guards found "considerably to our horror" that they had to camp next to the Tigers. "Yet, singular as it may seem," recalled Handerson, "we never had the slightest difficulty with them, and in fact the regiment and battalion got along together so well that they were often jestingly called 'the happy family.'"[52]

People had good reason to fear Wheat's men because they proved to be a reckless lot. Shortly after the First Battle of Manassas, the Lynchburg *Virginian* reported, "Some 'Rifle Tigers' [sic] and other N[ew]. O[rleans]. soldiers had like to take the town on Saturday evening. The row, however, was confined to themselves though the peace of our streets was sadly disturbed and the safety of our citizens put in jeopardy. . . . It is a shame for the community to be left at the mercy of armed men influenced by passion and mean whiskey." The Tiger Rifles so threatened Lynchburg's safety that its citizens were finally compelled to organize an armed guard and forcibly jail the drunken mob before it wrecked the town.[53]

Wheat's men were involved in two other melees within a few months. Somehow, Wheat's Battalion and the 1st Kentucky Volunteers developed bad blood between them and had to be separated in camp to keep the peace. At one new camp near Centreville, however, this routine procedure was overlooked, and the two commands were bivouacked adjacent to each other. That night while out on the town, two gangs of drunken Tigers and Kentuckians engaged in a violent street battle and attacked each other with paving stones. The noisy rocks bouncing off the frame houses awakened the town folks and created such a ruckus that a company of infantry had to be sent from camp to separate the men.[54]

Later that winter a dozen Tigers took on an entire company of the 21st Georgia when the Georgians absconded with the Louisianians' whiskey after the Tigers offered them a drink from their bottle. The Georgians' Capt. James Nisbet emerged from his tent to investigate the row and found several Tigers crumpled in the snow. He gathered up the battered soldiers and took them into his tent where they were treated to a drink and an apology when Nisbet learned of the brawl's circumstances. As the Louisianians were leaving, however, the captain warned them that they could have been killed if he had not intervened. The Tigers were reluctant to leave an unfinished fight and called defiantly over their shoulders, "We are much obliged, sor, but Wheat's Battalion kin clean up the whole damn Twenty-first Georgia any time."[55]

Whiskey caused most of the lawless incidents among the Louisianians at Centreville and on the Peninsula. Enlisted men were forbidden to have liquor in the camps, but one soldier wrote that the "Louisiana Brigade, being mostly city or river men, knew the ropes; and could get it from Richmond. Our men could not." Once while stationed around Culpeper the Tigers bought wine out of the house Gen. Richard Ewell was using as his headquarters. The overseer claimed that he was afraid the Tigers would steal the valuable wine anyhow, so he agreed to sell it through the cellar window for a dollar a bottle. The 6th Louisiana's George Zeller simply had his sister mail him his liquor. In one letter, he thanked her for the latest shipment of whiskey and declared, "[W]e all got so tight drinking to your health that some of us went to bed and the rest were put in the guard house and didn't get out until next morning." In the same letter, Zeller told his mother that he and three friends had sworn an oath to quit drinking, but shortly afterward he wrote another letter to his sister asking that she send two or three more bottles of whiskey and to make sure that they were packed correctly so as not to break.[56]

Lieutenant George L. P. Wren of the 8th Louisiana claimed that boredom caused much of the drinking, especially during the winter when there was nothing to do because snow and inclement weather cancelled drills. In January 1862, he wrote in his diary that "fiddling and dancing are going on in an adjoining cabin. . . . Officers all drunk tonight and a man killed in 'D' Company." A week later, he noted that "Some of the boys seem on a 'bust' tonight." One of Wren's comrades, thirty-five-year-old Irishman Michael Maloney, paid a heavy price for his drinking when he froze to death after getting drunk and passing out in the snow.[57]

Officers seemed to have been the greatest abusers of liquor because they were able to purchase it from camp sutlers. The 7th Louisiana sutler's ledger shows that one captain bought eight and a half gallons and one canteen of whiskey in less than two weeks, and Col. Harry T. Hays purchased five bottles of brandy, one canteen of whiskey, and one bottle of wine in nine days. The account of Capt. J. Moore Wilson, however, put all of the others to shame. It reads:

> September 12—one canteen of brandy
> 19—one bottle of brandy
> 20—three bottles of brandy
> 22—one bottle of brandy
> 23—one bottle of brandy and one canteen of whiskey
> 24—three gallons of whiskey
> 25—one canteen of whiskey
> 26—one flask of brandy
> 28—two gallons of whiskey and four bottles of brandy
> 29—two gallons of whiskey[58]

Although some of these purchases may have been for other men, Louisiana officers like Wilson were famous for their heavy consumption of spirits. Colonel Isaac G. Seymour complained bitterly about his officers' drinking habits and reported to his son that "some dozen or so of them are low vulgar fellows . . . [who] habitual [sic] whiskey tubs." Drinking so affected the performance of the 6th Louisiana that Seymour once pointed out the offenders by name and publicly rebuked them in front of their men during dress parade. Some of the officers in the 2nd Louisiana were nearly as bad. During a patrol in December 1861 they left their men standing outside in freezing weather while they adjourned to a nearby house to get drunk. Officers were even known to take a nip before going into battle. Charles F. "Charley" Thompson described an incident when the 2nd Louisiana was put on alert before daylight one morning. "While scouts and skirmishers were out, I heard [Capt. William] Levy call to an officer and tell him that he had not neglected his canteen of whiskey and come over and take a drink with him. I called to him [and he] said that Charley Thompson and he must have a drink. I took one the first I had had in some time." A month later, General Magruder ordered Thompson to be discharged. Levy was elected the regimental colonel but resigned his commission after being defeated for reelection in April 1862.[59]

Because of the Tigers' recklessness and abuse of alcohol, courts-martial became a regular occurrence in the Louisiana camps. Fighting, often alcohol-induced, was one of the most common reasons for such trials. From August 3 to September 3, 1861, there were four reported fights within the 2nd Louisiana, two of which resulted in stabbings. Punishment was the same at Centreville as on the Peninsula and appears to have been cruel and unusual by today's standards. When convicted of killing a hog, some members of the 9th Louisiana were sentenced to carry a rail on their shoulders for alternating periods of two hours for eight days. Drunkenness was often punished by days of hard labor in the trenches, and insubordination usually carried sentences of wearing a ball and chain. One Louisianian found guilty of the latter offense drew twenty days at hard labor with a ball and chain, and one of Coppens' Zouaves had to wear the dreaded device for the duration of his three-year enlistment. Other common penalties for minor offenses were public reprimands, forfeiture of pay, confinement in the guardhouse, standing on the head of a barrel, and wearing a "barrel shirt" with a placard attached declaring the offense. On rare occasions men were cashiered from the service. When this occurred they were normally marched out of camp to the tune of the "Rogue's March." At the suggestion of Colonel Hays, however, the Army of Northern Virginia eventually substituted "Yankee Doodle" because, as Hays put it, more rogues marched to that tune on any given day than to the "Rogue's March."[60]

George Zeller experienced the harsh military justice firsthand. In a letter to his mother he admitted that he and four comrades in the 6th Louisiana had been punished for going "out on a stroll and stay[ing] five days." The men had made the rounds of farms and towns around Manassas enjoying nice meals and comfortable beds before returning to camp and being arrested. All were bucked and gagged, and three had to forfeit two months' pay. "[A]ll five of us were put out on the hill so every Person could see us," explained Zeller. The humiliating punishment apparently was ineffective, however, because Zeller told his mother "that night when we got loos three of us made it up to go to Richmond and we will have A fine time there we are going to go next pay day." Taking such "French leave" must have been a tradition in Zeller's Violet

Guards because nine men were reported absent without leave in October and November 1861.[61]

The military courts were not alone in enforcing discipline. James T. Wrigley, Wheat's sergeant major, was a former New Orleans prizefighter, who at six feet, six inches in height, had no need for such formalities. About once a month he simply lined up the battalion, stripped off his coat, and menacingly growled, "Now men, yez have seen me lay down me sthripes. If any of yez has anything agin me let him step out like a man and settle it with me." There were few takers.[62]

Lieutenant Colonel Charles de Choiseul found the Sulakowski method of discipline more effective. De Choiseul was the great grandson of Louis XV's chief minister and the grandson of the Duc de Choiseul-Stainville who attempted unsuccessfully to rescue Louis XVI during the French Revolution. He also had family ties to the Princess of Monaco and the French Prince and Confederate Gen. Camille de Polignac. After Major Wheat was badly wounded at First Manassas, de Choiseul was ordered temporarily to take command of Wheat's Battalion. "I am," he wrote a friend, "the victim of circumstances, not of my own will. . . . Whether the Tigers will devour me, or whether I will succeed in taming them, remains to be seen."[63]

De Choiseul's moment of truth came when "the whole set got royally drunk." During the day one drunken soldier twice snapped his loaded musket at the colonel's orderly when the orderly tried to arrest him outside the colonel's tent. Luckily the musket failed to discharge, and the orderly was able to subdue him. De Choiseul reported that other unknown Tigers later succeeded in "knocking down & badly beating & robbing . . . a washerwoman of the battalion in a thicket not a hundred yards from the guard house." The camp gradually settled down, and de Choiseul retired for the night, only to be awakened at 10:30 p.m. by a free-for-all at the guard tent. Grabbing his pistol, he rushed out and found his guards battling seven or eight Tigers who were apparently trying to free some of their comrades. De Choiseul slugged one man who approached him threateningly and finally restored order "with seven or eight beauties bucked & gagged in the guard tent."[64]

The next day de Choiseul noticed two Tigers casually walking out of camp toward Centreville. No privates were to leave without a signed pass, so he rode over to investigate and was told that the orderly sergeant had given them permission. Suspicious, de Choiseul then went to question the sergeant but ended up arresting him when the sergeant gave "an impudent answer" to his inquiry. Ordered to his quarters, the soldier was walking away uttering oaths under his breath when another Tiger came up to the colonel and began taking the side of the departing sergeant. When de Choiseul ordered this man to the guardhouse, as well, the soldier refused to go. Furious at such insubordination, the mounted colonel picked him up by the collar and threw him heavily to the ground. After picking himself up, the soldier still refused to leave, so de Choiseul knocked him to the ground a second time. By then several other Tigers had encircled de Choiseul and were pressing closer menacingly. Realizing that he was in danger, the colonel gripped his revolver and sternly warned that he would shoot the first man who "raised a finger." The words were no sooner uttered than a "big double fisted ugly looking fellow came at me & said 'God damn you, shoot me.'" De Choiseul immediately drew his pistol. "He turned as I fired & [I] hit him in the cheek, knocking out one upper jaw tooth & two lower ones on the other side & cutting his tongue." The other Tigers quickly broke their encirclement and recoiled from the obviously dangerous colonel. "That quelled the riot," de Choiseul nonchalantly recalled.[65]

Another violent incident involving Wheat's Battalion occurred a few weeks after de Choiseul's near-riot. On November 29, 1861, Tiger Rifles Pvts. Dennis "Red" Corcoran and Michael O'Brien got drunk and were involved in an incident within the camp of the 7th Louisiana. Apparently, when a lieutenant and guard tried to arrest them, a scuffle ensued and Col. Harry T. Hays was knocked to the ground. Hays pulled his pistol and pointed it at Corcoran, but Capt. Obedia Miller of Wheat's Battalion happened to be passing by and stepped between them and successfully diffused the situation.[66]

Corcoran and O'Brien were arrested a few days later and on December 5 were convicted of attacking an officer and sentenced to death. Wheat made an impassioned plea for leniency because one of the men had risked his life to carry the wounded Wheat from the Manassas battlefield. Brigade commander Richard Taylor, however, rejected Wheat's request. Taylor actually wanted to rid himself of the troublesome Tiger Battalion altogether and had previously asked Gen. Joseph E. Johnston to transfer it out of his command. Johnston refused on the grounds that no other officer in the army would take the battalion, but Taylor claimed Johnston did promise "to sustain me in any measures to enforce discipline." Apparently, Taylor decided the attack on the lieutenant and Colonel Hays provided an opportunity to make an example of Corcoran and O'Brien and to reign in the wild Tigers. Not only did Taylor refuse Wheat's plea for mercy, he even ordered that the firing squad be picked from members of the Tiger Rifles. Wheat warned Taylor that such action might cause the men to mutiny, but Taylor stood firm.[67]

Father Smulders attended to the two men's spiritual needs as they awaited execution. Numerous soldiers commented on how bravely Corcoran and O'Brien met their fate. One Mississippian claimed that, when they were put into the wagon to be taken to the execution site, "one of them danced all over his coffin and said that they would show them how Louisianians could die." George Zeller witnessed the execution and reported that the men emerged from the wagon laughing and talking, while an Alabama soldier wrote that they "marched up in the presence of fifteen thousand men as boldly as a Tiger ever walked among a flock of sheep." Later when their caps were pulled over their eyes as a blindfold, one of the condemned men took it off and declared, "I will die looking in the muzzles of those rifles."[68] Apparently, this did not sit well with the officers because witnesses claim both men were eventually blindfolded.

At 11:00 a.m., on December 9, the entire division formed a threesided square around a slight depression used as a natural amphitheater for the executions. Twelve Tiger Rifles chosen by Taylor were drawn up to serve as executioners. The silent division watched as a band played the "Death March," and a covered wagon escorted by two companies with fixed bayonets slowly approached the open side of the square. One witness described what happened:

> Then six men get out of the wagon—two "Tigers," a catholic priest in long black cassock and three-cornered cap, and three officers. These step forward a little when the Colonel rides up to them and, speaking to the "Tigers," reads to them the charges of which they have been found guilty and the sentence of the court condemning them to death. The two "Tigers" have their hands tied behind them with rope. They are then led backward a short distance and made to kneel with their backs resting against two strong posts driven into the ground. Their hands are also tied tightly behind them to the posts. The priest is seen going constantly from one to the other of the two criminals, comforting them in preparing them for the awful death. . . . He holds to their lips a crucifix, which they passionately kiss and over which they pray. In a

few minutes the signal is given, the priest leaves them alone with an officer, who put a bandage over their eyes and retires.[69]

Tiger Rifles Lt. Edward Hewitt had the sad duty of informing Capt. Alex White of the executions because White was on recruitment duty in New Orleans: "When brought to the place of execution Corcoran saluted the party who were detailed to execute the last office with a cheerful, 'good morning my little lads; don't grieve for us; we are going to a better world,' 'Don't mangle us; shoot at our hearts if you love us. Boys, God bless you, good-bye!' Oh, Captain, that scene! . . . Those strong, stern men. . . bowed their head upon their rifles, and it was plainly seen each head was bursting with agony; every eye moistened with sympathetic tears. Red says: 'Boys it was at the C's yesterday; it is at the D's today, and I am ready.' Both men asked to be allowed stand and not blindfolded but refused and Red said 'Father I kneel to God! Tigers a last good-bye. God receive our spirits!'"[70]

Despite the seriousness of the soldiers' crime, some of the onlookers were sympathetic to the two Tigers. As a final gesture, Corcoran and O'Brien had published a farewell letter in a local newspaper, pleading for others not to also fall victim to the vice of liquor and forgiving those who were involved in their execution. Many soldiers recalled this letter as they watched the twelve executioners advance to within ten yards of the condemned men. The firing squad was not aware of it, but one company of Col. Henry B. Kelly's 8th Louisiana was standing behind them with loaded muskets. Fearing the Tigers might refuse to fire when ordered, Colonel Kelly was prepared to execute the executioners if the need arose. His concern was unwarranted for at the order, "Ready! Aim! Fire!" a dozen muskets split the crisp December air with a thunderous volley. The two men were dead by the time the echoes faded into the hills. In the hushed silence that followed, Pvt. Daniel Corcoran broke ranks, ran up to his brother's body, and gently held and caressed it. "It was heart-rendering," a correspondent wrote, "to see the poor brother's agony." Wheat, the only man in the division excused from attending the execution, broke down and cried in his tent upon hearing the discharge of muskets. After the burial, some soldiers ghoulishly combed the execution site for pieces of posts and other relics until the distraught Tiger Rifles angrily dispersed them.[71]

Corcoran and O'Brien were the first soldiers to be executed in the Virginia army, and it appears that their harsh sentence was a conscious effort on the part of certain officers to bring the Louisiana Tigers under control. Truth be told, however, the Louisiana officers were also guilty of their own transgressions. For example, the 6th Louisiana's Capt. Arthur McArthur and Lt. John Orr were convicted of being absent without leave in February 1862. In addition to being relieved of duty and pay for two months and being confined to camp, their offense and punishment were read to each of the brigade's regiments at the end of dress parade. Some officers in the 9th Louisiana apparently were also guilty of physically assaulting their men on occasion. In January 1862, an order was issued stating that "no officer is justified in striking and beating men or in using abusive language." Any officer found guilty of such conduct would be dismissed from the service on charges of conduct unbecoming an officer. This order was read three times to each of the regiment's companies on the parade ground.[72]

The violent nature of some Louisiana officers is also evident in two duels that took place early in the war. One involved the Tiger Rifles' Capt. Alex White and will be discussed in chapter 3. The other was between Lt. Alfred H. Jones of the 5th Louisiana and a Dr. Forward who served as the regiment's sutler while it was camped near Young's Mill. The two men reportedly became embroiled in an argument over a candle, of all things, and agreed to settle it with a duel. Meeting on Christmas Eve 1861 and using Mississippi Rifles at forty yards, both men fired at the same time. Jones was killed instantly, and Dr. Forward died within moments.[73]

Some of the officers' incompetence and contentious personalities also caused turmoil within their units. In June 1861, the company officers of Coppens' Battalion met with General Magruder and threatened to resign and serve as privates if Coppens continued in command. They conceded that he was "a brave and good man" but claimed he was "entirely without energy or the faculty to command." Magruder tried to defuse the situation by adding two Virginia companies to the battalion, raising it to regimental strength, and bringing in a new colonel, but Richmond rejected the plan and Coppens remained in command.[74]

Lieutenant Colonel Charles M. Bradford of the 3rd Louisiana Battalion had similar problems. His officers complained to President Davis that he was unfit, immoral, and a drunkard, but Davis had personally appointed Bradford, so he remained in command. Captain Henry Gillum of the Quitman Rangers led the fight against Bradford. He was finally able to get his company transferred to the 14th Louisiana, but he and one of his lieutenants were ambushed and seriously wounded the night before their scheduled departure. Gillum believed Bradford was responsible for the attack, but there is no evidence to support his claim. In April 1862, Bradford was court-martialed on charges of conduct unbecoming an officer, contempt for a superior, disobedience, and being drunk on duty. Although he was acquitted of the latter charge, he was convicted of the others and was relieved of duty and pay for six months. Bradford resigned his commission two months later.[75]

The 2nd Louisiana seems to have had the most internal squabbling early in the war. Lieutenant Alfred Flournoy Jr. and Pvt. Benjamin Smith wrote that the men lacked confidence in the elderly Col. Louis G. DeRussy because he was a sluggish and inefficient officer. Flournoy described DeRussy as being a "good old man" but "almost unfit for service." After serving a few weeks in Virginia, DeRussy abruptly resigned his commission from fear he would have to fight an older brother who was in the Union army at Fort Monroe. That left the regiment under the command of Lt. Col. John Young, who Flournoy believed was "worse than nothing" and "the most complete *Ass* I ever saw." According to Flournoy, the regiment's officers repeatedly tried to convince Young to resign without success. The officers were at wit's end when Young took the regiment on an eight-mile march one morning without any breakfast, only to discover that he had marched to the wrong place. Fortunately, Capt. William Levy of the Lecompte Guards arrived about that time with a colonel's commission and took over from Young.[76]

Levy's path to promotion was not an easy one. When DeRussy resigned, Levy and Capt. Jesse M. Williams of the DeSoto Rifles ran for the vacant position. Williams won the election, but Levy somehow convinced General Magruder to order a new vote be taken. When Magruder recognized Levy as the new colonel after the second vote, Lt. Sidney Baxter Robertson claimed that Williams' friends "sulked," and the defeated Williams challenged Levy to a duel. Robertson took the challenge to the new colonel, and Levy told him, "I'll fight him but you know Lt. I'm near sighted & can't see far." Under the dueling code, Levy had the right to choose the weapons because he was the challenged party, so Robertson recommended that he choose swords. Levy said that he had carried a sword during the Mexican War but had never struck anyone with it. Robertson then suggested that he demand "ten paces wheel & fire and advance" because Williams was a deadly marksman out to sixty yards. When the shocked Levy stammered, "That would be murder," Robertson shrugged, "Well what's war?" Before daybreak, Colonel Levy sent word to Williams that he would not meet him on the dueling ground because he could not wave rank to fight a subordinate officer. Robertson declared that "Capt Wms comment cant be written here."[77]

Lieutenant Flournoy and Private Smith agreed that conditions in the 2nd Louisiana quickly improved when Colonel Levy began to personally lead the regiment in drill twice a day and to issue firm orders that made "some *lazy ones* crawl out of their *holes*." Wolf Lichenstein, however, claimed that over time Levy's harsh manner made him unpopular with the men. Lichenstein accused the colonel of "tyranny, cruelty and wanton malisciscnous, his egoticsm was only second to his cruelty and his friends in that regiment were only few." Levy resigned his commission on April 30, 1862, after failing to win reelection to colonel, but Lichenstein believed he did so because "undoubtedly threats that were going the round reached his ears."[78]

Captain Williams, who lost the colonel's position to Levy, was embroiled in another controversy that summer. Members of his Pelican Rifles openly rebelled in August when Williams refused to account for money the men contributed to the company fund. Thomas Phifer informed his mother that the captain was "acting very strangely," and that the men had elected a committee to ask him to account for any money spent and to report how much was still on hand. Williams, however, refused and replied "very disrespectful" that some of the men were a disgrace to their home parish and "fit for Yankee Bullets."[79]

The shocked committee members thought Williams must have misunderstood their request and sent another. Captain Williams then replied that he had received a "very insulting ungentlemanly and insubordinate document purporting to be from the company signed by a committee of seven." Williams accused the committee of lying and reminded it that he had never wanted to act as the company's treasurer but that the men had insisted he take charge. As for not keeping accurate records, he pointed out that some of the company members were also involved in the disbursement of funds but they did not keep records, either. The accusations grievously offended Williams, and he wished he could return the money "to the donars rather than give it to such unworthy and ungrateful wretches as a considerable portion of this company seem to be." The captain closed by stating that, since the committee had not complied with his request to appoint someone to receive the remainder of the company fund, he would continue to manage it until further notice.[80]

DeRussy's leaving the 2nd Louisiana was not the only command change made in the Peninsula Tigers during their first year in Virginia. Colonel Mandeville Marigny also quit in disgust at Richmond's favoritism toward certain officers, but the greatest shock was the resignation of the much respected Colonel Sulakowski. Many soldiers considered him to be the best officer on the Peninsula, and General Magruder had him construct some of the most formidable Confederate works of the war. Unfortunately, the Polish officer was impatient and ambitious, and when Howell Cobb was promoted over him to brigadier general, Sulakowski offered his resignation. After a bitter farewell to his men, the colonel left Virginia to continue his career in the Trans-Mississippi Department.[81]

The men of the 14th Louisiana responded to their colonel's resignation by rioting. Sulakowski's departure left Lt. Col. Richard W. Jones in command of the regiment. Lieutenant Robert H. Miller described Jones as "a whining methodist class leader" and claimed he was unpopular with the men. Nearly half of the regiment's officers tried to resign when Jones was appointed colonel, but army officials refused their request. According to Miller, when Sulakowski took his leave, "the Regiment became *wild* and *uncontrollable*," tore down the sutler's shop, and physically threatened Colonel Jones. The colonel reportedly took shelter in the surgeon's quarters while the soldiers ran amuck. Wisely, the sutler poured all of his whiskey out on the floor, and the officers were finally able to control "the same demoniac spirit that broke out at Grand Junction."[82]

Compared to the Tigers on the Peninsula, the Louisiana Brigade stationed near Centreville seemed to be more stable in its affairs. The only personnel controversy that occurred there was in October 1861 when a new commander was appointed to replace Gen. William H. T. Walker. Walker was a former officer in the old army who had been wounded in both the Seminole and Mexican wars. On Christmas Day 1837, he was wounded in the leg, arm, neck, and shoulder but continued to lead his men against the Seminoles until he was shot in the chest. These and another serious wound in Mexico caused Walker chronic pain while he commanded the Tigers. One Louisianian wrote, "The permanent evidences of his sufferings remained in a painfully spare frame and a pale cadaverous complexion, which always suggested a ghost on horseback."

The Louisiana Tigers admired General Walker and appreciated his attention to drill that made the Louisiana Brigade one of the best trained units in the army. Lieutenant Wren declared, "We are all proud of our General—Walker—he has the entire confidence of his men," and another soldier wrote in his diary, "Every soldier seems pleased with his new Brigadier."[83]

Despite Walker's ability and popularity, however, Jefferson Davis replaced him with Col. Richard Taylor of the 9th Louisiana. Taylor was well-liked within his regiment, but his appointment to brigade command was not welcomed by the other brigade officers because he was the junior of four colonels and, unlike two of the others, had no previous military experience. Adding insult to this perceived injury, Taylor was the president's former brother-in-law, and his appointment smacked of nepotism. Davis denied the latter charge, but his wife, Varina, once admitted that Davis' two faults were that he was "too fond of West Point officers and his first wife's relations."[84]

The Louisiana colonels had been through this before when it was rumored that Taylor, not Walker, was to command the Louisiana Brigade. At that time, Colonel Seymour wrote a friend, "The powers in Richmond would have given the place to Taylor but they did not dare to do it." Seymour was the brigade's senior colonel and had fought in the Seminole and Mexican wars, so it is not known why Walker was appointed brigade commander over him. Seymour claimed that he held no ill will about being passed over and wrote, "I never stood a ghost of a chance for it; never expected it and of course, I am not disappointed—cause—I can not be used as a politician."[85]

When Taylor was first considered, the brigade's colonels apparently had enough political clout to prevent his appointment—but now the situation was different. President Davis had decided that morale and unit cohesion would best be served by brigading regiments together from the same state. Thus, General Walker was transferred to command a Georgia brigade, and Taylor was promoted to brigadier general to lead the Louisiana Brigade. Furious at being transferred from the unit that he had trained so well, Walker wrote Secretary of War Judah P. Benjamin, "I will not condescend to submit any longer to the insults and indignities of the Executive." Walker tendered his resignation but soon relented and returned to duty, only to be killed on July 22, 1864, while leading Georgia troops in the Battle of Atlanta.[86]

Taylor learned of his promotion on October 30 when he returned to camp from extended sick leave. He suffered from chronic rheumatoid arthritis, which sometimes left him bedridden, and he had spent part of his leave resting in the house of Secretary of War Benjamin. The news of Taylor's promotion shocked many members of the brigade. One Tiger sent a letter to a New Orleans newspaper in which he wrote, "A more shameful piece of business has not transpired during the war." An editorial in the New Orleans *True Delta* claimed that Colonel Seymour should have received the promotion, but "he is not either a relative of any of the 'grand chiefs' or a rabid politician of the [John] Slidell camp."[87]

Taylor was embarrassed by the decision to promote him. Acutely aware of his delicate position, he traveled by ambulance to meet personally with Davis to ask that the appointment be canceled. Davis promised to consider the request, but instead wrote the other three colonels and explained that he had made the appointment for the good of the service. This personal note apparently soothed their ruffled feelings and persuaded them to support Taylor. Taylor then accepted the promotion and soon became one of the army's outstanding brigade commanders. As one man wrote, "Dick Taylor is superior to any [West Pointer] and [has] more brains than all of them put together. If Davis was too fond of his first wife's relations, tis a pity there were not more like Taylor." For his part, Taylor realized that much of his success lay in his having inherited a brigade that was already well disciplined and trained. "Owing to the good traditions left by my predecessor, Walker, and the zeal of officers and men," he wrote, "the brigade made great progress."[88]

Taylor seems to have had a natural talent for military command. One man declared, "Dick Taylor was a born soldier. Probably no civilian of his time was more deeply versed in the annals of war." The thirty-five-year-old Taylor may have inherited his military talent from his father, the former general and president Zachary Taylor, even though they rarely spent time together. Taylor spoke fluent French, studied at Harvard, Yale, and the University of Edinburgh, and was a life-long student of military history. He briefly served as his father's secretary during the Mexican War and was chairman of the Louisiana Military and Defense Committee during the secession convention. When war erupted, Taylor served as a volunteer aide to Gen. Braxton Bragg at Pensacola, and Bragg hated to see him leave when he was elected colonel of the 9th Louisiana. "He had become about a necessity to me," declared the general.[89]

Taylor's greatest weakness was his poor physical constitution. He suffered from headaches that would leave his limbs paralyzed and severe rheumatoid arthritis that sometimes left him in a wheelchair. In 1850, Taylor also suffered from what doctors diagnosed as "congestion of the brain" brought on by anxiety and exposure to the sun.[90] Wet, cold weather only exacerbated his condition. David Boyd, a Virginia native who taught ancient languages at the Louisiana Seminary of Learning under Superintendent William T. Sherman before the war, served on Taylor's staff and knew the general well. He wrote,

Often in Virginia in the wet, cold weather he had to be helped on and off his horse; and then his disabled leg would hang limp, like a rope, from his saddle. In his moments of intense bodily suffering he was cross and irritable; but at such times the excitement of battle seemed to soothe him, and he would become pleasant and playful as a kitten. . . . of excellent memory, genial, full of humor and very witty, his dark-brown eyes a-sparkling, and with his rich, melodious voice, he was the most brilliant and fascinating talker that I remember in the Southern army. What a treat it was to sit around the campfire at night and listen to Dick Taylor!—when he wasn't suffering! When he was sick he was "ugly," and we had to keep away from him.[91]

For the vast majority of Louisianians the first year in Virginia proved to be a bore. Inactivity bred restlessness and petty grievances, which often erupted into violent outbursts of lawlessness and mayhem. The thefts, drunken brawls, and unmilitary behavior engaged in by some forever branded all Louisianians as misfits and unruly "Tigers." To offset this dark image, most of the Louisianians were eager to meet the enemy and receive their baptism of fire to prove themselves in combat. Typical of their attitude was the 9th Louisiana's Sgt. Al Pierson, who wrote his father in early 1862: "The day is now dawning and will soon open bright and clear as a May morning, when we will be acknowledged as one of the best governments that holds a place in the catalogue of the nations of the earth. Let the unholy and base legions of Lincolndom pour forth their fury and rage in all its power—we will meet them [in the field and] we will defeat them or perish upon the soil of our loved and cherished southern republic. This is what southern men have vowed by their acts and not by words. Let us die a soldier[']s death or live a freeman[']s life."[92]

On the Peninsula, seventeen-year-old Thomas Phifer had been eager to meet the Yankees ever since arriving at Yorktown and explained to his mother how the 2nd Louisiana would handle the enemy. "Our programme for fighting will be as follows—Kill one man as soon as they come within rifle shot, which will be one hundred and fifty yards—load again by the time that they get within fifty yards and kill another—then out with pistols and kill another—-those who have repeaters will kill at least three here. Then out with your bowies and go to work. We have knives as long as my arm. The average execution with them will be five—so if every man attends to his business strictly and they stand us half an hour, we will kill every man of them."[93] Whether the Louisiana Tigers could live up to their own expectations remained to be seen.

CHAPTER 3

Baptism by Fire

WHILE ALL OF THE Louisiana Tigers were prepared to meet the Yankees on the battlefield, the men stationed on the Peninsula experienced the first baptism by fire when they engaged the enemy in several small skirmishes. Some of the fights, however, ended badly. William E. Trahern, a member of the 6th Louisiana's Tensas Rifles, recounted an embarrassing encounter with the federals that resulted in the loss of the company's flag. The ladies of St. Joseph had made the flag a couple of months earlier and had presented it to the men in a moving ceremony before they left their hometown. Made of silk, one side had a blue field with a golden cotton bale bearing the name "Tensas Rifles," while the reverse side depicted the First National Flag pattern. "It was too beautiful to be shot at," declared Trahern, "and never was."[1]

The regiment was camped near Fairfax Court House on June 1 when it received word that the Yankees were advancing. Confusion ensued when the men were ordered to retreat, and the company's color-bearer asked the captain to let him take possession of the flag to protect it. The captain refused, however, and ordered that the flag be put in the mess kit. When the regiment hastily abandoned the camp, the men took with them what they could. Trahern recalled, "The heads of hogs, hams, and barrels of sugar were smashed in, and as the soldiers filed by with bayonet fixed, plucked a ham, and filled their Army sacks with sugar . . . [but] not one of those men who seized this food, carried it to our next camp. The tramp down the middle of the track of the Orange and Alexandria railroad, in the broiling sun of a June day, was too much for human endurance, for all along the road they had cast it away." For some reason, no one thought to bring along the mess kit containing the flag, and Union cavalrymen captured it when they entered the camp twenty minutes

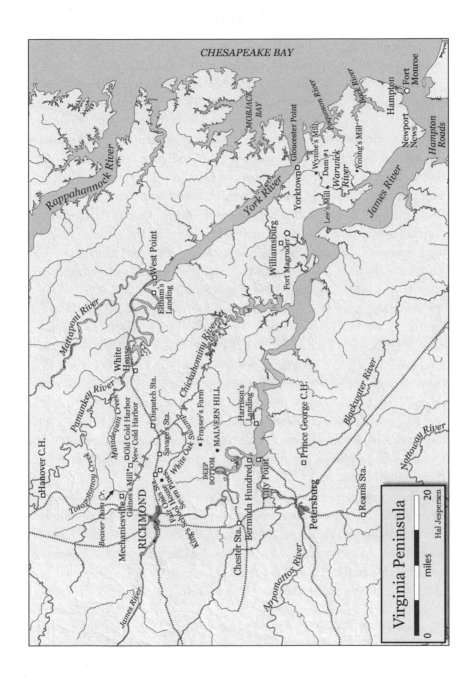

CHESAPEAKE BAY

Rappahannock River

MOBJACK BAY

York River

Piankatank River

Poquoson River

Back River

Hampton

Fort Monroe

Newport News

Hampton Roads

James River

Gloucester Point

Wynne's Mill

Yorktown

Dam #1

Warwick River

Young's Mill

Lee's Mill

Williamsburg

Fort Magruder

West Point

Mattaponi River

Eltham's Landing

Chickahominy River

Pamunkey River

White House

Matadequin Creek

Old Cold Harbor

New Cold Harbor

Dispatch Sta.

Savage's Sta.

Frayser's Farm

Harrison's Landing

Prince George C.H.

Blackwater River

Hanover C.H.

Totopotomoy Creek

Beaver Dam Cr.

Mechanicsville

Gaines's Mill

RICHMOND

Fair Oaks Sta.

White Oak Swamp

School House

Seven Pines

DEEP BOTTOM

MALVERN HILL

Bermuda Hundred

City Point

Petersburg

Reams Sta.

Chester Sta.

Appomattox River

James River

Nottoway River

King's

Virginia Peninsula

0   miles   20

Hal Jespersen

later. When the flag was returned to Louisiana after the war, the surviving Tensas Rifles agreed to donate it to Confederate Memorial Hall in New Orleans.[2]

Not long afterward, other Tigers played a supporting role in the much publicized, but quite small, clash at Big Bethel. The 2nd Louisiana was camped sixteen miles away when the fight began and was ordered to hurry to the battlefield to reinforce their comrades. Lieutenant William W. Posey wrote his parents that the regiment made a forced march to Big Bethel in less than three hours, "which is the best time that we ever been made and we then march[ed] back that night." A newspaper correspondent who saw the Tigers arrive on the field reported, "They are a fine-looking set of fellows." Despite their fast-paced march, however, the Louisianians arrived shortly after the battle ended. "We were just one hour too late," wrote Posey. "I got to see a good many of the dead Yankees laying on the battle field which we were as glad to find as I ever was to find a deer which I wounded and came upon."[3]

Union Maj. Theodore Winthrop was killed during the battle, and the 2nd Louisiana's Wolf Lichenstein claimed his body received special attention because Winthrop was the first officer to be killed in the war. "We all were eager for a sovenir [sic], so the soldiers with knives [in] hand cut off pieces of cloth from his uniform and all the buttons, of which I got one. The major's [illegible] chain & watch and all other trinkets he had in his pockets including family pictures, pocket bible etc. were all pilfered." The Tigers did not keep their souvenirs long, however, because when Confederate Gen. John R. Jones heard of the "dastardly pillage" he ordered all of the items to be returned "on pain of severe punishment."[4]

A few weeks later, the 5th Louisiana also visited the Big Bethel battlefield when it participated in a brief foray to Hampton. Sergeant John Charlton reported that the "trees & houses around are literally riddled with balls" and described how the men again scoured the area looking for souvenirs. Apparently, not all of the dead had been found earlier because Charlton wrote that "one of the Virginia Reg found a Revolver & Belt around the Skeleton of a Yankee." From Big Bethel the men continued with their mission to Hampton, where they exchanged some shots with the Union pickets before burning the town and withdrawing that night behind large bonfires that hid their movement.[5]

The Louisiana Tigers who were stationed in northern Virginia around Manassas also encountered the enemy occasionally. Captain Alex White's Tiger Rifles became the envy of its sister units when it made a raid to the Potomac River's Seneca Falls fifteen miles upstream from Washington and skirmished with the Yankees on June 28. White reported killing three enemy soldiers at the cost of one man wounded. The unfortunate Tiger was Pvt. James Burns, who was shot in the leg and had to undergo an amputation. He had the distinction of being the first of thousands of Louisiana battlefield casualties.[6]

Such clashes between the opposing pickets in northern Virginia seem to have been fairly common at the time. On July 2, the 8th Louisiana's John F. Geren wrote home about these small, but sometimes deadly, encounters. "The picket guards of each army are in sight of each other and they kill some of them occasionally [and] the Scout party bring in from three to ten nearly every day. We arrived here yesterday and they have brought several in since we came to this place. I went up to the guard house just a few minutes ago and took a peep at the Yankee prisoners, some of which are very fierce looking fellows and are no doubt very smart men sent out as spies."[7]

These small, insignificant clashes received a good deal of attention in newspapers and the soldiers' letters, but it was a skirmish on July 5 that made news across the Confederacy. Soon after arriving on the Peninsula, Lt. Col. Charles Dreux was placed in command of Young's Mill, an important link in General Magruder's defensive line that ran across the Peninsula from Yorktown to the Warwick River. Although Magruder intended for Dreux to stay on the defensive, the fiery young Creole and his men had other ideas. As William Moore put it, "The boys [are] all anxious for a pop at the enemy."[8]

By the time Dreux sponsored a Fourth of July celebration, the battalion was "in a fever of excitement" because of rumors that a battle was pending. In 1861, the South celebrated Independence Day as well as the North because the Confederates saw a great similarity between their struggle and the cause George Washington and other southerners fought for in 1776. To honor the occasion, Dreux invited General McLaws to a barbeque where the Declaration of Independence was read to the men, and patriotic speeches were made while whiskey flowed freely. Captain Samuel M. Todd presented Dreux with a jug of whiskey as a gift, and the colonel's martial spirit was running high when he made what McLaws described as "a most exciting, stirring speech." Standing before his battalion, the young officer closed his oratory by touching his sword hilt and solemnly promising the men that "this is our day, and we will have it." The tipsy crowd responded with enthusiastic cheers, unaware that Dreux fully intended to back up his pledge with action.[9]

The colonel was in a fighting mood by day's end and hastily made plans to cap off the festivities with a bold move against the enemy. His intended victim was a squadron of federal cavalry that regularly passed through a crossroads just outside Young's Mill. Dreux assembled twenty men from each of his five companies, about twenty Virginia cavalrymen, and one howitzer and its crew from the Richmond Artillery, and departed camp about 1:00 a.m. on July 5. By daylight, he had the men set in an ambush along the road that the Union cavalry used every morning. Dreux's plan was to wait until the enemy reached his position and then open fire with musketry, roll the cannon into the road and fire, and send in his cavalry to cause further confusion. If all went according to plan, Dreux expected to kill or capture all of the Yankee troopers.[10]

By daylight, Dreux had his infantry hidden in the brush alongside the road and posted the lone howitzer at the far end of the line. The eastern sky was rapidly growing lighter when he dispatched two scouts through the brush to see if the Yankees were coming. What happened next is unclear because those who left accounts disagreed on the details.

Jefferson Davis Van Benthuysen claimed the scouts had only gone about one hundred yards when they spotted mounted troops approaching. In the dim light, however, the scouts thought the riders were Confederates and revealed themselves. The Yankees then stopped short of the ambush and opened fire, killing Pvt. Steve Hackett of the Shreveport Greys. Dreux only had time to give the order, "Ready!" when a Union officer knelt down with a carbine and fired one shot at him. The bullet cut through Dreux's sword belt, shattered his pocket watch, and hit his spine. Dreux barely had time to mutter, "Steady, boys" before dying.[11]

Sergeant Daniel D. Logan wrote his sister that as soon as the firing began the Virginia cavalrymen "*cut & run* knocking down our men who were forming in the road scaring our horses, who ran off at full speed with the Howitzers, leaving their [men] in the road." Van Benthuysen reported that Pvt. Columbus Allen rushed forward and knocked out and captured the officer who shot Dreux, but Logan claimed one of his company members shot the officer. Logan also stated that Hackett killed another Yankee before he died and that one of Dreux's scouts killed two more. Besides Dreux and Hackett being killed, one man in the battalion was wounded.[12]

Other soldiers told a different story. According to some, the scouts hurriedly returned after seeing the mounted soldiers and told Dreux that a large cavalry column was coming their way. To ensure that the Yankees would ride into the ambush and get within range of the howitzer, word was quickly passed down the line not to fire until Dreux gave the signal. But then a single gunshot boomed on the left of the line in the direction of the approaching enemy. Realizing something had gone wrong, Dreux and some of his officers stepped out of the bushes into the dark road to investigate. With sword in hand, Dreux was straining to see through the dim light when several Union scouts suddenly appeared. The Confederate officers silently melted back into the underbrush but not before one Yankee spotted them and killed Dreux. At the sound of the shot, several of the hiding rebels and startled Yankees opened fire, as well. As bullets whistled through the air, rattled officers yelled confusing commands, and men ran frantically in different directions. The artillery officer ordered his gun rolled out on the road to fire into the Union cavalry, but the horses spooked in the confusion, broke loose, and galloped pell-mell in the opposite direction with the cursing artillerymen giving chase.

The "battle" was over, with Colonel Dreux and Private Hackett dead and little to show for the loss. Accusations over who was to blame for the fiasco soon flew as wildly as the Tigers' minié balls. Some men claimed the untimely shot that alerted the enemy was fired by one of Dreux's scouts who killed a snake at that crucial moment. Others accused certain officers of hiding behind trees when the shooting began, or worse, of shamelessly running away through the woods. Everyone agreed that the entire affair was badly mishandled, but few held the beloved Dreux responsible. Eugene Janin probably best summed up the incident when he wrote that "a 4th of July barbeque & a jug of whiskey presented to Dreux by [Captain] Todd had more to do with it than we like to have known out of the battalion."[13]

Dreux's death sent shock waves through the South, not only because of his high social standing but also because he was the first Confederate officer to be killed in the war. The members of Dreux's Battalion were so outraged that Maj. N. H. Rightor demanded satisfaction from the Yankees. He proposed sending a challenge to the enemy at Fort Monroe to pick five hundred of their best soldiers to meet on any field of their choosing so revenge could be exacted. General Magruder approved the measure and informed the Tigers that he would accompany them should the Yankees accept, but the secretary of war refused to endorse the challenge.[14]

A large portion of the Peninsula army paid its last respects to the slain

Tigers before their bodies were placed aboard a black-draped train for New Orleans. Accompanied by six honor guards, the train was met in the Crescent City by a huge crowd that silently watched as Dreux's coffin was unloaded and escorted to City Hall by a company of militia. There the colonel's body lay in state for several days and was viewed by thousands of mourners. On July 13, following a funeral service that involved forty Catholic priests, the casket was placed on a velvet-covered artillery carriage drawn by six coal-black horses and was escorted by a squadron of cavalry to St. Louis Cemetery. Buildings along the funeral route were draped in mourning, flags flew at half-mast, and church bells solemnly tolled every minute during the ninety-minute procession. Two hundred carriages carrying such dignitaries as Governor Moore and Mayor John Monroe followed along behind. An estimated sixty thousand people viewed the funeral procession, which was thought to be the largest ever held in New Orleans at the time. It was an event, one correspondent claimed, "which will never be forgotten . . . whilst one of the rising generation lives."[15]

Dreux's sudden and shocking death was only a harbinger of things to come. A week after the funeral, other Tigers were rushed into an intense firefight along the sluggish Virginia stream known as Bull Run. In mid-July, the war's first major campaign was underway as federal troops under Gen. Irvin Mc-Dowell left Washington and headed south toward Richmond. General P. G. T. Beauregard's Confederate Army of the Potomac was stationed along Bull Run near Manassas to guard its fords against any Union crossing. The long-awaited federal attack began on July 18 when Union Gen. Daniel Tyler cautiously advanced his division to feel out the Confederate positions at Blackburn's Ford. The federals first approached the camp of the 6th Louisiana at Fairfax Station, and the regiment had to retreat quickly. Private Andrew S. Herron wrote that the Yankees "were within two miles of us marching in three large bodies . . . so we had about 15 minutes to leave. . . . We retreated back along the rail road to Union Mills, burning the bridges as we came on." Captain William Monaghan, who commanded the regiment's picket line, was nearly cut off and captured, but, as Herron put it, he and his men made it back to camp "by some tall walking." Unfortunately, some nervous Mississippi troops shot and killed Sgt. Francis X. Demaign when he unexpectedly approached them.[16]

When Tyler's division reached Bull Run, a brisk fight erupted with Gen. James Longstreet's brigade, and Longstreet was forced to call on Jubal Early for support. Consisting of the 7th and 24th Virginia and Col. Harry T. Hays' 7th

Louisiana, Early's brigade was camped about a mile away. The three regiments were ready for action, Hays' men having already pocketed forty rounds of ammunition and pinned strips of red flannel to their shirts to identify themselves as Confederates because some of the companies wore blue uniforms. The Louisianians could hear the battle, but without orders there was nothing to do but patiently wait, listen to its roar, and watch the plumes of bluish-white smoke rise lazily above the tree-lined creek. Lieutenant George Wren's 8th Louisiana was camped nearby, and he also listened to the guns thundering along Bull Run. Later that day, Wren wrote, "Here, I heard, for the first time, volley after volley of musketry in actual engagement—The sound had a different charm upon me from that I expected and will no doubt more so when I come to experience it."[17]

After what seemed an eternity, Early finally received urgent orders to move his men and two guns of the Washington Artillery to the ford to shore up Longstreet's faltering line. Commands were quickly shouted around camp, and the brigade was soon up and shuffling down the hot, dusty road toward the sound of the firing. While marching to the battle, the men passed a small farmyard where Beauregard sat his horse watching them file past. Dressed in an impressive new uniform, the general took care to speak to each of the Louisiana companies as Hays' regiment hurried by. Bursting with pride, the men were anxious to enter the fray under the watchful eye of their commanding general. These thoughts were soon dispelled, however, when the brigade crested a hill and walked headlong into a stream of bloodied soldiers stumbling up the slope toward the rear. Some clutched shattered limbs and gaping wounds, but they urged the brigade on, nonetheless, for the federals were forcing a crossing at that very moment. Early quickly deployed the Tigers out front and sent them charging down the hill, with the Virginians following in support. The noise of battle and visions of the wounded so unnerved some of the Virginians that they fired volleys of musketry dangerously close over the Tigers' heads before reaching the ford. Luckily, there were no casualties, and Hays' men, according to A. J. Dully, arrived at the stream "just in time to save the day."[18]

Hays took up a position astride the ford while the Virginians filed in on his right. The brigade remained in this position for several hours, unable to advance and subjected to a heavy plunging fire from the blue-clad soldiers atop the much higher opposite bank. When it was evident that neither side could advance, the Yankees accepted the stalemate and withdrew, allowing

Early to send pickets across the stream to sound the alarm if they reappeared.

The Louisianians were pleased with their conduct, but the fight had not been the spectacular battle they expected. Hemmed in by brush and trees and having to hug the muddy creek bank for protection from the enemy's fire was hardly a heroic way to fight. Spirits were further dampened by the sight of the nine dead and fifteen wounded Tigers who lay strewn along the stream's edge. As the exhausted men glumly reflected on their first fight, a cold, steady rain set in for the night. Daylight was slow in coming through the overcast sky, and the creek was still shrouded in darkness when Hays' pickets trudged back to the ford from their all-night vigil across Bull Run. Mistaken for a Union advance by their jittery comrades, a shower of minié balls greeted the tired pickets that added one more Tiger to the fatality list.[19]

The skirmish at Blackburn's Ford convinced General McDowell that the ford was too heavily defended to force a passage. He then decided to move upstream above the Confederate left, cross over, and destroy the rebel army by smashing its left flank and steamrolling down the length of Beauregard's line. Guarding the Confederate left at the Stone Bridge was Col. Nathan G. "Shank" Evans with some Virginia cavalrymen, Wheat's Battalion, and the 4th South Carolina. Before daybreak on Sunday, July 21, Evans' pickets heard the low rumble of a massive troop movement beyond the bridge. Evans quickly advanced one company of Wheat's Battalion and some of his Carolinians as skirmishers while the rest of the brigade took up positions on nearby hills overlooking the bridge. Wheat also crossed over the creek to reconnoiter with a handful of men, but enemy fire soon forced him to withdraw. Not long afterward, a Confederate signal station informed Evans that a large Union force was moving upstream to turn his left flank. Evans and Wheat quickly consulted and agreed that their only option was to move to the left to try to hold back the enemy long enough for Gens. Beauregard and Joseph E. Johnston to send help. They then left Lt. Thomas Adrian to guard the Stone Bridge with a few Tigers while the rest of the brigade hurried upstream.[20]

With the South Carolinians on the left and Wheat on the right, Evans' line advanced through open fields and patches of woods to meet the enemy. On one occasion, the nervous Carolinians spotted the Tiger Rifles' blue striped pants and fired into them thinking they were Yankees. The Tigers immediately fired back. Wheat quickly rode into the woods and stopped the shooting, but not before two of his men were mortally wounded.[21]

At about 9:45 a.m., shortly after Wheat's Catahoula Guerrillas had been deployed as skirmishers near the base of Matthews Hill, Union Gen. Ambrose Burnside's Rhode Island brigade advanced through the forest with bayonets brightly reflecting the morning sun. Sporadic firing broke out along the line as Burnside's 2nd Rhode Island unexpectedly flushed out the Catahoula boys who were hiding in the brush and weeds at the edge of the timber. Sergeant Robert Ritchie wrote, "[T]he enemy opened on us, and we had the honor of opening the ball, receiving and returning the first volley that was fired on that day. . . . After pouring a volley, we rushed upon the enemy and forced them back under cover." Burnside's six artillery pieces and line of infantry poured a deadly fire into the advancing Tigers, and Catahoula Guerrilla Drury Gibson claimed, "The balls came as thick as hail [and] grape, bomb and canister would sweep our ranks every minute."[22]

Several sources reported that the Tiger Rifles and Catahoula Guerrillas threw down their Mississippi Rifles because they were not fitted for a bayonet and charged the federals with knives. One Alabaman, who called the Louisianians "the most desperate men on earth," claimed they threw their knives at the enemy, "scarcely ever missing their aim." According to the Alabaman, the "large knives" had strings attached, presumably so they would not be lost after being thrown. After the battle, one of the Tigers described this phase of the fight to a newspaper: "Flat on our faces we received their shower of balls; a moment's pause, and we rose, closed in upon them with a fierce yell, clubbing our rifles and using our long knives. This hand-to-hand fight lasted until fresh reinforcements drove us back beyond our original position, we carrying our wounded with us."[23] An English correspondent who witnessed the Tigers' attack also reported that the Louisianians charged with their bowie knives. "Now the battalion would keep up a lively fire from the woods, creep through brush, make a sudden charge, upset a cannon or two and retire. Again, they would maintain a death-like silence until the foe was not more than 50 paces off; then delivering a withering volley, they would dash forward with unearthly yells and [when] they drew their knives and rushed to close quarters, the Yankees screamed with horror."[24]

Recalling the fierce hand-to-hand fighting, Sergeant Ritchie wrote, "Our blood was on fire. Life was valueless. They boys fired one volley, then rushed upon the foe with clubbed rifles beating down their guard; then they closed upon them with their knives. I have been in battles several times before, but such fighting never was done, I do not believe as was done for the next half-hour, it did not seem as though men were fighting, it was devils mingling in the conflict, cursing, yelling, cutting, shrieking." When one Yankee fired at and missed a Tiger charging at him with a bowie knife, the two men grappled with one another and fell to the ground. A newspaper reported that "the Bengalese reached over and catching the Yankee's nose between his teeth, bit off close to his face, and then proceeded to perform a like service upon his cheeks, and thus he literally chewed his face into jelly." The mutilated Yankee was captured and treated in a Richmond hospital.[25]

Wheat claimed that he advanced and drove the enemy back on three different occasions, but superior Union numbers prevailed and all of Evans' men were finally forced to fall back. Wheat then consulted with Evans and was given permission to move to the left in an attempt to flank the Union artillery. During the maneuver, one group of Tigers mistakenly crossed an open hayfield and came under a murderous fire. Seeing that his men were in trouble, Wheat rode out to rally them. Dismounting, he held his reins in one hand and with the other drew his sword and waved it overhead, calling on the men to form around him. Handfuls of Tigers were beginning to respond to his call when there was the sickening thud of lead hitting flesh. The major collapsed, drilled through the body by a ball that grazed his left arm and then entered near his armpit and tore through one lung before passing out in front of the right armpit.[26]

Captain Buhoup rushed to Wheat's side and called on some of his Catahoula Guerrillas to roll the major onto a blanket and use it as a litter to carry him to the rear. The Delta Rangers' flag had been chosen by lot to serve as the battalion's colors, and color-bearer Austin Eastman tore it from the staff and draped it over Wheat. Grabbing the blanket's corners, the Tigers then headed to the rear, but a couple of the litter bearers were shot down, and Wheat tumbled hard to the ground. "Lay me down, boys," he gasped, "you must save yourselves." The Tigers adamantly refused to abandon him and called on others to lend a hand in removing the major from the field. After the battle, the Delta Rangers' Capt. Henry C. Gardner returned the flag to Eastman's sister, who had made and presented it to the company. With it was the message, "We have, dear Miss, baptized your gift in the din of battle and its folds have been wet with the blood of our gallant Major." Today, the bloodstained flag is on display in the New Orleans Confederate Memorial Hall.[27]

Although Wheat's and Evans' eleven companies had been steadily pushed back, they had maintained order and were effectively slowing the advance of thirteen thousand Yankees. However, the sight of Wheat being carried from the field, apparently mortally wounded, destroyed the Tigers' morale. Without his effective leadership, the battalion quickly disintegrated, and the men drifted away in small groups to continue the fight alone or attached to other commands. When Col. Robert Withers' 18th Virginia advanced toward the Henry House, it met some of the wounded men and stragglers leaving the fight. Withers tried to get the latter to return to the battle with his regiment and recalled that "all refused except two 'Tigers,' who, from their brogue were evidently Irish." Withers ordered his men to lie on the ground when they neared the Henry House while he tried to find out how the battle was going. "Just then," he wrote, "one of the 'Tigers' who had joined us ran up the slope to an orchard occupied by the skirmishers, got behind an apple tree, and fired two or three times, when he was shot through both legs. He squatted down, and turning his head over his shoulder called to his comrade: 'I say, Dennis, come up here and give them hell for they've got me!'"[28]

When the federals saw the growing confusion in the Confederates' ranks they pressed their attack with renewed vigor. By that time, Lieutenant Adrian, who had been left at the Stone Bridge with a small detachment of Tiger Rifles, arrived at the Matthews House and joined in a counterattack against the New York Fire Zouaves and Brooklyn Chasseurs. A musket ball shattered Adrian's thigh, but he raised himself up on one elbow as his men began falling back past him and shouted, "Tigers, go in once more. Go in my sons, I'll be great gloriously God damn if the sons of bitches can ever whip the Tigers!" Some of Tigers then rallied, turned, and met the Union charge along with two newly arrived Confederate brigades under Gen. Barnard Bee and Col. Francis S. Bartow.[29]

By noon, some order had been restored to the confused Confederate ranks, and a new line was established around the Henry House. After a series of charges and countercharges, the federals finally massed a determined assault in midafternoon that began to break the rebels' resistance. If not for the timely arrival of Early's brigade at this crucial moment, the entire Confederate army might have given way.

Since morning, Early's men had been marching from ford to ford, trying to block other threatened federal crossings. They never encountered much resistance, although the dust they kicked up did attract some enemy shells, one of which killed and wounded a handful of men in the 7th Louisiana. Early was several miles away at Blackburn's Ford when the battle began building to its climax around noon. Although his men were exhausted from having marched miles back and forth between the fords in the hot July sun, Early was ordered to move immediately to the left toward the fighting. With the 7th Virginia, 13th Mississippi, and the 7th Louisiana, Early headed for the sound of battle, which by now had increased to a sustained roar as the federals began their final push. At approximately 3:00 p.m., Early found General Johnston, who ordered him to locate the federal right flank and attack it to relieve some of the pressure on the Confederate front. Unable to obtain guides, Early had to judge where the Union flank was by the sound of firing. Hays' Louisianians "were much blown" from their earlier marching, but the column quickly moved away and soon found the Union flank positioned along a sharp ridge. Early placed the 7th Virginia in front, with Hays and the 13th Mississippi slightly behind it and to the left. When the order to advance was given, Hays reportedly shouted, "Hurrah for the Tigers! Charge for the Tigers and for Louisiana!" According to one of his men, they then rushed up and over the slope "whooping and yelling, like so many devils."[30]

McDowell's flank disintegrated before Early's assault, and Beauregard sent the rest of the Confederate line charging in, as well. Muskets, knapsacks, and other equipment littered the ground as the Yankees threw away their gear in their haste to escape. Hays' men scooped up discarded letters during the chase and amused themselves by reading aloud the Yankees' plans to hang Jefferson Davis and end the war in six weeks. Colonel Hays even stumbled upon and kept a complete set of elegant china that his men believed was abandoned by one of the northern picnickers who came to witness the Confederacy's downfall. Wheat's Tigers also helped themselves to the Yankees' discarded equipment. After the battle, one newspaper correspondent noticed the Tigers carrying knapsacks and haversacks stenciled with "US." When asked what it meant, a Tiger replied, "A few weeks ago . . . they meant 'Uncle Sam,' now they mean 'us.'"[31]

When darkness and confusion in the Confederates' ranks finally ended the chase, the exhausted but ecstatic rebels halted and huddled around sputtering campfires to recount their day's experiences. Both sides had about eighteen thousand men engaged in the battle, with the Confederates losing approximately two thousand men and the Union three thousand. Wheat's Battalion and Hays' 7th Louisiana could be proud of the role they played in this first great southern victory. Wheat's Tigers had helped hold back the Union on-slaught until Beauregard and Johnston could organize a defense, and Hays had helped break the federal flank at the most critical moment of the battle.

Losses among the Louisiana commands were surprisingly light considering the heavy fire to which they were subjected. Official reports show that Wheat had eight men killed, thirty-eight wounded, and two missing, while Hays lost only three killed and twenty-three wounded. A study of individual soldiers' records, however, indicate that Wheat had more men killed than reported. Historian Gary Schreckengost found that he actually lost twelve men killed or mortally wounded, thirty-one wounded, and four captured (one of whom was also wounded). The battalion's loss in officers was particularly heavy. Besides Wheat being wounded, Lt. Robert Dickinson, the battalion's adjutant, had his horse shot from under him, but he continued to fight on foot with his pistol and sword until he was wounded in the leg. Captain White of the Tiger Rifles was severely "stunned" when his horse was shot under him; Lieutenant Adrian of the Tiger Rifles was wounded in the thigh; Capt. Obedia Miller of the Old Dominion Guards was wounded in the ankle; and Lt. Henry S. Carey of the Old Dominion Guards was shot in the foot and then stabbed in the thigh by a Yan-kee officer while on the ground. Carey, however, managed to kill his attacker.[32]

The 79th New York captured one of Wheat's missing men and forced him to accompany the regiment on the retreat back to Washington. One of the sol-diers recalled, "Considerable astonishment as well as amusement was caused by the presence in our retreating ranks of a solitary prisoner, who plodded along with us and entertained us by his quaint remarks. His uniform attracted our attention: a Zouave cap of red, and jacket of blue, with baggy trousers made of blue and white striped material, and white leggings, gave him a rather rakish appearance; he announced himself as a member of the Louisiana Tiger Battalion, Major Wheat commanding."[33]

The Louisianians were hailed as heroes for their role in the First Battle of Manassas. Evans reported that Wheat's Battalion captured a stand of enemy colors, one of the most notable acts soldiers could accomplish, but did not identify to which Union unit the flag belonged. General Johnston also thanked the battalion in the presence of President Davis for its "extraordinary and desperate stand." Wheat, in particular, was singled out for praise. Beauregard sent a personal note to tell him that "you, and your battalion, for this day's work, shall never be forgotten, whether you live or die." Evans also appreciated

Wheat's service and wrote in his report, "I would call attention to the general commanding to the heroic conduct of Maj. Robert Wheat, of the Louisiana Volunteers, who fell, gallantly leading his men in a charge, shot through both lungs."[34]

In contrast to their comrades' praise, northerners accused the Tigers of unspeakable brutality after the fighting was over. An Ohio newspaper claimed that Union prisoners were generally treated well by the rebels, except the ones who fell into the hands of the Louisiana Tigers. The Tigers, which one newspaper referred to as the "Chain Gang Regiment," reportedly "displayed great brutality, cutting some of the captives' throats." A postwar Tennessee newspaper also claimed that a Tiger murdered a badly wounded Union soldier who begged him to relieve his suffering. The Tiger "coolly gratified him by cutting his throat with a dirk [and] then bowed to the other wounded men and blandly asked if 'he could accommodate any other gentlemen.'" A Wisconsin newspaper published the most sensational accusation when it reported, "It is said by Virginians who have come from the battle-field that these fiends in human shape have taken the bayonets and knives of our wounded and dying soldiers, and thrust them into their hearts, and left them sticking there; and that some of the Louisiana Zouaves have severed the heads of our dead, from their bodies, and amused themselves by kicking them about as footballs."[35]

The Tigers were also accused of desecrating the graves of Union soldiers. A year after the battle, a northern man who traveled to Manassas to retrieve his brother's remains discovered that his and several other graves had been dug up and the body parts scattered about. When a local resident was questioned about the matter, he claimed that the Louisiana Tigers were responsible for several such desecrations.[36]

After the dead had been buried around Manassas, the army's attention turned to treating the hundreds of soldiers who had been wounded in the battle. Among them was Major Wheat, whose surgeon did not believe he would recover from his dreadful wound. The night of the battle, Wheat asked the doctor about his chances of surviving, and the surgeon slowly shook his head and said, "Major, I will answer you candidly that you can't live 'til day." Wheat defiantly answered, "I don't feel like dying yet." "But," the surgeon replied, "there is no instance on record of recovery from such a wound." Thinking this over, the major resolutely declared, "Well, then, I will put my case on record" and astounded the surgeon by making a full recovery.[37]

While recuperating at James Barbour's Culpeper home, Wheat was treated as something of a celebrity. General Beauregard and other dignitaries visited him, and newspapers praised his contribution to the Manassas victory. Barbour wrote a letter to Virginia Gov. John Letcher seeking a promotion for Wheat, and rumors spread that he was to be made a colonel or perhaps even brigadier general. The praise was so widespread that one jealous friend declared, "Wheat, I would give a thousand dollars to stand in your shoes today." The major immediately turned to an aide and told him to give the man his shoes.[38]

While Wheat basked in glory, Capt. Alex White found himself embroiled in a bitter dispute with George McCausland. Sources disagree as to the feud's particulars, and there is actually little known about the twenty-four-year-old McCausland. He was from either Pointe Coupee or West Feliciana Parish, and his brief service record lists him as a private serving as an aide-de-camp to Gen. Richard S. Ewell. Most sources, however, indicate McCausland was a captain on the staff of either Ewell or Colonel Evans, probably the latter. One account of the incident claimed that Evans criticized White for not obeying his orders during the fight at Manassas, but White responded that he never received them. McCausland apparently was responsible for delivering the orders and took offense at White's insinuation that he failed in his duty and challenged him to a duel. Another source claimed McCausland accused White of cowardice for not immediately reentering the battle after his horse was shot under him, and White then called him a liar and challenged him to a duel. Whatever the cause, the two men chose Mississippi Rifles at "short range" to settle the matter.[39]

White and McCausland met on the field of honor just three days after the battle. According to a New Orleans newspaper, White fired first and shot McCausland through the hips, while McCausland missed. McCausland died from pneumonia on September 17, but it is not clear if the disease was a complication from his wound. White was arrested, but apparently a court-martial was never held. Such "affairs of honor" were not unheard of within the officer corps of both armies, and it is probable that the high command had little desire to prosecute such cases. Instead, White was sent to New Orleans under the guise of escorting the wounded Captain Miller back home and to recruit.[40]

The Louisiana commands that missed the Battle of Manassas were envious of their veteran comrades. Richard Taylor's 9th Louisiana heard of the impending clash while still in Richmond and managed to procure a train to try to reach Manassas in time to participate. Leaving the night of July 20, the men were shocked to find the locomotive so worn out that they had to get off in order for the train to make it over the steeper grades. Taylor's frustration grew as the morning dragged on. "At every halt of the wretched engine," he wrote, "the noise of battle grew more and more intense, as did our impatience." The men's worst fear was realized when they finally arrived at Manassas, only to find that the battle was over.[41]

Several of Hays' companies and all of the 6th and 8th Louisiana were particularly outraged because they had been detailed to guard supplies and act as reserves during the historic battle. Lieutenant Wren noted in his diary that it was not until after the enemy was routed that the 8th Louisiana was ordered to advance. "This was to my great satisfaction knowing that the enemy was fleeing, and it was a sad disappointment to me indeed when we were ordered to take our position in the breastworks without being permitted to pursue the enemy further, and this was the case with others in the company and especially with the captain who showed signs of anger that night after the battle."[42]

The 6th Louisiana was part of Gen. Richard S. Ewell's brigade and had spent the day marching and countermarching for miles. Ewell appreciated the stamina of Colonel Seymour's Irishmen and put that regiment at the head of the column. Lieutenant Campbell Brown, Ewell's aide and future stepson, wrote, "[T]he men, mostly hardy Irishmen, outfooted the less robust soldiers of the Ala. Regts. so much that we had twice to stop & wait for them. The day was excessively hot & dusty—yet those Irish marched over four miles an hour." Captain Monaghan recalled that it was a day "glorious to our sacred cause but full of bitter regrets to me and my gallant company, who, notwithstanding a march of over 25 miles, did not get a shot at the enemy. I hope for better luck next time." The men were so worn out by the end of the day that William Trahern reported they "drank water from swampy pools, with dead men's blood flowing into the water only a few feet distant."[43]

In contrast to those Tigers who were disappointed at missing the fight, some of the 6th Louisiana counted themselves lucky after visiting the battlefield. Private Herron wrote, "It was a sight that I will never forget and a sight that I would never care to see again." Lieutenant Jeremiah Hogan remembered that "the dead, dying and wounded lay in heaps with dead horses, arms and ammunition scattered all over the place, the wounded in agony crying for mercy and relief." Horrified at the human wreckage that lay scattered across the field and in nearby hospitals, these men quickly decided that combat was not the glorious excitement they previously thought.[44]

Wheat's Battalion and the 7th Louisiana had played key roles in the Battle of Manassas, but it was the latter regiment that made a lasting impact on southern history by helping to create the famous Confederate battle flag. General Beauregard took the lead in designing what became known as the "Southern Cross" and explained its origin to a select group of officers for whom he hosted a dinner party in November 1861. Beauregard explained that at the moment of victory at Manassas he spotted a column of troops maneuvering on his flank more than a mile away. "At their head waved a flag which I could not distinguish. Even by a strong glass I was unable to determine whether it was the United States flag or the Confederate flag. At this moment I received a dispatch from Capt. [Porter] Alexander, in charge of the signal station, warning me to look out for the left; that a large column was approaching in that direction, and that it was supposed to be Gen. [Robert] Patterson's command coming to reinforce McDowell. At this moment, I must confess, my heart failed me."[45]

Beauregard was considering a general retreat when he took one more look at the mysterious flag. It proved to be a fortuitous decision. "I took the glass and again examined the flag. . . . A sudden gust of wind shook out its folds, and I recognized the stars and bars of the Confederate banner." The flag turned out to be the Confederacy's First National Flag, which resembled the United States flag in both color and design. It was carried by Colonel Hays' 7th Louisiana, which participated in Jubal Early's counterattack on the Union right flank. Hays' second-in-command, Lt. Col. Charles de Choiseul, wrote home after the battle that the regiment just happened to be carrying the national colors that day instead of its blue regimental flag, but he did not explain why. Determined to avoid similar mistakes in the future, Beauregard decided that his men needed a distinctive battle flag. Collaborating with others, he settled on a blue St. Andrew's Cross on a red field, with white stars representing the southern states.[46]

After explaining the flag's origins, Beauregard had it brought out to show the officers. A reporter for the Richmond *Daily Dispatch* was impressed and wrote, "The flag itself is a beautiful banner, which, I am sure, before this campaign is over, will be consecrated forever in the affections of the people of the Confederate States." Not long afterward, Beauregard was transferred to the western Confederacy and the new battle flag took root there, as well. Today his original flag, which was first unveiled at a Virginia dinner party, can be seen in the Louisiana State Cabildo Museum in New Orleans.[47]

Shortly after the Battle of Manassas, the Louisianians along Bull Run were formed into the 8th Brigade under Gen. William H. T. Walker of Georgia. The only active campaigning conducted during the remainder of the year was in late September when Walker took his men to the Potomac River on a reconnaissance mission. The 6th Louisiana's George Zeller described the excursion to his family in his unique writing style:

> [O]ur Brigade had the pleasure of having a tramp for about one hundred miles to the river. . . . [T]hen we took six big Cannons and placed them in the woods rite acrossed from the Yankies. they where montin there guard at the same time when we fired our Canons at them and at A big store house they had fild with things for the winter. the first shot was fired amongst the guards then at the store house. you ought to have seen them running and hollering every wich way we shot the house down with three hot balls and set it A fire after that we come around another way we seen about one thousand Yankies on top of A high hill there we came out in an open field and marched around so the Yankies could see us they fired one canon ball at us it came within about one hundred and fifty feet the reason we don it was to get A fight but they would not come on the side we was there was five thousand of Yankies and there was only two thousand and one hundred of us they are to couward to come and fight us. . . . [W]e were very ancious at the time to have A fight but we could not get one no where so we had to come home again.[48]

For many Tigers this expedition was their first real experience in soldiering, and they found the outing to be quite pleasant. It was exciting to slip to the river's edge opposite Union encampments, bang away at surprised bathers, and then wave their flags in triumph and melt back into the woods. Such tactics were fun and relatively harmless, for the only casualties suffered during the sortie were foot blisters caused by the long forced marches.[49]

The Louisianians on the Peninsula joined in celebrating the victory at Manassas, but as the excitement faded they were left largely forgotten in their muddy trenches. Throughout the remainder of 1861, these men stoically performed the vital but dreary task of guarding Richmond against the enemy garrison at Fort Monroe. Colonel Sulakowski, who was placed in command of Magruder's entire left flank in January 1862, oversaw much of this important mission. Sulakowski's most lasting contribution to Richmond's defense was the building of a series of trenches and earthworks that were described by one Union engineer as the "most extensive known to modern times." Even mundane tasks like sprucing up the hamlet of Ship's Point came under the colonel's watchful eye. Lieutenant Miller wrote that Sulakowski turned the town "from the muddiest, and most miserable looking place, [into] a neat little village with every convenience of civilized life . . . including an *opera-house*" that was run by the 14th Louisiana's band members. Sulakowski's guiding hand was lost in February, however, when he resigned in a huff over real or perceived incidents of governmental favoritism.[50]

On October 19, thirty men in the 2nd Louisiana experienced their first taste of combat when they were among approximately seventy-five soldiers picked from several regiments to participate in a scouting expedition toward Newport News. The Tigers, along with some Georgia and Virginia troops who were chosen for their marksmanship skills, were led by a Lieutenant Causey. The next day the detachment set up an ambush in heavy brush alongside a road about three miles from Newport News. Thomas Phifer quickly realized the ambush would not succeed because the Georgians and Virginians "acted very bad jumping up and down making unnecessary disturbance." After the rebels lay in the mud for hours, three Union soldiers finally came down the road. Despite orders to remain hidden, one of the Georgians or Virginians rose up to get a better look, and the Yankees spotted him and took off running across an open field.

Phifer and several other men ran after the enemy and shot them down, but almost immediately, several hundred Yankees converged on the exposed Confederates out in the field and opened fire. One of the Georgians was hit, and a lieutenant with them ordered a retreat back to the main force. According to Phifer, everyone obeyed except some members of the 2nd Louisiana's Pelican Greys who wanted to collect a Yankee canteen and musket as souvenirs. They ran out to where the three enemy soldiers lay, bayoneted one who was still alive, and apparently collected their prizes. When they returned to their original position, Phifer and his friends discovered that everyone else had run away, leaving their overcoats and canteens behind. "All that we could hear of them was the noise that a drove of frightened hogs would make running through the woods." Phifer and his companions reluctantly joined the retreat and found the trail was littered with "their accoutrements upon the stumps and bushes in every direction."[51]

When the Tigers finally caught up with their comrades a half-mile away, Phifer claimed, "They were standing around in groups of ten or a dozen everyone talking at the top of his voice and no one listening to his tale." The brief encounter with the enemy apparently made an impression on those who participated in the ambush. William Posey reported that two men in his company were chosen for the expedition and informed his family, "The boys stood the fire very well but they said the balls whistled around them very thick and made them think there was a chance to be shot."[52]

In late March 1862, Union Gen. George B. McClellan's Army of the Potomac began arriving at Fort Monroe in preparation for a strike up the Peninsula toward Richmond. Badly outnumbered, General Magruder was forced to resort to trickery to delay McClellan's advance until Joseph E. Johnston could bring reinforcements from northern Virginia. Magruder shuttled trains back and forth to the front lines and had his men cheer the nonexistent reinforcements. Regiments were also split up and marched back and forth in view of the Yankees to give the appearance of a much larger army. Lieutenant Miller of the 14th Louisiana was impressed with the general's ingenuity and wrote, "The way Magruder fooled them was to divide each body of his troops into two parts and keep them travelling all the time for twenty four hours, till reinforcements came." Miller claimed that his regiment marched from Yorktown to the James River and back six times.[53]

The long-awaited Peninsula Campaign began on April 5 when McClellan's huge force lumbered up the Peninsula and probed both of Magruder's flanks. Although the Confederates easily repulsed these advances, the skirmishes kept them on edge while they prepared for the inevitable main assault. The tense waiting caused nerves to fray and sometimes led to tragic encounters. In separate incidents a sergeant in Dreux's Battalion, a Lieutenant Miller of Pendleton's Battalion, and Lt. Alfred Scanlon of the 10th Louisiana were killed by their own jittery men when they were mistaken for Yankees while inspecting the picket lines at night. Scanlon apparently became disoriented in the dark and went into no-man's-land. Upon his return, one of his pickets challenged him and opened fire when he did not hear Scanlon give the countersign. Lieutenant Miller was killed in a similar fashion. He and some men scouted beyond the lines on the night of May 14, and one of the pickets challenged them when they returned. Before Miller could give the countersign, however, the nervous picket shot him in the arm and he died shortly after surgeons amputated his shattered limb. The soldier who shot him was devastated, but Colonel Pendleton wrote, "I in some measure console myself with the thought that it will teach my men greater caution & circumspection."[54]

Daily shelling by huge Union siege guns further broke down Confederate morale. At Young's Mill, Eugene Janin reported that the federal gunners were "quite accurate" in lobbing shells into the works held by Dreux's Battalion. The men of the 14th Louisiana endured daily shelling for three weeks, during which time they never left their trenches and had only raw pickled pork and biscuits to eat. In one twenty-four-hour period, approximately three hundred shells were fired into the regiment's position, but, surprisingly, only three men were wounded. Lieutenant Miller found the incoming shells to be strangely intriguing. "The first thing we knew of them," he wrote, "is a shrill whistle unlike anything you or I ever heard before, then the sharp bell-like crack of the bomb—the whistle of the little balls like bumble-bees—then the report of the Guns."[55]

Father Hippolyte Gache noticed that the frequent shelling had a positive spiritual effect on the men. In reporting on one bombardment that took place on April 5, he wrote, "[D]uring the course of the day they fired on us some twenty times, but no one was injured or even really frightened, though many of their shells exploded in the midst of our troops. . . . I'm finally beginning to have a lot of work on my hands. The big fish, frightened by the sound of Yankee cannons, leave their deep holes and come up to where I can catch them."[56]

In addition to the frequent bombardments, cold rains drenched the exhausted Tigers almost daily. Wolf Lichenstein described the conditions that his 2nd Louisiana endured during the seven weeks it manned the Warwick Line: "[O]ften the ditch was full of water. . . . The enemies sharp shooters were on the alert and [illegible] a head was safe to be visible a second. We frequently would place a cap on a long stick and hold it up above the Earthworks, and the Cap would be riddled in a short time." On one occasion the Yankees unleashed heavy artillery and rifle fire in preparation for a rush across the river. "The limbs of trees came crashing & plunging down upon us," Lichenstein wrote. "The excitement was great." During the bombardment Lichenstein noticed that a friend was frantically shooting his weapon, but the musket was not discharging because in his excitement he forgot to cap the nipple. After pointing out the mistake, Lichenstein looked back and saw the man lying on the ground foaming at the mouth. Captain Ross E. Burke and others thought the soldier was either dead or wounded, but Lichenstein had known him since childhood and knew it was an epileptic seizure brought on by the excitement. Burke believed the soldier was "shamming" to get out of the fight, but Lichenstein was able to explain the situation and later escorted his friend to a Richmond hospital.[57]

Occasionally, the Confederates' artillery was as great a nuisance to McClellan as his was to Magruder. One such gun was a lone six-pounder stationed at Dam Number One on the Warwick River. The dam was one of several that Magruder designed to impede the Union advance by creating small lakes across McClellan's front. Colonel William Levy's 2nd Louisiana held Dam Number One, with General Howell Cobb's 15th North Carolina, Cobb's Legion, and the 11th and 16th Georgia strung out in trenches to Levy's right. On the morning of April 16, Gen. William T. H. Brooks' Vermont brigade was ordered to slip across the shallow, thirty-yard-wide pond and seize the annoying cannon and surrounding trenches.

At 8:00 a.m., several Union guns opened fire on Levy's position from a range of eleven hundred yards. With the Louisianians' lone six-pounder barking back with only limited effect, the artillery duel continued until 3:00 p.m., when eighteen federal pieces began blasting the Confederate works. At the same time, three companies of the 3rd Vermont eased into the waist-deep water, and the men began weaving their way through the flooded forest toward the opposite shore while holding their muskets and cartridge boxes high. The brush and timber clogging the pond concealed the approaching Yankees, but it also tripped up many and sent them tumbling headlong into the stagnant water. Under the covering artillery fire, the federals managed to reach the far shore undetected and surprise the 15th North Carolina on Levy's right and capture the trenches and cannon. The Tar Heels and 16th Georgia attempted a bold counterattack, but the death of the former's colonel and the arrival of two more Vermont companies forced the Confederates to retreat. Quickly reforming his line, General Cobb hurled the 7th and 8th Georgia, part of the

16th Georgia, and two companies of the 2nd Louisiana under Maj. Isaiah T. Norwood against the Yankees' position. This charge pushed the outnumbered federals back into the pond, where they were further cut up by devastating volleys from two other Louisiana companies that were stationed at the dam. The plucky Vermonters regrouped on the opposite bank and attempted a second crossing, but after suffering heavy casualties and having eleven balls riddle their flag they finally gave up the mission.[58]

After the bloody clash, the 2nd Louisiana's Lt. Sidney Baxter Robertson wrote, "The battle raged with great fury all day. The Vermonters charged desperately upon our battery, but they were hurled back bleeding and disordered, as many times as they advanced." One Alabama soldier raised the possibility that Levy's Tigers showed no quarter in the fight. According to William McClellan, when the 2nd Louisiana counterattacked it cut off the three Vermont companies and killed all but five of the men. McClellan heard a report that the enemy raised the black flag when they first attacked, but "Some say the Yankees never hoisted a black flag that the Louisiannans told they did so to justify them in Showing no quarter."[59]

The spirited fight at Dam Number One has received little attention from historians, but it was the Army of the Potomac's first assault on an entrenched position. The sortie carried a high price—63 of the Vermont men were dead and 127 wounded, along with 60 to 75 Confederates killed or wounded. For two days the federal dead lay sprawled along the muddy banks and bobbing in the putrid water before Colonel Levy crossed the dam under a flag of truce to arrange for their burial. Lieutenant Robertson reported, "[We] found thirty poor fellows horribly mutilated. We found another not yet dead. We delivered the dead to the Yankees under a flag of truce." Robertson wrote his mother that he hauled off six wagon loads of dead and wounded men, and criticized Colonel Levy for not retrieving some of their own wounded before they were captured. While the grisly work of removing the casualties was carried out, Levy inquired what regiment had made the initial assault that drove the Tar Heels from their trenches. When told it was only a "detachment" of the 3rd Vermont, the surprised Tiger declared, "It was lucky for us that you did not send over many such detachments."[60]

Thanks to Magruder's ingenious tactics, the rebels managed to hold their position on the Peninsula until General Johnston arrived with reinforcements. Johnston assumed command on April 12, but by the end of the month he still had only 60,000 men to face McClellan's 100,000-man army. To make matters worse, Johnston stood to lose a sizable portion of his army when the one-year enlistments for thousands of his men ran out that month. For some time, officials had been trying to get the soldiers to reenlist for the duration of the war, but the results were mixed. In February, Thomas Phifer of the 2nd Louisiana's Pelican Rifles informed his father, "The reenlistment question is very lively here. I would not be much surprised if they got the Pelicans yet. If I can get into a good company and enlist to advantage, I believe I will try it for two years longer anyhow."[61]

Many of those who did choose to reenlist did so because their officers promised them furloughs to visit home as a reward. Phifer reported that ten men in his company received reenlistment furloughs, although some were later cancelled. Some of the lucky men in the 6th Louisiana who got to go home had an encounter with LeGrand James Wilson, a Confederate soldier who had escaped from Fort Donelson, Tennessee. Wilson recalled trying to get on a train at Columbia, Tennessee, only to be told that no soldiers were allowed to board. He slipped into a car anyhow and was immediately surrounded by members of the 6th Louisiana. They were, Wilson claimed, the "roughest looking Irish soldiers I had ever met. . . . One of the roughest, knife in hand and half drunk, approached me as I entered the car." When the Tiger demanded to know why Wilson had disobeyed the order not to board the train, Wilson began to explain how he had escaped from Fort Donelson. The Louisianian's demeanor quickly changed. "The h—l you say, come back, comrade, have a drink, and tell us of the 'foit.'" According to Wilson, the Tigers shared their liquor with him, and "I was a lion among the 'tigers.'"[62]

Luckily for General Johnston, the Confederate Congress passed the Conscription Act on the same day the Vermont brigade attacked Dam Number One. This bill provided for the conscription of all eligible males from eighteen to thirty-five years of age and required those volunteer companies still on active duty on April 16 to reelect officers and reorganize for the duration of the war. The law had a sobering effect on the Louisianians because many of the men were tired of military life and eagerly looked forward to returning home. Complaints and oaths were loud and numerous in such commands as the 1st Louisiana, in which seven of ten companies were scheduled to disband in less than two weeks. A unique situation arose in Dreux's Battalion because five of its six companies were to disband before the law went into effect. General

Magruder personally appealed to its members to stay on the firing line until the immediate Union threat had passed. In a special order, he thanked the battalion for its faithful service and sympathized with the men's disappointment at not yet seeing combat. However, he hoped "that it may be never said that a La. Batl. . . . moved to the rear at the sound of the enemy's cannon." In closing, the general authorized the battalion's disbandment but stated that "he is satisfied that no co. will avail itself of it—at least until reinforcements have arrived."[63]

The Louisianians accepted Magruder's challenge and agreed to remain in the trenches an additional month without pay. On May 1, however, Colonel Rightor was told of Johnston's plan to evacuate the Yorktown-Warwick line and took the retreat as a release from the battalion's agreement. Calling the men together, Rightor gave a fiery speech before ordering the drummer boys to beat taps and the battalion to disband. The Shreveport Greys company was forced to remain on duty under the terms of the Conscription Act, so it was transferred to the 1st Louisiana. Most of the battalion members who were discharged returned to Louisiana, reorganized as Fenner's Louisiana Battery, and continued to fight in the western theater. The other Louisiana units in Virginia dutifully held elections for their officers in campaigns that were reportedly marred by "whiskey, promises and bribes of various sorts."[64]

During the army's 1862 reorganization, the War Department apparently approved the transfer of infantrymen to naval service because a number of Louisiana Tigers volunteered to serve on the CSS *Virginia* (formerly known as the *Merrimac*). The 2nd Louisiana's Thomas Phifer informed his sister, "The Merrimac is recruiting for six months. . . . Great excitement exists in camp about the Merrimac. About one hundred have just passed my tent to be sworn in." Records show that of twenty-four men in the 10th Louisiana who transferred to the navy, nine served on the *Virginia*, and at least two in Coppens' Zouaves did so, as well. Both of the latter were former sailors, and one had even served on the *Merrimac* before the war and declared he was glad to get back to her. A 1915 newspaper article claimed that a Louisiana Tiger named John McClellan was the last survivor of the *Virginia*'s crew, but there is no record of his having served in a Louisiana regiment.[65]

In northern Virginia, efforts had begun before the Conscription Act was passed to entice members of the Louisiana Brigade to reenlist for the duration of the war. In February, Lieutenant Wren reported that forty men in the 8th

Louisiana's Minden Blues had done so but that many others were "slow about deciding." After discovering that a number of his friends in the 9th Louisiana had reenlisted, he did so, as well, and was rewarded with a furlough home. After he returned to Virginia, Wren reported that "Quite an excitement was raised" when each company in his regiment elected new officers as required by the Conscription Act.[66]

While the Tigers reorganized in Virginia, recruiting efforts continued in Louisiana to supply the units with fresh troops. Sixteen new recruits from New Orleans joined one company in the 14th Louisiana, but two of the men deserted before reaching Virginia. Al Pierson, who was elected captain of his 9th Louisiana company during the reorganization, reported that an undetermined number of recruits had arrived in camp that spring and were being rapidly trained. What Pierson failed to mention was that his regiment suffered a heavy loss when the equivalent of an entire company of new men was captured on the way to the army. That April, several of the regiment's officers were returning to Virginia with about 125 men when they decided to take a shorter train route through Tennessee, even though the Battle of Shiloh had thrown the region into chaos. The trip came to an abrupt halt when Union cavalry captured the train and its passengers as they passed through Huntsville, Alabama.[67]

While Johnston's army reorganized under the Conscription Act, McClellan finalized his plans to move against Yorktown. When he advanced, however, McClellan discovered that Johnston had abandoned the Yorktown-Warwick line and withdrawn closer to Williamsburg. Sporadic skirmish fire broke out in the early morning of May 5 as the Union forces began probing this new rebel position in heavy fog and misty rain. On the Confederate right, Union Gen. Joseph Hooker charged through a rain-soaked forest and put so much pressure on the brigades of Cadmus Wilcox and George Pickett that Col. Richard Jones' 14th Louisiana and three Alabama companies had to be rushed in as reinforcements. Placed on the far right of the Confederate line, Jones sent two of his companies out as skirmishers and ordered the rest of the men to slip off their knapsacks and prepare to advance. When the order was given, the Tigers clambered over a rail fence and carefully picked their way through a tangled *abatis* of downed trees. After a great deal of slipping and falling on the slick logs, Jones' skirmishers finally made contact with Hooker's men but were blasted back onto the main line just as it was struggling through the jungle of wet, twisted foliage. Confusion reigned in the dark, wet woods. When Jones could not be found, other officers had to step up and deploy the regiment to meet the oncoming enemy. The Confederates attempted a counterattack, but they "were staggered and embarrassed for a moment" by the accurate Yankee fire. The Louisianians quickly rallied, however, and charged again, this time forcing Hooker's men back a mile. The rebels captured a number of prisoners, three pieces of artillery, and "a small mountain of knapsacks," which the famished Tigers put to good use.[68]

The Louisiana officers finally halted the advance from fear of overextending themselves and being cut off in the rear. While the Tigers laid down on the wet ground for rest and protection, other Confederate units drifted in and were quickly put into line next to Jones' men. Within minutes, the Yankees came crashing back through the dripping underbrush "with extreme fury." They sent volleys of musket fire tearing through the Tigers' ranks, seriously wounding several of Jones' men in the head, neck, and shoulders as they lay prone on the ground. After beating back this final assault, the Confederates pulled themselves together and withdrew to their original line. The Louisianians had played a crucial role in holding back McClellan's army during the Battle of Williamsburg, but they were badly shot up in the process. In the brutal fire fight on the Confederate right, the 14th Louisiana lost 194 men, with Lt. Col. Zebulon York and Maj. David Zable being among the wounded.[69]

In the center of Johnston's line, the 5th Louisiana and St. Paul's Foot Rifles saw action at an earthwork dubbed Fort Magruder. General Magruder had personally chosen the 5th Louisiana's Colonel Forno to command the rearguard, but Forno had to rush his troops back to the fort when they learned that the Yankees were fast approaching. Sergeant John Charlton wrote that, during the rapid retrograde, "Much baggage was thrown away thoughtlessly by the men it impeding their runing. I acknowledge throwing away my Canteen the very last thing I should have done. It was amusing to see the knapsacks. buckets. campkettles Etc jumping off the Artillery caisons, as the horses put to their utmost went tearing across the plowed fields. All this occurring under a heavy fire from the Yankees artillery." The 5th Louisiana and St. Paul's Foot Rifles did not engage any Union infantry that day but did lose twenty-nine men to heavy artillery and sharpshooters' fire. One of the dead in St. Paul's Battalion was Hiram Sample's "pardner." Sample and his unidentified friend were huddled under a rubber blanket that dark night trying to stay dry. When they stood up to change positions, a Yankee sharpshooter killed Sample's friend, and Sample was forced to leave his body in the fort's magazine when the army retreated the next day.[70]

During the retreat, a number of captured wounded federals were carefully laid out on the ground near Fort Magruder, and a large group of curious Confederates soon crowded around them to catch a glimpse of a real live Yankee. One pitiful Union soldier was shot through the abdomen and rolled in agony on the ground, pleading with the Confederate guards to kill him and end his misery. According to Virginia artilleryman Robert Stiles, Coppens' Battalion marched by at that time. Seeing the crowd, several curious Zouaves dropped out of ranks and walked over to see what was happening. They were, remembered Stiles, "the most rakish and devilish looking beings I ever saw." After hearing the poor Yankee's agonizing pleas, one Zouave elbowed his way through the crowd, stood over the wounded man, and asked, "Put you out of your misery? Certainly, sir!" He then swiftly brought down his musket butt and crushed the man's skull. The crowd gasped and moved back in horror from "this demon," but the Zouave simply looked around at the other wounded men and asked matter-of-factly, "Any other gentlemen here'd like to be accommodated?" When no one answered, he disappeared through the onlookers before anyone could react.[71]

In 1884, the Stanford (Kentucky) *Semi-Weekly Interior Journal* related a similar incident involving a wounded Confederate soldier. Exactly when this killing took place was not stated, only that it occurred while the Confederate army was retreating. A grievously wounded Confederate, "shot in a half dozen places, with both arms and both legs broken," was lying under a tree begging for someone to put him out of his misery. When a company of Louisiana Tigers marched by, one of the men broke ranks, and pulled out his large knife. "Taking him by the goatee the 'Tiger' raised his head and deliberate[ly] cut his throat from ear to ear, wiped the bloody blade on the grass and stepped back into his place, leaving the dead soldier leaning against the tree." This accusation and the earlier account of a Tiger killing a wounded prisoner at First Manassas are so similar that they all may be referring to the incident that Stiles witnessed.[72] Whatever the case may be, it is clear that by the spring of 1862 the Louisiana Tigers had become feared by their Confederate comrades as well as their Yankee adversaries.

CHAPTER 4

"Something to Boast Of"

JOSEPH E. JOHNSTON's Confederate army was reorganized after the victory at Manassas with Taylor's Louisiana Brigade and the brigades of Gens. George H. Steuart, Arnold Elzey, and Isaac Trimble being placed in Richard S. Ewell's division. The Louisianians found their new divisional commander rather odd—even by the Tigers' standards. An 1840 graduate of West Point, Ewell had served in the Mexican War and then led dragoons in the desert Southwest, where he performed so well that one of Arizona's original counties was named for him. Accustomed to commanding small units of men chasing Apaches, Ewell once claimed that he knew all there was to know about handling a squadron of dragoons but little else. This mindset was illustrated while his division was camped along the Rappahannock River in the early spring of 1862. Disappointed that his men were reaping few supplies from such a rich area, Ewell went foraging himself and returned to camp with a fine bull. When he proudly showed it to Taylor, the Louisianian admired the animal but pointed out that it would hardly feed the division's eight thousand men. Ewell's face went blank, then he sighed, "Ah! I was thinking of my fifty dragoons." Such idiosyncrasies endeared Ewell to many of the Tigers, and his very appearance drew sympathy. Taylor wrote of him, "Bright, prominent eyes, a bomb-shaped bald head, and a nose like that of Francis of Valois, gave him a striking resemblence to a woodcock, and this was increased by a bird-like habit of putting his head on one side to utter his quaint speeches." According to Taylor, Ewell was also extremely nervous and had the peculiar habit of sleeping "curled around a camp-stool, in positions to dislocate an ordinary person's joints."[1]

Taylor came to admire Ewell's considerable military abilities and aggressive tendencies. In describing his commander, Taylor wrote, "Superbly mounted, he was the boldest of horsemen, invariably leaving the roads to take timber and water." Like many other Civil War generals, Ewell preferred to be in the thick of the action and often appeared on the front lines. Twice during the 1862 Shenandoah Valley Campaign, he called on Taylor to accompany him to the skirmish line and afterward confided that he hoped "old Jackson would not catch him at it."[2]

Ewell also had a reputation for cursing like a sailor and was said to have been able to "swear the scalp off an Apache," but his slight lisp sometimes dulled its edge. The general's manner softened in 1863 when he became a Christian and married his widowed first cousin Lizinka Brown, for whom he had pined for decades. Ewell never seemed able to adjust to married life, however, and repeatedly introduced Lizinka as "Mrs. Brown." "With all his oddities," claimed Taylor, "perhaps in some measure because of them, Ewell was adored by officers and men." When Ewell visited Taylor after the war, Taylor wrote, "Dear Dick Ewell! Virginia never bred a truer gentleman, a braver soldier, nor an odder, more lovable fellow."[3]

In turn, Ewell came to respect Taylor and appreciate his natural grasp of tactics. On one occasion, Ewell burned a bridge across the Rappahannock after the Yankees drove the Confederates back across the river. As Taylor and Ewell sat their horses on a hill and watched the bridge burn, Ewell sensed that Taylor disapproved of his actions and quipped, "You don't like it." Drawing on his deep knowledge of military history, Taylor explained that it was easier to defend one bridge than several miles of possible river crossings. Recognizing the wisdom of Taylor's statement, Ewell simply asked, "Why did you keep the story until the bridge was burnt?"[4]

Perhaps one reason the Tigers were so fond of Ewell was because they were used to strange behavior. As it turned out, Taylor had as many personality quirks as his commander. He, too, was twitchy and was often afflicted with "nervous headaches," rheumatism, and strokes of paralysis that left his right side so weak that he sometimes had to be helped onto his horse. Such seizures made him ill-tempered, and David F. Boyd remembered, "Taylor well was charming company [but] Taylor sick was not a pattern of patience and amiability." Taylor's famous temper at times even caused friction with Ewell. On one occasion he was sitting in Ewell's quarters when a courier arrived with a report. When the courier remarked, "I passed Taylor's Brigade," the proud Louisianian shouted out, "How dare you speak in that manner! I am General

Taylor, sir." Ewell glowered at Taylor and silenced him by coldly replying, "This is my courier, sir," and then directing the embarrassed cavalryman to continue. "Taylor was undoubtedly a splendid officer," recalled the courier, "but he was proud as Lucifer, and therefore unpopular . . . and not one of the men would have acted as courier for Gen. Dick Taylor, if they could have avoided it."[5]

After the army's reorganization, General Johnston decided to abandon Manassas and Centreville in early March 1862 and fall back behind the Rappahannock River to be in a better position to defend Richmond from any Union thrusts up the Peninsula or out of Washington. Rumors of the withdrawal circulated through the rebel camps for days, causing Taylor's brigade hastily to assemble all the possessions it had accumulated over the last few months. Private Herron of the 6th Louisiana worriedly wrote, "It will be very hard on us to leave our fine houses now and go and lay out on the cold ground, after all of our trouble in building them." But orders were orders, and by the day of the evacuation small mounds of items lay scattered around the men's quarters as each soldier attempted to stuff his knapsack and blanket roll with the numerous little conveniences he felt he could not live without.[6]

On March 8, 1862, the army began pulling back, and two days later Wheat's Battalion torched the cherished winter huts. The Louisiana Brigade then abandoned Camp Carondelet and served as rearguard when the army headed south in a cold, drizzling rain. Thus began a long, arduous night march over roads that the late-winter rains had turned into quagmires. "We had," summed up W. G. Ogden, "a wet, miserable time of it." The Irishmen of Seymour's 6th Louisiana brought up the army's rear and soon noticed pots, pans, clothing, boots, and various equipment littering the darkened roadside as the exhausted Confederates discarded their precious cargo. By daylight most men carried only the clothes on their backs—their tents, blankets, and cooking utensils had been burned at Manassas or thrown away during the night. As the cold rains continued, they came to regret discarding so much gear. On March 17, Herron reported, "The weather is terribly disagreeable—raining almost constantly, and the troops are without tents. . . . I have been sleeping on the damp ground for several nights with no protection but a tent fly & fear that the exposure will cause a relapse of my sickness. . . . [T]he weather, our falling back, and everything disagreeable combined has given everyone the 'blue devils.'"[7]

Many of the Tigers collapsed from exhaustion on the muddy roadside. Taylor stopped the brigade several times to let these stragglers catch up and finally rode in the rear to give them some respite by carrying their muskets—a gesture other officers soon copied. Taylor further garnered respect by giving friendly advice on how to bathe blistered feet and readjust ill-fitting shoes during the short halts. The men appreciated these helpful hints and came to take pride in their improved marching ability. In the months to come, Taylor's brigade often set the pace for Stonewall Jackson's "foot cavalry," and one soldier claimed the Tigers "soon held it a disgrace to fall out of ranks."[8]

Northern newspapers took note of Johnston's evacuation and falsely reported that "the Louisiana Tigers, mounted, are scouring and devastating the country" beyond Manassas. In fact, the footsore Tigers never wandered from the road before they finally crossed the Rappahannock and got some much-needed rest. Ewell's division was then left to guard the river crossings while the bulk of Johnston's army bivouacked around Orange Court House. The Tigers saw little action during this time because heavy spring rains halted most maneuvering, but in April they were forced to destroy one bridge after Union cavalry threatened to cross the river.[9]

The torrential rains continued, and many of the men frequently wandered out of camp to seek more substantial shelter than their scanty tent flies offered. During one particularly bad storm, a number of Tigers went into a nearby church to keep dry. The cozy chapel was soon crowded with soldiers, who began joking and singing as they dried out. One man sang a vulgar little tune that drew chuckles from his comrades. When another soldier followed suit, however, James T. Wrigley, Major Wheat's huge sergeant-major, slowly rose in the pulpit, where he had been smoking quietly. "See here boys!" he said sternly. "I am just as bad as any of you, I know. But this is a church and I'll be damned if it's right to sing any of your smutty songs in here, and it's got to be stopped!" A hush fell over the crowd, and the men went back to their subdued chatter. Three months later, Sergeant-Major Wrigley was taken from the Gaines' Mill battlefield mortally wounded through the abdomen.[10]

In early April, Johnston moved most of the army to the Peninsula to block George McClellan's advance on Richmond, but Ewell's division was left behind with orders to continue guarding the Rappahannock line and to cooperate with Gen. Thomas J. "Stonewall" Jackson in the Shenandoah Valley to the west. Jackson's mission was to prevent the forty-five thousand federals in the Valley from sending reinforcements to McClellan on the Peninsula. If called upon, Ewell was to join him.

On April 18, Jackson did call for Ewell's division, and it left that very day for Gordonsville. The Louisiana Brigade's move to the Valley was even more trying than the Manassas evacuation. Marching orders stipulated that the men could carry only the barest of necessities, but this was hardly necessary because most of them possessed very little following the Manassas withdrawal. General Taylor took only one change of underwear and a tent fly, and most of his Tigers carried one blanket, two pairs of socks, and an extra shirt and pair of drawers and shoes. Sergeant Edmond Stephens packed a typical knapsack, and he complained, "I have but one suit of clothes & them now on my back and have been for a month."[11]

As the men departed the Rappahannock line, a steady, soaking rain set in that once again turned the Virginia roads and fields into bottomless morasses. Eighteen miles were covered the first day, but the rain turned to sleet and then snow. The freezing precipitation continued to lash the men for the next ten days and caused considerable grumbling. "We have nothing," wrote a miserable T. A. Tooke, "but march, march, and halt and sleep in wet blankets and mud." On the third night, an early spring blizzard blanketed the Tigers as they camped in an open field. In exasperation, Tooke told his wife, "I thought that I knowed something a bout Soldiering, but I find that I had never soldiered it this way."[12]

On April 30, Taylor's brigade led the division into the Blue Ridge Mountains' steep, winding Swift Run Gap to link up with Jackson, who was reportedly on the other side. After hours of struggling up the mountain, a violent storm pounded the men as they passed through the clouds. The air grew heavy and dark, lightning crashed all around, and thunder reverberated across the rocks and hollows. Some of the Tigers were scared senseless, and each peal of thunder brought a "moan and groan" from the men. Then, as suddenly as it began, the storm subsided and the brigade emerged above the clouds into brilliant sunshine. The regimental bands began playing "Listen to the Mockingbird," and jokes and good-natured ribbings were spun at the expense of those who had been frightened.[13]

After twelve torturous hours, Swift Run Gap was behind them, and the division camped that night at the western base of the mountain, only to find that Jackson had moved farther into the Valley. Jackson's departure further unsettled Ewell and Taylor, who had been having concerns about serving under the eccentric Stonewall for some time. Jackson's secretiveness irritated Ewell because the general would not explain his plans or even share intelligence on the enemy's disposition. According to Maj. David Boyd, neither Ewell nor Taylor wanted to serve under Jackson because his dismal winter campaigns and earlier defeat at Kernstown had damaged his reputation. "Ewell didn't like it," Boyd claimed, "and Dick Taylor didn't like it . . . they were afraid Jackson would lead them into some awful scrape." Although suffering from a flare-up of his rheumatoid arthritis, Taylor agreed to speak to President Davis about their concerns. He departed camp that evening and took an ambulance to Richmond to meet with Davis and Secretary of War Judah P. Benjamin. After hearing Taylor out, Davis and Benjamin agreed that it might be best to put a more senior officer over Jackson and mentioned the possibility of appointing Gen. James Longstreet to the position. Such a move was satisfactory to Ewell and Taylor, and the Louisianian headed back to the Valley, thinking the matter was settled.[14]

When Taylor returned to camp to share the good news with Ewell, he found that Jackson had ordered most of the division to move farther west to Conrad's Store. Wandering about the nearly deserted campground, Taylor found Boyd and asked where Jackson's army was located. When Boyd replied that he had no idea, Taylor exclaimed, "Well, this is strange! Nobody at Richmond knows anything about it. But there is one consolation. We won't be under this damn old crazy fool long. Gen. Longstreet is coming up here to take command." Taylor was mistaken, however, for he, too, was ordered to join the rest of Ewell's division at Conrad's Store, and Jackson remained free to act on his own. Apparently, Gen. Robert E. Lee, Davis' military adviser, had confidence in Jackson and convinced Davis to leave him in command. Boyd remembered years later that Jackson was not only skilled in outflanking Union armies but was also adept at slipping around "two of his own best Generals and the 'folks' back at Richmond."[15]

During the difficult march from the Rappahannock River to the Shenandoah Valley, some of the units in Taylor's brigade were forced to elect new field officers under the terms of the Conscription Act. One was the Bedford Artillery, a Virginia battery that had recently been assigned to Taylor's command. Taylor wanted the artillerymen to reelect Capt. Thomas M. Bowyer, but they voted in Lt. John R. Johnson, instead. According to Ewell's aide Campbell Brown, this disobedience "caused much swearing" by Taylor, and he declared the whole battery to be worthless. Every artilleryman was relieved of duty and sent back to Richmond, and Taylor replaced them with the 6th Louisiana's

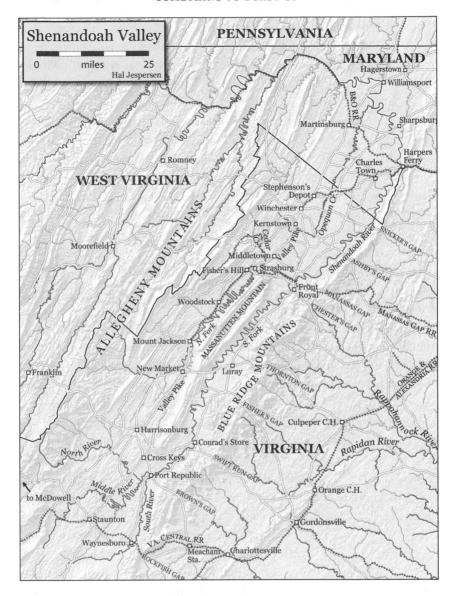

Mercer Guards, who were put under Bowyer. While in Richmond, the irate Virginians persuaded Confederate officials to countermand Taylor's order, and they eventually reformed the battery under Johnson but not before missing the Valley Campaign.[16]

The 6th and 9th Louisiana regiments also elected new field officers during this time. While near Gordonsville, the officers in the 9th Louisiana declined to stand for reelection, perhaps because they realized they would not win. As a result, Capt. Leroy A. Stafford was elected colonel, Capt. William R. Peck lieutenant colonel, and Capt. Henry L. N. Williams major.[17]

The 6th Louisiana chose new officers soon after the brigade camped at Conrad's Store, but the election was thrown into turmoil when the elderly Col. Isaac G. Seymour announced that he would not stand for reelection. Privately, the colonel informed his son that his horse had recently thrown him into cold water, which caused his rheumatism to flare up. He claimed that he might use that as an excuse to resign his commission honorably, but that was probably not the real reason for his decision. Undoubtedly, Seymour was angry at being passed over for the brigade command, and he seemed to be among a small group of Tigers who had little respect for General Ewell. In the letter to his son, Seymour claimed, "We are all exceedingly dissatisfied with Gen. Ewell, who is very eccentric and seems half the time not to know what he is doing."[18]

To make matters worse, Seymour did not get along with some of the regiment's company officers because of their heavy drinking. He explained to his son, "I am attached to my regiment, and I like the men, and the feeling is reciprocated, but with a number of my officers I am utterly disgusted. Some dozen or so of them are low, vulgar fellows and habitual whiskey drinkers. . . . I cannot have any respect for them but rather feel a loathing for them, and I cannot conceal this feeling and they well know my opinions of them." On one occasion, Seymour rebuked the officers during parade. "I told them in the plainest language that it was not the commission [that] made the gentleman, but on the contrary, commissions often by accident fell into the hands of those [who] where [sic] not and never could become gentlemen." Although Seymour did not mention it, his decision not to seek reelection may also have been based on the fear that his estranged officers would not support him.[19]

On May 8, the day before the election, Seymour appeared before the regiment in his dress uniform and explained that he would not seek reelection. The enlisted men looked upon the silver-haired Seymour as something of a father figure and referred to him as "the old man." Like a father, Seymour sometimes even used a switch on soldiers who misbehaved. According to one newspaper reporter, the soldiers "wept like babies" at the unexpected news and tried to convince the colonel to change his mind. Afterward they even borrowed a band from one of their sister regiments and serenaded Seymour at his tent. Although touched by the gesture, Seymour refused to change his mind and told the men that he would be leaving in the morning.[20]

The next day, as Seymour was preparing to depart, the regiment assembled as if for dress parade but without any of the officers being present. Their purpose was to read a petition to General Taylor written by Capt. William Monaghan and signed by all of the regiment's first sergeants. A second petition signed by "The members of the 6th Regt. La. Vols." was addressed to General Ewell. The petitions claimed that "some difficulty has arisen between the company officers and our colonel" and that Seymour was leaving because of "the petty aspirations of subordinate officers." They closed with a request that Taylor convince Colonel Seymour to stand for reelection. This outpouring of support from the rank and file caused Seymour to change his mind and run for the position. When the vote was announced to the men, a New Orleans newspaper claimed "such shouting as now took place can hardly be imagined." Seymour had been reelected colonel, Capt. Henry Strong was chosen to fill the vacant lieutenant colonel position, and Arthur McArthur defeated the incumbent for major.[21]

While camped at Conrad's Store, the Tigers scouted the countryside and occasionally encountered the enemy. According to Campbell Brown, Wheat's Tigers came close to "losing their laurels" during one skirmish on May 7 when they engaged the 13th Indiana and some federal cavalry near Somerville. Wheat was picketing the Shenandoah River with two of his companies, one company of the 9th Louisiana, and part of the 6th Virginia Cavalry when the Yankees attacked him. The Hoosiers were driving Wheat's men back in confusion when Maj. Davidson Penn came running to the rescue with several of his 7th Louisiana companies. Penn, a Virginia native, was a descendant of King Edward III and a distant relative of Confederate Gen. Patrick Cleburne. He was probably the most educated of all the Louisiana Tigers, having studied at Alabama's Spring Hill College and the University of Heidelberg, and graduating from both the Virginia Military Institute and the University of Virginia. Penn also had a keen sense of humor and often tormented his professors with annoying questions, but he turned out to be an outstanding officer who was wounded twice and captured once.[22]

When Penn arrived with the reinforcements, he assumed command, drove the Yankees back to the river, and forced the Union cavalry to swim across to escape. In the skirmish the Tigers inflicted about thirty casualties on the Hoosiers at a loss of two dead, four wounded, and one deserter. The latter was described as a "crazy Greek" who took several enemy prisoners and fought gallantly until the Yankees broke and ran. Campbell Brown claimed he then threw down his musket and "ran off after them as hard as he could go [and] has not been heard from since."[23]

On May 19, Ewell finally received orders to join Jackson, who had defeated Union Gen. Robert Milroy at McDowell and sent him fleeing to Franklin to link up with Gen. John C. Frémont's army. Jackson was now heading north toward Gen. Nathaniel Banks' army at Strasburg and Front Royal to defeat him before he became aware of the extent of Milroy's rout. Ewell had been expecting orders to join Jackson but was surprised when Jackson instructed him to split his command for the march. Ewell was to take most of the division north to Luray, but Taylor's brigade was to move west around the southern end of Massanutten Mountain to Harrisonburg and then north on the Valley Pike to join Jackson at New Market. Jackson never explained why he had Taylor make such a circuitous route, but it may have been an attempt to confuse any Union scouts observing Ewell's movement.[24]

Taylor left Conrad's Store at dawn on May 20 and reached Jackson's camp in a large open field outside New Market that afternoon. Many men in Jackson's Army of the Valley had never seen the famous Louisiana Tigers and were curious about them. The road on which Taylor marched passed through the middle of the Valley Army's camp, and Jackson's men began lining up alongside the road to catch a glimpse of the Louisianians. Taylor's brigade was the largest in Ewell's division with more than three thousand men, and it was among the best drilled and disciplined of any Confederate unit. The band of Wheat's Battalion led the brigade, playing "The Girl I Left Behind," and the Zouaves of the Tiger Rifles marched in step close behind. The rest of the brigade followed with their regimental flags flapping lazily in the breeze.[25]

According to Capt. James Nisbet of the 21st Georgia, "Each man, every inch a soldier, was perfectly uniformed, wearing white gaiters and leggings, marching quick step. . . . The blue-gray uniforms of the officers were brilliant with gold lace, their rakish slouch hats adorned with tassels and plumes. Behold a military pageantry, beautiful and memorable. . . . It was the most picturesque and inspiring martial sight that came under my eyes during four years of service." The Tigers' uniforms also caught the eye of John Worsham, who recalled, "This brigade made an unusually good appearance, as the mean were more regularly uniformed than any we had seen." In silent tribute, the hundreds of soldiers lining the road snapped an impromptu "present arms" salute as the Tigers marched by.[26]

As soon as the brigade made camp, the 8th Louisiana's band began playing lively polkas and waltzes, and the men grabbed partners and danced exuberantly as the astonished Valley Army watched. Taylor remembered the murmurs of disapproval from the pious Virginians who frowned upon "the caperings of my Creoles, holding them to be 'devices and snares.'" The Virginians in one of Jackson's artillery batteries certainly came to hold the Tigers in contempt, although for reasons other than their dancing. The artillerymen had a pet dog named Stonewall Jackson that could do an array of tricks, such as sitting up at roll call and holding a small pipe between its teeth. The gifted canine caught the eye of Taylor's Tigers, and they tried several times to "liberate" him from the battery. At last, one artilleryman sadly wrote, "the cunning thieves succeeded in hiding him," and the dog passed permanently to Taylor's brigade. A love of pets seemed to be universal among the Tigers. Later, when the 2nd Louisiana Brigade was formed, it had a mascot named Sawbuck that would follow the men into battle until it was wounded in the foreleg. Thereafter, it fell behind when the shooting began—playing "old soldier," the men quipped.[27]

After bivouacking his men, Taylor sought out Jackson, whom he had never met. Taylor was somewhat apprehensive about meeting his new commander because of Jackson's eccentric personality. Taylor found him perched atop a rail fence thoughtfully sucking on a lemon as he watched the Tigers make camp. With his best military bearing, Taylor approached the fence, snapped a crisp salute, and spat out his name and rank. While awaiting a response, he had a chance to size up the general. "A pair of cavalry boots covering feet of gigantic size, a mangy cap with visor drawn low, a heavy, dark beard, and weary eyes" caught his attention. Eyeing the Louisiana camp, Jackson asked in a low, gentle voice how far the brigade had come that day. Twenty-six miles, Taylor proudly replied. "You seem to have no stragglers," Jackson responded. "Never allow straggling," Taylor remarked, thinking how well the brigade's training during the Manassas evacuation had paid off. "You must teach my people," the general said, "they straggle badly." As Taylor nodded politely, one of the brigade's bands suddenly started a waltz that drew Jackson's attention back to the dancing Tigers. Sucking slowly on his lemon, he silently watched the men for a minute and then muttered, "Thoughtless fellows for serious work." Coming to his men's defense, Taylor responded that he hoped their gaiety would not affect their performance, but Jackson made no reply and continued studying the Tigers silently.[28]

Taylor took his leave and returned to camp, but late that night Jackson appeared unexpectedly at his campfire and stayed for several hours. Before lapsing into a prolonged silence, he told Taylor that the army would move out at daybreak and asked more questions about the Tigers' marching ability. It appeared that Jackson was impressed with them, but the same could not be said for some of the Tigers. One soldier recalled, "The remark was made by one of us after staring at him a long time, that there must be some mistake about him, [for] if he was an able man, he showed it less than any of us had ever seen." Some months later, the 14th Louisiana's Private Snakenberg got his first look at Stonewall Jackson when he heard men cheering the general as he rode by the camp. According to Snakenberg, Jackson was "a very ordinary looking person, riding a small sorrel horse, like a house on fire, along the road, about 100 yards off, who looked like a Jew peddler [sic]. He had on an old, faded, long-tail coat and a military cap with the peak pulled down over his eyes and set stooped forward in the saddle."[29]

The Tigers' suspicions of Jackson deepened before they recognized his brilliance because Jackson confided in no one, and his apparently aimless marching enraged many. "I don't know!" was Ewell's response to Taylor's inquiry of the meaning of one of Jackson's marches. "If Gen. Jackson were shot down I wouldn't know a thing of his plans!" "What!" exclaimed Taylor in disbelief. "You, second in command, and don't know! If I were second in command, I would know!" "You would, would you?" Ewell smilingly asked in his peculiar way of cocking his head to one side "like a sap-sucker peeping around a tree." "No, you wouldn't know any more than I do now. You don't yet know the man." The frustration of trying to decipher the meaning of Jackson's maneuvers prompted Ewell once to confide to Taylor that he "was certain of [Jackson's] lunacy, and that he never saw one of Jackson's couriers approach without expecting an order to assault the north pole."[30]

Milroy's army had already been defeated and chased to Franklin, where a second army was garrisoned under Frémont. The main body of General Banks' third Union army was at Strasburg, due north of Jackson, with his left flank anchored east of Massanutten Mountain at Front Royal. Taylor was ordered to lead the army out of New Market early on May 21, and Jackson joined him as he was getting the men formed before dawn. To Taylor's surprise, Jackson told him to head east through a pass in Massanutten Mountain to Ewell's position at Luray rather than north to Strasburg where Banks' main force was located. It was not until later that Taylor came to understand Jackson's plan. His cavalry would keep Banks' attention focused on the Valley Pike, while the infantry launched a surprise attack on the Yankees' isolated left flank at Front Royal. Because of Jackson's skillful maneuvering and diversionary tactics, neither Banks nor the Front Royal garrison had any idea that the latter was in danger.[31]

The army reached Luray that evening, and the next morning Taylor again took the lead in the march to Front Royal. Jackson probably kept the Tigers in the vanguard because his Valley Army was exhausted after weeks of campaigning while Taylor's brigade was relatively fresh. Jackson also appreciated the Tigers' marching abilities and used them to set the pace for the entire army. Pushing his men hard to keep up with the Louisianians was in keeping with Jackson's philosophy that "it was better to lose one man in marching than five in fighting."[32]

The small town of Front Royal sits on the east bank of the Shenandoah River's South Fork, just upstream from where the North Fork joins it to form the Shenandoah River proper (the Shenandoah River system runs in a general south-to-north direction). Two bridges crossed the South Fork in the rear of town. A wagon bridge was on the upstream side, and a railroad bridge paralleled it a few yards downstream. Union artillery placed on a ridge in the angle formed by the rivers' juncture had a clear view of the town and wagon bridge.

Following the east bank of the Shenandoah's South Fork, Taylor was approaching Front Royal on May 23 when a local woman named Belle Boyd rushed forward to inform him that the enemy had artillery covering the wagon bridge but none trained on the railroad bridge. A short time later, Jackson attached Col. Bradley Johnson's 1st Maryland to Taylor's command and ordered Taylor to put skirmishers out front and move slowly toward Front Royal. Jackson knew that the 1st Maryland (Union) was defending the town and that his rebel Marylanders would be eager to fight their Yankee counterparts. That is why Jackson called the 1st Maryland to the front of the column to lead Taylor's brigade forward. When the regiment marched past the Louisianians, Taylor ordered, "Present arms!" to salute them, and the Tigers shouted, "Give 'em hell, Maryland!" and other encouragements. Wheat's Battalion, with the Tiger Rifles in front, fell in behind the Marylanders, and the rest of Taylor's brigade followed.[33]

At about 2:00 p.m., Union pickets sounded the alarm when they spotted the 1st Maryland emerge from a belt of woods about a half-mile from town. As the Union soldiers began forming a line of battle, Taylor rode alone to the river's edge for a closer look at the enemy's defenses. Exhausted from the long day's march, his horse stepped into the stream to drink and instantly drew the Yankee sharpshooters' fire. The shower of balls splashed in the water all around Taylor's thirsty horse, but the general was reluctant to beat a hasty retreat. "I had not yet led my command into action," Taylor recalled, "and, remembering that one must 'strut' one's little part to the best advantage, sat my horse with all the composure I could muster. A provident camel, on the eve of a desert journey would not have laid in a greater supply of water than did my thoughtless beast." Finally getting his fill, Taylor's horse raised its head, looked around nonchalantly, and slowly ambled up the bank back toward the Louisiana Brigade. The Tigers wildly cheered their plucky leader, but their chorus was answered by a volley of Yankee musketry that knocked over several soldiers.[34]

The 1st Maryland soon advanced, and the Union line crumbled and fell back through town. When Wheat's Battalion was sent in to support Johnson, Ewell's aide Captain Brown watched the Tigers rush into battle: "I shall never forget the style in which Wheat's Battn. passed us, as we stood in the road. [Wheat] was riding full gallop, yelling at the top of his voice—his big sergeant-major [Wrigley] running at top speed just after him, calling to the men to come on—& they strung out according to their speed or 'stomach for the fight,' following after—all running—all yelling—all looking like fight. Their peculiar zouave dress & wild excitement made up a glorious picture. Wheat himself looked in a fight as handsome as any man I ever saw. One forgot his dissipated, debauched life in seeing the grandly reckless way in which he faced death."[35]

Johnson saw Wheat enter the fight just as his Marylanders headed toward a building the federals were using as a hospital. "Major Wheat shot by like a rocket, his red hat gleaming, revolver in hand, and got in first, throwing his shots right and left. The hospital was taken." The Yankees hurriedly abandoned Front Royal and retreated across both the South and North Fork rivers to make a stand on Guard Hill. Jackson expected to capture numerous prisoners in the frantic retreat but was infuriated when he saw many of Wheat's Tigers abandon the pursuit to loot the enemy's camp.[36]

Wanting to keep pressure on the enemy, Taylor suggested taking his brigade across the railroad bridge because it was sheltered from the Union artillery fire. Jackson nodded his consent, and Taylor ordered Col. Henry Kelly to send his 8th Louisiana across. With Kelly in front, the regiment rushed down to the bridge and began tiptoeing across the railroad ties under a brisk rifle fire. Two men tumbled off into the turbulent, rain-swollen water below and drowned after being shot or losing their footing. The rest of the regiment made it over without incident, and their success encouraged others to run across the nearby wagon bridge.[37]

By this time, the Union forces had set fire to the bridge across the North Fork, and Taylor realized that all of the Yankees would escape if it was lost. Looking inquisitively at his commander, Taylor again received an approving nod from Jackson and called on Wheat's men and the Moore Fencibles, a 9th Louisiana company that was attached to Wheat's Battalion as sharpshooters, to charge across the burning span. Kelly's 8th Louisiana followed close behind. Captain Brown watched as Wheat led the men across the bridge and later wrote, "He put spurs to his horse, galloped through the already kindled flame in face of the enemy's fire, & saved the bridge." Wheat's Tigers followed him across, but Colonel Kelly plunged into the river below and yelled "Come on, boys! We will yet have them!" Robert Rowe of the Opelousas Guards wrote, "Into the stream we went, and came near being taken away by the swiftness of its current. The enemy was firing into us from an almost perpendicular hill [Guard Hill] which we had to surmount ere we could reach them, but seeing we were determined to do so, at all hazards, he vamosed."[38]

Wheat's pursuit slowed when many of his men were forced to cross the bridge in single file after the fire caused part of the flooring to give way. When some of the Tigers began throwing burning timbers into the river, Colonel Kelly formed a bucket brigade and handed hats full of water to those on the bridge to douse the fire. The bridge was saved, Taylor recalled, "but it was rather a near thing." The flames singed and scorched the clothing of Wheat, Taylor, and the rest of the Tigers, and "smoke and fire had decidedly freshened up [Jackson's] costume" as he rushed across the bridge to join the Louisianians.[39]

Once over the river, Jackson sent Wheat's Battalion, the 1st Maryland, and what cavalry he had on hand in pursuit of the enemy. Major Aaron Davis, Taylor's commissary officer, was so caught up in the excitement that he gathered a number of mounted orderlies and chased after the enemy until a sudden return volley unhorsed him with a fatal bullet through the chest. Taylor wrote of Davis, "He was much beloved by the command, and many gathered quietly around the grave. As there was no chaplain at hand, I repeated such portions of the service for the dead as a long neglect of pious things enabled me to recall." Commissary officers like Davis were usually in the rear during battle, which prompted one soldier to admit, "I never heard of nary other quarter-master [or] commissary . . . being killed." Campbell Brown described Davis as "a very fine Officer" who had joined the pursuit "by way of a frolic." According to Brown, "The poor fellow was intoxicated, for the first time since entering the Service."[40]

When darkness and increased resistance from the Union troops finally ended the chase, the jubilant Louisianians took count of their losses. During the three-hour battle, eight men had been wounded, with Davis and the two luckless Tigers who fell from the railroad bridge being the only fatalities. Jackson had liberated Front Royal and captured seven hundred prisoners and a large quantity of badly needed supplies at a small loss to himself. Events had developed so quickly that most of the Tigers never even got into the action. In fact, Lt. George Wren of the 8th Louisiana claimed that the brigade's skirmishers were the only Tigers who fired a shot.[41]

Not long after the Confederates secured Front Royal, a Union supply train chugged into the station, its crew unaware that the rebels had taken the town. Major Wheat jumped onto the slow-moving locomotive, captured the train, and blew its whistle in celebration. Local resident Lucy Buck wrote in her diary that some of the Tigers then "doffed their uniforms and donned the Yankee blue. Then they got on the cars and steamed off to Markham." The Union garrison at Markham was not aware that Front Royal had been captured and assumed the Tigers were Union soldiers. After mingling with the Yankees for a while, the Louisianians even persuaded a few of them to return with them to Front Royal for an extended "visit."[42]

As the tired but victorious Louisianians settled in for the night, Jackson showed his appreciation of the Tigers by again coming to Taylor's sputtering campfire. After a lengthy silence, Jackson mentioned that Taylor's brigade would accompany him in the morning but gave no hint as to their objective. Taylor knew it was useless to pry for more details so he and Jackson spent the rest of the night in silence.

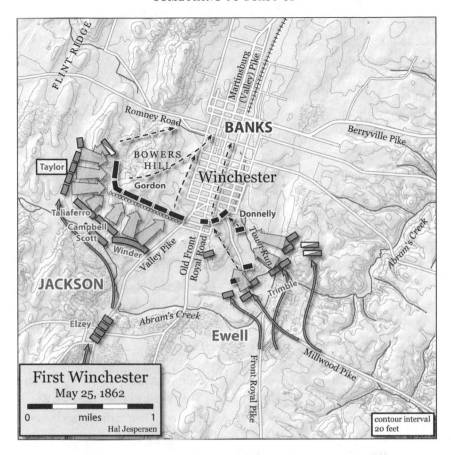

At approximately 8:00 a.m., May 24, Jackson received intelligence that Banks was retreating rapidly northward on the Valley Pike. After ordering Ewell to continue toward Winchester with the main body of men, Jackson took one hundred of Wheat's Tigers, a detachment of Gen. Turner Ashby's cavalry, and the Rockbridge Artillery as an escort, and headed west to Middletown to intercept Banks' fleeing column. Taylor wrote that Jackson ordered Wheat's men to stick close to the artillery, so they "trotted along with the horses and artillery at Jackson's heels" like a pack of devoted hounds despite the fast pace set by the horse-drawn pieces. The rest of Taylor's and Elzey's brigades followed, but the men were exhausted and gradually fell about a mile behind Jackson's entourage.[43]

At midafternoon, Jackson topped a ridge overlooking Middletown and saw federal wagons filling the pike as far as the eye could see. He quickly deployed his escort and began raking the clogged road with shot and shell. Jackson wrote that within minutes "the turnpike, which had just before teemed with life, presented a most appalling spectacle of carnage and destruction. The road was literally obstructed with the mingled and confused mass of struggling and dying horses and riders." Riding at the head of his brigade some distance behind, Taylor heard the shooting and hurried his men toward the battle. When he arrived, Taylor found "the gentle Tigers were looting right merrily, diving in and out of wagons with the activity of rabbits in a warren; but this occupation was abandoned on my approach, and in a moment they were in a line, looking as solemn and virtuous as deacons at a funeral." While gathering up prisoners, the Louisianians let out whoops of laughter when they found a number of apparently inexperienced troopers strapped to their saddles. Other Tigers were surprised to find Yankees wearing antiquated breastplates, including some of the federal dead with neat, round bullet holes drilled through the armor.[44]

Taylor's brigade arrived at Middletown just as a squadron of federal cavalry came charging down the road in an attempt to cut through Jackson's small band blocking the way. The Tiger escort quickly overturned a wagon in the middle of the road and together with the lead elements of the brigade took shelter behind a stone fence alongside the pike. With sabers slashing, the Yankee troopers thundered down the road in a cloud of dust but were blasted out of their saddles. Henry Kyd Douglas recalled how the Louisianians' volley shattered the charging column, and the rear element "plunged on, in, over, upon the bleeding pile, a roaring, shrieking, struggling mass of men and horses, crushed, wounded and dying. It was a sickening sight." When some Union cavalry in the rear of the column tried to escape by jumping a stone wall that lined the pike, Wheat ordered Captain White's Tiger Rifles to open fire with their Mississippi Rifles. A Virginia artilleryman saw a mounted Yankee captain leap across a fence, waving his sword overhead and calling on his men to follow suit. "[The Tigers] opened fire on him with their long-ranged rifles. I saw him fall soon after, and heard some of the Tigers say: 'That will do him. Fire at the others in the road.' It was fun for the Tigers to fight cavalry, but it looked a shame to shoot down the lone Yankee captain as he was vainly trying to rally his men . . . but alas! Such is war."[45]

With the enemy's column now split in two, Jackson took Wheat's Battalion, part of the 7th Louisiana, and Ashby's cavalry and pursued those Yankees fleeing north to Winchester, while Taylor and the rest of his brigade pushed south to drive the rear of the enemy column back toward Strasburg. Taylor had advanced barely a mile when he saw that some of the Union troops had taken a side road and were now in position on a ridge to the west. He formed a battle line and was advancing toward this new threat when the enemy's artillery opened fire and took out several men in the 7th Louisiana. A second round exploded under Taylor's horse. Taylor later wrote, "The saddle cloth on both sides was torn away, and I and Adjutant Surger, who was just behind me, were nearly smothered with earth; but neither man nor horse received a scratch." Then, as suddenly as they had opened fire, the enemy limbered up their guns and continued their western retreat. At the loss of only three dead and twelve wounded in the Middletown action, Taylor helped capture or destroy several hundred Union supply wagons and seize nearly one hundred prisoners. In addition, the 6th Louisiana took two Union battle flags, and Hays' 7th Louisiana captured four guidons, but it is not known to which Union units they belonged.[46]

Once the enemy withdrew from his front, Taylor reversed course and headed north to catch up with Jackson. By that time, Jackson had brought the Yankees to bay with his artillery, but he had no infantry within reach to press the attack. Riding back toward Middletown, his chief of artillery found one hundred or so men from the 7th Louisiana, but they were "much broken down by fatigue and heat." Nonetheless, he urged them to keep moving forward and continued on until he found some Confederate cavalry and a group of Tigers who were busily looting the captured wagons. Threats and pleas failed to dissuade them from their activity, and Banks made good his escape to Winchester. Jackson was furious over his men's failure to pursue the enemy. A few days later he issued General Order No. 54 stating that "the shameless pillaging practised by numbers of cavalry and infantry, who were intrusted with the advance in pursuing the enemy . . . so reduced [Ashby's] command as to render it necessary to discontinue the pursuit." That same day Jackson ordered Ewell to investigate the pillaging conducted by his men, "especially by members of General Taylor's command," but there is no record of anyone being punished.[47]

Expecting a rest when they finally joined Jackson, the Tigers were disappointed when he ordered that the pursuit continue. According to Henry Handerson, "The excitement of battle had begun to wear off, and we soon felt the fatigue and hunger of men who had been marching all day with little or no food. Yet our orders were to press forward to Winchester, distant some thirteen miles." The men pushed on even though the road was littered with burning wagons, pontoon bridges, and equipment that the fleeing Yankees had set ablaze to keep it from falling into the rebels' hands. The march continued past dark, and the men began to suffer from the cold as well as hunger. Douglas recalled that the army "was exhausted, broken down, and apparently unfit for battle," but Jackson pushed on, nonetheless. After the war, Taylor recalled, "Without physical wants himself, [Jackson] forgot that others were differently constituted, and [he] paid little heed to commissariat; but woe to the man who failed to bring up the ammunition!" So many men began to fall out from exhaustion that Jackson finally called a halt late that night two miles south of Winchester and let the men get some much needed rest. The pause was brief, however, because Jackson ordered Ewell to attack Winchester at daylight on the parallel Front Royal–Winchester Road to the east.[48]

Some of the Tigers had received only an hour's rest when they were rousted early on Sunday, May 25, to prepare for battle. Handerson recalled, "[W]e . . . arose from the ground . . . stiff and sore" but fell in line, nonetheless. A dense fog blanketed the landscape, and heavy skirmish fire began building along Ewell's line to the east when Taylor led his men down the road to get into position. Suddenly, Kyd Douglas came galloping out of the fog and told Taylor to hurry on with his brigade because the Union artillery was pounding the Stonewall Brigade in front, and Ewell was bogged down on the right. As the Tigers hurried forward, Jackson came down the road to meet them, and the Tigers respectfully lifted their hats in a salute which Jackson returned. Jackson quickly found Taylor and asked, "General, can your brigade charge a battery?" "It can try," responded Taylor. "Very good," said Jackson, "it must do it then. Move it forward." Taylor rode ahead with Jackson and found that the federal guns were hammering the Confederate artillery. Jackson pointed to the left where the enemy's artillery was positioned in a hilltop fortification and told Taylor, "You must carry it." Taylor later admitted, "I felt an anxiety amounting to pain for the brigade to acquit itself handsomely, and this feeling was shared by every man in it."[49]

Taylor was leading his men along the base of a ridge toward the enemy's battery when Jackson overtook him to make sure all was well. Upon seeing their general, the Tigers let out a spontaneous cheer, but Jackson instantly hushed them lest they give away their position. At that moment the Louisiana

Brigade was marching across a slight depression within view of the federal guns, and one veteran recalled that shells came screaming toward them and "almost took our hats off." The shrieking missiles hit several men, and the rest ducked involuntarily when the shells whizzed overhead. A Virginia artilleryman who was passing by at the time wrote, "I heard a colonel chiding his men for dodging, one whom called out, in reply, 'Colonel, lead us up to where we can get at them and then we won't dodge!'" Taylor also saw the Tigers ducking and was embarrassed that Jackson witnessed it. "What the hell are you dodging for?" he screamed. "If there is any more of it, you will be halted under this fire for an hour." Taylor claimed the men quickly straightened up "as if they had swallowed ramrods," but Jackson was unimpressed. With a sorrowful look, he leaned over to Taylor, clasped his shoulder, and said, "I am afraid you are a wicked fellow." When Jackson turned and rode away, the Tigers again cheered him, and this time he responded with a rare smile.[50]

Taylor finally reached a place where the ridge and fog hid the men from the Union soldiers manning the hilltop fort. He then deployed the brigade in a column formation with the 8th Louisiana in front. Honored at being chosen to lead the attack, Lt. Col. Francis T. Nicholls told his men, "Now boys, let this Regiment be the sledge-hammer of the Brigade! Give them the d—l." The Tigers began their advance at about 7:00 a.m. just as the sun rose over the Blue Ridge Mountains. As if on cue, the fog suddenly lifted and the previously hidden Louisiana Brigade was thrust into view of both armies. The men moved steadily up the hill in a walk with Taylor in the lead on horseback, occasionally turning in his saddle to check the formation. It was the first time he had led the brigade into battle, but he was as calm as a veteran. Major Boyd came to recognize this trait in his commander and wrote, "The excitement of battle seemed to soothe him, and he would become pleasant and playful as a kitten."[51]

The Tigers continued marching in step even after the enemy's artillery began inflicting casualties. The 8th Louisiana's Lieutenant Wren wrote in his diary, "I commenced seeing for the first time our own men from the Regt being wounded here I felt different from any thing I had ever felt before." Two Union regiments were supporting the artillery, with some of the men being posted behind one of three stone walls and fences the Tigers had to pass over. These advanced Yankees opened fire, as well, and one remembered, "Here at Winchester, the range was so good, and the enemy so massed, that with any aim at all, it was simply impossible to miss."[52]

In preparation for the final assault, Taylor ordered the brigade to wheel from column formation into a battle line. Robert Dabney, who watched from a distance, wrote, "Under a shower of shells and rifle-balls, this magnificent body of troops [performed the maneuver] with the accurateness and readiness of a parade." Then, according to another witness, Taylor stood in his stirrups and "in a loud commanding voice, that I am sure the Yankees heard," gave the order to advance at the double quick. With their comrades to the east cheering them on, the Tigers rolled over the stone walls. Robert Rowe wrote, "We rushed forward, whooping and yelling, [even] as they poured volley after volley into us." A Union officer remembered, "For a moment, the enemy seemed to stagger, but only for a moment; for feeling confidence in their great strength, they charged . . . with deafening cheers." Winchester was the first time the Louisiana Brigade raised the rebel yell, and it became one of their battlefield trademarks. From that moment on, the Tigers were known for their enthusiastic rebel yell. One veteran recalled that they were excellent "whoopers." "They would charge up a hill yelling at the top of their lungs. They would cross a field with a weird yell that began the minute that the order to 'charge' was given. . . . They never quit whooping."[53]

The Irishmen of the 6th Louisiana swept forward behind the aging Colonel Seymour. With his silver hair blowing, the colonel was flushed with excitement as he ran toward the enemy, waving his sword in one hand and hat in the other, yelling, "Steady men! dress to the right!" "I have rarely seen a more beautiful charge," wrote Kyd Douglas. "This full brigade, with a line of glistening bayonets bright in that morning sun, its formation straight and compact, its tread quick and easy as it pushed on through the cloves and up that hill was a sight to delight a veteran." The charge of the Louisiana Brigade was one of the most spectacular assaults of the Civil War, and it was forever etched into the minds of those who witnessed it. Bradley Johnson claimed the Louisiana Brigade swept over the hill "with the swiftness and regularity that a wave advances to the shore," and a Virginian remembered, "There was all the pomp and circumstance of war about it that was always lacking in our charges."[54]

When Taylor was about halfway to the enemy's artillery, part of the 4th Michigan Cavalry charged his left flank with drawn sabers. Colonel Kelly's 8th Louisiana became the first Tigers to open fire when it broke up the cavalrymen with a well-aimed volley that Rowe claimed emptied eighteen saddles and killed eight horses.[55]

From her home behind the federal lines, Cornelia McDonald watched as the Union position suddenly unraveled.

> I could see from the front door the hill side covered with Federal troops, a long line of blue forms lying down just behind its crest, on the top of which just in their front a battery spouted flame at the lines which were slowly advancing to the top. Suddenly I saw a long even line of grey caps above the crest of the hill, then appeared their heads! The cannon ceased suddenly, and as the crouching forms that had been lying behind the cannon rose to their feet they were greeted by a volley of musketry from their assailants that scattered them. Some fell where they had stood but the greatest number fled down the hill side to swell the stream of humanity that flowed through every street and by way, through gardens and over fences, toward the Martinsburg turnpike, a confused mob of trembling, fainting objects that kept on their flight till they were lost in the clouds of dust their hurrying feet had raised.[56]

Slowly at first, then in a rush, the entire right flank of Banks' line gave way. Jackson quickly ordered the rest of the army forward, and Ewell's men to the east joined in the attack. Winchester was bedlam as the Confederates chased the defeated Yankees through its streets. One rebel remembered that the civilians "shouted to our men from their doors and windows and cheered them on." Another wrote, "The pavement was crowded with women, children and old men, waving their handkerchiefs, weeping for joy and shouting as we passed at double-quick." One woman, however, was upset that so many Yankees were escaping and shouted to the Tigers, "Oh! You are too late—too late!" A tall, lanky Cajun in the 8th Louisiana broke ranks, swept her up in his arms, and planted a kiss upon her lips. "Madame!" he exclaimed, "*je n'arrive jamais trop tard!*" (I never arrive too late!). He then swaggered back to his cheering regiment and left the woman "with a rosy face, but [a] merry twinkle in her eye." The Cajun's comrade, Robert Rowe, was not so lucky. He wrote, "I really believe I lost several kisses by not stopping for them."[57]

The thankful townspeople poured into the streets and invited the soldiers in to visit and eat. Mrs. McDonald remembered, "Baskets of food were brought from the houses and passed hastily among the thronging soldiers, who would snatch a mouthful and go on their way." Some of Wheat's men also enjoyed a cache of liquor that they discovered. A newspaper reported, "Opposite the Taylor House [Hotel] the Louisiana Zouaves were fast becoming inebriated over some one hundred and fifty bottles of brandy, which the Medical Purveyor thought he had destroyed, but had not." The men heartily enjoyed the street celebration, but it slowed up Jackson's army and allowed most of the Yankees to escape. Major Wilder Dwight was not one of them because Major Wheat captured him after he lagged behind to help some wounded men. A Baltimore newspaper reported, "The rebels treated him with the greatest kindness and consideration. Major Wheat advised him to go to the Taylor House and get some breakfast; and all the Confederate officers behaved in a very gentlemanly manner."[58]

The Louisiana Brigade was the toast of the army. Immediately following the grand charge, Jackson galloped up to Taylor and gratefully shook his hand in a silent gesture that the Louisianian claimed was "worth a thousand words from another." The 6th Louisiana's Lt. George P. Ring, who had a bullet pass through his hat and another hit his boot heel, claimed that Jackson told Taylor that "he never saw or read of such a charge made by us at Winchester. . . . All the Virginia troops in this Army say that we beat any body they ever saw at a charge and now they say we can stand as long under a murderous fire as any troops in the World."[59]

The victory at Winchester was not without cost. The Tigers had fourteen men killed, including the 6th Louisiana's Maj. Arthur McArthur, a native of Maine, and eighty-nine wounded. Some of the soldiers who brought the latter in for treatment asked Mrs. McDonald and another woman if they would look after McArthur's body. McDonald recalled walking into the room where "four or five rough looking soldiers" sat with their dead officer:

A sad sight met our eyes when we went into the room where the dead man was. I could not at first believe he was dead—so natural were his features and so easy and restful was his posture. He was dressed in a beautiful new uniform, grey and buff; a splendid red silk scarf was around his waist, and his sword was lying by his side. He was very tall and slender with regular features and dark hair—very fine soft hair— his face was noble looking and must have been very handsome. . . . No wound could be seen, and not a drop of blood stained his clothing. The poor soldier who watched him, and who wept constantly, showed me a small gun shot wound in his chin hidden by the long jet black beard. It looked not larger than a pea, and only a drop or two of blood stained his beard. . . . It was his regiment that I had seen charge and take the battery, and I remembered having heard my boys say that they had seen an officer of the regiment as he galloped over the crest of the hill, fall backward from his horse.[60]

McDonald prepared McArthur's body and put some flowers in his hand. The men of the 6th Louisiana then raised enough money to purchase a metallic coffin from the local undertaker and buried him that evening.[61]

While Jackson's army praised the Tigers' valor at Winchester, the enemy once again accused them of committing acts of atrocity. One Union report claimed that Taylor's men "glutted their vengeance for the loss of New Orleans" by giving no quarter in the fight. Ordinarily such a charge would be dismissed as wartime propaganda, but one Louisianian wrote home a few weeks after the battle that some of the Tigers' wounded were bayoneted or clubbed to death at Winchester. In the future, he vowed, "Jackson's army will . . . take few prisoners." Although it is not likely that the fleeing Union soldiers had an opportunity to kill any wounded Confederates, it is possible the reverse could have occurred.[62]

After Banks' defeat at Winchester, the Union army retreated toward the Potomac River and safety. The Louisiana Brigade pushed five miles out of town after it and then let the cavalry take over the pursuit. Reflecting on the day, Lieutenant Wren wrote, "This was glory enough for me, right here I wanted the war to close. I did not wish to risk the chance of gaining any more honors in it. When I looked back upon the past I could but lift up my heart in thankfulness to Him that doeth all things well. I had been spared with health, had under gone all hardships and now had gone through a battle unhurt."[63]

Jackson was furious that so many of his men enjoyed Winchester's hospitality rather than pressing after the enemy, but he still allowed them to rest all day Monday, May 26, so that religious services could be held to make up for having to fight on a Sunday. Taylor took the opportunity to visit his sister, Elizabeth Dandridge, who happened to live in Winchester. Ewell's division was back on the road the next day chasing after the enemy but halted when Banks took refuge in the heavily fortified stronghold of Harpers Ferry.[64]

So far, Jackson's campaign had been a brilliant success with his 15,000 men besting three times their number in marching and fighting. Now, however, his army was in danger of being trapped in the Valley. Lincoln was worried that the victorious rebels might make a move on Washington and ordered Gen. James Shields' 20,000 men to march to the Valley from Fredericksburg. Frémont's army was also in route from Franklin to cut off Jackson at Strasburg. On May 30, elements of Shields' force recaptured Front Royal, deep in Jackson's rear, along with 156 men of the 8th Louisiana and 12th Georgia who were guarding the captured supplies there. In addition to this double threat was the remnant of Banks' army now regrouping at Harpers Ferry to the north of Jackson. Stonewall was caught in the middle of a triangle, with Banks at the northern apex and Frémont and Shields at the southern base angles.[65]

On Saturday, May 31, Jackson began retreating back to Strasburg in an attempt to escape before the two converging Union armies closed the back door. The Louisiana Brigade was camped just six miles shy of the Maryland border, and the 8th Louisiana's Robert Rowe was anticipating the moment they would cross over the Potomac River and head into Union territory. "We were highly elated at the thought," he wrote. "When our joys were at their highest pitch, they soon were dampened by the announcement of a 'fall back' to be made by us. Then you could see disappointed faces, officers and all."[66]

Taylor's brigade was ordered to serve as rearguard and clear the stragglers out of Winchester. The weather was rainy and disagreeable, and the retreat back through town depressed everyone. Mary Greenhow Lee wrote in her diary that the Louisiana Brigade stopped for some time in the street and that several of the Tigers came over to visit. Among them was the 7th Louisiana's Lt. Col. Charles de Choiseul, whom Lee described as being "particularly pleasant." Lee optimistically believed the army would return on Monday and invited de Choiseul to stay and visit. When the Louisianians informed her they would not be back, she found it difficult to believe that the soldiers who had helped liberate Winchester would abandon the people to the Yankees. Mrs. Lee reported that the Tigers were "grave" at having to retreat and that the news of Gen. Benjamin "Beast" Butler's Woman's Order insulting the ladies of New Orleans "has shocked them, & they leave us with a fear they had not felt before." When the brigade was finally ordered to resume the march, Rowe reported, "We took our leave of the city with cries and wailings from the ladies, imploring us to remain and give them protection from the invaders."[67]

While in Winchester, General Taylor visited the 8th Louisiana's Lieutenant

Colonel Nicholls, whose left elbow had been shattered six days earlier during the charge against the Union fort. Taylor wanted to take Nicholls with the brigade, but surgeons had amputated his arm that morning and forbade his removal. Nicholls and several other badly wounded Tigers were captured soon afterward. Rumors circulated in the following weeks that Nicholls was arrested as a spy while dressed as a civilian and that he was not being treated as a prisoner of war, but these stories proved false, and he and the other wounded men were later exchanged.[68]

The 9th Louisiana's Capt. David Workman, another of Sherman's Louisiana Seminary students, was also left behind after being badly wounded in the attack on Winchester. Sometimes later while he was in a Union hospital, one of his men came calling. When the soldier addressed him as "Captain Workman," a dying Yankee on the cot beside him raised his head and asked feebly, "Are you Capt. Workman . . . Capt. Dave Workman of the 9th Louisiana regiment?" When Workman assured him that he was, the soldier said he had something for him. Two weeks earlier his captain had been mortally wounded and gave him a package and asked that he send it across the lines at the first opportunity. "I didn't think . . . I would be able to deliver it so soon in person; but here it is." Puzzled, Workman asked, "And your captain, who was he?" "Your brother, Capt. James Workman, of the Ninth New York Cavalry." With that, the Yankee gasped and fell back on his cot dead.[69]

The Tigers marched about thirty miles before joining the rest of the army at Strasburg and drawing half-rations. An exhausted Taylor immediately searched out Jackson and found his commander huddled by a smoky campfire in a rare talkative mood. Staring into the flickering flame, Jackson informed Taylor between long pauses that Frémont's army was only three miles west of them and Shields was to the south on the other side of the Shenandoah River threatening to cut the army's escape route. The only way to safety, Jackson said, was to prevent Shields and Frémont from linking up. To do this, Taylor would rejoin Ewell's division and they would hold back Frémont in the morning while Jackson personally led the precious booty-laden wagon train to the south before Shields could cut the road. To help keep Shields on the opposite bank of the Shenandoah, Jackson also sent his cavalry as far south as Port Republic to burn the bridges on the river.[70]

By the time the sun peeped over the Blue Ridge on Sunday, June 1, Jackson was on the road with his wagons, and Ewell's men were deploying on the hills west of Strasburg to meet Frémont. Ewell's entire line was soon engaged in heavy skirmishing and coming under artillery fire. In a rare admission, Taylor claimed in his memoirs that he was a nervous wreck that morning. "Whether from fatigue, loss of sleep, or what, there I was, ducking like a mandarin. It was disgusting, and, hoping that no one saw me, I resolved to take it out of myself [at] the first opportunity." Ewell called for Taylor and noticed that the artillery fire was causing him to visibly shake. Taylor apologized and claimed he was like a frightened deer. "Nonsense!" snorted Ewell, "'tis Tom's strong coffee. Better give it up."[71]

Tom Strother was Taylor's slave. Three years older than the general, Strother always rode a horse at Taylor's side and did his cooking and washing. In describing Strother, Taylor wrote, "Tall, powerful, black as ebony, he was a mirror of truth and honesty. Always cheerful, I never heard him laugh or knew of his speaking unless spoken to." At Strasburg, Strother endured the Yankees' artillery fire better than his master. Earlier in the day, Taylor had ordered him to wait on a hill while he rode forward, but shells soon began to rain down around him. Strother stayed put, nonetheless, even after Jackson rode by and suggested that he move out of the area. Strother declined and explained that Taylor had instructed him to stay there and that "he did not believe [the] shells would trouble him." Strother's obedience and bravery apparently impressed Jackson. A few nights later, when Strother brought Taylor some coffee while Jackson was visiting, the general stood up, solemnly shook Strother's hand, and told Taylor of the incident on the hill.[72]

Taylor was not the only one addled by the artillery fire. According to the general, "Many slaves from Louisiana had accompanied their masters to the war, and were a great nuisance on a march, foraging far and wide for 'prog' for their owners' messes." When the brigade went into action at Strasburg, the slaves were ordered to remain in the rear of their respective regiments. Several score had assembled under a large tree to cook breakfast when a shell exploded in the treetop and showered them with leaves and limbs. The slaves quickly departed, but it is assumed that they rejoined the brigade later in the day.[73]

Despite the heavy artillery fire and skirmishing, the superior Union force was strangely passive, and Ewell was puzzled as to why. While pondering what to do, Taylor nervously suggested that the Louisiana Brigade be allowed to circle around the Union left flank to gain information on the Yankees' plans.

Ewell readily consented and told Taylor, "Do so, that may stir them up, and I am sick of this fiddling about." Taylor led his men to the Confederate right, where a Mississippi colonel told him the Union flank appeared to be weak. When Taylor deployed his men and advanced, the Yankees immediately broke and ran, and the Tigers wheeled down the Union line and began scooping up prisoners by the score. Many of the federals simply laid down their arms in surrender, which prompted Taylor to write, "Sheep would have made as much resistance as we met." The brigade's only casualties were a few men shot by other Confederates who mistakenly thought they were the enemy. The rest of the division soon joined in the chase, but Ewell finally called a halt after he realized he had fulfilled Jackson's instructions to delay Frémont's advance.[74]

Ewell's division soon caught up with Jackson's wagon train, and Taylor was ordered to pull his brigade off the road and serve as the rearguard once the army had passed. Jackson did not appear overly concerned about the Yankees pursuing. He told Taylor that Frémont would not advance until morning, and that Banks' rattled men would not get within striking distance until the next day. Taylor was making a mental note of this when Jackson suddenly turned and rode off without telling him how long he was to remain on the side of the road or if there was any cavalry farther back to notify him should Banks beat Jackson's predicted timetable. With these questions racing through his mind, Taylor watched over his men as they prepared to camp fireless in the cool spring air.[75]

Throughout the night Taylor could hear Jackson's retreating army rumbling along the road. He finally retired but a few hours later was jolted awake by what he thought was the sound of distant gunfire drifting in from the north. In a few minutes the sound was unmistakable—and getting closer. Wondering if Banks was moving faster than Jackson had anticipated, Taylor mounted his horse and rode out of the sleeping camp to investigate. On the dark road, he met some Confederate cavalrymen who informed him that most of the army, including the rearguard, had long since passed him by. Apparently, no one had noticed the Tigers sleeping off the side of the road in the dark. General Charles Winder's Stonewall Brigade was the closest unit Taylor could call on for support, but it, too, had marched by hours earlier. To Taylor's chagrin, the troopers told him that only one squadron of cavalry stood between him and the fast-approaching Yankees.

Galloping back to camp, Taylor quickly roused his sleeping men and got them out to the road after much kicking, grumbling, and cursing. Taking two Irish companies of Colonel Seymour's 6th Louisiana, he formed a hasty rear-guard and sent the rest of the brigade hurrying along the pike to catch up with Jackson. This had barely been done when a confused mass of screaming, shooting, saber-hacking Confederate and Union cavalry came crashing into the Irishmen and knocked several men hard to the ground. The Yankee troopers were soon beaten back, and one of the badly bruised Tigers was allowed to ride the horse of the lone prisoner taken during the clash.

To keep a better watch over his Irishmen, Taylor dismounted and stayed with them for the remainder of the long march. According to the general, the night was so dark that "owls could not have found their way across the fields," and only the dim glow of the roadbed kept them on the right path. Cavalry charges and rounds of searching artillery fire occasionally shot out of the blackness, but they caused little damage. The Irishmen remained cheerful despite the miserable conditions and passed the time joking about their predicament. It was a "fine night intirely for divarsion" they laughed, and many eagerly talked of meeting Shields' Irishmen at the end of their march. Frémont's Germans "is poor creatures," they told Taylor, "but Shields' boys will be after fighting." Taylor laughed and declared that he would bet on them in any upcoming fight. "You may bet your life on that, sor," they shouted. When Taylor considered bringing back another regiment to relieve them, the men scoffed at the idea. "We are the boys to see it out," one said. In his memoirs, Taylor wrote, "As Argyle's to the tartan, my heart has warmed to an Irishman since that night."[76]

At dawn of June 2, the footsore Tigers came upon Winder's brigade drawn up across the road to relieve them. Winder had heard the shooting during the night, realized the Louisianians were holding the rear alone, and took his brigade out of line to wait for them. Throughout the morning, Winder held the rear and skirmished with Banks' cavalry until Ashby's troopers finally arrived to take over that duty. With only an hour's rest, Taylor's brigade marched all day without any rations and finally camped a mile shy of Mount Jackson in a drenching rain. Rain, in fact, soaked the men every day and night from May 30 to June 5.[77]

The march was resumed at 5:00 a.m., but the men were allowed to stop and rest a few hours later after they crossed the Shenandoah's North Fork. With the river between it and the pursuing Yankees, Jackson's small army was safe for the moment. The 7th Louisiana's Henry Caldwell wrote in his diary,

"[A]ll took a swim in the river and washed our clothes. The first rest for 9 days. Were to get extra rations of mutton but left camp before it was given out. Consequently got no rations that day. And marched six miles to New Market and six miles on the other side."[78]

After a thirty-six-hour rest, Jackson continued the retreat on June 5 along a road that Caldwell claimed was six inches under water. Spirits were raised later in the day, however, when two days' rations of flour and bacon were issued and the exhausted men finally reached Harrisonburg. There the intrepid band turned eastward toward Port Republic and the only standing bridge across the Shenandoah River. Behind them Frémont and Banks had joined forces, crossed the West Fork, and were pressing the Confederate rearguard. On June 6, most of the Valley Army took refuge between the North and South rivers, two tributaries that met at Port Republic to form the Shenandoah's East Fork. To prevent Banks and Frémont from following, Ewell's division camped just west of North River at Cross Keys to burn the bridge once all of Jackson's men had crossed. It appeared that Jackson had placed himself in the jaws of a trap. Ewell's division, on the same side of the river as Frémont and Banks, was separated from the main army, and Shields was rapidly approaching from the north to cut off Jackson at Port Republic.[79]

On the morning of June 8, Frémont hit Ewell's division at Cross Keys and drove in his pickets. As Ewell attempted to make a stand, he received urgent orders from Jackson to send Taylor's brigade to Port Republic. While Ewell held off Frémont, the Louisianians rapidly marched toward Jackson, thinking that Shields must be attacking him. The brigade double-quicked a couple of miles, but then Jackson sent Taylor back to Ewell because the threatening force at Port Republic turned out to be only a small detachment of Union cavalry and artillery. The Tigers reversed themselves, hurried back to Cross Keys, and halted next to Gen. Isaac Trimble's brigade.[80] One of Trimble's Georgians wrote, "The Louisiana Brigade marched up in quick line, by the flank, each fours in perfect line, arms at 'right shoulder shift.' The 6th Louisiana was near us. Their old Colonel, Isaac Seymour, a martial man with long, silvery locks, whirled his horse and gave the command: 'Battalion Halt. Front! Right Dress!' Every rifle was quickly brought to 'Shoulder Arms' and the alignment perfected without a wobble. At the command 'Order Arms' the rifles of 800 men struck the ground as one man. 'Fix Bayonets. Stack Arms! Break Ranks!'"[81]

Ewell's men had defeated Frémont during the Tigers' absence, and the

Yankees had now withdrawn. The Louisianians were told to be prepared to move out in a few minutes and not to wander off, but Seymour's Irishmen broke ranks and shocked the Georgians by scurrying through the woods and fields in search of dead Yankees to loot. One Tiger turned over a body and told a Georgian, "This fellow will not need his watch where he has gone, as time is nothing there, and the burial corps will soon get everything that's left." While watching another Tiger go through the pockets of a dead man, a Georgia soldier asked if he and his comrades were prepared to fight Shields' army, which contained a large number of Irishmen. Of course, came the distracted reply. The Louisianian then straightened up and complained of how little booty the Germans of Frémont's army yielded. He hoped the Yankee Irishmen would prove more profitable.[82]

After the war, General Trimble claimed that he wanted to pursue Frémont to destroy or capture the entire enemy force and tried to get Taylor to support his plan. According to Trimble, Taylor refused because his men were too exhausted and hungry after days of marching and countermarching. Furious at Taylor's lack of aggressiveness, Trimble went to Jackson, who told him that he had no objections but that it was up to Ewell to decide. When Trimble returned to Cross Keys, he again pressed the issue with Ewell and Taylor, but both officers opposed the idea. Ewell even dismissed Trimble's offer to attack with just his brigade because even a minor reversal might disrupt whatever plans Jackson had for the next day. Trimble fumed over the decision and criticized Taylor in his report for being too timid and not backing his proposal. Taylor, in turn, never even mentioned the controversy in his writings.[83]

On the morning of June 9, Jackson left two brigades near Cross Keys to watch Frémont and sent Winder's men across South River to look for Shields. Taylor's brigade and the rest of the army crossed over North River by the lone bridge left standing and South River by a rickety, makeshift footbridge. Union prisoners had constructed the latter bridge during the night by laying a half-dozen wagon axles on the streambed to serve as a base and then laying planks from axle to axle. The bridge was so narrow that it could only be crossed by the men marching in single file. Taylor's slow progress frustrated Jackson because he badly needed the Tigers at the front. To make matters worse, Taylor did not receive several messages Jackson sent to him because he remained at the bridge to make sure all of the men got across. Colonel Kelly was leading the brigade, and the messages were delivered to him, instead.

The Tigers halted for breakfast when finally across the last river, but their meal was cut short by the sound of heavy gunfire in the direction Winder had taken. After leaving orders for the brigade to follow, Taylor rode forward and found Jackson calmly sitting his horse, watching Shields' Yankees advance across an open field against Winder's lone brigade. "Delightful, excitement," was Jackson's only comment.[84]

The terrain decidedly favored the enemy. The lush green Blue Ridge to the east sloped down to within a thousand yards of the river before leveling out into an open plain. Shields skillfully deployed his men perpendicular to the river along a rift where the plain rose abruptly to form a plateau overlooking Winder's position. With his flanks solidly anchored on the river and mountain, it was a formidable line, and Winder's brigade was being badly shot up trying to dislodge Shields from it.

A six-gun battery posted at a coaling on the federal left near the mountain was wreaking havoc on Winder's men. When Taylor did not arrive as planned, Jackson sent the 2nd and 4th Virginia regiments to attack the battery, but they were repulsed. Colonel Kelly's 8th Louisiana, which arrived some time before Taylor, was sent toward the coaling, as well. Now that the rest of the Louisiana Brigade was on the scene, Jackson ordered Taylor to push on to the mountainside and silence the battery. Without bothering to tell Taylor, however, Jackson jerked Hays' 7th Louisiana out of line as the brigade filed off toward the coaling and sent it to reinforce Winder's brigade struggling on the plain.[85]

While the rest of the brigade moved to the right, Hays led his men out onto the broad plain to join Winder. Hays was given command of the Confederate left, with his own 7th Louisiana and the 5th and 27th Virginia under his direction. No sooner had he established a defensive position than the federals began advancing across the plain to finish off the outnumbered Confederates. Knowing well that his thin gray line stood little chance of stopping the enemy's attack, Hays tried to throw the Yankees off balance by ordering his three regiments to charge. With a yell, the Virginians and Louisianians advanced under a murderous fire of artillery and musketry. Unfortunately, the bold assault was totally ineffective. Hiding behind tall spires of wheat, the 7th Ohio opened fire on the rebels from close range. "This shower of lead," wrote the regiment's historian, "made a fearful gap in the lines of the advancing column."[86]

Seeing their fire stagger Hays' line, the federals renewed their charge, and a ferocious fight erupted when the two lines collided. Colonel Hays was knocked out of action by a ball to the chest, and Lt. Col. Charles de Choiseul collapsed, mortally wounded. De Choiseul tried repeatedly to stay with his men but was finally carried off the field insensible. After the war, a veteran of the 29th Ohio claimed that the Yankees also captured the 7th Louisiana's flag after the color-bearer was shot down, but his claim is not supported by any other evidence.

The Confederates were dropping at a fearful rate before Major Penn took over and managed to place the men behind a fence that afforded some protection. But even there the Tigers were subjected to a concentrated fire that raked the rails and sent showers of splinters into their faces. At first in small groups, then in a rush, the 7th Louisiana finally broke and ran to escape the slaughter. The Virginians had no choice but to follow the Tigers, and soon the entire Confederate line was bolting for the rear where Ewell was forming his division. Major Penn succeeded in rallying some of the men around two Confederate cannons, but it was obvious that this handful of soldiers stood no chance against the blue wave rolling toward them. Suddenly, one Virginian recalled, there was heard "a mighty shout on the mountain side . . . and in a few minutes I saw General Dick Taylor's Louisianians debouching from the undergrowth, and like a wave crested with shining steel rush toward the . . . deadly battery with fixed bayonets, giving the Rebel yell like mad demons." Another Virginian recalled that at that critical moment the Tigers pounced on the enemy battery "like a hawk on a chicken."[87]

Exactly how Taylor's brigade approached the enemy's battery is unknown because the primary sources are contradictory. Most accounts of the battle simply state that Taylor moved around the edge of the mountain to the enemy's left flank, but the march was difficult and it is something of a wonder that the Tigers even got into the proper position. In his memoirs, Taylor claimed that Jackson gave him the order to attack the battery and provided Lt. Robert English to guide him along a narrow path. In his official report, however, he simply wrote that the route was thick with brush and did not mention having a guide or any details of how he received the order. After the war, Jackson's engineer Jedediah Hotchkiss claimed that Taylor never saw Jackson before making the move and that it was he who carried the order and guided Taylor to the battery. Colonel Kelly, who apparently was bitter because Taylor did not give him more credit for his service in the battle, took issue with some of

Taylor's claims and wrote his own postwar account of the battle. In it, Kelly criticized his superior and claimed that Dabney and Major Wheat brought him Jackson's orders to attack the battery and that he personally led the brigade through the woods. According to Kelly, Taylor was in the rear with the 6th Louisiana and was guided by Hotchkiss along a road while Kelly led the 8th and 9th Louisiana, and Wheat's Battalion through the woods without a guide. Kelly wrote that he was acting under direct orders from Jackson and that Taylor did not arrive on the scene until after Kelly already had the other regiments in position and had opened the attack.[88]

One Tiger who wrote an account of the battle for the New Orleans *Daily Picayune* described the march through the woods: "The enemy now opened a tornado of shot and shell in the supposed direction of the advancing column, but the random and ineffective fire did not impede their progress. . . . The nature of the ground was a great obstacle to the preservation of the column, and frequent halts were made to maintain a compact front and correct the alignment. The musical whistle of the minie bullet, those deadly messengers, as they now and then coursed their way through the thick foliage overhead, induced the belief that the movement now in progress was not entirely unknown to the enemy."[89]

However the Tigers managed to do it, they succeeded in getting into position under difficult conditions without the enemy discovering them. Unfortunately, once they were ready to attack, the Louisianians discovered that they had not moved far enough to flank the guns completely. To make matters worse, a deep gorge separated them from the Yankee artillery, and the enemy's pickets were posted above them on the side of the mountain. There was no time to readjust the line, however, because the cheers of Shields' victorious soldiers suddenly rose over the plain, and a frontal attack had to be made immediately. Through whispered orders, a strong skirmish line was sent out, and the brigade deployed in the brush with the 6th Louisiana on the far left where the ground was lowest, and Wheat's Battalion, the 9th Louisiana and the 8th Louisiana extending to the right up the mountain slope. Both Taylor and Kelly claimed to have ordered the attack, but when it began there was still some confusion in the ranks, and the thick woods further disorganized the men as they advanced. Nonetheless, the brigade raised the rebel yell, burst from the woods, and charged headlong toward the cannons. One of the Tigers later wrote, "Who that has ever heard that unearthly yell will forget it? The preface

to a charge, it was always the certain index of success, the spontaneous out-
burst of the soul." A Union artilleryman remembered that the battery had just
opened fire on the 7th Louisiana in the open field to their right and "mowed
them down in acres" when the Tigers suddenly emerged from the woods. With
little infantry support and having already suffered heavy losses in both men
and horses, the guns could not be withdrawn, and the artillerymen had to
stand and fight.[90]

Racing into and over the ravine, the Tigers were upon the startled artillerymen before they could wheel the guns around to fire at them. Union Surgeon
Henry Capehart claimed the Louisianians emerged from the woods just one
hundred yards from the battery and charged across the meadow with such
force "that they carried with them bodily a rail fence well out into the field."
Leading the charge was Colonel Kelly, who was described by one of his men
as "one of the best commanders in the Confederate army—always at home
when in the scene of action." Lieutenant Albert Moore, one of Kelly's officers,
was also out front leading his company forward with a cheer until he received
a mortal wound. Some of Moore's friends rushed to his side and asked if he
had any final message for his family. Moore replied weakly, "Tell my friends at
home I died with my face to the foe, doing my duty."[91]

All organization had been lost during the rush across the gorge, but the
Tigers succeeded in capturing the battery. Elated, the men climbed on the gun
tubes, laughed hysterically, and slapped one another's backs as they celebrated
their victory. Suddenly, artillery fire from another federal battery 350 yards
away cut men down by the score. Sergeant Edmond Stephens, whose musket
was shot in two in his hands, wrote that the Yankees "poured grape into us like
smoke." Seeing Union infantry massing for a counterattack behind this battery, William "Big" Peck, the 9th Louisiana's huge, six-foot, six-inch lieutenant
colonel, yelled for the men to kill the artillery horses of the captured guns to
prevent the enemy from recovering them. Major Wheat drew out his knife
and began slashing the throats of the horses nearest him. One man recalled
that blood spurted over the major as he carried out the grisly task, making him
"as bloody as a butcher." Others reached out, placed their muskets against the
poor creatures' heads, and fired. The horses were still shrieking and jerking in
their death throes when the Yankees charged into the battery and began clubbing Taylor's men with their musket butts. Colonel Kelly claimed the federals
"swarmed like so many hornets . . . about the lost battery," and another Tiger

wrote, "It was a sickening sight, men in gray and blue piled up in front of and around the guns and with the horses dying and the blood of men and beasts flowing almost in a stream."[92]

These Yankees were members of Gen. Erastus Tyler's brigade. After breaking up Hays' attack across the open plain, the brigade had turned its attention to Taylor. A number of soldiers left accounts of the ensuing hand-to-hand fight, which was one of the fiercest of the war. One Union soldier wrote, "The opposing forces fired in each other's faces. Bayonets gleamed in the morning sunshine one moment and the next they were plunged into living human flesh and dripping with reeking blood. . . . For a while the hand-to-hand conflict raged frightfully, resembling more the onslaught of maddened savages than the fighting of civilized men." Another witness declared, "Panting like dogs—nine tenths of them bareheaded . . . men beat each other's brains out with muskets which they have no time to reload." In a postwar newspaper article, an anonymous soldier claimed, "It was not war on that spot. It was a pandemonium of cheers, shouts, shrieks and groans, lighted by the flames from the cannon and musket—blotched by fragments of men thrown high into trees by the shells. . . . In every great battle of the war there was a hell-spot. At Port Republic, it was on the mountain side. . . . Men ceased to be men. They cheered and screamed like lunatics—they fought like demons—they died like fanatics." The battle roared so loudly that the soldiers on the plateau heard it above their own thunderous fight. A reporter claimed, "They hear this pandemonium of shrieks and screams on the mountain-side and they halt. It is a sound ten times more horrible than the whistle of grape or the hiss of canister. Men cease firing to look up. They can see nothing for the smoke, but what they hear is a sound like that of hungry tigers turned loose to tear each other to death."[93]

Tyler's men drove the Tigers out of the battery and back to the ravine, where they regrouped and charged the Yankees a second time. A postwar chronicler wrote, "They reach the guns again, and again men shoot, stab, cut, hack—aye! They grapple and roll under the wheels of cannon so hot that they would almost blister." One of the Louisianians acknowledged the Yankees' bravery when he wrote, "The cannoniers fought with their pieces to the last; no words can to [sic] justice to their heroism." Around the cannons five color guards of the 5th Ohio were shot down in rapid succession, and the Tigers wrenched away the regiment's battle flag and captured it. Despite such losses, however, the federals managed to hold on and again succeeded in bludgeoning Taylor's men back to the ravine.[94]

By now the Tigers were in disarray. Some companies of the 6th Louisiana managed to maintain order, but most of the brigade was mixed together. Colonel Kelly noticed Taylor and a few other officers with small groups of men searching for cover in the woods. "None of the other regimental colors were there, men and officers of the brigade being dispersed, in irregular bodies, on the hillsides along the road, and on both sides of the ravine." Adding to the confusion were the forgotten Union pickets farther up the mountainside who began taking pot shots at the Tigers. Taylor was forced to pull two companies of Col. Leroy Stafford's 9th Louisiana out of line and send them to silence the sharpshooters before he could launch his third attack on the battery. Luckily for the Tigers, General Ewell suddenly came crashing through the underbrush with the 44th and 58th Virginia regiments. One of the Virginians noticed that the Louisianians were in some confusion and that many were bleeding from various wounds. Then the soldier spotted Major Wheat, still holding the knife he had used to kill the artillery horses. "His sleeves were rolled up. In one hand was a revolver; in the other a great butcher knife. He was bloody to his elbows, actually dripping gore!" One soldier recalled that Ewell asked, "What troops are these?" When told that it was the Louisiana Brigade, the general exclaimed, "Men, you know me. We must go back to that battery." The Tigers responded with enthusiasm. "The men rose to their feet, a shout—the death knell of the enemy—burst spontaneous from the line, and without further orders they again dashed forward to the battery, over the ground already strewn with their dead comrades." The Tigers' fighting blood was up, and even the brigade's drummer boys joined in the final charge.[95]

Tyler's men were dragging the cannons away when the Tigers and Virginians rushed upon them for the third time. The day's fighting had cost Tyler more than two hundred men thus far, and he was unable to stop the charge. For a few desperate moments the battle raged around the guns, but the Yankees finally broke and pulled back to their own lines. With the cannons in hand once again and Ewell serving as a crewman, the rebels wheeled the guns around to fire at the retreating enemy. There was no cheering this time because across the field more federal brigades could be seen veering away from Jackson's line and charging toward Taylor and Ewell. Taylor knew they could not hold out against any more attacks and resolved "to set our backs to the mountain and die hard." Fortunately, Shields' line was by then in total confusion as a result of his left flank being smashed, and a renewed advance by Jackson's entire army put the Yankees to flight.[96]

The carnage around the battery proved the Louisiana Irishmen's earlier prediction that Shields' boys were looking for a fight. After witnessing four years of bloody warfare, Taylor wrote in his memoirs, "I have never seen so many dead and wounded in the same limited space." A Virginia artilleryman agreed. "I think there must have been eighty or ninety [horses] on less than an acre; one I noticed standing almost upright, perfectly lifeless, supported by a fallen tree." Union Surgeon Capehart concurred with his rebel counterparts and declared, "I have seen some of the bloodiest fields of the war, but I never saw dead and wounded men lie thicker than in the meadow."[97]

More than 300 Yankees and Tigers lay jumbled together among the dead artillery horses. In the short contest, Taylor had lost 165 men at the battery, while Hays lost another 123 on the open plain (his 7th Louisiana suffered the highest casualties of any of Jackson's regiments). The 19 officers and 269 men that the Louisiana Brigade reported losing during the two-hour Battle of Port Republic was the highest casualty rate among Jackson's brigades, and even those numbers may be too low. Historian Robert Krick studied the battle in detail and concluded that the Louisiana Brigade suffered 53 dead and mortally wounded, 270 wounded, and 27 missing. Not included in these figures are the men who broke down on the retreat or could not keep up because they were barefooted. Lieutenant Ring of the 6th Louisiana wrote his wife at the end of the campaign, "We have lost out of this Brigade during our retreat from Winchester nearly three hundred men by their straggling behind." Port Republic's blood bath affected the Tigers for some time. A Georgian who saw Taylor's brigade a couple of weeks later wrote, "The bullet marks and the blood-spattered guns showed the nature of the fighting at the hands of the Louisiana Tigers." The soldier recalled that the men's clothing, equipment, and wagons were also worn out, "But the soldiers! How lean and ragged, yet how game and enthusiastic! And when they stood up in line on dress parade under their tattered colors, their regiments were not larger than companies."[98]

Despite his heavy losses, Jackson had again emerged victorious from the two days' fighting around Cross Keys and Port Republic. With a loss of a little over one thousand men, he had inflicted more than seventeen hundred casualties on Shields and Frémont and had captured thousands of muskets and an abundance of other equipment. More importantly, Jackson had succeeded in making his escape from the Valley and was now in a position to aid in the defense of Richmond. Jackson knew who to thank for this success. Riding up to the captured battery at Port Republic "with an intense light in his eyes," he looked over the bloody ground surrounding the guns and told the men of the Louisiana Brigade that the six captured pieces would be presented to them as a tribute. "I thought the men would go mad with cheering," Taylor wrote, "especially the Irish." One huge Irishman in the 6th Louisiana, "with one eye closed and half his whiskers burned by powder," straddled the tube of one gun and yelled to Taylor, "We told you to bet on your boys!"[99]

Ewell wrote in his campaign report that to the Tigers belonged "the honor of deciding two battles—that of Winchester and [Port Republic]." In fact, the Louisiana Brigade played a key role in almost every engagement of Jackson's famous Valley Campaign. Taylor's men saved the crucial bridge at Front Royal, cut the federal column at Middletown, pushed the enemy out of Winchester, rolled up the Union line at Strasburg, and broke the Union flank at Port Republic. Much of the credit for Jackson's success in capturing or tying down thousands of federal troops in the Valley, plus taking ten thousand muskets, nine artillery pieces, and thousands of dollars' worth of supplies belonged to the Tigers.[100]

In a post-campaign letter to his wife, Lieutenant Ring pointed out that the Louisiana Brigade's contribution to victory came at a high price. "You cannot think, darling, how much we have suffered. One meal a day and that only bread and meat, from five to six hours sleep and two-thirds of the time it rains every night. When it did not it was very cold and our sleep did us little good. Were it not for the oil cloths we captured from the enemy, I do not know what we would have done as a good many times our wagons did not catch us in time to get our blankets." Such harsh conditions broke the health of many Tigers and the morale of others. Desertions in the Louisiana Brigade increased dramatically during the campaign as soldiers found the warmth of Union encampments strongly appealing. The Pemberton Rangers, a foreign-dominated company in the 6th Louisiana, had eleven men (about 10 percent of its complement) desert during May 1862.[101]

Despite the desertions, the Tigers were aware of their contributions to the campaign and claimed that Jackson had begun referring to them as his "Iron Brigade." Taylor could not have been more proud of his men and later wrote,

"Though it had suffered heavy loss in officers and men, it was yet strong, hard as nails and full of confidence." In return, the Louisianians now worshiped the man who only a month before they had considered crazy. Ring proudly declared after the campaign ended, "It will be something to boast of hereafter that I was one of Stonewall Jackson's Army. . . . I had rather be a private in such an Army than a Field Officer in any other Army. Jackson is perfectly idolised by this Army, specialy this brigade and he is as much pleased with us as we are with him."[102]

Jackson recommended Taylor's promotion to major general the day after the Battle of Port Republic. "The success," he reported to Richmond, "with which he has managed his Brigade in camp, on the march, and when engaged with the enemy at Front Royal, Middletown, Winchester, and yesterday near Port Republic makes it my duty as well as my pleasure to recommend him for promotion." The Tigers' gallantry also did not go unnoticed by the Richmond *Whig*, which reported, "This brigade . . . has crowned the Pelican flag with undying glory. . . . The world produces no better fighters than the Louisianians. . . . When a thing is to be done that nobody else dares do or can do, it is the very thing Louisianians insist upon doing, and always do it. The fact is, there is little touch of the very devil in the Louisianians—as some people on the other side of the Potomac will discover, one of these fine days."[103]

After burying the dead at Port Republic, Jackson's army moved in a steady rain to the southeast and up into the mountains by way of Brown's Gap. Taylor, who had already taken a meal from a dead Yankee's haversack, rode ahead of the brigade in search of a supply train to get rations for the men. He found it near the top of the mountain and berated the wagon master for moving so far ahead of the men. When he returned, the general found the men had camped on a very steep slope and were hunkered down among the rocks and logs trying to keep from sliding down the mountainside. According to Major Boyd, Taylor took in the situation and "made things 'blue' around him. The rest of us were more resigned and began to make the most of our unique camp . . . but our General only got the madder and 'cussed' the louder."[104]

Taylor's faithful slave, Tom Strother, made a bed of leaves, covered it with blankets, and the general finally retired for the night. Before morning, however, Boyd was awakened by Taylor furiously yelling for Maj. T. R. Heard, the brigade's quartermaster. "Taylor in his sleep had turned in his steep bed, and he, bed, and all were sliding down the mountain!" When Heard rushed to

Taylor's side and explained there were no other camp sites available, it "only made Taylor swear the more and the louder." By this time the entire camp was awake and laughing at "the wordy duel 'twixt General and quartermaster." Things eventually quietened down, but Taylor began calling for Boyd about dawn. Expecting to get a dressing down like Major Heard, Boyd was surprised to find Taylor in a good mood once again. "[H]e was as gentle as a lamb. . . . Taylor was happy again, and all the more pleasant and agreeable to everyone, as was his custom after explosions of temper, for his ugly mood and fretfulness the night before." All Taylor wanted was for Boyd to seek out Jackson to get permission to move the camp.[105]

As Boyd made his way through a pouring rain, he passed Ewell's ordnance train and heard fiddle music coming from one wagon. Curiosity got the better of him, and he peeked inside to see nineteen-year-old Sgt. Asa Olen Blackman of the 9th Louisiana sitting on an ammunition box, smiling and fiddling. "Olin [sic]," Boyd exclaimed, "what on earth are you doing here?" "Fiddling, sah! Fiddling!" Without stopping his music, Blackman explained that he had been assigned to the ordnance train but had a slave to drive the wagon. "I ride in the wagon and play the fiddle, sah!" When Boyd said he would put an end to that, Blackman cried out, "For Gawd's sake, Major, don't do that. This is the easiest job I ever had in the army. Don't, please don't tell Colonel Stafford." Boyd did inform Stafford and several weeks later during the Seven Days Campaign, he spotted Blackman, covered in dust, marching with his regiment. Boyd smiled at him, but Blackman just looked up with an expression of anger and sadness and declared, "if you had minded your own business I wouldn't be here packing this musket!" An oppressive feeling of guilt then weighed on Boyd when he wondered if Blackman's parents would forgive him should their son be killed. Afterward, Blackman was reduced to private for disobedience and was transferred to the 28th Louisiana in his home state, but he survived the war and became a planter afterward.[106]

On June 12, Jackson moved his army back into the Valley and camped at Weyer's Cave near Port Republic. There the Tigers enjoyed their first prolonged rest in weeks. Private Caldwell wrote in his diary that "all of us took a swim in the Shenandoah River for the second time . . . every thing quiet the sun shines beautiful all the men busy washing and drying their clothes." Henry Handerson shared Caldwell's sentiment and recalled how "we enjoyed the luxuries of a good bath, an abundance of food, clean clothes, and the rest which we all so much needed." Taking advantage of the quiet time, several officers got permission to visit Staunton, including Capt. Campbell Brown who accompanied Lt. Col. John Marshall Jones on a visit to see his girlfriend. Jones was known in the division as "Rum," and while in Staunton he lived up to his nickname. According to Brown, "[W]e had hardly reached the town when he met an old Army comrade [Col. Henry Kelly of the 8th Louisiana] & was tempted to take a drink with him & 'Big Peck' [of the 9th Louisiana] . . . . In two or three hours, I saw Kelly lying fast asleep on a bench in the hall of the hotel, evidently drunk and just afterwards Jones reached his room in a perfectly limp state."[107]

While the Tigers enjoyed their down time at Weyer's Cave, some of their comrades were making their way northward as prisoners of war. They were among the first of hundreds who would later share the same fate. Many of the men had been captured when they straggled behind during the retreat up the Valley, but some, like the 8th Louisiana's Lt. George Wren, had been captured at Port Republic. Late on June 9, Wren wrote in his diary that it had been "A memorable day to me." He gave few details of the fight but explained that, about the time the Tigers captured the enemy battery, "a boy of my size was taken prisoner. This was quite unexpected to me. When I started into the fight I thought of getting killed or wounded, but the idea of being taken prisoner had not entered my head. . . . I felt mad with my self for ever being caught in such a swap, but there was no remedy for it now. I was a prisoner and had surrendered when there was no alternative left."[108]

Wren's company comrade John P. Murrel was also captured, and the two accompanied the Yankees when they retreated from the field. When the column passed through Winchester two days later, Confederate spy Belle Boyd was able to tell them secretly that fellow Tigers William S. Lewis and Marshall Montgomery had eluded capture and were hiding out in town. When the prisoners were marched through Washington, D.C., some days later, an Irishman from the 69th New York recognized the Louisiana Irish prisoners as the men he had fought at Manassas. The Yankee Irishman asked one prisoner if he was the last of the Louisiana Tigers. "Are you the last of the Pittsburgh Zouaves?" came the reply. When the Yankee replied that no, he was not, the Tiger declared, "Well, we whipped you at Bull Run!" "If we were whipped it was not by you," snorted the Yankee, "for when I last saw you, you were running like the divil [sic]."[109]

In Alexandria, Virginia, Wren began throwing uniform buttons to women who seemed eager to get them. One particular beauty blew him a kiss in return for a button, prompting Wren to write, "[I] would have been willing to cut the last one off my coat for her." Wren declared that the women of Alexandria were the kindest he had met, which made it even more difficult when he saw a woman who had supposedly cheered for Jefferson Davis being escorted by soldiers to the guardhouse.[110]

After being exchanged at Fort Monroe in early August, Wren met a friend in Richmond who informed him of the heavy losses the company had suffered during his absence. Wren learned that four comrades had been killed and several others wounded at the very spot where he was captured at Port Republic. Another five had been killed later in the Seven Days Campaign, and some of his best friends had died of their wounds. Wren wrote in his diary, "I don't know when I had met with such a shock."[111]

Back at Weyer's Cave, the Louisiana Brigade's well-deserved rest came to an end on June 17 when it was once again put on the road. The men reached the top of Brown's Gap at midnight and stopped long enough to wolf down some bread and biscuits before continuing. On June 19, the army camped just outside Charlottesville, where large numbers of troops were arriving by rail. Soon it became apparent that their destination was Richmond, and rumors spread that a large offensive was being planned against McClellan on the Peninsula.[112]

An early war photograph of the
8th Louisiana's Thomas Taylor
(American Civil War Museum)

Coppens' Battalion at Pensacola, Florida. Vivandière
Amelia Riliseh is fourth from the left.
(*Library of Congress*)

Postwar photograph of Gen. Richard Taylor
(*Library of Congress*)

Col. Eugene Waggaman
(Gordon Berl)

Edwin Jemison of the 2nd Louisiana,
killed at Malvern Hill
(Library of Congress)

George L. P. Wren
(Rose Library, Emory University)

Gen. Harry T. Hays
*(Camp Moore Photo Collection, Center for Southeast
Louisiana Studies, Southeastern Louisiana University
Archives and Special Collections)*

Gen. Francis T. Nicholls
(Library of Congress)

Louisiana Tigers holding the line at Second Manassas
(from *Battles and Leaders of the Civil War*)

Louisiana dead of Starke's Brigade at Antietam
(Library of Congress)

Postwar photograph of
Capt. William J. Seymour
(Author's private collection)

Alfred Waud's sketch of the Louisiana Tigers' twilight
attack on Cemetery Hill
(Library of Congress)

Gen. Leroy A. Stafford
(Confederate Memorial Hall Museum)

Gen. Zebulon York
(Library of Congress)

Postwar photograph of
Gen. William Raine "Big" Peck
(American Civil War Museum)

CHAPTER 5

"I Have Got My Fill of Fighting"

WHILE TAYLOR'S BRIGADE was marching to glory in the Valley, the Tigers on the Peninsula were engaged in an exhausting fight themselves. Following the Battle of Williamsburg, Joseph E. Johnston's Confederate army made a nightmarish retreat toward Richmond. The 14th Louisiana's William Snakenberg remembered, "The fall back from Williamsburg was very bad marching. It had rained a great deal, and the soil (red clay) was very soft and cut up very bad by the wagons and artillery." Colonel Theodore Hunt's 5th Louisiana served as the army's rearguard, and Sergeant Charlton recalled that the duty was exhausting "in consequence of our marching in line of battle most of the time across fields ditches rail fences &c the latter over grown with thorny briars & the like. . . . The suffering from want of rations was a continual complaint from us, often being glad to have the opportunity of stealing the corn from the horses feed boxes & eating the same after parching it."[1]

The men in St. Paul's Foot Rifles were fortunate to have Hiram Sample serving as the battalion's commissary officer. He rode a mule ahead of the battalion and discovered a wagon full of bread parked at a deserted house. The bread had been sent for a Virginia unit, but Sample decided to commandeer it because his men had been living on parched corn for days. He informed the teamsters that he was a member of the Virginia unit they were seeking, but then warned them that "the Louisiana troops were ahead and they would take the horse, wagon and bread so they had better unload the bread and get back to Richmond as soon as they could." The teamsters readily complied, Sample proudly declared, "and my boys had a fine feast of good bread."[2]

After days of constant skirmishing with pesky Union cavalry and infantry, Hunt's weary men finally crossed the Chickahominy River at New Bridge and encamped for a well-deserved rest. Colonel Hunt then left for Richmond on official business and left Maj. William T. Dean in temporary command. On May 24, the 4th Michigan discovered Hunt's camp while on a reconnaissance and surprised the men. Charlton recalled that some of the Tigers had climbed trees to get a look at the enemy and spotted the approaching Yankees, but officer of the day Capt. James M. Coffey ignored their warnings. As a result, Charlton wrote, "We were surprised, and were idling away the time playing cards &c when we were fired upon at close range."

While part of the 4th Michigan traded shots with the Tigers, the rest of the Yankees silently waded across the river upstream and swept down upon the unsuspecting camp. The Louisianians hurriedly set fire to New Bridge and fell back in confusion, leaving numerous dead and wounded behind. Charlton claimed that the men stampeded, and that Major Dean was the "most prominent in running." Fortunately, Lt. Col. Henry Forno arrived on the scene and quickly began organizing the men. The 10th Georgia also came to help, and the Tigers rallied and finally forced the Yankees to withdraw across the river. After burying their dead, the dejected Tigers settled in for the night. According to Charlton, "The arrival of Lieut Nicholas Caufield [Canfield] from Richmond with a gallon or so of Apple Jack revived us considerable, it being a wet and dreary night."[3]

The Yankees took with them the regiment's records, rifles, swords, assorted souvenirs, and a number of prisoners. The Union soldiers reported that fifteen of the latter were wounded and were surprised at being treated so well because they had been told that they would be killed if captured. When General McClellan learned that the victorious Michigan soldiers were returning with their spoils, he rode out to shake the colonel's hand and congratulate him and his men on a job well done. McClellan then proudly informed President Lincoln that the 4th Michigan had "about finished [the] Louisiana Tigers." At a loss of only ten men, the Michigan boys had killed or wounded fifty Tigers and captured forty-three.[4]

Only a week after this humiliating defeat, other Louisiana commands were thrown into a savage fight along the Chickahominy River. While pursuing Johnston up the Peninsula, McClellan split his army across the sluggish stream, posting three of his army corps north of the river and two south of it around Seven Pines and Fair Oaks. Seeing a chance to smash these two isolated corps, Johnston ordered the divisions of A. P. Hill and Magruder to demonstrate against the three Union corps north of the river while Longstreet led his own and the divisions of Gens. D. H. Hill, Benjamin Huger, and Gustavus Smith against the two Union corps south of the Chickahominy.[5]

The battle opened at approximately 2:00 p.m., May 31, when Longstreet's men advanced against Gen. Erasmus Keyes' IV Corps. The battle raged all afternoon, but Longstreet's units became confused in the unfamiliar territory and the fight quickly deteriorated into a series of uncoordinated attacks by individual Confederate brigades. As the sun was setting over the smoky woods, Gen. Richard H. Anderson was ordered to take his men into action. Anderson's brigade was an eclectic mix of Alabamans, Floridians, Virginians, and Louisianians, with the latter consisting of Coppens' and St. Paul's battalions, which had been consolidated under Coppens' command.

Anderson galloped up to Coppens' consolidated battalion while the men lay in the woods under a heavy fire. Federals, strongly posted on a hill fronting the Tigers, had just repelled a Tennessee brigade, but Anderson calmly rode down the length of the prone gray line and shouted over the din of battle that the Louisianians must take the hill. "Remember Butler and New Orleans," he yelled, "and drive them into hell!" The Tigers sprang to attention, and one Georgia soldier recalled hearing the Zouaves' officers issuing their orders in French. In the growing darkness, a nearby band struck up "Dixie" as the Zouaves and Foot Rifles silently crept through a belt of timber to within fifty yards of the first Union line.[6]

Shouting "Picayune Butler," the Tigers broke into a run and routed two Pennsylvania regiments with a sudden volley of musketry from a distance of only fifteen yards. One of the more stubborn Yankees held his ground and engaged in a personal fight with an unidentified captain in St. Paul's Foot Rifles. Witnesses claimed that the two men were so close that it looked like they were about to engage in a fist fight when the Union soldier suddenly pulled a pistol and fired in the Tiger's face. Fortunately, the bullet missed, and the captain drew his own revolver and killed him, to the cheers of the battalion. The soldiers' elation was short-lived, however, because when the surprised Yankees discovered just how few Confederates there actually were, they halted their retreat, turned, and cut down the first line of Tigers with a well-aimed barrage of minié balls. The Pennsylvanians were severely thrashing the outnumbered Louisianians when more Confederates arrived to help push the enemy back again.[7]

When darkness ended the battle, both sides began strengthening and rearranging their lines in preparation for the next day's clash. Many of Coppens' men used the cover of night for more rewarding endeavors. One witness wrote, "These Louisianians seem to be great epicures, for scarcely one came off the field without having a well-filled haversack, and a canteen of liquor." While making the rounds of his position early on June 1, Gen. George Pickett blundered upon several Zouaves "who had evidently been on a plundering expedition." Loaded down with booty, the surprised Tigers tried to outmaneuver the irate officer by riding around him on their awkward mules. Pickett, however, was able to grab the reins of one mule and demanded an explanation from the cornered Zouave. The Tiger blurted out in fright that the Yankees were right behind them and begged Pickett to let go of his mule. The general reluctantly obliged so he could alert his superiors of the approaching enemy.[8]

Soon after Pickett's surprise encounter, D. H. Hill's division opened the second day's battle by fiercely assaulting the federal line. The stubborn Yankees held, however, and then counterattacked. The 14th Louisiana reportedly took an active part in beating back this last Union advance, and the battle finally died down. Both sides lay bruised and bloodied from the two-day struggle with little being accomplished strategically to justify the 6,000 Confederate and 5,000 Union casualties. The most significant result of the battle was the wounding of General Johnston on the first day of fighting. President Davis put Gen. Robert E. Lee in charge of the army, which he immediately renamed the Army of Northern Virginia.

The losses within the Louisiana commands were unquestionably severe but difficult to verify because their casualty lists were apparently lost. Coppens, who was seriously wounded in the battle, entered the fight with 225 men and left more than half of them dead or wounded on the field, including 11 officers. One source claimed that St. Paul's Foot Rifles started the battle with 200 men and came out with only 73, another reported it lost approximately 100 of 196 men, and yet a third put the casualties at 57. The latter source also claimed that 310 of the 380 men in Coppens' and St. Paul's consolidated battalion were casualties.[9]

Among the dead was a Lieutenant Bourges (possibly V. E. Bourges), who had been elected to his position in St. Paul's Foot Rifles a month earlier. John L. Rapier recalled sleeping next to him the night before the battle and of Bourges talking about his home and loved ones. According to Rapier, "I came to him three minutes after he fell. His eyes were shut. I raised his head and kissed hm. He opened his eyes and smiled—and said: 'John, I am mortally wounded; but it's all for my country. Drive them from our soil when I am dead.' He was shot through his sword belt, on the right side, just as he was drawing his sword & calling at the top of his voice, 'Charge! Charge! Chasseurs!' We were much scattered at the time, and few heard him or saw him fall."[10]

Despite their heavy losses, the Tigers' gallantry was noted by others. According to Rapier, "The praise of St. Paul's Battalion of Louisiana Foot Rifles is in the papers, amongst the citizens, and through the army." The Richmond *Daily Dispatch* reported on the battalion's actions and claimed it captured the colors of the 54th Pennsylvania, but that regiment did not participate in the battle. If the battalion did capture a flag, it is not known to whom it belonged. The newspaper also reported that General Longstreet honored St. Paul's Foot Rifles with a battle flag at a ceremony on June 13. After General Anderson read a note from Longstreet to the assembled men, one of his aides asked him to make a few remarks. Anderson smiled and declared, "Speech?—oh, the Louisianians require no speeches; they know what to do!" The battle flag was described as having a pink field, blue cross and stars, and the inscribed battle honors "Williamsburg" and "Seven Pines."[11]

Although no major action took place for several weeks following the Battle of Seven Pines, the Louisiana commands continued to man the front lines and engage in frequent skirmishes. Lieutenant Colonel Edmund Pendleton, the thirty-eight-year-old Virginian who commanded the 3rd Louisiana Battalion, wrote his daughter how four of his men walked beyond the picket line on June 17 and unexpectedly encountered five Yankees bathing in the Chickahominy. A quick exchange of gunfire left two Union soldiers dead. "So you see," he declared, "we are not on very neighborly terms with them."[12]

Paul J. Semmes' brigade, which included the 5th and 10th Louisiana, entrenched around the York River Railroad after Seven Pines. Jefferson Davis once visited the camp, and Sergeant Charlton proudly reported that he had the honor of escorting the president to the front lines. The regiment's position was in woods so thick that the men had to blaze trees just so the pickets could find their way to and from their outposts. While there, someone devised a plan to have Colonel Forno lead a "forlorn hope" mission. Forno was to take two large cannons, nicknamed "Long Tom" and "Charley," on ironclad railroad cars to a forward position where they could shell a Yankee battery that had been bombarding the area. "Happily," reported Charlton, "the undertaking was never carried out or very few if any would have returned to tell the tale."[13]

A few weeks after the Battle of Seven Pines, General Lee saw an opportunity to cripple McClellan's Army of the Potomac. McClellan had shifted all of his forces south of the Chickahominy River with the exception of Fitz-John Porter's corps, which was strongly dug in behind Beaver Dam Creek near Mechanicsville. In a maneuver similar to the one Johnston used at Seven Pines, Lee planned to concentrate two-thirds of his men north of the river to smash Porter's isolated corps, while Magruder and Huger remained to the south to hold the bulk of McClellan's army in place. After Lee crushed Porter, McClellan would be forced to retreat and could be overwhelmed while in motion.[14]

It was to participate in this offensive that Jackson's veterans were recalled from the Valley. Jackson would help force Porter's corps out of its Beaver Dam Creek line by attacking the Union right flank from the north. Longstreet, A. P. Hill, and D. H. Hill would strike from the west and southwest when they heard Jackson begin his attack. Lee planned to make his knockout blow on June 26, but McClellan beat him to the punch when he sent forward the left of his army on June 25 to secure an area from which to launch his own assault. The Yankees drove Huger's pickets back, and Ambrose R. Wright's brigade was rushed forward with others to shore up the line. Wright deployed Lt. Col. William R. Shivers' 1st Louisiana on the right side of the road with the 22nd and 4th Georgia to the right of Shivers. When the federals were seen emerging from thick woods in front, Wright's men surged forward. The Tigers reportedly yelled "Butler! and New Orleans!" and helped drive the Yankees back through the woods and into a cornfield. There they were surprised to encounter more Union brigades, including Thomas Francis Meagher's Irish Brigade and Dan Sickles' Excelsior Brigade. The Louisianians and Georgians retreated to the far edge of the field, regrouped, and then charged through the corn again. The enemy's deadly volleys rattled through the cornstalks and thinned the advancing rebel line. Colonel Shivers fell out with a ball through his right arm, leaving Capt. Michael "Jim" Nolan to lead the Tigers onward. Crouching as they advanced through the storm of lead, the Confederates finally made it across the deadly field and drove the Yankees back.[15]

The men in the 1st Louisiana were ecstatic, for this was their first fight and they had captured the battle flag of Sickles' famous Excelsior Brigade. In the midst of backslapping congratulations, however, minié balls peppered the regiment as a new Union charge came crashing through the timber. As Wright's men were driven back across the cornfield a second time, Yankee shells and canister tore through their backs, and the fighting raged near a small building called King's School House before finally sputtering out at dark. Captain Nolan's Tigers were then able to slip back out with some Georgians and Tar Heels and restore the original picket line.

That night, Pvt. James Henderson volunteered to help collect the wounded that were stranded between the lines. Henderson found Colonel Shivers, hoisted him onto his back, and carried him to the rear, and then returned to the cornfield to retrieve Shivers' sword and other personal effects. While doing so, he discovered other wounded men and carried them off the field, despite being fired upon by the Yankees. In reporting Henderson's heroic deed, the Richmond *Daily Dispatch* declared that "this fine soldier stole through the grass upon his hands and knees, and actually stole our wounded men from under the enemy's guns! We always delight to record the deeds of privates, but can any words of ours add to the honor of such a brave fellow as Henderson?"[16]

The 1st Louisiana's initiation into combat had been devastating. Among the dead and wounded were 16 of the regiment's 27 officers and 128 of the 328 men who took part in the fight. The unit suffered more casualties than any other regiment in the battle, but its performance did not go unnoticed. In his report, General Wright wrote, "I beg leave to bring to your notice the gallant conduct of the First Louisiana Regiment in their charge" across the cornfield. With the general's blessings, the Tigers had "King's School House" emblazoned across their battle flag to show that they were now combat veterans.[17]

Despite McClellan's bloody probe, Lee went ahead with his plans to pounce on Porter's exposed corps at Beaver Dam Creek. His instructions were simple—when A. P. Hill heard Jackson open the fight on Porter's right flank, he was to begin the western attack by clearing the federals out of Mechanicsville and then assaulting the Beaver Dam Creek line. All through the morning of June 26, Hill waited, straining to catch the sound of gunfire to the north. It was ominously quiet, however, for Jackson was uncharacteristically slow in getting into position. When 3:00 p.m. came and there was still no sign of Stonewall, Hill decided to advance on his own lest the day be wasted. Mechanicsville was quickly cleared of the enemy, and Beaver Dam Creek was reached. After studying the frowning cannons and musket barrels along the Union line, Hill decided the only chance for a breakthrough was to send Gen. Joseph R.

Anderson's brigade circling to the left to try to capture a particularly deadly battery on the Union right flank.[18]

After slowly snaking through the woods, Anderson's men finally reached the Union right flank only to find themselves facing a formidable obstacle. The federals were dug in behind earthen and rail breastworks with several batteries of artillery posted on the crest of a hill behind them. In addition, they had dammed up the creek in their front, turning the normally ten-foot-wide stream into a fifty-yard pond. Despite the odds, Anderson silently deployed the 14th and 35th Georgia and Pendleton's 3rd Louisiana Battalion along the densely covered creek bank. Under a devastating fire, the Georgians and Tigers then rushed through a nearly impassable briar thicket and tumbled down the slippery five-foot creek bank into the water. Many of the men were shot in midstream or as they struggled up the opposite muddy bank, but a sizable portion of the attacking line managed to cross the pond. Bleeding and torn from the briars, the Confederates rooted out the Yankees, seized a segment of their breastworks, and sent back a frantic plea to Anderson for reinforcements. Unfortunately, Union artillery was pounding the rest of the brigade on the far side of the pond, and Anderson was unable to send help. The men had to hold on alone until they could safely wade back across the pond under the cover of darkness.[19]

That night the question on everyone's mind was why Jackson had not fulfilled his part of the planned offensive. The great Stonewall was supposed to have launched the first attack against Porter, but the day ended without his men firing a shot. Historians have long pondered why Jackson's "foot cavalry" failed to get into position on time, but it was probably a combination of vague orders, lack of communication, fatigue, and Union obstructions in his path.[20]

Fresh from their Valley victories, Jackson's men were eager to mete out the same treatment to McClellan's boys that the federals along the Shenandoah River had received, but they had been on the move for days in terrible conditions. The 8th Louisiana's Isaiah Fogleman reported that his regiment traveled by train to Beaver Dam Station on June 23 and then began marching. "[I]t rained very hard and all night. After wading creeks and gulleys for some time, we became very wet and cold. Brigade scattered in every direction. It was the darkest night I ever wittenesed [sic]." On June 25, the Louisiana Brigade finally made it to Ashland, just twelve miles north of Richmond, but by that time the rigors of the last six weeks had completely broken down General Taylor. His rheumatoid arthritis was so severe that he could no longer mount his horse, and he suffered excruciating pain in his head and loins. Taylor was forced to relinquish command to Colonel Seymour and was put on the floor of an abandoned house while the brigade cooked three days' rations of fresh beef and prepared for the last push to the battlefield.[21]

When the Tigers moved out about 5:00 a.m. the next day, Taylor was almost paralyzed and had to be left behind. During the afternoon the men could hear the long, rolling thunder of artillery and musketry coming from their right. It was obvious that A. P. Hill was meeting stiff resistance at Beaver Dam Creek, but Jackson inexplicably had his men camp before sundown rather than racing to the fight.[22]

The night of June 26 was dark, and tension ran high in the Louisiana Brigade as the men lay on their arms. Around midnight the jittery command was jolted awake by what Henry Handerson described as "the most unearthly and terrible shriek that ever greeted mortal ears. It seemed that every man in the division was aroused by same cry." As the nervous soldiers jumped to their feet, fumbled with their muskets, and tried to form a line in the pitch blackness, a crazed mule came braying through the camp. Muffled laughter and curses spread down the line as word was passed that the screams were from the horses of Colonels Stafford and Peck, which had suddenly started fighting and sent the frightened mule bolting through camp. It was, declared Isaiah Fogleman, a "Stampede."[23]

After a restless night, Ewell's division resumed the march at 3:00 a.m. The men now followed A. P. Hill's division, and Private Caldwell reported that there was "heavy cannonading and musketry ahead constantly." Cautiously the Louisiana Brigade picked its way through abandoned federal camps that were littered with discarded equipment, dead horses, and shattered bodies. Some of the Tigers passed the time by picking up letters from the debris and reading them aloud to their comrades. Major Wheat, however, was not amused. Since the preceding day, when the brigade lay listening to the rumble of battle along Beaver Dam Creek, he was strangely subdued—even melancholy. His friends attributed this mood to the earlier deaths of his brother at Shiloh and a cousin in the Valley, but this was not the cause of the major's depression. Wheat was about to die, and he knew it.[24]

To all who would listen, the major talked of his impending death and made them promise to bury him where he fell. When he awakened on June

27, Wheat passed his brandy flask to Major Boyd and Colonel Stafford and read aloud a prayer from a small prayer book that his mother had given him. Then, Boyd recalled, Wheat would "cry like a child, take another drink and read from his little book again." Later in the day, Wheat met Maj. Moxley Sorrel and told him, "Moxley, something tells old Bob that this is the last drink he'll ever take in the world and he'll take it with you." Later, while riding beside Lieutenant Colonel Peck, Wheat declared emphatically that he would die before sunset and talked at length about his parents, especially his mother. An Alabama officer recalled hearing Wheat also instruct Peck to make sure that his mother received some certain property after his death. Throughout the day's march, Wheat continued to pull out his prayer book and read aloud from it. One prayer in particular seemed to hold special meaning for him. Titled "Joyful Resurrection," it began, "Lord, I commend myself to Thee. Prepare me for living, prepare me for dying." At first, the Tigers made light of Wheat's tearful farewells, but as they saw his growing melancholy, they, too, began to feel an oppressiveness.[25]

Porter withdrew his corps from Beaver Dam Creek during the night and fought a series of delaying actions throughout the morning of June 27. One of these bloody clashes was an unexpected attack on Gen. Roger A. Pryor's brigade early in the morning. When twelve Union cannons placed in a redoubt began inflicting heavy casualties on the brigade, the 14th Louisiana's Col. Zebulon York asked Pryor for permission to attack the position with his regiment. According to Private Snakenberg, Pryor refused, telling York, "No, you cannot get there alive." York insisted on trying and assured Pryor, "My men will go with me." To Snakenberg's relief, Pryor again refused permission. "Had he done so, I do not believe any would have lived to come back. A Brigade had charged it the evening before and failed." The 14th Louisiana stayed in place, and the men loaded and fired as fast as they could through dense smoke and fog that hid objects thirty yards away. Snakenberg reported that before the fight every man had been issued sixty rounds of ammunition instead of the normal forty, and now they were going through it quickly trying to suppress the fire from the enemy they thought was a short distance away across a deep gully.[26]

Men were dropping rapidly from the unseen foe's musketry when screaming rounds of artillery suddenly began exploding along the gray line. Major David Zable quickly realized that a friendly battery atop a hill in the rear was shelling the brigade by mistake in the fog. He dispatched a courier to silence the guns, but a bullet dropped him before getting far. Zable then spurred his horse and galloped back to the battery himself and pointed out his brigade to the artillerymen. While up above the fog, Zable was astonished to see that the previously unseen Yankees who were cutting his regiment to pieces were posted far up the slope and not directly ahead of his men as thought. For an hour the Tigers had been subjected to a murderous fire while harmlessly pumping volley after volley into the side of a hill. Zable rushed back down into the smoke-shrouded valley and ordered the men to aim higher. Cadmus Wilcox's brigade arrived soon afterward and got the advance rolling again by throwing a makeshift bridge across the gorge fronting the brigade.[27]

By midafternoon, Porter had skillfully set his men in two lines along a series of ridges overlooking a boggy creek bottom known as Boatswain's Swamp. Taking cover behind log breastworks and with batteries of artillery higher up the hill behind them, the Yankees were in a position to slaughter Lee's men as they crossed the swamp. As Longstreet put it, the Confederates were being forced to attack from a position "the enemy wished us to attack from." At 2:30 p.m., A. P. Hill made first contact with Porter and sent his brigades charging against the enemy's strong defensive position. After an hour and a half of savage bloodletting, however, Hill called a halt to the futile attacks and withdrew to let Longstreet and Jackson continue the fight.[28]

Although nearly thirty-six hours late, Jackson had finally arrived on the field and by 2:00 p.m. had Ewell's division in position to attack Porter's right flank around Gaines' Mill. When Jackson came riding down his line to make sure all was ready, Wheat spurred his horse to greet his commander, having snapped out of his despondent mood as soon as he heard the battle begin. Approaching Jackson, Wheat told him the front was no place for the commander and begged Jackson not to expose himself in this battle as he so often had done in the Valley. Leave the fighting to his Tigers, he exclaimed. Touched by the major's concern, Jackson reached out, grasped Wheat's hand, and told him he appreciated the thought, but that it was Wheat who would be in the most danger and he hoped the major would not be hurt. Wheat, however, apparently was no longer concerned about himself. Riding up to David Boyd, he scanned his ragged wharf rats and jokingly exclaimed, "Major, just look at my Louisiana planters! I'd like to see any 5,000 button makers stand before them this day."[29]

Heavy firing continued to build on Jackson's right, clearly indicating that Hill's attack was running into stiff opposition. To relieve some of the pressure,

Jackson ordered his brigades forward against the Union position anchored on a hill across Boatswain's Swamp. One soldier in the 6th Louisiana wrote, "The necessity for prompt action was so great that we were hurriedly formed in line of battle . . . and were rapidly marched under a terrific fire from the artillery as well as the infantry." With his officers prodding the troops past tempting Union encampments, Colonel Seymour quickly pushed the Louisianians across an open field and into a thick wood. As the brigade swept through the timber, searching rounds of artillery fire shattered treetops and rained limbs and shrapnel on the men. Smoke hung heavy in the foliage, and brush impeded the advance, but the Tigers trotted down into the swamp's knee-deep water. Henry Handerson wrote that they still could not see the enemy, "though the occasional whiz of a bullet assured us that the foe was not far distant." Officers became confused in the acrid smoke and thick brush and were not sure if they were still on course after sloshing through the water to the base of a hill. They quickly found they were when a barrage of bullets ripped through the formation. According to Handerson, "the intensity of the fire far exceeded all that we had experienced in the Valley."[30]

Seymour pitched over dead from bullets to his head and body, and the 6th Louisiana's color sergeant was badly wounded. Sergeant Benjamin Stagg quickly grabbed the flag and rushed thirty yards ahead of the battle line only to be shot through the heart and killed instantly. One of Stagg's comrades wrote, "Many of us were wounded, and all within a space of thirty yards, and that was as far as our brigade went." Unsure what to do, a few of the men fell back into the swamp, but most of the leaderless men simply halted on the hillside.[31]

Major Wheat became furious when he saw his Tigers falling back. Apparently in an attempt to inspire them to rally, he rode beyond the lines and threaded his way through the brush toward the Union position. Suddenly, both horse and rider collapsed in a heap only forty yards from the smoking enemy works. Caught in the open, Wheat was killed instantly by a ball that tore through one eye and out the back of his head. As at Manassas, the Tigers became demoralized after seeing their beloved major fall and began running back down the deadly slope. Major Boyd stopped one man and demanded to know why he was running. "They have killed the old Major," the Tiger sobbed, "and I am going home. I wouldn't fight for Jesus Christ now!" Several sources claim that, even though he was shot through the brain, Wheat cried out, "Bury me on the field, boys!" just as he died. Eyewitnesses, however, state that Wheat died instantly and there was no one around him to hear any last words. The story probably originated from Wheat's asking earlier in the day that he be buried where he fell.[32]

With Seymour and Wheat dead, the entire Louisiana line was in confusion and ready to bolt for the rear. Handerson declared, "Now was the critical time when a voice of authority to guide our uncertain steps and a bold officer to lead us forward would have been worth to us a victory. But none such appeared." Stafford was the senior colonel, but he was not aware that Seymour had been killed. As a result, no one stepped forward to take command while the hidden enemy continued to knock scores of Tigers out of line. Handerson wrote, "Four of my companions fell dead, and four severely wounded, within ten steps of me in the short space of fifteen minutes, while I escaped with a bullet hole in my hat." Unable to stand under the murderous fire any longer, the brigade finally broke and fled back down the slope to the swamp. Desperate comrades dragged and carried as many of the wounded with them as possible, but a number were left between the lines. With the help of others, Lt. B. T. Walshe, an Irishman in the 6th Louisiana, dragged Colonel Seymour's body back down the hill to the edge of the swamp and huddled next to it.[33]

The Yankees' bullets kicked up mud and water as most of the Tigers splashed back across the stagnant swamp just as Trimble's brigade came charging through to plug the gap left by their retreat. The Georgians shouted, "Get out of our way! We will show you how to do it!" to which a Tiger replied, "Boys, you are mighty good but that's hell in there." Lieutenant Walshe, who was also wounded, wrote, "I was [mistakenly] told it was Hood's brigade, and the fire given by them and returned by the enemy was terrific, making the water in which we lay spurt up like it does in a very heavy rain." Despite its heroic charge, Trimble's brigade also suffered heavy losses and failed to crack the strong Union line.[34]

While riding to the front, General Ewell's aide Campbell Brown encountered the Tigers running out of the bushes. He found that the 9th Louisiana and part of the 7th and 8th regiments were still in some order and took it upon himself to rally them and two companies of the 15th Alabama. Brown claimed it took forty-five minutes "of hard work," but he, and probably Colonel Stafford, finally got the men formed behind a ridge on Trimble's flank. Trimble, however, soon ordered Stafford to withdraw out of fire "as he found his men somewhat nervous where they were." About the same time, Gen. John B.

Hood's Texas brigade of Longstreet's command came whooping through the swamp on the Tigers' right and accomplished what the other brigades had failed to do. Lieutenant Walshe, who was still hunkered down next to Colonel Seymour's body, recalled, "We lay there between the fires of friend and foe for fully half an hour, when the Confederate yell was heard, and we knew that the position had been carried." By not stopping to return fire until they were within easy range, the Texans broke through the federal breastworks and precipitated a Union retreat that Pryor's brigade and others took advantage of on the far right.[35]

Pryor's brigade had actually begun its own attack shortly before Hood. Pryor came trotting down his line at 4:30 p.m., halted before the 14th Louisiana, and ordered it to follow him toward the Union works. The brigade pushed across a wide field, first walking, then breaking into a run down a gentle slope toward Boatswain's Swamp. Federal gunners sprang to their pieces and pounded Pryor's line for several minutes before the Confederates got within range of the Union infantry. The enemy's musketry tore ragged holes through the Louisiana line, and one bullet passed through Lt. Robert Miller's sword scabbard and killed a man running beside him. "The bullets came so thick," Miller wrote, "that I felt a desire to see how many I could catch with my open hand stretched out."[36]

As the brigade neared a gully in Boatswain's Swamp, the shrill rebel yell rose over the roar of battle. Jumping and clawing their way across the gorge, the Louisianians reformed their line on the other side, fired one volley, and charged once again. By now, the entire Union line was unraveling as a result of Hood's successful attack. The Tigers quickly reached a federal battery and in ten minutes killed half of its crew and captured the guns in some of the fiercest fighting of the day. The Louisianians then wheeled the cannons around to fire salvos at the retreating Yankees and renewed the chase.

When darkness ended the fighting, the Confederates held the field, but Pryor's brigade had lost 860 men out of 1,400 engaged. The 14th Louisiana counted 51 dead and 192 wounded, with one company of 45 men losing 29 members. Coppens' and St. Paul's battalions fared a little better with 5 dead and 46 wounded. Among the dead in the 14th Louisiana were two color-bearers and their color guards. According to Private Snakenberg, one of the men rolled up in the flag as he fell without anyone noticing during the fierce charge. It was not until that night that he and the flag were discovered missing, but the regiment had advanced so far by then that it was not possible to go back to search for them. Fortunately, a soldier in another unit retrieved the colors and returned them to the regiment two days later. They were then given to Irishman James McCann to carry.[37]

The day's carnage shocked the surviving Tigers. Lieutenant Miller lamented, "I have got my fill of fighting, I want no more of it." Miller blamed poor tactics on Pryor's part for the brigade's heavy losses at Gaines' Mill. "He is a politician general and merits the contempt of all soldiers. He hoped by displaying the largest number of men killed and wounded in his Brigade to obtain a promotion. He succeeded, by placing us in exposed positions and by getting his regiments confused in producing the longest list of killed and wounded. . . . It is not necessary to say that in all the fight, Brig. Gen. Pryor was at a distance to the rear which precluded the possibility of an accident to him."[38] In fairness to Pryor, the confusion Miller referred to was present in nearly all of the Confederate brigades, and several other soldiers mentioned Pryor often exposing himself to enemy fire. How much of Miller's complaints were shared by other Tigers and how much was personal spitefulness is not known.

To the left of Pryor's shattered brigade, Stafford was trying to pull his disorganized command back together. Darkness came quickly in the timbered swamp, and lanterns were used to search out the 142 wounded men, many of whom lay propped up out of the water against stumps and logs, moaning and crying for help. For the 29 dead, there was no hurry—they could be found and buried in the morning. By then the ill General Taylor had caught up with the brigade in an ambulance. The heavy losses affected him greatly, and he admitted after the war, "I had a wretched feeling of guilt, particularly about Seymour, who led the brigade and died in my place."[39]

Later that night a number of Tigers sought out Wheat's body to pay their respects. The next morning, when Major Boyd returned to make sure the body had been recovered, he found Lt. Samuel P. Dushane of the Tiger Rifles and several other battalion members already there, burying the major. When the task was completed, Dushane asked Boyd to say a prayer, but he declined. Dushane then declared, "Well, if I must, here goes it. Kneel down, boys." Boyd was moved by the lieutenant's words and wrote, "And never before or since have I heard such a prayer—so short, so telling—commending the spirit of his beloved commander and friend to the tender mercies of God."[40]

While the dead and wounded were collected, many of the Tigers took the opportunity to wander over the battlefield. Captain Al Pierson of the 9th Louisiana described to his father what he saw. "Where the battle raged the fiercest every twig was riddled and many trees not more than a foot in diameter had as many as forty balls in its truck. The yankee wounded was still lying on the ground and begging for water and food of all who passed by. The dead wore as many different faces as the living. Many seemed to have expired laughing while others cinched their teeth and hands and seemed to have perished in awful agony. Some were still clinging to their guns as if they died fighting. Language would in no way express the true picture as it really was."[41]

Private Caldwell of the 7th Louisiana also examined the battlefield and wrote in his diary, "[W]e are still on the battlefield the dead and wounded are strewn for miles all along the line of battle we drew no rations living on the enemy's deserted camps." During his walk, Caldwell found and apparently kept a Colt rifle that one of the Pennsylvania Bucktails had left behind. Billy Singleton, another member of the 9th Louisiana, examined the area on which the New York Fire Zouaves had fought. A friend later wrote, "At first sight he thought it was in reality a field of blood, the Zouaves having worn red trousers, and thousands of them lay dead on the field." According to this friend, Union Gen. John Reynolds suddenly stepped out of the bushes and surrendered to Private Singleton with the explanation that he was cut off from his own army and did not want to get shot. Singleton dutifully turned the general over to his superiors.[42]

June 28 was spent skirmishing and maneuvering as Porter pulled back to the south side of the Chickahominy River to join the rest of McClellan's army. The Confederates followed and marched through the burning wagons and supplies left behind by Porter's retreating men. Jackson's command continued to follow up the enemy the next day, but Stonewall again failed to live up to his reputation when he did not press the enemy vigorously enough. He was supposed to push across the Chickahominy and attack the Yankees around Savage's Station, but Jackson's unusual lethargy and confusing orders prevented him from even getting across the river. After spending much of the day tearing up the railroad, Taylor's brigade approached the Chickahominy only to find a burning Union munitions train roaring toward them. The Yankees had set fire to the train at Savage's Station and sent it barreling toward the rebels across the river. Captain Brown wrote that "an Engine & train came full speed towards the bridge, loaded with bursting shells, powder barrels etc. The troops on the road were hurried away for fear that the train might possibly leap the gap in the bridge—but instead of doing so it went down with a grand crash, thirty miles an hour, into the river. It was one of the grandest sights I ever looked at." No damage was done, but the explosion did frighten the ambulance horses and sent them galloping away with the wounded men.[43]

On the south side of the Chickahominy, Lee's troops continued to press after McClellan. Later in the day, the Confederates discovered that Union Gen. Edwin Sumner's corps had set up a new defensive line at Savage's Station to cover McClellan's crossing of White Oak Swamp. Magruder was the first to advance against this new position, but he was bloodily repulsed. McLaws then deployed and sent in Semmes' and Joseph B. Kershaw's brigades along the Richmond & York River Railroad. Advancing through a dense wood, Colonel Hunt's 5th Louisiana in Semmes' brigade suddenly halted after hearing someone issuing commands to an unseen force hidden in the undergrowth ahead. Hammers clicked and muskets were brought up, but several of Semmes' officers stayed the nervous men, thinking the unseen soldiers might belong to a stray Confederate brigade. Hunt, however, could see the mysterious men forty yards ahead and was not at all certain they were friendly. General Semmes finally sent Pvt. John Maddox of the 5th Louisiana out to investigate. "Who are you?" yelled Maddox. "Friends!" came the reply. "What regiment?" Maddox inquired. "Third Vermont!" Semmes ordered the brigade to open fire, and a roaring battle broke out in the dark woods.[44]

The 3rd Vermont was part of the Vermont brigade that had battled Colonel Levy's 2nd Louisiana so furiously at Dam Number One ten weeks earlier. This fight was no different. In the growing twilight, the Tigers and Yankees sent thousands of minié balls tearing through the brush. Charlton wrote, "The night was pitch dark. Our only guide being the flashes from the muskets." Hunt's men used "buck and ball," a combination of a minié ball and two buckshot, in their smoothbore muskets. With a scant forty yards of brush and timber separating the lines, this load was particularly deadly. When darkness finally ended the fight twenty minutes later, the Vermont brigade had lost a staggering 358 men—one-half of its effective force—and the Confederates claimed to have counted 100 Union bodies in front of Hunt's position. Semmes counted just 64 casualties. The 5th Louisiana lost only 6 men, perhaps because after their first volley the Tigers dropped to their knees to continue the fight.[45]

During the battle, Magruder sent a courier to Taylor asking that he bring up his brigade to help, but Taylor was unable to get there in time because a heavy rain that turned the ground into a "lake" slowed him down. Taylor's health also began to deteriorate once again, and he was forced to relinquish brigade command to Colonel Stafford and return to his ambulance the next day.[46]

The Yankees withdrew from Savage's Station during the night and established a new defensive position around Glendale and Frayser's Farm on June 30. Once again the rebel brigades were thrown into piecemeal attacks, and the entrenched federals chewed them up. Pryor's brigade was lying along the edge of a field under heavy artillery fire when the general came riding down the line to prepare for the advance. Pryor's presence seemed to attract even more shells—one exploded in the midst of the 14th Louisiana, taking out a half-dozen men, and another cut off the leg of Pryor's horse. When the charge was finally sounded, the brigade pushed across the field into devastating artillery fire and musketry. James McCann, who had been designated the 14th Louisiana's color-bearer just the day before, fell dead with seven bullet wounds, but another soldier snatched up the flag and the advance continued. The desperate charge accomplished little, and the rebels paid a staggering price for their bravery. The 14th Louisiana began the advance at Frayser's Farm with 900 men and left 243 littered across the field. One Tiger claimed that of 42 men in one company that entered the fight, "only nine men came out without bullets in their hides." For good reason, the soldiers dubbed Frayser's Farm the "Slaughter House."[47]

Those who survived the killing field were exhausted and almost completely broken down. In describing the men, Private Snakenberg wrote, "That night after the fight, we hardly knew each other, because we were so black. It was a very warm day and we had run so far, in a charge, that the perspiration poured out of us, and at that time of the war, the bullets we used were greased with tallow. So after handling the cartridges, biting the ends off to the powder, and wiping the perspiration from our faces, we got everything well mixed and left a good coat of tallow and powder on our hands and faces."[48]

Father Gache, the 10th Louisiana's chaplain, walked over the battlefield the next day and wrote a friend:

> The place where the battle had begun was covered with the dead, Confederate dead for the most part. . . . About a half mile further on we began to see the wounded lying alongside the dead, and from here

on it was all Federal troops. . . . Many of them were pitifully mutilated, lying in the dust under a fierce sun. Some of them didn't even have the strength to turn their faces to the shade. Here they had lain, anywhere from fifteen to twenty-six hours without so much as even a sip of water for their burning thirst. . . . I must remark that our soldiers who are depicted by the newspapers of the North as cruel, barbaric monsters, acted with great kindness toward the wounded. The Irish lads of my own 10th were especially outstanding in this respect. Each time the brigade came to a halt, dozens of men broke ranks and ran to cut down branches to provide shade for the wounded. Sometimes they would fix those branches into the ground beside the poor unfortunate Yankees; sometimes they would even gather up four muskets and bayonet them into the ground as a framework to support the branches. They would then give the men water, biscuits, and other bits of food that they happened to have. I have said that the Federals generally reacted with surprised gratitude to this kindness from their enemies; there was one, however, who just about died of panic when he saw the Confederates approaching him. The poor boy, frightfully mutilated and weakened by a great loss of blood, imagined that our troops were coming to put him out of the picture for good. In spite of all their solicitude and friendly words, three or four of our boys were not able to reassure him of their good intentions.[49]

The Battle of Frayser's Farm ended as had those on each of the preceding days—thousands of Confederates were lost, but McClellan's army was left intact and withdrew during the night to establish a position on Malvern Hill near the James River. Lee's weary command approached this new line cautiously and spent most of July 1 encircling it, preparing for yet another assault. The Union defenses were as strong as any the Army of Northern Virginia had seen. Several lines of blue infantry were arranged along the hill's slope, with batteries of artillery positioned behind them with a clear view of any approaching rebels. Lee planned to throw most of his army into the attack, but once again poor staff work and confusion resulted in only individual brigades advancing against the nearly impregnable line.

At 4:45 p.m. Huger's division ran out of the woods surrounding the hill and charged up the slope. "Remember Beast Butler and our women!" cheered the 1st Louisiana as it trotted toward Union Gen. George W. Morell's position. Federal gunners touched off their pieces and tore holes in the gray line with canister, while the Yankee infantry took out a number of men with long-range volleys of musketry. When three hundred yards from the enemy line, Wright's brigade found cover in a shallow depression. While the men were regrouping for the final assault, a detachment of federal infantry suddenly came swarming down the hollow on Wright's left, and it took forty-five minutes of fierce fighting to beat it back.[50]

It was almost dark when Wright's brigade and the other Confederate units emerged from the hollow for the final charge. The three hundred yards of open ground were quickly covered, and the rebels smashed into the Union infantry posted in front of the artillery. In the savage fighting that followed, the Confederates cut down the 62nd Pennsylvania's flag five times, the 12th New York's four times, and killed the colonel of the 4th Michigan. The Tigers thus gained some revenge for this latter regiment's rough handling of the 5th Louisiana six weeks earlier at New Bridge. Wright's brigade was finally able to push the Yankees back to their artillery, but then collapsed, too exhausted and shot up to continue any farther. Fewer than three hundred of Wright's original 1,000 men were left to man the firing line when darkness finally enveloped the hill. Approximately 362 men in the brigade were dead or wounded, and the rest were scattered in confusion among other brigades.[51]

To Wright's left, a number of Magruder's regiments were also being slaughtered. One of them was Col. Eugene Waggaman's 10th Louisiana in Semmes' brigade. The thirty-five-year-old Waggaman was born into a prominent New Orleans family and was a cousin of the regiment's first commander, Mandeville Marigny. Waggaman's Swiss grandfather came to Louisiana during the Spanish colonial period as the commander of a company of Swiss infantry, and his father, George Augustus, was a powerful Whig Party leader who had served as a federal judge, Louisiana's secretary of state, and a U.S. senator. George Augustus also was a cousin and close friend of President John Tyler, who planned to appoint him the U.S. minister to France. Unfortunately, the mayor of New Orleans mortally wounded Waggaman in a politically motivated duel before Tyler could do so. Colonel Eugene Waggaman graduated as valedictorian from Maryland's Mount St. Mary's College and was a sugar planter and former legislator when the war began. He joined the 10th Louisiana as captain of the "Tirailleurs d'Orleans" and rose through the ranks to become colonel when Marigny resigned his commission. A popular officer and devout Catholic, Waggaman would command all of the Louisiana Tigers before the war ended.[52]

The 10th Louisiana had been marking time for five days because it was kept in reserve during each of the preceding battles. Perhaps thinking his time to fight had finally come, Waggaman visited Father Gache the night of June 30 and said, "Father, I'd like to make another short confession." The two men found a private place where Gache heard the colonel's confession, and the next morning the chaplain noticed that Waggaman spent an extraordinarily long time at prayer. When Father Gache learned that Waggaman was missing in action a few days later, he declared, "This much is for sure: if he has to face death in some Yankee prison, he'll not be unprepared."[53]

On July 1, Waggaman and his regiment were once again left in the rear to act as reserves. The men in the 10th Louisiana were bitter and were openly expressing their anger at not being allowed to fight when one of Semmes' couriers galloped up to Waggaman and handed him a note. "Fall in!" the colonel roared as he scanned the order. Most of the men's spirits lifted as they realized they were to take part in the attack and that Colonel Hunt's 5th Louisiana was to be the reserve. Private Isaac Williams, a former teacher, was not among them. He shot himself in the foot to avoid the fight and later deserted to join a cavalry unit.[54]

After advancing for some distance, Waggaman halted his men at a fence that skirted a large field. The Yankee line could be seen five hundred yards away, and the only protective cover for charging troops was a shallow ravine halfway there. Crossing the open ground in a run, the regiment made it to the ravine but not before the Yankee artillerymen knocked out numerous men with their accurate fire. Waggaman regrouped his shaken line, had his Tigers fix bayonets, and then walked to the center of the regiment. "Men," he shouted, "we are ordered to charge the cannon in our front and take them. The Tenth Regiment has been in reserve all week, and every other Louisiana regiment has been in action. Not a shot must be fired until we get to the guns. Now, men, we are going to charge. Remember Butler and the women of New Orleans. Forward, charge!"[55]

When the regiment emerged from the hollow, hundreds of Union muskets and thirty-six cannons blasted the men, and a bullet or shell fragment cut in two Color Sgt. Joseph LeBleu's flag staff. Waggaman believed that some of the flanking fire was coming from a Confederate unit and sent Leon Jastremski to order it stopped. Jastremski did so but found to his surprise that it was Union soldiers doing the shooting and quickly surrendered.[56]

From the woods at the base of the hill, a member of the 5th Louisiana watched Waggaman's men advance "to within short distance of the guns of the Enemy [where] they became enshrouded in Smoke calling to mind 'Dante's Inferno.'" Those Tigers who survived the murderous fire and still had heart for the fight closed in on the Irish Brigade's 69th New York. Waggaman and a handful of soldiers penetrated the Union line and engaged the Yankees in hand-to-hand combat. One of Waggaman's Irishmen was bayoneted through the neck beside the colonel, and Waggaman knocked a Yankee's musket out of his own face before it could be fired. Cries of "Bayonet him!" and "Kill him!" rose all around as Waggaman continued to hack his way through the enemy line with his family's 150-year-old heirloom sword. It was a short fight, however, because the colonel and the few men with him were quickly over-whelmed. Moments before the 69th New York's Pvt. Richard Kelly captured Waggaman, the colonel threw away his sword to prevent it from falling into enemy hands. Another Union soldier picked it up, and when Waggaman was exchanged some weeks later, Union Gen. Winfield Scott Hancock had the sword returned to him. Afterward, Waggaman may have become more pro-tective of his sword because it was said that he often led his men into battle carrying a cane. Today, one of Waggaman's descendants owns the sword.[57]

The 10th Louisiana was the only regiment in Semmes' brigade that man-aged to penetrate the federal position, and it advanced farther than any other regiment in Lee's army. The following day Maj. Joseph Brent found a line of rebel dead that marked the attack's high-water mark. Beyond that was the body of an unidentified Louisiana lieutenant lying where the Union artillery had been set up. Moved by the sight, Brent felt that a monument should be erected there to honor the unknown officer's bravery.[58]

Of the 10th Louisiana's 318 men engaged in the fight, 18 were killed, 35 wounded, and 18 missing. That number, however, may not be accurate. Lieu-tenant Edward Seton informed his mother that the regiment lost 124 men in the battle, and modern researchers have found evidence that 20 men were killed, 36 wounded, and 26 captured. Half of the casualties were Irishmen, and one who was captured was left near the tent of Irish Brigade commander Gen. Thomas Meagher while his two captors got some coffee. Meagher came out and asked the prisoner why he had joined the rebellion. "I came with many of my neighbors," the Tiger replied, "and maybe you'd do the same if you were there." Recognizing his accent, Meagher pulled out a flask and offered the prisoner a drink, saying, "You are an Irishman. We can be friends, anyhow." The two captors then returned and were escorting their prisoner away when a rebel sharpshooter killed him.[59]

To Waggaman's left, the 2nd Louisiana suffered even greater losses. Colonel Isaiah T. Norwood led it across a twelve-hundred-yard-wide field against sixteen Union cannons that were supported by two brigades of infantry. Like Waggaman, Norwood also told his men to "Remember Butler and their homes" as they started forward over ground that was swept by shell, canister, and bullets. Private Lichenstein wrote, "The word was given to charge and a mighty yell went up and into the jaws of death we plunged. . . . Many of my friends fell right and left of me. Many of the flag bearers who were picked [off] by the sharp shooters and light artillery fell but [the flags] were not left to be dragged in the dust fast held in death's embrace its snatched [up] and hoisted again & again by those who would not let it be dishonored until again claimed by a [illegible]." When a third color-bearer was struck down, Maj. Richard W. Ashton grabbed the falling flag with one and was killed while waving his sword with the other. Lieutenant James B. Culpepper of the Vernon Guards was also lost. When he realized the wound was mortal, Culpepper slowly raised himself from the ground into a kneeling position, apparently to pray, and died upright. At some point during the charge, Colonel Norwood was also mortally wounded and Lt. Col. Jesse M. Williams took command. Lichenstein claimed that, by the time they neared the Union batteries, the line was so "tattered and torn" that they were forced to retreat. The regiment's 182 casualties, 5 of whom were color-bearers, exceeded all other Confederate regiments at Malvern Hill.[60]

Among the 2nd Louisiana's dead was Pvt. Edwin Francis Jemison of the Pelican Greys. Jemison volunteered when he was seventeen years old and for a brief time was attached to General Magruder, probably as an orderly. An officer who claimed to have witnessed Jemison's death said that he was killed when one of the huge gunboat shells exploded overhead. The shell decapitated young Jemison and "spattered his brains and blood all about the uniform" of the captain. "I turned suddenly . . . and saw that man standing headless, with bayonet drawn as at the charge, his blood spurting high in the air from the jug-ular vein, and it seemed to me an hour before he r——d and fell, still holding on to his gun." Jemison's portrait is one of the most reproduced photographs of the Civil War because it is a haunting image of a baby-faced soldier doomed to die on the battlefield.[61]

After the battle, Private Lichenstein counted himself lucky to be among the living. Before the attack began, his good friend William "Billy" Malloy confided that he did not believe he would live through the battle. Malloy was a good-natured Irishman who enjoyed pulling pranks, so Lichenstein told him, "Billy you are getting scared," to which Malloy calmly replied, "You get right long side of me & and I'll go as far as you." The two friends stayed together and were almost across the field when Malloy was shot through the bowels. Lichenstein continued on until a gunboat shell as large as a "flour barrel" exploded over his head and knocked out him and several other men. Captain Ross E. Burke, who had always looked out for Lichenstein, believed him dead and ordered that his body be taken to a nearby ravine so it would not be trampled. Some soldiers picked him up but then simply rolled Lichenstein down the slope into a stream of water. Stretcher bearers discovered him alive the next day and took him to a field hospital. Lichenstein wrote, "I had bled from mouth nose & ear & half of my side of head & cheek was black from the congealed blood caused by the enormous concusion [sic]. My hearing has never adjust[ed] itself to its normal condition." Malloy also survived his wound but was discharged from the army about a month later.[62]

While Waggaman's and Norwood's Tigers joined in the doomed assaults, Taylor's Louisiana Brigade, once again under the command of Colonel Stafford, lay under heavy artillery fire. Private Caldwell of the 7th Louisiana wrote in his diary, "[W]e laid under fire of their cannons for two hours. Loosing [sic] a great many men in the brigade Lieut [Louis Edward] LeBlanc of Co C 8th Reg was killed with a Minnie ball through the head our reg suffered considerable loss." The 9th Louisiana's Henry Handerson was exposed to the same deadly fire, but he found some of the shells strangely fascinating. "Here . . . for the first time I saw a shell in its course from the mouth of the cannon until its explosion. Coming directly towards me, it appeared as a small black object apparently enlarging as it approached, until it burst perhaps a hundred yards in my front." One man near Handerson sought protection behind a sixteen-inch oak tree, but a solid shot easily passed through the trunk and killed him while he sat whittling.[63]

Stafford was not supposed to take part in the deadly assaults on Malvern Hill, but several of his regiments mistakenly did because of a misdirected order. According to Campbell Brown, General Ewell was surprised to hear heavy firing on Stafford's front late in the afternoon. He at first thought the enemy was attacking but then learned that "Stafford [had] advanced mysteriously without orders." Ewell later discovered that a staff officer thought to be attached to Gen. William Whiting "had in an excited manner ridden up to one or two of the left reg'ts. & inquired why they didn't charge with the troops on the left—& had ordered them to charge." The Louisiana Brigade had been ordered to cooperate with Whiting, so a couple of Stafford's regiments joined in the assault. Brown claimed the attack was repulsed quickly but not before the Tigers "had silenced & very nearly captured a battery that stood in advance of the enemy's main line. The whole affair was over so soon & the uselessness of the attack so evident at once, that fewer lives were lost than might have been expected." Handerson was asleep on the extreme left of the line when the attack was made and was surprised to find most of the men around him gone when he woke up. He later wrote, "We . . . heard nothing of the movement and were left in our places. . . . Indeed the whole battle of Malvern Hill seems to have been conducted . . . without system or mutual cooperation, and with the natural result of a complete defeat." For the Louisiana Brigade, the cost of the mistaken charge was twenty-four dead and ninety-two wounded.[64]

When the battle ended, several Confederate units remained in position close to the Union line to hold the ground they had so dearly won. That night an informal truce was arranged with the Yankees to collect the wounded, and small parties of men began roaming the field with lanterns to retrieve as many as possible. The Union forces soon withdrew back to the James River, leaving the Confederates to continue the grisly work the next day. Private Caldwell wrote that July 2 was "a very disagreeable day it commence raining about day light and continued all day without ceasing. All of our men busy and ambulances in carrying off the dead and wounded and burying the Yankees loss on both side very great it is thought that it was the severest fight of the five days previous." Lieutenant Seton, who had survived the 10th Louisiana's gallant charge, took the opportunity to collect souvenirs from the field. Among his finds were a gold dollar and a Bible with the photograph of Col. William L. Brown of the 20th Indiana inside. Brown must have accidentally dropped his Bible because he survived the battle.[65]

Although the Battle of Malvern Hill cost the Tigers more than four hundred casualties, it also enhanced their fierce reputation and added to the men's notoriety. In General Meagher's Irish Brigade, the 88th New York clashed either with the 1st or 10th Louisiana, although they mistakenly thought it was Wheat's "desperadoes." After the battle, the regiment was licking its wounds and searching for new muskets to replace the ones damaged during the hand-to-hand fight. Corps commander Gen. Edwin Sumner at first refused to issue new weapons, thinking the men had discarded them during the lengthy retreat. He changed his mind, however, when he was shown a "pile of muskets with cracked and splintered stocks, bent barrels and twisted bayonets"—evidence of the fierce clash with the Tigers. One of the soldiers told the general, "The boys got in a scrimmage with the Tigers, and when the bloody villains took to their knives, the boys mostly forgot their bayonets, but went to work in the style they were used to, and licked them well, sir."[66]

The Battle of Malvern Hill ended the Seven Days' Campaign. McClellan was bottled up on the James River and no longer seriously threatened Richmond, but his position was too strong to be attacked. In the campaign, Lee lost about 20,000 men and inflicted approximately 16,000 casualties on the enemy. Just how many men the Tigers lost during that bloody week is uncertain, but their casualties were among the highest of any state. The official returns for the campaign list 179 dead, 797 wounded, and 73 missing. These records, however, do not mention Pendleton's Battalion and are less than the total of individual units' reports.[67]

Whatever the number, the Louisianians' losses were frightening. Father Gache spoke for many Tigers when he wrote, "I do love to see an army in battle array. I thrill to the thunder of artillery cannon and to the crack of infantry rifles; my blood tingles when I watch cavalry manoeuvers. . . . But alas, the events of Monday, Tuesday, Wednesday and Thursday have surfeited my appetite for war. I have now seen enough carnage to last me for life." Hiram Sample perhaps saw more of the suffering than most because he was detailed as an ambulance driver. He recalled, "The ambulances were dead axle wagons and had to go over corduroy roads and you can imagine how the poor wounded fellows suffered and the curses were something awful. I got them there all right but they were not all alive."[68]

Captain Pierson wrote to his father a month after the campaign ended to describe what he had gone through. "We have all seen some of the horrors of war and they are terrible indeed. I have seen the dead and wounded lying in piles, the ground literally covered with blood. I have heard the groans of the dying, pitifully crying for help in the last agony of death. I have seen the fire blazing forth from the enemies['] battery and heard the balls whiz around from their lines. Everything is very different from what I had imagined it to be; a man can rush heedlessly on through battle over the dead and dying with as little remorse of consciences as he could shoot a wild beast."[69]

In a letter published by a Mobile newspaper, Lt. Fred Richardson provided a detailed casualty list for his 5th Louisiana and revealed the terrible toll the campaign had taken on the Louisiana Tigers. "I have been through the 'mill,' and thank God, am thus far unhurt. . . . Such marching and such fighting—great God, I never expect to see the same again. Our men charged and captured batteries at the point of the bayonet. . . . The Louisiana troops are horribly mangled. . . . It may well be said that Louisiana's sons have poured out their heart's blood for our glorious cause. . . . The Federal prisoners are all imbued with awe for our Louisiana troops, and I am confident that they ever will be."[70]

The Seven Days proved to be Richard Taylor's last campaign in Virginia because Stonewall Jackson recommended his promotion to major general. When Captain Pierson heard the news, he wrote home, "It is currently reported in camp that we will be sent to La. in the fall. . . . As we are his old regiment we think he will carry us with him; but this is all speculation and amounts to nothing." Colonel Stafford and the officers of Taylor's old 9th Louisiana also wanted to go home and wrote the general, "You have made soldiers of us. Wherever you go, we desire to go and let your destiny be our destiny." When it was confirmed that Taylor would be transferred back to Louisiana, the Louisiana Brigade even petitioned President Davis for permission to accompany him. Taylor endorsed the request, but his former brother-in-law refused to allow it. Major Boyd was chosen to go with Taylor, but the rest of the Tigers stayed in Virginia, and Taylor was ordered to raise recruits for the Louisiana regiments once he got home. In approving Taylor's transfer to Louisiana, General Lee wrote Davis, "In regard to detaching Genl. Taylor, his presence in La. will no doubt hasten the enrollment and expedite the recruiting of regts. If it should establish his own health, it would be an additional benefit to the service. I would therefore on the latter ground alone recommend it." Jackson was concerned about the weakened condition of the Louisiana Brigade, but

Lee informed him, "The regiments assigned to you are those that will be first filled up with recruits from Louisiana. Genl. Taylor, still an invalid, will go to Louisiana to hurry on the men." As for Taylor, leaving Virginia was bitter-sweet. After the war, he admitted that he looked forward to returning home but wrote, "In leaving Virginia I was separated from my brigade, endeared by so many memories. . . . A braver command never formed line of battle."[71]

The Seven Days Campaign was also the beginning of the end for Wheat's Battalion. Major Wheat impressed Taylor in the Valley Campaign, and just a week before the major's death Taylor had recommended to Davis that all of the Louisiana battalions be consolidated into a regiment with Wheat serving as colonel. "Nothing could be more just. I am happy in the belief that [Wheat's] habits have materially changed for the better, and this belief is founded on the experience of several past months." Despite this praise, Taylor had never wanted Wheat's Battalion to be in his command, and Wheat's death provided him the opportunity to break up the unit. Taylor probably did so because the battalion only had sixty-four men present for duty and was too small to con-tinue as a separate command. Thus, Taylor recommended that the enlisted men be transferred to the other Louisiana regiments and all of its officers except Capt. Robert Atkins be dismissed from the service. (Taylor apparently believed that Atkins was the only officer who had earned the right to keep his commission.) Taylor's recommendation was approved, and the battalion was disbanded while it was stationed on the Rapidan River near Raccoon Ford in August 1862. One veteran wrote after the war that the individual members of Wheat's Battalion were allowed to choose which unit they wished to join, and a number of the former Tigers are known to have served in the western theater. Therefore, it appears that not all of the men transferred to the other Tiger regiments as ordered.[72]

General Lee was also forced to reorganize the Army of Northern Virginia after the Seven Days' Campaign. This was partly because of the heavy losses it had suffered and partly because President Davis had decided that morale would be strengthened if brigades were composed of regiments from the same state. As a result, the Louisiana regiments were shuffled around to create a second Louisiana brigade. The 5th and 14th Louisiana were added to the 1st Louisiana Brigade, and the 9th Louisiana was assigned to the new brigade. No explanation has been discovered as to why Colonel Stafford's 9th Louisiana was transferred, but it might have been to make sure the new brigade had a colonel with extensive command experience. The 1st Louisiana Brigade in Ewell's division now consisted of the 5th, 6th, 7th, 8th, and 14th Louisiana and the Louisiana Guard Battery. On Taylor's recommendation, Col. Harry Thompson Hays of the 7th Louisiana was promoted to brigadier general on July 25, 1862, and assumed command. The forty-two-year-old Hays was a native of Tennessee who had moved to New Orleans in his youth. After distinguished service in the Mexican War, the prominent attorney entered politics and became an active member of the Whig party. A hard drinker and tough fighter, Hays was respected by all and proved to be an excellent choice for the command.[73]

The new 2nd Louisiana Brigade was placed in Jackson's old division, now commanded by Gen. William Taliaferro. St. Paul's Foot Rifles and Pendleton's Battalion were disbanded, and their companies were combined to form a new 15th Louisiana regiment. The 15th Louisiana was then brigaded with the 1st, 2nd, 9th, and 10th Louisiana and Coppens' Battalion. The new 2nd Louisiana Brigade was placed under the command of Gen. William E. Starke, a Virginia native who had moved to New Orleans before the war and became a prominent cotton dealer. Although Starke had resided in Louisiana for years, he left the state to become colonel of the 60th Virginia when the war began. Because of his Virginia background, the Louisianians viewed his appointment with hostility because they believed one of their own colonels should have been chosen to lead the new brigade. Starke would have to win the Tigers' confidence through courage and ability. He quickly received the opportunity to demonstrate both because Robert E. Lee was about to resume the offensive.[74]

CHAPTER 6

Dark and Dismal Fields

W HEN MCCLELLAN refused to resume his offensive after the Seven
Days Campaign, President Lincoln sent Gen. John Pope and his
Army of Virginia across the Rappahannock River to attack Richmond from the north. To counter this new threat, Lee began shifting the Army
of Northern Virginia to Gordonsville on July 13. Because Harry Hays was still
recuperating from his Port Republic wound, the 5th Louisiana's Col. Henry
Forno assumed temporary command of the 1st Louisiana Brigade. Forno, a
sixty-two-year-old veteran of the Mexican War, was a former militia colonel
and New Orleans police chief. While not particularly popular with some of
the men, he proved to be a skillful leader. Late in the war, he was placed in
command of the notorious Andersonville Prison guard, but it is not certain
whether he arrived at the prison before it was closed.[1]

The Tigers' journey northward is a good example of the myriad threats
Civil War soldiers faced off the battlefield. One troop train derailed near Gordonsville and killed five men and injured twenty-six. In a separate accident at
Charlottesville, a member of the 7th Louisiana was killed when the cars ran
over him and cut off his head. As the 8th Louisiana's Isaiah Fogleman noted
in his diary, marching in the hot weather was equally dangerous. "[S]un very
hot," he scribbled on July 7, "several deaths in brigade by sun stroke."[2]

On August 9, Jackson pounced on Gen. Nathaniel Banks' command at
Cedar (or Slaughter) Mountain. The two Louisiana brigades were not heavily
engaged in the fight, but Union artillery still inflicted some casualties. Forno
reported no fatalities in his brigade and only eight men wounded, but that
apparently is not accurate. According to Lt. Robert Miller, one shell took out
six men in the 14th Louisiana and "scattered the brains and blood of poor
Ralph Smith all over a dozen of us." Starke's brigade had six men killed and

twenty-eight wounded. In an incident similar to the one described by Miller, a shell exploded in the midst of the 10th Louisiana and killed four men and wounded two others.[3]

After the battle, Father Gache watched members of Starke's brigade rob the Yankee dead and wounded. Afterward he wrote a friend, "These wretched men (and their number was greater than you might suppose) were not concerned with bringing help to the wounded, but in emptying their pockets and stealing their clothes. . . . There were some who went so far as to strip a dead man of every last piece of clothing to leave his body lying naked in the dust. I came upon two of these ghouls kneeling on either side of a corpse they had just despoiled fighting about who should keep the poor man's canteen."[4]

Jackson's victory at Cedar Mountain stopped Pope's advance and forced him to withdraw to the north side of the Rappahannock River. When Lee's army reached the river on August 20 and encamped, eight of the Tigers dressed in Zouave uniforms decided to take an excursion to nearby Stevensburg. W. E. Doyle, a town resident, recalled that they looted several houses while looking for liquor, and then procured a jug of whiskey and some hams at the local store. The female owner called on a Confederate soldier who was in town on furlough (one of only four men present at the time) to intercede, but when he admonished the Tigers they stretched his neck over a fence rail and were about to cut his throat when several women stopped them.

After draining the whiskey jug, the Louisianians then went to a shuttered hotel in search of more liquor and smashed out the windows to gain access. The hotel owner's sixteen-year-old son unloaded a shotgun into one Tiger, and a sick soldier who was staying there also shot at him with his pistol. The soldier was mortally wounded, and his friends carried him across the street to a house, all the time swearing they were going to burn down the town. The Tiger quickly died, and his friends spent some time burying him in a shallow grave. Fortunately, a Confederate courier came through town about that time and took word of the incident to the army encampment ten miles away. A squadron of cavalry was rushed to Stevensburg, and the Tigers were arrested. Doyle claimed the Tigers belonged to Wheat's Battalion and were returned to him for punishment, but that cannot be true because Wheat was already dead and his battalion disbanded. The Tigers in question could have been former Tiger Rifles who had been assigned to other units or members of Coppens' Battalion.[5]

After pushing Pope back across the Rappahannock, Lee wanted to attack the enemy quickly, but realized it was foolhardy to try to force a river crossing in Pope's front. Instead, he devised a daring plan that took advantage of Jackson's swift-moving "foot cavalry." Lee had Longstreet's corps remain in position to watch the Yankees on the Rappahannock while Jackson made a long march upstream and crossed over the river to sweep into Pope's rear unobserved. Jackson would then draw Pope away from the Rappahannock by cutting the Orange and Alexandria Railroad and threatening his supply line. While Pope focused on Jackson, Lee and Longstreet would follow Jackson's route and link up with him to destroy the Union army.

Ewell's division led Jackson's grueling march and covered twenty-four miles the first day, but many of the barefooted men found it difficult to keep up with their units. The 2nd Louisiana's Wolf Lichenstein wrote, "The road to Hay Market [and] Salem was literally packed with stragglers and not withstanding great efforts of our officers to get these men to their respective Regiments it was slow work." Lichenstein was among the fortunate soldiers who had shoes, but his feet became so "blistered & bleeding" on the march that he, too, was forced to fall out with his friend James W. Manney. The next morning they were roasting corn for breakfast when two cavalry officers rode up. One was a major who ordered Lichenstein and Manney to start marching, and they replied that they would as soon as they finished cooking their corn. When the major angrily drew his pistol and declared, "I will make you go," Private Manney, who had already been jailed once for an unknown offense, leveled his musket at the officer and ordered him to drop his pistol. The major turned pale, but hesitated, so Manney told him again to drop the pistol or he would make "daylight through him." The officers quickly rode away, and the two Tigers finished their breakfast.[6]

After covering fifty-five miles in thirty-six hours, Jackson's men approached Bristoe Station at sunset on August 26. The cavalrymen leading the advance encountered a handful of Union defenders and called on Forno's brigade to help drive them away. The Louisianians double-quicked three miles to the station and managed to capture the few Yankees who had not already fled. The Tigers suffered no casualties in the skirmish, but Lt. Col. David Zable had a close call when a shell exploded over his head and threw him to the ground in a somersault.[7]

While the exhausted Tigers lay gasping for breath, they heard the shrill whistle of a train down the double-tracked rails. Before they could hide, the train came chugging out of a belt of timber and began picking up speed when the engineer spotted the rebels and opened the throttle. As the cars rumbled past Forno's men, they fired a volley that killed the engineer and riddled the locomotive, but the train failed to slow and disappeared down the track to spread the alarm in Washington. As soon as the train barreled out of sight, Jackson called on the 21st North Carolina to help the Tigers barricade the track in case another train approached. The men barely had time to throw up some crossties before a second train was heard coming from Pope's base at Warrenton. While the Tar Heels and Tigers took cover, Jackson strolled along the rails and ordered the men to hold their fire until the train hit the barrier. Some of the Louisianians, however, disregarded Jackson's orders and peppered the train with musket balls when the engineer slowly approached the station. Smoking and wheezing through a score of bullet holes in its boiler and stack, the engine smashed into the crossties and careened with its twenty cars into a muddy ravine.

The Tigers swarmed down the embankment to inspect their prize and cheered when they saw that the locomotive bearing the name "Abe Lincoln" had a bullet hole through the likeness of the president painted on the engine. Suddenly, off in the distance, a third train was heard approaching and it, too, hit the barrier and tumbled off the track with its load of cars. The steam had barely cleared when yet a fourth train approached the scene. However, upon seeing the deserted station and twisted wreckage, its engineer wisely stopped the locomotive out of musket range and ignored the "all clear" signal that a Tiger blew on the whistle of one of the wrecked locomotives. The frustrated Louisianians then fired at the distant train and sent it chugging back to Warrenton to inform Pope of the rebel raiders.[8]

Knowing that Pope would soon send his infantry to investigate, Jackson left Ewell's division at Bristoe Station to watch for the Yankees while he took the rest of the corps to capture Pope's supply depot at Manassas Junction. Early on the morning of August 27, Ewell dispatched Forno's brigade, with the 60th Georgia and one cannon, two miles down the track in Pope's direction to destroy the bridge across Kettle Run. A detachment of Yankees arrived about the same time by train, but several well-placed cannon shots sent them retreating back down the track. The 6th Louisiana, commanded by the Irish-born Col. Henry B. Strong, and Maj. Trevanion Lewis' 8th Louisiana were left to burn the bridge, while Forno led the rest of the force back to Bristoe Station.

Lieutenant George Wren claimed that his 8th Louisiana was in the process of burning the bridge when Gen. Joseph Hooker's Union division arrived to drive off what was thought to be mere cavalry raiders. Wren's regiment fell back a few hundred yards to form a battle line and proceeded to fend off an entire Union brigade for an hour before running out of ammunition. The Tigers then abandoned their handful of dead and wounded and retreated back to Bristoe Station. The fight at Kettle Run had been short, but Wren declared that it "was about the tightest place we had ever been in. The act of retreating amidst a perfect hail storm of bullets was most alarming to me. I dreaded the idea of being shot in the back, which was the fate of many who started out with me. . . . I never felt more thankful in life than I did when I left this place in safety. I felt like dropping upon my knees and praising God for being delivered from such a dreadful conflict."[9]

The 6th and 8th Louisiana regiments stopped in a pine thicket next to the railroad about four hundred yards in front of Ewell's main line at Bristoe Station, and the 60th Georgia advanced and extended the Tigers' line to the left, or south. The unsuspecting enemy soon approached with two brigades in column on either side of the track. The 8th Louisiana took the Yankees by surprise when it suddenly opened fire from a range of fifty yards and charged from the thicket. The 5th and 6th Louisiana and 60th Georgia joined in and soon had the Yankees running "like Turkeys," one rebel claimed. The brief encounter was bloody, but the four Confederate regiments managed to hold back Hooker's fifteen regiments before breaking off the engagement and rejoining Ewell's main line.[10]

The two Union brigades that bore the brunt of the fight lost 408 men in the ambush, but the Louisianians' losses are not known for certain. One source claims the Tigers lost ninety men and the Georgians forty-two, but another puts the 5th Louisiana's losses at twenty-six killed and fifty-eight wounded, and the 8th Louisiana's at two dead and twenty wounded. N. Wayne Cosby, an 8th Louisiana historian, has also documented seven men from the latter regiment who were killed or mortally wounded, rather than two.[11]

Under orders to rejoin Jackson if hard pressed, Ewell quickly disengaged from Hooker and marched to Manassas Junction. When the men tramped into the station well past dark, they were incensed to find that Jackson's soldiers had already looted most of the supplies. Having lived off roasted corn and apples since crossing the Rappahannock, the hungry rebels had made the most

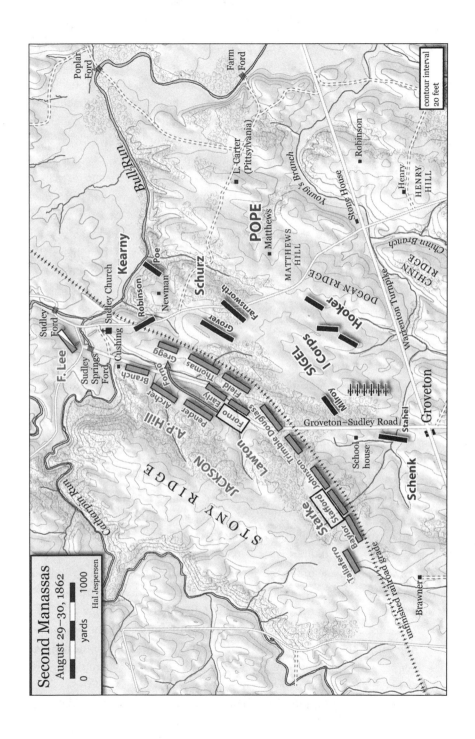

Second Manassas
August 29–30, 1862

0   yards   1000
Hal Jespersen

contour interval
20 feet

Poplar
Ford

Farm
Ford

Bull Run

L. Carter
(Pittsylvania)

Robinson

Kearny

Sudley Church

Poe

Newman

Robinson

Schurz

POPE

Matthews

MATTHEWS
HILL

Henry

HENRY
HILL

Stone House

Young's Branch

Sudley Ford

Cushing

Farnsworth

Grover

Hooker

DOGAN RIDGE

CHINN
RIDGE

Chinn Branch

Sudley
Springs Ford

F. Lee

Branch

Gregg

Thomas

Field

SIGEL
I CORPS

Warrenton Turnpike

Archer

Pender

A.P. HILL

Forno

Early

Forno

Milroy

Stahel

JACKSON

Trimble Douglass

Lawton

Johnson

Groveton–Sudley Road

School
house

Groveton

STONY RIDGE

Starke

Stafford

Schenk

Catharpin Run

Baylor

Taliaferro

unfinished railroad grade

Brawner

of the occasion and spent the better part of the day ransacking the vast Yankee warehouses. One Confederate wrote, "To see a starving man eating lobster salad & drinking rhine wine, barefooted & in tatters was curious; the whole thing is indescribable." "We got any amount of sugar and coffee, bacon and salt," declared Sergeant Stephens of the 9th Louisiana. "Though we could not take anything off except what little we could put in our haversacks."[12]

Despite their late arrival, Forno's brigade found one supply train that had been left untouched. Father James Sheeran of the 14th Louisiana described the scene when Ewell's men were turned loose on the cars: "I had often read of the sacking of cities by a victorious army but never did I hear of a railroad train being sacked. I saw the whole army become what appeared to be an ungovernable mob, drunk, some with liquor but the others with excitement. . . . Just imagine about 6,000 men hungry and almost naked, let loose on some million dollars worth of [supplies]. . . . Here you would see a crowd enter a car with their old Confederate greys and in a few moments come out dressed in Yankee uniforms; some as cavalry; some as infantry; some as artillerists; others dressed in the splendid uniforms of Federal officers."[13] The men became so excited during the looting that officers found it difficult to control them. The 5th Louisiana's John Charlton recalled, "I remember seeing some half a dozen Louisianians fighting over a bundle of blankets. And when Genl Ewell rode up & commanded the men to return to their regiments no more attention was paid to him than if he had been one of them."[14]

Manassas Junction was fired at midnight to destroy what supplies could not be carried off, but some soldiers continued to search through the burning cars for booty. "It was a very dark night," wrote Campbell Brown, "& the scene as wild & grand as I ever imagined. Many of the men were gathered around the burning cars & buildings, examining their contents—throwing back into the flames what they did not want—looking dark & strange against the fiery background." When the order was given to fall in, however, the mob became an army once again and moved out to take up a new position around the hamlet of Groveton. Forno's brigade camped in line of battle that night and used the Yankee tent flies captured from Manassas Junction for shelter. Sergeant Charlton found the scene to be surreal and wrote, "It was a comical sight. The men wrapt in the white [tent] Fly's and it being a bright moonlight night looked more like an army of ghosts than anything else."[15]

Knowing that Pope would soon move against him, Jackson decided to wait in ambush beside the Alexandria Warrenton Pike. Late in the afternoon of August 28, Gen. Rufus King's division casually marched past Jackson's position, unaware of the rebel trap. When Gen. John Gibbon's brigade passed the waiting Confederates, Taliaferro's division swept over a ridge to the Yankees' left and savagely attacked the blue column. For several hours the brigades of W. S. H. Baylor, Alexander Taliaferro, Isaac Trimble, Alexander Lawton, and William Starke struggled unsuccessfully to overwhelm Gibbon's "Iron Brigade." Taliaferro claimed that it was "one of the most terrific conflicts that can be conceived." As a blood-red sun slowly set, the two lines stood erect in an open field beside the road and blasted each other from a range of less than one hundred yards. At dusk Taliaferro's men rushed across the field and pushed Gibbon back toward the road, but the stubborn Yankees refused to break. The battle raged well into the night, with only the muzzle flash of muskets revealing the opposing line. Eventually, Taliaferro fell wounded and then Ewell was knocked out of action with a shattered kneecap. Starke took command of the battered division and turned the 2nd Louisiana Brigade over to Colonel Stafford, who fought to maintain his position in front of the scrappy 7th Wisconsin and 56th Pennsylvania. Not until 9:00 p.m. did the federals slowly withdraw back to the turnpike and the firing finally died out.[16]

The bloody clash at Groveton was Starke's initiation as a brigade commander, but his superiors praised his performance. Taliaferro later wrote that the Louisiana Brigade's "gallantry was conspicuous, and the ability of its commander, Brig. Gen. W. E. Starke, was a guarantee that it did all that the gallant Louisianians . . . were required to perform." It is not known how many Tigers fell during the twilight fight, but it had to have been a considerable number judging from the losses sustained by the federals. General King lost 751 men, or more than one-third of his command, and the 7th Wisconsin lost every one of its field officers in front of the Tigers' position.[17]

Knowing that Pope would send more troops against him, Jackson sought out a strong defensive position from which he could make a stand until Lee and Longstreet arrived with reinforcements. He found it on the old Manassas battlefield, where the cuts and embankments of an unfinished railroad provided some protection for his men. By the early morning of August 29, Jackson had placed A. P. Hill's division on the left near Bull Run, Ewell's division under Lawton in the center, and Taliaferro's division, which was still under Starke's command, on the far right. Pope soon had most of his army on hand to crush

Jackson and began preparing for an assault at 10:00 a.m. by pounding the railroad grade with artillery fire. General Early was put in command of his and Forno's brigades and spent the early morning on the far right protecting Jackson's flank. However, when Longstreet's corps began to arrive on the battlefield later that morning, Jackson moved Early's command behind the center of his line to act as a reserve.[18]

A young Virginian who was lost from his unit stumbled across Forno's Tigers and was told by a Louisiana major, "Better stay with us, my boy, and if you do your duty I'll make it right with your company officers when the fight's over. They won't find any fault with you when they know you've been in with the 'Pelicans.'" The young soldier did remain awhile with the Tigers and marveled at their unique appearance. "Such a congress of nations," he recalled, "only the cosmopolitan Crescent City could have sent forth, and the tongues of Babel seemed resurrected in its speech. English, German, French, and Spanish, all were represented, to say nothing of Doric brogue—and local 'gumbo.'" The Virginian remembered how the Tigers passed the time by quietly playing cards "with a greasy, well-thumbed deck, and in smoking cigarettes, rolled with great dexterity, between the deals." Before leaving, the young soldier was shocked to see the Louisianians cheerfully play a hand of cards with the loser having to fill his friends' canteens by running to a nearby spring across a bullet-swept field.[19]

Wolf Lichenstein, who had straggled behind on the march to Manassas Junction, finally found his regiment that morning, only to have a shell explode in his face as he lay in line. Blinded and feeling blood covering his head, he jumped up and ran around panic-stricken until he slammed into a tree and "nearly knocked myself sensless [sic]." Two friends rushed to the semi-conscious Lichenstein and helped him to a nearby stream to wash. "My clothes & face & head was full of blood & brains & I wondered if I wasn't dead." No wound was found, however, and the trio concluded that the gore must have come from another soldier. When the men returned to the line, they discovered that the shell that had stunned Lichenstein had killed or wounded thirteen other men. The soldier who had been lying next to Lichenstein was missing his head.[20]

At 2:00 p.m., Pope launched a strong attack against Gen. Maxcy Gregg's brigade on the far left of Jackson's line. For an hour and a half, the South Carolinians held out against overwhelming odds before being forced to fall back from the railroad grade after exhausting their ammunition. Forno's brigade was summoned to help and came crashing through the timber at 3:30 p.m. According to Sergeant Charlton, "Henry Forno . . . performed a brilliant movement that went much towards gaining the day, namely a Brigade Wheel." The details of Forno's maneuver are not known other than his Tigers slammed into Gen. Cuvier Grover's brigade—one of the commands Forno had faced earlier at Bristoe Station—and sent it reeling back to the railroad grade in confusion. Colonel Zebulon York was in front of his 14th Louisiana with sword in one hand and hat in the other, crying out, "Come on, boys, come on." When he staggered and fell, his men thought he had been hit, but York jumped back up and yelled, "Never mind, boys, I am not hurt. Come on." Shortly afterward, he went down again and declared, "Well boys, they got me now." A bullet had torn through York's neck, and he would be absent the next seven months recuperating.[21]

With the screaming Tigers hot on their heels, Grover's men stumbled back across the railroad grade and onto Gen. Nelson Tyler's brigade. When the Louisianians collided with Tyler, they wildly bayoneted and clubbed the federals and captured several officers by leaping onto the horses and dragging them from their mounts. After the Tigers wrenched away their colors, the Yankees finally withdrew and left the railroad grade to Gregg and Forno. No sooner had the Confederates bellied up to the embankment than another Union battle line pushed through the smoky woods and captured a portion of Jackson's position to Forno's right. Forno helped seal the breakthrough by stubbornly holding his ground and then assisted in stopping yet another attack with point-blank volleys of musketry. The Tigers' muskets were fouling from the rapid fire and were almost too hot to handle, but they received no respite. Still more Union soldiers surged forward over the shattered bodies of their comrades and planted their battle flags just ten feet from the Louisianians' position before falling back. With their ammunition exhausted and casualties mounting, Gregg and Forno were near the breaking point. At that moment, one of Gregg's men recalled, "[A] shout behind [us] paralyzed us with dread." The Confederates whirled around to face an expected attack from the rear but saw, instead, that it was Early's brigade charging through the underbrush to their aid.[22]

Early was in the rear when he received word of the Union breakthrough on Forno's right. Snatching up the 60th Georgia and 8th Louisiana, which also was in the rear replenishing its cartridge boxes, he attached them to his Virginia brigade and hurried toward the front. Early's charge knocked the Yankees from the railroad grade and sent them tumbling back to their own lines. Just as Early rolled past the Louisianians, however, a Yankee sharpshooter wounded Forno and put him out of action. Command of the brigade fell to Colonel Strong, but by then the fighting on that part of the field was mostly over.[23]

Early, Gregg, and Strong were relieved that night and withdrew to rest and count their losses. For the Tigers the butcher's bill was thirty-seven dead, ninety-four wounded, and four missing. However, Gen. A. P. Hill took note of the brigade's outstanding service in his battle report: "[M]y division, assisted by the Louisiana Brigade . . . commanded by Colonel Forno, with a heroic courage and obstinacy almost beyond parallel, had met and repulsed six distinct and separate assaults, a portion of the time the majority of the men being without a cartridge."[24]

Starke's 2nd Louisiana Brigade, which was still under Colonel Stafford's command, was far to the right of Forno's position near a deep gully that cut through the railroad grade. That afternoon, Pope began massing his men in some timber in front of the cut, a move not unnoticed by the 10th Louisiana's Henry Monier, who wrote in his diary that the "woods to the front [are] blue with Federals." When Pope launched his attack, the Yankees seized a portion of Lawton's line to the left of the Louisianians. Galloping up to his old brigade, Starke yelled for the men to fix bayonets and then led the Tigers out to join Col. Bradley Johnson's Virginia brigade to help relieve the pressure on Lawton's front. Monier claimed that the men responded to Starke's order "with a yell, and started off on a double quick on their own impulse."[25]

A chorus of rebel yells rose from the line as the two brigades swept over the unfinished railroad grade and charged into the Yankee-filled woods. Following Colonel Johnson, who placed his hat on the tip of his sword and vigorously waved the men onward, the Louisianians and Virginians collided with the first federal line and rolled it back upon Capt. R. B. Hampton's artillery battery, which had just arrived to try to stop the rebels. In the charge, Johnson's men trampled one of Gen. Daniel Sickles' color-bearers but continued on without picking up the flag. Following behind, several members of the 1st Louisiana stopped to claim the abandoned colors of the famed Excelsior Brigade. The capture came just two months after the regiment had seized the Excelsior Brigade's flag at the Battle of King's School House.

The federal artillerymen furiously loaded rounds of canister and blasted the Confederates when they stopped to dress their line only one hundred yards away. One Tiger recalled that halting under such a murderous fire "might have been heroic, but it certainly was not wise. However, not a man faltered." A Union officer who witnessed the fight wrote, "We slaughtered them at a great rait [sic]," but the rebels could not be stopped. Captain Hampton was finally ordered to withdraw his battery, but he had to abandon two guns because the horses for one had been killed and the recoil of the other had jammed its handspike into a stump and it could not be retrieved. Lieutenant Thomas Mills of the 10th Louisiana reached one of the guns first and claimed it for the Tigers, while Johnson's men overran the other. When General Starke ordered his victorious brigade to return to the railroad cut, the Louisianians were determined to bring back their trophy, dead horses or not. Members of the 15th Louisiana improvised by forcing some federal prisoners into the harnesses and then prodding them with bayonets back to the railroad cut. Father Sheeran reported, "The sight of some fifty Yankees hitched to a piece of artillery, with the 15th [Louisiana] charging bayonets, coming across the battlefield at a double quick drew forth a burst of laughter from our Confederate boys."[26]

By nightfall all of the Tigers were back in their own lines except for the 8th Louisiana's Minden Blues company, which was ordered to remain out front as pickets. Lieutenant Wren wrote that he and his men spent the night "amid the groans of the wounded Yankees. This was the most distressing sight I have ever witnessed. Many of them we gave water that were in our reach but many suffering who we were afraid to approach, as the enemy's pickets were near us." When dawn broke, the Tigers discovered that they were within sight of the Union pickets, and a sharp skirmish erupted all along the line. The Minden Blues captured a number of prisoners, but Wren remembered, "I never wanted to be relieved worse in my life for we had been up all night and then upon our feet fighting half the day without anything to eat." To his relief, the company was finally withdrawn about noon.[27]

On the morning of August 30, Stafford's brigade was behind the railroad embankment to the left of the deep cut under orders from Jackson to hold that position at all costs. The Tigers were formed in two lines, with the second line in a supporting position about two hundred yards behind the first. The 42nd and 48th Virginia of Bradley Johnson's brigade were to their right with the former regiment holding the deepest part of the cut. At 3:00 p.m., wave after wave of blue infantry were thrown against Jackson's position. The men of Stafford's brigade were resting with stacked muskets when they saw the first attack approaching and scrambled to get into line. The Tigers lay along the top of a hill which kept the federals mostly hidden from sight until they suddenly popped into view over the crest only fifty yards away. Sergeant Edmond Stephens wrote, "We cut them down as they threw themselves in sight," but when the 24th and 30th New York of Col. Timothy Sullivan's brigade returned fire and knocked out many of the men, Stafford had to bring up his supporting line to plug the gaps. As the Yankees approached the railroad grade, Maj. Andrew Jackson Barney of the 24th New York rode far out in front of his regiment, calling on it to follow. The gallant Barney surprised the Tigers by riding to the top of the embankment, and some of them yelled, "Don't kill him! Don't kill him!" but Barney fell almost immediately with a bullet through his head. His confused horse then stood there for a moment before continuing on into Stafford's lines. One of the Tigers crawled forward and dragged Colonel Barney to safety, but he died a few hours later.[28]

The New Yorkers took cover on the embankment's outer slope, separated from the Tigers by only a few yards of dirt. There, the federals were hidden from the Louisianians' view, but Trimble's brigade on Stafford's left opened a deadly enfilade fire on them. One soldier claimed that the Yankees were "simply jammed up against the embankment. . . . They were so thick it was impossible to miss them. . . . What a slaughter! What a slaughter of men that was."[29]

When other Union brigades attacked Bradley Johnson's position on Stafford's right, several hundred yards of the line blazed with ferocious musket fire. A member of the 24th New York wrote, "The yells from both sides were indescribably savage. . . . We were transformed . . . from a lot of good-natured boys to the most bloodthirsty of demoniacs." Johnson wrote, "I saw a Federal flag hold its position for half an hour within ten yards of a flag of one of the regiments in the cut and go down six or eight times, and after the fight 100 dead were lying twenty yards from the cut, some of them within two feet of it." The 14th Louisiana's Wolf Lichenstein described the fight as being "fierce and bloody. The field was strewn thick on both sides with killed & wounded. [The armies were like] two giants . . . bending to & fro for advantage."[30]

In thirty minutes, the Louisiana Tigers and Johnson's Virginians managed to beat back several enemy assaults, but losses were heavy, with Lt. Cols. William H. Spencer of the 10th Louisiana and R. A. Wilkerson of the 14th Louisiana among the dead. Ammunition was also running low, and Henry Monier claimed that "the brigade fired with the care of old hunters." William Singleton and Pinckney Lyon of the 9th Louisiana volunteered to go to the rear for more ammunition, but yet another Union attack was mounted before they returned. According to Sergeant Stephens, the ensuing clash was "the ugliyst fight of any." Groping frantically for ammunition from among the dead and wounded, the Louisianians managed to fight off the determined Yankees, who approached the very muzzles of the Tigers' muskets. Sergeant John Charlton, who had become separated from his 5th Louisiana and was now fighting with the 1st Louisiana, claimed that "there was no lack of guns laying around." Snatching up one to join the fight, Charlton loaded and fired so frantically that he once forgot to remove the ramrod "and consequently sent that at the Yanks."[31]

An Alabaman in Trimble's brigade remembered that, when the Tigers fired their last round, "the flags of the opposing regiments were almost flapping together." In desperation the Tigers finally resorted to throwing rocks at the enemy. One source claims that the 1st Louisiana's Lt. Col. Jim Nolan shouted for the men to make use of the numerous rocks that lay scattered around the embankment, while another source credits an Irishman named O'Keefe for standing up and yelling, "Boys, give them rocks." The Yankees were charging up to the base of the embankment once again when out of the smoke fist- and melon-size stones suddenly rained down upon them. "Such a flying of rocks never was seen," claimed one witness. A member of the 24th New York admitted that the shower of rocks was "an unlooked for variation in the proceedings. Huge stones began to fall about us, and now and then one of them would happen to strike one or another of us with very unpleasant effect."[32]

Some of the Yankees picked up the rocks and threw them back at the rebels, but their advance had stalled, and Col. John M. Brockenbrough's Virginia brigade of A. P. Hill's division was sent to reinforce Stafford. Colonel Robert M. Mayo of the 47th Virginia described what he saw as he approached the railroad cut: "[T]he minnie balls were rattling like hail against the trees, and as we debouched into the field through which the railroad cut ran, nothing could be seen between us and the smoke and fire of the enemy's rifles except the tattered battle-flag of the Louisiana brigade; the staff of this was stuck in the ground at the edge of the cut, and the brigade was at the bottom of it throwing stones."[33]

The unexpected "battle of rocks" briefly confused the Union soldiers, but within minutes they were regrouping to press on the attack. Fortunately for the Confederates, Gen. D. H. Hill had placed his artillery on high ground to the Louisianians' right and was able to enfilade the advancing federal lines. Soon after the Tigers began throwing their rocks, Hill's artillery broke up the attack. At about the same time, Singleton and Lyon returned to Stafford's brigade with badly needed ammunition, and the Union soldiers began concentrating their fire on them. Captain R. J. Hancock, the men's company commander, claimed that Stonewall Jackson also saw them approaching and "kept his hand raised as if in prayer until both of them reached the cut unhurt . . . [and a] Confederate yell went up."[34]

As this last Union attack collapsed, Pope's entire line began falling back. Lee and Longstreet had arrived on the battlefield the day before, but Lee held Longstreet's corps back until the most opportune moment to strike. Recognizing the moment had come, Lee sent both Longstreet and Jackson pressing after the enemy in a massive counterattack. General Stephen D. Lee saw the Tigers pour over the embankment they had held so tenaciously and watched them "tearing the cartridge boxes off the fallen Federals as they passed over them, while others with stones were actually pelting them as they pressed forward." Sergeant Charlton participated in the chase with his adopted 1st Louisiana and later talked with a Union prisoner who claimed that the Tigers had hit all of his comrades with their rocks. Charlton wrote that "he was so cut up about the head that he looked like an indian more than a white man."[35]

The Second Battle of Manassas ended as did the first with the federals being driven from the field. The victory, however, had been costly. Among Lee's 10,000 casualties were 5 generals and 10 colonels, and Stafford's brigade's share of the bloodletting was a devastating 110 dead, 269 wounded, and 6 missing. After the battle, the 2nd Louisiana's Thomas Phifer wrote his father, "Our loss was very severe at Manassas as our company went in with twenty men and came out with four, but hundreds of Yankees fell before our brigade." In another letter to his sister, Phifer gave a detailed list of the men in his company who were killed and wounded, and wrote, "There is, however, one consolation, that for every noble southern son, that bade farewell to home . . . a half a score of inhuman wretches crossed the fiery portal and now assist their companions who have gone from before Richmond in their devilish orgies. . . . The above report . . . will fall heavily upon our friends at home."[36]

The Tigers' fierce defense of the railroad embankment became well known throughout the South and made the 2nd Louisiana Brigade something of a legend. In fact, word of the heroic deed began spreading through the army that same day. General A. P. Hill reportedly rode up to an artillery battery during the battle and told the captain that "the Louisiana brigade, being out of ammunition, was holding the enemy in check with rocks." As the rock-throwing incident was retold over the years, the Louisianians' stand on the bloody embankment was seen as the epitome of southern bravado. Their heroism cannot be denied—the stoic Tigers did, indeed, hold onto their position long after others might have fled, and their reliance on the rocks is well documented. However, it was not their strong arms that broke up the last federal charge. The barrage of stones certainly surprised the Yankees, but the equally brave Union soldiers could not have been beaten back with rocks after they had clung so tenaciously to the embankment under deadly volleys of musketry. What finally broke the federal assault was Confederate artillery. When the Yankees seemed about to break through the Tigers' position, General Hill shattered the blue lines with enfilading artillery fire, and Brockenbrough's brigade rushed in to reinforce Stafford and Johnson at a crucial moment. It was this combination of events, not the Tigers' rock throwing, that forced the Yankees to withdraw.[37]

After the battle, Father Sheeran inspected the ground in front of Stafford's position and left a vivid description of what he saw. "Oh! May I never again witness such scenes as I saw this day. . . . The Yankees in front of the R[ail] R[oad] occupied by the La. troops were lying in heaps. Those in front of the R. R. had something of the appearance of men, for they were killed with rocks or musket balls and with their face to our men. But those scattered throughout the woods and fields presented a shocking spectacle. Some with their brains oozing out; some with the face shot off; others with their bowels protruding; others with shattered limbs. . . . They were almost as black as negroes, bloated and some so decomposed as to be past recognition."[38]

Most of August 31 was spent in burying the dead and collecting the wounded. Lieutenant Wren helped in the gruesome task and afterward wrote, "I never saw the dead lie half so thick as the Yankees did at this place. . . . I did not see a man but had been stripped of his shoes and pockets generally turned. Shoes being a very scarce article, there was a great demand for them, and a good pair would hardly escape the notice of a soldier, if they were not already in actual service." William Snakenberg was among the rebels who scoured the field for shoes. He finally found some on a wounded Union soldier who told him, "Well, take them. If I live, I can get more; and if not, I shall not need them."[39]

After helping to clean up the battlefield, Jackson's command was ordered east to Jermantown to intercept Pope's retreating army before it reached the safety of Washington. When Union cavalry discovered that Jackson was on the move, Pope sent Gen. Jesse Reno with his and two other divisions to stop the Confederates west of Jermantown near Chantilly. On September 1, Jackson learned that the Yankees were approaching him from the south and wheeled his three divisions to the right to meet them. Ewell's division, under General Lawton, was in the center with Col. Henry Strong's 1st Louisiana Brigade placed in the center of the division. Strong had a thirty-acre field in his front and a larger cornfield on his right flank with Trimble's brigade to the left and Early's and Lawton's brigades behind him, acting as a reserve.[40]

At about 4:30 p.m., Union Gen. Isaac Stevens ordered his division to advance just before a violent thunderstorm rolled in. Lightning flashed, thunder boomed, and, as George Wren put it, the "rain fell in torrents." The right of Stevens' division stretched across the field in Strong's front and the left through the cornfield to his right. When the Tigers opened fire they severely cut up the 79th New York "Highlanders," a regiment made up largely of Scot immigrants. When the Highlanders came to a halt in front of Strong's brigade, General Stevens grabbed the regiment's colors and led it forward once again. Just as he stepped over a broken-down rail fence, however, he was hit in the head by a bullet that was almost certainly fired by a Louisiana Tiger.[41]

Enraged at their commander's death, Stevens' division surged forward again, but by this time the downpour had drenched the cartridges on both sides and many muskets misfired. Nonetheless, the 79th New York managed to reach Strong's position at the edge of the woods, and a fierce hand-to-hand fight erupted between the Scot Highlanders and the Irishmen of the 6th Louisiana. Suddenly, the Louisiana line began to unravel, and the Tigers fell back in confusion.

What caused the Tigers to break is not clear. A newspaper claimed that the Louisianians retreated after the 6th Louisiana's commander, Maj. William Monaghan, was wounded, but the regiment's Lt. George P. Ring also blamed General Lawton for not supporting the brigade when it was attacked: "Our division being badly handled, our brigade had to bear the brunt of the battle unsupported for two hours. Our regiment after fighting against desperate odds for two hours fell back in confusion, when Maj. Monaghan was wounded." General Early, who was moving his brigade behind the Tigers to shore up Strong's right flank, blamed the rout on Colonel Strong's poor handling of his men. Early claimed that Strong was "entirely inexperienced on the management of a brigade." Captain Campbell Brown agreed with Early's assessment and wrote that Strong was "a brave gentleman but [an] inefficient, slow officer." According to Early, Strong was trying to realign his regiments to meet the Highlanders' attack, but "that his want of sufficient skill in the command of a brigade caused him to get it confused, so that it could present no front, and it therefore had to fall back." Father Sheeran further muddled the issue by claiming that a Georgia regiment precipitated the rout after "some Greenhorn, acting as Adjutant," came running down the line screaming that they had been flanked. It turned out to be a false alarm, but Sheeran wrote that it still "caused a panic among some of our regiment." Whatever caused the retreat, Maj. Trevanion Lewis' 8th Louisiana was able to retire in good order, and the rest of the Tigers quickly rallied and returned to the front to hold Early's left flank.[42]

Soon after the Tigers retreated, Stevens' division also withdrew and the battle shifted to Jackson's right. When Union Gen. Philip Kearny attacked through the cornfield, he rode ahead to reconnoiter, despite being warned that the Confederates were near. He was killed when he blundered into Edward Thomas' Georgia brigade, but the 9th Louisiana's Captain Hancock claimed that Pvt. William Singleton actually fired the fatal bullet. According to Hancock, Singleton was on the skirmish line wearing an oil cloth during the thunderstorm when Kearny approached him. Unable to see Singleton's uniform, Kearny thought he was a Union skirmisher and asked, "To what regiment do you belong?" Singleton raised his rifle, replied "Ninth Louisiana," and demanded the general's surrender. Kearny's head dropped as if he were in deep thought and then he twirled his horse around, leaned over its neck, and galloped away. Singleton shot the general and continued skirmishing but later told an ambulance crew where to find the body. After dark, Singleton was making coffee when he heard someone mention that the body of a Yankee officer had been discovered but it had not been robbed. When Singleton asked if the officer had one arm and then described the fatal wound, the soldier confirmed the details, and Singleton realized that he had killed General Kearny. Private Snakenberg partly corroborated Captain Hancock's account when he wrote in his memoirs that Kearny "was shot off in front of our Brigade pickets." If Hancock's story is true, it would appear that the Louisiana Tigers killed both Generals Stevens and Kearny at Chantilly.[43]

By the time the fighting at Chantilly died down after dark, Strong's brigade had lost thirty-nine men killed, ninety-nine wounded, and three missing. In fact, the 5th, 6th, 8th, and 14th Louisiana suffered the highest number of casualties of any of Jackson's regiments. All of those who survived the fight marveled at escaping the murderous fire, but Charles Behan of the 5th Louisiana was particularly lucky. He had a bullet splinter his musket stock as he took aim, four balls rip through his clothing, and most of his pants blown off by a shell. Nevertheless, he emerged unscathed—only to be killed two weeks later at Antietam.[44]

After the Battle of Chantilly, Pope continued his retreat to Washington and surrendered the initiative to Lee, who decided to take the war to the North by invading Maryland. Several factors led him to this momentous decision. A move northward would take the war out of Virginia and allow farmers to harvest their crops and feed the army through the winter. Lee also believed that his ragged men would find badly needed supplies and recruits in Maryland, and that a major victory on northern soil might win the Confederacy much sought-after foreign recognition and aid.

The invasion began on September 4 when Lee's forward units waded across the Potomac River after an exhausting twenty-six-mile march. Although tired and hungry, the men of the 1st Louisiana Brigade were in good spirits when they sloshed across the shallow river two days later as nearby bands played "Dixie" and "Maryland, My Maryland." Strong's brigade had not eaten all day, so his Tigers were dismissed briefly on the Maryland side to gather a meager meal from a cornfield before marching on to Frederick.

Huge crowds of curious onlookers lined the road to watch the rebels march by. Some earnestly waved and cheered, but most were either openly hostile or indifferent toward their "liberators." While passing by one farm, an inebriated member of Starke's 2nd Louisiana Brigade stopped at the front gate to get some bacon from the farm's mistress. During the exchange, the woman became irate and accused the soldier of not paying for the meat. The woman's wailing caused the entire column to halt and listen as she declared that she was a staunch Unionist "and must not be imposed on by any Confederate rebel." After much ranting, the woman finally discovered that she was mistaken and the Tiger had gained the bacon honestly. Father Sheeran then stepped forward, admonished her to be more careful in her accusations, and declared that the Tigers would forgive her if she gave three hearty cheers for Jeff Davis. Although the woman adamantly refused his suggestion, Father Sheeran claimed her ruffled feathers were somewhat smoothed by the time the brigade departed.[45]

Later that day Jackson's divisions arrived in Frederick, Maryland, and the people crowded the streets and balconies to watch as the rebels tore down the town's federal flags. Lieutenant Wren wrote in his diary, "The people here seem very much surprised at our suden [sic] appearance in Maryland. Some seemed pleased at seeing us while others seemed almost horror struck." Wren recounted how three elderly ladies walked three miles to town to see the great Stonewall Jackson and were disappointed when Wren informed them that they had just missed him. When the women said they had heard that Jackson's "foot soldiers" never tired while marching, Wren politely informed them that they did, in fact, "become a little wearied sometimes."[46]

The 14th Louisiana's William Snakenberg also wrote of the reception the Tigers received in Frederick. "We found a great many friends among the ladies, but they were afraid to show it, or let us have any food openly but many prepared food, and as we would pass their windows, would make some sign to attract our attention and get us there some way, so that we could get some of their good vituals [sic], such as milk and butter. Some, bolder than others, would display a Confederate flag, but numbers would have the stars and stripes hung out."[47]

The men in the 2nd Louisiana Brigade had a similar reception. The 2nd Louisiana's Thomas Phifer wrote his sister that Frederick was about the size of Shreveport, Louisiana, and that it had many Unionists residents.

But we were made to feel proud by our welcome here. The people did all they could for us, some brought water, some food, some clothing and they offered their services in every way they could benefit us. Some danced, some laughed, some cried. Fairy groups of beautiful girls skipped about the streets crying "Welcome, welcome brave Southerners, Sweet is our welcome of the brave." Some said they wished no better fate than to become the wife of a Southerner. They were shocked to see us so ragged and barefoot. They made many presents and things they sold cost only a trifle. Boots that would cost $25.00 in Richmond, were bought here for four and five. We cannot help but enjoy ourselves here, but it cost many precious lives to get here.[48]

The Tigers enjoyed bathing in the Monocacy River and eating the provisions Maryland had to offer. Lieutenant Wren wrote, "We get plenty of good butter milk to drink from the people who are settled thickly about. We have plenty of nice fruit to eat." Thomas Phifer agreed and wrote his father, "We get abundance of all kinds of fruits which is a great help to our army. Sometimes we have to eat fruit in order to make our rations hold out." Phifer also claimed that his company received four or five new recruits while at Frederick, but he did not elaborate as to whether they came from Louisiana or Maryland.[49]

Not long after Jackson left Frederick, a civilian delegation paid him a visit and accused some "foreign" soldiers of getting drunk and looting several establishments. The general immediately ordered Starke's 2nd Louisiana Brigade to return to town so the culprits could be identified. Starke, however, was incensed at Jackson's assuming the guilty soldiers were in his command and refused to obey the order unless the other brigades were also sent back. Jackson placed Starke under arrest, but a subsequent investigation proved the perpetrators were actually Virginians in the Stonewall Brigade. Starke had earned a reputation for being a strict disciplinarian and sometimes arrested his own officers when they failed to keep the men in ranks. He probably refused to obey Jackson's order because he was confident his officers had kept a close watch on the men while they were in Frederick. Starke was killed before he was brought to trial for defying Jackson, and Jackson's Virginians seem to have escaped any punishment for their misdeeds.[50]

On September 10, Lee dispatched Jackson to capture the federal garrison at Harpers Ferry while the rest of the army penetrated farther into Maryland to gather supplies. Private Snakenberg estimated the distance to the historic town to be only about fifteen miles as the crow flies, but Jackson led his men on a sixty-three-mile march to approach Harpers Ferry from the west while two other commands encircled the town from the north and east. Civilians along the way continued to turn out to watch the rebels march by, but Isaiah Fogleman and George Wren, both members of the 8th Louisiana, had different experiences with the locals. Fogleman claimed that the rebels created a "great deal of excitement, Marylanders volunteering loud cheers from all sides," and that the ladies of Martinsburg cheered them when they passed through that town. Lieutenant Wren, however, wrote that he "found the people looking very sour at us, all, very nearly, were union people."[51]

Early on the morning of September 11, after leaving the sick and barefooted behind, Jackson's command waded across the Potomac River at Williamsport. Three days later, Gen. Harry T. Hays, having recovered from his Port Republic wound, arrived and assumed command of the 1st Louisiana Brigade from Colonel Strong. That same day, Jackson surrounded Harpers Ferry and opened fire with his artillery. As Lichenstein put it, Jackson pounced on the garrison "like a hungry eagle on a lamb." The federals surrendered the next day, much to the relief of the Tigers, who were preparing to attack the fortified town. A jubilant Lieutenant Ring wrote that Hays' brigade was already in line of battle when the men saw the white flag being raised. The welcomed sight brought "hearty and sincere cheers" from the entire division because it meant they would not be ordered forward. Lieutenant Wren shared Ring's joy because he and his comrades in the 8th Louisiana were dreading the anticipated attack. "Oh! what a relief this was from suspense for the consequence would have been for the infantry to charge, had the artillery failed."[52]

Not far away, Thomas Phifer in Starke's Louisiana brigade joined in the celebration. He wrote his father, "We have been shelling this place of such renouned [sic] strength for two days. This morning about nine o'clock they run up a white flag about as large as a sheet and made an unconditional surrender. . . . Some of the boys have been compelled to march barefooted but they will get some shoes tonight from Harpers ferry." Phifer optimistically believed the capture was the first step to a Confederate victory. "Before you receive this you will hear of one of the greatest victories over the Yankees ever yet gained. Next you will hear of our taking possession of Baltimore, Philadelphia, Washington & Cincinatti unless peace be declared sooner."[53]

In addition to taking 11,000 prisoners, seventy-three cannons, thirteen thousand small arms, and an abundance of supplies, William Snakenberg reported that Jackson also captured 5,000 runaway slaves at Harpers Ferry. Lieutenant Ring, however, was disappointed that Jackson cordoned off the town rather than allowing the men the same free access to the bountiful supplies that they had enjoyed at Manassas Junction. Ring apparently believed the men deserved the reward as payment for the recent forced marches. "Since the 1st Sept.," he wrote, "after having fought every day for ten days we have made a circuit through western Maryland and are now here almost where we

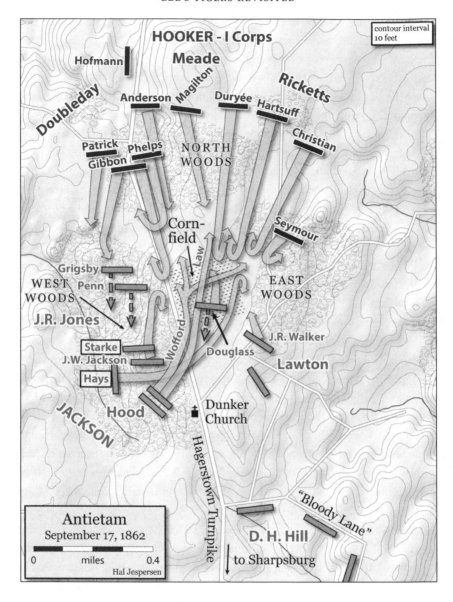

contour interval
10 feet

HOOKER - I Corps

Hofmann

Meade

Doubleday

Magilton

Anderson

Duryée

Ricketts

Hartsuff

Christian

Patrick

Phelps

NORTH
WOODS

Gibbon

Corn-
field

Seymour

Law

Grigsby

WEST
WOODS

Penn

EAST
WOODS

J.R. Jones

Wofford

J.R. Walker

Starke

Douglass

J.W. Jackson

Lawton

Hays

JACKSON

Hood

Dunker
Church

"Bloody Lane"

Antietam

September 17, 1862

Hagerstown Turnpike

D. H. Hill

0   miles   0.4

to Sharpsburg

Hal Jespersen

started from. It is too much as the state of our ranks show, and if Jackson keeps on at it, there will soon be no army for him to command." Four months earlier, Ring's company had 112 men on its rolls but now reported only 11 for duty. Another company in the 6th Louisiana had 2 officers commanding 2 men by the time Harpers Ferry fell, and the entire 1st Louisiana numbered just 121 men. The Tigers did not know it, but those numbers were about to be reduced even further.[54]

Although Jackson's envelopment of Harpers Ferry went smoothly, Lee's Maryland campaign had hit a snag. Lincoln restored General McClellan to command of the army in Washington after Pope's Manassas fiasco, and he was now once again threatening Lee with the Army of the Potomac. After a copy of Lee's campaign orders fell into federal hands, McClellan became privy to the Confederates' plans and began pressing Lee with uncharacteristic speed. To meet the Yankee threat, Lee decided to concentrate his army along Antietam Creek near Sharpsburg and ordered Jackson to rejoin him there. Jackson then left Gen. A. P. Hill at Harpers Ferry to parole the federal prisoners and put the rest of his corps on the road to Sharpsburg on the night of September 15.

Hays' brigade left Harpers Ferry around midnight and crossed the Potomac River at Shepherdstown about daylight. It was, declared Lieutenant Wren, "the third time, in less than two weeks," that the Tigers had waded across the river. Starke's 2nd Louisiana Brigade was farther back in the column and crossed the river about noon. Jackson's old division, now under Gen. J. R. Jones, and Ewell's division, commanded by General Lawton, arrived at Antietam Creek on the afternoon of September 16 and were placed on the left of the Confederate line. For the remainder of the day both armies exchanged skirmish and artillery fire as they jockeyed for positions along the small stream. Both Louisiana brigades were exposed to a heavy artillery bombardment that afternoon, and Lt. A. M. Gordon of the 9th Louisiana was mortally wounded when a shell ripped off both of his legs at the thighs. When the shelling ended at nightfall, the Louisiana brigades were moved forward and put into the line of battle.[55]

William Snakenberg had a fitful night as Hays' brigade lay behind the Dunker Church near the Hagerstown Pike. "That night I had got a notion in my head, that the next day I should be wounded. I never thought once that I would be killed, or fatally wounded, but was afraid that I might have to be cut into to get the ball [out]." Snakenberg considered seeking out Colonel Zable to ask that he keep an eye on him and not leave him on the field if wounded but then changed his mind because he did not want Zable to think he was trying to avoid the fight. Snakenberg decided to remain quiet and spent his time tearing up all of his letters and throwing away all of his possessions except what was absolutely vital. Just before dawn on September 17, he heard a single cannon fire and realized it was a signal gun to start the battle. Snakenberg calmly stood up, tied his blanket over his left shoulder to protect his chest, and then "set down in the ranks and ate up all my rations."[56]

When the signal gun fired, Jones' division was positioned west of the Hagerstown Road facing north, with Winder's and Jones' brigades on the front line and Taliaferro and Starke in reserve. Across the road to Jones' right was Lawton's division. Lawton had his own brigade, under Col. Marcellus Douglass, and Trimble's brigade stretched through David Miller's thirty-acre cornfield, supported by Hays' Tigers, who were in a plowed field three hundred yards in the rear. At first light, federal batteries far to the east opened a deadly enfilading fire upon Lawton's brigades as General Hooker's corps advanced down the Hagerstown Pike from the north. When the approaching Yankees came into sight, they were greeted by a chorus of rebel yells that rattled the cornstalks. Seeing the cornfield glistening with polished bayonets reflecting the early morning sunlight, Hooker halted and deployed his artillery to rake the field. "In the time I am writing," he penned, "every stalk of corn in the northern and greater part of the field was cut as closely as could have been done with a knife, and the soldiers lay in rows precisely as they had stood in their ranks a few minutes before. It was never my fortune to witness a more bloody, dismal battlefield."[57]

The fierce artillery fire cut to pieces the Confederate units in and behind the cornfield. Lieutenant Ring wrote his wife, "I thought, Darling, that I heard at Malvern Hill heavy cannonading, but I was mistaken." Several Tigers in Hays' brigade wrote of the terrific bombardment, and Snakenberg described it as a "severe cannonading" that killed and wounded many men. "One shell burst and wounded three men at my side and another killed and wounded thirteen on my left, some of whom I went to school with only a few years before." Lieutenant Wren wrote that his 8th Louisiana was "under the most terrific artillery fire that ever happened . . . the shells bursting over up and around us till the whole heavens was illuminated with flashes of light from the exploding shells."[58]

The 5th Louisiana's Capt. Fred Richardson recalled Hays ordering the brigade to lie down to escape the exploding shells, but it helped little.

> Our company was small, and we (the officers) laid down behind
> it. William, Lieutenant [Nicholas Canfield's] brother, was leaning

immediately in his front. Nick [Canfield] was reclining on his elbow, conversing with Lieut. [James] Gubbins of our camp. Lieutenant [John Fitzsimmons], of Company B, by the side of him, was struck, and Nick remarked: "Fitz, you are hit." Many of those surrounding us were uttering exclamations of "Oh," etc., as they were shot, when, all at once, a shell from the enemy plunged through my poor camp, passing first through the body of William, then cut off the leg of John Fitzsimmons, then both feet of D[avid] Jenkins, and passed through my poor friend Nick, entering at the small of the back, coming out at the breast, tearing out and exposing his heart. . . . By the one shot I lost three killed.[59]

Richardson did not mention it, but a shell also killed the 5th Louisiana's Charles Behan on this his eighteenth birthday.[60]

The exploding shells quickly covered the woods and fields with a thick grayish haze, giving the advancing Yankee lines a ghostly appearance as they emerged through the smoke. By 6:45 a.m., Colonel Douglass was dead and his men were falling back before the advancing enemy. Called to the front lines, Hays' brigade raised the rebel yell as it rushed past Douglass' men into what Lieutenant Wren described as a "dense fog of smoke" at the edge of the cornfield. Wren was in command of his company and admitted that the cacophony of sights and sounds left him shaken. "[I] had to put on a strong nerves just at this time for I never had seen so many falling in as little a time in any instance before, death seemed depicted in many countenances yet there was a continued shout of forward from different commanders until we were near the enemy and had commenced firing."[61]

Approximately 550 Louisianians charged into the cornfield and collided with Union Gen. George Hartsuff's brigade. The historian for the 12th Massachusetts described the Tigers' musketry as "the most deadly fire of the war." Another Union soldier recalled, "It was a hot time for us and most all of our Regt. were used up in a very short time." With the help of Douglass' Georgians, the Tigers drove Hartsuff's men out of the corn and back to the edge of the East Woods, where they made a stand. One of the Yankees wrote, "Never did I see more rebs to fire at than at that moment presented themselves."[62]

Hays was within 250 yards of the enemy when Lieutenant Wren realized that the brigade had advanced into an angle in the Union lines and was being swept by a cross fire from two sides. Hays ordered the brigade to close the gaps in the line by shifting to the right. Wren wrote that, after he accomplished the maneuver, "I found but three men out of eighteen [in my company] standing, several had just fallen wounded and in one moment more a ball passed through the calf of my left leg and on the top of my right just cutting the skin. The balls were coming so thick at this time that I feared that I should never be able to get off of the field." Unable to lead his men effectively, Wren headed to the rear "through a perfect storm of shot and shell" but managed to reach safety.[63]

As he had foreseen, Private Snakenberg was also wounded in the deadly cornfield. He was loading his rifle "when I felt something burn me and seemed to paralyze me on the left side. I stood still trying to think of the matter, not knowing I was wounded and put my right hand to left side of waist and pulled my clothes away from my body, when everything seemed to turn green to me and I staggered for 20 feet and fell." Snakenberg's friend Mike Clark, an Irish immigrant, heard his cries for help and rushed over and helped him from the field. Snakenberg had been shot three times with "one ball through the folds of my blanket on right side, one striking my left hand and one through my body on left side."[64]

Among the Tigers killed in the cornfield were Sgt. John Heil, the Irishman who carried the 6th Louisiana's colors, and Col. Henry Strong, the regiment's commander. Strong and his milky-white steed made easy targets and were quickly knocked down by the whistling balls. Henry Richardson, also in the 6th Louisiana, was shot from his horse and dragged helplessly around the bloody field by his foot until another bullet killed the frightened animal. Lieutenant Ring, who was shot through the knee and arm and had two bullets smash his sword, rushed to Colonel Strong's body to recover his personal effects, but Hays yelled for the brigade's survivors to withdraw to the Dunker Church before he could accomplish the task. With a shout the victorious Yankees charged through the corn in pursuit, and one soldier stopped to pick up Colonel Strong's gloves and wave them triumphantly over his head. Just as Hays made it safely to the church, Hood's Texas Brigade charged past and drove the enemy back through the corn once again.[65]

At the Dunker Church, a shocked Hays found that only about 40 men rallied around him after the thirty-minute engagement. Isaiah Fogleman wrote in his diary later that day that "our brigade shot up very much. . . . Our Brigade so small, all put under one flag." Some stragglers rejoined the unit overnight, but Hays' brigade still numbered only about 100 men the next day.[66]

The Tiger brigade was not the only unit that suffered heavy losses in the cornfield. When the 12th Massachusetts returned to the rear, there were only 32 men with its colors, although some stragglers showed up later. When an accurate casualty count was finally tallied, it was discovered that the regiment's commander had been mortally wounded and 224 men had been lost out of 334 engaged. The 12th Massachusetts' 67 percent casualty rate was the highest of any Union regiment at Antietam.[67]

About noon, Hays took his small band of Tigers and returned to the front to support Hood's Texans, who were lying on the ground under a heavy fire. Captain H. Bain Ritchie, who had assumed command of the 6th Louisiana after Colonel Strong's death, was then killed, and Lieutenant Ring took over the regiment. Hays' men were forced to lay under the murderous fire because it was too dangerous to try to advance or retreat. Thus, Lieutenant Ring wrote, "We remained in the front exposed to frequent shelling from the enemy until 5 o'clock p.m. when we fell back to a less exposed position."[68]

Approximately 61 percent of Hays' brigade was lost at Antietam, with 45 men killed, 289 wounded, and 2 missing. All of Hays' staff officers and regimental commanders had been shot down, including the 14th Louisiana's Colonel Zable, who would be out of action for six months. The 7th Louisiana lost 14 officers, while the 6th Louisiana entered the fight with 12 officers and had 5 killed and 7 wounded. Among the brigade's dead were Pvt. George Zeller, whose letters chronicled the 6th Louisiana's activities early in the war, and the Zouaves' Col. Gaston Coppens, who was temporarily commanding the 8th Florida. Coppens was mortally wounded when his regiment was sent into action at the sunken road that became known as "Bloody Lane." He was sent back to Richmond but died while being cared for in a private home.[69]

Lieutenant Wren was amazed that he escaped with just a leg wound. "When I was once out of danger," he wrote, "I never felt so thankful in all my life. I had come out of a place that it really seemed to me that a person could not stand in at all and at one time think I was in fifty yards of one line of the enemy, but could see them, only, indistinkly [sic] on account of the smoke." Reflecting on his miraculous survival when so many others were killed, Wren was convinced that God had been watching over him and wrote in his diary, "This was a wonderful day on the Potomac."[70]

Private Snakenberg also counted himself among the lucky ones. He later wrote, "It was a very hard fight and many thousands were wounded and killed.

. . . I have said, and I believe it, that in the battle of Sharpsburg, the bullets were flying so thick in the air, that if a person could hold up an iron pot with safety, that it would soon fill." Snakenberg was especially thankful when a surgeon assured him that the bullet had passed through his body, and he would not have to be cut on as he had feared the night before. Taken back to Virginia, he spent the next five weeks in a hospital.[71]

While Snakenberg was being treated behind the Confederate lines, his brigade comrade, Michael Sullivan of the 6th Louisiana, was in a Union field hospital. Sullivan had been shot five times in the attack through the cornfield but miraculously survived and was captured. One bullet hit him near the left kneecap and broke his femur, two went into his left thigh, one fractured his right femur, and one struck him in the back. Before he died seven months later, surgeons splinted his broken bones, probed for minié balls, removed bone fragments, and lanced abscesses. Union surgeons considered Sullivan's case significant enough to be included in the postwar publication *Photographic Atlas of Civil War Injuries.*[72]

On the western side of the Hagerstown Pike, Starke's 2nd Louisiana Brigade was subjected to the same artillery barrage that raked Hays' men before they entered the cornfield. When one shell knocked General Jones out of action, Starke took command of the division and turned the brigade over to Colonel Stafford. This change in command came at a critical moment when Winder's and Jones' brigades were beginning to fall back before Hooker's juggernaut, and Stafford and Taliaferro were advancing to take the place of those two shattered brigades. Although directing the actions of the entire division, Starke grabbed one of the Tigers' flags and led the brigade out toward the enemy. Sweeping up the western side of the road, the gray line quickly moved through a patch of woods and charged into the Yankees. A terrific roar filled the air as each side cut loose with long, rolling volleys of thunderous musketry. Colonel Jesse M. Williams of the 2nd Louisiana fell badly wounded with a bullet through his chest, and three balls hit Starke almost simultaneously, and he died within the hour.[73]

Stafford continued to push the brigade up the western side of the pike through what Lt. Col. Edmund Pendleton described as a "murderous fire which thinned our ranks at every step." On the other side of the road was Gen. John Gibbon's famous Iron Brigade, the same midwestern soldiers who had stood toe to toe with Starke's brigade at Groveton a few weeks earlier and had just helped drive Hays' Tigers out of the cornfield. When Gibbon's men opened a deadly fire into Stafford's right flank, Stafford wheeled the brigade to face the threat and advanced to a post-and-rail fence that ran alongside the road. There he ordered the men to lie down and open fire on the Iron Brigade, which was about thirty yards away behind the fence that ran along the other side of the pike. As the two brigades traded volleys, two regiments of federal sharpshooters began picking apart the 1st Louisiana on Stafford's left flank. A Union artillery battery also unlimbered seventy-five yards from the road and shattered the gray line with canister that blew fence rails and body parts high into the air. Some of the Tigers climbed over the fence and attempted to rush the enemy but were quickly cut down in the middle of the road. Like Hays in the cornfield, Stafford was caught in a deadly cross fire, but one Tiger claimed the men stood their ground for fifteen minutes before the Virginia brigades on the left "run and left our Brigade alone." Within minutes, the federals poured into the gap created by the Virginians' retreat and forced the Tigers to pull back toward the Dunker Church.[74]

Scores of dead and wounded were left behind, as was the 1st Louisiana's battle flag. When a Yankee sharpshooter killed the color-bearer, the flag fell across the rail fence. Lewis C. Parmelee, the 2nd U.S. Sharpshooters' adjutant, retrieved it, but five bullets riddled his body before he could make it safely back to his side of the road. Major Alfred Turner and Sgt. Isaac Thomas of the 80th New York engaged in a foot race to capture the colors, but Thomas won out and carried the flag away. Robert Strom, the 10th Louisiana's color-bearer, was also killed next to the fence, but comrades saved his flag.[75]

At the Dunker Church, Stafford was forced to relinquish command of the brigade because shell fragments had badly bruised his foot. Finding a successor was difficult because every one of the brigade's field officers had been killed or wounded, and 9 of the line officers were dead. Lieutenant Colonel Edmund Pendleton finally took over even though a shell had badly bruised his ankle when it passed between his legs. Like Hays' brigade in the cornfield, the 600 men of the 2nd Louisiana Brigade were only in combat for about thirty minutes, but they had 81 men killed, 189 wounded, and 17 missing. Some companies almost ceased to exist, and Sgt. Edmond Stephens reported that the 9th Louisiana was "almost destroyed." That regiment's Bienville Blues lost 20 of 32 men, and all 18 members of the Moore Fencibles were killed or wounded. Lieutenant Seton wrote his mother that the 10th Louisiana's best officers had been lost in the recent battles and that only four of his company's sixteen men escaped Antietam unhurt. The battle, in fact, proved to be the costliest of the war for the 10th Louisiana, which lost 35 percent of its men.[76]

McClellan's tough Yankees had shattered both Louisiana brigades in less than an hour. Fortunately, the battle soon ended on that part of the field, and the fighting drifted farther south and finally ended when A. P. Hill's division arrived from Harpers Ferry and stabilized Lee's line. That night and next day truces were arranged to bury the dead and retrieve the wounded. The carnage along the Hagerstown Pike, where Starke's brigade traded volleys with the Iron Brigade, was particularly horrifying. One Union soldier wrote that "the piles of dead . . . were frightful" and claimed that a path had to be made through the road by dragging away the bodies and placing them along the fences. The Iron Brigade's Edward S. Bragg reported, "I counted eighty Rebels in one row along the fence in front of us, lying so thick you could step from one to the other."[77]

Although the horrific battle along Antietam Creek ended in a draw, McClellan could claim victory because Lee began withdrawing back to Virginia the next night. From his ambulance, Lt. George Wren summed up the fighting when he wrote in his diary, "Yesterday will ever be an epoch in the history of our country that can never be forgotten by the American people. The Sharpsburg fight much the bloodiest that ever occured [sic] on the American Continent." Lee's army was battered, but McClellan discovered that it was still dangerous when he attempted to cross the Potomac near Shepherdstown on September 20. After Hays' brigade and other units were rushed back to stop him, Lieutenant Ring wrote his wife, "After a fight of a few hours . . . we drove them back and through the river, killing and drowning a large number. [It ended] all ideas and desire for another attempt on the part of our Yankee friends to pay us another visit."[78]

The heavy casualties Lee suffered at Antietam, and in particular his loss in officers, again made it necessary to reorganize some of the army's brigades. The late George Auguste Coppens' younger brother, Marie Alfred, was promoted to lieutenant colonel and assumed command of the seventeen surviving members of Coppens' Battalion. The unit was renamed the Confederate States Zouave Battalion and was detached from the other Tiger commands to serve on various garrison duties for the remainder of the war. During that time, Coppens was convicted on two counts of dereliction of duty. Colonel Pendleton continued to command the 2nd Louisiana Brigade on a temporary basis, but in January 1863 Col. Francis T. Nicholls of the 8th Louisiana was promoted to brigadier general and assumed command even though he had never served with the brigade. Colonel Stafford's 9th Louisiana was returned to the 1st Louisiana Brigade, and the 14th Louisiana was transferred to Nicholls' brigade. Why Lee made these changes in the 2nd Louisiana Brigade is unknown, but Stafford had the unique experience of having temporarily commanded both Louisiana brigades and seems to have led them well. The fact that he was later promoted to brigadier general and given command of the 2nd Louisiana Brigade indicates he had Lee's confidence, so it seems curious that Lee would promote and bring in Nicholls, an outsider, to lead the brigade when he could have left the 9th Louisiana in place and promoted Stafford.[79]

Many of the Tigers who were wounded at Second Manassas and Antietam were granted furloughs to return home to recuperate. Lieutenant Wren was among them. While on a train heading west, he wrote in his diary that "little did I expect to get to see my friends in Louisiana, so soon when, I left last spring, and little did I expect, to, have ever, passed through what I have and be permitted to see them so well as I am. . . . I fear it may be the last opportunity I will have, as I feel confident that I shall never go through the same danger again without finding a worse fate." That troubled thought is the last entry in Wren's diary. As the cold winter set in, he and the other Tigers contemplated what new hardships lay ahead. For Wren it included another wound and suffering in a Yankee prison camp.[80]

CHAPTER 7

Fighting the Good Fight

O NCE THEY WERE safely back in the Shenandoah Valley following the Antietam Campaign, the Louisiana Tigers encamped near Winchester, Virginia. The only action of note that took place there was a five-day foray by Hays' brigade to the Martinsburg area in October to tear up more than twenty miles of the Baltimore and Ohio Railroad. Lieutenant Henry Handerson wrote, "I never thought I should ever become such a 'bridge-burner!'" but Lieutenant Ring shrugged the duty off as simply some "civil engineering."[1]

While in the Valley, some of the Louisiana Zouaves, probably members of Coppens' Battalion, had a surprise encounter with Union staff officer Maj. S. A. Defoe. Defoe blundered into the Zouaves while scouting toward the Confederate lines. When he heard the approaching soldiers speaking French, Defoe realized they were Louisiana Tigers and decided to bluff his way out of his predicament rather than flee. Before the war, he had spent time in south Louisiana and had learned to speak what he called the "Creole 'Gumbo' French." It was also helpful that Defoe's staff officer's uniform appeared somewhat "Zouavish." He spurred his horse to meet the Zouaves, and the Louisiana captain snapped a sharp salute when he saw the major's uniform. Defoe returned the salute and asked in French what the captain was doing there. When the captain explained that he had been ordered to put out a picket line, Defoe replied, "Well, just move your men back over the crest of the hill and wait there until I examine the ground, and if things look safe I will signal you to advance." "But Monsieur," the captain protested, "the Yanks are said to be thick around here." Defoe said he would take the responsibility, to which the Tiger captain replied, "Very good, Monsieur," and marched his men away. Once they were out of rifle range, Defoe spurred his horse in the opposite direction. It was only then that the Louisiana officer realized he had been duped and ordered his men to fire, but Defoe escaped.[2]

When the two Louisiana brigades first encamped around Winchester, they were in a pitiful condition. On September 22, 1862, Hays' brigade had only 693 officers and men present for duty, with 480 being absent without leave and 1,401 on sick or wounded furlough. So many noncommissioned officers absented themselves for "frivolous excuses" in Colonel Penn's 7th Louisiana that Penn ordered any noncom who left his post without permission to be reduced to the ranks. Fortunately, the number of men present for duty increased rather quickly as the slightly wounded, sick, and stragglers returned to camp. By the middle of October, Hays had approximately 1,500 men present for duty, but an astonishing 2,310 were still listed as being absent sick or wounded. Even if more men had managed to report for duty, it is doubtful whether Hays could have provided them arms. It is not known whether soldiers lost or threw away their muskets during the retreat from Antietam or the weapons had become defective after months of hard service, but on November 3 Hays reported that 400 of his men were completely unarmed.[3]

Nicholls' brigade appears to have fared better in maintaining its strength than its sister unit. Father Sheeran reported that the 2nd Louisiana Brigade was in excellent condition that fall and winter because many of the wounded and stragglers had returned to their regiments. An October report showed that the 1st, 2nd, and 14th Louisiana had 1,406 men present for duty, but the brigade's true strength was probably around 2,000 because there were no reports found for the 10th and 15th regiments. However, Nicholls' brigade also suffered from a number of desertions and the ever-present sickness. In October alone, the brigade's surgeons treated 680 cases in just three of the brigade's five regiments.[4]

Sickness greatly weakened both brigades that autumn, but the men also suffered from hunger and a lack of shoes and clothing. Sergeant Stephens of the 9th Louisiana wrote, "The Boys are shivering & huvering around their little chunk fires. Though as meny as black birds, we are sadly in need of clothing & Piticularly in Blankets & Shoes." Stephens claimed the regiment's quartermaster was selling "Confederate shoes" for five dollars a pair but did not explain why the officer was selling government supplies rather than issuing them free of charge. Few men could afford the exorbitant price, and Stephens reported in November that "our whole Army is very near Shoeless."[5]

In a series of letters home, Capt. Al Pierson corroborated Stephens' bleak report. "Our living now is very hard," he wrote his brother, "nothing but beef and flour and nothing to cook that with." Pierson complained that the daily salt ration was just two tablespoons for every five men, bacon could not be found anywhere, and fresh pork and butter were too expensive for soldiers to purchase. James Carrington also informed a friend that "Nothing can be bought in this country except sometimes a chicken for which one dollar is the price." Carrington proudly reported that he did succeed in acquiring nineteen pounds of honey for his company, but at a cost of nineteen dollars. "So you see," he grumbled, "how much of our confederate 'money' it took to get anything in this part of the state."[6]

In November, rations in Hays' brigade consisted of ten pounds of wheat per one hundred men, issued once a week, and a small quantity of beef distributed the other six days. This near-starvation diet caused some of the Tigers to resort to theft. Georgia Col. Clement Evans informed his wife that about a dozen of Hays' men went to a nearby farm at sundown and informed the owner that they had been detailed to guard his property. The appreciative farmer provided them a hearty supper but during the night "his bee gums, and sundry fat turkeys, went the way of all the earth along with his curly tailed pet pig, and the self appointed guard." Evans claimed that three members of the 6th Louisiana later pulled the same trick and asked the farmer if they could borrow his watch so they would know when it was time to relieve each other from guard duty. "He sent it out and in a short while he found that his guard had departed, and so had his watch."[7]

After spending two months around Winchester, Jackson's corps left the area on November 21 and began making its way to Fredericksburg to join the rest of Lee's army in stopping another Union threat to Richmond. Lincoln had relieved McClellan of command of the Army of the Potomac when he failed to take the offensive after Antietam and replaced him with Gen. Ambrose Burnside. Burnside developed a plan to move the army rapidly to the Rappahannock River at Fredericksburg and cross over before Lee could react. If successful, Burnside would then be between Lee and Richmond and could either strike out for the city or dig in and force Lee to attack him. Unfortunately for Burnside, however, the movement bogged down unexpectedly, and Lee had time to concentrate his army on the high ground south of Fredericksburg to block his path.[8]

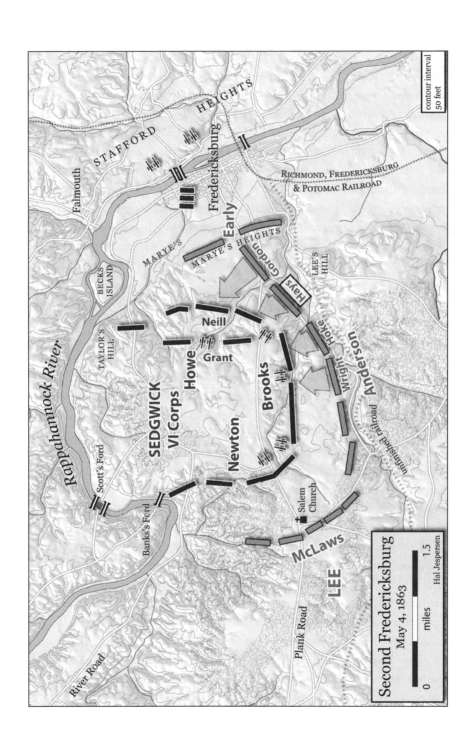

contour interval
50 feet

STAFFORD HEIGHTS

Falmouth

Fredericksburg

RICHMOND, FREDERICKSBURG
& POTOMAC RAILROAD

BECKS ISLAND

MARYE'S

MARYE'S HEIGHTS

Early

Gordon

Hays

LEE'S HILL

Rappahannock River

TAYLOR'S HILL

Neill

Grant

Howe

Brooks

Hoke

Wright

Anderson

SEDGWICK
VI Corps

Newton

unfinished railroad

Scott's Ford

Banks's Ford

Salem
Church

McLaws

LEE

Plank Road

River Road

Second Fredericksburg
May 4, 1863

0   miles   1.5

Hal Jespersen

Jubal Early's division, which included Hays' Louisiana brigade, brought up the rear as Jackson marched for Fredericksburg. When Gen. D. H. Hill's division passed through New Market, Hill thought it prudent to leave a regiment behind to protect the town from the notorious Louisiana Tigers. This did not sit well with the 7th Louisiana's Sgt. John F. "Fred" Gruber, a well-educated German immigrant and former New Orleans fire chief. Known in the army as the "New Orleans Dutchman," he was a humorous and good-natured man. According to Maj. David Boyd, Gruber "was the life of the Louisiana brigade—I may say of Early's division." As the brigade's commissary sergeant, Gruber was allowed to ride a horse and to come and go pretty much as he pleased. Several generals in Jackson's command enjoyed the sergeant's company and often requested that he ride with them on night marches because his good humor kept them awake.

Boyd claimed that Sergeant Gruber knew everyone who lived along the well-traveled Valley roads, including a Mr. Siebert who owned the only tavern in New Market. On the morning that Early's division entered town, Gruber and some friends paid a visit to Siebert's tavern but were confronted by a squad of General Hill's North Carolina troops. Gruber was about to dismount when one of the Tar Heels stopped him and declared, "We-uns belongs to Gineral Hill's command, and we-uns be put here to keep you-uns out!" Gruber rode away without arguing but then turned down an alley to approach the tavern from the rear. Mr. Siebert let the Tigers in and even filled their canteens with whiskey. Gruber stayed to visit, but the other soldiers returned to the brigade to inform the men that they could get a drink at the tavern's back door. By the time Gruber left Siebert's with two canteens of whiskey for himself and one for Generals Hays and Early, other Tigers were lined up in the alley to get their liquor.[9]

The men began showing the whiskey's effect as they marched over the Massanutten Mountain later that day. Major Boyd declared, "And such a day that was! . . . the road was lined with drunken men who had fallen out of ranks. Nearly everybody in the Louisiana brigade, and many in other brigades, had taken a drink too many; and old Jubal was merry and a-grinning." Jackson took notice of the spectacle and sent a note that night to Early demanding to know why he had seen so many drunken men while riding in the rear of Early's command. Early, who may have still been tipsy himself, replied that he "presumed the reason why the Lieutenant General commanding, when riding in the rear of his command, saw so many drunken men, was because he did ride in the rear of his command!" Jackson immediately ordered his aide Sandy Pendleton to place Early under arrest, but Pendleton convinced him to wait until morning. When dawn broke, Jackson declared that he would take care of the matter himself, but he never did arrest Early.[10]

The 175-mile forced march to Fredericksburg was brutal because of the men's poor physical condition and the snow and freezing rain. Captain Pierson wrote his father, "We had the hardest march when leaving the Valley that we have ever taken since we have been in the service. We averaged over twenty miles every day for more than a week. Many of the boys gave out on the road but most of them have come up lately." Pierson chose not to tell his father about another drunken spree that occurred along the way, but he wrote his brother, "We crossed the Blue Ridge where there was a distillery and all hands both offi-cers and men got on a general binder and merry yes very merry was the times."[11]

When Jackson's corps arrived at Fredericksburg, Lee placed it on the Con-federate right while Longstreet's corps was put on Marye's Heights to the left. Burnside managed to fight his way across the Rappahannock on December 11 and launched a series of attacks on Lee's position two days later. The federals had some success on Jackson's front where his line crossed a low swampy area, but all of Burnside's attacks on Longstreet's position at Marye's Heights were thrown back with great slaughter. In what turned out to be one of the Union's worst defeats of the war, Burnside lost more than 12,000 men to Lee's 5,300 casualties. The 2nd Louisiana's Wolf Lichenstein watched the slaughter and wrote, "It was a sad sight to see those brave Yankees flee & fall before Lee's fierce fire."[12]

Neither of the Louisiana brigades was actively engaged in the Battle of Fredericksburg, although both came under heavy artillery fire while held in reserve. Lieutenant Handerson recalled a solid shot hitting the road in front of the 9th Louisiana and ricocheting over the head of the men. It looked so harmless that Handerson admitted it was "almost tempting . . . try to catch it." While under the heavy fire, General Jackson rode up and calmly sat his horse next to a battery that was engaged with the Union artillery. Hander-son claimed that Stonewall looked like the "incarnation of war" and silently watched the duel while shrapnel cut the air around him. All of the Tigers were hugging the ground to avoid the deadly missiles and were finally moved back to a sunken road that offered some protection.[13]

Reubin C. Macon of the 13th Virginia had an encounter with some Tigers that morning although he did not know to which brigade they belonged. Macon's regiment was getting into position along a ridge and could see that the advancing Union soldiers were dressed in what appeared to be brand-new uniforms. At that moment the Louisianians passed by. According to Macon, "The battalion was made up principally of Irishmen from the wharves, brave fighters, but equally noted for their love of plunder." Macon heard two of the Irishmen in conversation as they marched. "'Pat, look over yonder. The whole face of the earth is covered with Yankees.' 'Faith,' said he, 'if they come this way, I will have an overcoat before night.'" Unfortunately for Pat, the enemy never got close enough for him to plunder their dead.[14]

The Irishmen could have used the overcoats because the night was clear and bitterly cold. Unable to sleep, Handerson stood to get warm and noticed that frost had covered his comrades' blankets. As he looked down the long line of men under the bright moon it struck him that they appeared to be bodies laid out for burial. Adding to the eerie feeling was the unusually quiet night and a rare aurora borealis that danced across the sky. The plain below where the enemy's dead and wounded lay was covered in a veil of fog. According to Handerson, "[T]he solemn stillness of the night was broken by a faint and gostly wail, which located itself at no special point, but seemed to rise like a mist from the face of the whole field of battle and conveyed the impression of wide spread and terrible anguish."[15]

While exposed to the Yankees' artillery fire, Hays' brigade lost forty-five men and Nicholls' brigade thirty-nine. Nicholls' brigade also lost an officer when he resigned under a cloud of suspicion. For reasons unknown, soldiers in the 14th Louisiana accused Capt. Henry M. Verlander, the regiment's temporary commander, of cowardice. Father Sheeran claimed that Verlander "had disgraced himself and the regiment by his cowardice and that the men publicly denounced him." Sheeran visited Verlander and hinted that he should resign his commission, but the captain replied that, while he knew some of the men did not like him, he would not resign. Sheeran later wrote, "I told him he was mistaken for it was not only a few who accused him of cowardice, but every man in the regiment." Verlander then resigned, and Sheeran claimed "the 14th got rid of the biggest coward that ever played soldier." Afterward, someone wrote on Verlander's service record, "Resigned and deserted to the enemy."[16]

After Burnside retreated across the Rappahannock on December 15, both Louisiana brigades spent the next several months picketing the river. The duty was a welcomed respite because the opposing pickets usually agreed to informal truces and fraternized and traded with one another. William Snakenberg recalled the unwritten rule of behavior during such times:

> We used to do picket duty on the banks of the River, and while we were not doing active campaign duty did not fire on each other. This seemed to be a general rule in winter when in quarters and the pickets used to have long talks with each other and always in good spirits. We used to change tobacco, which was scarce with them, for coffee, which was very scarce with us. We even swam in the same water or bathed in spring, if not too cold; and if either side got orders to fire on the pickets, we generally gave each notice to go in their holes. . . . I have talked for an hour at a time with them, each on our own side of the river, which was not a wide stream—we could easily throw a square of tobacco across and they could sling a pound of coffee across by fastening a string or strap to the package.[17]

Some of the Tigers used miniature hand-carved boats to ferry the trade goods across the river. One soldier even managed to get a letter delivered home in occupied Louisiana by sending it over for a Yankee to mail. The only drawback to such illicit fraternizing was the discovery that the federals were not too adept at sailing, and the return cargo often drifted downstream out of sight.[18]

A number of Tigers, like the 9th Louisiana's Ezra Denson, even accepted the Yankees' invitation to cross the river for a visit. Upon his return, Denson told his messmates that the Yankees hailed from the Old Northwest and were as tired of the war as the Louisianians. "They expressed a hearty desire to witness its termination," Sergeant Stephens reported Denson as saying, "for they were disgusted, discouraged and dissatisfied and could not digest old Lincoln's actions calling for negro troops. They said they would be willing to meet us in the middle of the river . . . and shake hands with us and never fire another gun."[19]

On another occasion a New York native in the 6th Louisiana learned that the federal regiment across the river contained some old acquaintances and swam over to see them. Shocked at his emaciated condition, his friends urged him to desert and stay with them. Captain William J. Seymour described what happened next:

The ragged, half-starved "Rebel" drew himself proudly up, his eyes flashing and face all aglow with patriotic fervor, and contemptuously spurned the dishonorable offer; he told his tempters, that he had often times braved danger and death side by side with those dirty, ragged "rebs" over the River, and shared with them the exposure and suffering of the march and privations of the camp—was fully aware of the supreme condition of the Federal troops; but that he would not desert his colors for all the gold that the Federal Government could command. He declared that he had embarked in what he considered a righteous cause, and if it would be the will of God, he would die fighting for it.[20]

As the winter dragged on, conditions in Hays' brigade began to deteriorate. Smallpox broke out later in December, but most of the men had been vaccinated, and those who contracted the disease were quickly sent away. That same month, one company in the 6th Louisiana reported thirteen men being excused from duty because they were barefooted, and all of the Tigers suffered from a lack of shelter with which to ward off the biting Virginia cold. On December 20, a member of the 8th Louisiana actually froze to death after getting drunk and lying exposed to the elements all night. Hays' brigade was stationed at Port Royal at the time and fought the cold by burrowing into the ground like animals and using blankets and tent flies to cover what they dubbed "Camp Hole in the Ground."[21]

Snow and subfreezing temperatures were common throughout the winter of 1862–63. Captain Pierson wrote his father in December, "The weather is very cold here now. The ground is covered with snow and the sun melts it but little during the day though the weather is quite clear. Some of the boys are still without shoes and consequently have to keep themselves about the fire. Most of them have good clothes and none of them are without a good blanket." A week later Pierson wrote his brother, "It is clear today but water freezes in a few minutes after it is brought up. Some of the boys are still barefooted and others have no good clothes." The brutal weather continued into the early spring, with a foot of snow still covering the ground on April 5, 1863.[22]

Nicholls' brigade fared no better. Major Francis Rawle reported in December that none of the men had any tents and that there was a shortage of wagons and horses to gather supplies.[23] A few weeks later, the 10th Louisiana's Sgt. Oliver Moss described to his fiancée how difficult it was to keep the brigade supplied: "The snow is one foot deep on level land. Previous to 36 hours snowing it rained for 6 days which caused the rivers to rise, and also made the roads very bad. We cannot haul our commissaries from the depot as fast as we consume them. In fact, we are short of rations right now on account of bad roads. I have just returned from the depot with 2 wagons loaded with quartermaster's stores. I had an awful time of it. If you were to see me and my teams you would think there is some mud in Virginia as well as in Calcasieu [Parish]. There is over 200 wagons broken and mired between here and the depot which is only 6 miles away."[24]

Moss also denounced men in other units who were grumbling about the difficult conditions. "If General Jackson's troops do not complain I do not think that any others have the right to do so for we have had more marching and fighting to do, and less to eat than any troops in the service. There is over half of the Louisiana troops that are killed or wounded since they came to Virginia and what is left is ready and willing to meet the Yankees at anytime or place."[25]

Constant food shortages exacerbated the miserable living conditions. By early 1863, *weekly* rations ranged from one and three-quarter pounds of meat for some men, to one-third pound of bacon, one and one-eighth pounds of flour, and three ounces of sugar for others. Colonel Pendleton lamented that coffee cost him $4.75 per pound and prices were so high that his food bill was $100 per month. Pendleton, however, apparently ate rather well because Capt. Thomas G. Morgan of the 7th Louisiana tallied his food bill for April 1863 at $12.52. With this he purchased six and a half pints of beef, fourteen and a half pints of bacon, fifty-four pints of flour, six pints of rice, nine pints of sugar, two pints of salt, three pints of molasses, and three pints of peas. Lowly privates, of course, could ill afford extra food at any price and were forced to supplement their diets by poaching on neighboring farms.[26]

Surviving reports for the Louisiana brigades show what a heavy toll the winter took on the men. When newly appointed general Francis T. Nicholls returned to duty in January 1863 following his arm amputation at Winchester, he discovered that his brigade had shrunk significantly. According to a January 26 morning report, there were 1,062 men present for duty (or about half of the October number) with 164 of those sick and 37 under arrest. Another 455 men were absent sick, 102 were on approved leave, 346 were absent without leave, and 25 were serving on detached duty.[27]

The deplorable conditions in Hays' brigade can be seen in the reports of Hays' assistant adjutant general, John H. New. His inspection for January 10, 1863, notes discipline as being "good" in the 5th and 9th Louisiana but "poor" in the 6th, 7th, and 8th regiments. The men's competence in drilling was little better. The 6th and 7th regiments were rated moderately good, the 9th "tolerable," the 8th "miserable," and the 5th was excused from drill entirely for a lack of shoes. The 9th Louisiana had 103 barefooted men on January 30, but all of the regiments suffered from a shoe shortage, as well as underclothing and blankets. No tents were available for constructing a hospital, and the brigade's prisoners were detained in the open air because there was no guardhouse. The men's muskets were described as being in "sad" condition, and there were hardly any bayonets in camp. New reported that there were "not more than three camp kettles" in the entire brigade with which to cook the meager rations, and that some companies had only one skillet which all of the men had to share. In concluding his gloomy report, New exclaimed, "There is a painful apathy and indifference among company officers, [who] understand a few stereotyped movements in the Battalion drill, [but] take them out of them and they are at Sea."[28]

Because of the "enormity of the suffering" in Hays' brigade, New wrote Louisiana Rep. John Perkins to ask his help in securing supplies. New claimed that of the brigade's 1,500 men, 400 had no footwear of any kind and many were without blankets. "There are some," he added, "without a particle of underclothing, having neither shirts, drawers, nor socks; while overcoats, from their rarity, are objects of curiosity." Government officials blamed the military for the brigade's deplorable condition and claimed that all of the army's requisitions sent to Richmond had been filled. New's plea for help apparently worked, however, because the army's quartermaster finally filled an order for 1,000 shoes for Hays' brigade.[29]

Apparently Hays and New also made a concerted effort to improve conditions in camp because each succeeding inspection showed clear gains. A guard tent was erected by February 28 to house the two officers and twenty-one men still under arrest, and a few log huts were constructed by winter's end. Additional shoes and blankets eventually arrived, as well, and discipline improved as the weather warmed and daily drills resumed.[30]

The Louisiana officers also worked hard to bring more troops into the ranks. Colonels Waggaman and Forno were dispatched to Louisiana and Mobile, respectively, to gather recruits, and some government officials lobbied Lee to send one of the brigades home to collect badly needed replacements. Lee refused but did allow additional officers to return to Louisiana to round up deserters and to collect volunteers and conscripts. Lieutenant Seton asked his family to tell those soldiers who had overstayed their furloughs that they should return to duty immediately "or they will be published as diserters & orderd to be arrested & tried for such in the Western department by a lat[e] order of the Secretary of war. I am also happy to see that all thoes damt cowards at home on the North bay [illegible] are to be arrested & sent back." When the badly needed reinforcements arrived in camp, the Tigers welcomed those who had volunteered but shunned the draftees. "The conscripts of La.," wrote Thomas Newell, "has got a bad name in Virginia, especially among the troops. They say that they run in Bull Run style as soon as attacked."[31]

The harsh conditions during the winter of 1862–63 had a demoralizing effect on the Tigers, and many men slipped out of camp without authorization for rest and recreation. Colonel Pendleton, in fact, claimed that nearly half of Nicholls' brigade was absent without leave in Richmond that December. One member of the 10th Louisiana known only as "Patrick" even deserted in order to join a different unit, but he was caught, convicted of desertion, and sentenced to be shot. As Patrick faced the firing squad, Adj. Henry Puissan read the verdict which stated that the "whole" court had concurred in the death sentence. Puissan then read a separate document from General Lee that pointed out an error in the court's conviction. The Articles of War stipulated that if more than two-thirds of the court's members agreed to a sentence, the report should simply state that two-thirds agreed so as not to reveal how the members voted. By stating that the whole court had concurred with the death sentence, the report revealed that all of the members had voted to execute Patrick. Lee ordered that the verdict be set aside and Patrick freed and returned to duty because a man could not be tried twice for the same crime. Patrick's comrades cheered the announcement and rushed to congratulate him. "How lucky it was that all the members of the court found me guilty," Patrick exclaimed. "If a single one of them had voted otherwise, my days would have been numbered."[32]

To make the dreary winter camps more bearable, some Tigers turned to religion while others played in the snow, skated on ice, or had snowball fights. Lieutenant Seton reported that his 10th Louisiana engaged in a snowball fight with another brigade and "we wiped the Virginians out. . . . It was conducted the same as a regular battle commanded by Colonels etc. only it was with snow balls & to day the 1st & 2nd Brigs tried to come & whip us [illegible] but they could not succeed we ran them back to their camps it was exciting times we have fun every time it snows." Captain Pierson reported that his 9th Louisiana also enjoyed playing "a game of ball," although it is not known if he was referring to baseball. He wrote, "This is quite a show sometimes. As many as one hundred are engaged at once." Other forms of entertainment apparently did not meet the officers' approval. Although the details are not known, more than twenty Irish noncommissioned officers in the 7th Louisiana were reduced to the ranks for a wild celebration they held on St. Patrick's Day.[33]

Some Tigers also began robbing civilians who came into camp to get money to purchase various things that made the winter camps more bearable. This criminal activity became so prevalent in Hays' brigade that special orders were issued on December 20: "The Brig. Genl. comdg. painfully regrets having to call the attention of the officers and men of this command to the frequent occurrence of late of theft and robberies committed within the limits of this camp upon unoffending citizens. He had hoped that there was sufficient pride among the soldiers from Louisiana to put down any such disgraceful acts that . . . bring reproach, if not disgrace, on all. . . . The Brig. Genl. comdg. therefore wishes it distinctly understood that the next instance of robbing brought before his attention committed by any member of this Brigade will be punished with the severest penalty known to military law."[34]

The Tigers' persistent preying upon the local people brought numerous delegations of irate citizens to General Early's headquarters because he had temporary command of Ewell's division. Early, in turn, constantly pestered Hays to stop the depredations and probably pressured him to issue the above order. However, Hays apparently did not believe his men were responsible for all of the crimes attributed to them and finally tired of Early's unrelenting accusations. Calling his colonels to his tent, Hays told them he was drawing up a petition requesting that the 1st Louisiana Brigade be transferred out of Early's command. Colonels William Monaghan, Leroy Stafford, and Trevanion Lewis signed the document with Hays, but Davidson Penn, a native of Virginia and an old friend of Early's, refused to do so.

Hays sent the petition to Early and requested that it be forwarded to Jackson and Lee. Early's famous temper exploded, and he ordered all of the colonels to his quarters. Eyeing the group sternly as they sat silently around him, Early declared, "Gentlemen, this is a most remarkable document that I have had the honor to receive from you; but I am glad to see there is one man of sense among you—Penn didn't sign it." He then cited example after example of how the Tigers' misdeeds had disgraced the division. His voice rising, Early exclaimed that after patiently bearing this outrageous behavior, he was now being insulted by a petition asking that he transfer the Tigers. Finally, Early exclaimed in a shrill voice, "Who do you think would have such a damn pack of thieves but me? If you can find any Major General in this army such a damn fool as to take you fellows, you may go!" A tense quiet fell on the group as the words sank in, but then the keen-witted Stafford exploded in laughter over the ridiculous scene. The tension was broken, and all were soon laughing at themselves over drinks from Early's jug.[35]

Hays' brigade was not alone in preying on the local civilians. The men of the 2nd Louisiana frequently bought supplies from a nearby farmer, including wheat to make a coffee substitute. According to Private Lichenstein, the Tigers eventually tired of the farmer's unreasonable price and became so "boisterous" that General Jackson ordered a squad of soldiers be placed at the farm at all times. On one occasion when Lichenstein was in charge of the guard, the farmer authorized him to sell the wheat and turn the money over to his wife. Lichenstein did so, but his comrades became angry at the farmer's price gouging and suggested stealing the remaining wheat. Lichenstein agreed, and they took as much wheat as they could carry from several barrels. Not long afterward, someone stole two of the farmer's pigs, and he discovered the "wheat swindle." According to Lichenstein, the man rushed to Jackson's headquarters "raging & foaming & frothing, he was so overcome he could scarcely tell his woes." Lichenstein claimed that nearly every man in the regiment had taken some of the wheat, but no one would admit to anything. Jackson finally gave the farmer a certificate of damage that could be redeemed by the government after the war, and "he was happy enough."[36]

After picketing the Rappahannock River at Port Royal for some time, Hays' brigade returned to the Fredericksburg area and camped near Hamilton's Crossing. There the men were constantly reminded of the slaughter that had taken place back in December. Sergeant Stephens wrote, "It is no trouble to see a half buried Yankee with one arm, leg or head sticking out from under the dirt and any quantity of dead horses." Stephens claimed that such sights were so commonplace that the men paid no more attention to them than if "they were so many chunks." Captain Pierson agreed and informed his father that the half-buried Yankees "are still exposed to view in many places, some with their hands and arms sticking out, while others['] heads are projecting and present the most hideous pictures, their teeth glistening as though grinning at the passers by."[37]

The men's spirits finally lifted as the winter slowly released its cold grip on the Virginia countryside. In early March 1863, Captain Pierson wrote his father that not only had the living conditions improved but more recruits were also arriving in camp. "The troops are generally well clad & shod and in fine spirits. The rations are very light but the men seem to enjoy them. They have learned to be quite shifty and will get along with less than half than they could have done when we first came out." Soon after this letter was posted, rations considerably improved in Hays' brigade, and Pierson wrote, "[T]hanks to Mas Jeff Davis I get plenty of bacon and biscuit with an occasional mess of rice and now and then some sugar & molasses. We can purchase but few articles of food extra of what we draw. Our Sutlers have a few beans & peas which we buy and have a feast of liquor about once a week. We can procure Oysters here at from five to ten Dollars per gallon of which we are all passionately fond (the best and healthiest diet for a soldier in the world)."[38]

Pierson also claimed that the long winter encampment had allowed the army to receive much-needed training. "All of our Brig. Gens. are striving to have the best drilled and disciplined Brigades, hence the improvement has been very great this winter." Apparently, army officials also were able to acquire badly needed equipment that spring. In April, Private Caldwell reported that many of the men in his 7th Louisiana had received new gear. "Napsacks and haversacks furnished to all new [illegible] who have none. Bayonets furnished."[39]

Along with the warmer weather, spring also ushered in a new campaign season. General Joseph Hooker, the new commander of the Army of the Potomac, was laying a clever plan similar to the one Lee used against Pope in the Second Manassas Campaign. He would create a diversion by leaving part of his army to demonstrate in Lee's front at Fredericksburg, while the bulk of his force secretly marched upstream to cross the river and sweep into Lee's rear. Lee would then be cut off from Richmond and forced to fight on ground of Hooker's choosing.

When the Union army began breaking camp on April 28, 1863, Capt. William Seymour and Col. Leroy Stafford climbed up the steeple of Fredericksburg's Episcopal Church to get a better look. Seymour recalled seeing "the hosts of the enemy, drawn up in battle array, their burnished arms glistening in the sunlight and their banners floating proudly in the breeze."[40] Hays' brigade was called into action at 6:00 a.m. the following day when Gen. John Sedgwick's corps began laying pontoon bridges across the Rappahannock in a dense fog. Captain Seymour, the son of the late Col. Isaac Seymour, had recently joined the brigade as a member of General Hays' staff, and this was to be his first action in Virginia. He recalled his camp sendoff:

> When the Brigade had been formed and I was sitting on my horse at the head of the column. . . . An Irish woman rushed out of her hut in the camp of the 6th Regt., in demi-toilette, with her red shock of hair unkempt and disorded, and coming up to me, raised her long, bony arms to Heaven and fervently called upon the Almighty to cover me with His shield in the day of battle and preserve me from the hands of the enemy. Though the woman was hideously ugly, there was an earnestness and solemnity in her manners that produced a profound impression on the minds of all who saw and hear her. She was a laundress in my Father's Regt. & revered his memory—hence her blessing upon me.[41]

According to the 7th Louisiana's Private Caldwell, the men received no rations before being ordered to advance to the railroad under artillery fire. While the rest of the brigade remained there, Col. William Monaghan took his 6th Louisiana out to the rifle pits at the river's edge under intense artillery and rifle fire to aid the 13th Georgia in delaying the enemy's crossing. Captain F. J. Montgomery's Moore Fencibles of the 9th Louisiana advanced, as well, to act as sharpshooters. The Georgians, however, soon exhausted their ammunition and left the Tigers to dispute the landing alone. As the skirmish fire increased, General Jackson rode out to Monaghan's position to check on the situation. The federal balls whistled through the air, and the Tigers feared the general would be hit, but after calmly surveying the river he cased his binoculars and rode back to the main line unhurt.[42]

Forno's 5th Louisiana was soon sent in to reinforce Monaghan, and together they stubbornly contested the laying of the bridges. From his position at the railroad, Captain Seymour watched the two regiments stand their ground. "The noble fellows strove manfully to hold their position and keep the enemy from effecting a crossing and caused many a Yankee to bite the dust by their cool and well directed fire." Once again, the Tigers were facing the Union's Iron Brigade which rowed across the river in small boats to establish a beachhead to protect the engineers laying the pontoon bridges. One Yankee claimed that the "water fairly boiled" from the Tigers' rifle fire, but the boats finally landed and the federals jumped out and climbed up a ravine to drive the rebels away.[43]

By 10:00 a.m. the Tigers' wounded filled the rifle pits, and eighteen-year-old Nathan Cunningham, color-bearer for the 5th Louisiana, laid down his flag and volunteered to return to the rear to bring them fresh water. As he departed, the federals effected a landing below the Louisianians' position and moved into their rear. The order to withdraw was yelled over the roaring battle, but the men on the far flanks failed to hear it and remained in the trenches long after the others fell back. One member of the Iron Brigade wrote that the Tigers were "gobbled" up as they retreated, and another claimed, "It was amusing to see our men too rush on. Two of them pushed up the bank alone and took them out of the smaller pits; they would only take their muskets away from them, tell them to run to the rear, and then, throwing down the captured muskets, rush on to the next pit." An officer in the 6th Louisiana claimed that the Yankees surrounded his company so quickly that only three men were able to make a run for it, and one of them was killed.[44]

Young Cunningham was racing back to the river with his canteens when he met his comrades heading for the rear and discovered that no one had thought to bring the regiment's flag. Ignoring his friends' advice to fall back with them, he ran to the rifle pits, passed the canteens to the wounded, and retrieved the colors. As he turned to go back, Cunningham found his path blocked by a company of federals who demanded that he surrender. When the young soldier bravely declared that he could never give up as long as he carried the regiment's flag, an impressed Union officer waved down his men's muskets and allowed the plucky youngster to continue on his way.[45]

Officially, the 5th and 6th Louisiana lost eighty-nine men along the river, with most of the casualties being taken prisoner, but that figure is probably low. James Gannon, a 6th Louisiana historian, has found evidence of seven dead, twelve wounded, and seventy-nine missing in that regiment alone. Among the captured were Lt. Col. Joseph Hanlon and Capt. Frank Clark, both of whom had just rejoined the regiment after being wounded at Winchester and Antietam, respectively. Clark was wounded again on the river bank, but he and the other Tigers had delayed the Yankees' river crossing for two hours.[46]

Rain set in during the afternoon and continued the next day, soaking the Tigers who were left exposed in their forward position. On the morning of April 30, the 7th Louisiana relieved the 5th Louisiana on the picket line, but the field remained quiet. Hays' brigade spent the next two days strengthening its works and, according to Captain Seymour, watching the federals "working like beavers on their fortifications." There was little firing except for opposing batteries that dueled with one another across the river. The only Louisiana casualties were the result of one federal shell that exploded in the 9th Louisiana and wounded two men, and a Confederate round that burst prematurely over the regiment and injured three more.[47]

By now, Confederate cavalry had informed Lee of Hooker's maneuver upstream. Realizing that Sedgwick was only a demonstration, Lee left Early's division and Gen. William Barksdale's brigade to watch him at Fredericksburg while the rest of the army hurried west to intercept Hooker. Fighting broke out around Chancellorsville on May 1 as Lee and Hooker collided in the Wilderness, an immense area of dense thickets. Neither side won an advantage, but the Confederates discovered that Hooker's right flank was unprotected and vulnerable to attack. In a hurried conference that night, Lee agreed to leave the divisions of McLaws and Anderson along Hooker's front while Jackson took his entire corps on a circuitous route to the left to strike the federal flank.

It took most of May 2 for Jackson's men to make the long march, but he was finally in position by 6:00 p.m. Jackson deployed his corps in three one-mile-long lines, with Gen. Robert Rodes' division in the front line; Gen. Raleigh Colston, who now commanded Jackson's old division, in the second; and A. P. Hill in the third. Nicholls' brigade was in Colston's division, and the 2nd Louisiana's William Clegg wrote that after a day-long forced march the brigade got into position about an hour before sundown. Clegg claimed they were given no rest before being ordered forward through "the thickets and most difficult bushes to get through I ever saw." The rebels advanced blindly, guided only by the Orange Turnpike, until they suddenly burst out of the woods onto the unguarded federal flank. Jackson's men completely surprised and routed

Gen. Oliver O. Howard's XI Corps just as it was preparing supper. The 14th Louisiana's William Snakenberg recalled that "many of them never got their guns and ran like sheep and we after them until dark. They were kind enough in their hurry to leave us all of their provisions, partly cooked only, but we did not then have time to stop to eat any." Apparently, discipline in the 2nd Louisiana was not as strict because Clegg wrote that the men helped themselves to the Yankees' abandoned suppers.[48]

It was not until a half-hour after the attack began that the federals began making defensive stands in some rifle pits. Clegg recalled that "the musketry was very heavy and continuous," but the rebels quickly drove the enemy back. The Yankees fled for two miles, unable to halt the onslaught until they reached the Union artillery around the Chancellor House. There they put up a stubborn defense until darkness ended the first day's fight.[49]

The three Confederate battle lines had merged into one during the headlong charge and were a confused mass of men milling about when the fighting ended at dark. Some semblance of order was attained about 8:00 p.m., and the rebels began moving forward along the turnpike in bright moonlight. Suddenly, Union artillery opened fire from close range, and screaming shells raked the road. Men and horses were blown apart, soldiers panicked and began firing wildly, and horses galloped blindly through the regiments. One Virginian recalled that the artillery fire was "the most terrific and destructive shelling that we were subjected to during the war. We could hear someone scream out every second in the agonies of death."[50]

William Clegg was caught in the barrage and later wrote, "[W]hen the shells & grape shot came tearing through the ranks the scene is indescribable. the men seemed almost panic stricken, the groans & shrieks of the wounded was heart rending artillery horses riderless came thundering back with pieces & caissons. horsemen dashing about, shells bursting in the ranks & grape shot tearing through the woods all combined presented a most horrible spectacle." Lieutenant Colonel Burke managed to get the men of his 2nd Louisiana to lie on the ground, where they were relatively safe from the shelling. Clegg recalled that when the order "steady Second" was passed down the line "every man was upon his face in a minute at his proper place. . . . I have been under a good many shellings but that was the most severe of any."[51]

General Nicholls was mounted on his horse and trying to bring order to his confused brigade when a solid shot ripped through his mount's abdomen and tore off his left foot. The general managed to throw himself free from his horse when it collapsed, but he lay unnoticed in the cluttered road while shells and canister whizzed overhead. When the barrage finally lifted, ambulance crews searched for the wounded but were forced to crawl around in the dark because the enemy fired at any visible lanterns. Some of them found Nicholls a half-hour after he was hit and began patting him down in the dark in search of wounds. When they found both his left arm and foot were missing, they apparently believed he was mortally wounded and left him in the road. Fearing he would soon bleed to death, Nicholls felt his leg but "found to my utter surprise that the wound did not bleed at all." After a long wait, some Tigers finally discovered the general, wrapped him in a blanket, and carried him to the rear. Nicholls recovered from his wound but never returned to the brigade, serving, instead, in various administrative positions.[52]

Although the day's fighting had gone extremely well for the Confederates, the loss in field-grade officers had been high with Gens. A. P. Hill and Jackson being wounded about the same time Nicholls lost his foot. Some North Carolina troops reportedly shot Jackson when they mistook him and his entourage for the enemy as they returned from a nighttime reconnaissance. In 1901, however, former Louisiana Tiger Frank S. Rosenthal claimed that he wounded Stonewall. According to Rosenthal, twenty Louisiana soldiers were on the picket line that night under orders to let no one pass even if they knew the countersign, which was "I don't know." Not long after taking up their positions, a group of horsemen rode down the Tigers' line, responded with the proper countersign, and turned to enter the lines. Following orders, Rosenthal and eight other Tigers opened fire and hit Jackson three times. There is no record of a Rosenthal serving in Nicholls' brigade at that time, but that is not unusual. Some veterans ridiculed Rosenthal's story, but his claim that Jackson rode parallel to the line before being shot does match the historical record. Also, the 2nd Louisiana's William Lichenstein lent some credence to the story when he wrote that he was within twenty feet of Jackson when he was wounded.[53]

General J. E. B. Stuart took command of Lee's left wing after Jackson's wounding and realigned the divisions to continue the push at daybreak. Colonel Jesse M. Williams, having recovered from the chest wound he received at Antietam, replaced the wounded Nicholls and led the brigade when it was put on the far left of Colston's line. By dawn on Sunday, May 3, Stuart had

Hill's division in front, with Colston and Rodes in support. The 2nd Louisiana's Clegg wrote, "Next morning by sunup tired & as sleepy as we were, we went at it & were fighting all day, driving them from their rifle pits." When the advance began at 6:00 a.m., Hill quickly made contact with the enemy and touched off a roaring battle. Colston's division was soon called up and advanced past Hill's bloodied men straight into the heavy Union fire coming from around Chancellor's Hill. Colonel Williams' men became hotly engaged in a close-quarter fight with the 7th New Jersey and had five color-bearers of the 10th Louisiana killed in the smoky thicket. The 2nd Louisiana's Pvt. Richard Knight, an Irish immigrant, was also killed while holding a Union flag that he apparently had captured. In turn, the 7th New Jersey claimed to have seized the 1st Louisiana's flag when the Union soldiers flanked the Tigers and forced them to fall back two hundred yards. Fortunately for Williams, the Yankees failed to press their advantage, and he had time to place his brigade behind some abandoned Union breastworks before the next attack came.[54]

The Louisianians had just settled in when they caught glimpses of Union soldiers easing toward them through the underbrush, and the woods exploded again as the Tigers and Yankees exchanged volleys of musketry. The enemy's fire began arching around the Tigers' left as the federals tried to flank them, but the 2nd Louisiana matched the maneuver and protected the brigade's flank by bending back perpendicular to the main line in a tactic known as "refusing the line." The federals were then content to keep their distance and trade long-range shots with the Tigers. By then Williams' ammunition was almost gone and the men were beginning to give way, but Gen. Alfred H. Colquitt's brigade came running through the woods to reinforce them. Despite their dwindling ammunition, the Tigers surged forward with Colquitt's men against Gen. Erastus Tyler's Union brigade. The Pennsylvanians put up a stubborn fight, killing one Tiger when he grabbed a battle flag and shooting off Colonel Pendleton's finger. Eventually, the Yankees were forced back through the forest, which by now was engulfed in brush fires caused by the flaming muskets and exploding artillery shells.[55]

The Tigers were then pulled out of line and sent to the rear to replenish their cartridge boxes and eat lunch. After only a few hours' rest, however, they were ordered to join the division for yet another attack. Once again Williams was placed on the far left of the line and sent against a battery of twelve Union guns that was posted on a hilltop with infantry support. The brigade gamely pressed forward, but murderous rounds of artillery fire tore into the men when they emerged into a field three hundred yards from the enemy position. One soldier claimed the 10th Louisiana was particularly hard hit by "a perfect storm of grape and shells." The regiment lost fifty men in less than ten minutes and had its sixth color-bearer of the day killed. Before the battle was over, six more of the regiment's color-bearers would die.[56]

One shell ripped open Scotsman John M. Legett, the 10th Louisiana's unpopular colonel, and almost tore him in half. Incredibly, he lived long enough to ask some of his men for forgiveness of his shortcomings and to receive their assurances that they held no ill will against him. Lieutenant Colonel Henry Monier assumed command of the battered regiment, which had begun to falter under the deadly fire. The entire brigade might have broken and run had it not been for the courageous efforts of General Colston and the regimental officers who held the men in line. Soon, however, Colonel Williams realized that it was suicidal to hold his position any longer and ordered the brigade to pull back into the woods and entrench.[57]

After scratching out some makeshift earthworks, the Louisianians were stunned to see just how fierce the federal musketry had been. Charles and J. M. Batchelor of the 2nd Louisiana both counted five holes in their clothing and skin. The latter wrote home, "I was struck five times and once a ball flattened on my sword belt buckle (which would have gone through my stomach) which I have and will send to you by the first opportunity, the 2nd ball cut the skin of my throat. A third on my left cheek the fourth through my coat on my side fifth through the fleshy part of my hand inflicting a severe flesh wound." A canister shot struck Batchelor's brother Charlie in the back during the withdrawal, but the spent ball did no damage after passing through his knapsack. A bullet also tore through his blanket roll and knapsack only to be deflected by a small box he had snatched from a Yankee's knapsack. Other Tigers poked fingers through similar holes in their blanket rolls and slouch hats and marveled at their good fortune.[58]

The Batchelors' regimental comrade, Charles C. Davenport, was not as fortunate. Although slightly wounded in the foot by a shell the night before, he went into battle on May 3 and was blinded by a bullet that went through his right eye and out his left temple. Davenport was left behind when the regiment was driven back, but he was found the next evening lying in a small stream. He survived the horrific wound and wrote, "My coat was almost burned off me, having caught fire from the battle field. . . . I have a faint recollection of the Federals coming to me while I lay on the battle ground and searching my pockets." Davenport never regained his sight.[59]

Lieutenant Seton of the 10th Louisiana was among the missing. He was shot in the right calf in the first charge that morning and was captured when the brigade was forced to fall back to its breastworks. Seton wrote his sister, "I was left between both fires for along while until a Yankee came & got me out. I was verry glad for not three hours after the woods caught on fire & burnt a great many the Yankees treated me kindly while I was in their hands."[60]

About a month later, Seton wrote his mother about the battle: "Our company stood on the field the last & fought with the Yankees at 30 yards distance they [the company] did not leave until I told them to go." Seton then cautioned his mother, "you must not say anything & I will [name] you the boys who runned & was not in the co. at the fight." He then named two soldiers who ran away, one of whom "has always runned." But Seton also mentioned those who stood with him under the terrific fire. One was "poor Jim Reeves," who was killed standing next to Seton. When Reeves fell, Seton picked up his rifle to give to Frederick Sark, a German immigrant whose musket had misfired, but when he turned around Sark was also dead. Sadly, Reeves' younger brother, John, was shot in the face and permanently blinded while standing alongside Jim. At almost that same moment, John Reeves' wife died in childbirth back in Louisiana. The Reeves' last brother, Isaac, was killed two months later at Gettysburg.[61]

The Tigers remained in their works and skirmished with the federals throughout the night of May 3 and all of May 4. During this lull, the smoke cleared from the woods and they were able to see the ghastly fate of many of their comrades. One Virginian who walked through the thickets where the Louisianians faced Tyler's brigade wrote years later:

> I witnessed the most horrible sight my eyes ever beheld. . . . The scene beggers description. The dead and badly wounded from both sides were lying where they fell. The woods, taking fire that night from the shells, burnt rapidly and roasted the wounded men alive. As we went to bury them we could see where they had tried to keep the fire from them by scratching the leaves away as far as they could reach. But it availed not; they were burnt to a crisp. The only way we could tell to

which army they belonged was by turning them over and examining their clothing where they lay close to the ground. . . . It was the most sickening sight I ever saw during the war.[62]

Father Sheeran examined the entire eight miles of battle lines and claimed the part occupied by the Tigers "was the most shocking of all." Raging fires "for nearly half a mile burned the dead bodies and many of the wounded to a crisp."[63]

While the 2nd Louisiana Brigade fought in Chancellorsville's thickets, Hays' brigade was helping to hold the precarious line at Fredericksburg. Early's division was stretched along the hills overlooking the town, but the thin gray line was manned by an average of only one soldier every twenty feet. After Lee departed for Chancellorsville, these badly outnumbered Confederates kept up a brave front by constantly shifting units, cheering nonexistent reinforcements, and lighting thousands of campfires at night to inflate their numbers.

On May 2, Hays placed the 6th and 9th Louisiana near Barksdale's Mississippi brigade on Marye's Heights in the rear of Fredericksburg while the 5th, 7th, and 8th regiments dug in on the right at Hamilton's Crossing. As the sun slowly set, a deep rumble could be heard toward Chancellorsville, where Jackson was making his flank attack, but at dusk the sound of the distant battle was drowned out by a lively skirmish that erupted between the 7th Louisiana and a federal unit.[64]

Soon after dawn on May 3, Barksdale reported that the Yankees were moving out of town toward his position. To shore up this threatened point, Early ordered Hays to double-quick his men from Hamilton's Crossing to the Confederate left. The 6th and 9th Louisiana had departed Barksdale's front at 3:00 that morning to rejoin the brigade and now had to turn around and march back again. Following the trench line, the Tigers began the eight-mile jaunt as the sun ushered in a warm spring day. Soon scores of men began falling out from exhaustion and heat stroke, and others were struck down by federal shells that peppered the column from across the river. As the brigade passed behind Barksdale's command, Colonel Monaghan's 6th Louisiana was dropped off to take up a position on the Mississippians' right and in front of the New Orleans Washington Artillery. One Tiger wrote, "On going into the trenches we found we had so large a space to cover that we were placed in one rank, with an interval of about a pace between the men." Only two hundred Tigers were still with Hays when he finally reached the Confederate left. One soldier recalled that the men were "Breathless, drenched with perspiration and utterly fagged-out" when they collapsed into the rifle pits just as the federals launched their attack.[65]

From atop their hill, the Tigers had a spectacular view of the enemy's advance and watched as the blue lines swept toward Marye's Heights. They were soon broken up by the Washington Artillery and Barksdale's brigade, the latter being positioned behind the stone wall made famous in the first Battle of Fredericksburg. The 9th Louisiana's J. R. Williams later wrote that "our Brave Boys Shot them Down by the hundreds." Smoke boiled up above the battle, and the shouts and firing of the combatants carried over the field as far as Hays' position. Twice the rebels cut down the Union soldiers before the wall, but on the third try they rushed in without stopping and clubbed Barksdale's men back. Suddenly, the entire Confederate line collapsed, and Barksdale's Mississippians were driven up the slope. Monaghan's Tigers had to abandon their exposed position, as well, and lost twenty-seven men captured as they fled before the victorious Yankees.[66]

After the battle, the Confederates claimed that the federals took the position after violating a truce to collect their wounded. The Mississippians reportedly allowed a Union officer to get too close to Barksdale's line, and he was able to see how thin the Confederates were spread and that a ravine on Barksdale's right had been left unguarded. When the Yankees made their third attack, they swarmed up the ravine and took the rebels by surprise. A soldier in the 6th Louisiana reported, "We were so intent watching the enemy in our front that we did not discover them on our flank and rear until it was almost too late. The brave boys of the Washington Artillery stood to their guns to cover the retreat, and actually poured two rounds of canister into the Yankee columns after the Stars and Stripes had been planted on the works." Many of the men in the Washington Artillery were captured, but they had played a critical role in helping the one thousand or so Confederates hold off approximately seventy-five hundred Yankees for so long.[67]

Although they were far from the action, Hays' men also had to beat a hasty retreat to prevent being cut off by the speedy federals. Meanwhile, Lee had dispatched General Wilcox from Chancellorsville to help the hard-pressed Early. Wilcox encountered Hays' retreating brigade and tried to convince Hays to join him in blocking the road west to Chancellorsville. Hays agreed that it would be a wise move but explained that he had to follow his orders to join

Early farther south on the Telegraph Road. Disappointed, Wilcox deployed his men across the Chancellorsville road alone, and Hays continued on to link up with Early.[68]

For a brief moment the road to Lee's rear was open, but Sedgwick chose to follow the retreating rebels southward instead. By the time he corrected this error and began moving west toward Chancellorsville, Sedgwick found Wilcox had blocked the road with his and other Confederate brigades that had been rushed back to Fredericksburg. By nightfall Lee was in control of the Chancellorsville battlefield and dispatched McLaws' and Anderson's divisions to join Early. Private Williams recalled that the news of the reinforcements "flew like lightning along our lines. a New life had Sprung up in us."[69]

On the afternoon of May 4, the three Confederate divisions had Sedgwick's corps hemmed in against the Rappahannock River. On the Confederate right, Hays' brigade was in the center of Early's line, facing a Union-occupied hill, and waited impatiently for orders to attack. One member of the 6th Louisiana wrote, "We maneuvered around until the afternoon, when, finally we thought, we had the enemy in a trap, and anticipated a complete bagging arrangement, but we found out afterwards that the bag had a hole in it." During the day Lee arrived on the field to take charge, and the 9th Louisiana's J. R. Williams wrote that he "Rode along our lines looking as calm as though Nothing unusual [w]as going on. . . . [W]e all Knew there was a grand Move on foot for Gen Lee Himself Superintended the forming of our lines." Lee, Early, and Hays then held a conference next to the Tigers to discuss the necessity of taking the hill in Hays' front. A 6th Louisiana soldier reported, "Gen. Lee asked who had a brigade that could do it. Gen. Hays, it is said, promptly announced that he had a brigade that would charge Hell, but I doubt it, the General [Lee] being a pious man."[70]

Lee finally decided to make the attack. One Tiger claimed that, as word spread among the other units, "we consequently had hundreds of spectators, among whom were Gen. Lee and staff, several newspaper reporters, etc." Hays placed the 7th and 9th Louisiana on the left under his command and the 8th, 5th, and 6th on the right under Colonel Forno. At about 4:00 p.m. the booms of three cannons echoed over the hills to signal the attack. Private Williams remembered that at that moment the order was given to cap muskets and fix bayonets. "That convinced the men that the Ball was about to open." Some Union prisoners who were standing nearby later told one of the men that "they know hot work was coming when they saw us obey that order."[71]

In loud, clear voices, Hays and Forno yelled, "Forward, double-quick!" and the brigade sprang forward with what was described as "a cheer as Louisianians alone can give." One Tiger claimed the men clawed their way up the steep slope, screaming "like a legion of 50 ton locomotives." "Our boys were so eager to go," wrote Sergeant Stephens, "[they] were more like a pack of pampered negro dogs just lost from the halter on a fresh track. They went not at a double quick but as hard as they could run, squalling & hollering as loud as they could ball . . . every man for himself and Old Yank got up and dusted, leaving things behind as they went."[72]

Captain Pierson wrote his father:

> The yankees could not stand the La. yell but broke before we got within long range distance of them. They were posted in a very strong position, having a long chain of hills in their rear, and a road which formed an excellent breast work besides several fences which would have afforded sufficient shelter . . . all these they ran off and left in the most shameful and confused style. They ran before we got in sight of them. Even the yell of the demon Louisianans as they call us was more than they could bear; all the pris[o]ners who were captured said they knew that we were the La. boys as soon as we screamed. They said they had rather fight a whole Division of Virginians than one of the La. brigades.[73]

Hays' men pressed on, and the federal line melted away. As they advanced, the Louisianians snatched ammunition from the Yankee dead and plundered their bodies. One Tiger declared, "Their well-packed knapsacks furnished us with clean shirts and socks, both of which we needed badly." The federals fell back half a mile to a sunken road that was lined by a chest-high brush fence. Jumping over the fence into the eight-foot-deep roadbed, they then clawed and struggled to get up the other side. Henry Handerson of the 9th Louisiana was close on their heels and jumped over the brush, as well, even though he did not know what was on the other side. Landing hard in the roadbed, he found himself surrounded by a group of startled Union soldiers. Handerson wrote, "It is hard to say which of us was most surprised, and for a moment I thought my time had come." Fortunately for Handerson, more Tigers followed suit, and the Yankees quickly surrendered and "gladly obeyed" their orders to head to the rear. Other Union soldiers tried to make a stand farther up the hill, but one of the Tigers claimed "they did not wait till we got up, but merely satisfied themselves that we were really coming, and off they went again, the boys after them, shrieking at them as a steam car does when a cow is on the track."[74]

Hays and Forno stayed with the men and continued to urge them forward. One Tiger described the officers' conduct as being "splendid": "[T]hese men surely know no fear. They seemed to be everywhere at once—in the road, where the shell from Stafford Heights seemed to fairly sweep everything before it, they galloped up and down, urging the men up the other side. Col. Forno's fierce voice could be heard above the yells, carrying a [*illegible*] every command. Both, with steeds covered with foam, would, where the line appeared to slack from exhaustion, dash to it, and with words of cheer urged the men to keep up, that they were driving the enemy. Away they would start again. . . . Their actions and words infused a confidence in the men, that few men have the faculty of imparting."[75]

After reaching the top of the hill, the Tigers swarmed over an open plateau toward a third Union line drawn up on an even higher hill covered with felled trees. Sergeant Stephens claimed that the men had lost all organization in the long charge, and the brigade now "formed simply a howling, rushing and firing mob." Hays' brigade had rushed so far ahead of its sister units by then that the Tigers' comrades were actually firing into them from the flank and rear. One newspaper reporter wrote that Hays' men had "walked over the enemy as giants over pigmies," but the brigade then collided with Col. Lewis Grant's fresh Vermont Brigade, dug in behind strong breastworks of knapsacks and felled trees. A year earlier, the Vermont Brigade had fought it out with the 2nd Louisiana at Dam Number One and the 5th Louisiana at Savage's Station. Now it waited until the Louisianians were within twenty feet before rising up and delivering a staggering pointblank volley of musketry. For the first time, Hays' men halted their advance to fire back. One Tiger recalled that, after dragging himself over deep gullies and felled timber to reach this last Yankee line, "to stand and fight was a rest that was truly refreshing."[76]

Thousands of muskets and three batteries of artillery opened fire on the Tigers, one shell alone killing and wounding seventeen men in the 9th Louisiana. "Such a scene as ensued never entered my imagination," declared Stephens. "A wall of fire on three sides. The air was fairly hissing with round shot, shell, grape, canister and minie balls."[77] Watching from the rear, another soldier claimed, "The enemy opened everything they have on us at once. Their missiles ploughed the ground in front [of us] as we advanced as though an earthquake [was] about to bury us alive. The shells burst over our heads, and the fire from the thousands of small arms, caused such a cloud of smoke that until the men advanced further nothing could be seen of them. I thought that they [Tigers] had been swept from the face of the earth at one blast, but hearing that unearthly yell, I knew that they had not faltered, and [that] they had no such intention."[78]

In fact, Hays' brigade had actually shot its bolt by this time, and the Vermont Brigade cut it to pieces. One soldier in the 2nd Vermont wrote, "[T]heir dead covered the ground as grey as a badger in front of us." Some of the Tigers tried to flank the enemy, but artillery firing canister ripped them apart. The Vermont soldier claimed, "The air was full of arms and pieces of men blown to pieces. . . . They fairly melted like dew on the grass in the noon day sun." When Grant's brigade finally fell back across a field, the die-hard Tigers chased after them. According to the Vermont soldier, they "came on mad with joy till the field in our front was literally covered with them." Another Union soldier claimed that the 12-lb. Napoleons tore through the Louisianians' ranks and "piled the dead and wounded knee deep to the horses."[79]

By now half of Hays' men had dropped out from exhaustion. To escape the Yankees' rapid fire, some soldiers hugged the ground behind captured Union breastworks, while others hid in the numerous gullies that cut through the hillside. Finally, the Tigers began giving way and retreating toward their own lines. Some were shot down as they ran, but many others were so tired they simply collapsed and were captured. The 9th Louisiana's exhausted Colonel Stafford was seized when he sat down on a log, gasping for breath, and Colonel Grant personally nabbed the 7th Louisiana's Colonel Lewis, who sullenly handed over his sword.[80]

Early and Lee watched the attack from a high hill and became ecstatic when they saw the Tigers break through the first two enemy lines. Early grabbed his hat, threw it to the ground, and yelled, "Those damned Louisiana fellows may steal as much as they please now!" Lee simply clasped his hands together and sighed, "Thank God! the day is ours." Their elation was short-lived, however, because Hays' charge was broken up on the last hill, and the other Confederate brigades failed in their attempts to break Sedgwick's line. Nonetheless, according to Private Williams, General Lee declared that "it was the grandest Charge Made in this war." Early entertained the thought of renewing the attack and rode out to meet Hays as he was reforming the remnants of his brigade, but darkness and the complete disarray of the Confederate units dashed any hope for a second assault.[81]

Captain Pierson believed Early made the right decision because the Tigers were in no condition for a second attack. "Most of the men are entirely broken down having been under arms for eight days in succession and having neither rested nor slept but little during the whole time. Many men fainted by the wayside and had to be borne off the field by the litter bearers. This has been one of the most trying times I have ever witnessed since I have been out. . . . Still they bear it all almost without a murmer."[82]

The Chancellorsville Campaign ended when both Sedgwick and Hooker withdrew safely across the Rappahannock, leaving Lee's men to bury the dead and collect the wounded. The two Louisiana brigades accounted for about 10 percent of Lee's 10,281 casualties. In the deadly thickets around Chancellorsville, Nicholls lost 47 killed, 265 wounded, and an unreported number of missing, with 48 officers being among the lost. In the six days that Hays confronted Sedgwick's corps at Fredericksburg, he lost 63 men killed, 306 wounded, and approximately 300 captured, or about 45 percent of the 1,500 men who started the battle. Fortunately, nearly all of those who were captured were exchanged within a month and returned to their units.[83]

Most of the Louisiana wounded were taken to the Louisiana Hospital in Richmond, which a reporter for the Richmond *Examiner* visited a month later.

> Nearly all the beds are occupied by some maimed and disabled defender of his country. Among them are a number of very serious and interesting cases, three of which struck us particularly. One has both eyes forever destroyed by a ball, and another has a wound penetrating both liver and right lung, and the third is suffering from a most serious vessical wound. These cases, we were informed, are rare, and generally fatal, but it is the opinion of the Surgeon in charge that they will recover. Not a single death has yet occurred. . . . Citizens should recollect that these men have successfully exposed their forms as a barrier between the foe and this city, with its homes and property. Men there are languishing in the hospitals who have only been horribly mutilated, but who have lost all but life in the country's service. It is certainly not now too much to

ask that they be not forgotten by the Government, and cared for by the people, their valor helped to save from vandal invasion.[84]

The heavy casualties among field-grade officers once again forced the Army of Northern Virginia to undergo a reorganization. The greatest loss was that of General Jackson, who lingered for several days before dying from complications from an amputated arm. To the Tiger's delight, Lee chose General Ewell to replace the fallen Stonewall as their corps commander. Sergeant Stephens wrote that Ewell "was the choice of all the soldiers as well as the officers," and Sergeant Fogleman claimed that, when the men learned the news, "We gave him three cheers."[85]

General Edward Johnson eventually replaced Colston as commander of Jackson's old division, and a new III Corps was formed around the divisions of Richard Anderson, Henry Heth, and William D. Pender and placed under A. P. Hill. Then there was the task of choosing General Nicholls' successor. Hill recommended Colonel Forno, but that officer was transferred to Mobile for recruitment duty and then retired from the army in 1864. Edmund Pendleton had commanded the brigade temporarily while at Fredericksburg, but he apparently had not impressed his superiors. Pendleton, Lee reported, "is not highly considered, and its [Louisiana Brigade] service, I fear, will be lost to the army" if he was promoted. Other officers were rejected, as well, so the matter was left unresolved, and the 2nd Louisiana's Col. Jesse M. Williams remained in temporary command.[86]

Despite the Confederates' impressive victory at Chancellorsville, Jackson's death depressed the army. "The loss of no one man of our Confederacy would be more lamented than that of this great and good man," wrote W. B. Colbert. Sergeant Stephens echoed this sentiment when he reported that Jackson's death "cast a gloom throughout this Army and peticularly in this Corps, for he was our Comd. Gen'l. and we had every confidence in him." Many Tigers attended Rev. Beverly Tucker Lacy's funeral service on May 17 at Jackson's former headquarters. The text for the moving service came from II Timothy 4:6–8 with verse 7 being the main theme: "I have fought a good fight, I have finished my course, I have kept the faith." Afterward, Captain Pierson wrote that the sermon "caused many veteran soldiers to shed a tear. This army is wrapped in mourning and sad are the countenances of everyone at the mention of the great hero's name."[87]

The Tigers seem to have had different opinions on how Jackson's death would affect the war effort. Some, like the 9th Louisiana's J. R. Williams, did not think it would make a difference: "[T]he Enemy May think that Now Gen Jackson is Dead that they Can whip us but whenever they attempt it they will find that Though Jackson is Dead his Spirit is with his Men and whenever they go into Battle they will feel that the spirit of the Departed Hero is hovering over them and the bare Thought of him will incite them to Deeds of Daring that will adorn the Pages of history for time Immemorial. Dead Yes he May be Dead to Some People but he Never will be Dead to the army of Northern Virginia for he will live in the Hearts of his Men So long as one of them Continues to Breathe."[88]

On the other hand, Jackson's death and the slaughter at Chancellorsville and Fredericksburg shook the faith of some soldiers. Soon after Jackson's funeral, General Hays and several of his officers sat in a Richmond hotel room discussing with Gen. John Bell Hood and others the likely fate of the Confederacy. When J. H. Cosgrove asked Hays and Lieutenant Colonel Burke whether the Confederacy would survive, both "seemed to express a doubt, although they explained that it did not imply ultimate disaster." Chancellorsville had been a resounding victory, they said, but it resulted in no great military advantage. Hays also complained that the civilian government had assumed near-despotic power but still seemed unable to win the war. It could not even make good use of its available manpower because Longstreet's corps had been detached to Suffolk throughout the late campaign. For the first time, it appeared, the shadow of doubt was creeping into the minds of some Louisiana Tigers.[89]

CHAPTER 8

"Going Back into the Union at Last"

D ESPITE THE SHOCK OF JACKSON'S DEATH and the army's heavy losses at Chancellorsville, the Army of Northern Virginia was soon once again in excellent condition. Its manpower steadily increased in late May and early June as those soldiers who were captured in the Chancellorsville Campaign were exchanged, and the slightly wounded returned to duty. Captain Al Pierson reported that all of the men in his 9th Louisiana company who had been captured and all but 3 who had been wounded had returned by June 1. Fifty Tigers rejoined Hays' brigade on June 3 alone, and by mid-month the brigade had an impressive 137 officers and 1,495 men present for duty.[1]

While Hays' brigade rested at Hamilton's Crossing, it was visited by Louisiana's Sen. Thomas J. Semmes, whose brother Andrew served as Hays' brigade surgeon. Hays honored the senator by assembling the brigade to listen to him give a speech. When Semmes finished, the appreciative men applauded loudly, and then Hays made a few remarks. A newspaper reporter described the general's speech as a passionate one. "The affair was quite interesting—the feelings excited being the more heartfelt under the recollection that speakers and men were cut off from their homes, and far away from them were fighting the foe who had carried desolation and misery to those homes. Gen. Hays told them that though they had not the pleasure of fighting the enemy on their own soil, they could yet fight him here on a soil consecrated by the blood of a Seymour, a Wheat, and a host of brave Louisianians."[2]

With his army once again ready for battle, Lee decided to launch a second northern invasion that summer to relieve the enemy pressure on Virginia, disrupt any offensive plans Hooker might have, and encourage the northern peace movement by defeating the Union army on Union soil. The increased camp activity and orders to be prepared to move out at a moment's notice alerted the Tigers that something was brewing. One soldier wrote that when the men were instructed not to fish on picket duty "we knew that something would happen soon." The anticipated offensive began on June 3, and Capt. George Ring wrote home that he hoped this would be the "final campaign" to end the war.[3]

Lee ordered Ewell's corps to lead the way into Pennsylvania, but it first had to drive Gen. Robert H. Milroy's Union forces out of the Shenandoah Valley. Early's division broke camp on the night of June 4, and John Gordon's brigade lit large fires to hide the movement from Hooker's observation balloons across the Rappahannock River. The men were also forbidden to light fires on the first night of the march lest the enemy spot them. Ewell's corps marched rapidly through a sometimes drenching rain and quickly reached the Blue Ridge Mountains. Upon seeing the familiar heights, the men cheered when they realized they were heading back to the roads and towns they knew so well. One Virginia artilleryman wrote, "[W]e heard, at first indistinctly, toward the front of the column continued cheering. Following on, it grew louder and louder." Puzzled at first, the artilleryman realized the reasons for the cheers when he, too, saw the Blue Ridge ahead. "We had thought that the love for these old mountains was peculiar to us who had grown up among them; but the cheer of the [Louisiana] Creoles who had been with us under Jackson was as hearty as our own."[4]

As they passed through the mountains, several Louisianians dropped out of ranks to ask for a meal at a nearby farm. While conversing with the lady of the house, she revealed that some rowdy soldiers had passed by earlier—probably Louisianians, the woman declared. The Tigers said nothing until she asked from where they hailed. Thomas Reed recalled that when they replied, "Louisiana," the woman "turned pale as death, then she flushed up as red as scarlet. Then she would turn pale again, then red again." When she finally found her voice, the woman exclaimed, "I tell you the very name of [a] Louisiana soldier is a horror to me, and I hope while you are under my roof you will behave yourselves." They did.[5]

Pushing rapidly down the Valley, Early's and Rode's divisions surprised Milroy's men and by sundown on June 13 had pushed them back to Winchester. The Confederates approached the town from the south and began skirmishing with the enemy, but Milroy believed he was facing only a small harassing force and sent his cavalry out of a large fort to drive them off. One Confederate wrote that it was "one of the most splendid spectacles I have ever seen . . . with their shining swords drawn and other equipment reflecting the bright sunshine. They formed so as to occupy the entire width of the pike, intending to cut their way out by a sudden and overwhelming dash through our lines. . . . The rattle of their steel scabbards, the clanking of their spurs, and the noise of the iron shoes of their horses as they struck the hard surface of the pike were awe-inspiring."[6]

Colonel Stafford sent the 9th Louisiana's Moore Fencibles, who often acted as sharpshooters, out to a stone wall that ran near the road. Private Reed recalled the captain telling the men, "Now, boys, don't shoot until you hear the report of my pistol; then each man be sure he strips a saddle." When the Yankees trotted into range, the captain fired, and the men opened up with their muskets, knocking a half-dozen troopers off their horses and sending the rest galloping back to the fort. Unfortunately for the rebels, the cavalrymen managed to capture one Tiger who informed Milroy that both Ewell's and Longstreet's corps were near Winchester. Milroy now realized he was badly outnumbered, but he was unable to call for reinforcements because the rebels had cut the telegraph wires.[7]

After a night of drenching rain, Ewell continued his march to Winchester by sending Early's division down the Valley Pike, while Johnson's men followed the parallel Front Royal Road. The federal defensive works at Winchester were impressive. A huge earthen fort blocked the direct route into town, and a smaller redoubt known as the West Fort covered the approaches to the main fort from a hill northwest of Winchester. Colonel J. Warren Keifer commanded the West Fort and its garrison, which included the 110th Ohio, one company of the 116th Ohio, and six three-inch ordnance rifles of the 5th U.S. Artillery's Battery L. After studying Keifer's formidable defenses, Ewell decided the West Fort was the key to Winchester because its artillery commanded the main fort.[8]

Ewell left Gordon's brigade and the Maryland Line to demonstrate against Winchester while Early's other three brigades moved toward the left to capture the West Fort. Local guides led the men on a winding, but quick-paced, eight-mile hike to approach the bastion unseen. Because the day was brutally hot, the exhausted soldiers were allowed an hour's rest when they reached the attack position while Early, Hays, and Captain Seymour crept forward to get a better look at their target. After working their way to the edge of some woods, the officers were amazed to find that the Union sentinels were focused on Gordon's men skirmishing south of town and were completely ignoring their part of the field. The Confederates had done such a good job staying out of sight that Milroy believed the main enemy force had already bypassed him. One of Keifer's men later wrote, "Everything was quiet on Sunday the 14th. The boys were laying on the parapets in the sun. We came to the conclusion the confederates had all went to Church to get Religion, but they were only fixing to kill all of us."[9]

Hurrying back to his waiting men, Early ordered Hays to prepare for action while twenty pieces of artillery were rolled silently by hand into two fields flanking the woods. Hays' brigade would have the supporting fire of thirty cannons, but the 5th Louisiana's Capt. Samuel H. Chisholm claimed the officers did not know that at the time or even what the plan of action was until Hays called them together to discuss the attack. One anonymous Tiger recalled, "The scene was one of the most solemn and soul-stirring that occurred during the war," and Chisholm wrote, "I have never seen men look so serious, but we knew that General Hays would lead the charge and we were willing to follow. I stepped back to my company and ordered the boys to throw off their blankets, etc. and in a moment all hands knew that the ironclad brigade had to make good again its name." By 5:00 p.m., Hays had his Tigers in two lines, with the 7th Louisiana on the left, 9th in the center, and 6th on the right, and the 5th and 8th regiments in a second supporting line. The brigades of Isaac Avery and William Smith were farther in the rear to support the attack if necessary.[10]

Finally, at about 6:00 p.m., Early gave the signal and the roar of artillery made the ground tremble. One of the Ohio defenders recalled, "All at once, Oh! Here came a shower of shot and shell. The boys tumbled off the parapets like turtles drop off a log into the water." The small redoubt immediately disappeared from view as the shells tore huge craters in its earthen walls and kicked up geysers of dust and smoke. The federal cannons fired back, and for several minutes a deafening artillery duel ensued that could be heard for miles around. Hays claimed that Early's gunners quickly knocked out four of the six Union cannons and killed fifty horses, and that "scarcely a head was discovered above the ramparts." The federal artillerymen, in turn, mostly fired too high and inflicted little damage on the rebels.[11]

Taking advantage of the artillery cover, Hays led his men through the forest to the base of the hill. Although the Tigers were scarcely two hundred yards from the West Fort, the Yankees still could not see them because of the dust and smoke. Anxious to start the attack, Hays asked Early three times for permission to begin, but Early told him to wait until all of the federal guns had been knocked out of action. When Hays began taking sporadic enemy fire, he decided to launch the assault on his own initiative before the Yankees could concentrate their guns on him.[12]

With their colors flapping in the breeze, Hays' two lines of Tigers silently emerged from the woods. In a repeat of the previous year's battle at Winchester, groups of civilians clambered onto rooftops to watch the Louisianians tangle once again with the Yankees. Cavalryman Harry Gilmor was at Ewell's headquarters at the time and heard the attack begin. "[A]mid the thunders of thirty or forty guns, there broke on our expectant ears heavy volleys of musketry and the terrible, long, shrill cry of the . . . 'Louisiana Tigers.'" The two gray lines charged past Lizzie and Alma Yonley, who stood watching from the doorway of their farmhouse perched on the grassy slope. Years later Lizzie wrote of the thrill she felt as the Tigers rushed by "with banners flying and our own and the enemy's shells screaming over. . . . The storming of those breastworks was the grandest sight my eyes ever beheld." In 1900, the surviving Tigers presented Lizzie with a medal to honor her and Alma for caring for the Louisiana wounded after the battle. Among them was Pvt. Henry Caldwell, whose diary chronicles life in the 7th Louisiana.[13]

When Hays' yelping men reached the *abatis* protecting the fort, Early's artillery fell silent, and the five hundred Union defenders opened fire. Lorenzo Barnhart wrote, "They came in desperate order. We gave them a volley low down in their legs. They dropped out of ranks. We made large gaps in their lines, but they did not stop, for they closed the gaps shoulder to shoulder. . . . They had been in such scraps before." When James Stewart, the 9th Louisiana's color-bearer, fell dead from a ball through his head, Hays yelled, "Hoist those colors in the Ninth!" and the flag was grabbed up again. The Tigers pressed on and did not return fire until they were just twenty yards from the enemy. "They gave us a volley," Barnhart recalled, "then came onto us with bayonets and a yell like Indians." Stunned by the artillery barrage and with only two guns still in service, the federals were barely able to fire a couple of volleys before the rebels scaled the wall and jumped on top of them.[14]

Lieutenant John Orr of the 6th Louisiana and Maj. J. Moore Wilson, commander of the 7th Louisiana, were the first to enter the redoubt. Wilson was yelling, "Come on boys!" and Orr hacked away with his saber at the Union color guards until he was run through with a bayonet. Barnhart wrote, "They overcrowded us, but we made it hot for them for a moment. [We] were clubbing with the butts of guns, and thrusting the bayonet at and through each other. For a moment it looked like H——l." The Union gunners and some of the Ohio infantrymen fought valiantly around the cannons, but Lt. J. Warren Jackson of the 8th Louisiana claimed that most of the Yankees "were rather too nimble for us." Captain Samuel Chisholm agreed and wrote, "But few of them dared to cross bayonets with us, the balance outrunning quarterhorses. All those who stood their ground were soon rolling in their own blood and many who ran were shot in the back."[15]

After shooting the artillery horses to prevent the crews from taking away the guns, the Tigers proceeded to kill or capture the stubborn artillerymen. Working around the sixty-odd horse carcasses that littered the redoubt, some of the Tigers managed to turn the two working pieces around and fire several salvos at the fleeing enemy. In another small redoubt to the left, federal gunners tried to drag away their two guns but were foiled when a volley from the 7th Louisiana killed their horses. With the West Fort safely in hand, the Louisianians began helping themselves to the ample supply of coffee, soup, and bread abandoned by the Yankees. As the men enjoyed their meal, the 9th Louisiana's huge Col. William Raine Peck collapsed on the wall after struggling up the hill. Wheezing and gasping for breath, he drew cheers and laughter when he yelled, "Bully! Bully! by God! Bully!! for the old Ninth, by God!!"[16]

After the battle, the Louisiana Tigers were again honored for capturing the key to Winchester. Early wrote in his report, "The charge of Hays' brigade upon the enemy's works was a most brilliant achievement," and one of the Confederate artillerymen claimed, "Our command witnessed many great and gallant charges during the operations of the Army of Northern Virginia (including Pickett's at Gettysburg and the Irish Brigade at Fredericksburg) yet we were generally agreed that for intrepidity, steadiness, and all other qualities which made up the veteran soldier we never saw this charge excelled, even in Lee's army."[17]

Ewell was particularly impressed with the Louisianians. As he watched from a nearby hill, his view of the battle was obscured by the dust and smoke that hung over the West Fort. After the Tigers rushed into the works, Ewell could see small groups of Union soldiers fleeing out the back, but the struggle inside the bastion was hidden from view until a sudden breeze dramatically cleared the air. Ewell then saw the Tigers' flags flying from the parapets and yelled, "Hurrah for the Louisiana boys!" Captain Seymour remembered that Ewell was still "very profuse in his praise of our Brigade" several days later. Father Sheeran claimed that Ewell acknowledged "the daring courage displayed by [the Tigers] in storming and capturing the enemy's breastworks. He said, next to God he was indebted to them for the almost bloodless victory." To show his appreciation, Ewell issued orders for the hills west of Winchester to be named "Louisiana Ridge" or "Louisiana Heights" on all military maps. The people of Winchester also owed a debt of gratitude to the Tigers for liberating them twice during the war. They paid it on July 4, 1896, when a monument was dedicated to the sixty-nine Louisiana dead who were buried in the Stonewall Jackson Cemetery. Former Tiger general and Louisiana governor Francis T. Nicholls, various Louisiana veterans, and an estimated ten thousand people attended the ceremony.[18]

Despite having charged over open ground, Hays' casualties were moderate at twelve dead and sixty-seven wounded. Among the latter was the 6th Louisiana's Captain Ring, whose letters are some of the most informative written by any Tiger. He was wounded in the ankle and was out of action for six months. The Yankees lost about seventy men, plus the eight cannons that were captured. Milroy and the fort's commander later claimed that ten thousand rebels stormed the fort and that the Confederates lost four hundred men.[19]

With the West Fort in Confederate hands, Milroy realized that his main fort was now untenable. Anticipating the inevitable evacuation of Winchester that night, Ewell dispatched Johnson's division down the Martinsburg Pike to the rear of town to cut off the enemy's retreat. Temporarily commanded by Col. Jesse M. Williams, the 2nd Louisiana Brigade led the division down the dark road and arrived at Stephenson's Depot as the eastern sky began to glow. Johnson had just finished deploying his men behind a stone fence alongside the road when Milroy launched a vigorous attack to cut his way through the rebels. Johnson's men had depleted nearly all of their ammunition but were clinging stubbornly to the wall when they were subjected to thunderous cavalry charges on both flanks. Luckily, the Stonewall Brigade arrived in time to drive the cavalry back from Johnson's right flank, but Milroy and a thousand of his troopers continued to maneuver around the Louisiana regiments on the left. Seeing the enemy's cavalry slipping around their flank, Lt. Col. Ross

E. Burke and Maj. Thomas N. Powell led the 2nd and 10th Louisiana, respectively, along a parallel route to head them off. Henry Monier wrote that an intervening ridge separated the two columns for a short distance, but then the ground leveled out, and "after a race of about 200 yards we faced into line, jumped over a fence, fired into the enemy and charged."[20]

This deadly volley and supporting artillery fire broke up Milroy's formation and sent it fleeing back down the road. The federal retreat then became a rout when Johnson rode out and led the Tigers in pursuit. As he often did in battle, the general carried a heavy hickory club instead of a sword, a habit which led the soldiers to call him "Club" Johnson. The 2nd Louisiana's Pvt. Joseph Moreau captured a flag most likely belonging to the 67th Pennsylvania, and a member of the 10th Louisiana took another unidentified flag. A third Tiger caught one Union lieutenant and returned to his regiment with the officer's sword and pistol and nineteen of his men who had surrendered. At the cost of only a handful of casualties, Williams' brigade had captured about six hundred of the approximately two thousand Union prisoners taken at Stephenson's Depot.[21]

The first phase of Lee's invasion was now completed. Ewell's corps lost just 269 men in clearing Milroy's army from the Valley and opening the way to Pennsylvania. In addition, 28 cannons, 300 wagons, 4,000 prisoners, and a large number of small arms were also seized. To prepare them for the long march ahead, Lee allowed his hungry men free rein on much of the captured goods. Sergeant Stephens wrote his parents, "Such plundering of sutler wagons and all fancy notions of the Yankees. Our soldiers were just turned lose & told to go [to] it. I have as many nice clothing as I want, Sugar & coffee, rice & Everything else we wanted. I captured a fine lot of paper & Envelopes. I am writing to you on Yankee paper, pens, ink & envelopes."[22]

Within days of Milroy's rout, the confident Confederate army reached the Potomac River at Shepherdstown, and Hays' brigade had the honor of being the first infantry unit to cross over into Maryland. Watching from the bank, Captain Seymour laughed when the Tigers screamed and shouted "most boisterously" as they entered the cold water. "It was amusing," he wrote, "to see the long lines of naked men fording it—their clothing and accoutrements slung to their guns and carried above their heads to keep them dry." Nicholls' brigade was equally enthusiastic when it crossed later. Charles Batchelor wrote his father, "Never did soldiers appear more buoyant and cheerful than Lee's army" as it headed north. Forty years later, Col. David Zable asked a gathering of veterans, "Don't you remember with what confidence we entered into our enemy's country; how we believe[d] we could surmount every obstacle; that there was no foe we could not defeat; such was our faith in our commander and our power to do so."[23]

Lieutenant J. Warren Jackson of the 8th Louisiana claimed that, when they reached the Pennsylvania state line, "[We] shook Md dust off of our feet and marched into the union to the tune of 'Dixie.'" In a scene reminiscent of the previous year's incursion, scores of civilians stood alongside the road to watch the invaders pass by. Amused by their startled looks, Lieutenant Jackson said the Louisianians told them with a smile "that we had Eat up the last mule we had and had come over to get some beef & bacon. Others simply proclaimed that we were going back into the union at last." Southern Pennsylvania soon was swarming with haggard-looking rebels who destroyed bridges, railroad tracks, and government property and confiscated anything that might be useful.[24]

Ewell spread out his corps to cut as wide a swath as possible. The general accompanied Rodes' and Johnson's divisions (which included Nicholls' brigade) to Carlisle, Chambersburg, and Shippensburg, while Early marched on a parallel road to Greenwood, Gettysburg, and York. All along their route, the rebels helped themselves to Pennsylvania's bounty. The 2nd Louisiana's William Snakenberg recalled how the men ate the farmers' cattle and gorged themselves on ripe cherries that grew alongside the roads. His comrade Charles Batchelor wrote, "[N]ever did men fare more sumptuously than they up to the battle of Gettysburg—The people of Penn. gave apple butter, rich yellow butter, chickens, ducks and vegetables in abundance. This they always did apparently with cheerfulness only asking that their barns and dwellings could be spared. This we always did in fact we did them as little damage as possibly could be done. . . . Probably thirty thousand men were afflicted with sore mouth caused from want of fresh meat and vegetables before we marched into the state. It was not long however after we marched there before every man was in perfect health."[25]

While Pennsylvania's rich countryside was a popular topic in the Tigers' letters and memoirs, none of the extant sources mention the other commodity being confiscated—African Americans. The rebel army captured a large number of blacks, both runaway slaves and free people, and sent them back South to serve as slaves. Several Louisiana Tigers wrote about their time in Pennsylvania in great detail, so it is rather odd that they never discussed this aspect of the campaign. They must have known of the policy, but whether they never got the opportunity to capture blacks or just did not think it worth mentioning is not known. W. G. Loyd of the 2nd Louisiana recalled seeing only two African Americans during the campaign, and they were an old couple who stood on the side of the road as the brigade passed by. "One of my company asked the negro man if he was 'secesh,' and he replied 'Yes, sir, massa; I sees you now.'"[26]

Waynesboro was the first significant Pennsylvania town the rebels visited, and one resident described Early's division as it came down the street on June 23. "The soldiers were well armed, in perfect discipline and moved as one vast machine. Not many stragglers were to be seen. . . . The Southern soldiers were supposed to be uniformly clothed in grey, but not these soldiers who came through Waynesboro. Their dress consisted of every imaginable color and style. Some even wore blue clothes, which they had doubtless stripped from the Union dead in former battles. Most of them were of necessity ragged and filthy, showing that they were sadly in need of new outfits." John Arthur Taylor, who had joined the 8th Louisiana when he was just sixteen, described the reception Hays' brigade received: "[I]t was right touching to see how frightened the women were—some could be seen crying and wringing their hands, while others could be seen at a distance standing in crowds looking at us, with every appearance of fear, very much in the same manner as the wild beeves of Louisiana gather round a person creeping through the grass in hunting ducks."[27]

Sixteen-year-old Lida Welsh, however, discovered that the much-feared Louisiana Tigers did not live up to their fierce reputation. "The men all seemed cheerful. [S]poke kindly to the children on the porches; no doubt many of them were fathers of little ones. When a 2-year-old boy, left alone for a short time, stood on a rocking-chair and rocked with all his tiny strength until the chair moved along to the very edge of the porch, a dozen men broke ranks and rushed to save the little fellow." That evening, Hays' brigade camped at the end of Walsh's street, and she recalled hearing hundreds of Tigers "singing familiar old hymns." Other residents reported listening to rebel chaplains delivering sermons to the men.[28]

It appears that most of Waynesboro's people were pleasantly surprised at the rebels' good behavior. They could thank General Early for taking the precaution of closing all of the saloons while his division was in town. Many years later a local historian claimed that, while the town's residents greatly feared the Louisiana Tigers, "there is no record that the soldiers harmed any one along the line of march, but they needed food, and a chicken or a pig running at large was not safe during this invasion." One elderly resident recalled, "Those southern boys were polite and courteous but ragged and dirty." In fact, the men were so friendly that young girls readily engaged them in conversation and cherished as keepsakes the little knickknacks they received from the notorious Louisiana Tigers.[29]

Part of the reason for the Tigers' good behavior was Lee's orders that the men respect private property and pay for personal items with genuine, albeit worthless, Confederate money. For the most part, it appears the soldiers in the Army of Northern Virginia obeyed the order, and officers kept detailed records whenever horses, cattle, and other property were confiscated for the army. One civilian claimed that the Confederate officers "told our people that if they won the war, their government would pay their bills and redeem their currency in gold, but if they lost the war, the Federal government would be obliged to make settlement."[30]

Even the Louisiana officers seemed surprised at their men's lack of plundering. Lieutenant Jackson claimed that the Tigers "behave worse in Va. than they did in Penn.," and General Ewell wrote, "It is wonderful how well our hungry, foot sore, ragged men behave in this land of plenty—better than at home." Captain Seymour agreed and declared, "During our march the inhabitants were treated with the greatest kindness and consideration. . . . Everything that was taken for the use of the army was paid for, except in some cases when the tender of the money was refused. Stragglers would sometimes make predatory excursions into barnyards and dairies belonging to the persons who were disposed to be inimical and unaccommodating—this was unavoidable; but I did not hear of a single instance of a citizen being insulted or his property damaged."[31]

Unlike in past campaigns, some Tigers actually made good public-relations officers during the invasion. Father Sheeran wrote that the Pennsylvanians told him that the rebels' kind treatment of the civilians had gained them new friends, and one Virginian recalled watching a touching encounter between a young boy and a rough Louisiana Tiger. The boy rushed breathlessly up to his mother, crying, "Mother, Mother! May I go to the camp with the rebels? They are the nicest men I ever saw in my life. They are going to camp right out here in the woods, and they are going to have a dance, too!" Standing by the front gate was "a bowing, smiling, grimacing, shouldershrugging Frenchman" from Hays' brigade. In broken English, he promised the mother he would look after the boy. The woman had already seen the Virginian befriend her younger son, so she reluctantly consented. The soldier wrote years later how he watched the boy and his Tiger chaperone disappear down the road: "If the brigade did have the dance, then the lad saw what was really worth seeing, for if there was anything Hays' Creoles did and loved to do better than to fight, it was to dance, and their camp stag dances, sandwiched in between a big march and a big battle were said to be the most 'utterly utter' performance in the way of faunlike pranks that grown and sane men ever engaged in."[32]

Of course, not all of Waynesboro's citizens looked kindly upon the Tigers. A member of the 7th Louisiana discovered just how frightened some of the locals were when he walked into a home and politely asked if he could have some food. The mistress of the house agreed and told him to be seated and she would prepare a meal. While busying herself in the kitchen, she made light conversation and asked the soldier to what regiment he belonged. When the man replied "Seventh Louisiana!" the woman passed out. The Tiger rushed to her side and was kneeling over her when the husband walked in. He angrily demanded an explanation, and the shocked Tiger told him of their short conversation. The husband then relaxed and revealed the cause of his wife's fright. The Confederate cavalry had galloped through town a short time before and informed everyone "that the La. Tigers would kill, burn & destroy everything & every body in the country."[33]

Charles Batchelor and John Taylor had similar experiences when dealing with the Pennsylvanians. According to Batchelor, the citizens readily gave food to passing soldiers, "only asking that their barns and dwelling be spared." Taylor wrote his father that the men had no trouble getting food from the people because they were so frightened that "they told the boys they might have everything they had, if they would only not destroy their property. It seems they were told by the authorities of the State that if we ever came over there we would burn everything we could lay our hands on." Some of Early's men even went out of their way to promote their savage reputation. A few days later when Hays' and Robert Hoke's brigades marched through York, the Tigers and Tar Heels overheard a group of children ask their father, "Why Papa I thought the Rebs had horns, where are they?" Turning toward them as they passed, the soldiers jabbed their bayonets at the children and scowled, "Here are our horns!"[34]

Early's division left Waynesboro early on the morning of June 24 and marched sixteen miles to Greenwood, where it rested the next day. Resuming the march on June 26, the men then headed for Gettysburg. Along the way, Early ordered the destruction of abolitionist Thaddeus Stevens' ironworks, which was located between Greenwood and Cashtown. Besides railroads, the Caledonia Iron Works was one of the few instances where the rebels deliberately destroyed a large amount of private property.[35]

Gordon's brigade and a detachment of cavalry led the march and drove some Union militia out of Gettysburg before the rest of the division arrived late in the day. Hays' brigade camped about a mile northwest of the town, which Fogleman described as being "beautiful." Resident Fannie Buehler claimed that, except for a little looting and a few stolen horses, "so far as could be done, the officers controlled their men." Controlled or not, the Tigers still managed to create a stir. Two men, described as being "Irish soldiers," met some Irish residents in town who agreed to sell them some liquor. Soon a fight broke out between the Tigers and the locals because, as one Georgia soldier put it, the former were "beating up the old citizens." One woman was so frightened of the rebels that when Thomas Reed approached her she begged, "Spare me and my children, and you shall have everything we have got on the place!" She was, Reed recalled, "the worst scared woman I had ever seen." When Reed explained that all he wanted was something to eat, the woman invited him into her house for a meal. Before she was finished, however, other famished Tigers wandered in to partake of her hospitality, and Reed claimed that by the time they took their leave "the little woman was almost crazy."[36]

Early's division departed Gettysburg for York on June 27, but the 9th Louisiana's Pvt. John D. Shackleford was left behind with a local farmer because he was too sick to travel. The farmer brought in a doctor to treat the soldier, but Shackleford died and was buried on the side of the road. The following day Pvt. Charles Brown, a German serving in the 8th Louisiana, straggled behind on the column and was never seen again. A comrade wrote on his service record, "supposed to have been killed by the citizens of Penn." Shackleford and Brown were the first of many Tigers to die in Pennsylvania.[37]

On the march to York, Early split his division, with Hays making a circuitous march northwest by way of Mummasburg and Hunterstown, while the rest of the division took the direct route. Hays' march was exhausting because recent rains had turned the road into a quagmire. According to Lieutenant Jackson, "The mud [was] nearly Knee deep & [men were] straggling by the hundreds." The rebels had confiscated a large amount of whiskey in Gettysburg, and Hays generously gave each of his men a pint. What apparently was meant to be a kind gesture, or perhaps a necessary measure to prepare the men for the day's grueling march, actually touched off a four-day drunk. Those men who did not drink gave their whiskey to friends who did, and soon numerous Tigers were tight as a drum. "The whole brigade got drunk," wrote Lieutenant Jackson. "I never saw such a set in my life." As the brigade's number dwindled with every muddy mile, Captain Seymour hit upon a solution to the straggling. Whenever a soldier began to fall behind, Seymour pulled the man out of line and threw him into the cook wagon atop "the sharp sides and projecting legs of pots & kettles, which sobered them speedily. These drunken fellows would not ride far before they begged most piteously to be taken out and allowed to walk."[38]

During the morning, two whiskey-ladened Irishmen in the 7th Louisiana began to argue and threaten one another. When the brigade stopped for a rest, Colonel Penn had the men tear down a rail fence and build an impromptu boxing ring so the two Tigers could settle things before the march resumed. Penn ordered them to "get in there and fight it out," and they did for several rounds, cursing the entire time. Penn finally stopped the bout and ordered the two men to clean up at a nearby stream. Within minutes they were laughing about the fight and were good friends once again. Two days later, more fisticuffs erupted when an entire company of the 9th Louisiana got drunk and engaged in what was described as "a general family fight" that left one officer badly injured and several men under arrest.[39]

As Hays' brigade struggled along the muddy road, company commanders were ordered not to allow their men to leave the ranks while carrying a musket. When Captain Pierson discovered that one of his 9th Louisiana men, who "was somewhat intoxicated," had walked out of the road to avoid a big mud hole, he immediately put him under arrest. Colonel Stafford then arrested Pierson for not keeping his men in line but released him the next day. Being arrested for such a trivial matter insulted Pierson, and he demanded a court-martial to clear himself of wrongdoing. He technically remained under arrest until November, even though he was allowed to rejoin his company and fight at Gettysburg. The charges were eventually dropped because the regiment could not afford to lose an experienced company commander over such a minor infraction.[40]

The rebels passed through East Berlin and camped just outside York on June 28. James Gall Jr., an agent for the U.S. Sanitary Commission, visited Hays' camp and described what he found. "The supply wagons were drawn up in a sort of straggling hollow square, in the center of which the men stacked their arms in company lines, and in this way formed their camp. There were no tents for the men and but very few for the officers. Their whole appearance was greatly inferior to that of our soldiers. The men were busy cooking their dinner, which consisted of fresh beef, part of the York levy, wheat griddle cakes raised with soda, and cold water. No coffee or sugar had been issued to the men for a long time."[41]

When Gall asked one of the Tigers how he managed to ward off the rain without a tent, the soldier explained that he got along just fine. Rather than carrying the extra weight of a tent, he and a friend shared a gum blanket when it rained. They simply spread one of their wool blankets on the ground to lie on and covered themselves with the other and put the waterproof gum blanket over it. Gall noticed that nearly everyone in the rebel army followed this method, and that the few tents that existed were reserved for the highest ranking officers. "Everything that will trammel or impede the movement of the army is discarded, no matter what the consequences may be to the men." One of the Tiger officers also revealed to Gall that all of the soldiers in Hays' and Hoke's brigades were well-armed with British Enfield rifles that had been captured from Milroy at Winchester.[42]

York was crowded with refugees who had fled ahead of the rebels to save their livestock and what belongings they could carry. Their fears apparently were well founded because the Tigers seem to have foraged more around York than any other Pennsylvania town. Squads of soldiers roamed the countryside looking for anything the army could use. One gristmill owner claimed the Tigers paid him a visit and left with eight barrels of flour, fifteen bushels of corn, and fifteen meal bags. At another mill, members of Hays' brigade reportedly took twenty-five bushels of flour, sixty bushels of corn, and fifty bushels of wheat, and also burned the owner's fence rails for campfires and destroyed twenty acres of grass by camping on it. Other bands of Tigers confiscated three horses from some civilians who were trying to hide them in a field and waylaid the Kessler family as they rode in a wagon and forced them to return to Hays' camp. The rebels eventually allowed them to leave but kept the wagon and five mules. The Kesslers walked home, only to discover that they were missing two horses and numerous bushels of oats, corn, and horse feed.[43]

It soon became a game of hide-and-seek between local farmers who were determined to protect their livestock and the rebels who were equally determined to ferret them out. As Captain Seymour recalled: "Horses were found in bedrooms, parlours, lofts of barns and other out of the way place[s]. Major [John G.] Campbell, Acting Quartermaster of our Brigade, called at a large, finely furnished house, the owner of which he had learned was possessed of a splendid horse. The proprietor stoutly denied that he had such an animal but, unfortunately for him, a neigh from an adjoining room gave the nay to his assertion and revealed the hiding place of the much desired quadruped. The Major quietly opened the door and there in an elegant parlour, comfortably stalled in close proximity to a costly rosewood piano, stood a noble looking horse."[44]

In addition to plundering the local farms for supplies, General Early also demanded that the townspeople comply with a "levy" of $100,000, 2,000 pairs of shoes, 1,000 hats, 1,000 pairs of socks, and 3 days' rations. When the citizens came up with only $28,600 and about 1,200 shoes, hats, socks, and rations, and insisted that was all they could raise, Early believed them and ordered no retribution.[45]

While camped outside York, numerous Tigers took the opportunity to stock up on personal items. Private Thomas Reed wrote, "Some of the boys made a raid on the merchants of York and got a lot of hats and shoes. I got a nice hat, which I was very proud of." Other Tigers robbed a dry goods store of shoes, hats, and writing paraphernalia. When one Louisiana officer visited a store, the owner claimed he had nothing left to sell but was enticed to open the door when the officer offered to purchase some shirts with gold. Afterward, the officer told his men that they, too, could get shirts at the store, but the store owner would not accept their Confederate money. Undeterred, the Tigers barged in and were delighted to find some liquor as well as shirts. When the owner refused to sell them the liquor, they pushed him out the door, locked it, and started to "indulge on a great spree." The soldiers made so much noise that a crowd had gathered by the time they walked out with armloads of goods. The men then asked the store owner what they owed and settled their bill with Confederate money. The dismayed businessman reported the incident to the Tigers' officers, but they simply told him "that the day would come when he would be glad to have some Confederate money in his possession."[46]

Captain Seymour recalled how many of York's citizens seemed exceedingly friendly and expressed sympathy for the rebel cause. In fact, from the day the rebels entered Pennsylvania, numerous people claimed to be Copperheads and members of the pro-southern Knights of the Golden Circle and shared with the Confederates their secret signs, countersigns, and handshakes. According to Seymour, "Much to our surprise, hundreds of people in the towns through which we passed greeted us with these signs and we joyfully accepted them as proofs of the anti-war feeling that pervaded the country." It was not until they reached York that Seymour discovered that two men had traveled ahead of the rebels claiming to be members of the Knights. They informed the people that the enemy would not molest anyone who was a Knights member and agreed to show them the secret signs for five dollars. Impressed with the con men's ingenuity, Seymour wrote, "In this way thousands of people were induced to pay their money for the privilege of being accounted as friends of the South; hence our apparently cordial greeting along our line of march. A shrewd Yankee trick that."[47]

While Hays' brigade enjoyed York, Colonel Williams' 2nd Louisiana Brigade marched toward Harrisburg. As is often the case, these Tigers' activities are not as well documented as the 1st Louisiana Brigade, but it can be assumed that they acted in a fashion similar to Hays' men. S. Herman Dinkgrave of the 2nd Louisiana described some of the men's adventures in a letter he wrote on June 28. "There has been scarcely any injury to private property save in a few instances done by straglers [sic] to houses that were deserted but those that have habitants suffer no injury at all. I think we aught to retaliate for when the [enemy] invade our soil he spares nothing. Not even the women and children. . . . The valley we are in is one of the richest I ever saw and we are living off the fat of the land and no expense of the Government!" Dinkgrave went on to describe how a captain and guard were sent to a nearby house to protect it, "but as soon as the old woman saw them coming she fainted and when she came to she began begging not to kill her. Several have fainted on seeing a rebel. Nearly all the houses along the road have been deserted."[48]

Ewell had hoped to capture Harrisburg, but on June 29 he received orders from Lee to start concentrating his scattered corps. Lieutenant Michael

Murray of the 6th Louisiana wrote, "On the morning of the 30th, we turned back towards Gettysburg, where important business awaited us." After the rebels had departed York, a local man wrote his brother, "The County people are beginning to come in. They were plundered indiscriminately particularly by a Louisiana brigade. Horses and mules taken, houses broken open, and everything the thieves fancied stolen." By the turn of the century, however, even the citizens of York had forgiven the Louisianians for their depredations. On Memorial Day, May 17, 1906, some of the locals came to the Providence Church cemetery to hold a memorial service and lay flowers on the graves of eight Louisiana Tigers who were buried there after the Battle of Gettysburg.[49]

Later in the day, Early received a message from General Ewell informing him that he was with Rodes' division marching for Heidlersburg and for Early to join them there. By the time Early's men camped three miles east of the town, they had covered twenty-six miles that day but were still in good humor. Captain Seymour recalled that "it was inspiring to see the spirits of the men rise at the prospect of a fight. We all knew that, were Meade's Army to be defeated, the roads to Washington, Philadelphia and Baltimore would be open to us." That night Lee sent orders to Ewell to proceed to either Cashtown or Gettysburg the next day as conditions warranted. Lee wanted to concentrate his army quickly because the fluid situation was changing rapidly. Throughout most of the invasion, General Stuart's cavalry had been cut off from Lee on a raid behind the Union lines, thus depriving Lee of badly needed intelligence as to the Yankees' whereabouts. Stuart's silence led Lee to believe that Hooker's Army of the Potomac was unaware of the invasion and was still in Virginia. Thus, it came as a shock when he learned on the night of June 28 that the Yankees had not only crossed the Potomac River but were closing in on his scattered army. It was to meet this threat that Lee ordered his far-flung divisions to begin concentrating at Cashtown or Gettysburg. Although slowed by the muddy roads, A. P. Hill reached Cashtown on June 30 and dispatched one of his brigades to Gettysburg to look for supplies. It withdrew after encountering Union cavalry, but Hill planned to return the next day with his entire division.[50]

General George Meade had replaced Hooker as commander of the Army of the Potomac after Hooker resigned in a huff over a dispute involving the Harpers Ferry garrison. When Meade learned that his cavalry had encountered rebel infantry outside Gettysburg, he hurried reinforcements there. The two armies collided in the rolling fields northwest of town on July 1, and a major battle developed as more and more units were sucked into the fight. As Rodes' and Early's divisions approached the battlefield from the northeast, Hays' Tigers began to hear the unmistakable sound of artillery in the distance. Seymour recalled, "The heavy booming of cannon told us that the conflict had begun and we pushed on with great rapidity." Rodes arrived first shortly after noon and was placed on the left of Hill's line. After Rodes became hotly engaged with the enemy that afternoon, Early arrived on the Harrisburg Road to Rodes' left after a twelve-mile march. Purely by chance, he was in a perfect position to strike the Union right flank held by Gen. Oliver O. Howard's XI Corps.[51]

Early formed a battle line behind Rock Creek with Gordon on the right, Hays in the center, and Hoke and Smith on the left. Hays' brigade was astride the road, with the 7th, 8th, and part of the 9th Louisiana on the eastern side and the 9th, 5th, and 6th regiments on the west. Early then ordered Gordon's brigade forward into a patch of timber to support Rodes' left flank. One of the Tigers remembered how the Louisiana and Georgia officers took the time to bid one another farewell before Gordon led his men to the front. The Tigers watched as the Georgians disappeared into the woods and then listened to their heavy firing for an hour before seeing groups of Union soldiers retreating from the woods up a hill in their rear. Hays was then ordered forward and advanced against a long stone wall behind which many of the Yankees had taken shelter. The federals managed to fire one volley before the Tigers mounted the wall and forced their surrender. One Louisianian wrote that he and his comrades realized they had won when they saw "the uplifted hands of thousands of blue-coats for as far as they eye could see on either side."[52]

Gordon and Rodes quickly broke the Union line on what became known as Barlow's Knob and began driving the enemy back toward Gettysburg. Captain Seymour wrote, "The musketry was very severe and we feared that Gordon would be borne back; but in a few minutes the firing ceased, & the smoke lifting from the field, revealed to our sight the defeated Federals in disorderly flight, hotly pursued by the gallant Georgians." Lieutenant Jackson declared that Gordon was "driving the Yankees before [him] like sheep. It was the prettiest sight I ever saw." From the rear, Campbell Brown watched as Hays joined Gordon in chasing after the enemy. "Then came one of the most warlike & animated spectacles I ever looked on," he recalled. "Gordon & Hays charged across the plateau in their front, at double-quick, sweeping everything before them & scattering the extreme right of the enemy."[53]

Early advanced the rest of his line across Rock Creek and smashed Leopold Von Gilsa and Adelbert Ames' Union brigades. Hoke's brigade, which was temporarily commanded by Col. Isaac Avery, joined Hays in attacking a Union artillery battery that was supported by infantry. Although those federals put up a stiffer fight than the ones Hays encountered earlier, they were also finally forced to retreat. Gradually, Avery pulled ahead of Hays and opened fire on the Union infantry behind a rail fence at a range of about forty yards. The Yankees answered the volley with one of their own and appeared as though they were going to make a stand. However, when the Tigers caught up with Avery, they leaped over the fence, and scattered the enemy. Thomas Reed wrote that "the Yankees were running across an old field and looked to be as thick as you ever saw black birds fly, and as they ran I took three fair cracks at them. I don't know whether I killed one or not, but I hope I did not."[54]

After the war, Capt. J. R. Hancock of the 9th Louisiana claimed that Pvt. William Singleton, the same soldier who was said to have killed Gen. Philip Kearny at Chantilly, killed Union corps commander Gen. John F. Reynolds at Gettysburg. According to Hancock, Singleton was out front serving as a skirmisher when he noticed a Yankee officer to his right using field glasses to watch some Confederate units approaching his left flank. Using a hedge that ran alongside the road for cover, Singleton slipped within rifle range and shot Reynolds. Singleton reportedly had captured Reynolds a year earlier at Gaines' Mill, and Hancock claimed that he "expressed himself afterwards on several occasions that it was with sincere regret that it was Reynolds and not some other Northern officer who had been killed." Reynolds, however, could not have been Singleton's victim because he was killed several hours before Hays' brigade even entered the fight and at a location far away from the Tigers' position. However, it may be that Singleton shot Gen. Francis Barlow, who commanded the troops which Early attacked and was severely wounded on the knoll that came to bear his name.[55]

According to Virginia artilleryman Robert Stiles, a big Irishman in the 9th Louisiana by the name of Burgoyne did not participate in the dramatic charge outside Gettysburg. Burgoyne liked cannons and often left the ranks to help out any nearby artillery crews that were shorthanded. On the afternoon of July 1, he attached himself to Stiles' battery and served as a rammer during the fight. Stiles claimed Burgoyne gave "vent to his enthusiasm in screams and bounds that would have done credit to a catamount." When a huge Irish prisoner who was standing nearby recognized Burgoyne's accent, he asked the Tiger why he was serving with the rebels. Burgoyne replied that he was a free Irishman and could fight with whomever he chose, to which the Yankee declared, "I had the plizure of kicking yez out from behind Marye's wall, that time Sedgwick lammed yer brigade out o' there!" "Yer a d——n liar," responded Burgoyne, "and I'll jist knock yer teeth down yer ugly throat for that same lie." The two Irishmen then lit into each other, much to the amusement of the bystanders. After they exchanged a few blows, Stiles noticed that a bullet had shattered two fingers on the Yankee Irishman's right hand and that it was a bloody mess. He yelled to Burgoyne, "Hold! Your man's wounded!" The Tiger immediately stopped fighting and declared, "You're a trump, Pat'; give me your well hand. We'll fight this out some other time. I didn't see you were hurt." The two then shook hands, and Burgoyne returned to his regiment.[56]

The Union XI Corps disintegrated when Early's charge shattered its right flank and beat a hasty retreat back toward Gettysburg. Lee then ordered a general attack, and the entire Union line collapsed. Hays' men were actually closer to town than many of the Union soldiers, and it became a foot race to see which side would enter its streets first. The Tigers met virtually no resistance from the beaten Yankees, and Lieutenant Jackson claimed, "We shot them down, bayoneted them & captured more prisoners than we had men." When one mounted Union officer was spotted trying to rally his men, some of the Tigers were impressed with his bravery and shouted, "Don't shoot that man." It was a futile gesture, however, because a volley of musketry soon killed him, and his men ran away. General Hays witnessed the incident and was said to have "expressed his deep regret when the gallant hero fell." Before the battle ended, Private Reed saw another act of enemy bravery. "While we were chasing the Yankees and getting in behind the houses, I saw their flag fall nine times. We would shoot it down and they would grab it up and run, till finally them scoundrels got it behind the houses and were gone. I will say right here that a man will stay longer and stick closer to his colors than he will to his brother."[57]

Hays' brigade had cut off the retreat of at least five thousand Union soldiers, and they surrendered in droves. Captain Seymour, who barely escaped serious injury when a shell exploded near his head, was responsible for one large capture. He wrote, "One Dutch Colonel at the head of about 250 men came up to me and cried out that he surrendered. . . . I made him throw his sword upon the ground and sent the whole party back to our rear guard under the escort of only one Confederate soldier." Hays reported that so many Yankees laid down their arms that he was uncertain what to do with them all. The general later claimed that he had no choice but to point the prisoners toward the rear and send them on their way unescorted. By the time the Tigers finished combing the streets of Gettysburg, they had lost seven men killed, forty-one wounded, and fifteen missing but had taken an estimated three thousand prisoners—approximately twice the brigade's strength. Many of the captives were wounded, so Colonel Penn had Abraham Stout, a captured surgeon with the 153rd Pennsylvania, set up a hospital in the German Reformed Church on High Street to treat them.[58]

The Union survivors rallied on Cemetery Hill, a large prominence just south of town that offered an excellent defensive position. Within an hour of taking Gettysburg, Hays, Gordon, Early, and Rodes met with Ewell and urged an immediate advance before Meade could fortify the hill. There were still several hours of daylight left to accomplish this task, and it was obvious that the high ground dominated the area. Ewell, however, was under orders from Lee to attack Cemetery Hill only if he was certain of success because Lee had no reserves to support him if the battle did not go well. In addition, Ewell had received reports, later proved erroneous, that a Union column was approaching his rear. After weighing all the factors, he decided to postpone the attack until Johnson's division arrived from Carlisle. When Hays persisted in pushing for an advance, Ewell reportedly laughed and asked if his Tigers never got a bellyful of fighting. Hays bristled and replied testily that his only concern was to prevent the unnecessary slaughter of his men in a later assault. After the war, General Longstreet claimed that Hays told him that his brigade could have taken Cemetery Hill that afternoon without losing ten men. Early, however, denied that Hays ever said such a thing and maintained that Longstreet's claim was ludicrous because several thousand Union soldiers with artillery were on Cemetery Hill by the time an assault could have been launched.[59]

Ewell actually had good reason to delay the attack on Cemetery Hill, but Hays' men were angry, nonetheless, and watched as more and more Union troops arrived on the hill in their front as the afternoon wore on. Oaths and curses were muttered along the line, and many men openly exclaimed their wish "that Jackson were here."[60]

Once Gettysburg was secured, Hays deployed his brigade along its streets. The men gathered hay and straw for bedding from nearby stables and covered the sidewalk of Middle Street before cooking supper. Town resident Sallie Myers claimed, "'The Louisiana Tigers' were feared the most, because of their reputation for lawlessness, and so the people avoided them as best they could." A curious William McLean looked out his window and observed some rebels, who were probably Louisianians, sitting on the curb rummaging through captured Union knapsacks and reading aloud the letters they found. Suddenly, his five-year-old daughter began singing "Hang Jeff Davis on a Sour Apple Tree" from an open window, but the rebels paid her no attention.[61]

Rufus Northrop, a member of the 90th Pennsylvania who escaped capture by hiding in a church steeple, had a close-up view of the enemy's activity in Gettysburg during the battle. He wrote afterward, "The rebels had thousands of muskets which they had captured from us . . . collected in stacks in the street. . . . The rebels seemed to be having a good time generally and their rail fence gait told of empty whiskey barrels. They appeared perfectly happy and inclined to treat every body with attention."[62]

Some of the Tigers wandered off to forage for food and loot, which prompted one Confederate soldier to declare, "I assure you that city is well plundered. The Louisianians left nothing that human hands could destroy." One group of Tigers visited Catherine Foster's home early the next morning and woke her as they were trying to break in the back door. When she opened it, "Two toughs, supposed to be Louisiana Tigers," demanded a light so they could search the house for Union soldiers. Foster gave it to them but explained that rebel officers had already searched the house. Her husband then came in, and one of the Tigers pointed his musket at him and demanded fifty dollars. When he said he did not have that much money, the Louisianian said, "Give me what you have!" Foster handed over three dollars, and the Tigers cursed him and left. If the men had searched the house, they might have found the Union soldier the Foster family was hiding in the cellar.[63]

Another woman, known only as "Mrs. M," also left an account of her encounter with the Louisiana Tigers.

> To say that we were terrified when the rebel army entered town is
> to speak mildly. Rough, ragged men appeared on the streets; they took
> the chickens and pigs from the barns, and then they entered the houses

and laid their hands on all the food. Our house was searched again and again. What one overlooked the other found. They were very polite . . . but they took everything, just the same. . . .

"You are not as much afraid of the rebels as you thought you would be," said one of them to me one day, for my heart was really filled with compassion for these dirty, hungry young fellows who took possession of the kitchen and gorged themselves with half-baked bread.

"[N]o," I said, "I am not afraid of you, but I think I would be afraid of the "Louisiana Tigers." The kitchen was filled with an uproar of delighted laughter as they cried out: "You need not fear any longer, madam: we are the 'Tigers.'" And then the cannon boomed and the guests rushed out, with their mouths filled with hot dough, and I, their unwilling hostess, hastened to hide in the cellar again.[64]

Justus Silliman, a member of the 17th Connecticut who had been wounded in the head and captured, was treated at the Tigers' field hospital. He informed his mother two days later that "we had every attention shown us, our wounds promptly attended to and received kind treatment. those who a short time previous had been hurling death at us, now assisted our wounded, bringing them water, crackers etc."[65] While at the hospital, Silliman also witnessed the plundering of Gettysburg.

The rebels occasionaly came in bringing sheep, chickens, etc captured at the neighboring farm houses. They all seemed perfectly confident of success as they were concentrating nearly the whole of their army of Va at this place. Occasionally some of the rebs would come up from the city with carpets, collars, shoes and other articles taken from the stores in Gettysburg. . . . The rebels with whom I conversed seemed anxious to close the war and all were anxious to see Jeff Davis and Abe Lincoln hung and many looked forward to our next presidential election [1864] in hopes that it would either bring about a *reconstruction of the union* or come to some terms of peace.

There were several darkees around the hospital who were waiters on rebel officers, one of these was quite friendly and was a true union man. he said the rebels tried to make their case as good as possible but that they were hard up.[66]

Johnson's division, which included Colonel Williams' 2nd Louisiana Brigade, had farther to march to reach Gettysburg than Ewell's other divisions. It was near Carlisle when Johnson received the order to concentrate and did not arrive on the battlefield until late on July 1 after an exhausting twenty-five-mile march. Charles Batchelor wrote his father that the men started early in the morning and marched in quick time to get to Gettysburg by sundown. Colonel Zable recalled that during the exhausting march "the men as usual [were] in good humor and enjoying the full rations afforded by the fertile country we were marching through." The first indication the men had that a battle was in progress was the distant boom of a cannon during the morning that sounded "as a distant tap on a bass drum." When Johnson finally arrived in Gettysburg, he was ordered to the east side of Rock Creek and settled into a position near Culp's Hill about two hours before dark. Zable claimed that, as his men rested, they also wondered why no attack was being made on the high ground. "We though it strange that we were not taken into action at once having learned the success of the other Divisions of our Corps. We might have captured a wagon train we saw on a hill and held that hill. The troops realized there was something wanting somewhere, there was an evident feeling of dissatisfaction among our men, we were not doing Stonewall Jackson's way."[67]

When darkness finally enveloped the field, the Yankees were left undisturbed along Cemetery and Culp's hills and other high ground south of town. As a full moon rose that night, small groups of Confederates went back over the battlefield to bury the dead and collect the wounded. Alice Powers, however, noticed that the Louisianians did not bury everyone. Referring to some Union dead that lay near the Presbyterian Church, she wrote, "These dead soldiers lay on the sidewalk until Saturday morning [three days later] as the squad of Louisiana Tigers who guarded the street would not permit the citizens, who begged that privilege, to bury them at night. . . . Restless and uneasy we slept in our clothes that night getting up often to watch that no harm came to the dead who lay in sight of our doors."[68]

During the night, Early ordered Hays to locate a good position between Gettysburg and Cemetery Hill from which he could attack. Hays found such a place about six hundred yards beyond town and returned at 2:00 a.m. to awaken the brigade and move it to Winebrenner's Run near William Culp's farmhouse. In the dark, the men were placed behind a low ridge that Hays thought would protect them from any enemy fire coming from Cemetery Hill.

Isaac Avery's North Carolina brigade came up, as well, and took a position on Hays' left.[69]

The rest of Lee's and Meade's lines slowly took shape that night. On the Confederate side, Ewell's corps held the left wing stretching from Culp's Hill to Cemetery Hill and Gettysburg. Hill's corps was in the center facing Cemetery Ridge, and Longstreet was on the far right facing Cemetery Ridge and the hills known as Little and Big Round Top. Lee was determined to renew the attack on July 2, but it took him all night and much of the next day to hammer out the details. It was finally decided that Longstreet would open the attack from the right flank. When Ewell heard Longstreet's guns, he was to demonstrate against Meade's right flank by bombarding Culp's and Cemetery hills with artillery fire and then follow up with an attack if possible. The stage was set for two of the bloodiest days in American history.

CHAPTER 9

Gettysburg

WHEN THE SUN rose over Gettysburg on July 2, 1863, it quickly became apparent that the ridge behind which Hays had placed his Tigers the night before did not protect them entirely from the Union sharpshooters. The regiments on the far right along Weinbrenner's Run, which were probably the 5th and 6th Louisiana, were particularly exposed because the ridge flattened out there and offered no protection at all. The hours ticked by, and Captain Seymour claimed that General Ewell "expressed great anxiety to withdraw our Brigade." Ewell even rode out to inspect Hays' position but decided that the men could not be withdrawn without exposing them to the Union artillery posted on Cemetery Hill. The Louisianians were forced to stay put, and one soldier claimed they "stretched on the ground . . . and spent the afternoon in eating, sleeping and card playing."[1]

"So we had to remain there," remembered Captain Seymour, "more than five hundred yards in advance of Ewell's main line of battle—hugging the ground behind a very low ridge which only partially covered us from the enemy's fire. It was almost certain death for a man to stand upright and we lost during the day forty-five men in killed and wounded from the fire of the enemy's sharpshooters." Lieutenant Jackson's and another company that were serving as skirmishers had been placed even closer to Cemetery Hill during the night. After the battle, Jackson wrote, "and there we had to stay—if any one shewed themselves or a hat was seen above the fence a volley was poured into us." Jackson finally had enough and decided to withdraw his skirmishers back to the regiment. "We had to crawl about 60 yds in the bushes then jump & run like '240' for about 30 yds. We all got into town & round to the regt."[2]

Those Tigers who could do so kept up a steady fire at the Yankees. The 17th Connecticut's Lt. Albert Peck wrote, "As soon as it was light . . . we could see the Johnnies moving along the fences in our front, keeping out of sight as much as possible. . . . It was not long before 'zip' came the bullets from them, and our boys promptly returned their fire, although it was difficult to see them. Our boys took shelter behind the rail and board fences and apple trees, and once in a while the bullets would peel the bark from the trees, and there were a good many close shaves."[3]

Some of Hays' sharpshooters were posted around a brickyard and in the town's buildings. They engaged the 153rd Pennsylvania's skirmishers and sometimes placed hats on sticks to draw the enemy's fire and reveal their position. The Union prisoner Justus Silliman, who had been moved to the German Reformed Church, watched the sharpshooters at their deadly work: "The La brigade were in a hollow in front of us, where they lay close until nearly dark though they had their skirmishers out nearly all day. [T]hese were occasionally picked off by our sharpshooters. Bullets frequently whistled around our hospital but I have not heard of any one being injured by them."[4]

James Patrick Sullivan of the Iron Brigade was another wounded prisoner being held by the Louisiana Tigers. According to Sullivan, the Louisianians "felt very jubilant over yesterday's battle, exultingly told [us] that 'you uns' were whipped and they were going to take Washington, Baltimore, and Philadelphia and end the 'wah.'" Sullivan, however, "took the brag out [of them]" when he pointed out that it had taken half of Lee's army to defeat a relatively small Union force and that it would be much more difficult to whip Meade's entire army.[5]

It was not until 4:00 p.m. that Ewell finally heard Longstreet's attack begin on the far right and ordered his artillery to open fire on the enemy positions fronting him. In its forward position, Hays' brigade found itself caught between a roaring eighteen-gun Confederate battery and several Union batteries on Cemetery Hill. When the federal guns thundered back in defiance, the Louisianians had a spectacular view of the duel. It was, Seymour wrote, "a most exciting and thrilling spectacle. . . . The roar of the guns was continuous and deafening; the shot and shell could be seen tearing through the hostile batteries, dismounting guns, killing and wounding men and horses, while [occasionally] an ammunition chest would explode, sending a bright column of smoke up towards the heavens."[6]

To the left, Johnson's division was expecting orders to attack Culp's Hill. Nicholls' Louisiana brigade, still under the temporary command of Col. Jesse

Williams, was at the base of the hill on the far left of Johnson's division. Throughout the night the men listened to Union reinforcements arriving on Culp's Hill and all afternoon heard the Yankees felling trees and digging earthworks along its crest. As the enemy's activity increased about sundown, a twelve-pound shell suddenly struck the ground in front of the 14th Louisiana. By then, Colonel Zable wrote, the men were becoming "anxious."[7]

The thirty-year-old Zable was a native of New Orleans and a former California Forty-Niner. When he failed to strike it rich, he toured Central and South America and then returned to the California gold fields for eight years before traveling to Europe. He was working as a New Orleans grocer when the war began and immediately organized a volunteer company called the Lafayette Guards. Elected captain, Zable and his company became part of Colonel Sulakowski's 14th Louisiana. Zable had already fought in numerous battles and was wounded at Williamsburg, but Gettysburg would prove to be one of his most desperate fights.[8]

Late that afternoon, General Ewell decided to follow up his artillery bombardment with attacks on both Culp's and Cemetery hills. When the order finally reached Williams' brigade to prepare to advance, Sikes Phillips of the 2nd Louisiana felt an ominous foreboding when he found himself standing in the front line. R. C. Murphy, who stood behind him, noted his friend's uneasiness and offered to exchange places. Phillips gratefully accepted, and soon afterward the deafening cannons fell silent, and orders were given to advance. When the men crossed Rock Creek at dusk, a Union sharpshooter almost immediately killed Lt. Col. Michael "Jim" Nolan of the 1st Louisiana. Nolan was Irish-born and had just returned to the regiment earlier that day after being away on furlough. Father Gache claimed that he had been chosen to take command of the brigade and had been appointed a brigadier general but was killed before receiving the commission. Nolan was a popular officer, whom one man described as "the best, bravest and grandest soldier I ever met." Another Tiger wrote on the colonel's service record, "A most gallant officer."[9]

The Louisiana regiments reformed on the far side of the creek and then advanced against the Union pickets. According to Colonel Zable, when they reached the base of Culp's Hill the Tigers raised the rebel yell and rushed "as best they could up the steep hillside over rocks and through the timber." As the men struggled up the steep slope, the hilltop suddenly exploded in smoke and flame. From behind their barricades, the New Yorkers of Gen. George Greene's

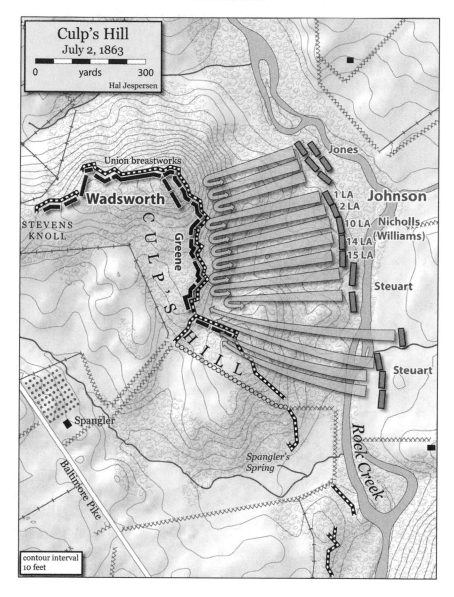

Culp's Hill
July 2, 1863

0   yards   300

Hal Jespersen

Union breastworks

Wadsworth

STEVENS
KNOLL

C U L P ' S

Greene

Jones

1 LA
2 LA

Johnson

10 LA   Nicholls
         (Williams)
14 LA
15 LA

Steuart

H I L L

Steuart

Spangler

Spangler's
Spring

Rock Creek

Baltimore Pike

contour interval
10 feet

brigade unleashed a murderous fire, and Sikes Phillips was mortally wounded in the groin even though he stood behind his friend R. C. Murphy.[10]

Williams' men became confused on the dark hillside and soon lost all semblance of order. On the right, the 1st Louisiana forced the Yankees out of part

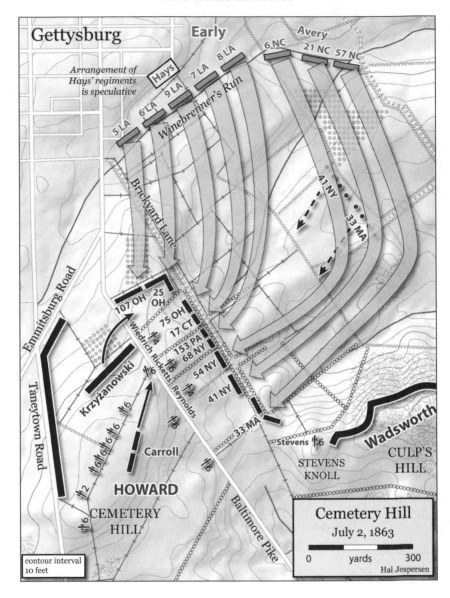

Gettysburg

Early

Avery

6 NC 21 NC 57 NC

Hays

8 LA

7 LA

*Arrangement of
Hays' regiments
is speculative*

9 LA

6 LA

5 LA

Winebrenner's Run

Brickyard Lane

41 NY

33 MA

107 OH 25 OH

75 OH

17 CT

153 PA

68 NY

54 NY

41 NY

33 MA

Krzyżanowski

Wiedrich Ricketts Reynolds

Carroll

Stevens

STEVENS
KNOLL

CULP'S
HILL

Wadsworth

HOWARD

CEMETERY
HILL

Baltimore Pike

Emmitsburg Road

Taneytown Road

Cemetery Hill
July 2, 1863

0   yards   300

Hal Jespersen

contour interval
10 feet

of their breastworks, but the angle and topography of the hill caused most of
the Tigers to crowd toward the center, which prevented them from fighting
effectively. When the enemy's fire became unbearable, the Louisianians sought
cover among the trees and rocks forty to one hundred yards from the Union

line. For four hours Johnson's Confederates clung to the rocky slope, banging away at the enemy. The Tigers fired so many rounds that muskets fouled from excessive use and had to be replaced with weapons snatched up from the dead and wounded. It was not until past midnight that the firing slackened enough for some of the rebels to collect what dead and wounded they could and withdraw a short distance down the hill. Others were too close to the enemy to disengage and had to remain in place. W. G. Loyd of the 2nd Louisiana hid behind a small rock but carelessly stuck his right leg out too far and was hit by a bullet. According to Colonel Zable, "The night of July 2 was one never to be forgotten, our lines were so close together that we were compelled to speak in a whisper."[11]

Some of the braver Tigers silently crept through the smoky woods in search of wounded comrades who had been left behind. Friends of Wolf Lichenstein found him with a shattered arm, wounds in his legs, and his uniform torn from bullets. He was lying within talking distance of the Yankees, and it was impossible to move him without drawing the enemy's fire. All the men could do was strap a canteen to Lichenstein's chest to alleviate his horrendous thirst and leave him where he was. Before daylight, three bullets ripped the canteen apart, and Lichenstein had to suffer through an entire day without water.[12]

Lieutenant Charles Batchelor was shocked to find his younger brother, Albert, also lying on the bloody slope. Three Batchelor brothers served in the same 2nd Louisiana company. Madison was the company captain, but he was absent, recovering from a wound received at Chancellorsville. Charles served as a second lieutenant, and Albert, the youngest, had only joined the company three weeks earlier. Albert had been shot about 8:00 p.m., but it was not until three hours later that the firing died down enough for Charles to go searching for him. Charles, who had taken command of the company because all of the senior officers were either dead or wounded, eventually found his brother. After the battle he wrote the family, "Finally I came to poor Albert lying on the ground wounded under the left eye, the ball passing through and under his nose bulging out his right eye and coming out [near] the temple. He also had a ball shot through his left leg." With the help of a captain who had lost all of the men in his company, Batchelor carefully carried Albert to an ambulance in the rear. After a tearful embrace, Charles returned to Culp's Hill to seek out the other nineteen casualties among his twenty-six-man company. Of his brother, he wrote, "He fought most gallantly . . . being shot down . . . in the advance on the enemys breastworks. Poor fellow, it was his first fight and he made me proud of him."[13]

Left on Culp's Hill in the hands of the enemy were the color-bearers of the 1st and 14th Louisiana. Charles S. Clancy carried the former regiment's flag through what was described as "a perfect tornado of shell and bullets." When he became separated from the regiment and realized that he was about to be captured, Clancy tore the flag from its staff and hid it under his shirt. Clancy kept the flag throughout his imprisonment at Forts McHenry and Delaware and faked an illness in order to be exchanged early. He was the regiment's sixth color-bearer, the previous five having been killed or wounded, and he dutifully returned the flag to his regiment. Nearly two hundred bullets, one shell, and one shell fragment were said to have perforated the flag during the nighttime battle on Culp's Hill. The identity of the 14th Louisiana's color-bearer is unknown. Private Snakenberg simply stated in his memoirs that the soldier, like Clancy, was cut off during the withdrawal and hid the flag on his body before he was captured. He, too, returned the colors to the regiment after being exchanged.[14]

During the night, the Tigers began to fear that the Yankees would launch their own attack in the morning to drive them off the hill. According to Zable, "It was decided after consultation among the officers of the Brigade that our best plan to mask our weakness would be to open fire on the enemy before daylight . . . so as to cause them to believe that we were about to make another effort to capture their works." Zable claimed the Yankees' return fire "was the most terrific and defeaning [sic] we ever experienced," and the smoke was so dense that the Tigers could only see the enemy's position by the flash of their muskets, even though they were only twenty yards apart in some places. Nonetheless, the plan worked, and the federals remained behind their breastworks.[15]

Outside Gettysburg, Harry Hays had been ordered to make his own attack on Cemetery Hill whenever he heard Johnson begin his assault on Culp's Hill. Hays had also been given temporary command of Hoke's North Carolina brigade, which was positioned on his left, and was told that Gordon's brigade would support him should he make a breakthrough. The Louisianians had been in position for the assault since dawn, but, like Johnson's division, were forced to wait until Longstreet opened his attack on the right. Most of the Tigers were quiet and pensive, well aware of the reception awaiting them on Cemetery Hill. Throughout the previous night they had listened to the federals on the high ground "chopping away and working like beavers." Captain Seymour remembered, "The quiet, solemn mien of our men showed plainly that they fully appreciated the desperate character of the undertaking, but on every face was most legibly written the firm determination to do or die." Reuben Ruch, a prisoner from the 153rd Pennsylvania being held in the German Reformed Church, claimed to have watched while some of the Tigers steeled their nerves below his window. "I . . . saw them drinking out of a barrel. The head of the barrel was knocked in. One would get a tin cup full and three or four would drink out of the same cup until it was empty. It could not have been water, for a tine of water would not have had so many drinks in it. It was straight whiskey, and they were getting ready to charge the Eleventh Corps."[16]

As the sun descended in the west, Hays' Tigers finally heard the growing roar to their left that signaled Johnson's attack on Culp's Hill. About that time, General Early rode up to Hays' position. Captain Seymour watched him approach. "Just before dark the solitary figure of old Gen. Early is seen emerging from one of the streets of the town and, riding slowly across the field in the direction of our position, the little puffs of dust that arise from around his horse's feet show that the Federal sharpshooters are paying him the compliment of their special attention." Ignoring the bullets, Early sauntered up to Hays and asked if he was ready. Receiving an affirmative reply, he ordered the two brigades forward to seize the heights.[17]

Hays had no delusions about the difficult task that lay ahead. His men had always appreciated the fact that he never deceived them when it came to a dangerous assignment. Now, with the time at hand, the general galloped along the Tigers' line to steel the men for the assault, shouting that Early said they must silence the artillery on Cemetery Hill. As encouragement, he promised that Gordon's brigade would come up to reinforce them once they had taken the guns. Hays then dismounted so as not to attract the enemy's fire and prepared to advance. Nearly every other officer followed his example.[18]

Just after 6:00 p.m., a lone bugle from the 57th North Carolina wailed over the field, signaling the advance. "I felt as if my doom was sealed," wrote Lieutenant Jackson, "and it was with great reluctance that I started my skirmishers forward." An anonymous member in Jackson's 8th Louisiana recalled General Hays yelling, "Rise up, brigade! Forward! Double quick! Stop when you reach the first batteries! Our friends will be there to meet us!" Watching from the rear, Private Ruch wrote, "The Johnnies started stooped over, scattered like a drove of sheep, till they got to this ridge. Then every man took his place." Exactly how Hays aligned his regiments is not known except that the 57th North Carolina was on the far left near Culp's farm, with the 21st and 6th North Carolina stretching to the right. The Tigers then continued the line farther to the right. It is probable that the 8th Louisiana was on the brigade's left and the 7th, 9th, 6th, and 5th regiments extended the line to the right. Once their lines were set, the rebels lunged forward and popped over the ridge.[19]

Near Cemetery Hill, the men in Capt. Greenleaf T. Stevens' battery had been listening to the fight rumbling on Culp's Hill a quarter of a mile to their right. The sun had gone down and everything was peaceful in their sector until a sergeant jumped up and yelled, "Look! Look at those men!" as he pointed to the left toward Culp's farm. Glancing in that direction, the artillerymen could see the Tar Heels of Avery's brigade and the left wing of Hays' Tigers climbing fences and forming a line. Stevens quickly opened fire and was soon joined by the other batteries.[20]

According to Lieutenant Jackson, when Hays' line swept over the ridge, the Yankee cannon "vomited forth a perfect storm of grape, canister, shrapnel, etc. But 'Old Harry' shouted forward! and on we went over fences, ditches and through marshy fields." Avery's men on the left suffered the most from the artillery fire because they were exposed in an open pasture. Hays' Tigers, however, were largely protected when they went down into a ravine, and the Union gunners mostly fired over their heads in the growing darkness. Hays admitted afterward that "we thus escaped what in the full light of day could have been nothing else than horrible slaughter." Captain Seymour agreed and wrote, "The Yankees have anticipated this movement and now thirty pieces of cannon vomit forth a perfect storm of grape, canister, shrapnel, etc., while their infantry pour into us a close fire from their rifles. But we are too quick for them and are down in the valley in a trice, while the Yankee missiles are hissing, screaming & hurtling over our heads, doing but little damage." Silas Schuler, a member of the 107th Ohio, agreed that the gunners' aim was inaccurate. He wrote home that the "Artillery fired but they fired too high. Then we began to fire, but too high also." Unfortunately, the artillery fire also endangered some Union skirmishers out front. Lieutenant Milton Daniels of the 17th Connecticut wrote, "I remember the lead wadding from one shot killed one of our men, which demoralized us worse than the enemy in front."[21]

Apparently, the Yankees' aim improved in time because Private Ruch wrote that "our grape and canister began to plow gaps through their ranks. They closed up like water, and advanced at the double quick. . . . To see grape and canister cut gaps through the ranks looks rough. I could see hands, arms, and legs flying amidst the dust and smoke. . . . It reminded me much of a wagon-load of pumpkins drawn up on a hill, and the end gate coming out, and the pumpkins rolling and abounding down the hill. . . . The slaughter was terrible."[22]

Many of the Union infantrymen who were defending Cemetery Hill had been sent to reinforce Culp's Hill against Johnson's attack. Now there were barely twelve hundred men of the XI Corps' 1st Division posted behind a low rock wall that ran alongside Brickyard Lane (modern-day Wainwright Avenue) at the base of the hill. Adelbert Ames had assumed command of the division the day before, and his brigade was now led by Col. Andrew Harris. Harris had the 107th and 25th Ohio on the far left facing northwest, with the right wing of the 25th Ohio making a sharp ninety-degree turn to the right, or southeast, to follow the rock wall. The 7th Ohio and 17th Connecticut continued the line to the right and connected with the 153rd Pennsylvania and 68th and 54th New York of Leopold Von Gilsa's brigade. About two hundred yards behind Ames' infantry on top of Cemetery Hill were, from left to right, the artillery batteries of Capt. Michael Wiedrich of the 1st New York Light Artillery and Capt. R. Bruce Ricketts of the 1st Pennsylvania Light Artillery. When Ricketts was brought into position that afternoon, Col. Charles Wainwright, commander of the I Corps artillery, told him, "Captain, this is the key to our position on Cemetery Hill, and must be held, and in case you are charged here, you will not limber up under any circumstances, but fight your battery as long as you can."[23]

One Union officer claimed that Hays' men screamed, "We are the Louisiana Tigers!" as they rushed toward the stone wall at the base of Cemetery Hill. Hays' Louisiana Brigade took aim at Wiedrich's battery, which had begun firing canister as soon as the Tigers swept over the ridge. After the war, Colonel Harris wrote of the rebels, "They moved forward as steadily, amid this hail of shot shell and minie ball, as though they were on parade far removed from danger. It was a complete surprise to us. We did not expect this assault as bravely and rapidly made. In fact, we did not expect any assault." The regiments on Hays' right hit the 107th and 25th Ohio, while the center and left wheeled to the right to strike the main federal line along the stone wall. Avery's Tar Heels also had to make a right wheel to attack Ricketts' battery. Lieutenant Edward Whittier, who watched from his position near Culp's Hill, later wrote that it was "a movement which none but the steadiest veterans could execute under such circumstances." It first seemed to the Yankee artillerymen that the Tar Heels were heading for Culp's Hill, but then as Avery made his wheel, the line suddenly turned and charged straight for them.[24]

The thin Ohio line facing the Tigers numbered no more than five hundred men. Colonel Harris rode his horse up and down the wall, urging the men to hold their position while Wiedrich's cannons fired shells over their heads. Sergeant Frederick Nussbaum of the 107th Ohio remembered, "Our orders were to shoot low, and we mowed the Tigers down as they came up the hill." Crouched behind the stone wall, Lt. Oscar Ladley noticed that the Tigers' flags and officers were out in front of the men as they approached the hill, and Lt. Edward Culp recalled, "On they came, with their wild, diabolical yells, up to our first line of stone fence . . . and the carnage began. I cannot describe the scene that followed. Nothing would stay the progress of the rebels."[25]

Men from the 9th Louisiana hit the 75th Ohio and fought their way across the wall and captured the regiment's flag. According to Union Capt. Ben Fox, "A 1st Lieut[enant] was first to enter. I had no pistol and not having my sabre drawn, I hit him with a rock. He not over ten feet at the farthest from me. A private of Co. D was ready for him with cold steel, or the bayonet, and making a lung[e] at him, ran it through up to the hub, putting an end to the Lieut. The Reb Colors next came with a lot of mad men—did not stop. Up and on they went, the battery was what they wanted." The Tigers slammed hard against the angle in the Union line, and hand-to-hand fighting, described as "obstinate and bloody," broke out and spread down the wall from north to south. Schuler wrote, "They kept coming up the hill. . . . Then we opened up our fire on them. Some of them fell. They came within about fifteen feet of our location. Our Adjutant asked their Captain, 'Will you surrender?' 'No, Sir!' So the Adjutant shot the Captain." One of the Tigers recalled the close-quartered fight years later. "[T]he Yankees [were] on one side and we on the other side of the wall—knocked each other down with clubbed guns and bayonets. This is the first fight in which I felt certain of killing a Yankee."[26]

After the battle, Lieutenant Jackson admitted that that some of the federals fought furiously at the wall. He wrote, "mr yank . . . did not want to leave. But with bayonets & clubbed guns we drove them back." Raising the rebel yell, Hays' men finally broke through the angle where the 25th Ohio was positioned. Sergeant George S. Clements recalled that the Tigers "put their big feet on the stone wall and went over like deer, over the heads of the whole regiment." With their line breached, many of the Yankees withdrew back up the hill to Wiedrich's battery so as not to be cut off. To the right, however, the 75th Ohio and 17th Connecticut were in a stronger position on a slight knoll that was somewhat higher than the rest of the line. The two regiments opened fire on the Tigers at 150 yards and thinned the rebel ranks, but the Tigers closed in and another wild hand-to-hand fight broke out. This time the determined Yankees held the line, and one Connecticut captain actually grabbed a Louisianian and dragged him over the wall as a prisoner.[27]

Meanwhile, the North Carolina Tar Heels had advanced under heavy artillery fire and struck Von Gilsa's brigade on the Union right. Colonel Avery, however, never made it that far. A bullet hit him in the right side of the neck and knocked him off his horse, but no one noticed in the smoke and confusion. Realizing that he was mortally wounded, Avery took out a piece of paper and managed to scrawl a note to Maj. Samuel Tate before dying. "Major," it read, "tell my father I died with my face to the enemy."[28]

The 33rd Massachusetts, which had been posted out front as skirmishers during the day, had withdrawn to the far right when the rebels first advanced out of Culp's Meadow. Colonel Adin Underwood watched in the growing darkness as the North Carolinians moved forward and later wrote, "The roar and shriek of the shot and shell that ploughs through and through their ranks is appalling. The gaps close bravely up and still they advance. Canister cannot check them." The 57th North Carolina got within fifty yards of Underwood before his men opened fire. The rebel line was staggered but kept moving forward, and the Massachusetts men braced for the impact. The Tar Heels' flag was almost at the wall when off to the right Stevens' battery opened an enfilading fire, and the enemy colors fell. When the smoke cleared, the Tar Heels were piled up in heaps.[29]

To the left of the Massachusetts boys, Von Gilsa's 68th and 54th New York held a relatively low spot, and knolls and swales in their front protected the rebels until they popped into view only a short distance away. Two months earlier at Chancellorsville, these same rebels had flanked and routed the New Yorkers, and only the day before they had been flanked again at Gettysburg and suffered terrible losses. It was the perfect place for the Tar Heels to make a breakthrough. Sweeping over the wall, the North Carolinians killed the 54th New York's color-bearer and then wounded two men in quick succession who dared to pick up the fallen flag. When the 57th North Carolina's Col. Archibald Godwin climbed over the wall, a huge Yankee swung his musket, but Godwin parried the blow with his arm and hacked down with his sword, splitting the man's skull. One federal claimed that "clubs, knives, stones and fists—anything calculated to inflict death or pain was resorted to." A Confederate color-bearer, perhaps from the 6th North Carolina, carried his flag in one hand and a rifle in the other and jumped up on the wall farther to the right in front of the 153rd Pennsylvania. "Surrender you Yankees!!" he yelled, but a Pennsylvanian ran him through with a bayonet and fired into him at the same time. A soldier nearby remembered how the minié ball blew out the back of the rebel's uniform as it blasted through his body at point-blank range. The Tar Heel fell, and the flag lay draped across the wall. A soldier from each side grabbed it, and a tug-of-war ensued until the Confederate finally was able to bring it back to his side. Not far away, when the 21st North Carolina lost its color-bearer, a major picked up the flag and was shot, and two more men were killed in rapid succession as they tried to retrieve the colors. "The hour was one of horror," remembered one soldier.[30]

Most of the Union line finally gave way and retreated up Cemetery Hill except for the 33rd Massachusetts and 41st New York, which stood firm on the far right, and the 75th Ohio and 17th Connecticut, which continued to hold the center. Some witnesses mistakenly believed that all of the federals ran away after little resistance. Captain Ricketts accused the defenders of panicking and fleeing so frantically up the hill that they ran into the canister he was firing at the enemy. It was an ungracious comment on Ricketts' part, considering the stubborn fight put up by those federals who held their positions. The smoke and darkness undoubtedly hid many brave acts, and only those soldiers who fled were easily visible.[31]

It was now time for Hays' men to make their final push up the hill, but the task was not easy. As one Tiger recalled, "we could look up and see the Yankees far above us, pouring down a fire from both artillery and musketry." On top of Cemetery Hill, Union artilleryman August Buell noticed that the rebels never halted to return fire in their climb toward him. "If they had fired a volley at us then there is little doubt that the remnant of our poor ole Battery would have been wiped out; but for some reason they came on with cold steel alone. It may be imagined that we gave them the best we had, but artillery fire does not have its best effect upon troops coming straight on, and it is plain that we could not have stopped them with our four guns unaided."[32]

Generals Carl Schurz and Oliver O. Howard were near the cemetery when they heard the Tigers raise what Howard called "the shrill and ominous" rebel yell as they charged the wall. Schurz ordered two of Wladimir Krzyzanowski's regiments to fix bayonets and rush through the cemetery to help Wiedrich defend his battery, and General Howard appealed to Winfield Scott Hancock for reinforcements. Hancock sent him Col. Samuel Carroll's II Corps brigade, the same regiments that had fought some of the Tigers a year earlier at Port Republic. Carroll had only three regiments available—the 14th Indiana, the 4th Ohio, and the 7th West Virginia—but he rushed them through the cemetery at such a rapid pace that soldiers had to discard their knapsacks and blankets just to keep up with him. It was so dark and smoky that some men ran into grave markers, and others heard the ominous sound of bullets splattering against the headstones. The first thing one of the men witnessed when he arrived at Ricketts' battery was an artilleryman using a rock to kill a Tiger who had climbed on top of one of the gun tubes.[33]

By now, the Confederates had lost all cohesion and were little more than two armed mobs rushing into the batteries—the Tigers on the Union left heading for Wiedrich's battery and the Tar Heels and a few Louisianians on the right aiming for Ricketts. Like water rushing around a rock, the rebel line was split by the stubborn stand made by the 17th Connecticut and 75th Ohio at the stone wall. The 8th Louisiana's Lieutenant Jackson claimed it was so dark by the time the final rush was made that "we couldn't tell whether we were shooting our own men or not." Major Tate estimated that only 75 of his men and maybe a dozen of the 9th Louisiana were still with him when he climbed over the wall, and Colonel Godwin reported that there was so much confusion in the smoke and darkness that only about 50 men accompanied him for the final rush to the Union guns. Thus, in all probability, no more than 150 rebels made the final charge against Ricketts' battery. Leroy A. Stafford, colonel of the 9th Louisiana, was one of them, and he sprinted ahead to be the first to reach the guns. Major John Hodges, however, passed up Stafford, followed closely behind by the 9th Louisiana's color-bearer, who defiantly jabbed his flag next to a cannon.[34]

One wounded Ohio soldier who was headed to the rear reached the top of Cemetery Hill about the same time the rebels did. He later recalled, "The bullets seemed to come criss cross from every way, but I was just ahead of them. . . . As I ran up the hill between the cannon which were belching war, and on across Cemetery Hill I looked to my left and saw the rebs right among our guns and noted through the smoke hand to hand fighting. . . . Dear me but that was a terrible place just at that time!" The wounded soldier then encountered Krzyzanowski's reinforcements running toward Wiedrich's battery and claimed, "I came near being run over." From that point on, there is conflicting testimony about the fight for the guns. The Confederates claimed they captured the two batteries and held them for some time. The federal artillerymen, however, said there was a brief but fierce hand-to-hand fight, during which the rebels entered the batteries, but they remained only briefly.[35]

General Schurz claimed that, when he reached the batteries, he discovered "an indescribably [sic] scene of mêlée." Some of the Confederates were among the guns, and an intense hand-to-hand fight was raging, with the federal gunners using rammers, fence rails, hand spikes, and rocks to knock down the enemy. The Tar Heels and Tigers captured Ricketts' left guns and tried unsuccessfully to spike them. A Confederate lieutenant grabbed for the battery's guidon on the lunette, but a pistol-wielding artilleryman who was nearby on horseback shot him down. The artilleryman then took the banner and turned to retreat, but a bullet tore through his body and shattered the flagstaff. Dismounting, the stricken man staggered to Captain Ricketts and cried, "Help me captain!" before collapsing dead.[36]

When the Confederates tumbled into the battery, a Yankee lieutenant saw a rebel point a rifle at one of his sergeants and demand his surrender. The officer quickly threw a rock into the rebel's head, and the sergeant grabbed the man's rifle. As the Confederate fell, the sergeant shot him in the stomach and began clubbing him with the rifle's butt, breaking his arm as he tried to parry the blow. The bloodied man then cried for quarter. The lieutenant excused the sergeant's excessive zeal by noting that in the dark it was not clear how badly he had hurt the enemy soldier with the gunshot, and the sergeant simply was not taking any chances. While this bloody fight raged among Ricketts' left guns, incredibly the cannons on the right, only a few feet away, continued to fire. Major Tate claimed that Ricketts' artillerymen fought "with a tenacity never before displayed by them, but with bayonets, clubbed muskets, sword, and pistol, and rocks" the Confederates finally loosened their grip on the battery and forced them out. Ricketts lost six dead, fourteen wounded, and three missing during the short fight.[37]

To Tate's right, the Tigers were also storming Wiedrich's battery. When one Louisiana officer reached the guns, he waved his sword and yelled, "This battery is ours!" but a German artilleryman declared, "No, dis battery is unser" and knocked him down with a sponge staff. Another officer threw himself across one of the cannons and cried out, "I take command of this gun!" A federal holding the lanyard screamed out in German, "You can have this!" and literally blew the rebel to bits.[38]

The Louisiana color-bearers suffered particularly heavy losses in the charge up the hill. The 6th Louisiana's color-bearer, Sgt. Phillip Bolger, was badly wounded, and the 5th Louisiana's was killed. Private Arthur Duchamp carried the 8th Louisiana's flag and made it across the stone wall but was wounded during the final rush to the guns. Corporal Leon Gusman, a twenty-one-year-old former student, picked up the flag and entered the battery with a number of comrades. Lieutenant Jackson wrote afterward that Gusman "was then wd or taken & our colors lost," but what actually transpired was much more dramatic.[39]

When Gusman reached the guns, he waved his flag triumphantly overhead. Lieutenant Peter Young of the 107th Ohio claimed the enemy were "yelling like demons" around the cannons when Sergeant Nussbaum pointed out to him a flag-waving rebel who was surrounded by a small group of men. Young ordered his Buckeyes to fire on the flag, and all of the Tigers ran away except Gusman, who fell to one knee, still clutching his colors. Young wrote:

> I ran forward, revolver in hand, shot down the rebel Color bearer (8th La. Tiger Regt. as it proved by the inscription on the vile rag) and sprang for the colors, at the same time a rebel, seeing his comrade fall, sprang forward and caught them but fell to the ground, where I wrested them from him. These in one hand and revolver in the other, I was in the act of turning towards our men, when a rebel bullet pierced my left lung and arm. . . . I kept on my feet till I reached our men when all strength left me and my Sergt. Maj. Henry Brinker caught me in his arms as I was falling. . . . I learned subsequently that a rebel Lt. followed me with drawn sword and was about to strike me, when Lt. F[ernando] C. Suhrer of our Regt. gave him a saber cut on the shoulder, which brought him down.[40]

After Gusman was killed, the Yankees searched his body. Sergeant Nussbaum wrote: "We made a quick examination of the color-bearer's body and found seven bullet holes through him; we also examined the contents of his canteen which, being nearly full, contained whiskey and gun powder, and which we judged accounted for his desperate bravery. I took his knapsack which was a very neat one, made of leather with a goat-skin cover, and which contained a single biscuit lately baked being yet warm; being minus my own knapsack, I carried it a while, but the Comrades made so much fun of me that I threw it away for which act I have been sorry ever since."[41]

Maryland cavalryman Maj. Harry Gilmor accompanied Hays' brigade and witnessed another fight for a flag.

> While advancing on the main line of works, I saw one of our colour-bearers jump on a gun and display his flag. He was instantly killed. But the flag was seized by an Irishman, who, with a wild shout, sprang upon the gun, and he too was shot down. Then a little bit of a fellow, a captain, seized the staff and mounted the same gun; but, as he raised the flag, a ball broke the arm which held it. He dropped his sword, and caught the staff with his right before it fell, waved it over his head with a cheer, indifferent to the pain of his shattered limb and the whizzing balls around him. His third cheer was just heard, when he tottered and fell, pierced through the lungs.[42]

The anonymous officer's men scooped him up and brought him downhill to the wall, and Gilmor carried him back to the main line.

Hays' Tigers had, for the moment, seized Wiedrich's battery, and Avery's Tar Heels and a few Louisianians had captured part of Ricketts' battery, but the support needed to expand the breakthrough was not at hand. Rodes' division was supposed to have joined in the attack on Hays' right, but Rodes never got into a position to do so. Before the attack even began, Hays was concerned that he would not be supported as promised and sent an officer to impress on Rodes the importance of his role in the attack, but the officer found Rodes "completely choked up in the narrow streets of the town with his division, and consequently he could not aid us."[43]

Left alone on the hilltop, Hays' men squirmed into position around the captured batteries, checked their cartridge boxes, and waited for the coming

Union counterattack. Out in the darkness the Tigers could hear the sound of massed men on the move and could occasionally see shadowy figures coming their way. The ghostly movement proved to be the two regiments General Schurz had sent to help—the 119th and 58th New York of Krzyzanowski's brigade. Hays, however, was not certain if the approaching men were the enemy because he was still hoping that Rodes might come up on his right. But when the Yankees were only twenty yards away they fired three volleys into the battery, and Hays saw by the muzzle flashes that they were Yankees. When the rebels responded with a volley of their own, Hays could see three more Union battle lines approaching and realized he was hopelessly outnumbered. Outgunned and unsupported, he yelled for the Tigers to fall back to the stone wall, and a general withdrawal began at about 10:00 p.m.[44]

The Tigers and Tar Heels on Hays' left also found themselves overwhelmed. The few men who had followed Major Tate into Ricketts' battery could hear Carroll's brigade maneuvering in the dark. As Carroll's three regiments approached the battery, one of the artillerymen shouted, "Glory to God! We are saved!!" Carroll wrote, "It being perfectly dark, and with no guide, I had to find the enemy's line entirely by their fire." Twice the Confederates dispersed the advancing Union counterattack with well-aimed volleys, but Major Tate finally ordered the men to make a run for it through the ever-increasing hail of bullets. During the retreat, the 9th Louisiana's Billy Singleton and the Irish-born Patrick "Mib" McGee helped one of their wounded officers back down the hill. McGee was then shot through the hand but continued to help, despite the officer's protests. McGee had taken only a few more steps when a canister shot shattered his ankle, and he fell to the ground. Singleton then hoisted the officer up onto his back and carried on alone for two hundred yards before another Tiger saw him by the light of the cannons' flash and came to his assistance. McGee apparently made it back to Gettysburg but later died of his wounds.[45]

Carroll sent his men rushing after Tate and captured a few of the slower rebels. The pursuing Yankees then stopped at the stone wall and fired blindly into the darkness after the retreating enemy. No one fired back, but out of the blackness came a deep Irish voice identifying himself as a federal and pleading for them to stop firing. When told to come over the wall, a large, burly Irishman climbed over and yelled, "Thank Jasus, I'm in the Union again."[46]

The Tigers who returned to Gettysburg that night were in a foul mood. It was generally believed that Rodes' failure to advance had ruined an excellent opportunity to cripple Meade's army. The men ranted that once again the Louisiana Tigers had breached the Yankee line, but others had failed to take advantage of it. "A madder set of men I never saw," wrote a federal prisoner who witnessed their return. "They cursed their officers in a way and manner that showed experience in the business. . . . It was simply fearful. . . . They said their officers didn't care how many were killed, and especially old Hays, who was receiving his share of the curses." A civilian who had watched Hays' men rout Howard's corps the day before wrote, "There seemed now to be an entire absence of that elation and boastfulness which they manifested when they entered the town on the evening of the first of July." Gates Fahnestock, a young Gettysburg resident, also witnessed the rebels' return: "What was left of the Louisiana Tigers were not so jubilant—they were tired, exhausted, and discouraged; and what they said of the Germans in Howard's command on Cemetery Hill was not complimentary." Those Tigers who were captured on Cemetery Hill were equally dejected. A Union soldier recounted how one of them declared that he had been in twenty-two battles but "had never been whipped before and that they had never seen such desperate fighting as they had met with that night; that they were the worst whipped men I had ever seen."[47]

Hays was among those who were angry and frustrated. About the time he decided to retreat, his quartermaster arrived with news that Gordon's brigade was coming up to reinforce him. Hays began reforming his line to make another try for the batteries and sent an officer back to find Gordon, but the officer was unable to locate the Georgia brigade. Hays then went back down the hill himself and found Gordon waiting at Winebrenner's Run, where the advance had begun. Realizing that Rodes had not advanced, either, and that it now was too late to make a second attempt on Cemetery Hill, Hays reluctantly gave up and brought his men back to a position alongside Gordon.[48]

For a brief moment, Lee's men had succeeded in breaking the Union line on Cemetery Hill and clearing a path to the rear of Meade's army. The Yankee defenders realized they had won by the narrowest of margins and could not help but respect the rebels' bravery. One of them described Hays' attack as "a grand, though gory, example of the heroism of the American soldier," while another wrote that it was "another fruitless display of magnificent bravery, in which life and zeal were thrown away." The failed attack cost Hays 21 dead, 119 wounded, and 41 missing, while the Tar Heels suffered about 200 casualties. Among those lost were some of the Louisianians' most effective officers. Colonel Trevanion Lewis, Maj. Henry L. N. Williams, and Capts. Victor St. Martin and Louis Cormier were killed or mortally wounded, and many others were wounded and put out of action for the foreseeable future.[49]

Colonel Lewis was a former clerk from New Orleans who had been wounded at Antietam and captured during the Valley Campaign and at Second Fredericksburg. On his service record someone wrote, "He was an excellent officer and very much regretted by his regiment. A gallant, brave and military man." Nineteen-year-old Captain Cormier of the 6th Louisiana was shot in the stomach and taken to a barn that served as one of the Tigers' field hospitals. The next day, several local women came to help the wounded and paid special attention to him because of his youth. Cormier declared that he knew he was mortally wounded and asked if they would return later "to see him die." They did, and Cormier talked of his mother and two sisters before asking the women to kiss him goodbye. He then died.[50]

Apparently, a truce was arranged sometimes in the next forty-eight hours that allowed the Louisianians to retrieve some of the wounded men who had fallen into enemy hands. Charles Moore of the 5th Louisiana was shot in the foot during the charge up Cemetery Hill and woke up in a Union hospital, where a surgeon removed the ball and bound his wound. Later a Confederate ambulance came to the hospital, picked up Moore and Capt. St. Clair Johns, also of the 5th Louisiana, and carried them to Hays' hospital. Johns was captured after being left behind when Lee retreated, but he was soon exchanged.[51]

Hays' attack on Cemetery Hill was one of the most dramatic moments in a battle filled with drama, but it has not received the same attention as the fight for Little Round Top or Pickett's Charge. It should, however, because participants viewed it as a critical moment in the Union victory. General Schurz claimed, "The fate of the battle might have hinged on the repulse of the attack," and historian Douglas Southall Freeman wrote, "The whole of the three days' battle produced no more tragic might-have-been than this twilight engagement on the Confederate left." Even Union Pvt. Luther Mesnard wrote that Cemetery Hill was "the place where the battle of Gettysburg came nearer being lost than at any other point of time."[52]

Two mistakes caused the Confederates' defeat. First, Early erred in not having Gordon immediately follow up Hays. From the edge of town, Early had watched as Hays moved his men forward and ordered Gordon to advance from the railroad. But by the time Gordon reached Winebrenner's Run, where Hays' assault began, wounded men were already returning from the front. They told Gordon that the attack was going well, but that no one could see Rodes anywhere to the right. Realizing that Rodes had not moved up to support Hays, Early ordered Gordon to halt because he believed that putting him into the fight without support on the right would have only added to the casualty list and gained no benefit. If Early had put Gordon closer to the front and sent him in immediately behind Hays, perhaps he could have reinforced Hays when the batteries were captured and then held them against the Union counterattack.[53]

The Confederates' greater mistake was Rodes' failure to support the attack. As Hays and Avery advanced, Early sent a staff officer to hurry Rodes forward, but there was no coordination between the two divisions. Rodes, who was positioned inside Gettysburg, wrote that he had been ordered that afternoon to cooperate with Longstreet's attack on the far right as soon as an opportunity presented itself. When Longstreet advanced that afternoon, Rodes saw movement on top of Cemetery Hill and consulted Early, and both agreed to act together in an advance. Rodes began making preparations but found out too late that it would require considerable time to move his division out of town and get into position on Hays' right. He never explained why he did not move out earlier in the day when he was first ordered to cooperate with Longstreet. General Stephen Ramseur, whose brigade was to lead the attack, crept forward in the dark to reconnoiter and reported seeing a heavy line of enemy artillery and infantry. By that time, Early's attack was over, and Rodes decided not to assault the Yankees' strong position in his front.[54]

The fight for Cemetery Hill received a great deal of attention, at the time, and the participants began bickering over who did what soon after the battle ended. Major Tate quickly realized that the North Carolinians' role in the attack was being ignored in favor of the more famous Louisiana Tigers. On July 8, 1863, he informed North Carolina Gov. Zebulon Vance that just a few members of the 9th Louisiana accompanied his 6th North Carolina to Ricketts' battery. When no one came to support them as promised, Tate assumed the responsibility of ordering a retreat. Upon reaching the Confederate lines, he angrily asked why he had not been supported and "was coolly told" that no one knew he had made it into the battery's works. Tate went on to tell the governor that he expected General Early would claim that it was impossible to take the hill when, in fact, the Tar Heels would have succeeded if only they had been properly supported. "All we ask is, don't let old North Carolina be derided, while her sons do all the fighting." Long after the war ended, another North Carolina veteran took issue with the Tigers receiving all of the credit for the twilight attack. He denounced those "lying writers who have reported the charge as that of the 'Louisiana Tigers'" and correctly pointed out that the three North Carolina regiments lost more men in the attack than the five Louisiana regiments combined.[55]

On the Union side, veterans of Krzyzanowski's and Carroll's brigades argued after the war about who should receive more credit for turning back Hays' attack. Carroll's men and at least one of Ricketts' artillerymen believed it was Carroll's brigade that saved Cemetery Hill. Krzyzanowski's supporters, however, claimed that his three German-dominated regiments did most of the fighting while few of Carroll's soldiers even fired a shot. The truth is that both brigades played a key role in the victory. Krzyzanowski's counterattack focused on saving Wiedrich's battery on the left while Carroll recaptured Ricketts' battery on the right. In the dark and confusion it is understandable that the men in the separate brigades saw little of the other that night.[56]

There is an interesting postscript to the struggle for Gettysburg's high ground. On December 8, 1941, Richard C. S. Drummond, secretary of the Cayuga County (New York) Historical Society, wrote Louisiana governor Sam Houston Jones to inform him of the existence of what was claimed to be the 8th Louisiana's battle flag that was captured atop Cemetery Hill. Drummond did not say how a flag captured by an Ohio regiment had made its way to New York, but he explained that the last member of the local Grand Army of the Republic (GAR) post had passed away and that the flag was found among the post's property. He sent Jones a photograph of the flag and offered to return it to the people of Louisiana. The flag itself was unusual, for it had a white background (instead of the normal red), a red St. Andrew's Cross (instead of blue), and the words "Louisiana Tigers" painted on it in blue letters. Because of its unusual coloring and the lack of a unit designation, many historians doubt its authenticity. The point is now moot, however, for apparently World War II distracted the authorities, and the colors were never returned to the Bayou State. Attempts to relocate it have failed, but perhaps somewhere in a dusty attic or an old trunk there remains a relic of the bitter fighting for Gettysburg's Cemetery Hill.[57]

Other flags also disappeared atop Cemetery Hill that bloody night. The 9th Louisiana's flag was captured, and Union soldiers may have torn it to pieces for souvenirs. A member of the 17th Connecticut recalled looking at the dead and wounded strewn about and seeing "a rebel color bearer lying dead near our batteries. . . . I picked up a couple of stars that had been torn from a rebel flag and a piece of the flag also." The stars he collected may have been all that remained of the 9th Louisiana's flag. Private Nathan Holmes Willis of the 9th Louisiana apparently captured the 75th Ohio's flag, and Capt. A. L. Gusman presented it to General Hays, although he mistakenly identified it as belonging to the 57th Ohio. In 1889, Hays' widow contacted the GAR and offered to return an unidentified Union flag that was captured at Gettysburg. Unfortunately, there is no record of what transpired after that, and the flag is still missing.[58]

After spending a restless night just outside town, Hays' brigade rested on July 3, but it was still subjected to the federal sharpshooters' frightfully accurate fire. When Ewell and Early's engineer, Capt. H. B. Richardson, rode past the prone brigade, the two officers were warned of the sharpshooters, but Ewell scoffed at the danger because the federals were at least half a mile away. Within moments, Ewell was hit in his wooden leg, and Richardson was shot through the body.[59]

Early finally had Hays move his men back into the streets to act as a reserve force, but some of Hays' men remained on skirmish duty at the edge of town. Lieutenant Henry E. Handerson of the 9th Louisiana had just rejoined his regiment that morning after being on wounded furlough. To reach his company on the south side of Gettysburg, he had to sprint across Baltimore Street while dodging the sharpshooters' fire. Weaving his way through backyards and gardens, he finally reached the house where his company was holed up. "Here an amusing sight met my view. Around a table at the center of the room were gathered the majority of my company, engaged in discussing a generous meal, apparently procured by ransacking the pantry and cellar of the mansion, while at each of the front windows a couple of men were occasionally exchanging shots with the enemy, being relieved at intervals by their comrades and retiring to join the feast until their turn once more came around. Of course I was met with a hearty welcome."[60]

The Union sharpshooters on Cemetery Hill also harassed Handerson's regimental comrade Thomas Reed when he accompanied a detail to cook rations. "While we were getting ready, and while I was going into a house, whack! went something. Then I heard something drop on the floor on the other side of the house. I went and picked it up, and it was a ball shot from one of those globe-sighted guns. The ball had struck the wall of the house some two feet from the door, and about two feet up from the floor. He had come that nigh getting me, and I knew he was at least half a mile away. The way those devils did [it] was to climb up trees with their guns and spy-glasses and then pop away at us." Private William H. Poole, also of the 9th Louisiana, was not so lucky. While skirmishing, he took up a position at a second floor window that provided a good view of Cemetery Hill. Poole rested his rifle across an overturned table, but a Union sharpshooter fired a bullet that went through the table and into his chest. The homeowners found Poole dead the next morning and buried him.[61]

Major Eugene Blackford of the 5th Alabama commanded Rodes' sharpshooters to the right of Hays' men and had an encounter with the Louisianians that day. Blackford recalled how at mid-morning an officer who claimed to command Hays' sharpshooters came to him and said he was ordered to get directions from Blackford on where to find his post. The major instructed the Louisianian on how to reach a particular house and later went to check on him. When Blackford reached the Tigers' position, he found a "truly amusing scene. His quarters were in a very [nice] house, and he had selected the parlor as his own bivouac. Here one was playing the piano, which sounded sadly out of harmony with the roar of musketry. Without, several men were laying around on the sofas, and the room was full of prints & engravings which the rude fellows examined, and then threw down on the floor. On the table there was a doz[en] brands of wines and liquors, of which all partook freely. The commanding officer thought it was very strange that I at once insisted upon his visiting his post, and making the men fire."[62]

At the end of the day, Hays' pickets were forced to fire on one of their own men, a deserter who suddenly abandoned the picket line and took off running toward the federal positions on Cemetery Hill. The anonymous Tiger made it safely to the Union soldiers stationed at the stone wall where so much blood had been spilled the night before and was sent to the rear. He explained that he was a sailor from Pittsburgh who had joined the Confederate navy in 1861 while drunk in New Orleans and was later conscripted into the 5th Louisiana. During the twilight attack, he attempted to desert by feigning a wound in the hope of being left behind, but his comrades picked him up and carried him back down the hill. One other Tiger is known to have taken the opportunity to desert at Gettysburg, and he went on to join the Union army.[63]

While Hays' pickets dueled with their Union counterparts near town, the fighting on Culp's Hill renewed at 4:00 a.m., July 3, when the Yankees opened fire on the rebel units that had gained a foothold there. Tens of thousands of minié balls ripped through the trees, killing an entire forest and raining limbs on top of Colonel Williams' Tigers. Colonel Zable recalled that "the roar of musketry was so intense that it was useless to attempt to give a command unless shouted into the men's ears. . . . [H]ad the enemy fired with more deliberation they would have annihialated [sic] the Brigade, as it was, our loss was severe. Our foes were evidently demoralized, shooting wild into the tree tops so that the leaves and limbs were falling so thick and fast that it seemed it was raining." It was, Zable declared, "the most terrific [firing] we ever experienced." When Confederate reinforcements were finally sent to help the Tigers, they made the mistake of raising the rebel yell as they came up the hill. Alerted to their presence, the federals quickly focused their fire on the reinforcements and cut them to pieces. Williams' men were so close to the enemy that they were fairly well protected by the hill's slope, but their fellow soldiers were completely exposed. Colonel Zable wrote, "As we looked behind us and saw our comrades coming to relieve us being killed and wounded to no purpose, we regretted that we were being relieved." Years later, Zable still remembered the horrific rifle fire and claimed, "Perhaps no other Confederate troops were under longer continuous fire than was that part of Johnson's Division, commencing on the evening of July 2nd, and with a four hour intermission, continuing until late the following day."[64]

When Gen. George Pickett's desperate charge on the afternoon of July 3 failed to crack Meade's defenses, Lee decided to pull back to McPherson's and Seminary ridges to a stronger, shorter line in hope that Meade would attack him the next day. After Williams' 2nd Louisiana Brigade withdrew to a position north of Gettysburg, a local woman surprised Colonel Zable when she emerged from the house she had been holed up in since the battle began. According to Zable, she asked "when this foolishness was going to stop, saying she had not milked her cows in three days."[65]

Hays' brigade vacated Gettysburg by 2:00 a.m. on July 4, but not all of the Tigers made it out of town. When Union troops cautiously advanced at daylight, they captured about three hundred Confederate prisoners, many of whom were Tigers who had slept through the withdrawal. The wounded Justus Silliman reported that the Confederates departed so quickly that they even left behind thousands of captured rifles that were neatly stacked in the streets. He proudly reported home, "I have captured a La tiger belt plate also a piece of a reb flag." Someone also picked up an abandoned Tiger drum in the street which was later displayed in California's Sutter's Fort museum.[66]

When Hays reformed his brigade on McPherson's Ridge about two miles northwest of town, he had the men construct defensive works to meet the expected Union attack. Unfortunately, the ground the Tigers occupied was where much of the first day's battle had taken place, and bodies still littered the area. Captain Brown of Ewell's staff recalled, "Corpses so monstrously swollen that the buttons were broken from the loose blouses & shirts, & the baggy pantaloons fitted like a skin—so blackened that the head looked like an immense cannon ball, the features being nearly obliterated—& that the necks were almost undistinguishable, being marked only by a sharp line between head & body. I saw one or two heads actually forced from the body by the swelling of both."[67]

When Meade declined to attack the rebels, Lee decided it was time to withdraw back to Virginia. The retreat began on the night of July 4, with Early's division acting as rearguard. For the thousands of wounded who were hauled off in wagons, the nightmare that followed was sheer torture. R. J. Hancock wrote that he was in agony when his shattered thigh swelled to twice its normal size, and he was bounced around in a rickety wagon for eighteen days. One twice-wounded Louisiana officer became delirious from pain and grief over his brother's death and committed suicide in a hospital by slitting his own throat. Others were more fortunate once they reached Virginia. Wade G. Chick of the 7th Louisiana wrote a friend months later to tell her that his hospital had fresh milk from fourteen cows that were brought back from Pennsylvania.[68]

Hundreds of Lee's wounded men were left behind in Union hands because they could not survive the trip back to Virginia. Some, like the 6th Louisiana's Captain Cormier, received competent care in hospitals or private homes. Others, like Wolf Lichenstein, suffered untold horrors. He was among a number of Tigers who were left unattended in a barn owned by a "Dutch" farmer who hated the rebels. Lichenstein paid the farmer "hard money" to help them, but the more seriously wounded soon began to die. One of Lichenstein's friends wrote, "In time the accumulated dead bodies decayed, the stench was something awful, and, in this condition those alive remained for seven days!" Lichenstein finally bribed the farmer to alert Union soldiers to their predicament, and the men were taken to the Seminary for treatment. His friend claimed that "Wolf was a sight. Covered with dirt, vermin and dried blood, his wounds foul and reeking, weak from lack of attention and nourishment, he was at death's door, and he looked it." The surgeons advised amputating his shattered arm, but Lichenstein refused and survived his ordeal.[69]

Lichenstein's comrade Albert Batchelor was also among the wounded who were left behind. Incredibly, he recovered from the bullets that tore through his head and leg. About six weeks later, Albert wrote his father from a hospital near Gettysburg to let his family know that he was alive. "It has pleased the God of battles that I should number among the many wounded of the great and hotly contested battle fought near this place." By that time, Albert had recovered enough to move about on his own, and he marveled at his "almost miraculous escape." About two months later, he wrote his brother Charles to tell him "that he has entirely recovered being not in the least disfigured."[70]

Some of the dead Tigers were buried in unmarked graves, and in 1949 someone discovered a skull, along with a Louisiana breastplate, on property that housed a field hospital. In 2014, an auction company put the skull and some accompanying artifacts up for sale with the hope of getting $50,000 to $250,000 for the gruesome relics. Fortunately, there was such a public outcry that the company canceled the sale and turned the remains over to the Gettysburg National Military Park.[71]

Lee lost more than 20,000 men during the three-week invasion. In the Battle of Gettysburg, Hays' losses were reported to be 36 dead, 201 wounded (at least 8 of whom died in Union hands), and 76 missing, and Williams counted 44 dead, 309 wounded, and 36 missing. The two brigades' casualty lists, however, are not consistent. Another puts Hays' total losses at 194 and Williams' at 291, but even these numbers do not tell the entire story. On June 19, when the invasion was young, Hays had 1,626 officers and men on duty. On July 8, only 945 answered roll call—the rest were casualties or straggling somewhere on the muddy roads. Losses were so severe that officials took rather desperate measures to rebuild the brigades. During the campaign, the Richmond *Daily Dispatch* ran an official notice offering amnesty to all Tigers who had been left behind because they were under arrest. They were to report to the recruiting headquarters by the end of July to be placed back on active duty.[72]

Even northerners noted the heavy losses in the Louisiana brigades. An Ohio newspaper declared, "The 'Louisiana Tigers,' who include the scrapings of New Orleans, and were perhaps as desperate a band of outlaws as were ever gotten together—always excepting the Texas Rangers . . . have been nearly annihilated in the late battle of Gettysburg." A Pennsylvania newspaper agreed and reported, "There was lately a great slaughter of tigers in Pennsylvania. Of the 1,200 'Louisiana Tigers' that made a charge at Gettysburg only 300 saved their spotted skins."[73]

Despite their heavy losses, the Confederates retreated from Pennsylvania in high spirits. Herman Dinkgrave wrote home on the day the retreat began and reported that the 2nd Louisiana had marched 463 miles since June 12. "So you can imagine how wearied we must be though the boys keep in good spirits and are confident of success." Colonel Zable noticed the same determination and later recalled, "The Army of Northern Virginia had passed through a fiery furnace [but] they still believed our great Lee would lead us to final victory." The men were convinced that it was the Yankees' strong position, and not any superior fighting skills, that had led to defeat. Campbell Brown probably summed up most of the Tigers' feelings when he wrote, "It would be ridiculous to say that I did not feel whipped—or that there was a man in that Army who didn't appreciate the position just as plainly. But the 'fight' wasn't out of the troops by any means—they felt that the position & not the enemy had out done us. . . . Such at least were the feelings of all with whom I talked."[74]

Father Sheeran was amazed at the Tigers' good spirits despite "wading to their knees in the mud and mire." The troops, he claimed, "were as cheerful a body of men as I ever saw, and to hear them, you would think they were going to a party of pleasure instead of retreating from a hard fought battle." Even when exhaustion overcame them on the miserable march, they did not lose their sense of humor. Private Reed wrote that after an extended period of silence someone would yell out, "Hello! John! How would you like to be a soldier boy?" "Knock that fool in the head!" another would answer, and a good laugh would perk them up for a while longer.[75]

The men's morale remained high because they knew the campaign had accomplished some of its goals and had enhanced the reputation of the Louisiana Tigers. From Hagerstown, Maryland, Captain Pierson wrote home, "The men are generally in fine spirits and would give the Yankees a hearty welcome with bloody hands if they were to attempt to drive us from our present position." He went on to say that the invasion was worth the sacrifice because the army was bringing back from Pennsylvania hundreds of cattle, huge amounts of bacon, more than one thousand horses, badly needed medicine, captured artillery, and "an immense amount of small arms and ammunition." While

Pierson admitted that the army had suffered a tremendous loss in men, he argued that they would have been lost anyhow if the fighting had taken place in Virginia, but the army would have not acquired the material gains it did in Pennsylvania. "With such men as Lee, Ewell, Hill & Longstreet," he wrote, "I am willing to tie my future destiny in this war. They have already proven themselves worthy of the confidence of their men and now they have the whole matter in their own hands."[76]

As for their reputation, the Tigers knew that they had fought well against overwhelming odds. Hays' men were particularly cocky. "Need I mention," wrote John F. Gruber to David F. Boyd, "that your gallant little Brigade won laurels upon laurels." In addition to briefly breaking the federal line on Cemetery Hill, he claimed, "At Winchester the[y] stormed a fortification with eight cannons scattering the rather bluish looking inmates in every direction. . . . Whatever stain the conduct and misdeeds of a few may have made upon its name, Hays' La. Brigade ranks second to none in bravery and daring, the ——— Stonewall [Brigade] not excepted." Gruber also claimed that Gettysburg had greatly enhanced Hays' reputation, as well. "[Hays] is growing more popular in the army and disappointment is manifested, that he is not been ere this made a Major General. He has wonderfully improved, he handled his Brigade at Winchester & Gettysburg very skillfully, while the great requisite to keep cool, is more with him a matter of course; add to this his gallantry and the majical [sic] influence it has over his men, it is not to be wondered at, that [the Tigers] look for some appreciation of them and their leader's service."[77]

The gallantry of Hays and his men did not go unappreciated. In his official report, General Ewell wrote that Hays' attack on Cemetery Hill "was worthy of the highest praise. In this and at Winchester the Louisiana brigade and their gallant commander gave new honor to the name already acquired on the old fields of Winchester and Port Republic, and wherever engaged." General Early also commended Hays, but he did not let it influence his stormy relationship with the Louisiana brigade. Shortly after returning to Virginia, he and the Tigers resumed their usual bickering, which prompted Gruber to write, "Just now a little feud is going on between old Jubal and our Brigade. Using an insignificant incident as a protest, he again denounced the Brigade in unmerciful terms and was impudent enough . . . to write a note embracing in substance his charges." The note so enraged Hays' officers that they once again pulled their trump card. "The officers unwilling to have their men [labeled] as thieves very promptly took the matter in hand and by a unanimous vote requested Gen. Hays to petition for a transfer to some other division." As expected, this action brought Ewell into the spat on the side of his Tigers. "Gen. Early is at present for once on the stool of penitence," reported Gruber, "he having avowed his willingness to retract anything said calculated to wound the feelings of either officers or men."[78]

Lee succeeded in making his escape across the rain-swollen Potomac River, although it was a difficult maneuver. Seymour wrote, "The passage of the Potomac was a very hazardous undertaking. The waters were very high, and the crossing was effected in the face of a watchful and powerful enemy. But it was accomplished with no loss of material except a few disabled wagons & two pieces of cannon which the horses were unable to drag through the deep mud. . . . The rain descended in torrents during the whole night and we all were soaked through to the skin."[79]

In early August, the army finally halted and took up a position on Virginia's Rapidan River to rest and reorganize. With only 713 officers and men left in Colonel Williams' shattered brigade, the Louisiana officers petitioned Lee either to apprehend the brigade's numerous deserters to refill the ranks, consolidate it with another command, or send it someplace for garrison duty where the small brigade could perform a valuable service while its officers recruited replacements. Colonel Williams disapproved of garrison duty but did forward the petition through channels in the hope that his officers would be allowed to recruit. Johnson, Ewell, and Lee all rejected the proposal, however, on the grounds that the Army of Northern Virginia could ill afford to lose, even temporarily, any of its brigades.[80]

In October, the 2nd Louisiana Brigade finally received a permanent commander when Col. Leroy A. Stafford was promoted to brigadier general and transferred from the 9th Louisiana. The forty-one-year-old Stafford had earned a reputation for being among the best of the Tiger officers. Born and raised in Rapides Parish, he was educated at the finest schools in Kentucky and Tennessee and had been a prominent planter near Cheneyville, Louisiana. After being elected parish sheriff in 1846, he served in the Mexican War as a private and received the only military training he had before the Civil War. Stafford opposed secession in 1861 but organized the Stafford Guards when some neighbors predicted that conservatives such as he would not fight if war came. Lieutenant Handerson described Stafford as being "Fond of a glass of liquor" and an avid card player who was normally a pleasant man but could become "violent and somewhat tyrannical when aroused." General James A. Walker claimed that Stafford was "one of the bravest and best men I ever knew," a sentiment Gen. Edward Johnson shared. According to General Ewell, Johnson believed Stafford "was the bravest man he ever saw. Such a compliment from one himself brave almost to a fault and habitually sparing of praise needs no remark."[81]

Lee's choice of Stafford to command the 2nd Louisiana Brigade is puzzling and was unpopular at the time. The brigade's officers and men looked upon him and his staff as "interlopers," who stole the command from Jesse M. Williams, the brigade's senior colonel and the officer who had led it through the bloody Gettysburg Campaign. It is not known why Lee chose the outsider Stafford to replace Williams, just as it is not known why Lee shuffled Stafford's 9th Louisiana into and out of the 2nd Louisiana Brigade earlier in the war. Stafford was an outstanding officer, but no criticism can be found of Williams for the way he handled the brigade during the Gettysburg Campaign. Although Lee no doubt had good reasons for choosing Stafford, the brigade's officers were angry at the decision, and it took time for the new commander to be accepted. To his credit, it appears that Williams never displayed any resentment at being passed over for promotion.[82]

For several months following the Battle of Gettysburg, Lee's Tigers rested and licked their wounds. The campaign had left their ranks severely depleted, but it had not broken their spirit. If anything, they were more determined than ever to carry on the struggle, although it must have been apparent to most that the outlook was bleak. To his father, Charles Batchelor wrote: "Like true patriots who are willing to loose life, property and all else they now hold [illegible] their rights, honor, and freedom. Unlike the weak kneed croakers of Mississippi and Louisiana (who are willing to abandon all their countrymen have so nobly struggled for just because Vicksburg or Port Hudson have fallen into the hands of the enemy) they still bare their noble breasts to the storm and with one voice shout we will never give over the struggle till Each one of us shall have been captured and borne away to dark and filthy dungeons to die—No, as long as there is one man left of Lee's noble army the enemy will never possess themselves of our soil."[83]

CHAPTER 10

Into the Wilderness

T HE ARMY OF Northern Virginia, except for Longstreet's corps, which was temporarily detached to the western theater, settled along the Rapidan River following the Pennsylvania campaign to guard its fords against a possible Union crossing. Captain Pierson informed his father, "The army here is in excellent health and spirits and wo[u]ld fight a much harder fight tomorrow than they would have done before the retreat from Penn. All of the convalescents have returned to their post and [the] army is much recruited." Noting that his Bienville Blues company had increased to fifty or sixty men, Pierson boasted, "All of them are in the best of health and can whip twice their number of Yankees any day."[1]

From mid-September to early October 1863, Hays' brigade picketed Raccoon Ford and listened to the Yankee drums beating in the camps across the river. The only significant action that took place during that time was when federal cavalry drove in the Confederate cavalry pickets in mid-September. The Tigers were rushed to the river to prevent the enemy from crossing, and a lively skirmish took place over the next two days, in which three men in the 6th Louisiana were killed. On September 16, Capt. Frank Moore slipped two companies of the 5th and 9th Louisiana across the Rapidan and surprised the 5th New York Cavalry. Several federals were killed in the raid, including the commanding officer, and forty-two were captured. The Yankees accused Moore's men of murdering their major after he was captured, but the Tigers claimed they killed him when he kept shooting after being ordered to surrender. Bolstered by this small success, Hays' confident men wished daily that the enemy would try to force a crossing; as William Oliver put it, "It is getting cold and we stand in need of blankets and overcoats."[2]

The 6th Louisiana's Capt. Michael O'Connor wrote that such picket duty was "severe" and that the men were forced to remain in their rifle pits from September 14 to October 8 without any cover to shield them from the weather. Frequent Union artillery fire also resulted in about fifty casualties during their stay there, with the 8th Louisiana once losing ten men in a few minutes because it was ordered to march over an exposed hill rather than around it. Nevertheless, the Tigers still found opportunities to enjoy themselves. Isaiah Fogleman reported on October 3 that a series of horse races were held in camp with "a great many spectators." The main event was Colonel Peck, commander of the 9th Louisiana, riding regimental surgeon William S. Love's horse against a mount belonging to one of the regiment's company captains. Peck lost the twenty-two-dollar bet but made it up on some of the other races.[3]

The army slowly regained its strength during this relatively quiet period as numerous sick and wounded men, and even some deserters, returned to their units. In early October, Lee took advantage of his men's improved condition and lashed out at the enemy when he learned that Meade had weakened his army by sending two corps to Tennessee. The eager Confederates swung north of the Rappahannock River and spent days on forced marches trying to bring the retreating Meade to bay. Captain O'Connor reported that it was "the most severe march we have had during the war," and Lt. Joseph G. Davis wrote that more than half of his 6th Louisiana company was barefoot during the campaign. The maneuvering came to a climax on October 14 when A. P. Hill's corps attacked the enemy at Bristoe Station and was defeated. Hays arrived on the field late in the day and managed to capture a few prisoners, but the fighting was over.[4]

The following day, the men in Hays' brigade watched as Generals Lee, Ewell, Hill, Stuart, and Early gathered together on a hill in their front to discuss what they should do next. Lee decided it was futile to continue chasing Meade and contented himself with destroying the enemy's rail line before crossing back over the river on the lone pontoon bridge located at Rappahannock Station. After the withdrawal, he ordered that an infantry brigade be posted on the north bank to guard the bridge in the hope that he would be able to resume the offensive in the near future. Johnson's and Early's divisions camped on the south bank and took turns posting brigades on the other side in some old federal earthworks. By that time, the Tigers were much broken down from the autumn campaign, and an officer in the 6th Louisiana wrote that his men were lacking in "Shoes, Blankets, pants, shirts, drawers, socks and overcoats."[5]

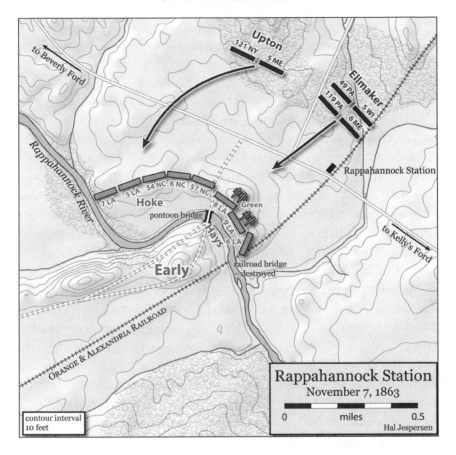

Rappahannock Station
November 7, 1863

On November 5, Meade took the offensive by sending his infantry against Rappahannock Station and Kelly's Ford, another crossing on the Rappahannock farther downstream. Seeing an opportunity to cripple one of the columns, Lee ordered Early to hold the enemy in check at Rappahannock Station's pontoon bridge while Rodes and Johnson pounced on the Yankees crossing at Kelly's Ford. At sunrise on November 6, Col. Davidson Penn, who was acting commander while Hays was serving on a court-martial, led the 1st Louisiana Brigade across the bridge to the earthworks. Captain Antoine L. Gusman's 8th Louisiana and Col. William Monaghan's 6th Louisiana were sent out in front of the center and right flank to act as skirmishers, while Peck's 9th Louisiana and Col. Thomas M. Terry's 7th Louisiana occupied the trenches.

The 5th Louisiana was away on picket duty, but Penn did have four guns of the Louisiana Guard Battery, which were placed in two redoubts within Peck's and Terry's position.[6]

Occupying the old works was a gamble because they had several weaknesses. The semicircular trench line was anchored on the river above and below the bridge and bulged out about two hundred yards in the center. A higher ridge several hundred yards in front commanded the entire position. Attacking troops could mass behind it, advance unseen behind a railroad embankment that ran near the rebels' right flank, and then suddenly attack by way of a road that ran under the embankment near the Tigers' position. There were also several "dead points" in front of the works that the Louisianians' fire could not reach. To make matters worse, a downstream dam turned the river into an unfordable lake, making the narrow pontoon bridge the only avenue of quick escape should the Tigers run into trouble.[7]

At about noon on November 7, the enemy began massing in front of the Louisianians. After watching the buildup for several hours, Colonel Penn and Captain Seymour were convinced that Meade's entire V and VI Corps were facing their lone brigade. Urgent messages were sent across the river to Early, but it was not until 3:00 p.m. that he and Lee arrived with reinforcements. Early rode across the bridge to inspect the Tigers' position and realized that the nine-hundred-man Louisiana brigade and the Louisiana Guard Artillery's four guns could not hold out against the thirty thousand Yankees that were massing in front of them.

By that time, Penn had withdrawn the 6th and 8th Louisiana back to the trenches and Capt. John G. Angeli's 5th Louisiana had arrived from picket duty downstream. At 4:00 p.m., Hays also returned to resume command and was soon reinforced by the 6th, 54th, and 57th North Carolina of Hoke's brigade, under Col. Archibald C. Godwin, which he placed in the center of his line. The Tar Heels' arrival increased Hays force to about two thousand men. Lee wanted to send another cannon over, as well, but had to cancel the order when he realized the federal sharpshooters would cut down the crew before they could get into position. No more help would be coming from Lee, but he believed the Union activity was simply a demonstration to mask the attack at Kelly's Ford. The general was convinced that Hays and Godwin could hold their position unaided because the Yankees could only advance on a two-brigade front because of the terrain's restrictive nature. Even if Hays did have to retreat, Lee thought he could pull back across the bridge under Early's protective fire from the south bank.[8]

Subsequent events proved Lee wrong, for rather than a demonstration, Meade was preparing a full-scale assault. By dark, six artillery batteries were bombarding the pontoon bridge, and the enemy's infantry had virtually surrounded Hays' position. Captain Seymour had the unenviable task of ferrying messages back and forth across the bridge while "the balls whistled around my head in a manner that was not musical in the least." After successfully running the gauntlet several times, Seymour finally had to abandon his work and take cover in the trenches when his horse, "Dick Ewell," was hit in the leg.[9]

Just before dark, Seymour realized the Tigers and Tar Heels were in trouble when he saw Union skirmishers and two lines of battle advancing toward them. Afterward he wrote, "This movement revealed to us the overwhelming numbers of the force opposed to us." As darkness enveloped the river, Lee and Early watched Hays' trench line suddenly erupt in jagged flashes of musket fire, although a strong wind drowned out the sound of the shooting. When the flashes abruptly ceased, Lee dismissed it as a skirmish and told Early that "it was too late for the enemy to attempt anything serious that night." Lee retired for the evening, still convinced that the action was nothing more than a demonstration. Early had no reason to believe otherwise until an aide sent to check on Hays' rations came galloping back, saying that the Tigers were streaming across the bridge in an apparent retreat. Early quickly alerted his men on the south bank and rode to the river to investigate.[10]

For once the Yankees had completely fooled Robert E. Lee. Masked by their artillery fire and a howling wind, two brigades of the VI Corps with fixed bayonets had swooped down on the Confederate line with a vengeance. Colonel Emory Upton's brigade hit Hays' left, and Col. Peter Ellmaker's brigade the center and right. The muzzle flashes Lee and Early saw were the surprised Tigers fighting back. Captain Pierson wrote home, "Our boys fought them, killing nearly all of their first line and fighting the 2nd line with the butts of their guns until they were finally overpowered and compelled to surrender." Scores of Yankees were cut down, and others tried to surrender, but the momentum of the mass of charging men pushed them into Hays' position. Without firing a shot, the federals pierced the rebel line in two places, cutting off the 6th, 8th, and 9th Louisiana on the right from Godwin's regiments and the 5th and 7th Louisiana on the left.[11]

The 6th and 49th Maine and 119th Pennsylvania hit Hays' right. Major George Fuller of the 6th Maine wrote, "The fire grew heavier as the line neared the works, and the men were struck down with fearful rapidity, but unwavering with wild cheers, the survivors reached the fortifications and springing over them engaged the enemy in hand-to-hand combat." Both sides fought furiously, and Charles Batchelor reported, "Our men clubbed their muskets and used them freely over Yankees heads." The Louisiana Guard Artillery, which was posted a little advanced of the right center, fired its last two rounds just as the enemy reached the guns and bayoneted two men. Sergeant Otis Roberts of the 6th Maine was the first to enter the trenches, and several Tigers quickly surrounded him. The sergeant yelled that he surrendered, but when five of his comrades jumped in, he cried out, "I take it back!" Roberts then led a charge against the 8th Louisiana's color guard and after a brief bayonet fight captured the flag and forced the color guard to retreat. Not far away, the 6th Louisiana's color-bearer, Godfrey Gaisser, realized he was about to be captured and tore his flag from its staff and hid it under his shirt.[12]

Major Fuller claimed that the Tigers seemed "astonished and bewildered" at the suddenness of the attack and either ran for the river in the rear or to their left, where the federals had not yet broken through. When it became apparent that all was lost, the Confederates tried to make their escape as best they could. A scowling federal slapped Charlie Stewart, Hays' courier, on the back and ordered him off his horse. Stewart complied, but the Yankee left after noticing that the animal was wounded and not likely to go anywhere. Stewart quickly remounted and managed to lash his wounded mount across the bullet-swept bridge, although the poor horse was shot five more times in the process. Surrounded by screaming Yankees, Hays was resigned to capture but could not sheath his sword in the mob of fighting men. When his horse bolted for the bridge, he simply hung on and was able to escape through a hail of gunfire. Peck and Seymour made similar escapes, and Monaghan, Terry, and Maj. William Manning swam to safety. Unfortunately, most of the Tigers were not so lucky. Scores of Louisianians and Tar Heels tried to swim the river but were shot in midstream or else retreated from the freezing water and surrendered. On the other side of the river, a horrified Early watched as the flash of muskets and yells of the combatants marked the fight's progress. "I had the mortification," he wrote, "to hear the final struggle of these devoted men and to be made painfully aware of their capture, without the possibility of being able to go to their relief."[13]

Within minutes after Hays' collapse on the right, Upton overwhelmed Godwin's North Carolina regiments and the 5th and 7th Louisiana on the left. When the 7th Louisiana's Colonel Penn heard cheering, he at first believed the Confederates were winning the battle, but a Union officer stepped out of the darkness and demanded his surrender. Brandishing his sword, Penn warned the Yankee to stay back, but the officer explained that Penn was hopelessly outnumbered and that he would be treated properly if he surrendered. Penn then lowered his sword in submission. Lieutenant Charles Pierce, one of Penn's officers, also carried a sword that he had taken from a Yankee officer at Winchester, but rather than give it up, he broke it over his knee and then handed the hilt to his disappointed captor.[14]

Colonel Clark C. Edwards, whose 5th Maine attacked Hays' left wing, tricked some of the rebels into surrendering. After taking the works in his front, he and a handful of men made their way to the river where the 5th Louisiana was posted. When Edwards suddenly realized he had walked right up on the Tigers' rifle pits in the dark, he brashly asked for the regiment's colonel and demanded that he surrender. When the officer said he would confer with his comrades, Edwards cut him off and pointed to a hill in the rear. "Not a moment I will allow sir," he barked. "Don't you see my columns advancing?" A large body of troops could be seen silhouetted on the hill, but they were actually Confederate prisoners being escorted to the rear. The rebel officer surrendered and then asked if he could keep his sword "which had never been dishonored." Edwards agreed but then pointed to some others standing nearby and said, "but I will take the swords of those officers."[15]

Seven Confederate battle flags were captured at Rappahannock Station, but Leon Bertin followed Gassier's example and saved the 7th Louisiana's colors by tearing it from the staff and hiding it under his shirt before surrendering. The Yankees later found a staff with bits of flag still clinging to it but apparently never searched the prisoners for the hidden colors. That night while huddled around a campfire as a prisoner, Bertin followed Colonel Penn's advice and burned his cherished flag to prevent it from falling into enemy hands.[16]

The action at Rappahannock Station was one of the Civil War's relatively rare bayonet charges and hand-to-hand fights. One of the Union participants wrote, "Here the unusual sight of death by bayonet wounds was witnessed, a dozen or more Confederate soldiers showing bayonet wounds, as well as some Union dead." Two tough, determined federal brigades had attacked and captured the entrenched Confederates, but the Tigers found it hard to accept the defeat and made exaggerated claims about the battle. Following the fight, one soldier wrote that they had "made many a Yankee bite the dust," and another claimed, "The ground for 150 yards up to the very breastworks was literally covered with their dead and in some cases they were piled upon each other. . . . [Hays] certainly saw over one thousand dead upon the field."[17]

In fact, the two Union brigades had captured nearly 1,600 rebels, four cannons, and seven stands of colors at a loss of only 348 men. Muster rolls show that on November 10 fewer than 500 of Hays' men were left on duty while 699 were reported captured. Some regiments had almost disappeared. Of the 122 men in the 5th Louisiana, only 1 captain answered roll call following the debacle. The 6th Louisiana's Colonel Monaghan admitted, "The affair was disastrous to our Army," and J. S. Dea declared that there was little left of "that skeleton Brigade of Louisianians. Her ranks cannot be swelled again. . . . [And] one or two more charges, I dare say, who will fill there ranks—there ghosts, I presume." The brigade was so reduced in numbers that there was even talk of consolidating it with Stafford's brigade. This did not happen although the remnants of Hays' and Hoke's brigades were temporarily combined under Hays' command. It was a decision that so rankled the North Carolina officers that Early had to separate the Tigers' and Tar Heels' camps to keep the peace.[18]

At the time, it seemed as if Hays' famous command was lost forever. In a glowing editorial, the Richmond *Whig* wrote:

> We must be permitted . . . to express our sincere regret at the capture of a large portion of Hays' brigade. Decimated as it was, the nine hundred remaining Louisianians were worth their weight in gold to the army. . . . There is nothing to show that Hoke's brigade did not fight as bravely in the late affair as that of Hays', but the imperishable record of the . . . [latter] in the great campaign in the Valley and in all the mighty battles in Virginia, Maryland and Pennsylvania, had endeared it to the whole country and particularly to the people of Virginia—Before they were trained, the Louisianians gave evidence of pluck and elan of the soldier by nature. . . . If now they are lost to Lee's army, we know not where the material will be found to replace them.[19]

The hundreds of captured Tigers and North Carolinians were taken to the rear and put aboard trains for northern prison camps. One Union soldier who watched them march by wrote, "Some of the prisoners were the famous Louisiana Tigers, a fine lot of men physically, and as they marched by, in the best of humor, some of them remarked, 'We're going to see Father Abraham and get some soft bread.'" Having become used to seeing rebels in ragged uniforms, the federals were surprised to find Hays' men well dressed. Another Union soldier reported, "The Prisoners taken here were better clothed then any we had seen before. All were provided with overcoats and jackets of a much better material than our own. They were made of English manufacture, much darker than the United States uniform, and this furnished conclusive evidence of successful blockade running."[20]

The 5th Louisiana's Sgt. John Charlton was among the prisoners taken at Rappahannock Station, and he later recalled, "It was a queer sensation I felt on being captured, but the Yankee I first saw, Shook hands and acted like a gentleman to me during the night." Before surrendering, Charlton took apart a pistol his father had given him and hid it in his pants. The next day he and forty-four other prisoners were put in a small box car that he claimed was "worse than the black hole of Calcutta."[21] On one train, trouble broke out among the prisoners. A New York newspaper reported, "The North Carolinians and the Louisiana Tigers had a fight in the cars, on their way to town . . . the former boldly saying they were heartily sick of the war and did not wish to be exchanged. The latter called them 'paltroons,' and at length the two parties came to blows."[22]

Some of the Louisiana prisoners were placed in the notorious Point Lookout prison camp. Sergeant Payton P. Maddox sent Captain Pierson a letter from there, and Pierson forwarded the news to his father. Pierson wrote, "[T]he boys' treatment is anything but good—[Maddox] writes 'our rations are short and we are very much in need of clothing. I thought that I had seen hard times before but I have never known what hard times were before. I would give my right arm to get away &c.' He also writes that 'none of our brigade are taking the oath.' Poor fellows. I feel for them and wish I could share my clothing, blankets and food with them as scanty as my supply is."[23]

Although two Union brigades had crushed Hays and Godwin, few people seem to have held the soldiers responsible for the defeat. One exception was the editor of the Richmond *Enquirer,* who wrote a disparaging piece about the Tigers' role in the fight. Colonel Peck was so enraged that he wondered aloud if the editor would foolishly challenge him to a duel if he wrote the paper "a very insulting letter." Lee did not share the editor's views and told his staff that none of the officers directing the Rappahannock Station defense should be blamed. He wrote in his report that "the courage and good conduct of the troops engaged have been too often tried to admit of question." The poor layout of the earthworks, darkness, and the surprise of the assault were the most widely accepted reasons for the defeat, although Lee also felt that sharpshooters should have been stationed far enough in advance to warn of the attack. The consensus of the men, however, was that Lee was to blame for not foreseeing what was developing and either sending Hays more reinforcements or withdrawing the two brigades. One Tiger wrote home, "You and everyone else will wonder why those brave men were not reinforced in time to save them from destruction, nobody knows but Genl. Lee, who I hope will account satisfactory for it." In fact, Lee did admit to Early that the attack had surprised him, and to his staff he "rather intimated whatever blame there was must attach to himself."[24]

In the final analysis, it did little good to second-guess anyone, although one Tiger held on Johnson's Island could not help but complain "at the fate, which through the stupidity of some one, placed me here." Lee put the incident aside and proceeded with the war. When he met Hays the following day, Lee said, "General, this is a sad affair. How do you feel today?" "I feel, sir," the dejected Hays replied, "as well as a man can feel who has lost so many men." "That is all over now and cannot be helped," Lee assured him. "The only thing is to try to get even with them today."[25]

The Union victory at Rappahannock Station was matched by a successful crossing at Kelly's Ford. To avoid being trapped along the Rappahannock, Lee burned his pontoon bridge and fell back across the Rapidan. On November 26, Meade continued to pressure the rebels by crossing the river on Lee's right and marching for his rear. The weather was bitterly cold when the army began shifting to the right to block the enemy's path. Captain Seymour wrote, "[W]e suffered severely during the march. Those of us who were on horseback were so benumbed by the cold that we were compelled to dismount whenever the column halted and dance around on the frozen ground in order to restore circulation." Because Ewell was on extended sick leave, Early temporarily commanded the II Corps, and Hays led Early's division. The next day, Hays found the federals in force around Locust Grove and began skirmishing while the rest of the army got into position.[26]

On Lee's left, Johnson's division was shuffling down a narrow road, not expecting any immediate enemy resistance, when its wagon train came under heavy fire from a patch of woods to the left. Taken by surprise with unloaded muskets, the division's infantry had to hurry back to the wagons and form a battle line in the thick woods. Suspecting the enemy to be merely cavalry raiders, the men charged through the narrow belt of timber with a cheer, but heavy volleys of musketry staggered them when they emerged onto a field surrounding Payne's Farm. Instead of cavalry, the outnumbered rebels were facing the entire federal VI Corps solidly emplaced behind a low rail fence 350 yards on the other side of the clearing.[27]

The woods had badly broken up the Confederates' formations, and they had to hastily take cover behind a rail fence. When ordered to charge, Stafford's men tore down the fence and rushed with the rest of the division across the bullet-swept field. After covering only 150 yards, however, Stafford found that the other brigades had fallen behind and he was forced to retreat. The Louisianians tried three times to cross the field but were bloodily repulsed on each occasion. Fortunately, Lt. Henry Handerson remembered, the federals "were about as bewildered as ourselves at the unexpected conflict" and failed to press their advantage. The Tigers lost heavily in the attacks, although for some reason most of the wounded were hit in the extremities and not seriously hurt. An exception was S. A. Johnson, who was shot through the back when the brigade retreated. After dragging the badly wounded soldier to safety, Johnson's comrades discovered that his only concern was that people back home would think he was a coward when they learned where he had been hit. "He would not care for his wound," wrote J. M. Batchelor, "if it was only in front."[28]

Captain D. T. Merrick, the brigade's inspector-general, and John S. Boykin, the 10th Louisiana's color-bearer, were also among the wounded. Merrick survived a bullet that unhorsed him when it hit the right side of his face and cut off his left ear lobe when it exited the other side. Boykin was shot in the thigh after advancing his colors to within fifty yards of the enemy, but his gallantry earned him a commendation in Lt. Col. Henry D. Monier's after-action report.[29]

While the brigade sought shelter behind the jumble of fence rails, Stafford constantly galloped up and down the firing line on his horse, "Harry Hays." It was not until later that he disclosed to friends the reason for his recklessness. Stafford's horse was so badly frightened by the raging gunfire that the only way the general could control him was by staying in motion. Although some uninformed spectators marveled at this apparent bravery, Stafford found one who was not impressed. When he rode back to an artillery battery to redirect its fire, one of the crewmen remarked, "General, who was that crazy fellow on horse-back trying to get himself killed and at the same time show off by prancing his horse up and down the line of fire?" Stafford smiled as he rode off and said "Oh! that was one of the officers in my brigade."[30]

When the firing slackened at dark, a number of Tigers crept into the field to search for wounded men trapped between the lines. Unfortunately, federal skirmishers had slipped onto the contested ground, as well, and prevented the Tigers from collecting their men. When Stafford withdrew back to the road after dark, he was greatly dismayed at having to abandon most of his dead and wounded. Subsequent roll calls showed that the brigade had suffered nearly half of the division's fatalities with thirty dead, ninety-six wounded, and two missing.[31]

Finding the federals too strongly entrenched to assault, Lee retired behind Mine Run, dug in, and dared Meade to attack him. Meade, however, refused to take the bait and settled in on the opposite side of the creek. For several days the two armies shivered in their cold, wet ditches under a steady rain and exchanged volleys of musketry. When the Tigers finally received orders to advance against the enemy's trenches, they were surprised—and relieved—to discover Meade had pulled out.[32]

During the standoff at Mine Run, Stafford's and Hays' men had the additional displeasure of watching several of their comrades dragged beyond the lines to be shot. Stafford's scheduled execution had a bizarre ending when the two condemned men suddenly bolted for the Union lines and escaped. One soldier claimed that their comrades fired at them but missed intentionally "for we did not want to see any of the soldiers executed." It is not known for what crime they were to have been executed.[33]

Hays' shooting had a more predictable ending. Twenty-year-old John Connolly, an Irish member of the 6th Louisiana's Violet Guards and former New Orleans newsboy, had deserted his company several months earlier. Described as "a sullen, cross, ugly fellow, who seemed to be entirely devoid of pride and sensibility," Connolly had hired out as a substitute for three hundred dollars and joined the Union army. He had the misfortune of being captured by his old company during the Bristoe Station Campaign and was sentenced to be shot for desertion. On November 30, the Tigers stood along the earthworks as a shackled Connolly was led to the head of a grave dug fifty yards away. When his shackles were removed, Connolly's hands were tied behind him, and twelve of his former comrades stepped forward with muskets. While a priest stood by whispering prayers and offering Connolly a crucifix to kiss, Captain Seymour read the charge and sentence and asked Connolly if he had any last words. The doomed man quietly replied that he had never "pulled a trigger against his old comrades" and had resolved never to do so when he joined the enemy. He added that he harbored no ill will against Seymour or the firing squad because he knew they were only doing their duty. Seymour then turned to the executioners and told them it would be an act of mercy if they aimed well. Seconds later, Connolly was killed by nine balls through his head. "I hope," Seymour wrote, "that I may never witness a like scene again."[34]

When Meade finally tired of the stalemate and withdrew from Mine Run, the Louisianians returned to picket duty along the Rapidan River. The winter of 1863–64 was miserable, although the men at first remained in good spirits. Captain Pierson wrote his father on January 5, 1864, "The boys are all in excellent health and much more cheerful than any one could expect when we consider their condition. Many of them are as good as barefooted, otherwise their clothing is very good—they get ¼ pound of bacon or 1 pound of beef; and 1 pound of flour per day which you know is a very slim allowance for a stout hearty man—notwithstanding all this they are very cheerful and merry all the while."[35]

One reason morale remained high was that furloughs were more liberally handed out that winter. With the Mississippi River in Yankee hands and mail to Louisiana having been virtually halted, the Tigers used the furlough system to stay in contact with loved ones. Furloughed soldiers were loaded down with letters and delivered them if they were successful in slipping across the river. Lieutenant Seton wrote his mother that winter, explaining that he sent her letters regularly but was unsure if she was receiving them. "[W]hat will you say when I tell you that its [sic] been ten months since I herd [sic] from you or any one from home?" The haphazard postal system was exposed in a November 1864 announcement in the Opelousas (Louisiana) Courier that declared, "Those who have letters to send to Virginia may leave them (until the 1st December) with Mr. Posey, in Opelousas, or Mr. Millspaugh in Washington. Lt. Thomas D. Cooke, 8th Louisiana Infantry, will forward to their destination."[36]

Unfortunately, the high morale Captain Pierson described began to erode as the winter dragged on, and food and clothing became scarce. At times, a daily ration in Stafford's brigade consisted of a quarter-pound of meat and one pound of cornmeal, with an occasional small amount of coffee and sugar. As early as October, a number of soldiers in the 6th Louisiana claimed they were "totally barefoot & nearly naked," and in December, 250 of Hays' men reportedly had no blankets. Coal was in such short supply that the army began issuing corn shucks for fuel at a time when the weather was often so cold that ink froze in the men's pens as they wrote home. "It is a great wonder," wrote Captain Seymour, "that these men do not freeze to death these terribly cold nights. Many of them use pine leaves and boughs wherewith to shield them from the cold, while others sit up by the fires all night, and, borrowing the blankets of their more fortunate comrades, sleep during the day."[37]

The Tigers' writings detail the suffering. Lieutenant Michael Murray of the 6th Louisiana wrote in his December company report, "The men are suffering for want of blankets and shoes, there being only four men now in the company who have shoes fit to leave camp with on any duty." Frustrated by this lack of clothing, the regiment's Colonel Monaghan complained, "Overcoats would be too great a luxury to mention."[38]

Private William Trahern, also of the 6th Louisiana, wrote years later that the winter of 1863–64 was the only time he recalled actually going hungry during the war. He claimed that floodwaters often disrupted the supply line, and the men were left without rations for days. "It was a trying time, and we lived solely on wild onions and watercress—I mean of course the private soldier only underwent this tribulation." During the winter, Trahern temporarily served as the regimental quartermaster and was shocked at how much better the officers lived. "Just to think of the private soldier almost starving, whilst his highest Commanders in his own regiment were feasting upon the best of old-time foods, such as coffee and tea, ham and eggs, bacon, flour and corn-bread, and I am almost certain that there was a goodly supply of old Bourbon." Trahern's disappointment in the officers' behavior, however, did not prevent him from enjoying the same privileges while he served in the quartermaster position. "Everything in this rich manner was for a time in my possession, and it pleased me to take full advantage. If it could have been possible, I would have conveyed some of it to my suffering comrades."[39]

To supplement their meager rations, some soldiers once again began preying on the local people. Colonel Clement Evans wrote that guards had to be placed at every house in the area because of the theft. When two of Hays' Tigers were arrested for possessing "unlawfully acquired pork," Evans admitted that such activity could not be stopped. "These depredations upon the property of citizens is very difficult to be restrained, impossible to be entirely suppressed. Patrols travers the country in all directions, guards remain at every house, yet the hogs, the sheep and even the cows disappear. It must not be understood from this that this army is composed of rogues and highway robbers. Among so many thousands there will be scores of evil men capable of any act of meanness. In comparison with the Yankee army in this particular our men are angels of light."[40]

Some relief for the clothing shortage was found by seeking outside help. General Stafford appealed to the people of Louisiana to send his men whatever clothing they could spare, but it is not known if he was successful. Hays had better luck with the Virginians, who, Sergeant Stephens claimed, "seem to regard this Brigade as a big muscle in Lee's Army." In Richmond, people contributed money to a committee that was formed to aid the 1st Louisiana Brigade. The committee provided Hays with 256 overcoats, about 250 pairs of yarn socks, and some blankets and shirts. Stephens reported that the citizens of Lynchburg also raised twenty thousand dollars "on behalf of the band of Exiles, as we call ourselves," but it is not clear if they donated the money or were forced to contribute. The Richmond *Whig* reported that Lynchburg sent the Tigers 170 blankets, ten overcoats, and twenty-five pairs of socks but asked that more donations be made because not enough money had been raised to pay for it all. Records of the 6th Louisiana indicate such items were collected through a "levy" that was placed on Lynchburg to supply each of Hays' men with a coat and blanket.[41]

Conditions improved somewhat that Christmas when the government issued coffee, sugar, and "other delicacies" that Sergeant Stephens claimed were "quite a treat for the soldiers." Log cabins also were constructed in January for winter quarters, and they helped ward off the bitter cold. Captain Pierson informed his father that the buildings were "covered with good oak boards—well chinked and daubed with mud and have also good chimneys and warm fire places."[42]

Nonetheless, the Tigers' morale remained low. Reflecting on his time in the army, one soldier complained, "I am almost wild. I do not think that I will ever be fit again to associate with respectable people. I have not spoken to a lady for two years [for] I have been in the woods since I left home." Father Sheeran claimed that the war-weary men in Stafford's command became susceptible to "the enemy of peace and charity," and that so many men deserted to escape the suffering that it "even threatened to break up the organization of our brigade."[43]

On February 18, 1864, General Lee wrote Secretary of War James Seddon to express his concern about the desertions in Stafford's brigade. He claimed that no one could account for it because "every attention is given to the wants of the men and every effort [is] made to supply them with food and clothing." Lee also wrote to General Ewell on the subject. "I am much concerned at the desertions in the [Louisiana] brigade—Can you ascertain the cause & remove it? Perhaps some changes of position in the 14th Regt: might be beneficial. The use of corn meal seems to me too trivial to account for it—If there are men whom it disagrees with, it might be changed by Drs prescription." Apparently, the 14th Louisiana was suffering from a higher desertion rate than its sister regiments, but it is not known why Lee believed a shakeup in the regiment's command structure would make a difference. David Zable led the 14th Louisiana, and he seems to have been an exemplary officer. There is also no explanation for how the use of cornmeal affected desertions. General Stafford was on leave in Richmond for an unspecified operation at the time, and Lee hoped his return "may produce some change in the disposition of his men." Whether it did or not is not known.[44]

Despite the numerous desertions, there remained a solid core of Louisiana Tigers who were undaunted by the hardships and refused to go over to the hated enemy. H. Evans wrote a friend, "I do not care about knowing the doings of the Yanks in your part of the world. You can't learn me anything about them—I know the beasts too well. I know their nature as well as I do my door. I know that in the whole catalogue of crimes they have left nothing undone to change their well deserved reputation of cowardly dogs."[45]

Hays' and Stafford's brigades did find ways to combat the loneliness, hunger, and battle fatigue that winter. Both brigades built wooden theaters and organized minstrel shows. One Tiger claimed that Hays' troupe "perform Every night, and it is crowded. Some times all the Generals in the Corps is in with their wife to see the performances." A minstrel troupe established by Stafford's and Walker's brigades charged a dollar admission to raise money for the Confederate widows and orphans. Writing their own material, the soldiers put on several musicals and satirical plays, with the most popular performance being a skit depicting army surgeons drinking and playing cards while nearby wounded suffered.[46]

Baseball was another popular pastime. On one occasion Hays' and Stafford's brigades played one another for a thousand-dollar prize, with each brigade putting up half the money. After a two-and-a-half-hour contest, Hays' "Ironclad brigade" won although the score was not recorded.[47]

One of the most popular forms of entertainment in the rebel camps was snowball fights. Each dusting of snow brought out squads of men from the Deep South, who laughed and chased one another until exhausted. In describing one clash between Stafford's brigade and two brigades of Virginians and North Carolinians, Private Snakenberg wrote, "[T]he fight was contested all day about as hard as any fight and many hard knocks were given and taken during the day."[48]

On March 23, after a particularly heavy snowstorm, an epic snowball battle occurred when the 15th Louisiana's Maj. McGavock Goodwyn gathered up members of Stafford's brigade and the Stonewall Brigade and challenged Gens. George Doles' and Stephen Ramseur's brigades to a fight. The Georgians and Tar Heels surprised Walker's and Stafford's men by taking up the gauntlet and chasing them for over a mile before breaking off the engagement. Major Goodwyn, however, refused to accept defeat and sent out "conscript officers" to round up reinforcements while he sought out Gen. James Walker, the Stonewall Brigade's commander, to come take charge of a new offensive. Battle flags began to unfurl, drummers beat the long roll, and staff officers galloped through camp shouting orders, and soon there were eight thousand men ready to take part in the mock battle. Stafford arrived to lead his brigade, while more of Rodes' division assembled on a nearby hill with Doles and Ramseur to make snowballs and scream threats of annihilation at Johnson's division forming below.

Walker accepted the Louisianians' request to lead a new charge and devised an elaborate battle plan. While Stafford hid his brigade in a patch of woods on the right, Walker would lead the rest of Johnson's division against Rodes' line, briefly engage it, and then retreat to draw them from their hilltop. When the "enemy" passed the woods, Stafford would strike their flank, and Walker would turn to counterattack.

When Walker began his advance, Father Sheeran wrote, "The lines were so regularly formed, the movements so systematic, the officers displaying so much activity at the head of their commands, their men fighting so stubbornly, now advancing on the opposite column, now giving way before superior numbers that one would forget for a moment that it was merely a sham." Walker rode directly into Rodes' division and was pelted by hundreds of snowballs. A Virginia soldier wrote, "The snow-balls fell like hail; for a time the surrounding scenery and the combatants were completely obscured." Within seconds, Walker and his horse were covered with snow. "Retreat! Retreat!" he yelled, and the men, stumbled back down the slope with Rodes' men chasing them "almost exhausted with laughter." At the critical moment, Stafford rushed from the woods and "once more there was a vast cloud of snow from breaking balls that filled the whole air." The Virginia witness wrote, "Down they came with a terrific yell, led on to the charge by their gallant Brigadier [Stafford], who rode in front of his line, crying out, 'Boys, charge the tar heels!' He had scarcely got the words out of his mouth, when a snow ball, as large as a 36-pound ball, struck him directly in the mouth with such force that he came near vacating his saddle. Then came a yell which could be heard for miles, and the General was carried off the field hors du combat." The "enemy" continued to press Walker's men back across a narrow bridge until from out of nowhere some Mississippians and Texans came to the rescue. According to the Virginian, "[T]hey swarmed from the woods like bees from a hive, every man with his hat or cap full of snow-balls. Rhodes' men were in a bad fix now—between two fires.—As soon as Johnson's men saw that their allies had arrived, they turned round and ran Rhodes back to the bridge, which, however, the Mississippians had barricaded, and he had to surrender just when he thought his victory was complete.—Gen. Rhodes acknowledged that Johnson had completely out-generaled him."[49]

One source claimed that Walker's men also chased some of their adversaries for over a mile back through their own camps. "Many prisoners were captured and sent to the rear," remembered one soldier, and another claimed, "Some of the Louisianians . . . stole some cooking utensils from Rodes' men and kept them." After five hours of fighting, the exhausted soldiers finally called it quits, and the victorious Tigers "came home as proud as if they had gained a victory over the Yankees."[50]

Such outdoor activity was good for morale, as was the arrival of five hundred of Hays' men who were exchanged after being captured at Rappahannock Station. Among them was Godfrey Gaisser, the 6th Louisiana's color-bearer who had hidden the flag under his shirt for safekeeping. When Gaisser was safely within Confederate lines, he hoisted his colors on a sapling and "flaunted it defiantly in the face of Yankees on board the other boats."[51]

The 7th Louisiana's Alexander Belcher was also among the exchanged Tigers. At Rappahannock Station, Yankee soldiers chased him and Lt. Col. Thomas M. Terry to the river. Terry shucked off his boots and overcoat and dove into the icy water, but Belcher could not swim, and the water was so cold that he immediately cramped up and had to surrender. "The Yankees fished me out with their bayonets," he wrote, "and I was wet and shaking with cold." Belcher's captors had him put on Terry's boots and coat and took him away. He was still wearing the colonel's garb when he returned to the regiment four months later, and Colonel Terry was the first person he met in camp. Terry asked him, "Belcher, did you happen to find a pair of mittens in those pockets?" As it turned out Belcher had, and he told Terry, "I knew you thought a heap of them and they are as good as new." Terry gently took the mittens and then said, "God bless you. I value those mittens more than anything I possess, for my dear mother knit them and sent them to me."[52]

As the weather warmed and more men returned to camp, the Tigers were filled with a new fighting spirit, which prompted J. R. Garcia to declare, "I am very glad to see that we will have a good Brigade once more to make the Yankees Skedaddle from the Valley." J. S. Dea shared Garcia's enthusiasm: "I hope with the blessings of God if nothing happens to me I will witness another Yankee run in that sweet Valley of Virginia." The Louisianians especially wanted to test the mettle of the highly touted Ulysses S. Grant, who had taken command of the Union armies. The Army of Northern Virginia, wrote Charles Batchelor, was "anxious to meet the Yankees' greatest general under the immortal Robert E. Lee." Although Batchelor firmly believed peace would come if the South could only win a few more battles, he understood the dangers that lay ahead and added, "Pray continually and fervently for us my dear sister."[53]

The Tigers soon got their chance to strike the enemy because on May 4, 1864, Grant began crossing the Rapidan on Lee's right to draw the rebels into battle. Lee hoped to intercept the federal column as it passed through the tangled Wilderness and ordered Longstreet to join the army from his camps near Gordonsville, while Ewell's and Hill's corps hurried eastward along the parallel Orange Turnpike and Plank Road, respectively. The Louisianians abandoned their winter camps on a beautiful spring morning and fell in line with the rest of Ewell's corps. The rebels advanced cautiously, knowing that the Yankees were now on their side of the river, and stopped at nightfall at the edge of the Wilderness. When the march resumed on May 5, the Tigers were in high spirits because they were approaching Chancellorsville and the scene of their great victory the year before. "I never saw our men so cheerful," wrote Father Sheeran. "The poor fellows had little idea of the terrible conflict in which they were about to engage."[54]

After deploying Johnson's division astride the Orange Turnpike, with Rodes and Early in support, Ewell began inching his way into the dark Wilderness. He moved slowly because Lee had ordered him not to bring on a general engagement until Longstreet arrived and to regulate his advance to Hill's progress on the Plank Road to his right. At 11:00 a.m., the column suddenly halted when word was passed quietly down the line that the Yankees had been spotted ahead. As the ambulances and wagons began pulling off the road to make room for the infantry to deploy, Stafford took his men into the woods north of the Plank Road and formed a line of battle with Steuart's brigade to his right, facing Saunders' Field, and Walker's Stonewall Brigade on his left toward the Rapidan River. Stafford then sent out his sharpshooters and waited.

Shortly afterward, Union general Gouverneur K. Warren's corps viciously attacked the right center of Johnson's division. Smoke boiled above the green foliage as Johnson's entire line began firing blindly toward the sound of the cheering Yankees. The federals killed Gen. John M. Jones when they smashed into his brigade and sent it reeling back down the road. Ewell desperately threw Rodes' division and Gordon's brigade into the melee and after a bitter fight managed to push the enemy back. When the Union brigades withdrew three hundred yards, both sides hurriedly dug in and tried to retrieve some of the wounded men from the path of several brush fires begun by the intense firing.[55]

Taking advantage of this temporary lull, Ewell straightened out his confused line by withdrawing Jones' shattered brigade from the south side of the road and replacing it with Rodes' division. Most of Johnson's division was shifted north of the road, and Ewell sent Early through the woods to extend Johnson's left. Impatient for orders, Stafford rode back to get his instructions while his men scratched out makeshift earthworks, cooked dinner, and quietly smoked in the thicket. The woods around the Louisianians seemed to come alive with wild game flushed out by the noise and fires. Colonel Zebulon York brought peals of laughter when he chased a frightened fox down the trench line, and a turkey that bolted from the underbrush was greeted with rebel yells and a volley of musketry. Even a skittish rabbit was run down and caught by some of the more nimble soldiers. This entertainment was cut short, however, when several of the sharpshooters came rushing back through the brush shouting breathlessly that federal skirmishers were only a short distance away. The soldiers grabbed their muskets and scrambled to their feet just as Stafford arrived. When told of the situation, he ordered the brigade to fall back a short distance and reform. After the men got into position, hundreds of ramrods rattled down musket barrels as officers gave the order, "Load!" When all was ready, Stafford rode out in front of his men and cautiously picked his way through the bushes to meet the expected Union assault.[56]

Lieutenant Henry Handerson recalled that the brigade had advanced about a quarter of a mile when off to the right erupted "the most tremendous roll of musketry it was ever my fortune to hear." It was about 3:00 p.m., and the Yankees were advancing across Saunder's Field toward Ewell's line. The woods in Stafford's front remained eerily quiet, but William Snakenberg recalled how the men poured a murderous oblique fire into the enemy's right flank. "Their flank was exposed to our Brigade and the way we poured lead into them was a sin. We were placed on a high ridge and we could see every move they made, also, Johnson leading his line when they made the charge. The enemy's ranks were as thick as blackbirds in the field and there was no reason for any men in our line to throw away any bullets. All could see where to shoot. We fired as long as they were in sight, then fired into the woods where they had gone."[57]

Stafford's own front was soon crawling with Yankees who stopped along a low ridge and pumped volleys of heavy musket fire into the Louisianians. With hat in hand, Stafford spurred his horse across a gully fronting the brigade and waved his men forward. The federals quickly retreated across a narrow field and drew up in a new position along the opposite tree line. Stafford was preparing to push across the field when a courier came galloping out of the thickets, pointing frantically to the left, and screaming, "They are coming!" Stafford at first did not believe the excited aide because Walker's brigade was supposed to be on the Tigers' left flank. As Walker was advancing, however, the Yankees had attacked both of his flanks and forced him to withdraw, and now Col. Henry Brown's New Jersey brigade was pushing into the gap. Snakenberg recalled, "We were so busy shooting at those in our front, that the enemy got a line of battle in our rear, and fired a volley into our backs before we had any idea that the enemy was behind us. By that volley many were killed and wounded in our line."[58]

Stafford hurriedly ordered the fifty men of the 1st Louisiana to refuse the left flank and hold off the charging Yankees. The commanding officer there, however, either misunderstood his orders or panicked and simply waved his sword overhead and yelled for his men to rally around him. The resultant mob could offer no resistance against the aggressive enemy and succeeded only in making themselves an easy target. Realizing he could not hold off the flank attack, Stafford yelled over the roar of battle for Lieutenant Handerson to make his way to the right, find Steuart's left flank, and guide the brigade to it. Handerson, however, had barely ridden out of sight when he was captured after blundering into another Yankee line sweeping through the woods.

By then, resistance was hopeless. Cut off from both Confederate brigades on his flanks, surrounded by nearly impassable thickets, and blinded by smoke from the woods fires, Stafford could only order his men to withdraw to the right and make their way back to the original line. Snakenberg and two comrades made a run for it, but only Snakenberg made it out safely. "I kept on at angles to the enemy's line of battle, with their balls cutting all around me, and why I was not hit I never will know." His friends could not understand it either. They saw the bullets kicking up dirt at his feet and watched him tumble to the ground several times, even though Snakenberg did not remember falling.[59]

General Stafford was not so fortunate. He sat his horse and calmly waited until the last man of the 1st Louisiana filed past before turning to bring up the rear. Suddenly, the general was knocked from his horse by a bullet that severed his spine when it cut through his body from armpit to shoulder blade. Several men scooped up the paralyzed general and carried him back to the trenches, where others were busily reinforcing the position. It is not known how many men Stafford lost in the thirty-minute clash, except that the 10th Louisiana had six killed, nineteen wounded, and eight missing.[60]

While the brigade dug in along an old woods road, Hays' men came rushing by on their way to extend Johnson's left. These Tigers, especially the men of the 9th Louisiana, were shocked to see "poor Stafford" laid out under a shady tree beside the road, suffering from the agonizing wound. Although in a hurry to reach their assigned position, the men slowed as they passed, and each one spoke a few words of encouragement and sympathy to the stricken officer. Stafford, in turn, told them he was ready to die if need be and urged them to fight to the last man. Many of the soldiers left the general believing he might recover from the ghastly wound, but Stafford died in Richmond on May 8. His death was said to have "cast a gloom over the city." President and

Mrs. Davis attended the funeral and watched as the Louisiana general was laid next to Maj. Roberdeau Wheat.[61]

Hays' brigade soon arrived on Walker's left and prepared to counterattack through the woods. Captain Seymour was dispatched to inform Walker of the impending assault, but the 25th Virginia was the only regiment that actually joined in the attack. When all was ready, Hays pushed the men into the thickets, past the dead and wounded littering the ground, and almost immediately engaged the enemy. Firing as they slowly advanced, the Tigers drove the Yankees through the woods with ease, although the dense timber and smoke broke up the brigade's alignment and disorganized the men.[62]

After advancing half a mile, the Tigers suddenly emerged onto a field and spotted a long line of federals partially hidden in the woods on the other side. The two Union brigades of Gens. David Russell and Thomas Neill heavily outnumbered Hays' small band, but the Louisianians were caught up in the excitement of the chase and recklessly pushed on through the field. The Yankees patiently waited, leveled their muskets, and cut down the advancing gray line. Russell and Neill then sent their men swarming around Hays' flanks, completely cutting off the 25th Virginia and capturing 300 of its members. Hays frantically extracted his command from the slaughter and withdrew back across the field "under a murderous fire." The retreat continued through the thickets, finally halting at the original line. There the shattered brigade used tin cups and bayonets to throw up some hasty earthworks and nervously scanned the underbrush in front for any sign of the enemy. John Pegram's brigade slid in on Hays' left and came under a heavy attack late in the day but managed to beat it off with the help of the 6th Louisiana. When the Tigers could finally take stock of their losses, they discovered that they had lost 250 men in the brief charge, or more than one-third of Hays' command. Some units literally ceased to exist. When the day began, there were only 5 men left in the 6th Louisiana's Tensas Rifles, and all of them were captured.[63]

The day had cost the two Louisiana brigades some of their best men. Among the wounded were Capt. Al Pierson, Corp. William Trahern, and Sgt. Edmond Stephens, whose writings tell so much about the Tigers' activities. Pierson wrote that a ball cut across the top of his right hand leaving "a gash across the back about 2½ inches long and the depth of a large Minnie bullet. At the same time I had one hole through my coat & four through my pants so you may judge that I feel very thankful that I escaped as well as I did." When Stafford ordered the retreat, Trahern discovered blood running down his leg from a severe flesh wound near the knee. He remembered there was "a large ragged hole torn by the bullet striking the bone," but fortunately the bone was not broken. Trahern collapsed from the loss of blood, but two fellow soldiers used a blanket for a litter and carried him to the rear. Sergeant Stephens was not as fortunate. He was a little beyond the main firing line, kneeling on the ground to shoot under the brush when a comrade accidentally shot him from the rear. The bullet entered near his anus and exited his lower abdomen, ripping his intestines as it passed through his body. Stephens remained conscious as he was carried to the rear and lingered for over a week before he finally died.[64]

With darkness rapidly approaching in the smoky woods, the opposing lines dug in a few hundred yards apart along parallel ridges. Isolated sorties and constant skirmish fire were kept up well into the night as brave soldiers on both sides ventured into the smoldering no-man's-land to drag the helpless wounded to safety. The day's fighting had been much like the Battle of Chancellorsville, fought a year earlier on the same ground. The dense woods prevented the use of artillery, and the battle degenerated into a series of scattered fire fights. When darkness finally ended the battle, the Wilderness glowed for miles as hundreds of fires spread among the dead and wounded trapped between the lines.

On Ewell's right, Hill's corps had also become heavily engaged along the Plank Road but managed to hold its position. On the morning of May 6, however, the federals renewed their attacks and routed Hill, but Longstreet arrived just in time to save the army from defeat. Later in the day, Longstreet fell to the curse of the Wilderness when he was mistakenly shot by his own men, almost a year to the day after Stonewall Jackson suffered the same fate. Ewell's line was comparatively quiet while the fighting raged on Hill's and Longstreet's fronts. Deadly sniper fire and occasional probes kept the men alert, but the bloody assaults of the previous day were lacking. Captain George Ring of the 6th Louisiana found time to jot a note to his wife during this interlude. In closing, he wrote: "With a trust in Providence for his continued favors, and the Hope abiding that this will be the last fight and that I may escape safely, with all my love—I had got this far when the enemy made a severe attack on us, which was for a half hour, when they fled to the shadows of obscurity. I am now out with my company skirmishing and the bullets are whistling all around me. I have just had another man killed, but this is nothing when you get used to it."[65]

The only major development on Ewell's front came late in the day when Gordon discovered that Grant's right flank was unprotected and attacked. The surprise blow came just at dark, and the federal flank was thrown back nearly a mile before darkness finally ended the pursuit. Hays was supposed to join the attack once the enemy was dislodged, but Neill's Union brigade in his front refused to abandon its works, and the Tigers' participation was limited to heavy skirmishing.[66]

After a second hellish night of fires and screaming wounded, May 7 dawned strangely quiet. It was soon apparent that Grant had abandoned his Wilderness line and was moving southeastward toward Spotsylvania to turn Lee's right flank. While other units moved out to intercept him, the Tigers were left behind to help collect the dead and wounded. "Never was there a more grim and ghastly spectacle of the horror and terrible destructiveness of War," wrote Captain Seymour. Father Egidius Smulders, who discovered packs of wild dogs devouring the dead, visited a field hospital where some of the wounded told of being "horrified as they . . . heard the shrieks of hundreds of the wounded enemies who were burned in their field hospitals."[67]

Fanning out into the scorched woods, Hays' men soon had a large number of badly wounded federals laid out along the trenches. "A ghastly exhibition of torn and mutilated humanity it was," recalled Seymour. Those who could be moved were taken to field hospitals, but the mortally wounded "were left to die on the ground where they laid." By nightfall, all were dead—the last to succumb being a frightened German who spoke no English. As he gasped for breath, the Tigers crowded around him out of morbid curiosity. When tears began to roll down the man's face, one Tiger blandly remarked that he must be thinking "of his vrow and little ones." Shortly afterward, the man appeared to be dead, and a soldier knelt down and began rummaging through his pockets. A bystander was horrified at such callousness and warned the man that the Yankee's ghost would haunt him if robbed before he was actually dead. When the Tiger backed away, his concerned comrade bent over, felt the pulse, and declared that the German was indeed "dead as a door nail." The second Tiger then removed all the valuables from the body, much to the chagrin of the other but "to the amusement of the bystanders."[68]

While the Tigers collected the wounded along the front lines, Trahern was being treated in the rear. Many soldiers criticized the surgeons for being rough and uncaring, but Trahern appreciated their service: "With star candles mostly in use, they performed wonderful operations. . . . [T]his Corps of able, hard-working officers, halted at the tent next to mine, and immediately took off a leg of an infantry soldier. My turn came next, and to my delight they pronounced my wound not at all dangerous. Although the night had long since shaded the earth, bullets were still flying through the trees, and sometimes through the tents." Trahern was loaded into a wagon with a soldier whose leg had been amputated at the hip and sent off to Richmond. "My suffering was nothing to be compared to that of my comrades. We were tossed about often, and sometimes violently, and every time this occurred, a solemn wail came from my companion of such a sorrowful nature as to almost break my heart."[69]

While racing toward Spotsylvania on May 8, Lee was forced to make command changes to fill the positions of the five generals who were killed or wounded in the Wilderness. General Richard Anderson replaced the disabled Longstreet, and Early was given temporary command of the III Corps because A. P. Hill was too ill to continue. Lee then had to decide who would command Early's division. The logical choice was Hays because of his seniority, his temporary command of it at Mine Run, and his outstanding war record. Lee, however, chose John B. Gordon instead. Although it is generally believed that Gordon won the promotion because of his initiative in launching the flank attack on May 6, that alone cannot explain Lee's decision. Gordon was without question an excellent officer, but he was nearly one year Hays' junior in rank, and his combat record could not be considered better than the Louisianian's. Perhaps Lee blamed Hays for the disaster at Rappahannock Station or, more likely, he acted out of sheer intuition. Whatever the reason, the promotion created a difficult situation.

Not wanting to offend Hays, Lee had to find a graceful way to pass him over. In a confidential note to Ewell, Lee ordered Hays' brigade transferred to Johnson's division and consolidated with Stafford's men. Lee justified this move by claiming the two brigades were so small that they could no longer function well independently, and it would place all of the Louisianians in one unit. Moving Hays out of the division also conveniently opened the way for Gordon's promotion and perhaps soothed Hays' feelings by putting all of the Tigers under his command.[70]

While Hays was to exercise overall command, Lee's order called for both brigades to keep their separate organization, with Colonel York commanding Stafford's men and Colonel Peck leading Hays'. There had been talk of consolidating the brigades over the winter, but Hays' men had opposed the idea. At

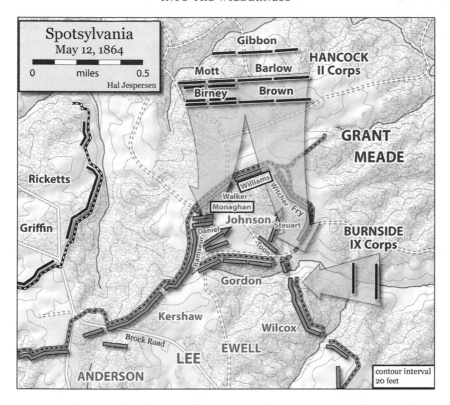

Spotsylvania
May 12, 1864

0 miles 0.5
Hal Jespersen

Gibbon

Mott Barlow HANCOCK
II Corps

Birney Brown

GRANT
MEADE

Ricketts

Williams
Walker
Monaghan
Johnson Steuart
Daniel
Griffin
Toon
BURNSIDE
IX Corps

Gordon

Kershaw

Wilcox

Brock Road
EWELL
LEE
ANDERSON

contour interval
20 feet

that time Captain Pierson wrote his sister, "[O]ur Brig. is now reduced to less than a good regiment and all of the men are bitterly opposed to being consolidated with the second La. Brig. for many of the regiments are composed of foreigners, and hence the difficulties arising out of consolidation." There is no record of Hays' thoughts on the subject, but most of the Tigers in both brigades felt the same as Pierson. After the deed was done, Maj. Edwin L. Moore wrote, "The discipline in this command is lax. . . . [It] is composed of the discontented fragments of Hays' and Stafford's brigades. . . . Both officers and men bitterly object to their consolidation into one brigade. Strange officers command strange troops, and the difficulties of fusing this incongruous mass are enhanced by constant marching and frequent engagements." Assistant Adjutant General H. E. Paxton best summed up the Tigers' feelings when he wrote, "The troops of the old organizations feel that they have lost their identity, and are without the chance of perpetuating the distinct and separate history of which they were once so proud. This loss of prestige must excite to some extent a feeling of discontent." Discontented or not, the Louisianians had to live with the decision and spent the last year of the war together as one unit. With a total strength of barely a thousand men, Hays' consolidated brigade was a pitiful remnant of the twelve thousand eager Tigers who had come to Virginia three years earlier.[71]

Grant withdrew from the Wilderness on the night of May 7 and headed south toward Spotsylvania. Fortunately for Lee, Anderson reached the strategic crossroads just minutes before the enemy and managed to hold it until the rest of the army arrived. The Louisiana Tigers remembered the march to Spotsylvania as a difficult one. One unidentified officer wrote, "It was the most fatiguing march I have ever made. We were all Saturday night [May 7] moving about 7 miles; we had to feel for the enemy all the way, and yesterday was exceedingly hot, not only from the sun, but part of the forest was on fire, and we had to march often through a wall of fire and smoke. I am nearly broke down from the want of sleep."[72]

By sundown of May 9, the weary rebels had thrown up three miles of trenches and had settled confidently behind their earthworks to await any federal assault. Although formidable, their position had a weak link in its right center, where the line jutted out northward in a great bulge. Johnson's division held the tip of this so-called "Mule Shoe," with Jones' brigade at the apex, Steuart on the eastern side, and Hays and Walker on the western side. Sporadic skirmish fire throughout May 9 hampered the Louisianians' attempts to strengthen their part of the line. Private Snakenberg claimed that "we worked on our breastwork and cut off the boughs of the trees that were down in our front, making the ends of the limbs sharp." Beyond this *abatis* the men dug rifle pits in a two hundred fifty-yard-wide field to protect the brigade's sharpshooters and skirmishers. The Yankees were hid in thick woods at the far edge of the field.[73]

While supervising the earthworks construction, Hays was struck by a stray ball or sharpshooter's bullet and collapsed in the ditch, seriously wounded. He was taken to the rear and never rejoined his Tigers. Hays recovered from the wound in Virginia but then was transferred to Louisiana, where he served out the rest of the war. Captain Seymour claimed that Colonel Monaghan assumed control of the consolidated brigade and kept the Tigers at their work. If so, Colonels Peck and York must have been absent during the battles around Spotsylvania because they were senior to Monaghan in rank. Further evidence of their absence is that Col. Jesse M. Williams led York's brigade during much of the Spotsylvania fight, and Col. Alcibiades DeBlanc took over the Tigers in late May when Monaghan fell ill.[74]

Lee soon realized that the Mule Shoe was vulnerable to attack and began constructing a new line across its base. Until the new works were finished, however, Johnson's men would have to remain alert against any Union assault. On May 10, Grant hit Gen. George Doles' Georgia brigade on the Mule Shoe's western side and punched a hole through the Confederate defenses. Although the rebels contained and eventually sealed the breakthrough, Lee became even more concerned about the salient's vulnerability. An inspection of the line on May 11, however, convinced him that Johnson could hold the Mule Shoe with the support of numerous cannons that were placed behind him. In the early afternoon, Ewell took a further precaution by ordering Monaghan to leave Colonel Williams' 2nd Louisiana Brigade in its position near the Mule Shoe's apex and move the 1st Brigade to where the Yankees made their breakthrough the day before.

In a steady rain, Monaghan slid his men to the left and occupied Doles' muddy works amid much grumbling from the Tigers over having to rely on strangers' defenses that had already been overrun once. Their outlook changed, however, when they were told that this was the weakest part of the line, and that Ewell had personally requested that the corps' most dependable brigade hold it. The danger of the position was dramatically shown when Ensign Arthur Duchamp, the 8th Louisiana's color-bearer, was killed when he thoughtlessly stood to plant the regiment's flag on the new works. Duchamp had been previously captured at Antietam and was severely wounded while carrying the colors in the Tigers' twilight assault on Cemetery Hill. He recovered in time to be captured again at Rappahannock Station and had just been promoted to ensign on May 4 for his gallantry at Gettysburg. Captain Seymour wrote of him, "Young Duchamp was naturally a mild, amiable man, but in battle he was as brave as a lion, and no man carried his flag closer to the enemy than he did." All heads remained low afterward when the brigade went about the gruesome task of removing the federal dead that still lay in and about the trenches. Every man was also able to collect at least three muskets each, but attempts to bury the bodies were abandoned when the Yankees fired on the Tigers' burial parties.[75]

When night fell, an ominous foreboding fell over the Confederates holding the exposed Mule Shoe. A gloomy fog and drizzle that enveloped the trenches could not muffle the low rumble of a massive troop movement somewhere out in the blackness. Officers strained in the night to decipher the meaning of the noise, and couriers rushed news of the mysterious movement to Lee. He believed Grant was again pulling out to make another run for the Confederate right flank and ordered Johnson's artillery to withdraw from the Mule Shoe so he could move quickly if that proved to be the case. Monaghan, however, was convinced that the rumbling was the Yankees preparing to attack and dispatched Captain Seymour at midnight to convey his fears to General Johnson. Johnson agreed with Monaghan and urgently requested that Ewell send the artillery back. Johnson and Monaghan proved correct, for rather than retreating, Grant was massing the twenty thousand men of Gen. Winfield Scott Hancock's II Corps for an attack.[76]

Throughout the predawn hours, the nervous Tigers peered anxiously into the darkness and prepared their muskets by pulling the loads to replace the damp powder. The 2nd Louisiana Brigade received some support after midnight when a Virginia regiment was brought up as reinforcements. "What's the matter here?" yelled one irritated Virginian. "You've had us waked up before day and brought out of our shelter into the rain?" "We will have the Yankees over here directly to take breakfast with us!" an unsympathetic Tiger shot back.[77]

Daylight on May 12 came slowly through the mist and fog. By that time, the rumbling out front had ceased, and a tense quiet had settled over the trenches. As objects slowly became visible, the Tigers anxiously listened for the expected gunfire from their pickets posted beyond the breastworks. It was barely light when the scattered popping of skirmish fire broke the silence. Private Snakenberg's company was scheduled to return to the picket line that morning and had risen early to get out to the rifle pits before daylight in order to avoid the enemy's fire. He recalled, "About the time we were ready to start for the skirmish line, those on the line commenced firing very fast and soon came running into the works, saying that the enemy were advancing. We went into the works, but on account of a very heavy fog we could not for some time see anything, but waited until all the skirmish line had got in our works and the enemy had come near enough to be seen, we commenced firing on them."[78]

Captain Seymour was with the 1st Louisiana Brigade farther to the left when the attack began. He heard the increasing tempo of rifle fire and then off to his right there "burst upon our startled ears a sound like the roaring of a tempestuous sea." All eyes turned toward an angle in the line at the tip of the Mule Shoe, and one of Monaghan's men jumped up, pointed in that direction, and yelled, "Look out, boys! We will have blood for supper!" Through a break in the fog in front of Jones' brigade could be seen wave after wave of madly cheering federals bearing down on the position that would soon be dubbed the "Bloody Angle." At the same time, Johnson's missing artillerymen came rushing back to their position just in time to be overwhelmed by the Yankees. Only two of the cannons managed to fire a shot. They unlimbered at the 2nd Louisiana Brigade's position but only got off one round each before being captured. According to Snakenberg, "Gen'l Ed Johnson fired the gun and Brigadier Gen'l George Hume Stewart was standing close to him. I was near enough to them to have touched them with my gun by reaching forward."[79]

The blue tidal wave washed over Jones' brigade with hardly a shot being fired. Grant's cheering Yankees then fanned out to both sides and came tearing down the trench line with fixed bayonets. The steady rain resumed as the Union assault slammed into the 2nd Louisiana Brigade and Steuart's brigade. Snakenberg wrote, "They came over the works where they were thin and then down behind our division before we knew anything. I was on the parapet and fired a number of times, as those of my Company behind me kept loading and passing me their guns." After only a few shots, however, Snakenberg reached back for another musket only to find that his entire company had fled. The only ready musket at hand was one he had loaded the previous day with twenty-one small balls. He picked it up and "fired it at the New York and United States color bearers in Gen'l Winfield Scott Hancock's corps who made the charge in our front and [they] threw [their] colors to the ground. . . . I did not know whether the color bearers were killed or not. This was the last shot I fired in the service of the Confederate States." Snakenberg was quickly captured and spent the rest of the war as a prisoner.[80]

Snakenberg was one of only a few Tigers who managed to fire their weapons before the federals overran them. Colonel Williams was killed in the brief struggle, but most of the brigade was captured. Among them was Lt. Edward Seton, whose poorly spelled letters help tell the story of the 10th Louisiana, and Leon Jastremski, who fell into the enemy's hands for the third time. Snakenberg and Jastremski survived the war, but Seton died from typhoid on February 11, 1865, in Fort Delaware. His family was devastated, and Seton's sister prayed every day for the rest of her long life for God to damn Abraham Lincoln to hell.[81]

The 2nd Louisiana Brigade also lost a number of its battle flags during the disaster. Private Phillip Schlachter of the 73rd New York and Sgt. C. H. Fasnacht of the 99th Pennsylvania earned Medals of Honor for capturing the 15th and 2nd Louisiana's flags, respectively. Only Sergeant Fasnacht left an account of his heroic deed. As he was charging the rebel line, he noticed the 2nd Louisiana's flag planted on the trench line and was determined to capture it. In the pouring rain, Fasnacht mounted the works with other men and knocked down one rebel with his musket butt because his weapon was empty. The Tiger color-bearer and color guard were just a few feet away, and Fasnacht ordered them to surrender, but they turned and ran into some nearby woods. The sergeant gave chase and finally caught up with them and demanded their surrender again. When the color-bearer agreed and let the flag drop to the ground, the others gave up, as well. None of the half-dozen Tigers ever fired on the lone Yankee, which led Fasnacht to believe that their muskets were also empty. Fasnacht ordered the prisoners to the rear and then ripped the flag from its staff and stuffed it into his shirt.[82]

Various sources claim that two other Louisiana flags were also captured at Spotsylvania, but their identity is uncertain. Archibald Freeman of the 124th New York was awarded a Medal of Honor for capturing the 17th Louisiana's flag, but that regiment never served in Virginia. A newspaper also claimed that Sgt. William Jones of the 73rd New York and a Corporal Reynolds of the 4th Excelsior Regiment captured the 13th Louisiana's flag, but that regiment was not at Spotsylvania, either. Jones was awarded a Medal of Honor for his actions in the battle, but it was for capturing the flag of the 65th Virginia. It is possible that the soldiers did seize flags belonging to the 2nd Louisiana Brigade, but army officials incorrectly recorded them when they were logged into the record.[83]

To the left of the breakthrough, Monaghan and the men of the 1st Louisiana Brigade watched as the brutal onslaught swept relentlessly toward them. Thinking quickly, the colonel ordered his men to move by the left flank to a small hill 150 yards away, where a traverse ran perpendicular to the breastworks and across the Yankees' line of advance. The Tigers moved quickly but not before the federals captured thirty-eight men on the right flank. Among them was Lt. George L. P. Wren, whose diary documents the 8th Louisiana's activities. The brigade had barely gotten into position when the federals were upon them "yelling like devils." Monaghan roared, "Fire!" and the Tigers obliterated the first blue line, but the mass of men continued pushing forward. Time after time, the federals attacked Monaghan, but, according to a London *Herald* correspondent, the Louisianians' new position behind the traverse "presented a front as firm as a ledge of rock [and] those houseless, landless warriors of Louisiana" held firm and managed to contain the Union penetration to the Bloody Angle at the Mule Shoe's apex. Some weeks later, Philip Collins wrote that Monaghan's shift in position was made "under a most terrific fire of musketry and shells, but our gallant little Brigade rallied and at the proper place and repelled the advance of the enemy and held them in check until reinforcements came up and drove them back which saved the day and gave us some rest for a few days."[84]

The fighting along Monaghan's line was among the fiercest of the war, with the two armies often embraced in deadly hand-to-hand combat. "I have been in a good many hard fights," wrote Captain Ring, "but I never saw anything like the contest of the 12th. We lay all day and night in the Breastworks in mud five inches deep, with every kind of shot and shell whistling over us, amongst us, in us, about us, so that it was as much as your life was worth to raise your head above the works."[85]

Fourteen officers in Monaghan's brigade were shot that day, with the 5th Louisiana's Col. Bruce Menger, whom one soldier called "one of the best field officers in our Brigade," being among the dead. The line held despite the heavy losses, and General Gordon soon rushed in reinforcements that pushed the federals back across the breastworks. Both armies then clung to opposite sides of the trench line and blasted each other from point-blank range. The steady rain filled the trenches with water, drowning some of the wounded, and the incessant firing shredded oak trees behind the rebels' line. Some men fired as many as four hundred rounds during the fight and had to pick up weapons from among the dead and wounded when their muskets fouled from excessive use. While Lee desperately tried to complete the new line along the Mule Shoe's base, the battle raged at the Bloody Angle, with neither side being able to dislodge the other. Finally, long after dark—sixteen hours after the fight began—the new works were completed and the exhausted gray defenders were able to disengage and fall back.[86]

When Monaghan reassembled the surviving Tigers the next morning, he found that the 2nd Louisiana Brigade had been almost annihilated. Precise numbers are not known, but most of the brigade was captured, with the 10th Louisiana alone losing four dead, seven wounded, and fifty-seven missing. The 1st Louisiana Brigade lost fewer men captured but had a larger number killed and wounded. The 9th Louisiana's Washington Rifles had twelve men killed and another dozen or so wounded while at Spotsylvania, and only sixty members of the 6th Louisiana answered roll call after the fight on May 12. The concentrated musket fire mutilated many of the dead, and they had to be buried without being identified. The scene along Monaghan's position defied description with mangled bodies lying in heaps among the works. "May God grant that I may never again experience such sensations or witness such scenes," wrote Father Sheeran. "The sights are shocking. The smell is still more offensive."[87]

The rifle fire was so heavy around the Bloody Angle that bullets whittled down mature oak trees. Two of them were located behind the position held by the 2nd Louisiana Brigade and the Stonewall Brigade. The largest was about sixteen inches in diameter and became something of a landmark which even Robert E. Lee visited. Its stump was eventually placed in the Smithsonian Institution.[88]

The Louisiana Tigers were able to contain Grant's breakthrough on the Mule Shoe's western side but have been given little credit for their stubborn stand. Most histories of the fighting at Spotsylvania treat the Louisiana brigades as if both were positioned with the 2nd Louisiana Brigade and were captured in the first moments of the battle. Virtually all accounts of the battle credit Gordon for saving Lee's army by rushing in reinforcements to seal the breach and ignore the critical role Monaghan's men played. If not for Monaghan's quickness in laying out a defensive position perpendicular to the trenches, the Yankees would have continued flanking the rebel brigades all the way down the western side. After the battle, a proud Captain Ring wrote his wife, "Genl. Ewell says our Brigade saved his left, by the determined stand we made which checked the enemy's advance. I hope he will mention it in his report." He did not.[89]

Lee's army was so badly shot up from the two weeks of slaughter that changes in the command structure were again necessary. Hill was well enough to return to the III Corps, so Early resumed command of his division. That displaced Gordon, but since Johnson was among those captured on May 12, the Georgian inherited his wrecked command. All of the Virginians remaining in the division were consolidated under Gen. William Terry, and the few surviving Louisianians were put under the 14th Louisiana's Col. Zebulon York, who must have rejoined the brigade shortly after the battle ended. There was little for York to command, however, for the Tigers had lost a staggering 808 men captured, besides several hundred killed and wounded, since the campaign began.[90]

Colonel York was a forty-four-year-old native of Maine and an original member of Tochman's Polish Brigade. Some sources claim he was of Polish ancestry, but there is no proof of it. York did, however, come from a prominent family; his grandfather served as an aide to George Washington during the Revolutionary War, and York graduated from both Kentucky's Transylvania University and the University of Louisiana. When the war began, he was one of Louisiana's richest men, co-owning six plantations and seventeen hundred slaves that produced forty-five hundred bales of cotton per year. York and his partner also reportedly paid the state's highest property taxes. As lieutenant colonel of the 14th Louisiana "Wildcats," York had earned a reputation for bravery "that amounted to rashness" and for profanity that put even some Tigers to shame. When the 14th Louisiana was stationed on the Peninsula early in the war, soldiers joked that it was the army's most favored regiment because it had York to damn the men and Father Sheeran to save them. It is not certain when York actually assumed command of the Tiger brigade because it appears Monaghan continued to lead it until he fell ill on or about June 1 and was forced to take extended sick leave. When York did take over, he was promoted to brigadier general, effective June 2.[91]

After a short rest, York's consolidated brigade was brought back to the line on May 14. Apparently some of the men were deployed earlier as skirmishers because Pvt. John B. Roden of the 7th Louisiana was wounded the day before. Roden, an Irish immigrant, had transferred to the regiment from Wheat's Battalion when it was disbanded and was captured at Rappahannock Station. Although there was nothing special about his being shot, Roden did leave one of the more detailed accounts of a wounded Tiger's hospital experience.[92]

After being hit in the arm on the skirmish line, Roden's first concern was making it back to the trenches safely because "the balls were flying pretty thick." When he reached the earthworks, some of the men began to joke about his wound and declared, "O, yes, don't play off that way; you just want a furlough." At the field hospital, a surgeon declared that he would have to operate on the wound but that amputation was not necessary "just now." "This was not very comforting," declared Roden, "as it left the impression that it might be later." He was then placed on a barn door that had been set up as an operating table and administered chloroform. Roden was later told that he sang "The Bonnie Blue Flag" and other patriotic songs while under the anesthesia.

Almost immediately after the surgery, it was reported that Grant had turned Lee's flank, and the hospital was quickly evacuated. "All who could walk were ordered to do so, the nearest station being Milford, some thirty miles distant." Roden walked twelve miles the first day and fourteen the next before finally collapsing in the middle of the road and being put in a wagon for the final leg to Milford. There he was transported by train to Richmond's Winder Hospital, where his wound was treated for the first time since the operation. Roden remained in the hospital for eight weeks, during which time he was poorly treated by an "insolent" nurse and threatened with the guardhouse for throwing his cornbread at the man. Roden survived the war but never fully recovered from his "shattered arm."[93]

Almost immediately after York returned to the trenches, the federals attacked once again. Afterward, Captain Ring wrote disgustedly that a number of soldiers threw down their weapons and surrendered to the Yankees without a fight. According to Ring, they believed the war would end that summer and being sent to a prison camp was "the safest way to escape the danger of the campaign."[94]

On May 18, Grant sent Hancock's II Corps to spearhead an even larger attack on Lee's new line at the base of the old Mule Shoe. One company of the 9th Louisiana and some Virginians from Col. John S. Hoffman's brigade had been sent out on picket duty near the Bloody Angle. Once again it was the pickets who first heard the sounds of a massive predawn troop movement, and officers whispered orders for the men to get ready for an attack. When the federal skirmishers advanced, the Confederate pickets quickly fell back to the main line to sound the alarm. After their bloody experience on May 12, the Tigers were nervous as to what was coming their way, but when the tightly packed Union brigades became visible, there was a sense of relief. One Virginia artilleryman wrote, "All were astonished at this and could not believe a serious attempt would be made to assail such a line as Ewell had, in open day, over such a distance." The Virginian declared that he and his comrades were eager "to pay off old scores." The Yankees advanced in four lines of battle, but the Tigers' and Virginians' accurate fire broke them up while they were still three hundred yards from the earthworks. Captain Henry Egan of the 15th Louisiana claimed that, when the enemy finally broke and fled, the Tigers mounted their works in jubilation and "called to them to come back, but they had no notion of coming again."[95]

Grant's persistent attacks and his heavy losses convinced the Louisianians that he would bleed the federal army white by summer's end. Philip Collins wrote a friend, "There has been some of the most desperate charges made by the Yankees this Campeign that I hav ever known them to make before but they hav been handsomely repulsed on every occasion with great slaughter as our army has don the most of their fighting behind breastworks." Captain Ring noted the same ferocity in the Yankee attacks and informed his wife, "We have met a man this time who either does not know when he is whipped, or who cares not if he loses his whole Army, so that he may accomplish an end. . . . He seems determined to die game if he has to die at all."[96]

Despite having fallen back closer to Richmond, some of the Tigers believed Lee actually held the upper hand because of the heavy losses Grant had sustained. In explaining the situation to a friend, Collins wrote, "Grant has got a good deal nearer Richmond than he was when he fought us in the wilderness but our army is just as far from being whipped now as it was then and from all accounts the Yankees are pretty badly whipped now and if they don't mind they will bee whipped wors than they hav ever been before they get out of this. Grant leaves his dead on the battle field to rot like buts[?] to rot on top of the ground. I hav seen a great many of them myself after they had decayed so much that the flesh had left their faces." On a similar note, Captain Egan wrote his brother, "I thank God they have at last got a leader (or rather I should say a master) who will drive them on to the slaughter and if he can only goad them on for a short time longer at the rate he has been doing it since the 5th of May; there will be but few of them left by the time this campaign closes. I think Gen. Grant's appointment to the command of the 'Grand Army of the Potomac' is a perfect God send to the Confederacy. . . . Grant is the only Yankee general who has ever given us the advantage of fighting on our own chosen ground. . . . Our cause never looked brighter."[97]

CHAPTER 11

All Played Out

G RANT'S HEAVY LOSSES in the Overland Campaign led some Tigers to believe that the Union army was on the verge of defeat. That was far from the case because, on May 19, Grant launched yet another offensive maneuver by withdrawing from Spotsylvania to turn Lee's right flank. When Lee discovered that the enemy was on the move, he ordered General Ewell to make a reconnaissance in force against the Union right flank to disrupt Grant's plans. General Gordon took the lead with York's brigade and a motley assortment of Virginians from what remained of Johnson's division. By chance, Gordon advanced through a gap in the Union lines and hit the Fredericksburg Road just as a Union wagon train was passing by. Almost immediately the hungry rebels broke ranks and swarmed over the wagons looking for food. The men were so distracted by barrels of pork that they did not notice Gen. Robert O. Tyler's Union brigade approaching. In the nick of time, however, Gordon regained order and withdrew from the road to a patch of woods to the west, where the men hastily threw up logs and brush for protection.

The 7th New York Heavy Artillery and 1st Maine Heavy Artillery were untried in battle, and one soldier wrote that they advanced across an open field, "just as you see them in pictures." The Tigers and Virginians cut the Yankees to pieces, partly because the federals stood their ground in the open and fired slow, methodical textbook volleys. Ewell then ordered his men to attack the green troops, but the artillerymen surprisingly held their ground and inflicted heavy losses on the rebels before reinforcements arrived. Some of the Virginians broke and withdrew, and it was only with difficulty that Gordon and Ewell were able to beat back the Union attacks in what became known as the Battle of Harris Farm. During the fighting, Ewell's horse was killed and fell on the general, and he had to be dragged out from under his dead mount. When the battle finally ended, Ewell's standing with Lee had suffered because what was intended to be a reconnaissance had ended in him getting something of a drubbing.[1]

After pulling out of Spotsylvania, Grant next confronted Lee at the North Anna River, but when he could gain no advantage there he headed south once again on May 27 to the crossroads at Cold Harbor. Lee and the exhausted Tigers followed in what Sergeant Charlton called "Rather a forced march" in occasional heavy rains. The following day, William Bayliss Tull and his two brothers joined the Louisiana Brigade. The Tull boys were from Livingston Parish, where the two oldest ones had joined the 9th Louisiana's Colyell Guards when the war began. William was only sixteen at the time, but he enlisted in the cavalry and saw action at the Battle of Baton Rouge. When his brothers returned home after a prisoner exchange, they visited young Tull's regiment with one of their comrades, and Tull offered to switch places with the married man.[2]

When the Tulls arrived in Richmond, the Overland Campaign was raging and the wounded had flooded the city. Apparently on a whim, the brothers decided to go sightseeing at the "Distributing Hospital." William wrote:

Thousands were being brought to this hospital by train loads every few hours from off the field of the Wilderness. The wounded who were in most need of care were first brought to this place, operated on and then sent to other hospitals for care and rest. . . . I can only make a feeble attempt to describe the scene that greeted our eyes at this distributing center. The hospital was a great tabernacle shaped building with a dirt floor. I am not able to say what its dimensions were, but there was room for at least one thousand operating tables, and on each of these a poor bleeding soldier lay stretched. Besides these were thousands of men on the ground on the outside of the building waiting their turn. The faithful surgeons bending over those bleeding suffering fellows were worn out from over work and loss of sleep, yet they toiled on unceasingly. Men in going under the influence of chloroform act differently, so in this case some of them were signing [sighing?], some cursing, others hollering, while yet others were praying. The horroring discord and confusion of sound seemed to intimate the mingled agony and suffering of the victims. All of this, together with the smell of blood and putrid flesh made it one of the most awful spectacles the mind could contemplate.[3]

When the Tulls arrived in camp on May 28, they received a warm welcome from the nineteen men still with the Colyell Guards. After the war, William recalled, "The sharp-shooters were out in front, and an occasional bullet would whiz over our heads." Few recruits were reaching the Tigers by this time in the war, so the men were particularly appreciative of William making the journey to Virginia. "The boys were glad to see us," he wrote. "At this stage of the conflict, every one who could find a pretext had fallen out of the service, and for this reason the old veterans knew how to appreciate the spirit of a man who would give himself in the service when others were faultering and falling out." Because William was still dressed in civilian clothing, the Tigers dubbed him "Coperas Breeched" and immediately sent him out to the picket line.[4]

When Early's corps reached Cold Harbor, it was put in the center of Lee's line. The Louisianians had been in contact with the enemy almost every day for the past three weeks and had covered many miles over muddy roads, but they found no respite in the trenches. Union sharpshooters shot three Tigers on June 1. One of the snipers hid in a distant tree near Meadow Bridge and killed Capt. Charles McLellan of the 15th Louisiana. The bullet first passed through the shoulder of a comrade and then hit McLellan in the back of the head. He died immediately after muttering, "Oh, Lordy!" The 8th Louisiana's Lt. Col. Germain A. Lester, a University of Mississippi graduate who had been wounded previously at Second Fredericksburg, was also killed.[5]

June 2 was another wet, dreary day with constant skirmishing. That afternoon Early discovered that Gen. Thomas Crittenden's Union division was shifting its position and attacked while it was in motion. Gordon's division engaged in a bloody fight with two Union brigades before the battle finally sputtered out. Casualties for the Louisiana Brigade are not known except that Pvt. Thomas Reed was shot in the right thigh. The impact of the bullet spun him around, and he accidentally jabbed Captain Ring with his bayonet. Raising his sword, the surprised Ring cursed Reed and threatened to slash him, but Reed brought up his bayonet and told the captain "to cut if he was ready." Ring walked away, and Reed received a wounded furlough. After volunteering to serve with Bedford Forrest's cavalry for a time, he realized the war was lost and went home to his wife and children.[6]

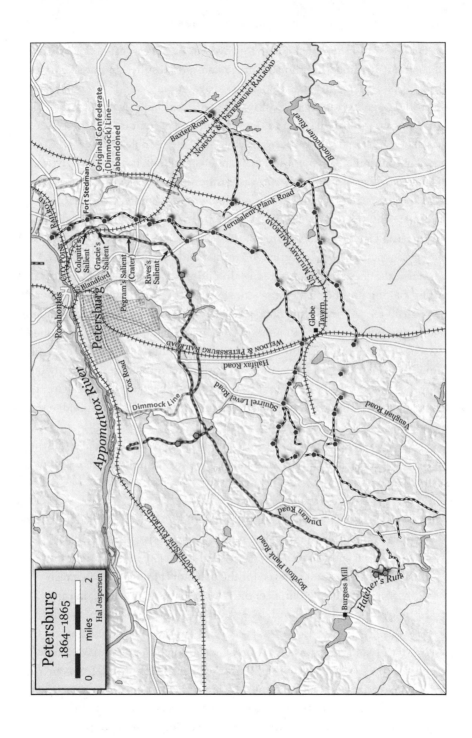

Petersburg
1864–1865

Hal Jespersen

miles
0   2

Appomattox River

Petersburg

Pocahontas

City Point Railroad

Blandford

Colquitt's Salient
Gracie's Salient
Pegram's Salient
Rives's Salient (Crater)

Fort Stedman

Original Confederate (Dimmock) Line — abandoned

Baxter Road

NORFOLK & PETERSBURG RAILROAD

Blackwater River

Jerusalem Plank Road

US Military Railroad

Globe Tavern

WELDON & PETERSBURG RAILROAD

Halifax Road

Cox Road

Dimmock Line

Squirrel Level Road

Vaughan Road

South Side Railroad

Duncan Road

Boydton Plank Road

Burgess Mill

Hatcher's Run

On June 3, Grant launched what proved to be his biggest attack at Cold Harbor, but it gained him no advantage and only resulted in massive casualties. It is not known what role York's brigade played in the repulse, but the 10th Louisiana reportedly lost its flag. Sources claim that, when the color-bearer was hit, the flag fell to the ground, and at least one Union soldier was shot while trying to retrieve it. Later, Lt. Peter Ambler of the 11th Connecticut found the flag, put it in his knapsack, and took it home after he was discharged. The 11th Connecticut was positioned more than two miles away from the Louisiana Brigade, so it is not known how Ambler came across the colors or why the Tigers did not retrieve it themselves. While the story is suspect, the Danbury Grand Army of the Republic post displayed the flag for many years before it was returned to Louisiana in 1925.[7]

When the federals disappeared again on June 9, Lee believed Grant was either making another short move to the right or withdrawing entirely to regroup. In fact, Grant was making a quick march to Petersburg, a city about twenty-five miles south of Richmond through which most of Lee's supplies passed. If Grant could capture Petersburg, Lee would either have to attack him on ground of his choosing or abandon Richmond in order to supply his army. Fortunately for Lee, General Beauregard managed to turn back Grant's lackluster attack on the city and bought enough time for Lee to respond to the enemy's bold move.

After weeks of campaigning, the Tigers were about played out from the constant fighting, marching, and manning the picket lines. Private Tull described the harsh conditions:

> There had been no such thing as rest for us. Real sleep had fled from us. If we found time in the trenches to lie down to sleep then it was not to rest. It was only a kind of restless semi-consciousness wherein the dread of battle was not relieved for the boom of cannon, the wild crash of musketry, the deadly shriek of the "Minny-ball," and the bursting and hizzing of the bombshell with its scattering death-fragments spattering in every direction, these were all the time haunting the restless sleeper like the cry of grim monsters in some hideous night-mare. . . . [W]e had ceased to look for any clothing, shoes, hats, or other apparel, from our poor Government. Our ration itself had been cut one half. We usually drew three days ration at a time, and as a rule we ate that up in one day, and often at one meal, trusting to Providence for the next supply.[8]

Unfortunately for the Tigers, there would be no rest. Just as Lee was preparing to meet Grant's new threat, he received ominous news on June 11 that Gen. David Hunter's Union army had defeated the Confederate forces in the Shenandoah Valley and was threatening Lee's supply line by moving against the important rail hub at Lynchburg. To stop Hunter, Lee had no choice but to dispatch the II Corps to reinforce Gen. John C. Breckinridge's small division that was defending the town. General Early had replaced a sick Ewell as the corps' commander, and Lee ordered him to destroy Hunter's army and then threaten Washington and Baltimore by moving down the Valley toward the Potomac River. Lee hoped Early's move would relieve some of the pressure on Petersburg by forcing the federals to detach part of the Army of the Potomac to stop him.

On June 13, Early pulled out of the trenches and led his men to the west. On the same day, eight Louisiana congressmen petitioned President Davis to allow the members of York's brigade a ninety-day furlough to return to Louisiana to gather new recruits. In their plea, they wrote, "These brigades are mere skeletons, the two hardly equal to half a regiment. . . . Three years of hardships and dangers ought to entitle the few survivors of this once magnificent corps to this small boon." Even though the entire brigade now numbered only a few hundred men, the army could not afford to lose the Tigers, and Davis rejected the petition. The consolidated Louisiana Brigade would accompany Early to Lynchburg and new battlefields.[9]

At Charlottesville, Early put some of his units on trains to speed their way to Breckinridge, but York's Tigers were forced to march. When Hunter arrived on the outskirts of Lynchburg on June 17, he found Gens. Francis T. Nicholls and Harry T. Hays, two of the Tigers' former commanders who were in Lynchburg recuperating from wounds, helping Breckinridge place troops to defend the city. The vanguard of Early's corps began arriving later that day, and Hunter retreated westward toward the Alleghany Mountains after a short fight.[10]

Early gave chase for three days but finally called a halt at Salem and gave his men a badly needed day of rest. On June 23, he began the second phase of his mission by making a rapid march down the Valley toward the Potomac River and Maryland. As the column neared Lexington, General Gordon's soldiers requested that they be allowed to make a ten-mile detour to visit the famous Natural Bridge. In return, they promised to march twenty-five miles a day thereafter to make up for the lost time. Somewhat surprisingly, Gordon agreed and then gave the men two hours to sightsee once they arrived at the landmark. Local residents acted as guides and took the soldiers down into the gorge, where, to their surprise, they saw that they had actually marched across the bridge without realizing it. Private Tull was impressed by the "millions of names" visitors had left scrawled on the canyon's walls, and he and many others followed suit. Tull claimed that "hundreds of our names, with our Company and Regiment, were left where future ages can see that the Natural Bridge was once in the possession of the Confederate army." Then, as they soaked in the peaceful scenery and drank from the cool creek water, officers began barking orders. "Word came to fall in line," Tull recalled, "but we were loath to obey, and our indulgent officers permitted us to loiter some time after [the] first orders."[11]

Later in the day, Early's corps reached Lexington and found that Hunter had burned the Virginia Military Institute. While there, the ragged rebels paid their respects to their fallen hero, Stonewall Jackson. According to Tull, "We marched around the grave at trail arms, flags lowered and drums muffled as in a funeral march. After this, we formed into a hollow square, then stacked arms and rested at will. One after another of the Generals addressed us, recounting the scenes of the many battles through which we had followed his leadership. . . . They admonished us to keep untarnished to the end of life the fame so dearly bought." General York later wrote how the return to the Shenandoah and the visit to Jackson's grave affected his men. "This Valley is for my Command classic ground," he wrote. "As they tread its highways, the Eagle eye, the nervous frame, the flashing genius of 'Stonewall Jackson' are incarnate before them. Each spot is to them a monument of his immortality. . . . With colors drooping, arms reversed & to the solemn dirge, my brave Louisianians filed past the grave of the dead hero at Lexington."[12]

As Early's corps continued its march toward the Potomac, local residents turned out in droves to welcome the men back to the Valley. Tull recalled:

> All along our march, the enthusiastic reception given us by the citizens was an inspiration next to the real sweets of victory. Great throngs of patriotic, Spartan-like mothers, lovely girls and bright lads gathered in the towns and along the highways to greet us. Flags and handkerchiefs could be seen fluttering from portico, window and doorway along our march. Crowds of these dear creatures would throng the sidewalks dispensing cold water and lunches to the hungry and famishing soldiers. Showers of roses and other fragrant flowers were thrown

upon us from the overhead balconies and windows. Wild shouts mingled with patriotic songs would fill the air. Every possible expression of hope and joy were indulged, seeing the old "Second Corps" again on their way to the front to so surely beat back the enemies of their homes. These expressions on the part of the people would call forth the most thrilling outbursts of that ever to be remembered and awe-inspiring "rebel yell."[13]

In contrast to this enthusiastic welcome was the shock of seeing how savagely Hunter's raiders had ravaged the Shenandoah Valley. According to Tull:

They had destroyed everything that the inhabitants of the country had to live upon. Pens full of cattle, sheep and hogs were killed and left to rot, wardrobes were robbed and the clothing of women and children were taken out and torn to shreds and left, feather beds were taken out into the streets of the villages and ripped open. In places the feathers were knee deep. Bed clothing and other household supplies were cut or torn into strips, while fine rugs were taken out and thrown into the roads and trodden under foot. Doors were taken off their hinges and broken to pieces, while gates were torn away and fences thrown down. Women and children were thus left desolate, frightened and distracted by the savage manner of the human brutes. These scenes greeted our eyes for miles.

The crowning shame of it all was overtaken later in the day. Our Colonel [Peck] haulted us to rest for a few minutes, as was our custom on a forced march. Standing by the road side near us was an old gray haired man and his wife weeping in great anguish. As soon as we stopped, the old man began to tell the cause of their grief. As well as I can remember it I will relate the sad story word for word: "This morning eleven Yankees came into our home acting roughly, and after plundering the house, they seized our two daughters and criminally outraged them and they have both died, poor things." Our Colonel rode up to[o] and viewed the corpses, then rode back to where we were and made us a brief speech. I do not now recall all he said but I do remember this much: "Catch the dogs and give them the bayonet. I charge you, take no prisoners."[14]

By that time, Early's men were pushing Union stragglers and small units ahead of them, and they began finding exhausted Yankees, abandoned equipment, and stolen loot along the roadside. Tull never mentioned whether the Tigers obeyed Colonel Peck's orders.

Tull was among many of Early's men who found it difficult to maintain the brutal pace. He had fallen ill but praised Colonel Peck, who was commanding the 1st Louisiana Brigade at the time; Lt. Col. John J. Hodges; and Maj. Singletary for frequently offering to carry his musket or other equipment to help him keep up. "This of course was contrary to military usage," Tull wrote, "but it was no unusual thing to see my Colonel riding at the head of the column with my gun on his shoulder." The brigade had outpaced its supply train, and the lack of food only worsened Tull's condition. He claimed that on one occasion the Tigers went three days without any rations and were forced "to live on green apples and other such fruit as we could find. All of the officers' horses had given out and they were compelled to walk. I venture the remark that history will record few instances where a pursuing army was reduced to such straits because of their disregard for self in their chase after an enemy."

Tull finally fell out from heat exhaustion just south of Winchester, and his two brothers left him on the side of the road in the shade of a willow tree. According to Tull, "My good and brave Colonel Peck stood guard over me till . . . the Ambulance Corps, came up." Peck helped load Tull into the ambulance and then instructed the driver to leave him with the chief surgeon in Winchester. Tull survived his ordeal but had a lengthy stay in the Staunton hospital, where food was in short supply. He wrote that "our ration consist[ed] of soup made from poor beef, thickened with flour and one thin slice of light bread. Our coffee was made from parched wheat and we had neither sugar nor milk to flavor it with." Eventually, Tull became so hungry that he often slipped out of the hospital and visited women in the countryside because they would feed him out of pity.[15]

The 9th Louisiana and the Louisiana Brigade's sharpshooters under Captain Workman and Lt. W. J. Reams led the way into Martinsburg on July 3 and drove the Yankees out of town after what General York described as a "short but sharp resistance." York complained that his starving brigade did not receive its fair share of the substantial supplies that were captured, but a member of the 8th Louisiana wrote that the regiment spent the next day "partaking of the good chear provided by the Yankees from their 4th of July celebration."

After the army crossed over the Potomac at Shepherdstown on July 5, the exhausted Louisiana Brigade lost a couple of men to artillery fire when it participated in an attack on Maryland Heights. In his report, York proudly wrote, "My sharpshooters as usual took a spirited part in the advance."[16]

Early's crossing of the Potomac River on July 5–6 marked the third time most of the Louisiana Tigers had carried the war to the enemy, but now the joyous enthusiasm that had accompanied the two previous Maryland invasions was lacking. The mood was more subdued because the men were exhausted and knew that the war had turned against them. For nearly half of Early's soldiers, the crossing was also physically painful because the sharp rocks cut their bare feet.[17]

Incredibly, Union officials in Washington were not even aware of the rebel threat. Hunter had failed to notify his superiors of Early's presence in the Valley when he retreated to West Virginia and, as late as July 3, General Grant reported that Early's corps was still at Petersburg. However, that same day, Gen. Lew Wallace learned that Hunter had abandoned the Valley and realized there was nothing to stop the enemy from invading Maryland. As a precaution, he began assembling troops along the Monocacy River near Frederick to block any rebel advance toward Washington.

Early made contact with Wallace on July 9 but knew that a frontal attack across the Monocacy bridge would be suicidal. Thus, he ordered Rodes' and Ramseur's divisions to demonstrate near the bridge while Gordon slipped his division across the river a mile downstream to hit the federal left flank. So as not to be detected, Gordon's men were told to discard anything that might make noise. Canteens, knapsacks, and all of the luxuries accumulated on the march were piled up and left behind—much to the dismay of the Louisianians, who knew they probably would never see their precious belongings again.

Gordon discovered a ford below the bridge and managed to wade his men across the Monocacy while the Yankees' attention was fixed on Ramseur and Rodes. Gordon could see the enemy behind a low rail fence on the other side of a field that was dotted with haystacks and laced with strong fences. After studying the federal position, he sent Clement Evans' brigade through a patch of woods on the right and had York deploy a battle line in the center, with Terry supporting his left rear. Gordon's plan was to attach in echelon, starting with Evans and then York and Terry.[18]

When all was ready, Evans burst out of the woods and hit the Yankees' flank with volleys of musketry, but Evans was wounded and his brigade suffered heavy losses. York's line then surged forward with Terry's brigade following on the left. Colonel Eugene Waggaman, who had recently returned to the 10th Louisiana after extended duty in Louisiana, was out in front of the 2nd Louisiana Brigade, cheering the men forward, and Colonel Peck led the 1st Brigade on horseback until his mount was killed from under him, and he was slightly wounded by a bullet to the chest. Gordon wrote, "As we reached the first line of strong and high fencing, and my men began to climb over it, they were met by a tempest of bullets, and many of the brave fellows fell at the first volley." Scores of Tigers and Virginians were cut down when the federals opened fire from 125 yards, but the two brigades then sent the Yankees scattering with their own volley. York was proud of his men's steadfast courage and wrote in his report that "the sight was more than imposing. My veterans marched under fire with the precision of automata." General Gordon was also in the thick of the action and had his horse killed under him, as well. York later wrote, "His escape was miraculous, his horse being killed under him at the very front of his Command, where his voice might be heard above the roar of Musketry."[19]

The rebels regrouped and then chased after the enemy, only to be hit hard by a second Yankee line when they reached a small branch at the bottom of the hill's back slope. Early later recalled that so many of his men were shot down along the creek that the water was red with blood for one hundred yards. Nonetheless, the Confederates kept up the pressure, and General York claimed that the enemy soon "ran like sheep without a Shepard." Falling back to a sunken road, the federals made a final stand and were able to check York's and Terry's advance. The 9th Louisiana came under a fierce fire, but color-bearers continued to wave the regimental flag proudly, even though four were shot down in rapid succession. Wallace finally withdrew from the field after leaving hundreds of prisoners behind.[20]

Gordon's division lost heavily in the attacks on Wallace's line, but York bragged that his Tigers had "stood their ground" against a "withering" fire and drove the enemy from the field. "Too much praise cannot be awarded to my Officers & Men for their bearing in this engagement. Disciplined by the fire of 20 Battles, they so uniformly & so generally meet danger & death without fear, that it is almost impossible to discriminate in the record of gallantry." York reported losing 45 dead and 118 wounded at the Monocacy, which was between one-fourth and one-half of the brigade's total strength. The 14th New

Jersey and 151st New York, the two Union regiments which bore the brunt of the Tigers' attack, suffered the greatest number of dead in Wallace's army, with the 14th New Jersey reporting 140 casualties and the 151st New York 101.[21]

The Louisiana Brigade's officer corps suffered particularly heavy losses. Among the wounded were Lt. Cols. Joseph Hanlon, an Irish officer in the 6th Louisiana, and John W. Hodges of the 9th regiment, who was shot in the arm and underwent an amputation. York admired Hodges and wrote in his report, "He is one of the best Officers in the service." Hodges and many other Tigers who were too badly wounded to travel were left behind and captured by the Yankees. One six-year-old local boy who watched the battle from his house gathered up sheaves of wheat to make bedding for the wounded. As it turned out, Colonel Hodges was one of the men his family helped, and the boy remembered that he "had his upper arm bone shattered by a leaden bullet and suffered great pain."[22]

The Battle of the Monocacy is not one of the more famous Civil War clashes, but participants described it as among the fiercest. According to Captain Seymour, it was "one of the sharpest & most bloody fights of the war." Gordon agreed and declared, "This battle, though short, was severe," and York wrote, "The combat of the 'Monocacy' although short was a severe test of the endurance of my Command." At a cost of approximately seven hundred men, Early had inflicted two thousand enemy casualties, with most of the Yankees' losses occurring in front of the Tigers. Looking over the field the next day, Father Sheeran wrote, "On the crest of the hill where our men first attacked the enemy, we saw a regular line of dead Yankee bodies. A little in the rear they were to be seen lying in every direction and position, some on their sides, some on their faces, some on their backs with their eyes and mouths open, the burning sun beating upon them and their faces swarmed with disgusting flies."[23]

After the battle, Early acknowledged York's role in the victory when he rode up and simply said, "General, you have handled your command well and it has done its duty nobly." "This I shall ever consider a complament of note," wrote York, "coming from one of the most cross grained & faultfinding Gens. in the C.S. Army."[24]

With the way to Washington now open, Early resumed his advance at daylight and pushed his men thirty miles through oppressive heat and dust. July 11 was even worse, but on that day the Tigers finally approached Fort Stevens, one of many forts ringing the city, and could see the Capitol's dome in the distance. General Early claimed that he wanted to attack immediately, but "the men were almost completely exhausted and not in a condition to make an attack." York disagreed and wrote in his report, "The sight of its domes & fortifications fired anew my men, & they would have hailed with joy the command for an assault & moved with intrepidity to its execution."[25]

The rebels' approach threw the city into a panic. Fortunately for Lincoln, Wallace's sacrifice at the Monocacy had bought the time needed for Grant to rush reinforcements to Washington. Realizing that a successful assault was now impossible, Early withdrew on July 12 and headed back to Virginia. Union forces cautiously pursued, and numerous skirmishes were fought in the lower Valley over the next week. One at Castleman's Ferry on July 18 left two of the Tigers' sharpshooters wounded and Capt. Al Pierson dead. Pierson's letters are some of the most informative left by the Tigers, and General York lamented his death. He wrote that Pierson "was a pains-taking faithful & remarkably brave Man."[26]

Philip Collins and Felix A. Bledsoe wrote Pierson's father to give him the details of his son's death. Pierson had just returned to his company from furlough two days earlier and had taken command of the skirmish line along the Shenandoah River that morning. Bledsoe described how Pierson was putting the men in place when several well-hidden Yankees opened fire from the other side of the river at a range of about one hundred yards. Pierson's men immediately lay down and sought cover behind trees, but the captain "walked along perfectly regardless of dangers and exclaimed 'Boys see those Yankees behind that clay root—shoot them.'" Pierson remained in the open shouting orders in his usual loud voice until a bullet tore through his upper right arm and passed completely through his body. Falling to the ground, he yelled, "Collins, I'm killed take me out," but the enemy's fire was so heavy that no one could reach him, and he quickly died. Pierson's men had a coffin made and buried him in a nearby farmer's cemetery. Collins informed Mr. Pierson that he had taken possession of the captain's personal effects and at the request of Colonel Peck had also collected some buttons and a lock of hair to send to the family. "Capt P was a brave officer & much beloved by his company," Collins wrote. "He was true as steel—good and kind to his men. His bravery suited him well for the battlefield—while he was too boisterous and too much destitute of caution and craftiness to fight the Snake in the grass. His loss is felt greatly."[27]

On the same day that Captain Pierson was killed, the 5th Louisiana's Maj.

Alexander Hart arrived with reinforcements for York's brigade. Hart, who had been wounded at Antietam and Gettysburg, had been serving on detached duty in Richmond during the fighting at the Wilderness and Spotsylvania. When General Lee issued orders on July 4 for all members of the II Corps to report to their respective units, Hart assumed command of 250 soldiers. It is not clear if all of the men were Tigers, and surgeons later dismissed 35 of them for health reasons, but Hart led the remainder to the Valley.[28]

Early finally made camp near Strasburg, from which he could keep pressure on Washington. Although he had been successful in drawing away some of Grant's army from Petersburg, Early's raid also nearly ruined the Louisiana Brigade with its forced marches, severe losses at the Monocacy, and constant skirmishing. In addition, the men were still seething over the forced consolidation of the two brigades. On July 24, Richard Colbert wrote from the Valley, "I am tired of being pulled & hauled about as we are, no officers, no Brigade. [It is] not [right] taken all the flags out of our brig. but one, all out [of the] 2nd La. but one, only four line officers in our Regt., all played out, and the men are playing out fast too. Nearly every man is his own Gen. in our Brig. . . . Seventy-nine men in our regt. and some thirty or forty in the other Regt. . . . I tell you we have no discipline at all now. I am getting very tired of it. . . . I fear our brig. will lose all the glory it has won in Va."[29]

The 9th Louisiana's Private Tull agreed that morale was low and confidence in General Early was waning after the Washington Raid. "From this time on," he wrote, "the private soldiers began to lose confidence in our Corps Commander. By this time every veteran soldier in the ranks had become a Major General in his own knowledge of war-craft, and if there occurred any mismanagement on the part of the officers, they were sure to detect it and expose it in some way."[30]

Instead of losing their laurels as Colbert feared, however, the Tigers actually enhanced their reputation the same day he wrote his letter. Early believed that one more Confederate victory in the Valley might clear the federals out of the region. Therefore, when he learned that the Yankees under Gen. George Crook were converging on Winchester a few miles north of his camps, he did not hesitate to attack. At daylight on July 24, Early advanced toward the enemy with Gordon's division in the lead. The day was turning brutally hot when Gordon encountered a Union line of battle three miles southwest of Winchester at Kernstown. Encountering federals who were ready to fight surprised Captain Ring because the men had been told that the enemy had already fled the area. But then, he recalled, "the sharp, quick sound of the minie was heard, affording palpable evidence that there was work ahead for us." General Early deployed Wharton's division to the right of the road and Gordon to the left, with Ramseur swinging around Gordon's left flank. As Gordon's brigades moved into position, it occurred to Captain Ring that they were covering the same ground on which he was wounded in the Second Battle of Winchester. "Our Division filed off at exactly the same point as last year, and the thought struck me rather forcibly, I wonder if we will continue the coincidence and be fortunate enough to get another nice eight-month furlough wound."[31]

When Wharton and then Gordon attacked the federals, the Union line began to collapse just as it did a year earlier. Captain Ring wrote that his men also came under heavy artillery fire from the same hill from which he was wounded in the previous battle. "[W]e came up with our double-quicking friends and our sharpshooters gave them a fire that covered the ground with killed and wounded." Nearly all of the casualties the Tigers suffered were the result of the Union artillery, which prompted Ring to observe, "I must say that if all other branches of their service fought and was handled as well as their artillery, we would not have so easy a time."[32]

When the enemy retreated into Winchester, General Breckinridge put Captain Ring in charge of the sharpshooters and ordered him to push the Yankees out of town. Ring did so but then encountered a strong line of Union infantry beyond town and became concerned that a major battle might develop. Fortunately, at that moment the Confederate cavalry drove the enemy from the field. It was, Ring declared, the first time in three years of war that he actually witnessed a cavalry charge. Soon afterward the federals tried to make another stand, and Ring had his men take cover behind a stone wall. He expected to take considerable casualties when he ordered an attack, but once again the enemy broke and ran. "To my utter astonishment the moment our men emerged from the rock walls behind which they had been sheltered, then away start our Yankee friends. . . . [O]f all the tall traveling I have ever seen, they did some of the tallest from that time until night." The Tigers were relieved to see them go and followed along "with many humorous remarks about the race we were running."[33]

The Tigers lost only thirteen men in the fight, and Major Hart claimed they drove the enemy four miles beyond Winchester before finally stopping from sheer exhaustion. Richard Colbert declared, "The enemy just double quicked to Williamsport and I don't know but what they are going yet. They were perfectly demoralized, though we captured but few as they were Hunter's men & they think we will kill the last one of them as they treated our citizens so outragious down about Lynchburg."[34]

When the day ended, the men of the Louisiana Brigade had marched twenty-five miles, six while in line of battle. They then were forced to camp for the night in a steady rain without any tents for cover and spent the next day tearing up the Baltimore & Ohio Railroad as they advanced. After having some time to reflect on the running fight, Ring informed his wife, "It is a very singular coincidence, darling, that for three successive years our Army has driven the enemy out of Winchester, and each time on a Sunday, and also that the La. Brigade by the fortune of war have been the first to enter the city."[35]

Suffering only light losses, Early had inflicted more than fifteen hundred casualties on Crook and pushed him back to the Potomac River. For the rest of the summer, the rebels marched constantly to keep the Yankees occupied in the Valley and unable to reinforce Grant. On August 5, the Louisiana Brigade even crossed the Potomac River into Maryland for the fifth time in the war and engaged in a skirmish outside Sharpsburg. Major Hart took the opportunity to visit the Antietam battlefield and found the spot where he was wounded two years earlier. After returning to Virginia, the rebels suffered a slow trickle of casualties as they continued skirmishing around Winchester. One clash on August 25 claimed the life of the 6th Louisiana's popular and effective Col. William Monaghan, who had just returned to the brigade from sick leave a few weeks earlier and resumed command of the 1st Louisiana Brigade.

Early's corps had been marching toward the Potomac River that day with Gordon's division in the lead when it encountered Gen. Alfred T. A. Torbet's Union cavalry coming down the road. The Yankee troopers attacked, but the rebel infantry dispersed them in a quick, fierce engagement. The rest of the day was spent in what Major Hart described as a "rousing fight" that dragged on for nine miles between Leetown and Shepherdstown. Nearly all of the thirty or so casualties the Tigers suffered were hit by artillery fire, but Monaghan was shot through the head near Shepherdstown. He was buried the next day; General York, Colonel Waggaman, and Majors Hart and Alfred A. Singletary were among the pallbearers.[36]

The almost daily grind of marching and skirmishing continued, with another sharp fight taking place near Smithfield on August 29 that cost the Tigers thirty more casualties. The deadly routine was beginning to take a heavy toll on York's consolidated brigade. Numbering only a few hundred men, it was exhausted, clothed in ragged uniforms, poorly disciplined, and still aggravated over the consolidation of the two brigades. By the end of August, the Tigers had marched more than eight hundred miles since leaving Lee outside Richmond and had been engaged in seventeen battles and major skirmishes. An astonishing 764 men were listed as being absent without leave, and 971 were in northern prison camps. Inspections that month show that the consolidated Louisiana Brigade had 601 officers and men present for duty, with the 1st Brigade having 427 and the 2nd Brigade only 174. The 9th Louisiana was the largest regiment with 152 men and the 10th Louisiana was the smallest with 24. The inspecting officer described the men's clothing as being "bad," and claimed that 195 men (or 45 percent) in the 1st Louisiana Brigade were barefoot, 298 needed trousers, and 315 were without shirts or underclothes. On the other hand, the men's muskets were described as being "serviceable," and there was an ample supply of ammunition.[37]

General Philip Sheridan assumed command of the Union's Valley forces soon after the Kernstown debacle and attacked Early outside Winchester on September 19 when he learned that Early had weakened his army by sending part of it to Lee. The hard-driving Yankees were forcing Ramseur's division back when Gordon arrived on the field and deployed on Ramseur's left. York placed his Tigers along the edge of a large field, and General Early took up a position behind them. Captain Ring claimed they watched as Sheridan's men advanced toward them "in beautiful order with their bright gun barrels reflecting back the rays of the sun in a way to make your eyes water." Just before noon, Early ordered York to meet the enemy, and the gray line moved across the clearing toward the Yankees. Captain Seymour wrote that it was "the beautiful and rare sight of two opposing lines charging at the same time."[38]

Both sides proudly advanced without firing a shot. Then at two hundred yards they halted, took aim, and cut one another down with minié balls. "I had the pleasure," wrote Ring, "of seeing and participating in the prettiest stand up, fair open fight that I have ever seen." For ten minutes blue and gray traded volleys across the field, but Ring boasted, "Southern pluck was too much for our Yankee friends," and the federals retreated to the shelter of some timber. "We of course raised a Louisiana yell and [went] after them pouring a fire into their backs that soon made the ground black with their hateful bodies." Gordon's entire division took up the chase, but the Louisianians outran their sister brigades when they heard a false rumor that a Union regiment from Louisiana faced them. Finding himself in advance of the division, York was forced to fall back a hundred yards and then turn around to beat off two determined Union counterattacks. "I never saw our brigade fight better," wrote Ring. "The fact of these renegades being opposite to us seemed to nerve each man's arm and make [his] aim certain. . . . I think and firmly believe that every man in Hays' and Stafford's Brigades killed his man that day."[39]

Following these attacks, the battle settled into a prolonged skirmish until midafternoon, when Sheridan's cavalry rode roughshod over Early's horsemen on the far left. The Confederate cavalry screen folded and galloped for the rear, uncovering the flank of Early's infantry. "It soon became a rout on our part," admitted Ring, who stood seventy-five yards behind York's firing line, watching the Confederate brigades come unhinged regiment by regiment. Seeing the rebel line breaking up, the Union infantry charged across the field, but instead of fleeing, the Tigers stood their ground and shot down the advancing bluecoats. For crucial minutes, York's men fought alone to cover the panicked retreat of their comrades and littered the field with Yankee dead. One federal flag was seen to fall five times in five minutes, but the enemy kept coming and soon overwhelmed the Tigers. Every mounted officer in the brigade was wounded by the hail of bullets and shrapnel, including General York, who had to leave the field when a ball shattered his left wrist.[40]

Unable to withstand such a barrage, the Louisiana Brigade finally yielded and fell back through some woods. Ring wrote that the Tigers emerged onto another field and were startled to see "that the gig was over with us unless some extriordinary dispensation of Providence [intervened]. . . . All over the plain men could be seen flying to the rear, officers riding to and fro trying to rally and reform the men. It was a mortifying, but a very exciting scene." General Gordon did his best to stem the tide, which prompted Captain Ring to write, "I never saw as fine a sight in my life as our noble Gen. Gordon presented, as he galloped down the line with a stand of colors in his hand, his hat off and long hair streaming back in the wind." Ring was holding the colors of the 2nd Louisiana Brigade when Gordon rode up to him and shouted, "Form your men, Captain, I know they will stand by me!" But it was useless. Small groups of soldiers would halt and draw up a line, but then the charging Yankees would send them scattering. With the Louisianians bringing up the rear, Early's demoralized men fled through the streets of Winchester and finally halted miles away at Fisher's Hill.[41]

The army was humiliated at the Third Battle of Winchester (or Opequon Creek), although the Tigers' conscience was eased by the knowledge that they had covered the retreat and enabled most of the men to escape. The price for their heroism was high, however, for the brigade suffered 154 casualties. Among the wounded was Colonel Peck, who was hit in the right thigh by a shell fragment. Colonel Waggaman, who had recently rejoined the 10th Louisiana after a lengthy absence on recruiting duty in Louisiana, fought like a mad man with his horse's reins in his teeth before he, too, was wounded. And Major Hart, the officer who brought badly needed reinforcements from Richmond, was captured after three bullets mortally wounded his horse. With General York and Colonels Peck and Waggaman out of action for the foreseeable future, brigade command fell to the 6th Louisiana's Lieutenant Colonel Hanlon.[42]

As the men dug in on Fisher's Hill, they discussed the turn of events and speculated as to what caused the defeat. Captain Ring believed the lack of shoes weakened the army and informed his wife, "One of the principal causes of our defeat on Monday was the miserable condition of the Army in the way of shoes. I have heard from reliable authority that we had over four thousand men able to bear arms but who were not armed on account of being barefooted. And if we are forced once more to make a rapid retreat up this Valley, we will lose a great number of prisoners on this account alone. . . . Our men are shoeless, pantless, jacketless, sockless and miserable. . . . God grant that our leaders may soon learn that men cannot march and fight when they are half naked and with feet that leave bloody marks wherever they step."[43]

Being barefoot no doubt hampered the Confederates, but the real reason for their defeat was Sheridan's cavalry trouncing Early's troopers. "If the Yankee Infantry had fought half as well as their Cavalry," admitted Ring, "we would not have any army here this morning."[44] Early lost approximately one-fourth of his army at the Third Battle of Winchester, including Generals Rodes and Godwin killed. Demoralized over the defeat, the Confederates on Fisher's Hill were apprehensive as they watched a huge dust cloud slowly wind toward them on September 21. That morning Sheridan's victorious army began drawing up in Early's front, and skirmish fire erupted along the line. The Louisiana sharpshooters posted beyond Early's works were heavily engaged with their

Yankee counterparts throughout the morning. When it came time to relieve them, Seymour had Capt. Dave Workman put on a private's coat before going out so he would be less conspicuous. This precaution, however, proved worthless because just ten minutes after Workman reached the picket line he was killed by a federal sharpshooter.[45]

The next afternoon, Early was caught off-guard when Sheridan launched a heavy attack on his left flank. The Confederate army repeated its Winchester performance when regiment after regiment came loose from left to right and fled to the rear. Once again the Louisiana Brigade stood alone to cover the retreat of its sister brigades. The Tigers waited until they were almost surrounded before abandoning their line, but not before Pvt. James Connor of the 43rd New York earned a Medal of Honor for capturing the 2nd Louisiana's flag. Captain Seymour claimed that all organization was lost because escape "required the greatest fleetness of foot." Early lost another twelve hundred men, but by holding the federals at bay for crucial minutes the Louisianians prevented the loss from being higher. After withdrawing safely up the Valley, Early reportedly told the Tigers, "I saw you at Fisher's Hill and pointed to you as an example for others to take pattern by. If all had stood as you did, the issue would have been different than from what it was."[46]

Confederate artilleryman John H. Lane could attest to the Tigers' fighting spirit at Fisher's Hill. Cut off from his own unit during the retreat, he fell in with the Louisiana Brigade as it withdrew slowly from the field. One Tiger, with tears running down his face, told his comrades, "I say, men, for God's sake let us stop and fight them right here! We are ruined forever." Lane wrote, "Of course they did not stop for it would have been madness for a hundred men to attempt to make a stand against the whole Yankee army in daylight." Later that night, Lane again visited the Louisianians "under circumstances that made my heart warm towards them and caused me to think if our whole army had been composed of such men, then it might truly be said that 'we might all be killed, but never could be conquered.'"[47]

Fortunately for Early's shattered army, Sheridan abandoned his pursuit to lay waste to the Valley to ensure that it would never again serve as the breadbasket of the Confederacy. This further deprived Early's men of badly needed food, a fact Sergeant Charlton came to realize when he returned to his 5th Louisiana on October 4 after extended sick leave. Arriving after dark, he ate the meager rations that were called supper and wrote in his diary, "Realized what a fool to return to camp." Three days later, Charlton reported that the men had been put on half-rations, no doubt because of Sheridan's destruction. "Yankee devastation. Very bad," he wrote. "I counted no less than 14 fires burning."[48]

Sheridan's campaign to destroy the Valley's resources gave Early some precious time to regroup, and by October 18 he was once again ready to attack the enemy bivouacked north of Cedar Creek. Learning that Sheridan was absent from his army, Early believed it was the perfect time to hit the enemy while they were leaderless, but the 6th Louisiana's Lieutenant Trahern had concerns when he got his first look at the huge Union army: "It was the largest encampment of soldiers I ever looked upon. They were stretched across the pike for a distance of five miles on each side." The Confederate plan called for Kershaw's and Wharton's divisions to pin down the enemy at the main crossing on Cedar Creek while Gordon's division moved to the far right where it could strike the federal flank at daylight. As at the Monocacy, surprise was of the utmost importance, and Lieutenant Trahern wrote that "it was ordered in camp that no officer should allow his sword to beat against anything, nor the private soldier to carry his tin cup. It was to make the march as silent as possible." Gordon's men were forced to strip down, and canteens, knapsacks, and equipment that might clank or rattle were piled up and left behind when they headed toward the Yankees' left.[49]

Following the circuitous route along a narrow mountain trail took most of the night and required the men to wade the Shenandoah River four or five times. Daylight was rapidly approaching by the time Gordon was in position and began deploying in a thick fog. As the men stumbled into line, officers began calling for two volunteers from each company. When the men stepped forward, they were solemnly told to follow behind the attacking line and shoot any soldier who tried to retreat. Every attempt was being made to prevent another rout.

Soon after Kershaw and Wharton began their diversion on the enemy's front, Gordon's men raised the rebel yell, exploded out of the fog upon the Union flank, and sent the federals reeling back through their camps. Trahern recalled that only one Union picket managed to fire a shot before the rebels were inside the lines. Running forward "with an almost hurricane speed," the Tigers killed any soldier who tried to make a stand. "Some were in the death ranks, without pants or shoes. . . . It seems to me they were ushered into eternity, with only a moments warning." Many others were killed inside their tents as volleys of minié balls tore through the canvas.[50]

The rebels were victorious all along their line and captured thirteen hundred prisoners and eighteen cannons. But then, Early's attack fizzled. The well-supplied Yankee camp, which even included milk cows, awed the starving rebels, and they could not help but fall out of line to loot. Trahern estimated as many as five thousand men abandoned their comrades for that purpose. "The desperate condition of our army at this particular junctive, was an overwhelming argument in defense of those who participated in taking over for their own use, the vast amount of food-stuffs, and other goods chattels. . . . We were ending this great battle, by 'fighting on our stomachs.'"[51]

The rebels' plundering was a godsend to the Yankees because it gave them time to regroup and make a stand. Gordon urged Early to continue the attack and finish off the enemy, but Early believed the federals would withdraw on their own. It was a fatal mistake because Sheridan hurried back to his army, rallied his defeated men, and launched a devastating counterattack that afternoon. By that time, Evans' brigade was on the far left with a quarter-mile gap between it and the Louisiana Brigade, a gap which neither Gordon nor Early took any steps to close. Sheridan's counterattack crushed Evans' brigade, and then George Custer's cavalry charged the Louisianians' left flank and wrecked it as well. Colonel Hanlon was captured for the third time in the war, and Captain Ring was seriously wounded.[52]

Once again it was the Union cavalry that played the key role in Early's defeat. According to Trahern, the Yankee troopers "came down like an avalanche. . . . Completely routed, we were scattered like sheep." Sheridan captured several hundred prisoners and pushed Early's disorganized mob back to Fisher's Hill once again. That evening, Sergeant Charlton wrote in his diary, "Everything in confusion. Whole brigades take to the mountains. . . . lost one of my shoes and was compelled to run barefooted some two miles on the rocky pike." Total losses for the Louisiana Brigade are unknown, but the 10th Louisiana had one man killed, three wounded, and nine missing, and a company in the 6th Louisiana entered the fight with two men, and both were shot.[53]

General Evans blamed Early for the disaster. He wrote his wife, "There was plundering done on this as on every other battle field but it was Early's miserable Generalship which lost the battle. If history does not say so it will not speak the truth." Lieutenant Trahern agreed. "There was an unhappy charge circulating through the rank and file of our joyous Command. The report was that our Commander-in-chief General J. Early was so overcome by alcoholic stimulant, that he would not listen to General Gordon's advice to fall back to Fisher's Hill, and immediately fortify."[54]

Early's defeat at Cedar Creek ended the fighting in the Valley for the year. This was fortunate for the Louisiana Brigade because it was in no shape to participate in any more campaigns. With only 563 men present for duty, the command was reorganized into a battalion for easier handling, although it officially remained on the books as two separate units constituting a consolidated brigade. The ten regiments were combined to make six companies—Company A, for example, being made up of the 5th, 6th, and 7th Louisiana under Maj. William Manning. So many officers had been lost that some of the consolidated regiments were commanded by lieutenants. A new Tiger commander also had to be selected because York never returned to the brigade after his mangled arm was amputated. Colonel Peck of the 9th Louisiana was chosen for the position. The Madison Parish native who was known in the army as "Big Peck" had risen swiftly through the ranks from a private in the Milliken Bend Guards to colonel of the regiment. He was well liked by the men and proved to be a capable leader.[55]

A concerted effort was made that winter to secure new recruits for Peck's undermanned brigade, but it was not successful. One bizarre scheme was a plan that sent General York to Salisbury, North Carolina, to raise recruits from the German and Irish Catholics who were held in the prisoner-of-war camps there. Louisiana was the only Confederate state with a predominantly Catholic population, and officials believed it would be easier to convince the Union prisoners to serve in the Louisiana Tiger regiments than in Protestant-dominated units. When word of the plan reached the Tigers in Virginia, Theodore Woodard wrote his father, "Genl York is raising a brigade of yankee prisoners to fight the yanks but I don't think it is a very safe business, for I think they are too treacherous however, York is willing to try it."[56]

The recruitment plan was the brainchild of Father Egidius "Giles" Smulders, a Dutch native who served as the 8th Louisiana's chaplain. In an October 1864 letter to President Davis, he wrote, "I understand that there are now in our hands a large number of Irish Catholic prisoners of war, who I think may be induced to enlist in the Confederate Army. . . . I respectfully request that [these prisoners] be collected in one locality, that facilities may be offered me and some other Catholic Priests for conducting religious exercises amongst them and for holding other incourse [sic] with the view of bringing them over to the Confederate cause."[57]

In November, Secretary of War James Seddon informed General Lee of the attempt to raise recruits from the Yankee prisoners. Seddon wrote, "Among others, General York, while wounded here, has obtained this permission and proposes to visit the prisons, taking with him one or more Catholic chaplains, whose influence, he thinks, may be profitably exercised upon those of the same religious persuasion."[58]

York traveled to Salisbury with Fathers Smulders and James Sheeran and set up a separate camp for the so-called "Galvanized Rebels." The Louisianians were optimistic because the federals, who had no hope of being exchanged and were dying at a rate of thirty men a day, seemed grateful to have Catholic priests minister to their religious needs. On January 17, 1865, York wrote Secretary Seddon:

> We have now in our camp between 600 and 700 recruits. The great obstacle has been the difficulty of procuring clothing and supplies from the quartermaster's department. We have also been interfered with by the recruiting officers of Lieutenant-Colonel Tucker. If we could have the exclusive privilege of recruiting in all the prisons for a few weeks we have no doubt but that we could shortly muster a brigade, composed of such material as would reflect no discredit on our noble army. We hope that you will be so kind as to foster this enterprise, and to see that the necessary clothing, etc., be furnished by the quartermaster's department, as we can do nothing without the uniforms.[59]

Unfortunately, controversy soon ensued as officials bickered over who had the authority to recruit the Yankees and why uniforms could not be secured. General Lee even waded into the dispute and questioned by what authority Colonel Tucker was involved in the plan. "General York," he affirmed, "is recruiting for the Louisiana brigade."[60]

After a brief flurry of activity, the attempt to raise Yankee recruits failed, but no record was left to explain why, other than Father Smulders' explanation that "few availed themselves of the opportunity." One can only speculate that the prisoners just pretended to be interested in joining the Tigers as a way to get transferred to the special camp and receive preferential treatment. Whatever the reason, all were returned to the main prison.[61]

With so few Tigers left on duty, the men hoped they would be furloughed and allowed to visit home that winter, but it was not to be. On December 7, the brigade boarded a train in Staunton to join the rest of Gordon's division in leaving the Valley to reinforce Lee's beleaguered army at Petersburg. J. H. Cosgrove remembered that when they arrived "the men were cheerless, and though disheartened, determined to 'stay to the finish.'" Peck's brigade was placed outside Petersburg on Lee's extreme right near Hatcher's Run, but little is known of its activities there. Sergeant Charlton reported that the Tigers lived in what they christened Camp Stafford and that it was "laid out into Streets & numbered viz Monahan, Lester, Williams &c in memory of our lamented officers."[62]

A February 1865 inspection revealed that the Louisianians continued to persevere through the harsh conditions. In part, the report read, "The appearance of the troops is good considering the state of their clothing, which is much worn. . . . The arms are in fair condition. Accoutrements are greatly needed." Discipline was also described as being good, but the number of men present for duty was appalling. Company A (5th, 6th, and 7th Louisiana regiments) only had 3 officers and 133 men present for duty, while a surprising 355 were absent with leave and 310 were absent without leave. When Private Woodard rejoined his 6th Louisiana as an exchanged prisoner in January 1865, he discovered that Company A had dwindled to about 60 men, with only 4 of them belonging to his Tensas Rifles.[63]

The only major battle the Tigers are known to have engaged in while near Hatcher's Run took place on February 5–6, 1865, when Grant attempted to move around Lee's right flank to cut his supply line on the Boydton Plank Road. Peck's brigade was shuffled back and forth throughout the day before the battle finally began about 4:00 p.m. in a heavy snowfall. Heth's division bore the brunt of the fighting before both sides withdrew about dark. The battle resumed on February 6, with Gordon's division entering the fray. Peck's Louisiana Brigade numbered approximately 400 men, but only about 250 were engaged because the rest had been left on picket duty along the Petersburg trenches. Gordon's division advanced near a sawmill and sawdust pile with Terry's brigade on the left, Peck in the middle, and Walker's brigade of Pegram's division on the right. The fighting focused on the sawdust pile with attacks and counterattacks swirling around it. Gordon's men were forced back twice, but the general ordered a third attack, and a newspaper reported, "With a yell, Peck's Louisianians struck the heap of saw dust and carried it." Sergeant Charlton, who described the fight as "a perfect hurricane of balls," came across a pine sapling that had seventeen bullets in it. Peck later wrote that he eventually had to withdraw from the hard-won sawdust pile because "many of my men had by this time been killed and wounded and the command was short of ammunition." Charlton reported that, when the federals withdrew shortly afterward, the "half naked" Tigers took the opportunity to grab badly needed clothing from the enemy's dead.[64]

Officially, the Tigers lost six killed and seventeen wounded in the fierce Battle of Hatcher's Run. Among the dead was Lt. John S. Dea, who had joined the 8th Louisiana in 1861 when he was twenty years old. Dea was with the regiment throughout Jackson's 1862 Valley Campaign and apparently fell in love with Marguerite Williams, the daughter of the Winchester farmer who took care of Lt. Col. Francis T. Nicholls after he was wounded. Promoted to 1st lieutenant, Dea was wounded at Antietam, captured at Second Fredericksburg, and severely wounded again at Spotsylvania. He was serving as acting adjutant of General Gordon's sharpshooters when he was killed at Hatcher's Run. On his service record was written "a brave and gallant officer, present at all actions."[65]

The day after the Battle of Hatcher's Run ended, Maj. William Owen Miller of the New Orleans Washington Artillery learned that Peck's Louisiana Brigade had been assigned to his unit as infantry support. Owen recalled, "Soon after, a small body of troops, not over 250, came marching towards me through the ice-covered pines, and I recognized at the head of the column the giant form of Col. Peck. And this was all that was left of the "Louisiana brigade" that had numbered over 3,000 muskets before Richmond in the Seven Days' battles! . . . This extraordinary diminution of numbers showed plainly what it had gone through, and the truly gallant, unconquerable Louisiana brigade, now of 250 brave hearts, tempered like fine steel in the fiery blasts of battle, was all that was left for me to depend upon to support my guns."[66]

After Hatcher's Run, the Louisiana Brigade was put into the Petersburg trenches near the "Crater," a large mine crater that was the focus of a fierce July battle. In recalling this new position, William Trahern wrote, "[W]e were soon in a mess of debris, called winter quarters. We didn't march, it is true, a great deal, but oh! the discomforts from rain and snow, without protection, except the open flier tents captured at Strausburg [sic]." The hunger, atrocious weather, and deadly Yankee fire made the weeks spent on the Petersburg line among the worst of the war. The Tigers often lay exposed to sleet and rain for days at a time, and food was nearly nonexistent. Gordon's men sometimes fed themselves by picking corn feed out of horses' tracks, but on one occasion a starving Tiger in the 9th Louisiana found the Yankees were a convenient commissary. When a federal picket shouted across no-man's land to ask what the Louisianians were having for supper, the Tiger replied that they would not be fed until late the next day. The sympathetic federal then held up a big chunk of meat and told the rebel that if he wanted it he could come over safely. The Tiger's companions were convinced it was a trick, but that night the hungry soldier yelled, "Yank, don't shoot! I came after that piece of meat!" and slipped out of his trench. The friendly federals guided him into their lines and loaded him down with meat, hardtack, bread, and coffee before sending him on his way.[67]

In describing his soldiers stuck in the Petersburg trenches, General Lee wrote, "The physical strength of the men, if their courage survives, must fail under this treatment." The dreadful conditions certainly took a heavy toll on Peck's brigade. Apparently both physical strength and courage failed many Tigers, for desertions again plagued the command. Nine men crossed over the lines on February 19, and at least 19 others abandoned their comrades that winter. Sickness was also rampant, and the brigade began to wither away at an alarming rate. By the end of February, only 401 men were left on duty, with several regimental companies having only 2 members and some having completely vanished. The brigade also lost Colonel Peck in February when he was promoted to brigadier general and transferred to the western theater. Normally, David Zable of the 14th Louisiana would have assumed brigade command as the senior colonel, but he and about 80 Tigers were ordered to North Carolina to join General York. Zable and his men assisted York in defending a bridge against several Union cavalry attacks and then were assigned as bodyguards to President Davis after he fled Richmond in April 1865. With Peck and Zable gone, brigade command fell to the 10th Louisiana's very capable Col. Eugene Waggaman.[68]

Perhaps sensing that the end was near, Louisiana Gov. Henry Watkins Allen sent orders to Virginia for each of the state's regiments to compile a history of its service. The task of summarizing the 6th Louisiana's activities fell to Major Manning. On March 20, under the heading "done in the trenches near

Petersburg," Manning first listed the regiment's most prominent dead—Colonels Seymour and Strong, and Major McArthur—and proudly reported that "there has not been any great event in the History of the Army of Northern Virginia in which this Regiment has not rendered Material Service." He continued: "Originally over one thousand men strong, it has been reduced by the fortunes of war to a mere skeleton of its former numerical strength. More than three hundred of the rank and file of this command attested their devotion to the Cause in which they embarked by surrendering their lives on its behalf. Hundreds of its brave men, maimed and crippled, scattered broadcast throughout the land, bear on their persons living evidence of duty and fidelity to their Country, while the few surviving brave and true men who are still left to do battle in a Just Cause exhibit still the same stern devotion which actuated them in the outstart of the war."[69]

Short entries were also made for each of the 6th Louisiana's companies. In regard to Company E (Mercer Guards), which had suffered the regiment's highest desertion rate, Manning wrote, "This roll contains a black list of Deserters but still it only shows to more advantage the few (though not many) that did stand by the cause they vollenteered [sic] to support through all misfortunes and all disasters." Less than a month later, there were only fifty-five men still with the regiment to surrender at Appomattox.[70]

For a month the Tigers lay in their cold, muddy trenches near the Crater under constant artillery and sharpshooters' fire. Everyone, including Lee, knew the fight was at an end unless a miracle saved them from the tightening siege. Then in March, about the time Manning was writing his regimental history, General Gordon proposed to Lee a bold plan to break out of Petersburg. Gordon recommended punching a hole through the Union encirclement to force Grant to shorten his line and provide an opportunity for Lee to send part of the army to North Carolina to link up with Gen. Joseph E. Johnston to continue the fight. Lee gave his approval, and Gordon soon found a weak spot in the Union line to make the attack.[71]

By that time, Gordon had been promoted to command the II Corps, and Gen. Clement Evans led Gordon's old division, which included Waggaman's Louisiana Brigade. On March 14, Gordon shifted his men to the left and placed Evans' old brigade on the left near Colquitt's Salient, Waggaman's Tigers in the center, and Terry's brigade on the right at the Otey Battery. Fort Stedman, the Union position Gordon had chosen to attack, was opposite Colquitt's Salient.

The opposing works were barely 150 yards apart at Fort Stedman, and the winter rains had weakened the fort's walls. If the federal pickets and obstructions protecting the approaches could be removed without alarm, Gordon believed the fort could be captured and Grant's line broken. Lee concurred, and the breakout was scheduled for the predawn hours of March 25. Gordon assembled about 11,500 men from his corps and Bushrod Johnson's division for the attack, and another 8,200 men from other units were waiting in support. In all, approximately one-half of Lee's army was committed to the breakout attempt.[72]

During a strategy meeting with his officers, Evans suddenly turned to Waggaman and declared, "On account of the valor of your troops, you will be allowed the honor of leading off in the attack. This you will make with unloaded arms." Waggaman did not record his thoughts on the honor bestowed upon him and his Tigers. General Lee was to provide guides who would lead three "bold colonels" and their companies of one hundred handpicked men each across no-man's land. Based on Evans' remark to Waggaman, it is presumed that the three companies were Louisiana Tigers. They were to follow some ax-wielding North Carolina soldiers who would clear away the obstructions. Out in front of everyone would be a small group of Louisianians who were to pretend to be deserters and capture the Union pickets once they were within the federal lines. The three colonels would then assume the names of known Yankee officers and disorient the federals by issuing confusing orders in the dark. Once the fort was taken, the rest of Gordon's men would follow up, fan out to either side to enlarge the breakthrough, and cut a path to Grant's rear, where Lee could either wreck the Army of the Potomac or make a break for North Carolina.[73]

As Gordon's line was preparing for the attack at 3:00 a.m., a Yankee picket suddenly shouted, "What are you doing over there, Johnny? What is that noise? Answer quick or I'll shoot!" Hearts raced as it appeared the movement had been detected, but a rebel huddled next to Gordon hollered back, "Never mind, Yank! Lie down and go to sleep. We are just gathering a little corn. You know rations are mighty short over here." This seemed to satisfy the curious Yankee, and the works again fell silent. Shortly afterward, Gordon turned to the same soldier and ordered him to give the signal for the assault. The man hesitated for a moment, and then yelled, "Hello, Yank! Wake up; we are going to shell the woods. Look out; we are coming!"[74]

After this chivalrous warning, the Tigers started the attack. One Confederate soldier recalled how the men went forward "with unloaded muskets and a profound silence, leaped over our breastworks, [and] dashed across the open space in front." The first men out of the trenches were Lt. R. B. Smith of the 2nd Louisiana and eight other Tigers who headed for Fort Stedman's south wall to capture the pickets. Silently making their way toward the enemy, they quickly accomplished their task, and the obstructions were cleared without a shot being fired. With the rest of Gordon's force following close behind, Lieutenant Smith and his small squad then scaled the fort's wall and leaped among the garrison.[75]

The Richmond *Whig* reported:

> Their situation was a critical and perilous one, but with remarkable coolness and bravery, they held it until reinforcements arrived, when the Fort was assaulted and its garrison captured or killed. . . . [T]he Louisiana brigade, being the head of the supporting column, was a short distance to the left, attacking works surrounding another battery of several guns, defended by a garrison of two hundred men. With their accustomed intrepidity and gallantry, the task assigned them was soon accomplished. In a moment they were at the base of the fortifications; they escaladed and stormed the breastworks, penetrated the Fort by forcing their way through the embrasures, while a shower of grape, canister and musketry was poured upon them from within, and captured every thing within the redoubt save the few who escaped under the cover of darkness or those who were slain.[76]

The two hundred Yankee defenders were caught completely by surprise, but they quickly rallied and fought back against the gray mob tumbling in on top of them. One Union officer claimed they had time to fire two three-inch rifled cannons at the attackers but were overrun before they could reload. "Small-arms were [then] brought into use, and for a short time the enemy were held in check by a hand-to-hand conflict." The soldiers rolled in the muddy trenches scratching and clawing, and one Tiger claimed that they fought "as if they had drank two quarts of brandy." Finally, at slight loss to themselves, the Louisianians captured most of the feisty Yankees, plus three mortars and four cannons. The guns were left in charge of Irish-born Capt. J. B. Bresnan of the 6th Louisiana, who turned them over to a company of artillerymen to fire on the fleeing federals. Bresnan, who had already suffered one wound in the war, was bayoneted through the stomach later in the morning and captured in the hospital when Grant took Richmond a week later.[77]

In a report written that afternoon, General Evans claimed that three groups of soldiers entered Fort Stedman: the division's sharpshooters, which were often commanded by Louisiana officers; the 13th and 31st Georgia; and Waggaman's Louisiana brigade. Terry's brigade, with support from Evans' brigade, also attacked the Union works as day was breaking and began clearing a path toward the rear, but it lost momentum when many of the soldiers started looking for food inside the Yankee works. By the time the sun rose over the horizon, about seven hundred yards of the enemy's trenches were in Confederate hands, along with several hundred prisoners and seventeen cannons and mortars. But the attack then stalled. Evans blamed the three guides General Lee provided because it turned out they were not very familiar with the ground and caused several units to get lost in the maze of earthworks or wander into other commands and disorganize the attack.[78]

The Yankees soon contained the breakthrough with a vigorous counterattack and began lobbing shells into the captured works. The Tigers took refuge in Fort Stedman and shot down a number of federals before the enemy swept over them. Gordon finally ordered a retreat, which Evans said took place "under a galling fire of artillery and small arms." Another frantic hand-to-hand fight raged in the trenches before the Tigers spiked the captured artillery and made a dash for their own lines "under a terrible fire of artillery and musketry." One source claims Waggaman lost half his men in the Battle of Fort Stedman, while Evans' unpublished report puts the Tigers' losses at 3 dead, 26 wounded, and 25 missing. Evans' entire division reported 43 killed and 122 wounded. When Waggaman finally reached safety, he met General Evans. Recalling the general's remark about the "honor" of leading the attack, Waggaman asked if the Tigers had done their duty, and Evans simply replied, "They did."[79]

The unsuccessful breakout at Fort Stedman sealed Lee's fate. Realizing that the Confederates must have stripped their defenses to mount the offensive, Grant launched a heavy attack on Lee's far right flank on April 1. The Yankees badly defeated Lee's men at Five Forks and tightened the noose around the Army of Northern Virginia. Evans reported that the Union heavy artillery opened fire on his position about 10:00 p.m. that night and continued almost without letup until daylight.

On Sunday, April 2, Gordon's corps occupied four miles of trenches, and the Louisiana line was so thin that the Tigers were spaced fifteen feet apart. At daybreak the Yankees managed to break through Gordon's line in three places and slammed into the Louisiana Brigade in its position at Graves' Salient. Colonel Waggaman was headed to church with Maj. Thomas Powell of the 10th Louisiana when the enemy attacked. While walking together, Waggaman jokingly asked if they would get there on time. Major Powell glanced at his watch and remarked, "Hardly, unless we leave quickly." His words were cut short by the whack of a minié ball striking his head. The major fell dead, and a thunderous roar swelled all around Petersburg as Grant launched his final assault.[80]

The Tigers stopped the attack at Graves' Salient and were then hurried to the Crater to reinforce the line there. Evans put the Louisiana sharpshooters in front to lead a counterattack to recapture some of the lost trenches, with Philip Cook's and Waggaman's brigades following behind. Evans wrote, "I pressed the attack along the trenches from traverse to traverse until I regained two hundred yards of the lost works, fighting often being hand to hand." An attempt by Evans to expand his position failed because his men had to charge across an open field against an entrenched enemy that was being constantly reinforced.[81]

During the day, Lee informed Gordon of the Five Forks disaster and instructed him to hold the federals back while the rest of the army evacuated the Petersburg line. Orders went out to Gordon's commanders not to waste men on retaking lost positions but simply to keep the enemy at bay. In the evening, the Union forces attacked again and captured the picket line on Evans' right, but he reported they "were immediately driven out by Col. Waggaman." For twenty-two hours the Louisiana Tigers hugged their breastworks under a constant fire from the federals, who still held the Confederate trenches on either side of them. As the day dragged on, all of the Confederate line in the area was either captured or abandoned, except for the small portion near the Crater that was held by the Louisiana Brigade. Waggaman's losses during this last-ditch stand are not known, but the 10th Louisiana's Lieutenant Colonel Monier wrote in his diary that all of the men who were killed were shot in the head, apparently when they carelessly raised above the trench line. At times, in order to gauge the strength of the enemy in front, soldiers would place a cap on a pole and then count how many bullets pierced it in a given amount of time. According to Monier, it was "just as the steamer tells of the number of feet it is drawing by its lead soundings."[82]

At about 10:00 p.m., Evans was ordered to withdraw his division and catch up with the rest of the army as it headed for Amelia Court House forty miles to the west. Lee planned to obtain badly needed supplies there and then turn south to join Joe Johnston's army in North Carolina. When Evans retired across the Pocahontas Bridge over the Appomattox River that night, the Louisiana Brigade apparently served as rearguard because it did not leave the trenches until 1:30 a.m., April 3. Lee made it safely to Amelia Court House on April 4 but found no supplies waiting for him as expected and was forced to continue his flight toward Farmville and Appomattox Court House. His plan now was to continue west to Lynchburg, where he hoped to be resupplied, and then move south toward North Carolina. While it appears Waggaman's Louisiana Brigade played an important role in the short Appomattox Campaign, the only substantive source of information on its activities comes from General Evans' unpublished report, which he wrote the day after the surrender.[83]

When Lee's army departed Amelia Court House on April 6, Evans' division formed the rearguard with the assistance of Gen. W. F. Lee's cavalry. Almost immediately, Union Gen. A. A. Humphreys' pursuing II Corps began pressing Evans from the front while dismounted Yankee cavalry attacked his flanks. To fend off the constant attacks, Evans formed his division in a crescent shape and kept it pointed toward the enemy. To keep relatively fresh troops in the rear, General Gordon moved along in a leap-frog manner by having Evans' and Bryan Grimes' divisions alternate at the rear of the column. One division would stop, throw up breastworks, and hold off the enemy for a while, and then hurry past the other division, which would do the same thing. In this manner the enemy was kept at bay. As Evans put it, "They were advanced again and again, broken in the same manner, the infantry and artillery both doing their duty in handsome manner." Although he provided no details, Monier scribbled in his diary that the Tigers retreated and fought all day, first on one side of the road and then on the other.[84]

Despite the trying conditions, the Louisiana Brigade continued to maintain incredible discipline during the retreat. Monier recalled an incident when the Tigers marched in cadence across Long Bridge. The structure began to sway to the point that it was about to collapse, but instead of panicking and running to get off the bridge, every man immediately stopped in place when the order was given to halt. They then waited patiently until the vibration and swaying ceased and continued on across in route step.[85]

During the day, Union forces exploited a gap that developed in the long rebel column and captured General Ewell and a good portion of the army at Sailor's Creek. Unaware of the disaster, Evans followed the wagon train in his front, which happened to take a different route. When Humphreys continued to attack his column, Evans placed Colonel Waggaman's Tigers in the rear, with Terry's and Col. John Lowe's (Evans') brigades staggered in support at eight-hundred-yard intervals. According to Colonel Monier, Waggaman's brigade was then ordered at dark to halt and support a lone cannon posted on a side road and to defend it while the rest of the army continued the retreat toward Farmville. The Tigers remained in their isolated position until 9:00 p.m. and then rejoined the column at High Bridge, where they were allowed to rest until daylight.[86]

Sometimes during that dreadful day, Col. Edmund Pendleton, commander of the 15th Louisiana, took out an envelope and hastily scrawled a message to his wife (who was staying in Virginia). Despite the setback at Sailor's Creek, Pendleton remained confident: "The whole army of Gen'l Lee is now within ten miles of Farmville. After a severe battle at Petersburg on Sunday 2nd April in which our lines were broken & our communications cut, we have been compelled to fall back to a more defensible line. I am sorry to think that this implies the abandonment of the greater part of Va. & it is not unlikely you & my dear children will be left in the Enemy's hands, tho' I hope not. I shall use my utmost exertions to come to see you. Our Army is not whipped—indeed it is strong & ready to fight today. . . . I write this hasty note on the march & will endeavor to write you more fully in two or three days. Love to all."[87]

When the retreat resumed on April 7, Lee allowed Gordon's exhausted men to lead the army rather than to continue fighting in the rear. During the day, Waggaman's brigade was temporarily attached to Gen. James A. Walker's division and joined it in a charge that successfully checked the enemy. No details are known about the fight, but Evans wrote that Waggaman gained Walker's "applause" for his service. Later in the day, Union forces managed to cross High Bridge after the Confederates failed to burn it and began pressing William Mahone's division at Cumberland Church. Elements of Longstreet's and Gordon's corps, including Waggaman's brigade, were sent back to help stop the Union pursuit, and the Tigers were placed on the far right of the line on some hills near the Appomattox River. There they skirmished and built fortifications out of fence rails but never came under a major attack. When the wagon train passed safely by, the Louisiana Brigade was taken out of line and resumed the march toward Appomattox Court House, periodically stopping to form a line of battle whenever the federals threatened to attack. The battle at Cumberland Church was one of the largest in the Appomattox Campaign, with Grant losing 571 men. The number of Confederate casualties is unknown.[88]

By this time, the Louisiana Brigade was nearly wrecked. For a week it had fought in the mud and rain and frequently served as the army's rearguard. Waggaman's men often held their ground against repeated federal attacks and then ran for safety only when nearly surrounded, sometimes running past Yankees scarcely twenty yards away. Ammunition ran low, and food was in such short supply that a daily ration for each Tiger consisted of only one biscuit and one ounce of bacon.

When Evans' division finally reached Appomattox on April 8, it was ordered to move beyond town and form a line of battle. After doing so, Evans sent out skirmishers and scouts and discovered that the enemy had blocked the road leading to Lynchburg, Lee's intended destination. That night Lee decided to meet with Grant the next day to discuss surrender, but in a conference with his generals it was agreed to make one last attempt to break through Grant's encirclement. Gordon's corps and Fitzhugh Lee's cavalry would make the attack while Longstreet's corps guarded the rear.

At 5:00 a.m., Sunday, April 9, the Army of Northern Virginia's last attack began. Gordon's battle line was to the northwest of Appomattox Court House, facing southwest with Fitzhugh Lee's cavalry on the right and Grimes' and Evans' divisions on the left. Waggaman's brigade, numbering only 178 men, was near the left flank. Gordon advanced at 8:00 a.m. and later wrote, "I take especial pride in recording the fact that this last charge of the war was made by the footsore and starving men of my command with a spirit worthy of the best days of Lee's Army."[89]

The dismounted Union cavalry that was first encountered offered little resistance, and Evans reported that "the enemy gave way in all points in front of the troops of the Corps." Soon, however, an order arrived to halt the advance because the Yankees were massing on the right and in the rear. When Union cavalry suddenly attacked Evans' rear, he turned the division around to face the new threat. Proud of how well his exhausted men rose to the occasion, Evans wrote, "These movements, ordinarily so difficult under fire, were executed almost as promptly and with almost as little confusion as if done on the drill ground." By that time it was obvious to Gordon that the enemy was succeeding in surrounding Lee's army, and he sent his chief a message that read, "Tell General Lee I have fought my corps to a frazzle, and I fear I can do nothing else unless I am heavily supported by Longstreet's Corps." When Lee received the note, he knew it was time to surrender.[90]

Unaware of Lee's decision, Evans led one more advance against an artillery battery that was firing on his division. The attack was made across a half-mile-wide freshly ploughed field, but the Tigers raised the rebel yell for the last time and stumbled dog-tired across the furrowed ground. One federal line was dislodged from behind a fence, and a Tiger bayoneted the color-bearer and seized his flag. Other elements of the division captured the artillery, and the Tigers apparently kept on going toward another battery until Waggaman received orders to disengage and fall back to the main line. The bewildered Tigers returned as ordered and lay exhausted on the ground, confused over why they had to break off a successful attack. Then the news was spread quietly through the ranks—Lee had surrendered.[91]

Although Evans never made the claim, others believed that his division made the Army of Northern Virginia's last charge. While Evans tried to avoid the controversy over who deserved that honor, he did write, "I do not want to make any special claim as to last fighting at Appomattox. All of us did the last fighting. But it does seem that my division had the good fortune to make this little battle after the moment of actual surrender."[92] No matter who made the last, desperate attack at Appomattox, for all practical purposes the war in Virginia was now over.

CHAPTER 12

A Louisiana Legacy

FOR WEEKS, the Tigers had known that the end was near, but the actual surrender came as a shock. For some, it was a relief. Shortly after a ceasefire was announced on April 9, the former enemies mingled together, and Capt. George W. Shealey of the 8th Maryland (Union) came upon a group of Union soldiers who were standing around a wounded rebel sitting on a cot with his head down and crying. In his hand was a cracker that one of the Yankees had given him, and more were piled on the cot. No one was talking. Shealey wrote, "He was a very badly war-worn veteran, indeed. His suit was frayed and dirty and his left trousers leg above his knee, showing a clean white bandage around his leg." Captain Shealey walked over and asked the rebel why he was crying. "I didn't expect this," the soldier replied. "Our officers told us if you Yanks caught us you would put out our eyes and cut off our ears. Now, I see they lied to us. I belong to the Louisiana Tigers. I am the last of four brothers. The others have been killed in the war. This is the third time I have been wounded. I love the old Flag. I am glad the Union is saved." Reflecting on the scene, Shealey wrote, "This man clearly understood that the flag that he had fought so hard for was destroyed—had no more place on the earth. He was done with it, and right there proclaimed his allegiance to the Union."[1]

On April 12, the Army of Northern Virginia formed ranks for the last time in preparation for the surrender ceremony. Regiments resembled squads as the worn-out Tigers crowded around their tattered banners on the hills outside Appomattox. The 9th Louisiana was Waggaman's largest command, and it had only 68 men present. The 10th Louisiana was the smallest with just 16, and junior officers were leading the 14th Louisiana because there were no field officers left. After the surrender, a total of 373 Louisiana Tigers signed parole oaths, and more than half of them had straggled into camp after the

fight on April 9. Apparently, many more were scattered around Virginia because Colonel Waggaman arrived in New Orleans by steamer on May 13 with
approximately 700 paroled Louisiana Tigers.[2]

All flags, government property, and weapons, except the officers' sidearms,
were to be surrendered. However, when Colonel Waggaman formed the brigade, he asked the men if he could have a piece of the 10th Louisiana's flag as a
memento. Permission was granted, and Waggaman used his family's heirloom
sword (which had been saved at Malvern Hill) to cut off the lateral side with
two stars. It became the colonel's most treasured possession, and after the war
he refused numerous requests from people who wanted pieces of it. Only once
did Waggaman agree and that was to give Robert E. Lee's daughter Mildred a
piece with one of the stars. In return, Miss Lee sent Waggaman a portrait of
her father.[3]

More than seventy rebel flags were surrendered at Appomattox, but none
was identified as belonging to a Louisiana regiment. It is known that Colonel
Pendleton hid the 15th Louisiana's flag on his person and took it home, and it
is possible that members of the 10th Louisiana followed Waggaman's lead and
cut up their colors. It is not known what happened to the flags of the other
eight regiments or even if they still had colors. Colonel Zable was in possession of the 14th Louisiana's flag in 1899 and carried it to a veterans' reunion in
Charleston. However, Zable was not at Appomattox so it is not known if it was
still in service at that time or was one that had been retired earlier. Whatever
the case, the newspaper that covered the reunion claimed that eleven Tigers
had been killed or wounded while carrying the flag into battle.[4]

Losses among the Louisiana soldiers in Virginia had been appalling. Casualty figures are not complete and vary with different sources, but of the
approximately 12,800 men who served with the Tigers, about 3,300 (or
around 25 percent) died during the war—approximately 2,000 being killed
or mortally wounded in battle and 1,300 dying from other causes. All of the
units suffered heavily, but some distinctions are the 13 lieutenants who were
killed or mortally wounded in the 2nd Louisiana during an eighty-day period
in the summer of 1862, and the 32 color-bearers killed or wounded in the
10th Louisiana—12 of whom were killed in the Battle of Chancellorsville.
The position of commanding officer in the 2nd Louisiana Brigade seems to
have been particularly jinxed. Within months after assuming command, all
5 executives—Starke, Nicholls, Stafford, Williams, and York—were killed or

seriously wounded. The 6th Louisiana was similarly cursed and had 3 commanders killed: Seymour at Gaines' Mill, and Strong and Ritchie at Antietam. The 9th Louisiana's losses are, perhaps, the best documented. Forty percent of the DeSoto Blues died in the war, and the Washington Rifles had nearly a 100 percent casualty rate. Of the 154 men who served in the latter company, only 8 were still on duty on January 16, 1865. Fifty had died of disease; 31 had deserted; 25 had been discharged for various reasons; 13 had been killed or mortally wounded; 13 had been retired for disabilities; 5 had been transferred; 4 were missing; 3 were on sick or wounded furlough; 1 had been promoted and apparently left the company; and 1 was a prisoner of war.[5]

Such losses often hit individual families hard. Four Fontenot brothers served in the 8th Louisiana's Opelousas Guards and all became casualties. Hippolyte was captured at Rappahannock Station and exchanged but then died in a Union hospital after being wounded and captured again at the Monocacy; Horthere was mortally wounded at Gettysburg; Denis was captured at Spotsylvania; and Alexander was captured when Richmond fell.[6]

The Confederate States Rangers of the 10th Louisiana had numerous relatives serving together. Among them were three Reeves brothers, their brother-in-law, and seven cousins. Of the brothers, James was killed at Chancellorsville at about the time his wife died in childbirth in Louisiana. His brother John was shot in the head and blinded in the same battle, and brother Isaac was killed two months later at Gettysburg. Of the cousins, one lost a leg at Antietam and one was killed at Fort Stedman.[7] Three Ryan brothers also served in the company. Asa's leg was shattered at Antietam, and Union surgeons amputated it after he was captured; his brother Isaac was wounded at Second Manassas and Chancellorsville, captured at Spotsylvania, and killed at Fort Stedman; and Joseph was wounded at Second Manassas but deserted to join the cavalry in Louisiana.[8]

Many Tigers, such as Lt. George Wren of the 8th Louisiana, were wounded in several battles and taken prisoner more than once. Wren was captured at Port Republic, wounded at Antietam and Chancellorsville, and captured a second time at Spotsylvania. The 10th Louisiana's Capt. Leon Jastremski was captured at Malvern Hill, exchanged, and then captured again at Cedar Mountain just four days after rejoining the regiment. After being exchanged a second time, he was shot in the throat at Chancellorsville and in the hand at Gettysburg, and then was captured a third time at Spotsylvania.[9]

The Tigers' field officers were not immune to the suffering. The 6th Louisiana's Irish-born Lt. Col. Joseph Hanlon was severely wounded at First Winchester (the wound would contribute to his death after the war) and captured. After being exchanged, he returned to the regiment, only to be captured again while contesting the Yankee's crossing of the Rappahannock River at Second Fredericksburg. Exchanged a second time, he was wounded again at Cold Harbor and then captured a third time at Cedar Creek.[10]

The Tigers' division and corps commanders recognized the great sacrifices the Louisianians made over four years of war and before leaving Appomattox thanked them for their service. On April 11, 1865, General Evans issued his farewell address to Waggaman's brigade:

> The sad hour has arrived when we who served in the Confederate Army so long together must part, at least for a time. But the saddest circumstances connected with the separation are that it occurs under heavy disaster to our beloved cause. But to you, Colonel, and to our brother officers and brother soldiers of Hays' and Stafford's Brigades, I claim to say that you can carry with you the proud conscience that in the estimation of your commanders you have done your duty. Tell Louisiana, when you reach her shores, that her sons in the Army of Northern Virginia have made her illustrious upon every battle ground, from first Manassas to the last desparate blow struck by your command on the hills of Appomattox, and tell her, too, that as in the first, so in the last, the enemy fled before the valor of your charging lines. To the sad decree of an inscrutable Providence let us bow in humble resignation awaiting IIis will for the pillar of cloud to be lifted. For you, and for your gallant officers and devoted men, I shall always cherish the most pleasing memories, and when I say farewell, it is with a full heart, which beats an earnest prayer to Almighty God for your future happiness.[11]

The next day, General Gordon followed suit:

> In parting with the Louisiana Brigade of this Army I cannot omit to offer the tribute which is due to as heroic a devotion, as ever illustrated the arms of any people.

Coming with glorious ardour into the support of a cause, which sacred in itself, is doubly consecrated to-day by its dead; you have carried your enthusiasm into a hundred battles, filling your comrades and Countrymen with pride and your enemy with fear.

Steadily and unshaken have you passed throughout the struggle, with untarnished record. Your name is without the shadow of a stain. Your conduct in the closing hours is as lofty as when with full ranks you struck and exulted in victory.

Take with you soldiers in parting the unfeigned admiration of my heart.[12]

The Louisiana Tigers were the Dr. Jekyll and Mr. Hyde of the Confederacy. Some were drunken, lawless renegades who plundered homes, businesses, and farms and often posed a greater threat to the South's civilians than did the Yankees. Montgomery, Alabama; Grand Junction, Tennessee; and Lynchburg, Petersburg, and Stevensburg, Virginia, felt the Tigers' wrath—as did countless farmers who suffered the loss of livestock and crops to the pilfering soldiers. The Tigers also gained a reputation for killing wounded prisoners and desecrating enemy graves. On February 18, 1863, the New York *Times* compared the Louisianians to wild Indians when it wrote that the "drunken rebel savages" in the Indian Territory attacked Unionist Indians "with a fury and ferocity which could not be surpassed by Louisiana 'Tigers.'"[13]

Yet when it came to fighting, the Tigers were rated among Lee's most dependable soldiers. Such battlefield exploits as Starke's brigade holding the line at Second Manassas with rocks were seen as the epitome of southern bravado and became an integral part of the mystique that surrounded the Confederate soldier. Stonewall Jackson owed much of his fame to the actions of Taylor's brigade in the Shenandoah Valley, and Confederate armies were saved from disaster by the little-known stand the 1st Louisiana Brigade made at Spotsylvania's Bloody Angle and the rear-guard action of York's brigade at Third Winchester and Fisher's Hill.

The same men who pillaged towns and delighted in drinking and fighting also knelt in knee-deep snow at Fredericksburg for Easter services, held frequent revivals and prayer meetings, and astonished everyone on the dreary Petersburg line by building a chapel which the Rev. John William Jones described as being "one of the best arranged, neatest and most comfortable chapels which I ever saw in the army." During the bitter winter of 1862–63, when General Early wanted to rid himself of the Tigers because of their thievery, Hays' brigade donated three thousand dollars for the relief of the destitute citizens of shelled-out Fredericksburg, and the hell-raising "Wildcats" of the 14th Louisiana raised twelve hundred dollars for the orphans in Richmond.[14]

Despite their exalted military record and devotion to duty, desertions plagued the Louisiana commands throughout the war. Exactly how many soldiers walked away is not known because no figures are available for some of the units, but of the 11,848 men for which there are some records, at least 1,049 deserted (or about 9 percent). Those commands with large numbers of foreign members suffered the most desertions, perhaps because their support for the cause was not so strong. The Irish-dominated 6th Louisiana led the regiments with 269 deserters out of its 1,215 members (22 percent). The 15th Louisiana (14 percent) and 5th Louisiana (11 percent) ranked second and third, respectively. The desertions sometimes wrecked entire companies. From May 1 to August 31, 1862, 98 men deserted the 15th Louisiana, with 27 of 55 members of the Bogart Guards abandoning the cause. Men taking leave without permission was almost as prevalent. The 2nd Louisiana's Floyd Guards had 15 of 33 men absent without leave at one time.[15]

Many of the Louisiana deserters and prisoners of war secured their freedom by swearing an oath of allegiance to the U.S. Constitution. At least 275 Tigers are known to have taken the oath before Appomattox, with the Irishmen of the 6th Louisiana again leading the regiments with 76. Although some men deserted and then took the oath, most were given after the soldier was captured. Inside both flaps of a diary belonging to the 5th Louisiana's Sgt. T. W. Reynolds is scrawled a message that most Tigers would have agreed with: "Daniel W. Linder, Co. F, 5th La. Regt. Took the Oath of Allegiance to the U.S. government Dec. 23, '63. The C[onfederate] S[tates] are willing to get rid of all such as he was. Branded in the Regt. as a damned coward." Linder was an Illinois native who worked as a lawyer before the war and took the oath after being captured at Rappahannock Station.[16]

A surprising number of Tiger deserters and prisoners of war who took the oath of allegiance joined the Union army and became what was known as "Galvanized Yankees." For some, this was probably just a way to escape the starvation and disease that accompanied captivity, but for those who had been forced to enlist in the rebel army it was a chance to serve the Union. One of the men from the 6th Louisiana who switched sides paid with his life at Mine Run when he fell back into the hands of his old comrades. Of the Louisiana Tiger regiments, the multinational 10th Louisiana provided the most Galvanized Yankees with fifty-two. Twenty Galvanized Yankees from the 1st Louisiana Brigade and thirty from the 2nd Brigade who had been captured at Gettysburg joined the 3rd Maryland Cavalry (Union). In fact, former Confederate prisoners made up half of this unique regiment, and 80 to 90 percent of them deserted again after the unit was sent to New Orleans.[17]

Victor Braud of the 7th Louisiana is the best documented case of a Louisiana Tiger who became a Galvanized Yankee. Although service records incorrectly list him as Victor Brand, he was a twenty-year-old barber from Baton Rouge when he enlisted in 1861. Braud was wounded in the face at Port Republic and then deserted at the Battle of Gettysburg and was put in the Old Capitol Prison in Washington, D.C. He took the oath of allegiance on December 13, 1863, and ultimately joined the 104th Pennsylvania as George Duke. The 104th Pennsylvania was placed in the Petersburg trenches in November 1864 shortly before the Louisiana Tigers arrived. M. L. Pemberton, the regiment's drum major and a friend of Braud, wrote after the war that they regularly listened to the Louisiana Tiger drum corps play on the other side of the lines. According to Pemberton, the Tigers' band was "one of the best I ever heard in the rebel army." One night the 7th Louisiana attacked the Pennsylvanians' picket line, and Braud had to fight his old comrades. Then during the April 3, 1865, Union attacks on Petersburg the 104th Pennsylvania captured some of the Louisianians, including the drum corps. Pemberton wrote that since his regiment did not have a bass drum, he confiscated the Tigers' drum and used it during the Appomattox Campaign. For a week, Pemberton wrote, Braud (aka Duke) "marched behind the same bass drum he had so often marched after when a member of the Louisiana Tigers." Pemberton still had the drum in 1907 and claimed, "I play 'Dixie' to-day on the drum just as we learned it from the Louisiana Tigers."[18]

For many of the weary Tigers, Appomattox ended their war but not their suffering. Thomas Reed, the 5th Louisiana soldier who decided to extend his wounded furlough permanently, found his wife and two children in dire straits and could only feed them by making shoes for a planter in exchange for a bushel of corn for each pair. Reed's wife died the next year, but he remarried and eventually settled in Arkansas to farm. Colonel Henry Forno, Reed's dependable regimental commander who was wounded at Second Manassas while commanding Hays' brigade, survived some of the war's bloodiest battles only to be killed in a railroad accident on January 31, 1866, at Amite, Louisiana. The 6th Louisiana's Capt. George P. Ring was wounded three times and wrote some exceptionally detailed letters that tell so much about the Tigers' battles. He returned to New Orleans to work as a cotton weigher but lived only two years after Appomattox. Wolf Lichenstein, whose diary chronicles the 2nd Louisiana's activities, survived into the twentieth century, but he never regained the use of his fingers on the arm that was shattered at Gettysburg and was forced to live out his final years with a daughter in New York City.[19]

Sergeant John H. Charlton, who left an interesting memoir of his service with the 5th Louisiana, made it back to New Orleans, married, and had nine children, only to die in a tragic incident in 1885 at the age of forty-three. The national press widely covered Charlton's death, although newspapers differed on the details of what happened. After separating from his wife, Nora, Charlton sank into a deep depression and began drinking heavily when the mercantile company he worked for as an accountant let him go. While drinking with a friend, he was seized by "a species of delirium tremens" and began arguing with the man. Charlton hit him, and when the friend picked up a chair to defend himself, the former Tiger drew his pistol and shot him in the side and neck. A reporter declared, "This seemed to sober him and thinking that he killed his friend turned the pistol on himself." The friend survived.[20]

Postwar life was difficult for the former Tiger generals, as well. William Raine "Big" Peck returned to his Madison Parish plantation, "The Mountain," but died in 1871 just nine days shy of his fifty-third birthday. Zebulon York, who was perhaps the richest man in Louisiana when the war began, came home to find that he was financially ruined because his slaves had been freed. Unable to rebuild his life as a planter, he opened a hotel called the York House in Natchez, Mississippi, and remained there until his death in 1900.[21]

After rising to the rank of lieutenant general and serving well in the Trans-Mississippi and western departments, Richard Taylor surrendered the Army of Tennessee in Alabama on May 4, 1865. He was immediately beset by both financial and personal difficulties. During the war, the Yankees had destroyed his plantation, two of his young sons had died of scarlet fever, and his wife's health was ruined. Taylor became active in Reconstruction politics and lobbied Presidents Andrew Johnson and U. S. Grant to help the former rebels rebuild their shattered lives. He supported Samuel Tilden in the contested 1876 presidential election and was involved in the backroom negotiations that led to the Compromise of 1877 that settled the election in the Republican Rutherford B. Hayes' favor. Having suffered from poor health all of his life, Taylor died in 1879 at age fifty-three from internal congestion brought on by chronic rheumatoid arthritis. Shortly before his death, he published his memoirs, *Destruction and Reconstruction,* which became a Civil War classic.[22]

A number of Tiger officers followed Taylor's lead and became politically active during Reconstruction. The 10th Louisiana's Capt. Leon Jastremski, who had survived being captured on three occasions as well as wounds in the throat and arm at Chancellorsville and Gettysburg, respectively, was elected Baton Rouge's mayor three times. He also served as a vice-president of Louisiana State University, chairman of the state's Democratic Party, state commissioner of agriculture, editor of the *Louisiana Review* and president of the Louisiana Press Association, brigadier general of the Louisiana National Guard, commander of the state's United Confederate Veterans, and the U.S. consul to Peru.[23]

Both Gen. Harry T. Hays and Col. Eugene Waggaman were elected sheriff of Orleans Parish after the war and fought the state's Republican administration during Reconstruction. Hays ended the war as a major general in the Trans-Mississippi Department (although the senate never confirmed the appointment) and was elected sheriff soon after returning home. In 1866, however, Gen. Philip Sheridan, the Reconstruction commander of Louisiana, suspected Hays of ordering his deputies to attack African American demonstrators in what became known as the New Orleans Riot and removed him from office. Hays then practiced law and became affiliated with the anti-Republican White League before dying of Bright's disease in 1876 at the age of fifty-six.[24]

Colonel Waggaman also joined the White League and bitterly opposed William Pitt Kellogg, the Republican candidate who was sworn in as governor after the disputed 1872 election. In an attempt to put Democratic candidates Gov. John McEnery and former Tiger officer Lt. Gov. Davidson Penn into office, Waggaman led the White League troops into New Orleans in 1874 and fought the city police in what became known as the Battle of Liberty Place. Waggaman defeated the police, who were under the command of former rebel comrade Gen. James Longstreet, but the U.S. Army intervened and forced Waggaman's men to withdraw. The following year, Waggaman was elected sheriff of Orleans Parish and remained a prominent state figure until he died of a stroke in 1897.[25]

The 8th Louisiana's Lieutenant George L. P. Wren, who was wounded at Antietam and captured at Port Republic and Spotsylvania, returned to his home near Minden, Louisiana, and became a schoolteacher before marrying and fathering seven children. He later worked as a successful planter and served eight years in the state legislature and four years in the senate. In announcing Wren's death in 1901, the local newspaper wrote, "[I]n all of the relations of life, whether in the discharge of his civic or religious duties, he measured up to the fullest standard of the faithful citizen and true christian."[26]

Lieutenant Henry Handerson, the educated Yankee tutor who joined the 9th Louisiana with his friends, exchanged his sword for a stethoscope. After graduating from the modern-day Columbia University Medical School, he suffered a terrible personal loss when his wife died after giving birth to their fourth child and his three oldest children, ages five through eight, contracted diphtheria and died over a five-day period. Handerson eventually remarried and fathered two more children and had a long and distinguished medical career. A devout and active member of the Episcopal Church, he stoically accepted going blind two years before dying of a stroke in 1918 at the age of eighty-one. In a posthumous biographical sketch for his last book, one of Handerson's colleagues wrote, "Seeing this tall venerable gentleman, sedate in manner and philosophical in mind, presiding over the Cuyahoga County Medical Society or the Cleveland Medical Library Association, few of the members ever pictured him as a fiery, youthful Confederate officer, leading a charge at a run up-hill over fallen logs and brush, sounding the 'Rebel yell.'"[27]

Captain William Seymour transferred out of the Louisiana Brigade late in the war and ended up serving in Georgia as inspector general for Gen. Pierce Manning Butler Young's cavalry. Returning to New Orleans after the surrender, he resumed working in the newspaper business and was able to honor one of his father's wishes. When Colonel Seymour passed through his hometown of Macon, Georgia, on the way to Virginia in 1861, he mentioned to some friends that he would like to be buried there should he be killed. In 1868, Captain Seymour traveled to Lynchburg, Virginia, and dutifully brought his father's body back to Georgia. Seymour was appointed colonel of the 1st Louisiana militia during the postwar period, and fathered eight children, although three died in infancy. He died in 1886 from chronic heart disease.[28]

Major David F. Boyd, who wrote extensively about Richard Taylor and Jackson's Valley Campaign, ended his military career in the Trans-Mississippi Department. After the surrender, he returned to the Louisiana Seminary in Pineville, where he had taught under William T. Sherman before the war. Boyd served as the school's superintendent and became known as the "Father of LSU" for his role in transferring the seminary to Baton Rouge and renaming it Louisiana State University. Boyd served as LSU's first president from 1870 to 1880 and was teaching there when he died in 1899.[29]

Of all the former Tigers, Gen. Francis T. Nicholls had the most successful postwar career. When running for governor on the Democratic ticket in 1876, he found his war record and devastating wounds to be a political asset in winning the veterans' vote. Nicholls reportedly asked them to support "all that is left of General Nicholls" and to vote for him for governor because he was "too one sided for a judge." Nicholls was elected governor in 1876 and 1888, and then became a judge after all when he served as the chief justice of the state supreme court from 1892 to 1911. In the latter position, Nicholls also had a professional relationship with former colonel Henry B. Kelly, who became a judge on the state court of appeals. Nicholls died from heart failure in 1912, and today's Nicholls State University in Thibodaux is named in his honor.[30]

Other Tigers who left accounts of the war years lived rather ordinary lives. The 14th Louisiana's William P. Snakenberg, who wrote one of the better Tiger memoirs, survived the infamous Elmira prison camp after being captured at Spotsylvania and settled in Wilson, North Carolina, after the war. He had been sent there to recuperate after being shot through the body at Antietam and married a local woman in November 1862. Snakenberg fathered six children and served as Wilson's chief of police but only returned to Louisiana once to attend a veterans' reunion in 1903. He died from Bright's disease in 1916 while living in a veterans' home.[31]

William Bayliss Tull's memoir abruptly ends with his falling ill during Early's Washington Raid, and it is not known if he ever returned to duty. He did survive the war and returned to Livingston Parish and married a few months after the surrender. Tull and his wife had six children, one of whom died as a child, and spent the remainder of their lives scratching out a living on rented farms in Louisiana and Mississippi.[32]

Louisiana Tiger chaplains Louis-Hippolyte Gache and James Sheeran continued their holy missions after the war. Father Gache was assigned to

Baltimore's Loyola College and then transferred to the Holy Trinity Church in Georgetown, Maryland. He served several other churches, as well, before retiring to St. Andrew-on-Hudson in New York and passing away in 1907 at the age of eighty-six. Father Sheeran returned to New Orleans and was praised for his selfless work in treating victims of the 1867 yellow fever epidemic. Soon afterward, he was appointed pastor of a church in Morristown, New Jersey. After overseeing the construction of a new church and parochial school, Sheeran died of a stroke in 1881.[33]

As the surviving Louisianians struggled to rebuild their lives after the war, they continued to fascinate Americans, and stories about Tiger veterans often appeared in newspapers. In 1866, the Jonesborough (Tennessee) *Union Flag* reported on a man who walked into a Pennsylvania bar and brashly boasted that he was a former Louisiana Tiger. The reporter claimed that the barkeep promptly knocked him to the floor and explained that the "barkeeper was a returned soldier, and the language of the 'Tiger' pleased him not." In 1889, another newspaper reported that German immigrant and former Tiger John Brown flew the American flag at half-mast at his Long Branch saloon on New York City's Broadway when Jefferson Davis died. Many people complained, but Brown simply said, "George Vashington vas a rebel, vat's the matter mit Jeff Davis?" Then there was W. S. Stubbs, a peddler who claimed to have graduated from Johns Hopkins medical school and sold medicinal gum drops on the streets of Richmond. When he was arrested for peddling without a license, the *Times-Dispatch* reported, "He swore and asseverated, and did it over again, that he once belonged to the Louisiana Tigers, and that he could fight anything from a wildcat to a buzz saw. He was prepared to prove it, but none wanted to see the proof. . . . He is a gentle soul at times. At other times—well at other times he is a Louisiana Tiger, and some tiger at that. The police reverence him greatly. They have arrested him time without number."[34]

The Tigers' war exploits were told and retold so many times in the postwar period, often with great exaggeration, that many people came to believe that they had served in all of the military theaters. Some western Louisiana units, such as Randall Gibson's brigade, were incorrectly labeled Tigers, and Union veterans claimed to have fought the Tigers in such far-flung battlefields as Shiloh, Farmington, Secessionville, Champion Hill, Missionary Ridge, and Atlanta. The Tigers received so much press that a Pennsylvania GAR post decided to adopt the nickname "The Lambs," in 1892 because, as the commander put it, "the post needed something to offset the famous 'Louisiana Tigers.'" Even some Confederate veterans began to take offense at the inordinate amount of attention the Tigers received. One wrote tongue-in-cheek, "Nearly every account of the war which I have read by Northern writers gives great prominence in every battle to the 'Tigers,' and I am of the opinion that every soldier in the Union Army actually thought he fought the 'Tigers.' I cannot estimate the number they must originally have mustered, according to the amount of fighting they are represented by the boys in blue to have done, but there was certainly more than a million of them, or they wouldn't 'go around.'"[35]

By the time the veterans began holding battlefield reunions, the Louisiana Tigers had attained near-mythical status. Hays' twilight fight on Gettysburg's Cemetery Hill, in particular, captured the people's imagination, while the role the North Carolinians played in the same attack and the longer and bloodier battle the 2nd Louisiana Brigade had on nearby Culp's Hill were largely forgotten. At the turn of the century, one Florida newspaper claimed, "The north end of Cemetery Hill is probably the most noted point on this famous battle ground, from the fact that at this place occurred the daring charge of the Louisiana Tigers." The Tigers' popularity was evident when a large veterans' reunion was held in 1888 to commemorate the Battle of Gettysburg's twenty-fifth anniversary. A reporter for the New York *Times* wrote, "The Louisiana 'Tigers' have arrived. . . . [F]or many hours the 'Tigers' were lions and from them none, no matter how celebrated, could divert popular favor." Another correspondent claimed, "[T]he few 'Louisiana Tigers' who were present were among the most popular men on the ground. The federal veterans made a rush to shake hands with them. The last time the 'Tigers' were at Gettysburg the federals were too busily engaged to think of shaking hands."[36]

Early one morning during the reunion, four men and two women were seen walking along Cemetery Hill. The men were pointing to the north and east as they walked, and some nearby Pennsylvania veterans overheard one say, "We rushed up that slope, had a hand-to-hand fight right here where those guns are; some of our boys got as far as the road back there, but it was of no use. We did our best, but were driven back, all who were alive." One of the women replied, "I think it's a wonder that any of you got back."

The Union veterans then approached, and one said, "We heard you say you had rushed up that slope, and the only men who reached the top, except the men who guarded it, were Louisiana Tigers." According to the reporter,

"A smallish man, of wiry frame, his hair and goatee flecked with gray, stepped forward a couple of paces and said, with a smile that was lamb-like, 'We are four of the Tigers, sah.'" The men then began shaking hands, and "the northern veterans welcomed the representatives of the most desperate fighters the south produced. The news jumped quickly from point to point that the 'Johnnies' had come. It was lamented on all sides that they had not come in greater numbers, but it was conceded that four Louisiana 'Tigers' would cover a multitude of short comings."

The four Tiger veterans were Frederick A. Ober, Thomas Higgins, John J. Wax, and L. J. Cordes. Ober and Higgins had served in the 5th and 2nd Louisiana, respectively, but there is no record of Wax and Cordes. A Confederate battle flag adorned Ober's personal card, under which were the words, "Louisiana Tigers. Here we are again." The reporter claimed that so many people wanted one of the cards that Ober ran out within an hour. He wrote, "Veterans of all ranks and all ages showed an immensity of interest in the four Tigers,"[37] while another declared, "The four 'Louisiana Tigers' who arrived yesterday continue to attract attention, and the veterans . . . were anxious to again meet the furious fighters of the South."[38]

Ober became even more popular when someone asked him why so few Louisianians had come to the reunion. He replied that it was because the veterans did not learn about it in time to make arrangements, but that he was instructed by Louisiana's United Confederate Veterans to tell the Gettysburg visitors "that if defenders for the stars and stripes were needed the Louisiana Tigers were and would always be ready to furnish their full quota. . . . I tell you, sahs, we are American citizens. I am an American citizen and I am proud of it, and if it ever becomes necessary, I will fight for that citizenship and for the men I once fought against, and for whom I now have a feeling I can not express. I am American born and I am for America." The crowd cheered Ober's response. Sadly, Ober was killed in a train wreck while returning home from the reunion.[39]

The reporter who covered the reunion noticed that, while everyone visited Little Round Top, Culp's Hill, and the Peach Orchard, "none of these points do visitors, either military or civilian, spend so much time as at East Cemetery hill, and all because of the desperate conflict that occurred on this hill between the Louisiana 'Tigers' in their mad attempt to demolish Weederich's [sic] and Rickett's batteries and their supports. Veterans never tire of telling how the gunners used the rammers upon the heads of the 'Tigers,' and how the latter fought like wild beasts. They never tire, of either listening to 'Tiger' Ober tell how disgusted the name of 'Tiger' made them when it was first applied to one company and then gradually spread to all Louisiana troops, and how proud they now were of the title."⁴⁰ Even Gen. John B. Gordon, the Tigers' old commander, noticed the attention the Tigers were receiving. He wrote, "I saw an old one-legged 'Louisiana Tiger' in charge of a dozen Union veterans, who were actually carrying him around and giving him a glorious time, eating, drinking, telling stories and presenting him to their friends."⁴¹

August Kissel, a former member of Capt. Greenleaf Stevens' battery, which helped repulse the Tigers' attack on Cemetery Hill, also had an encounter with one of his former enemies. He recalled that, while sitting on a gun tube at his old position east of Cemetery Hill at dusk, "I had the pleasure of meeting some of the Louisiana Tigers that tried to capture our battery 25 years ago at the same hour. I tell you, boys, we had a glorious clapping of hands, and a royal good time."⁴²

In November 1894, some of the Tigers returned to Gettysburg to help lay out the Louisianians' battle lines for the planned Gettysburg National Military Park. Louisiana, in fact, was the first southern state to send a delegation to help historian John B. Bachelder and the park's commission locate the rebels' positions. The 14th Louisiana's Col. David Zable, who became a prominent New Orleans businessman and a founder of both the United Confederate Veterans and Young Men's Christian Association, led the Tiger delegation. Accompanying him were Pvt. Eugene H. Levy of the Donaldsonville Artillery, Capt. Andrew J. Hero and Sgt. Maj. C. L. C. Dupuy of the Washington Artillery, Sgt. Hugh H. Ward of the 7th Louisiana, and Corp. Albert M. Levy of the Louisiana Guard Battery.⁴³

Upon their arrival, the delegation first retraced the route Hays' brigade took on the first day of battle and put out markers along the Harrisburg Road where it fought and on some buildings on Middle Street where the Tigers assembled afterward. After locating Hays' position outside of town near Cemetery Hill, Zable then led the delegation out to Culp's Hill, where the 2nd Louisiana Brigade engaged the Yankees on the second and third days of battle. Crossing Rock Creek, Zable pointed out where Col. Michael "Jim" Nolan was killed, and in the dead timber that covered the hill he found the oak tree behind which "the heroic" Pvt. John H. Ozier had picked off Union soldiers and some big rocks about fifty yards below the 29th Ohio's monument that sheltered the brigade's men. Zable then drove stakes in the ground where the individual regiments had been posted.[44]

In 1913, more Tigers returned to Gettysburg for the battle's fiftieth anniversary, or what one reporter dubbed the "love-feast." Among them was St. Francisville mayor A. B. Briant. While walking around Cemetery Hill, he encountered a Union veteran who asked if he had been there during the battle. When Briant replied yes, that he had served in the 7th Louisiana, the man declared, "Then it was you who took our cannon." "Yes," Briant replied, "but we couldn't keep them." "Well, I shall capture you then," said the stranger, and he took Briant around town and treated him to dinner. Although the newspaper identified the Union veteran as a Capt. Ripley, he may have been Bruce Ricketts, who commanded one of the two batteries the Tigers attacked. Upon returning home, Briant claimed that he and his fellow veterans received special attention while at Gettysburg because they had been members of the Louisiana Tigers. Even an unidentified Union general from Maine asked if could come to Briant's tent for a visit.[45] Dr. O. D. Brooks, another Tiger veteran who attended the reunion, received similar treatment. He wrote that "the attention given the Louisiana veterans was particularly cordial from Federal veterans, officials, and ladies alike. . . . Pretty girls willingly accepted and wore La. Div. badges as souvenirs." Tiger veteran T. R. Carroll, who served in the 5th Louisiana, was even chosen for a photo op. He and W. T. Shoemaker of Pennsylvania were photographed shaking hands across the stone wall that was the target of Pickett's Charge "as a symbol of everlasting peace and friendship between the blue and the gray."[46]

By the turn of the twentieth century, the Louisiana Tigers' reputation was sealed. In discussing Louisiana's multicultural Civil War soldiers, one writer declared that they were a mongrel set of men who deserved their fame because they were rarely defeated on the battlefield. "[T]oday in Louisiana to have belonged to that band of heroes in the rough is the highest distinction. Sometimes as a gray and bent man passes slowly along a quiet street in New Orleans loungers under the awnings on the other side point him out and say to each other: 'He is one of them.'"[47]

Some Union veterans also began to take pride in the fact that they once stood toe-to-toe with the fierce Tigers on the battlefield. One former soldier who enjoyed reading about the war in the *National Tribune* renewed his subscription in 1882 with the remark, "Your paper brings to mind things of the past—when we wished to see the elephant in the shape of a Tar-heel or a Louisiana tiger—when we heard that old rebel yell, and saw that long line of grey coming down for one last charge." On occasion, Union veterans even found that fighting the Tigers paid off in politics. When a Mr. Groll ran for treasurer in Napoleon, Ohio, in 1889, the local newspaper pointed out that he was a veteran of the 107th Ohio and "was one among those who fought the Louisiana Tigers at Gettysburg. He will make a good treasurer."[48]

As the Louisiana Tiger veterans became stooped with age, newspapers began holding an informal death watch to document the last living member. One of the first to claim the honor was a man who used the pen name "Solomon." In 1895, he made the outlandish claim that there were only eighteen Tigers left after the Battle of Malvern Hill and just three after Rappahannock Station. The *National Tribune,* the Union veterans' newspaper of choice, quickly published a rebuttal in an article titled "A Free-Going, Natural-Gaited Liar": "If he belonged to that [Louisiana Tiger] organization he comes by his mendacity naturally, for there has been more audacious and voluminous lying about that crowd than any half-dozen others on either side during the war."[49]

The *Tribune* was correct about the myths surrounding the Tigers, but the nation's interest in the Louisianians' demise did not diminish, and stories about the "last" Tiger continued to appear for the next thirty years. Perhaps the most interesting claim was made by Lamar Fontaine in 1896. He boasted that he fought in twenty-seven major battles and one hundred skirmishes, was wounded sixty-seven times (thirteen bullets "grazed" his lungs), was pronounced dead five times, once killed sixty enemy soldiers in sixty minutes in the presence of Robert E. Lee, and was such a Yankee-killer that the enemy put a $20,000 dollar reward on his head.[50] There is no record of a Lamar Fontaine having served with the Louisiana Tigers, which is not unusual, but one has to wonder if he ever meant for his story to be taken seriously. In fact, several newspapers began to treat the "last Tiger" claims as nothing more than a joke. In 1906, the *National Tribune* wrote:

> The Louisiana Tigers threaten to be as constantly with us as the poor and the survivors of the Light Brigade. Though we have reports of them being entirely wiped out at the second Bull Run, Malvern Hill, Gettysburg, and a score of other battlefields, they seem to have stood

wholesale killing in a most astonishing way, and few weeks pass without the last of the "Louisiana Tigers" dying somewhere in the country. . . . Remarkable men them Louisiana Tigers! They had the most astonishing faculty, never possessed by any other soldiers, of getting into every big battle, no matter by what army it was fought, and no matter how the battle went they were to be "exterminated." As a rule, other regiments, both North and South, did all their fighting in some one army, but the Louisiana Tigers were not restrained by any such narrow routine of military limitations. They were instantly shifted from the lines of the Potomac to those of the Tennessee and Mississippi, in order to be present at some great battle and be exterminated. Of course, the number of Yankees that they killed is far beyond anything that the Pension Bureau ever dreamed of, but that was a mere incident.[51]

About the time the *National Tribune* began reporting on the "last of the Tigers," the Louisianians' fame was given a boost when Dr. Charles Hunter Coates formed the first football team at Louisiana State University. Coates was the head of the Chemistry Department and took it upon himself to organize and coach the team in 1893. Thus, it fell to Coates to choose the school's colors and mascot. By necessity, the colors became purple and gold because it was Mardi Gras season, and those were the only colored ribbons the store had in abundance. Three years later, Coates decided the team needed a mascot name and settled on the "Louisiana Tigers." He later explained, "It struck me that purple and gold looked Tigerish enough and I suggested that we choose 'Louisiana Tigers,' all in conference with the boys. The Louisiana Tigers had represented the state in the Civil War and had been known for their hard fighting. . . . So 'Louisiana Tigers' went into the New Orleans papers and became our permanent possession."[52]

For the next fifty years, LSU's athletic teams were almost always referred to as the "Louisiana Tigers." It was not until the mid-1930s that sportswriters began using the terms "LSU Tigers" and "Louisiana State Tigers," but "Louisiana Tigers" remained the preferred name until the late 1950s when the simpler "Tigers" became more common. Today, few people outside LSU's loyal fans realize that the school's Tiger mascot is actually a reference to Louisiana's most famous soldiers.[53]

The "Tiger" nickname also attached itself to Louisiana's soldiers in the post–Civil War period. When the United States entered the Spanish-American War in 1898, the state's volunteers serving in Cuba were referred to as the Louisiana Tigers, and when Louisiana native and Marine Corps general John A. Lejeune became a popular hero in World War I, a newspaper declared that the "spirit of the Louisiana Tigers still lives."[54]

In modern times, the 256th Infantry Brigade of the Louisiana Army National Guard adopted the Louisiana Tiger name and today is referred to as the Tiger Brigade. Called up in 2004 to serve in Iraq, it was sent to Fort Hood, Texas, for advanced training. The 1st Battalion, 69th Infantry, New York National Guard, was also sent to Fort Hood at the same time. Known as "The Fighting 69th," it traces its ancestry back to the Civil War's 69th New York of the famous Irish Brigade. After the Civil War, the 69th New York was designated a National Guard unit and gained more fame while fighting in both world wars. At Fort Hood, the 69th New York was attached to the Tiger Brigade to bring it up to strength. The last time the New Yorkers and Louisianians came in close contact was during a desperate hand-to-hand fight at the Battle of Malvern Hill. Nearly 150 years later, they were heading off to war as comrades.[55]

Upon arriving in Iraq, the Louisianians dubbed its bivouac Camp Tigerland. Then on January 2, 2005, a roadside bomb destroyed one of the unit's Humvees and killed six of the modern-day Louisiana Tigers and one member of the 69th New York. By the time its tour of duty ended, the task force had lost fifteen men killed and fifty wounded. Those gallant soldiers represented two states that had fought one another in a vicious civil war nearly 150 years earlier, but they died together as brothers-in-arms. As Col. Mark Kerry said when the two units first merged, "I guess we can file this away under the heading 'The Civil War is Really Over.'"[56]

APPENDIX
Unit Numbers and Losses

Unless otherwise stated, statistical data on the number of desertions, oaths, places of birth, and deaths for individual units were obtained from original muster rolls. These rolls do not contain information for each soldier or even on every unit. Therefore, the statistics are not without error; they are simply a summation of the information that is available and should be used for comparison purposes. The lists of companies show the original captains at the time of organization.[1]

1ST LOUISIANA VOLUNTEERS

The 1st Louisiana was mustered into service for twelve months on April 28, 1861. The regiment's total enrollment was 960. Of these, 162 men were killed or mortally wounded, 74 died of disease, 1 was accidentally killed, at least 88 deserted, 12 took the oath of allegiance, and 8 were discharged under foreign protection. Twenty men were still on duty when the regiment surrendered at Appomattox. Almost all of the regiment's members were from the New Orleans area, and most were clerks, farmers, and laborers. Of the 843 members who gave a place of birth, 292 were born in states outside of Louisiana; 226 in Louisiana; 202 in Ireland; 59 in the Germanic states; 34 in England; 10 in France; 9 in Canada; 6 in Scotland; 2 in Poland; and 1 each in Belgium, Brazil, and Switzerland.

The regiment's original officers were Col. Albert G. Blanchard, Lt. Col. William G. Vincent, and Maj. William R. Shivers. Blanchard, an 1829 West Point graduate, served until he was promoted to brigadier general on September 21, 1861, and returned to Louisiana. Vincent succeeded him, but he was replaced by Samuel R. Harrison when the army was reorganized in April 1862. Harrison resigned two months later and was replaced by Shivers, who served until he was forced to resign in 1864 because of wounds. James Nelligan succeeded him.

During the war, 19 officers were killed or mortally wounded, 1 died of disease, 2 deserted to the enemy, and 2 were cashiered from the service.[2]

Company A: Caddo Rifles, from Caddo Parish, Capt. Charles Dailee commanding. This company had a 29 percent mortality rate.

Company B (first): Louisiana Guards (Co. B), from New Orleans, Capt. Camille E. Girardey commanding. At the request of the company members, it was formed into the independent Louisiana Guard Battery on July 5, 1861.

Company B (second): Red River Rebels, from Rapides Parish, Capt. James C. Wise commanding. This company replaced the Louisiana Guards (Co. B) after it transferred out of the regiment.[3]

Company C (first): Louisiana Guards (Co. C), from New Orleans, Capt. Francis "Frank" Rawle commanding. This company transferred to Dreux's Battalion on July 16, 1861.

Company C (second): Slocumb Rifles, from New Orleans, Capt. Robert W. Armistead commanding. This company replaced the Louisiana Guards (Co. C) when it transferred to Dreux's Battalion.

Company D: Emmet Guards, from New Orleans, Capt. James Nelligan commanding. Irish-born men dominated this company.[4]

Company E: Montgomery Guards, from New Orleans, Capt. Michael "Jim" Nolan commanding. Irish-born men composed 77 percent of this company, but only 10 percent deserted during the war.

Company F: Orleans Light Guards (Co. D), from New Orleans, Capt. Patrick R. O'Rourke commanding.

Company G: Orleans Light Guards (Co. B), from New Orleans, Capt. Thomas M. Dean commanding.

Company H (first): Davis Guards, from New Orleans, Capt. Ben W. Anderson commanding. This company was from Lexington, Kentucky, and was transferred to the 15th Kentucky on August 2, 1861.[5]

Company H (second): Askew Guards, from New Orleans, Capt. Andrew Brady commanding. This company transferred from the 3rd Louisiana Battalion to replace the Davis Guards when it moved to the 15th Kentucky. The Askew Guards transferred to the 15th Louisiana on May 22, 1862.

Company H (third): Shreveport Greys, from Shreveport, Capt. Capt. William E. Moore commanding. This company originally served in Dreux's Battalion, but when that battalion was disbanded it transferred to the 1st Louisiana on June 27, 1862, to replace the departing Askew Guards.

Company I: Orleans Light Guards (Co. A), from New Orleans, Capt. Charles E. Cormier commanding.

Company K: Orleans Light Guards (Co. C), from New Orleans, Capt. Charles N.
    Frost commanding.

The Tiger Bayou Rifles were ordered transferred from the 14th Louisiana to the 1st
Louisiana on August 5, 1861, but it is not known if they ever became an official company
of the regiment. The Catahoula Guerrillas may also have served in the 1st Louisiana.[6]

2ND LOUISIANA VOLUNTEERS

The 2nd Louisiana was mustered into service for twelve months on May 11, 1861.
The regiment's total enrollment was 1,297. Of these, 218 men were killed or mortally
wounded, 181 died of disease, 4 were killed accidentally, at least 88 deserted, and 4
took the oath of allegiance. Forty men were still on duty when the regiment surrendered at Appomattox, and 8 of those were musicians. The regiment consisted mainly
of farmers but also had a large number of clerks. Of the 1,020 members who gave a
place of birth, 655 were born in states outside of Louisiana; 263 in Louisiana; 41 in the
Germanic states; 37 in Ireland; 7 in Canada; 5 each in England and Scotland; 2 each in
Poland, France, and Italy; and 1 in Denmark.

The regiment's original officers were Col. Louis G. DeRussy, Lt. Col. John Young,
and Maj. Isaiah T. Norwood. DeRussy resigned in the summer of 1861, and William
Levy was elected to replace him. When the army was reorganized in April 1862, Norwood was elected colonel, but he was killed at Malvern Hill. Jesse M. Williams took
command afterward and led the regiment until he was killed at Spotsylvania. Ross
E. Burke was then promoted to colonel, but he had recently been exchanged from a
prison camp and never rejoined the unit. Senior line officers led the regiment for the
remainder of the war.

Company A: Lecompte Guards, from Natchitoches Parish, Capt. William M. Levy
    commanding.
Company B: Moore Guards, from Alexandria, Capt. John Kelso commanding.
Company C: Pelican Greys, from Monroe, Capt. Arthur H. Martin commanding.
Company D: Pelican Rifles, from DeSoto and Natchitoches parishes, Capt. Jesse M.
    Williams commanding. Of the 109 original members of this company, 33
    were students or teachers. A total of 151 men served in the company, but only
    32 survived the war. Of those, 31 were wounded.[7]
Company E: Vernon Guards, from Jackson Parish, Capt. Oscar M. Watkins com-
    manding.
Company F: Claiborne Guards, from Homer, Capt. John W. Andrews commanding.
    Of the 135 men who served in this company, 20 were killed or mortally

wounded, 20 died of other causes, 19 were wounded, and 40 were taken prisoner.[8]

Company G: Floyd Guards, from Carroll Parish, Capt. John W. Dunn commanding.

Company H: Atchafalaya Guards, from Pointe Coupee and Avoyelles parishes, Capt. Richard M. Boone commanding. Raised in Simmesport, this company was strongly supported by the area's planters and had many members who were quite wealthy. The company also appears to have served in the 10th Louisiana.[9]

Company I: Greenwood Guards, from Caddo Parish, Capt. William Flournoy commanding.

Company K: Vienna Rifles, from Jackson Parish, Capt. H. W. Perrin commanding. This company suffered a 37 percent mortality rate during the war.

5TH LOUISIANA VOLUNTEERS

The 5th Louisiana was mustered into service for the duration of the war on June 4, 1861. The regiment's total enrollment was 1,074. Of these, 161 men were killed or mortally wounded, 66 died of disease, 2 were killed accidentally, 1 was murdered, 1 was executed, at least 118 deserted, and 32 took the oath of allegiance. Seventeen men were still on duty when the regiment surrendered at Appomattox. The vast majority of the regiment's members were laborers and clerks. One member complained that most of the men were "uneducated Irishmen," but that was an exaggeration.[10] Of the 528 members who gave a place of birth, 200 were born in Louisiana, 121 in other states, 94 in Ireland, 59 in the Germanic states, 25 in England, 12 in France, 7 in Switzerland, 3 each in Canada and Scotland, 2 in Cuba, and 1 each in Mexico and Poland.

The regiment's original officers were Col. Theodore G. Hunt, Lt. Col. Henry Forno, and Maj. William T. Bean. General Lafayette McLaws described Hunt as being "an old gentleman of independent manner, and an open talker, was [a] member of Congress from Louisiana and has a considerable opinion of his influence and of his ability both as a soldier and a member of Society."[11] When Hunt resigned in August 1862, Forno was promoted to colonel, but he was transferred to Mobile, Alabama, in May 1863. Lieutenant Colonel Bruce Menger then assumed command, but he was sometimes absent sick or wounded. When Menger was killed at Spotsylvania, Maj. Alexander Hart took over. During the war, 13 of the regiment's officers were killed or mortally wounded, 4 died of disease, 1 was killed in a duel, 2 deserted to the enemy, and 1 was dismissed from the service for cowardice.

All of the companies, except for the Louisiana Swamp Rangers (St. Helena Parish), were from New Orleans.[12]

Company A: Crescent City Guards, from New Orleans, Capt. John A. Hall commanding.

Company B: Chalmette Rifle Guards, from New Orleans, Capt. A. E. Shaw commanding. Fifty-nine percent of the men in this company were foreign-born. It suffered a 28 percent desertion/oath rate and a 28 percent mortality rate.

Company C: Bienville Guards, from New Orleans, Capt. Mark L. Moore commanding. This company suffered a 19 percent desertion rate.

Company D: DeSoto Rifles, from New Orleans, Capt. William B. Koontz commanding.

Company E: Orleans Cadets (Co. B), from New Orleans, Capt. Charles Hobday commanding. Forty-six percent of the men in this company were foreign-born, and it suffered a 20 percent desertion rate.

Company F: Orleans Southrons, from New Orleans, Capt. Ossian F. Peck commanding. This company had a 34 percent desertion/oath rate, but only 22 percent of the men were foreign-born.

Company G: Louisiana Swamp Rangers, from St. Helena Parish, Capt. Edward J. Jones commanding. Seventy-two percent of the men in this company were foreign-born, and 39 percent deserted or took the oath of allegiance.

Company H: Perret Guards, from New Orleans, Capt. Arthur Connor commanding. It was claimed that this company consisted mostly of gamblers, and one soldier wrote that "to be admitted one must be able to cut, shuffle, and deal on the point of a bayonet."[13]

Company I: Carondelet Invincibles, from New Orleans, Capt. Bruce Menger commanding.

Company K: Monroe Guards (Rifles), from New Orleans, Capt. Thomas Dolan commanding.

Records indicate the Louisiana Greys also served in the regiment.[14]

6TH LOUISIANA VOLUNTEERS

The statistical figures for the 6th Louisiana come from James Gannon's book *Irish Rebels*. This regiment, also known as the Irish Brigade, was mustered into service on June 4, 1861, with eight companies for the duration of the war and two for twelve months. The regiment's official enrollment was 1,146, but Gannon has identified 1,215 men who served in the unit. Records indicate that 219 were killed or mortally wounded (Gannon could only verify 180), 104 died of disease, 5 were killed accidentally, 1 was executed for desertion, 1 drowned, at least 269 deserted, and 76 took the oath of allegiance. Fifty-two men were still on duty when the regiment surrendered at Appomattox. Of those, at least 30 were original 1861 volunteers and nearly half of them had been prisoners of war at some time. The regiment had a large number of New Orleans Irish laborers who were said to be "turbulent in camp and requiring a strong hand, but responding to kindness and justice, and ready to follow their officers to the death."[15]

Of the 949 members whose birthplaces are known, two-thirds were foreign-born. There were 468 born in Ireland; 164 in Louisiana; 135 in other states; 113 in the Germanic states; 25 in England; 14 in France; 9 in Canada; 7 in Scotland; 3 each in Italy and Switzerland; 2 in Norway; and 1 each "at sea" and in Belgium, Cuba, Malta, Mexico, and Sweden. Of all the Louisiana Tiger regiments, the 6th Louisiana had the highest known percentage of foreign-born members (68 percent) and desertions (22 percent).[16]

The regiment's original officers were Col. Isaac G. Seymour, Lt. Col. Louis Lay, and Maj. Samuel L. James. The 6th Louisiana had three successive commanders killed in action. When Seymour was killed at Gaines' Mill, Henry B. Strong took command and served until he was killed at Antietam. Captain H. Bain Ritchie took over in the midst of the same battle, but he, too, was killed later in the day. William Monaghan was promoted to colonel in November 1862 and led the regiment until he was given command of the consolidated Louisiana Brigade in 1864. Although not in command of the 6th Louisiana at the time, Monaghan was killed in a skirmish on August 25, 1864. Regimental command then fell to Lt. Col. Joseph Hanlon, and when he was captured at Cedar Creek, Maj. William H. Manning took over and surrendered the men at Appomattox.[17] In addition to these commanders, 15 other officers were killed or mortally wounded, 1 was killed accidentally, 2 died of disease, and 3 deserted to the enemy.

Company A: Union and Sabine Rifles, from Union and Sabine parishes, Capt. Arthur McArthur commanding. Fifteen percent of this company deserted and/or took the oath of allegiance.

Company B: Calhoun Guards, from New Orleans, Capt. Henry B. Strong commanding. Ninety-three percent of the men in this company were foreign-born, with 85 percent of those being Irish. Thirty percent deserted and/or took the oath of allegiance.[18]

Company C: St. Landry Light Guards, from St. Landry Parish, Capt. Nat Offut commanding. Eighteen percent of the men in this company deserted and/or took the oath of allegiance.[19]

Company D: Tensas Rifles, from Tensas Parish, Capt. Charles B. Tenney commanding. This company left home with 101 men, and another 25 joined later.[20]

Company E: Mercer (Rifle) Guards, from Orleans Parish, Capt. Thomas F. Walker commanding. This company was temporarily assigned to Capt. Thomas

Bowyer's Virginia artillery battery from April 17 to August 12, 1862. About one-third of the men were Irish-born, and an incredible 45 percent deserted and/or took the oath of allegiance.[21]

Company F: Irish Brigade (Co. B), from New Orleans, Capt. William Monaghan commanding. Ninety-one percent of the men in this company were Irish-born, and 35 percent deserted and/or took the oath of allegiance.[22]

Company G: Pemberton Rangers, from New Orleans, Capt. Isaac A. Smith commanding. Of the 104 men who served in this company, none was born in Louisiana. Ninety-eight percent were foreign-born, with 78 percent of those being Germans. The company suffered a 43 percent desertion/oath rate, and 20 men were killed, mortally wounded, or died.[23]

Company H: Orleans Rifles (Guards), from New Orleans, Capt. Thomas F. Fisher commanding. About one-third of this company was Irish-born.

Company I: Irish Brigade (Co. A), from New Orleans, Capt. James Hanlon commanding. This company contained no native-born Louisianians. It was 89 percent foreign-born and suffered a 38 percent desertion/oath rate.[24]

Company K: Violet Guards, from New Orleans, Capt. William H. Manning commanding. About half of this company was Irish-born. Twenty-three of the 125 men were killed, mortally wounded, or died.[25]

Records indicate the Southron Guards also served in the 6th Louisiana.[26]

7TH LOUISIANA VOLUNTEERS

The 7th Louisiana, sometimes called the Pelican Regiment, was mustered into service for the duration of the war on June 5, 1861. The regiment's total enrollment was 1,077. Of these, 190 men were killed or mortally wounded, 68 died of disease, 2 were killed accidentally, 1 was murdered, 1 was executed, at least 53 deserted, and 57 took the oath of allegiance. Forty-four men were still on duty when the regiment surrendered at Appomattox. The unit was composed mostly of clerks, laborers, and farmers and was described by Richard Taylor as being a "crack regiment."[27] Many of its members belonged to the prestigious Pickwick Club of New Orleans, which presented a flag to the regiment before it left for Virginia.[28] At least 60 percent of the unit was foreign-born, with about 43 percent of the men hailing from Ireland. Of the 980 members who gave a place of birth, 373 were born in Louisiana; 329 in Ireland; 179 in states outside of Louisiana; at least 123 in the Germanic states; 24 in England; 9 in Canada; 5 in France; 3 in Switzerland; 2 each in Scotland and Sweden; and 1 each in Hungary, Spain, Italy, and the West Indies.

The regiment's original officers were Col. Harry T. Hays, Lt. Col. Charles de Choiseul, and Maj. Davidson B. Penn. When Hays was promoted to brigadier general on July 25, 1862, Penn was promoted to colonel and assumed command of the regiment (De Choiseul was mortally wounded at Port Republic). After Penn was captured at Rappahannock Station, Lt. Col. Thomas M. Terry took command, although Maj. J. Moore Wilson also led the regiment whenever Terry was absent. During the war, 13 officers were killed or mortally wounded, and 1 died of disease.

The 7th Louisiana was an exception to the rule of foreign-dominated regiments having high desertion rates. The Virginia Guards had a 63 percent foreign makeup but only a 10 percent desertion rate, the Sarsfield Rangers was 75 percent foreign-born but lost only 10 percent to desertion, and the Irish Volunteers was 92 percent Irish-born but had a 17 percent desertion/oath rate.

Company A: Continental Guards (Co. A), from New Orleans, Capt. George Clark commanding.

Company B: Baton Rouge Fencibles, from Baton Rouge, Capt. Andrew S. Herron commanding.

Company C: Sarsfield Rangers, from New Orleans, Capt. J. Moore Wilson commanding. Seventy-five percent of this company was foreign-born.

Company D: Virginia Guards, from New Orleans, Capt. Robert P. Scott commanding. Sixty-three percent of this company was foreign-born.

Company E: Crescent Rifles (Co. B), from New Orleans, Capt. Samuel H. Gilman commanding.

Company F: Irish Volunteers, from Assumption Parish, Capt. William B. Ratliff commanding. Ninety-six percent of this company was Irish-born.

Company G: American Rifles, from New Orleans, Capt. William D. Ricarby commanding.

Company H: Crescent Rifles (Co. C), from New Orleans, Capt. Henry T. Jett commanding. Thirty-six percent of this company was foreign-born.

Company I: Virginia Blues, from New Orleans, Capt. Daniel A. Wilson, Jr., commanding. This company was 80 percent Irish-born and suffered a 23 percent desertion/oath rate and a 27 percent mortality rate.

Company K: Livingston Rifles, from Livingston Parish, Capt. Thomas M. Terry commanding.

8TH LOUISIANA VOLUNTEERS

The 8th Louisiana was mustered into service on June 15, 1861, with seven companies for the duration of the war and three for twelve months. The regiment's total enrollment was 1,321. Of these, 252 men were killed or mortally wounded, 171 died of disease, 2 were murdered, 1 was killed accidentally, at least 8 deserted, and 56 took the oath of allegiance. Fifty-seven men were still on duty when the regiment surrendered at Appomattox. Of the 1,114 members who gave a place of birth, 542 were born in Louisiana; 299 in other states; 141 in Ireland; 44 in the Germanic states; 26 in France; 21 in England; 8 in Canada; 5 each in Mexico and Denmark; 4 each in Belgium and Holland; 4 in Sweden; 3 each in Norway and Scotland; 2 each in Brazil and Switzerland; and 1 each in Cuba, Italy, Martinique, and Russia. The 8th Louisiana was composed mainly of farmers and laborers and was one of the most multinational Tiger regiments. For some reason, it also had the most known Scandinavians of any Tiger unit.[29]

In his memoirs, Richard Taylor inaccurately claimed that the regiment was raised from the Bayou Teche region of Louisiana and was composed of Creoles. Actually, few of its companies were from the Teche country. Judging from Taylor's description of the regiment, however, the Acadians were the most conspicuous element of the command because of their French language, lively music, and dancing.[30]

The regiment's original officers were Col. Henry B. Kelly, Lt. Col. Francis T. Nicholls, and Maj. John B. Prados. Kelly resigned in April 1863 and was succeeded by Trevanion D. Lewis, but he was killed at Gettysburg. Alcibiades DeBlanc was then promoted to colonel, but he never recovered from a Gettysburg wound and did not rejoin the regiment. Germain A. Lester was promoted to lieutenant colonel and took over, but he was killed at Cold Harbor, and command fell to Capt. Louis Prados, who surrendered the regiment at Appomattox. During the war, 19 of the regiment's officers were killed or mortally wounded, 1 died of disease, and 1 deserted to the enemy.

Company A: Creole Guards, from Baton Rouge, Capt. Leon J. Fremaux commanding. Only 34 percent of this company was foreign-born, but it suffered a 28 percent desertion/oath rate. Twenty-nine percent of its members died during the war.[31]

Company B: Bienville Rifles, from New Orleans, Capt. Augustin Larose commanding. This company had men from twelve foreign countries. Of its 142 members, 20 percent deserted or took the oath.[32]

Company C: Attakapas Guards, from St. Martin Parish, Capt. Alex. DeBlanc commanding. Twenty-nine percent of this company was foreign-born, but only 8 percent deserted.[33]

Company D: Sumter Guards, from New Orleans, Capt. Francis Newman commanding. Sixty-seven percent of this company was foreign-born, and it had a 27 percent desertion/oath rate.[34]

Company E: Franklin Sharpshooters, from Winnsboro, Capt. Germain A. Lester commanding. This company had a 33 percent mortality rate.[35]

Company F: Opelousas Guards, from St. Landry Parish, Capt. James C. Pratt com-
     manding.[36]
Company G: Minden Blues, from Minden, Capt. John L. Lewis commanding. This
     company had a 24 percent mortality rate.[37]
Company H: Cheneyville Rifles (Blues), from Cheneyville, Capt. Patrick F. Keary
     commanding.[38]
Company I: Rapides Invincibles, from Alexandria, Capt. Lee Crandell commanding.
     This company had a 26 percent mortality rate.[39]
Company K: Phoenix Guards, from Ascension and Assumption parishes, Capt. Law-
     rence D. Nicholls commanding. This company had a 29 percent mortality rate.[40]

9TH LOUISIANA VOLUNTEERS

The 9th Louisiana was mustered into service on July 6, 1861, with six companies for
the duration of the war and four for twelve months. The regiment's total enrollment
was 1,474. Of these, 233 men were killed or mortally wounded, 349 died of disease,
4 were killed accidentally, at least 115 deserted, and 25 took the oath of allegiance.
Sixty-eight men were still on duty when the regiment surrendered at Appomattox.
The regiment was composed mostly of North Louisiana farmers. Of the 1,168 members who gave a place of birth, 652 were born in states outside of Louisiana; 399 in
Louisiana; 85 in Ireland; 21 in the Germanic states; 5 in England; 2 in Canada; 1 each
in France, Norway, and Poland; and 1 listed as "Indian."

The regiment's original officers were Col. Richard Taylor, Lt. Col. Edward G. Randolph, and Maj. N. J. Walker. When Taylor was promoted to brigadier general in 1861,
Randolph took command of the regiment. Leroy A. Stafford defeated Randolph for the
colonel's position during the army's reorganization in April 1862 and led the regiment
until he was promoted to brigadier general in October 1863. William R. Peck was
then promoted to colonel, but he assumed command of the 1st Louisiana Brigade in
1864, and Lt. Col. John. J. Hodges took over the regiment. Hodges was captured at the
Monocacy, and senior line officers led the unit afterward. During the war, 19 officers
were killed or mortally wounded and 5 died of disease.

The 9th Louisiana claimed several honors during the war. It was the largest of the
Tiger regiments, and three brigadier generals were promoted from its ranks. It also
had the highest mortality rate and was the only regiment that had more men to die of
disease than in battle.

Company A: Moore Fencibles, from Homer, Capt. Richard L. Capers commanding.
     This company apparently was designated as sharpshooters because it fre-

quently was detached from the regiment to perform that duty. Its mortality rate was 30 percent, and 20 percent deserted, mostly to the Trans-Mississippi Department to join other military units.[41]

Company B: Stafford Guards, from Rapides Parish, Capt. Leroy A. Stafford commanding. The mortality rate of this company was 38 percent.[42]

Company C: Bienville Blues, from Bienville Parish, Capt. Benjamin W. Pearce commanding. Sixty-four percent of the men in this company were born in states outside of Louisiana. The mortality rate was 40 percent.[43]

Company D: Bossier Volunteers, from Bossier Parish, Capt. John J. Hodges commanding. Eighty-eight percent of the men in this company were born in states outside of Louisiana. The mortality rate was 38 percent.[44]

Company E: Milliken Bend Guards, from Madison Parish, Capt. William R. Peck commanding. The mortality rate of this company was 42 percent. This was the only company in the regiment with a large number of foreign-born members (55 percent), but only 1 man deserted and 15 took the oath of allegiance.

Company F: DeSoto Blues, from DeSoto Parish, Capt. Henry L. N. Williams commanding. This company's mortality rate was 40 percent.[45]

Company G: Colyell Guards, from Livingston Parish, Capt. John S. Gardner commanding. The total enrollment of this company was 147 men. It had a 39 percent mortality rate, with 13 men being killed or mortally wounded, and 44 dying of other causes.[46]

Company H: Brush Valley Guards, from Bienville Parish, Capt. William F. Gray commanding. Eighty-two percent of the men in this company were born in states outside of Louisiana. The mortality rate was 47 percent.[47]

Company I: Washington Rifles, from Washington Parish, Capt. Hardy Richardson commanding. The mortality rate of this company was 49 percent. Of the 140 men, 68 were killed, mortally wounded, or died, and 90 were wounded (the number of dead and wounded exceeds the number of members because some of the men who died were previously wounded).[48]

Company K: Jackson Greys, from Jackson Parish, Capt. James R. Cavanaugh commanding.[49]

10TH LOUISIANA VOLUNTEERS

The 10th Louisiana's muster rolls do not appear in the Bound Volumes at Tulane University, so much of the following information comes from Thomas Walter Brooks' and Michael Dan Jones' *Lee's Foreign Legion*, which has a tremendous amount of statistical information on the Tigers' most multinational regiment. The 10th Louisiana was mustered into service for the duration of the war on July 22, 1861. Its total enrollment was 953 men, of whom 138 were killed or mortally wounded, 59 died of disease, 5 were killed accidentally, 4 were murdered, 140 deserted (66 of those who deserted did so to join other Confederate units), and at least 163 took the oath of allegiance (42 of those joined the Union army). Sixteen men were still on duty when the regiment surrendered at Appomattox.

The regiment was composed of men from 21 nations (only three of the companies were predominantly Anglo-American), and most were laborers, farmers, and sailors. Of those giving a place of birth, 170 were born in Louisiana; 71 in states outside Louisiana; 249 in Ireland; 84 in the Germanic states; 44 in France; 26 in Italy; 24 in England; 20 in Spain; 9 in Canada; 7 each in Austria, Greece, and Mexico; 5 in Gibraltar; 4 in Portugal; 3 in Sicily; 2 in Norway; and 1 each in Corsica, Cuba, Martinique, Russia, Sardinia, and Switzerland.[50]

The regiment's original officers were Col. Mandeville Marigny, Lt. Col. Jules C. Denis, and Maj. Felix DuMonteil. Marigny was a former French army officer who patterned the 10th Louisiana after the French army regiments with which he had previous experience. The French language and manual of arms were used to train the unit.[51] Marigny resigned in July 1862, but he must have left the regiment at an earlier date because Lt. Col. Eugene Waggaman led the men during the Seven Days Campaign. When Waggaman was captured at Malvern Hill, Lt. Col. William Spencer took command, but he was killed two months later at Second Manassas. John M. Legett then took over, but he was also killed at Chancellorsville. Command fell to Henry Monier, but in mid-1864 Waggaman returned from extended duty in Louisiana and resumed his place. When Waggaman was promoted to command the consolidated Louisiana Brigade in February 1865, Monier again took command of the regiment and surrendered it at Appomattox. During the war, 13 of the officers were killed or mortally wounded and 2 died of disease.

Company A: Shepherd Guards, from New Orleans, Capt. Alex. Phillips commanding. This company's largest ethnic group was Irish.

Company B: Derbigny Guards, from New Orleans, Capt. Lea F. Bakewell commanding. Little is known of this company's ethnic identity.

Company C: Hewitt Guards, from Bayou Lafourche, Capt. Richard M. Hewitt commanding. This company's largest ethnic group was Irish.

Company D: Hawkins Guards, from New Orleans, Capt. Charles F. White commanding. This company's largest ethnic group was Irish.

Company E: Louisiana Swamp Rifles, from Pointe Coupee Parish, Capt. David M. Dickey commanding. This company's largest ethnic group was Anglo-American.

Company F: Louisiana Rebels, from New Orleans, Capt. John M. Legett commanding. This company's largest ethnic group was German.

Company G: Orleans Rangers, from New Orleans, Capt. Edward Crevon commanding. This company's largest ethnic group was Anglo-American.

Company H: Orleans Blues, New Orleans, Capt. William B. Barnett commanding.
This company's largest ethnic group was Irish.

Company I: Tirailleurs D'Orleans, from New Orleans, Capt. Eugene Waggaman commanding. This company's largest ethnic group was Italian.

Company K: Confederate States Rangers, from St. Landry Parish, Capt. William H.
Spencer commanding. This company's largest ethnic group was Anglo-American.

Records indicate that the Stars of Equality and the Atchafalaya Guards also served
in this regiment.[52]

14TH LOUISIANA VOLUNTEERS

The 14th Louisiana's muster rolls do not appear in the Bound Volumes at Tulane University. Therefore, some information is lacking. This regiment was created because
the Confederate government wanted to win the support of the South's foreign-born
population. Thus, it was decided to raise a Polish brigade in New Orleans. The 14th
Louisiana was originally known as the 1st Regiment, Polish Brigade (although hardly
any Poles were members) and was mustered into service for the duration of the war
on June 16, 1861. Ten companies made up the 1st Regiment, Polish Brigade, but the
Franco (Rifle) Guards was disbanded for its role in the Grand Junction riot. When it
was replaced in September 1861, the unit was renamed the 14th Louisiana Volunteers.

The regiment's total enrollment was 1,026. Of these, 184 men were killed or mortally wounded; 85 died of disease; 7 were killed or mortally wounded during the riot at
Grand Junction, Tennessee; and 1 each was killed accidentally, executed, and drowned.
It is not known how many men deserted. Twenty-three men were still on duty when
the regiment surrendered at Appomattox. The members were predominantly German,
French, and Irish, with many being Mississippi River boatmen. The 14th Louisiana was
difficult to discipline because of the soldiers' different nationalities and languages and
the malicious nature of many of its members. William P. Snakenberg declared that
three of the companies "could claim anywhere they were as home, men who worked
on the levee, loading and unloading boats all day, and spend their wages at night for
drink, sleep off their carousal under a canvas or tarpaulin until morning, then go to
work again."[53]

The regiment's original officers were Col. Valery Sulakowski, Lt. Col. Richard W.

Jones, and Maj. Zebulon York. Sulakowski, a Polish immigrant, served until his resignation in January 1862. He was succeeded by Jones, who also resigned in August 1862. York was then promoted to colonel and led the regiment until his promotion to brigadier general on June 2, 1864. Colonel David Zable assumed command, but he led some of the men to North Carolina for detached duty in early 1865. Senior line officers took charge of the men who were left in Virginia. Although no field officers died during the war, 10 line officers were killed or mortally wounded, 1 died of disease, and 5 deserted to the enemy.

Company A: Armstrong Guards, from Tensas Parish, Capt. Thomas P. Farrar commanding.

Company B (first): Franco (Rifle) Guards, from New Orleans, Capt. Robert Dalton commanding. This company was disbanded because of its role in the Grand Junction, Tennessee, riot.

Company B (second): Jefferson Cadets (Guards), from New Orleans, Capt. W. H. Zimmerman commanding. This company replaced the Franco (Rifle) Guards when it was disbanded. Forty-seven percent of the men were Irish-born, and 32 percent deserted. Records show that the Jefferson Cadets (Guards) also served with the 15th Louisiana.

Company C: Askew Guards, from New Orleans, Capt. John W. T. Leech commanding. This company also served with the 3rd Louisiana Battalion, 1st Louisiana, and 15th Louisiana. It is not known when it became part of the 14th Louisiana.

Company D (first): Empire Rangers, from Plaquemines Parish, Capt. Robert A. Wilkinson commanding. This company was later designated Company H.

Company D (second): McClure Guards, from New Orleans, Capt. Robert M. Austin commanding. This company was designated Company D when the Empire Rangers were redesignated Company H.

Company E: Nixon Rifles, from Pointe Coupee Parish, Capt. William H. Cooley commanding.

Company F: Concordia Rifles, from Concordia Parish, Capt. William H. Toler commanding.

Company G: Avegno Rifles, from New Orleans, Capt. P. F. Mancosas commanding.

Company H (first): Empire Rangers, from Plaquemines Parish, Capt. Robert A. Wilkinson commanding. The Empire Rangers originally were Company D but then were designated Company H. In December 1861, it changed places with the Quitman Rangers in the 3rd Louisiana Battalion.

Company H (second): Quitman Rangers, from New Orleans, Capt. Henry Gillum commanding. This company was originally part of the 3rd Louisiana Battalion, but Captain Gillum requested it be transferred after accusing Lieutenant Colonel Bradford, the commander of the 3rd Louisiana Battalion, of being unfit, immoral, and a drunkard. Thus, on November 27, 1861, the Quitman Rangers changed places with the Empire Rangers.

Company I (first): Tiger Bayou Rifles, from Carroll Parish, Capt. Field F. Montgomery commanding. This company was added to the regiment during the summer of 1861 but then may have transferred to the 1st Louisiana on August 5, 1861. It may have been replaced by the Catahoula Guerrillas.

Company I (possibly second): Catahoula Guerrillas, from Catahoula Parish, Capt. Jonathan W. Buhoup commanding. One source claims that this company replaced the Tiger Bayou Rifles when it transferred to the 1st Louisiana, but this is not corroborated by other sources. Either the Catahoula Guerrillas were added to the regiment in September 1861, or the records are in error on the date, and the Polish Brigade became the 14th Louisiana when the Tiger Bayou Rifles were added.[54]

Company K: Lafayette Rifle Cadets, from New Orleans, Capt. David Zable commanding. This company had 96 original members and was formed around Gretna's Hope Baseball and LaQuarte Team. Zable was president of the club. It had a heavy foreign influence with at least 31 members being born in the Germanic states, 20 in Ireland, 4 in England, and 1 in France. Sixteen men deserted, 4 of whom did so to join other Confederate units, and 3 took the oath of allegiance. This company is somewhat of an anomaly. Its members were predominantly foreign-born, but less than 12 percent of the foreign-born men deserted, while 30 percent of the native-born did. Not included in these statistics are 16 conscripts who were added later, 44 percent of whom deserted.[55]

15TH LOUISIANA VOLUNTEERS

The 15th Louisiana was originally known as the 2nd Regiment, Polish Brigade, although no known Poles were members (see the 14th Louisiana, above, for details on the Polish Brigade). The regiment was mustered into service with eight companies for the duration of the war on June 16, 1861. It was renamed the 3rd Battalion, Louisiana Infantry, on September 7 after it arrived in Virginia, with a promise to become the 15th Louisiana once two more companies were added. This occurred when the Catahoula Guerrillas and Crescent City Blues (Rifles) of St. Paul's Foot Rifles were added on August 2, 1862. The regiment's total enrollment was 901. Of these, 143 men were killed or mortally wounded, 98 died of disease, 1 was executed, at least 130 deserted, and 13 took the oath of allegiance. Eighteen men were still on duty when the regiment surrendered at Appomattox. The regiment was composed mainly of farmers, laborers, and clerks. Of the 520 members who gave a place of birth, 161 were born in Louisiana, 157 in other states, 118 in Ireland, 36 in the Germanic states, 17 in England, 11 in France, 10 were "Indians," 6 in Scotland, 3 in Canada, and 1 in Russia.

The regiment's original officers were Col. Francis T. Nicholls and Lt. Col. Edmund Pendleton, although Nicholls may never have actually served with the unit because he was recuperating from a wound when it was organized. When Nicholls was promoted to brigadier general on October 14, 1862, Pendleton succeeded him as colonel and surrendered the regiment at Appomattox. Nine of the regiment's officers were killed or mortally wounded during the war.[56]

Company A: Askew Guards, from New Orleans, Capt. Andrew Brady commanding. This company originally was part of the 3rd Louisiana Battalion and then served in the 1st Louisiana before being transferred to the 15th Louisiana on May 22, 1862. Records indicate it also served in the 14th Louisiana, but it is not known when it joined that regiment.

Company B: Empire Rangers, from New Orleans, Capt. Henry J. Egan commanding. This company originally served in the 14th Louisiana but was later transferred to the 3rd Louisiana Battalion and then the 15th Louisiana.

Company C: Grosse Tete Creoles, from Iberville Parish, Capt. William Bowman commanding. This company originally served in the 3rd Louisiana Battalion and had a 31 percent mortality rate.

Company D: St. Ceran Rifles, from New Orleans, Capt. Levi T. Jennings commanding. This company originally served in the 3rd Louisiana Battalion. It was 74 percent foreign-born and suffered a 25 percent desertion rate.

Company E: Grivot (Guards) Rifles, from New Orleans, Capt. Samuel D. McChesney commanding. This company originally served in the 3rd Louisiana Battalion.

Company F: St. James Rifles (Rebels), from New Orleans, Capt. Charles W. McClellan commanding. This company had a 45 percent desertion rate, but it is not known whether it had a large number of foreign-born members.

Company G: Davenport Rebels (Rifles), from Morehouse Parish, Capt. William C. Michie commanding. This company originally served in the 3rd Louisiana Battalion and had a 42 percent mortality rate.

Company H: Bogart Guards, from New Orleans, Capt. Joseph F. Wetherup commanding. This company originally served in the 3rd Louisiana Battalion.

Company I: Catahoula Guerrillas, from Catahoula Parish, Capt. Samuel W. Spencer commanding. This company previously served in Wheat's Battalion, St. Paul's

Foot Rifles, and Coppens' Zouaves. It transferred to the 15th Louisiana from the latter unit on August 2, 1862. Records indicate it also served in the 1st Louisiana.

Company K: Crescent City Blues (Rifles) (Co. B), from New Orleans, Capt. A. M. Ashbridge commanding. This company previously served with the 49th Virginia Infantry, St. Paul's Foot Rifles, and Coppens' Battalion. It transferred to the 15th Louisiana from the latter unit on August 2, 1862.

Records indicate the Jefferson Cadets (Guards) also served with the 15th Louisiana.

1ST SPECIAL BATTALION, LOUISIANA INFANTRY (WHEAT'S BATTALION)

The muster rolls for Wheat's Battalion do not appear in the Bound Volumes at Tulane University. Most of the following information comes from Gary Schreckengost's *First Louisiana Special Battalion* and Michael Dan Jones' *Tiger Rifles*. The 1st Special Battalion, Louisiana Infantry, commonly known as Wheat's Battalion, was mustered into service with five companies for the duration of the war on June 9, 1861. The total enrollment of the battalion was 550, of whom 17 were killed or mortally wounded, 11 died of disease, 4 were killed accidentally, 2 were executed, and 40 deserted.

Few Civil War commands consisted of companies as diverse as those of Wheat's Battalion. The Catahoula Guerrillas were largely made up of planters' sons (and was the only company that was not raised in New Orleans), the Walker Guards was a company of soldiers of fortune, and the Tiger Rifles had numerous criminals within its ranks. General Richard Taylor claimed that Wheat's Battalion was "so villainous . . . that every commander desired to be rid of it."[57] The unit was quickly dubbed the "Tiger Battalion" because of its unruly behavior, and the term was soon applied to all of the Louisiana infantry in the Army of Northern Virginia.

Roberdeau Wheat was appointed major and commanded the battalion until he was wounded at First Manassas. While he recovered, Lt. Col. Charles de Choiseul of the 7th Louisiana took temporary command. When Wheat was killed at Gaines' Mill, Robert Harris took over the battalion. Because of heavy casualties during the Valley Campaign and the Seven Days, the battalion was disbanded on August 21, 1862.[58]

Company A: Walker Guards, from New Orleans, Capt. Robert A. Harris commanding. Irish boatmen and stevedores dominated this company. Captain Harris was a former filibusterer, and it was claimed that every member of his company had served under William Walker during his filibustering expedition to Nicaragua in the 1850s. Of the 97 members, 1 was killed, 1 died of disease, and 9 deserted.[59]

APPENDIX

Company B: Tiger Rifles, from New Orleans, Capt. Alex White commanding. The Tiger Rifles became the most famous Louisiana company in Virginia, but specific information is known for only about 20 percent of its members. Of those, most of the foreign-born men hailed from Ireland, and most of the native-born came from Kentucky. This company was also raised on the New Orleans waterfront, and at least 40 of the men had prior military experience. Of the 101 members, 7 were killed or mortally wounded, 3 died in accidents, 2 were executed, 1 died of disease, and 8 deserted.

Company C: Delta Rangers, from New Orleans, Capt. Henry C. Gardner commanding. This company's flag was used as the battalion colors, and the other company flags were retired. Of the 92 members, 3 were killed or mortally wounded, 3 died of illness, and 9 deserted.

Company D (first): Catahoula Guerrillas, from Catahoula Parish, Capt. Jonathan W. Buhoup commanding. This company was organized with the intention of joining the cavalry but decided on the infantry because of the difficulties involved in transporting horses. Of the 129 members, 15 were killed or mortally wounded, 17 died of disease, and 9 deserted. When the Catahoula Guerrillas transferred to St. Paul's Foot Rifles on November 1, 1861, at Captain Buhoup's request, the Old Dominion Guards were designated Company D. It is not known why the Catahoula Guerrillas transferred from the battalion, but Hiram Sample claimed it was "owing to a disagreement between our officers." The company later transferred from St. Paul's Foot Rifles to Coppens' Battalion, and then to the 3rd Louisiana Battalion on August 2, 1862, to create the 15th Louisiana. Records indicate that the company also served with the 1st and 14th Louisiana. The Catahoula Guerrillas was the only one of Wheat's companies to serve throughout the war.[60]

Company D (second): Old Dominion Guards, from New Orleans, Capt. Obediah P. Miller commanding. Originally designated Company E, the Old Dominion Guards were designated Company D when the Catahoula Guerrillas transferred out of the battalion.

Company E (first): Old Dominion Guards, from New Orleans, Capt. Obediah P. Miller commanding. When the Catahoula Guerrillas left the battalion, the Old Dominion Guards were designated Company D. Of the 78 members, 2 were killed or mortally wounded, 1 died accidentally, and 1 deserted.

Company E (second): Wheat's Life Guards, from New Orleans, Capt. Robert Going Atkins commanding. This company was originally called the Rough and Ready Rangers but was disbanded when it could not fill its ranks and later reformed as the Orleans Claiborne Guards. It joined Wheat's Battalion in October 1861 to replace the departing Catahoula Guerrillas and replaced the Old Dominion Guards as Company E. At that time, Captain Atkins renamed the company Wheat's Life Guards. Of the 73 members, none was killed, 1 died of disease, and 4 deserted. Records indicate that the Orleans Claiborne Guards were also assigned to the battalion in June 1861.[61]

1ST BATTALION, LOUISIANA VOLUNTEERS (DREUX'S BATTALION)

The muster rolls of Dreux's Battalion do not appear in the Bound Volumes at Tulane University. Therefore, some information is lacking. The 1st Battalion, Louisiana Volunteers, commonly known as Dreux's Battalion, was composed of the first volunteer companies to respond to Louisiana's call for troops and was said to be made up of New Orleans' finest gentlemen.[62] In June 1861, five Louisiana companies stationed at Pensacola, Florida, were mustered into service for twelve months as the 1st Battalion, Louisiana Volunteers, with a sixth company being added in July. Total enrollment was 545, of whom 2 men were killed and 16 died of disease. The battalion was to muster out of service in April 1862, but the men volunteered to remain on duty until after the Battle of Yorktown. After the battalion was disbanded, most of the men reorganized as Fenner's Artillery and fought in the western theater.

Charles D. Dreux was elected lieutenant colonel of the battalion and served until he was killed in a skirmish on July 5, 1861. He was the first Louisianian and the first Confederate field officer to be killed in the war. N. H. Rightor succeeded him.[63]

Company A: Louisiana Guards (Co. A), from New Orleans, Capt. Samuel M. Todd commanding.

Company B: Crescent City Rifles (Co. A), from New Orleans, Capt. Stuart W. Fisk commanding.

Company C: Louisiana Guards (Co. C), from New Orleans, Capt. Francis Rawle commanding. This was the sixth company that was added to the battalion.[64]

Company D: Shreveport Greys, from Shreveport, Capt. James H. Beard commanding. After the battalion was disbanded, this company was transferred to the 1st Louisiana Volunteers on June 27, 1862.[65]

Company E: Grivot Guards (also known as the Terrebonne Rifles), from Lafourche Parish, Capt. Capt. F. S. Goode commanding.

Company F: Orleans Cadets, from New Orleans, Capt. Charles D. Dreux commanding. When mustered into service on April 11, 1861, this company became the first Louisiana volunteer company to enter the Confederate army. Of its 103 members, 37 were under eighteen years old, and it was claimed that Dreux was the only married man in the company.[66]

1ST BATTALION, LOUISIANA ZOUAVES (COPPENS' BATTALION)

The 1st Battalion, Louisiana Zouaves' muster rolls do not appear in the Bound Volumes at Tulane University. Therefore, some information is lacking. This battalion, commonly known as Coppens' Battalion, was raised under the personal authorization of Jefferson Davis, and he promised to increase the battalion to regimental strength should war come. It adopted the French Zouave uniform, French drill manual, and received all of its drill instructions in French. The battalion's six companies were raised in New Orleans, and, like Wheat's Battalion, it was rumored that some of the men were recruited from the city's jails. In reality, most of the members were laborers. About 20 percent of the battalion was said to be Swiss, and there was also a large number of Germans, Italians, Spanish, Irish, and English in the ranks. Coppens' Battalion mustered into service for twelve months at Pensacola, Florida, on March 27, 1861, but it was never increased to a full regiment.[67]

Of the 616 men who served in the battalion, 52 were killed or mortally wounded, 26 died of disease, and 2 were killed accidentally.[68]

Gaston Coppens was appointed the battalion's lieutenant colonel and served until he was mortally wounded at Antietam. His brother, Marie Alfred Coppens, then took command, and the battalion was eventually mustered into the regular Confederate army as the Confederate States Zouave Battalion. It was detached from the Army of Northern Virginia during the latter half of the war and performed various duties in Virginia.[69]

Company A: from New Orleans, Capt. Leopold Lange commanding.
Company B: from New Orleans, Fulgence De Bordenave commanding.
Company C: from New Orleans, Capt. Howard H. Zacharic commanding.
Company D: from New Orleans, Capt. Nemoura Lauve commanding.
Company E (first): from New Orleans, Capt. Paul F. DeGournay commanding. This company was detached from the battalion to serve as the Orleans Heavy Artillery.
Company E (second): 1st Company Foot Rifles, from New Orleans, Capt. Charles M. Rene commanding. This company transferred from St. Paul's Foot Rifles in August 1862 to replace DeGournay's company.
Company F: from New Orleans, Capt. Marie Alfred Coppens commanding.
Company G: Crescent City Blues (Co. B), from New Orleans, Capt. McGavock Good-

wyn commanding. This company transferred to the battalion from St. Paul's Foot Rifles in August 1862 and later transferred to the 15th Louisiana.

Company H: Catahoula Guerrillas, from Catahoula Parish, Capt. Samuel W. Spencer commanding. This company transferred to the battalion from St. Paul's Foot Rifles in August 1862 and later transferred to the 15th Louisiana.

3RD BATTALION, LOUISIANA INFANTRY
(BRADFORD'S OR PENDLETON'S BATTALION)

The 3rd Battalion, Louisiana Infantry, was originally mustered into service for the duration of the war on June 16, 1861, as the 2nd Regiment, Polish Brigade. It was renamed the 3rd Battalion, Louisiana Infantry, on September 7 after it arrived in Virginia but was usually referred to as Bradford's or Pendleton's Battalion. Its total enrollment was 678, but its losses are not known.

On June 21, 1862, the Catahoula Guerrillas and Crescent City Blues of St. Paul's Battalion were ordered to join the 3rd Louisiana Battalion so it could be designated the 15th Louisiana, but because of heavy fighting on the Peninsula this was not done until August 2.

Charles M. Bradford was elected lieutenant colonel when the battalion was organized, but he resigned on June 5, 1862, after being convicted of conduct unbecoming an officer, contempt for a superior, and disobedience. Edmund Pendleton then took command and served until the battalion was designated the 15th Louisiana Volunteers on August 2, 1862.

Company A: Askew Guards, from New Orleans, Capt. Andrew Brady commanding. This company transferred to the 1st Louisiana, probably in August 1861. It is not known what company replaced it as Company A.

Company B (first): Quitman Rangers, from New Orleans, Capt. Henry Gillum commanding. Gillum succeeded in getting his company transferred to the 14th Louisiana on November 27, 1861, after accusing Lieutenant Colonel Bradford of being unfit, immoral, and a drunkard.

Company B (second): Empire Rangers, from New Orleans, Capt. Robert A. Wilkinson commanding. This company was originally in the 14th Louisiana but exchanged places with the Quitman Rangers when Captain Gillum requested a transfer.

Company C: Grosse Tete Creoles, from Iberville Parish, Capt. William Patrick commanding.

Company D: St. Ceran Rifles, from New Orleans, Cap. Levi T. Jennings commanding.

Company E: Grivot Rifles, from New Orleans, Capt. J. S. West commanding.

Company F: St. James Rifles, from New Orleans, Capt. Adolphe Strauss commanding.

Company G: Davenport Rebels, from Morehouse Parish, Capt. William C. Michie commanding.

Company H: Bogart Guards, from New Orleans, Capt. George J. Mahe commanding.

7TH BATTALION, LOUISIANA INFANTRY (ST. PAUL'S FOOT RIFLES, CHASSEURS À PIED, WASHINGTON INFANTRY BATTALION, OR 19TH LOUISIANA INFANTRY BATTALION)

The muster rolls for the Washington Infantry Battalion do not appear in the Bound Volumes at Tulane University. Therefore, some information is lacking. This battalion was most commonly known as St. Paul's Foot Rifles. On April 19, 1861, the Confederate secretary of war accepted Belgian-born Henry St. Paul de Lechard's 1st Company of Foot Rifles (Chasseurs à Pied) directly into Confederate service. On October 1, the Crescent City Blues (Co. B) was added to St. Paul's company to form the battalion. The Catahoula Guerrillas were transferred from Wheat's Battalion to St. Paul's Foot Rifles on November 1.

The battalion's total enrollment was 316, but its losses are unknown. When the small unit was disbanded in August 1862, the companies were transferred to Coppens' Battalion, and later the Catahoula Guerrillas and Crescent City Blues were transferred to the 15th Louisiana. One veteran, however, claimed the battalion, or at least one of its unnamed companies, was detached from the Army of Northern Virginia after the Battle of Fredericksburg and was captured at Fort Gaines, Alabama, on August 5, 1864.[70]

Major Henry St. Paul originally commanded the battalion, but he resigned, although the date is unknown. Captain Edgar Macom was then promoted to take command.

Company A: 1st Company Foot Rifles, from New Orleans, Capt. Edgar Macom commanding. When St. Paul's Foot Rifles battalion was disbanded in August 1862, this company transferred to Coppens' Battalion.[71]

Company B: Catahoula Guerrillas, from Catahoula Parish, Capt. Jonathan W. Buhoup commanding. When the battalion was disbanded, this company transferred to Coppens' Battalion in August 1862 and later to the 15th Louisiana.[72]

Company C: Crescent City Blues (Co. B), from New Orleans, Capt. McGavock Goodwyn commanding. This company went to Virginia unattached and was temporarily attached to the 49th Virginia Infantry at the First Battle of Manassas.

In October 1861, the company was joined with St. Paul's Foot Rifles to form the battalion, and in August 1862 it was attached to Coppens' Battalion. The company later transferred to the 15th Louisiana. Of its members, 38 percent were foreign-born, and it suffered a 24 percent desertion rate.[73]

NOTES

ABBREVIATIONS

ANB	Antietam National Battlefield
CC	Centenary College
DU	Duke University
ECU	East Carolina University
EU	Emory University
FSNMP	Fredericksburg and Spotsylvania National Military Park
GNMP	Gettysburg National Military Park
HL	Huntington Library
HLW	Handley Library, Winchester, Va.
HNOC	Historic New Orleans Collection
JPC	Terry L. Jones Private Collection
LC	Library of Congress
LHAC	Tulane University, Louisiana Historical Association Collection
LSA	Louisiana State Archives
LSU	Louisiana State University, Baton Rouge
LSUS	Louisiana State University, Shreveport
MOC	Museum of the Confederacy
MSCA	Mansfield State Commemorative Area
MSU	McNeese State University
NA	National Archives
NSU	Northwestern State University
NYPL	New York Public Library
RNBP	Richmond National Battlefield Park
SHC	University of North Carolina, Southern Historical Collection
TU	Tulane University
UM	University of Michigan

USAERC   U.S. Army Education and Research Center
    UT   University of Texas
   VHS   Virginia Historical Society Library
   VSL   Virginia State Library

PREFACE

1. New Orleans *Times-Democrat*, in Reminiscences Division, n.d., Confederate Veteran Papers, DU.

2. Sidney J. Romero, "Louisiana Clergy and the Confederate Army," *Louisiana History*, II (1961), 280; Charles L. Dufour, *Gentle Tiger: The Gallant Life of Roberdeau Wheat* (Baton Rouge, 1957), 4.

3. Douglas Southall Freeman, *Lee's Lieutenant: A Study in Command* (3 vols.; New York, 1942, 1944), I, 87; Henry E. Handerson, *Yankee in Gray: The Civil War Memoirs of Henry E. Handerson, with a Selection of His Wartime Letters* (Cleveland, 1962), 33; Leon Jastremski to Robert H. Hemphill, June 8, 1901, in Hemphill Family Papers, DU.

4. Richmond, Va., *Times Dispatch*, June 6, 1915, *Chronicling America*, chroniclingamerica.loc. gov/ (accessed July 29, 2016); June 8, 1915, (accessed August 21, 2016).

CHAPTER 1
ON TO RICHMOND!

1. In this study, all direct quotations retain the soldiers' original grammar and spelling. Some punctuation, however, has been added for clarity. William E. Moore diary, May 26, 1861, typescript copy, in William E. Moore Papers, UT (first quotation); Andrew Newell to Robert A. Newell, June 20, 1861, in Box 1, Folder 2, Robert A. Newell Papers, LSU (second quotation); Andrew B. Booth (comp.), *Records of Louisiana Confederate Soldiers and Louisiana Confederate Commands* (3 vols.; New Orleans, 1920), III, 1271.

2. William E. Trahern, "A Biography of William E. Trahern, Written September 21, 1926," p. 16, RNBP.

3. W. E. Tull, "W. E. Tull's War Story," HLW.

4. "A Leaf from Memory," *Cosgrove's Weekly*, January 14, 1911, in Melrose Scrapbook 230, NSU.

5. William Lichenstein memoir, USAERC. There are no page numbers on the memoir.

6. Terry L. Jones, *The American Civil War* (New York, 2010), 82–85.

7. Natchitoches (La.) *Times*, April 12, 1929, in Melrose Scrapbook 1, NSU.

8. "Cheneyville (La.) Rifles' Flag Returned," *Confederate Veteran*, XIX (1911), 373–74.

9. Michael D. Jones, "Jeff Davis' Pet Wolves," *Civil War Times Illustrated* (March 1989), 30.

10. Bell Irvin Wiley, *The Life of Johnny Reb: The Common Soldier of the Confederacy* (New York, 1962), 21–22. Additional information on flags and flag ceremonies can be found at "Departure of the Baton Rouge Fencibles," *Camp Moore News*, Vol. 13, No. 2 (June 2011), Camp Moore

Museum, Kentwood, Louisiana; Trahern, "Biography," RNBP; "Company F, 8th Louisiana Flag Presentation," *Civil War Flags Message Board*, October 2, 2011, www.history-sites.com (accessed September 12, 2015).

11. Mrs. Roger A. Pryor, *Reminiscences of Peace and War* (New York, 1905), 172 (quotation); *The War of the Rebellion: A Compilation of the Official Records of the Union and Confederate Armies* (130 vols.; Washington, D.C., 1880–1901), Ser. IV, Vol. I, 194–95 (hereinafter cited as *OR*; unless otherwise indicated, all citations are to Series I); Lyle Saxon, *Fabulous New Orleans* (Gretna, La., 2004), 197–201; Jones, "Jeff Davis' Pet Wolves," 28.

12. Michael Dan Jones, *The Tiger Rifles: The Making of a Louisiana Legend* (Lexington, Ky., 2011), 43 (quotation); Gary Schreckengost, *The First Louisiana Special Battalion: Wheat's Tigers in the Civil War* (Jefferson, N.C., 2008), 34; Earl J. Hess, *Civil War Infantry Tactics: Training, Combat, and Small-Unit Effectiveness* (Baton Rouge, 2015), 32–33; Alison Moore, notes in 7-LA Louisiana Troops General Information, Louisiana Brigades Boxes, GNMP.

13. Lee A. Wallace Jr., "Coppens' Louisiana Zouaves," *Civil War History*, VIII (1962), 269–73; Jones, "Jeff Davis' Pet Wolves," 29–30.

14. Ross Brooks, "Red Petticoats and Blue Jackets: 1st Confederate States Zouave Battalion, or Coppens' Louisiana Zouaves," *Military Collector & Historian*, Vol. 45, No. 4 (Winter 1993), 148–52; Barry I. Mickey, "Coppens' Zouaves: A Louisiana Battalion in Lee's Army," *Military Images*, Vol. 7, No. 2 (September–October 1985), 10.

15. Edwin Albert Leland, "Organization and Administration of the Louisiana Army During the Civil War," M.A. thesis, Louisiana State University, 1938, 19–23, 31.

16. New York *Herald*, July 3, 1861, in *Camp Moore News*, Vol. 13, No. 3 (September 2011).

17. John F. Charlton diary, n.d., JPC (quotation); Atlanta *Constitution*, March 2, 1894, *Newspaper Archive*, newspaperarchive.com (accessed August 20, 2015).

18. Dufour, *Gentle Tiger*, 121, 212; New Orleans *Daily Item*, August 25, 1896, in David F. Boyd Scrapbook, David F. Boyd Papers, LSU; Thomas Cooper DeLeon, *Four Years in Rebel Capitals: An Inside View of Life in the Southern Confederacy, from Birth to Death* (Mobile, 1890), 66; Jones, *Tiger Rifles*, 20–22; Richard Taylor, *Destruction and Reconstruction: Personal Experiences of the Late War*, ed. Charles P. Roland (1879; rpt., Waltham, Mass., 1968), 17.

19. Jones, *Tiger Rifles*, 29–30, 41, 45–46, 48, 68; Schreckengost, *First Louisiana Special Battalion*, 41.

20. Jones, *Tiger Rifles*, 33; Schreckengost, *First Louisiana Special Battalion*, 5–31; Dufour, *Gentle Tiger*, 7–120.

21. Schreckengost, *First Louisiana Special Battalion*, 46 (first quotation), 171; Dufour, *Gentle Tiger*, 9 (second quotation); Leo Wheat, "Memoir of Gen. C. R. Wheat," *Southern Historical Society Papers*, XVII (1889), 47–54.

22. Taylor, *Destruction and Reconstruction*, 17; J. W. Buhoup to St. John R. Liddell, April 26, 1861, in Box 14, Folder 91, Moses and St. John R. Liddell Family Papers, LSU (quotation); Schreckengost, *First Louisiana Special Battalion*, 177; Taylor, *Destruction and Reconstruction*, 17; Dufour, *Gentle Tiger*, 120.

23. James G. Gannon, *Irish Rebels, Confederate Tigers: A History of the 6th Louisiana Volunteers, 1861–1865* (Campbell, Calif., 1998), iii, ix, 397.

24. Schreckengost, *First Louisiana Special Battalion*, 36.

25. John Francis Maguire, *The Irish in America* (London, 1868), 546 (quotation); Gannon, *Irish Rebels*, x–xii, 321–22; Ella Lonn, *Foreigners in the Confederacy* (Chapel Hill, 1940), 30–31; New Orleans *Daily Delta,* May 2, 1861.

26. Maguire, *Irish in America*, 576–77.

27. See the appendix for more information on the units' foreign-born soldiers. Gannon, *Irish Rebels*, xii, xiii.

28. Preface, Isaac G. Seymour Papers, in Schoff Civil War Collection, UM; New Orleans *Commercial Bulletin,* July 30, 1862, in New Orleans Civil War Scrapbook, Vol. 2, TU; Taylor, *Destruction and Reconstruction*, 39; Leland, "Organization and Administration of the Louisiana Army," 45–46; Lonn, *Foreigners in the Confederacy,* 107–8; Gannon, *Irish Rebels*, ii.

29. Thomas W. Cutrer and T. Michael Parrish (eds.), *Brothers in Gray: The Civil War Letters of the Pierson Family* (Baton Rouge, 1997), 27.

30. Sigmund H. Uminski, "Two Polish Confederates," *Polish American Studies*, XXIII (1966), 65–73; Lonn, *Foreigners in the Confederacy,* 101; Leland, "Organization and Administration of the Louisiana Army," 52–53.

31. William P. Snakenberg, "Memoirs of W. P. Snakenberg," 2 (first quotation), 7–8, JPC; Forrest P. Conner (ed.), "Letters of Lieutenant Robert H. Miller to His Family, 1861–1862," *Virginia Magazine of History and Biography*, LXX (1962), 71 (second quotation); Francis C. Kajencki, "The Louisiana Tiger," *Louisiana History,* XV (1974), 51–52 (third quotation).

32. "Fatal Affray Among the Soldiers," *Camp Moore News,* Vol. 13, No. 2 (June 2011).

33. John D. Winters, *The Civil War in Louisiana* (Baton Rouge, 1963), 34 (quotation); Bound #1, Record Roll, 1st Regiment Louisiana Volunteers, Army of Northern Virginia, in Association of the Army of Northern Virginia, LHAC; Sir William Howard Russell, *My Diary North and South,* ed. Fletcher Pratt (1863; rpt. New York, 1954), 137; Leland, "Organization and Administration of the Louisiana Army," 33.

34. Cutrer and Parrish (eds.), *Brothers in Gray,* 22.

35. Ibid.

36. Trahern, "Biography," 17, RNBP.

37. Leland, "Organization and Administration of the Louisiana Army," 33; Winters, *Civil War in Louisiana,* 24.

38. Buhoup to Liddell, June 7, 1861, in Liddell Family Papers, LSU.

39. Ibid. (first quotation); unsigned letter, but identified as St. John R. Liddell to son Moses, June 10, 1861, in Liddell Family Papers, LSU (second quotation); Schreckengost, *First Louisiana Special Battalion,* 46–47.

40. Barnes F. Lathrop (ed.), "An Autobiography of Francis T. Nicholls, 1834–1881," *Louisiana Historical Quarterly,* XVI1 (1934), 249–50; Ezra J. Warner, *Generals in Gray: Lives of the Confederate Commanders* (Baton Rouge, 1959), 224–25; C. Howard Nichols, "Some Notes on the Military Career of Francis T. Nicholls," *Louisiana History,* III (1962), 297–304.

41. Opelousas (La.) *Courier,* photocopy, September 6, 1862, RNBP.

42. Cutrer and Parrish (eds.), *Brothers in Gray,* 26 (first quotation); T. Michael Parrish, *Richard Taylor: Soldier Prince of Dixie* (Chapel Hill, 1992), 128 (second quotation), 133–34 (fourth

quotation); Handerson, *Yankee in Gray,* 91 (third quotation); Taylor, *Destruction and Reconstruction,* 8 (fifth quotation); for background information on Taylor, see Parrish, *Richard Taylor,* 5–123; Taylor, *Destruction and Reconstruction,* 4–8; New Orleans *Times-Democrat,* January 31, 1897, in Scrapbook, Boyd Papers, LSU; Warner, *Generals in Gray,* 299–300; Kenneth Trist Urquhart, "General Richard Taylor and the War in Virginia, 1861–1862," M.A. thesis, Tulane University, 1958, 1–17.

43. Handerson, *Yankee in Gray,* 9 (first quotation); Edward A. Seton to mother, July 20, 1861, in Seton Collection, MSU (second quotation).

44. Taylor, *Destruction and Reconstruction,* 40 (first quotation); W. G. Ogden to father, n.d., in Ogden Family Papers, TU (second quotation).

45. "The Delta Rifles, Part III," *Louisiana in the Civil War,* May 15, 2011, www.louisianacivilwar.org (accessed March 5, 2015).

46. "Excerpts About Camp Moore: Whit Martin, June 4, 1861," *Camp Moore News,* Vol. 13, No. 1 (March 2011).

47. "Wheat's Battalion," *Louisiana in the Civil War,* July 19, 2010, www.louisianacivilwar.org (accessed April 12, 2016).

48. Newell to Newell, June 20, 1861, in Newell Papers, LSU (quotation); Dufour, *Gentle Tiger,* 124.

49. R. S. Jackson to David F. Boyd, June 7, 1861, in Box 1, Folder 1, David F. Boyd Civil War Papers, LSU.

50. A. Meynier Jr., *The Life and Military Services of Col. Charles D. Dreux* (New Orleans, 1883), 11–14, in Civil War Manuscript Series, TU; Columbus H. Allen, "About the Death of Col. C. D. Dreux," *Confederate Veteran,* XV (1907), 307.

51. Sir William Howard Russell, *Pictures of Southern Life, Social, Political and Military* (New York, 1861), 45–48.

52. Moore diary, May 8 and June 2, 1861, in Moore Papers, TU; for details on the Louisianians' preparation for battle in Pensacola, see *Daily Delta,* May 24, 1861; J. W. Minnich article on Coppens' Zouaves, in Reminiscences, Executive and Army of Northern Virginia, LHAC; Taylor, *Destruction and Reconstruction,* 7–8.

53. Carrollton (La.) *Sun,* May 1, 1861, *Louisiana in the Civil War,* January 4, 2011, www.louisianacivilwar.org (accessed March 3, 2015).

54. Little Falls (Minn.) *Transcript,* July 16, 1886, *Chronicling America,* chroniclingamerica.loc.gov (accessed September 10, 2015).

55. The statistics on places of birth were obtained from Bound Volumes 1–10 and 12, in Association of the Army of Northern Virginia, LHAC, which include the Record Rolls of the 1st, 2nd, 5th, 6th, 7th, 8th, 9th, and 15th Louisiana Volunteers. See also the appendix for a breakdown by regiments of places of birth.

56. Charleston *Mercury,* July 10, 1861, in *Camp Moore News,* Vol. 13, No. 2 (June 2011).

57. Augusta (Ga.) *Dailey Chronicle & Sentinel* (October 10, 1861), in *Camp Moore News,* Vol. 13, No. 2 (June 2011).

58. Jones, "Jeff Davis' Pet Wolves," 30.

59. Ibid.; Brooks, "Red Petticoats and Blue Jackets," 148–49, 150 (quotation), 151.

60. Charles M. Blackford and C. M. Blackford (eds.), *Letters from Lee's Army; or, Memoirs of Life in and out of the Army of Virginia During the War Between the States* (New York, 1947), 23.

61. Jones, *Tiger Rifles,* 57, 66.

62. *Daily Delta,* May 6, 1861; Blackford and Blackford (eds.), *Letters from Lee's Army,* 23; Judith E. Harper, *Women During the Civil War: An Encyclopedia* (New York, 2004), 165.

63. "Catharine [sic] Hodges," *Find A Grave,* www.findagrave.com (accessed July 3, 2016); *Times Dispatch,* May 24, 1903, *Chronicling America,* chroniclingamerica.loc.gov (accessed March 5, 2015) (first quotation); Debra Nance Laurence, "Drury Gibson: Letters from a North Louisiana Tiger," *Journal of the North Louisiana Historical Association,* X (Fall 1979), 143 (second quotation).

64. Terry L. Jones, *Historical Dictionary of the Civil War* (2 vols., Lanham, Md., 2011), I, 283; list of chaplains, in Folder 5, Box 42, Bibliographic Material, LHAC; Egidius Smulders to Henry Kelly, March — 187–, in Folder 5, Box 42, Bibliographic Material, LHAC; Smulders' undated obituary, in Folder 5, Box 42, Bibliographic Material, LHAC; Rev. Joseph Durkin (ed.), *Confederate Chaplain: A War Journal of Rev. James B. Sheeran . . . 14th Louisiana, C.S.A.* (Milwaukee, 1960), ix, 6 (first quotation), 40–41; Romero, "Louisiana Clergy and the Confederate Army," 282–91; Alfred Flournoy Jr. to wife, July 8, 1861, in Alfred Flournoy Jr. Papers, LSU (second quotation); John William Jones, *Christ in the Camp, or Religion in Lee's Army* (Richmond, 1887), 516–17.

65. Introduction to Theodore H. Woodard Letters, typed copies, in J. D. Van Benthuysen File, MOC (first quotation); Charles Batchelor to father, October 18, 1863, in Folder 6, Albert A. Batchelor Papers, LSU (second quotation); see also Edward Seton to mother, August 11, 1861, in Seton Collection, MSU; Terry L. Jones (ed.), *The Civil War Memoirs of Capt. William J. Seymour: Reminiscences of a Louisiana Tiger* (Baton Rouge, 1991), 103–4; Taylor, *Destruction and Reconstruction,* 55–57.

66. New York *Times,* January 18, 1886, query.nytimes.com (accessed December 18, 2015); see also Eric J. Brock, "Honoring a Black Man Who Offered his Services to the Confederate Army," *Desoto Parish, Louisiana,* www.countygenweb.com (accessed December 18, 2015).

67. "Ed Merritt of the 8th Louisiana," *Louisiana in the Civil War,* April 13, 2010, www.louisianacivilwar.org (accessed December 18, 2015).

68. Lichenstein memoir, USAERC.

69. Arthur W. Bergeron Jr., "Louisiana's Free Men of Color in Gray," in Lawrence Lee Hewitt and Arthur W. Bergeron Jr. (eds.), *Louisianians in the Civil War* (Columbia, Mo., 2002), 100–119.

70. DeLeon, *Four Years in Rebel Capitals,* 71–72.

71. Mickey, "Coppens' Zouaves," 10–11.

72. DeLeon, *Four Years in Rebel Capitals,* 73 (quotations); Wallace, "Coppens' Louisiana Zouaves," 274–75.

73. Wallace, "Coppens' Louisiana Zouaves," 274–75.

74. Phoenix *Arizona Republican,* June 18, 1898, *Chronicling America,* chroniclingamerica.loc.gov (accessed December 18, 2015).

75. DeLeon, *Four Years in Rebel Capitals,* 80 (quotation); Wallace, "Coppens' Louisiana Zouaves," 274–75.

76. H. B. Cowles Jr. to unknown, June 20, [1861], in John Buxton Williams Papers, East Carolina Manuscript Collection, ECU.

77. Wallace, "Coppens' Louisiana Zouaves," 275 (quotations); Edward Porter Alexander to wife, June 8, 1861, in Edward Porter Alexander Collection, SHC.

78. Sallie A. Putnam, *Richmond During the War: Four Years of Personal Observation* (New York, 1867), 36–37; Alfred Hoyt Bill, *The Beleaguered City: Richmond, 1861–1865* (New York, 1946), 50–51.

79. Snakenberg, "Memoirs," 3, JPC; see also Lawrence Lee Hewitt, "A Confederate Foreign Legion: Louisiana 'Wildcats' in the Army of Northern Virginia," in Hewitt and Bergeron (eds.), *Louisianians in the Civil War.*

80. Memphis *Appeal*, n.d., in Browning Scrapbook, Amos G. Browning Papers, 64, DU.

81. Ibid.

82. Ibid. (quotation); Napier Bartlett, *Military Record of Louisiana* (Baton Rouge, 1964), 44–46; Compiled Service Records of Confederate Soldiers Who Served in Organizations from the State of Louisiana, War Record Group 109, Microcopy 320, Roll 253, NA; Snakenberg, "Memoirs," 3–4, JPC.

83. Snakenberg, "Memoirs," 4, 5 (quotation), JPC.

84. Ibid., 5.

85. Ibid.

86. Atlanta *Constitution*, March 2, 1894.

87. Schreckengost, *First Louisiana Special Battalion*, 49.

88. Charles de Choiseul to Emma Louisa Walton, June 30, 1861, in Folder 5, Walton-Glenny Family Papers, HNOC.

89. Thomas Walter Brooks and Michael Dan Jones, *Lee's Foreign Legion: A History of the 10th Louisiana Infantry* (Gravenhurst, Ontario, 1995), 9.

90. "Who Wouldn't Be a Soldier," *Camp Moore News*, Vol. 13, No. 4 (December 2011).

91. B. C. Cushman to David F. Boyd, May 16, 1861, in Box 1, Folder 1, Boyd Civil War Papers, LSU; see also Seton to mother, August 3, 1861, in Seton Collection, MSU; Cutrer and Parrish (eds.), *Brothers in Gray*, 31.

CHAPTER 2

THE LOUISIANA TIGERS

1. *OR*, Vol. V, 815, 961, 1030; Vol. XI, Pt. I, 569; Vol. LI, Pt. 11, 316; Vol. IV, 668–69; Vol. IX, 472. Taylor, *Destruction and Reconstruction*, 14–15.

2. Thomas H. Phifer to mother, May 27, 1861, in Thomas H. Phifer Letters, typed copies, 2nd Louisiana Folder, Louisiana Box, ANB; see also William W. Posey to mother, June 9, 1861, in *Camp Moore News*, Vol. 15, No. 4 (December 2013).

3. Clarksville (Tex.) *Standard*, June 15, 1861, in *Camp Moore News*, Vol. 13, No. 2 (June 2011).

4. Moore diary, September 24, 1861, in Moore Papers, UT.

5. Leon Jastremski to Charlie, September 2, 1861, in Folder 2, Leon Jastremski Family Papers, LSU.

6. Stephens was mortally wounded three years later in the Wilderness, an apparent victim of friendly fire. Edmond Stephens to William W. Upshaw, November 22, 1861, in Judge Paul

Stephens Collection, NSU; see also Francis Posey to sister, n.d., in *Camp Moore News,* Vol. 16, No. 2 (June 2014).

7. Cutrer and Parrish (eds.), *Brothers in Gray,* 39; for more on camp life, see letter of anonymous soldier in 1st Louisiana, May 18, 1861, in *Camp Moore News,* Vol. 13, No. 2 (June 2011).

8. Edmond Stephens and J. Monroe Thomas to Mrs. Pickens, November 21, 1861, in Stephens Collection, NSU.

9. Monier rose to the rank of lieutenant colonel and command of the 10th Louisiana. He was considered to be an outstanding officer and surrendered the regiment at Appomattox. Charles I. Batchelor to Albert Batchelor, October 10, 1861, in Box 1, Folder 4, Albert A. Batchelor Papers, LSU (first quotation); Bartlett, *Military Record of Louisiana,* 26 (second quotation); Brooks and Jones, *Lee's Foreign Legion,* 3; Alfred F. Flournoy Jr. to wife, typescript, September 22, 1861, in Alfred Flournoy Papers, LSU (third quotation).

10. Wren was captured at Port Republic, wounded at Antietam and Second Fredericksburg, and captured again at Spotsylvania. G. L. P. Wren diary, December 25, 1861, in Wren Collection, EU (first quotation); W. G. Ogden to father, June 26, 1861, in Ogden Papers, TU (second quotation); Booth (comp.), *Louisiana Confederate Soldiers,* III, 1166.

11. W. G. Ogden to father, January 24, 1862, in Ogden Papers, TU.

12. Richmond (Va.) *Daily Dispatch,* January 29, 1862, *Louisiana in the Civil War,* March 23, 2010, www.louisianacivilwar.org (accessed December 15, 2015).

13. Ogden to father, January 24, 1862, in Ogden Papers, TU (first quotation); Cutrer and Parrish (eds.), *Brothers in Gray,* 62 (second quotation); Edward Seton to mother, March 23, 1862, in Seton Collection, MSU (third quotation); see also Seton to mother, September 20, 1861, in Seton Collection, MSU.

14. George Zeller to family, January 1862, in George Zeller Letters, photocopies, 6th Louisiana Folder, Louisiana Box, ANB.

15. Urquhart, "General Richard Taylor," 25; Joseph T. Glatthaar, *General Lee's Army: From Victory to Collapse* (New York, 2008), 72–73 (quotation).

16. Record Book of the Hospital of the 7th Regiment of Louisiana Volunteers, 1861, in War Record Group 109, Chap. VI, Vol. 486, 1–4, NA; Edward Seton to John, December 5, 1861, in Seton Collection, MSU.

17. Dufour, *Gentle Tiger,* 153; Cutrer and Parrish (eds.), *Brothers in Gray,* 38 (quotation); Moore diary, August 2, 1861, in Moore Papers, UT; Cornelius M. Buckley (trans. and ed.), *A Frenchman, a Chaplain, a Rebel: The War Letters of Pere Louis-Hippolyte Gache, S.J.* (Chicago, 1981), 47; Ogden to father, January 24, 1862, in Ogden Papers, TU; J. B. Walton to Emma Walton, August 19, 1861, in Folder 7, Walton-Glenny Papers, HNOC; Taylor, *Destruction and Reconstruction,* 15.

18. Richard Colbert was captured at Rappahannock Station and declared missing after the Second Battle of Winchester. Richard Colbert to sister, August 11, 1861, in Folder 58, North Louisiana Historical Association Archives, CC (quotation); Edmond Stephens to unknown, January 9, 1862, in Stephens Collection, NSU; Booth (comp.), *Louisiana Confederate Soldiers,* I, 375.

19. Stephens to parents, September 14, 1861, in Stephens Collection, NSU (first quotation); Theodore Mandeville to Jose, August 24, 1861, in Box 2, Folder 12, Henry D. Mandeville Family Papers, LSU (second quotation); Glatthaar, *General Lee's Army,* 69–70 (third quotation).

20. Cutrer and Parrish (eds.), *Brothers in Gray,* 62.

21. Snakenberg, "Memoirs," 7, JPC; see also the shootings of Lts. Alfred Scanlon and Miller in chapter 3.

22. Jones, *Tiger Rifles,* 108, 189; Trahern, "Biography," 22, RNBP (quotation); Gannon, *Irish Rebels,* 9; Alfred Flournoy Jr. to wife, May 22, 1861, in Flournoy Papers, LSU; General Order, in Folder 2a, Box 48, LaVillebeuvre Papers, LSU; see Charlton diary, September 23 and 28, December 13, 1861, JPC, for similar incidents involving the 5th Louisiana.

23. Cutrer and Parrish (eds.), *Brothers in Gray,* 200.

24. Stephens to Mr. and Mrs. Paxton, January 14, 1864, in Stephens Collection, NSU (quotation); Boling Williams diary, 150, MSCA; see also Keith G. Bauer (ed.), *A Soldier's Journey: The Civil War Diary of Henry C. Caldwell* (Baton Rouge, 2001), 35; Flournoy to wife, typescript copy, May 22, 1861, in Flournoy Papers, LSU; Batchelor to father, October 18, 1861, in Folder 6, Batchelor Papers, LSU; James H. Beard to wife, August 21, 1861, in James H. Beard Papers, LSUS; Tull, "Tull's War Story," HLW.

25. Wiley, *Johnny Reb,* 281; see also Sallie Garland Young to Louis Marcel Rambin, September 23, 1864, in Young-Spicer Family Papers, ECU.

26. Benjamin Smith to R. H. Carnse, August 25, 1861, in Benjamin Smith Letter, LSU; Booth (comp.), *Louisiana Confederate Soldiers,* III, 602.

27. Conner (ed.), "Letters of Lieutenant Robert H. Miller," 83–84 (first quotation); Lafayette McLaws to wife, May 1, 1862, in Folder 5, Lafayette McLaws Collection, SHC (second quotation); Edward G. Randolph to David F. Boyd, June 1, 1862, in Boyd Civil War Papers, LSU (third quotation); Ben Hubert to Letitia, May 2, 1862, in Ben Hubert Papers, DU (fourth quotation); Isaac G. Seymour to William J. Seymour, May 2, 1862, in Seymour Papers, UM (fifth quotation).

28. J. H. Mackensie to Boyd, October 21, 1861, in Box 1, Folder 2, Boyd Civil War Papers, LSU; 9th Louisiana quartermaster document, Boyd Civil War Papers, LSU; W. Ezra Denson to John F. Stephens, November 16, 1861, in John F. Stephens Correspondence, LSU; J. M. Batchelor to Albert Batchelor, December 20, 1861, in Folder 4, Batchelor Papers, LSU; Richmond *Enquirer,* July 11, 1861; *OR,* Vol. VI, 748; see also Edward Seton to John, December 5, 1861, and Seton to mother, November 3, 1861, and January 6, 1862, in Seton Collection, MSU; William W. Posey to sister, October 24, 1861, in *Camp Moore News,* Vol. 16, No. 3 (September 2014).

29. B. C. Cushman to Boyd, May 16, 1861, in Box 1, Folder 1, Boyd Civil War Papers, LSU (first quotation); Cutrer and Parrish (eds.), *Brothers in Gray,* 65 (second quotation); see also William W. Posey to sister, October 24, 1861, in *Camp Moore News,* Vol. 16, No. 3 (September 2014); "Correspondence of Caddo Gazette," May 18, 1861, in *Camp Moore News,* Vol. 13, No. 2 (June 2011); Charles I. Batchelor to Albert Batchelor, August 25, 1861, Folder 4, in Batchelor Papers, LSU; Edmond Stephens to L. W. Stephens, January 4 and 19, 1862, in Stephens Collection, NSU; Mandeville to Rebecca Mandeville, August 27, 1861, Box 2, Folder 12, in Mandeville Papers, LSU; Fannie A. Beers, *Memories: A Record of Personal Experience and Adventure During Four Years of War* (Philadelphia, 1889), 229–30.

30. Thomas H. Phifer to mother, December 7, 1861, in 2nd Louisiana Folder, Louisiana Box, ANB; see also Edward Seton to mother, November 24, 1861, in Seton Collection, MSU; Brooks and Jones, *Lee's Foreign Legion,* 12.

31. Bauer (ed.), *Soldier's Journey*, 27–28, 34.

32. Kennedy died of disease less than a year later. Charlton diary, December 25, 1861, JPC (first quotation); Bauer (ed.), *Soldier's Journey*, 30; Booth (comp.), *Louisiana Confederate Soldiers*, I, 540; Cutrer and Parrish (eds.), *Brothers in Gray*, 73–74 (second quotation); George Zeller to family, January 9, 1862, in Zeller Letters, 6th Louisiana Folder, Louisiana Box, ANB (third quotation); Thomas H. Phifer to mother, January 19, 1862, in 2nd Louisiana Folder, Louisiana Box, ANB (fourth quotation).

33. Sample was captured at Gettysburg. Hiram Sample reminiscences, FSNMP (quotation); Booth (comp.), *Louisiana Confederate Soldiers*, I, 437; Thomas H. Phifer to unknown, June 9, 1861, in 2nd Louisiana Folder, Louisiana Box, ANB; Charlton diary, n.d., JPC.

34. Dufour, *Gentle Tiger*, 157 (quotation); New Orleans *Daily Item*, August 25, 1896, in Scrapbook, 96, Boyd Papers, LSU.

35. Jones, *Tiger Rifles*, 110–11; Grand Military Ball Handbill, www.archive.org/stream/grand-militaryba100rich#page/no/mode/1up, DU (accessed October 1, 2015).

36. William Cowan McClellan, *Welcome the Hour of Conflict: William Cowan McClellan and the 9th Alabama*, ed. John C. Carter (Tuscaloosa, 2007), 79 (first quotation); James Cooper Nisbet, *Four Years on the Firing Line*, ed. Bell Irvin Wiley (1914; rpt. Jackson, Tenn., 1963), 46 (second quotation); William C. Oates, *The War Between the Union and Confederacy and Its Lost Opportunities with a History of the 15th Alabama Regiment and the Forty-eight Battles in Which It Was Engaged* (New York, 1905), 75–76 (hereinafter cited as *15th Alabama*) (third quotation); John McGrath, "In a Louisiana Regiment," *Southern Historical Society Papers*, XXXVI (1908), 106 (fourth quotation).

37. Bartlett, *Military Record of Louisiana*, 26; New Orleans *Daily Picayune*, April 29, 1861; Buckley (ed.), *A Frenchman, a Chaplain, a Rebel*, 53.

38. Edward Seton to mother, July 20, 1861, in Seton Collection, MSU; Brooks and Jones, *Lee's Foreign Legion*, 2; McLaws to wife, August 18, 1861, in Folder 4, McLaws Collection, SHC (quotation).

39. Charles Moore diary, December 20, 1861, in Brake Collection, USAERC (quotation); John M. Coski, "When Louisiana Came to Virginia," *From the Collections*, Museum of the Confederacy (Spring–Summer 2002), 10, 12.

40. Billy Campbell cannot be positively identified. There is no record of anyone by that name in Dreux's Battalion, although several William or W. Campbells did serve. Col. R. G. Lowe, "The Dreux Battalion," *Confederate Veteran*, V (1897), 55–56; Beard to wife, April 4, 1862, in Beard Papers, LSUS; Booth (comp.), *Louisiana Confederate Soldiers*, I, 232, 237–39.

41. Lowe, "Dreux Battalion," 56; Col. R. G. Lowe, "Magruder's Defense of the Peninsula," *Confederate Veteran*, VIII (1900), 108; unidentified newspaper clipping in Civil War Scrapbook, 1862–64, TU; J. H. Cosgrove, "Reminiscences and Recollections," *Cosgrove's Weekly*, June 24, 1911, in Melrose Scrapbook 230, NSU; Booth (comp.), *Louisiana Confederate Soldiers*, III, 30.

42. Charlton diary, January 27, 28, 1862, and n.d., JPC; Booth (comp.), *Louisiana Confederate Soldiers*, II, 797.

43. Both Bunce and Trust later deserted the regiment, the latter in order to join a cavalry unit. Charlton diary, n.d., JPC; Booth (comp.), *Louisiana Confederate Soldiers*, I, 162, and II, 875.

44. McLaws to wife, August 18, 1861, in Folder 4, McLaws Collection, SHC (quotation); Register of Arrests, 1862–64, War Record Group 109, Chap. IX, Vol. 244, NA; Moore diary, Sep-

tember 1861–February 1862, in Moore Papers, UT; Fred Ober, "The Campaign of the Peninsula," in Reminiscences, Executive and Army of Northern Virginia, LHAC; James Stubbs to father, June 25, 1861, in Folder 1, Jefferson W. Stubbs Family Papers, LSU; list of charges against an anonymous private, 1st Louisiana Volunteers, October 1, 1861, in Box 1, Folder 1, James Calvert Wise Papers, LSU; Washington D.C. *Evening Star,* June 1, 1896, *Chronicling America,* chroniclingamerica.loc.gov (accessed October 1, 2015); see also "5th Louisiana: Trouble," *Louisiana in the Civil War,* June 18, 2012, www.louisianacivilwar.org (accessed October 1, 2015); 9th Louisiana's Order Book, December 22, 1861, MOC.

45. Snakenberg, "Memoirs," 6, JPC.

46. *Daily Picayune,* September 20, 1861.

47. Charles W. Turner (ed.), "Major Charles A. Davidson: Letters of a Virginia Soldier," *Civil War History,* XXII (1976), 20 (first quotation); anonymous letter, June 17, 1861, in Carrington Family Papers, VHS (second and third quotations); Manly Wade Wellman, *Rebel Boast: First at Bethel—Last at Appomattox* (New York, 1956), 62–63.

48. McLaws to wife, August 18, 1861, in Folder 4, McLaws Collection, SHC.

49. Lowe, "Magruder's Defense of the Peninsula," 105; also see Flournoy to wife, typescript copy, July 8, 1861, in Flournoy Papers, LSU.

50. Buckley (ed.), *A Frenchman, a Chaplain, a Rebel,* 43.

51. References to the Louisiana Tigers are found in *Newspaper Archive's* Dubuque *Herald,* April 13, 1862, newspaperarchive.com, and Perry (Iowa) *Chief,* December 3, 1886 (accessed October 13, 2015); and *Chronicling America's* Montpelier (Vt.) *Daily Green Mountain Freeman,* August 1, 1861, chroniclingamerica.loc.gov (accessed October 13, 2015); Alexandria (Va.) *Local News,* October 22, 1861 (accessed October 13, 2015); Iola (Iowa) *Register,* September 4, 1896 (accessed October 26, 2015).

52. Memphis *Daily Appeal,* December 19, 1862, *Chronicling America,* chroniclingamerica.loc.gov (accessed October 29, 2015) (first quotation); Oates, *15th Alabama,* 30–31 (second quotation); Nisbet, *Four Years on the Firing Line,* 56 (third quotation); Handerson, *Yankee in Gray,* 34 (fourth quotation); Lonn, *Foreigners in the Confederacy,* 105.

53. Leland, "Organization and Administration of the Louisiana Army," 37–38 (quotation); Ron Youngquist, "The Louisiana Tigers," in 7-LA-Brigades, Box 6, Folder 1, Louisiana Brigades Boxes, GNMP; New Orleans *Daily Item,* August 25, 1896, in Scrapbook, Boyd Papers, LSU.

54. W. G. Bean, *The Liberty Hall Volunteers: Stonewall's College Boys* (Charlottesville, 1964), 65.

55. Nisbet, *Four Years on the Firing Line,* 26.

56. Ibid. (first quotation); Terry L. Jones (ed.), *Campbell Brown's Civil War: With Ewell and the Army of Northern Virginia* (Baton Rouge, 2001), 162; Zeller to sister, n.d., and January 8, 1862, in Zeller Letters, 6th Louisiana Folder, Louisiana Box, ANB (second quotation).

57. Wren diary, January 22 and 31, 1862, in Wren Collection (quotations), EU; John Devine to mother, November 27, 1861, in John Devine Letters, MSCA.

58. Washburne and Hesler Ledger, LSU.

59. Isaac G. Seymour to William J. Seymour, May 2, 1862, in Seymour Papers, UM; Williams diary, notation for December 1861, in MSCA (first quotation); C. F. Thompson to brother, July 25, 1861, in *Camp Moore News,* Vol. 16, No. 1 (March 2014) (second quotation).

60. Williams diary, August 3–September 3, 1861, MSCA; unidentified newspaper clipping, in William H. Wharton Scrapbook, MSCA; Orders for October 10 and December 27, 1862, in Louisiana Troops, 7th Regiment Orderly Book, 1862–64, NYPL; Court-martial sentences signed by Lt. Col. W. G. Vincent, September 12, 1861, in Army of Northern Virginia Papers, Part I, LHAC; General Order #123, "Headquarters Army of Northern Virginia," October 28, 1862, LHAC; Mandeville to Ellwyn Mandeville, August 31, 1861, in Box 2, Folder 12, Mandeville Papers, LSU; General and Special Orders, 1861, 2nd Louisiana Infantry, in Box 48, Folder 2a, Jean Ursin LaVillebeuvre Family Papers, LSU; Thomas Benton Reed, *A Private in Gray* (Camden, Ark., 1905), 52.

61. George Zeller to family, November 7, 1861, photocopy, in Zeller Letters, 6th Louisiana Folder, Louisiana Box, ANB (quotations); "Mass AWOL in the ANV fall 1861?" *Louisiana in the Civil War Message Board,* July 3, 2011, history-sites.com (accessed March 15, 2015).

62. Handerson, *Yankee in Gray,* 34.

63. Bauer (ed.), *Soldier's Journey,* 4; Charles de Choiseul to Emma Louise Walton, September 5, 1861, in Folder 8, Walton-Glenny Papers, HNOC (quotation).

64. Charles de Choiseul to Emma Louise Walton, September 5, 1861, in Folder 8, Walton-Glenny Papers, HNOC.

65. Ibid., January 1, 1862, in Folder 1, Walton-Glenny Papers, HNOC; see also letter of November 6, 1861, Walton-Glenny Papers, HNOC.

66. Jones, *Tiger Rifles,* 102–3. Omaha *Daily Bee,* January 30, 1898, *Chronicling America,* chroniclingamerica.loc.gov (accessed October 6, 2015); *Home Journal* (Winchester, Tenn.), November 28, 1878 (accessed October 6, 2015).

67. Taylor, *Destruction and Reconstruction,* 17 (quotation); Parrish, *Richard Taylor,* 139–42.

68. Jones, *Tiger Rifles,* 105 (first quotation); Zeller to sister, n.d., in Zeller Letters, 6th Louisiana Folder, Louisiana Box, ANB; McClellan, *Welcome the Hour of Conflict,* 113 (second and third quotations).

69. Michael R. Thomas, "Confederate Firing Squad at Centreville," *Northern Virginia Heritage,* June 1980, 6 (quotation); unidentified newspaper clipping in Confederate States of America Archives, Army Units, Louisiana Volunteers, DU; 9th Louisiana Order Book, December 6, 1861, MOC.

70. Jones, *Tiger Rifles,* 104.

71. For text of the farewell letter, see Staunton (Va.) *Spectator,* April 1, 1862, *Chronicling America,* chroniclingamerica.loc.gov (accessed October 6, 2015); Michael R. Thomas, "Unearthing Two Tigers' Graves," *Northern Virginia Heritage,* June 1980, 7–8 (quotation); Dufour, *Gentle Tiger,* 160–63; Taylor, *Destruction and Reconstruction,* 17; New Orleans *Daily Item,* August 25, 1896, in Scrapbook, Boyd Papers, LSU; John Devine to mother, December 27, 1861, Mansfield Museum MSS., NSU; Richard Colbert to sister, December 26, 1861, in Folder 60, North Louisiana Historical Association Archives, CC; Zeller to sister, n.d., in Zeller Letters, 6th Louisiana Folder, Louisiana Box, ANB.

72. McArthur was killed at the First Battle of Winchester, and Orr was wounded at Antietam and Second Winchester and captured at Rappahannock Station; 9th Louisiana Order Book, January 17 (quotation) and February 13, 1862, MOC; Booth (comp.), *Louisiana Confederate Soldiers,* II, 1124, and III, 44.

73. Charlton diary, December 24, 1861, JPC; *Daily Dispatch*, December 30, 1861, Richmond *Daily Dispatch*, dlxs.richmond.edu (accessed October 8, 2015).

74. Wallace, "Coppens' Louisiana Zouaves," 276 (quotation); Mickey, "Coppens' Zouaves," 11.

75. Henry Gillum to B. F. Post, December 11, 1892, in Reminiscences, Executive and Army of Northern Virginia, LHAC; Buckley (ed.), *A Frenchman, a Chaplain, a Rebel*, 31; 9th Louisiana Order Book, April 24, 1862, MOC.

76. Smith was wounded at Malvern Hill and then wounded again and captured at the Wilderness, but he was exchanged and surrendered at Appomattox. Booth (comp.), *Louisiana Confederate Soldiers*, III, 602; Alfred Flournoy Jr. to wife, June 1 (second quotation), July 8 (first and third quotations), and July 21, 1861 (fourth quotation), in Flournoy Papers, LSUS.

77. Robertson memoir, USAERC.

78. Flournoy to wife, July 21, 1861, in Flournoy Papers, LSUS (first quotation); Smith to Carnse, August 23, 1861, in Smith Letter, LSU; Lichenstein memoir, USAERC (second and third quotations).

79. Thomas H. Phifer to mother, August 11, 1861, in 2nd Louisiana Folder, Louisiana Box, ANB.

80. Williams eventually became colonel of the 2nd Louisiana and was killed at Spotsylvania. "Messrs of the Pelican Rifles," August 10, 1861, 2nd Louisiana Folder, Louisiana Box, ANB; Booth (comp.), *Louisiana Confederate Soldiers*, III, 1100.

81. Bartlett, *Military Record of Louisiana*, 27; Eugene Janin to father, November 21, 1861, in Folder 1, Eugene Janin Collection, SHC; Flournoy to wife, July 8 and 21, 1861, in Flournoy Papers, LSU; Smith to Carnse, August 25, 1861, in Smith Letter, Flournoy Papers, LSU; Kajencki, "Louisiana Tiger," 52–53; Snakenberg, "Memoirs," 9, JPC.

82. Conner (ed.), "Letters of Lieutenant Robert H. Miller," 69–75.

83. Parrish, *Richard Taylor*, 133 (first and third quotations); Jack D. Welsh, M.D., *Medical Histories of Confederate Generals* (Kent, Ohio, 1995), 226–27; Wren diary, in Wren Collection, EU (second quotation).

84. Parrish, *Richard Taylor*, 136.

85. Isaac G. Seymour to unknown, September 2, 1861, in Seymour Papers, UM.

86. Parrish, *Richard Taylor*, 135.

87. Gannon, *Irish Rebels*, 13.

88. Parrish, *Richard Taylor*, 135 (first quotation), 137–38 (second quotation); Taylor, *Destruction and Reconstruction*, 14–16; Urquhart, "General Richard Taylor," 27–32.

89. Parrish, *Richard Taylor*, 137 (first quotation), 128 (second quotation); Taylor, *Destruction and Reconstruction*, 4–8; Urquhart, "General Richard Taylor," 1–17; T. Michael Parrish, "Richard Taylor," in William C. Davis (ed.), *The Confederate General* (6 vols., n.p, 1991), VI, 28–31.

90. Parrish, *Richard Taylor*, 42; Welsh, *Medical Histories of Confederate Generals*, 210–11; David French Boyd, *Reminiscences of the War in Virginia*, ed. T. Michael Parrish (Baton Rouge, 1994), 13.

91. Boyd, *Reminiscences of the War in Virginia*, 13.

92. Cutrer and Parrish (eds.), *Brothers in Gray*, 77.

93. Phifer to mother, May 27, 1861, in 2nd Louisiana Folder, Louisiana Box, ANB.

CHAPTER 3
BAPTISM BY FIRE

1. Trahern, "Biography," 16, RNBP.

2. Ibid., 18.

3. Posey was mortally wounded two years later at Chancellorsville. "Letters from Soldiers," W. W. Posey to parents, June 12, 1861, in *Camp Moore News*, Vol. 15, No. 4 (December 2013) (first and third quotations); Booth (comp.), *Louisiana Confederate Soldiers*, III, 178; William R. Cox, "Major General Stephen D. Ramseur: His Life and Character," *Southern Historical Society Papers*, XVIII (1890), 226 (second quotation).

4. Lichenstein memoir, USAERC.

5. Charlton diary, n.d., JPC.

6. Jones, *Tiger Rifles*, 72–73; Schreckengost, *First Louisiana Special Battalion*, 51; Dufour, *Gentle Tiger*, 126; *OR*, Vol. LI, Pt. I, 32.

7. John F. Geren died of typhus a few months after writing this letter. "The Trip to the Seat of War," John F. Geren to family, July 2, 1861, in *Camp Moore News*, Vol. 13, No. 2 (June 2011); Booth (comp.), *Louisiana Confederate Soldiers*, II, 5.

8. William Moore diary, June 28, 1861, in Moore Papers, UT.

9. William Clegg to parents, July 4, 1861 (first quotation), RNBP; Lafayette McLaws to wife, July 8, 1861, in Folder 4, McLaws Collection, SHC (second quotation); Lowe, "Dreux Battalion," 55 (third quotation); William Moore diary, July 4, 1861, in Moore Papers, UT.

10. J. D. Van Benthuysen to Wats [?], July 22, 1861, in Van Benthuysen file, MOC.

11. Ibid. (first quotation); Sgt. Daniel D. Logan to sister, July 8, 1861, in Letters of Sgt. Daniel D. Logan, MOC; Meynier, *Life of Col. Charles D. Dreux*, 15 (second quotation).

12. Van Benthuysen to Wats [?], July 22, 1861, in Van Benthuysen file, MOC.

13. Janinto Germain Vincent, August 2, 1861, in Janin Collection, SHC (quotation); *OR*, Vol. II, 188–89, 964–65, 990–92, 1003–5; Meynier, *Life of Col. Charles D. Dreux*, 11–17; "First Volunteers from Louisiana," *Confederate Veteran*, III (1895), 146; Lowe, "Dreux Battalion," 54–55; Allen, "Death of Col. C. D. Dreux," 307; Alfred Flournoy Jr. to wife, typescript copy, July 8, 1861, in Alfred Flournoy Jr. Papers, LSUS.

14. Meynier, *Life of Col. Charles D. Dreux*, 16–17.

15. Unidentified newspaper clipping in Civil War Scrapbook, 1861–62, TU (quotation); Meynier, *Life of Col. Charles D. Dreux*, 11–17; see also "Funeral of Charles Dreux, 1st Louisiana Battalion," *Louisiana in the Civil War*, www.louisianacivilwar.org (accessed December 15, 2015).

16. Gannon, *Irish Rebels*, 3–4.

17. Wren diary, July 18, 1861, in Wren Collection, EU.

18. A. J. Dully to unknown, July 19, 1861, in Army of Northern Virginia Papers, Part I, LHAC (quotation).

19. *OR*, Vol. II, 310–12, 440–50, 463–65; Jno. to Charley, July 28, 1861, in Army of Northern Virginia Papers, Part I, LHAC.

20. *OR*, Vol. II, 318; Schreckengost, *First Louisiana Special Battalion*, 55; Dufour, *Gentle Tiger*, 134–36; P. G. T. Beauregard, "The First Battle of Bull Run," in R. V. Johnson and C. C. Buel

(eds.), *Battles and Leaders of the Civil War* (4 vols.; New York, 1884–88), I, 207; Jesse Walton Reid, *History of the Fourth S.C. Volunteers, from the Commencement of the War Until Lee's Surrender* (1892; rpt. Dayton, Ohio, 1975), 23–25.

21. Schreckengost, *First Louisiana Special Battalion*, 56–58; Jones, *Tiger Rifles*, 81; OR, Vol. II, 558–62.

22. Jones, *Tiger Rifles*, 81 (first quotation); Laurence, "Letters from a North Louisiana Tiger," 132 (second quotation); see also Augustus Woodbury, *The Second Rhode Island Regiment: A Narrative of Military Operations from the Beginning to the End of the War for the Union* (Providence, 1875), 97–98.

23. McClellan, *Welcome the Hour of Conflict*, 53 (first three quotations); Jones, *Tiger Rifles*, 82 (fourth quotation); Schreckengost, *First Louisiana Special Battalion*, 58.

24. Jones, *Tiger Rifles*, 96.

25. Dufour, *Gentle Tiger*, 140–41 (first quotation); Jones, *Tiger Rifles*, 95–96 (second quotation); Schreckengost, *First Louisiana Special Battalion*, 73; for newspaper accounts about the use of knives see *Daily Dispatch*, August 6, 1861, *Chronicling America*, chroniclingamerica.loc. gov (accessed December 21, 2015), and Washington, D.C., *National Republican*, August 3, 1861 (accessed October 26, 2015); Richmond *Enquirer*, July 26, 1861.

26. Dufour, *Gentle Tiger*, 136–42; Jones, *Tiger Rifles*, 83–84.

27. Schreckengost, *First Louisiana Special Battalion*, 65 (first quotation); Jones, *Tiger Rifles*, 69 (second quotation), 86; unidentified newspaper clipping, in M. J. Solomons Scrapbook, 312, DU; Frank to "Darling," July 26, 1861, in Folder 11, John T. Wheat Collection, SHC.

28. Jones, *Tiger Rifles*, 88.

29. Ibid., 83 (quotation); Dufour, *Gentle Tiger*, 140–41; Richmond *Enquirer*, July 26, 1861.

30. Unidentified newspaper clipping in Civil War Scrapbook, 1861–62, TU (first quotation); Schreckengost, *First Louisiana Special Battalion*, 74 (second quotation).

31. Schreckengost, *First Louisiana Special Battalion*, 77 (quotation); unidentified newspaper clipping in Civil War Scrapbook, 1861–62, TU; OR, Vol. II, 488, 499, 555–58; De Choiseul to Walton, November 6, 1861, in Folder 8, Walton-Glenny Papers, HNOC; William B. Ratliff to P. G. T. Beauregard, July 4, 1884, in Pierre Gustave Toutant Beauregard Papers, DU; Jubal A. Early, *War Memoirs: Autobiographical Sketch and Narrative of the War Between the States*, ed. Frank Vandiver (1912; rpt. Bloomington, 1960), 16–27.

32. OR, Vol. II, 327, 570; Schreckengost, *First Louisiana Special Battalion*, 76.

33. Jones, *Tiger Rifles*, 91.

34. The Crescent City Blues, which later became part of St. Paul's Foot Rifles, temporarily served with the 49th Virginia at First Manassas, but nothing is known of its service there. *Daily Dispatch*, August 6, 1861, *Chronicling America*, chroniclingamerica.loc.gov (accessed October 26, 2015) (first and second quotations); OR, Vol. II, 559 (third quotation); *First Bull Run*, www. firstbullrun.co.uk/Potomac/Second%20Brigade/washington-battalion-artillery.html (accessed July 7, 2016).

35. The story of a Tiger murdering a prisoner may be apocryphal because a nearly identical accusation was made against a member of Coppens' Battalion during the Peninsula Campaign. Hillsborough (Ohio) *Highland Weekly News*, September 12, 1861, *Chronicling America*, chroniclingamerica.loc.gov (accessed July 7, 2016) (first quotation); Gallipolis (Ohio) *Journal*, June 26,

1862 (accessed October 26, 2015) (second quotation); *Home Journal,* June 17, 1869 (accessed October 26, 2015) (third quotation); Ebensburg (Pa.) *Alleghanian* August 1, 1861 (accessed July 7, 2016) (fourth quotation); see also Stanford (Ky.) *Semi-weekly Interior Journal,* February 1, 1884 (accessed May 18, 2016).

36. Plymouth (Ind.) *Marshall County Republican,* May 15, 1862, *Chronicling America,* chroniclingamerica.loc.gov (accessed October 26, 2015).

37. Wheat, "Memoir of Gen. C. R. Wheat," 55 (quotation); Section V in Henry T. Owen Papers, Accession 28154, Personal Papers Collection, Archives Branch, VSL; Richmond *Enquirer,* July 26, 1861; unidentified newspaper clipping in Civil War Scrapbook, 1861–62, TU; Dufour, *Gentle Tiger,* 143–46.

38. Schreckengost, *First Louisiana Special Battalion,* 78; Wheat, "Memoir of Gen. C. R. Wheat," 55 (quotation).

39. Jones, *Tiger Rifles,* 93–94; Schreckengost, *First Louisiana Special Battalion,* 77–78; Booth (comp.), *Louisiana Confederate Soldiers,* II, 1143; Alison Moore, *He Died Furious* (Baton Rouge, 1983), 78–79.

40. Jones, *Tiger Rifles,* 94.

41. Taylor, *Destruction and Reconstruction,* 9.

42. Wren diary, July 21, 1862, in Wren Collection, EU.

43. Jones (ed.), *Campbell Brown's Civil War,* 31 (first quotation); Gannon, *Irish Rebels,* 6 (second quotation); Trahern, "Biography," 19, RNBP (third quotation)

44. Nicholas Herron to Anne McCarthy, August 8, 1861, in Herron Family Correspondence, TU (quotation); Early, *War Memoirs,* 15; William F. Ogden to father, July 23, August 1, 1861, in Ogden Papers, TU; unidentified newspaper clipping in Civil War Scrapbook, 1861–62, TU; Jones (ed.), *Campbell Brown's Civil War,* 31–32; Taylor, *Destruction and Reconstruction,* 8–10.

45. *Daily Dispatch,* November 27, 1861.

46. Ibid. (quotation); Charles de Choiseul to Louisa Watson, November 6, 1861, in Walton-Glenny Family Papers, HNOC.

47. *Daily Dispatch,* November 27, 1861.

48. George Zeller to family, October (4?), 1861, in Zeller Letters, 6th Louisiana Folder, Louisiana Box, ANB.

49. Wren diary, October 2, 1861, in Wren Collection, EU; see also History of the 6th Louisiana Volunteers in Army of Northern Virginia Papers, Part II, LHAC; Bound Volume 8 in Association of the Army of Northern Virginia, LHAC; Frank E. Vandiver (ed.), "A Collection of Louisiana Confederate Letters," *Louisiana Historical Quarterly,* XXVI (1943), 942; "What Confederate Flag Was It?" *Confederate Veteran,* X (1902), 389; Fred D. Osborne, "Dumfries on the Potomac—Spring of 1861," *Confederate Veteran,* XVII (1909), 557; Compiled Service Records of Confederate Soldiers Who Served in Organizations from the State of Louisiana, War Record Group 109, Microcopy 320, Rolls 163, 175, NA.

50. Kajencki, "Louisiana Tiger," 52 (first quotation); Conner (ed.), "Letters of Lieutenant Robert H. Miller," 71–72 (second quotation); Special Order #580, January 6, 1862, in Association of the Army of Northern Virginia, Part I, LHAC; Moore diary, July 22, 1861, in Moore Papers, UT: McLaws to children, July 21, 1861, in Folder 4, McLaws Collection, SHC.

51. Phifer to mother, October 25, 1861, in 2nd Louisiana Folder, Louisiana Box, ANB.

52. Ibid. (first quotation); William Posey to Sister Lizzie, October 24, 1861, in *Camp Moore News*, Vol. 16, No. 3 (September 2014) (second quotation).

53. Stephen W. Sears, *To the Gates of Richmond: The Peninsula Campaign* (New York, 1992), 37; Conner (ed.), "Letters of Lieutenant Robert H. Miller," 71–72 (quotation).

54. Pendleton to "Lieut.," May 14, 1862, in Anderson File, MOC (quotation); Janin to father, April 11, 1862, in Folder 1, Janin Collection, SHC; Brooks and Jones, *Lee's Foreign Legion*, 20.

55. Janin to father, April 11, 1862, in Folder 1, Janin Collection, SHC (first quotation). Conner (ed.), "Letters of Lieutenant Robert H. Miller," 80 (second quotation). *OR*, Vol. IX, 405–6; Vol. XI, Pt. I, 403–4. Bartlett, *Military Record of Louisiana*, 27–28.

56. Buckley (ed.), *A Frenchman, a Chaplain, a Rebel*, 106.

57. Lichenstein memoir, USAERC.

58. G. G. Benedict, *Vermont in the Civil War: A History of the Part Taken by the Vermont Soldiers and Sailors in the War for the Union, 1861–5* (2 vols.; Burlington, 1886), I, 265; *OR*, Vol. XI, Pt. I, 363–67, 406–8, 415–21; B. M. Zettler, "Magruder's Peninsula Campaign," *Confederate Veteran*, VIII (1900), 197; Compiled Service Records, War Record Group 109, Microcopy 320, Roll 102, NA.

59. Sidney Baxter Robertson to mother, April 24, 1862, in Sidney Baxter Robertson memoir, USAERC (first quotation); McClellan, *Welcome the Hour of Conflict*, 160.

60. Sidney Baxter Robertson to mother, April 24, 1862, in Sidney Baxter Robertson memoir, USAERC (first quotation); Benedict, *Vermont in the Civil War*, I, 265 (second quotation); *OR*, Vol. XI, Pt. I, 363–67, 406–8, 415–21; Zettler, "Magruder's Peninsula Campaign," 197; Compiled Service Records, War Record Group 109, Microcopy 320, Roll 102, NA.

61. Thomas Phifer to father, February 4, 1862, in 2nd Louisiana Folder, Louisiana Box, ANB (quotation); see also Lt. Col. Edmund Pendleton to Gen. S. Cooper, March 3, 1862, in Anderson File, MOC.

62. LeGrand James Wilson, *The Confederate Soldier*, ed. James W. Silver (Memphis, 1973), 79–80 (quotation); Phifer to Lizzie, February 11, 1862, in 2nd Louisiana Folder, Louisiana Box, ANB.

63. General John B. Magruder's Special Order 701, March 27, 1862, in MC-3/MSS. 3, MOC (quotation); Jones, *American Civil War*, 89.

64. "First Volunteers from Louisiana," 146; "Dreux Battalion," 54–55; Paul E. Daugherty, "W. E. Moore in the Civil War," in Moore Papers, UT; *OR*, Vol. XI, Pt. III, 435; unknown to Colonel W. G. Vincent, April 2, 1862, in Box 1, Folder 1, Wise Papers, LSU; William E. H Huger to O. L. Putnam, July 20, 1899, in Flags, LHAC; Bound Volumes 1 and 2, in Association of the Army of Northern Virginia, LHAC; Thomas Taylor to Miles Taylor, April 12, 1862, in Box 1, Folder 3, Miles Taylor Family Papers, LSU (quotation); Williams diary, 119–21, 144, in MSCA.

65. Phifer to Lizzie, March 14, 1862, in 2nd Louisiana Folder, Louisiana Box, ANB (quotation); J. W. Minnich article on Coppens' Zouaves, in Reminiscences, Executive and Army of Northern Virginia, LHAC; Brooks and Jones, *Lee's Foreign Legion*, 14; Harrisburg (Pa.) *Star Independent*, April 12, 1915, *Chronicling America*, chroniclingamerica.loc.gov (accessed October 28, 2015).

66. Wren diary, February 8 and April 23, 1862 (quotation), in Wren Collection, EU; see also 9th Louisiana Order Book, April 24, 1862, in MOC.

67. Hewitt, "Confederate Foreign Legion," 126; Cutrer and Parrish (eds.), *Brothers in Gray,*

87; E. Russ Williams, "Retrospective," in anonymous newspaper clipping, Civil War Documents Collection, Folder 10, Box 77, USAERC.

68. Henry Gillum to B. F. Post, December 11, 1892, in Reminiscences, Executive and Army of Northern Virginia, LHAC (quotations); *OR*, Vol. XI, Pt. I, 275, 441–43, 450–60, 467, 475.

69. Gillum to Post, December 11, 1892, (quotation); Leon Jastremski, "Yorktown and Williamsburg"; Fred Ober, "The Campaign of the Peninsula," all in Reminiscences, Executive and Army of Northern Virginia, LHAC. McLaws to Adjutant General Right Wing, May 16, 1862, in Folder 5, McLaws Collection, SHC. John Y. Foster, *New Jersey and the Rebellion: A History of the Services of the Troops and People of New Jersey in Aid of the Union Cause* (Newark, 1868), 133; *OR*, Vol. XI, Pt. I, 487–91, 564–71, 581–89.

70. Fred Ober, "The Campaign of the Peninsula," Reminiscences, Executive and Army of Northern Virginia, LHAC; Charlton diary, n.d., JPC (quotation); Sample reminiscences, FSNMP.

71. Robert Stiles, *Four Years Under Marse Robert* (4th ed., New York, 1910), 80–81.

72. *Semi-weekly Interior Journal*, February 1, 1884, *Chronicling America*, chroniclingamerica. loc.gov (accessed May 18, 2016).

CHAPTER 4

"SOMETHING TO BOAST OF"

1. For details of Ewell's early life, see Donald C. Pfanz, *Richard S. Ewell: A Soldier's Life* (Chapel Hill, 1998); Taylor, *Destruction and Reconstruction*, 29, 31 (quotations).

2. Taylor, *Destruction and Reconstruction*, 29 (first quotation); Pfanz, *Richard S. Ewell*, 157 (second quotation).

3. Pfanz, *Richard S. Ewell*, 157 (second quotation), 268 (first quotation), 476 (third quotation).

4. Taylor, *Destruction and Reconstruction*, 32.

5. New Orleans *Times-Democrat*, n.d., in Confederate Veteran Papers, Reminiscences Division, DU (first quotation); Frank M. Myers, *The Comanches: A History of White's Battalion, Virginia Cavalry, Laurel Brig., Hampton Div., A.N.V., C.S.A.* (1871; rpt. Marietta, Ga., 1956), 39 (second quotation).

6. Gannon, *Irish Rebels*, 17 (quotation); Handerson, *Yankee in Gray*, 39; Taylor, *Destruction and Reconstruction*, 27–28.

7. W. G. Ogden to father, March 24, 1862, in Box 1, Folder 8, Ogden Papers, TU (first quotation); Gannon, *Irish Rebels*, 18 (second quotation); see also Thomas Taylor to Ann Steel, March 21, 1862, in Box 1, Folder 3, Taylor Papers, LSU; Edmond Stephens to parents, April 13, 1862, in Stephens Collection, NSU; Bartlett, *Military Record of Louisiana*, 32; Jones, *Tiger Rifles*, 114; Bauer (ed.), *Soldier's Journey*, 41; Ben Hubert to Letitia M. Bailey, March 17, 1862, in Hubert Papers, DU.

8. Taylor, *Destruction and Reconstruction*, 28 (quotation); J. E. B. Stuart to Joseph Johnston, March 12, 1862, in James Ewell Brown Stuart Papers, DU; Ogden to father, n.d., in Ogden Papers, TU.

9. Cleveland *Morning Leader*, March 21, 1861, *Chronicling America*, chroniclingamerica.loc.

gov (accessed October 29, 2015) (quotation); see also Columbus *Daily Ohio Statesman*, March 9, 1862 (accessed October 31, 2015); Pfanz, *Richard S. Ewell*, 151.

10. Handerson incorrectly identified the sergeant major as Tom Jennings. Handerson, *Yankee in Gray*, 40; Booth (comp.), *Louisiana Confederate Soldiers*, III, 1170.

11. Stephens to parents, May 12, 1862, in Stephens Collection, NSU.

12. T. A. Tooke to wife, April 26, 1862, in T. A. Tooke Letter, NSU.

13. Stephens to parents, May 12, 1862, in Stephens Collection, NSU; Oates, *15th Alabama*, 92–93; Taylor, *Destruction and Reconstruction*, 32–37; Reed, *Private in Gray*, 14 (quotation).

14. Boyd, *Reminiscences of the War in Virginia*, 7–8.

15. Ibid., 9–10; Donald C. Pfanz, Ewell's biographer, questions the veracity of Boyd's story concerning Taylor's meeting in Richmond. No other source has been discovered that supports Boyd's account. Pfanz, *Richard S. Ewell*, 166.

16. Jones (ed.), *Campbell Brown's Civil War*, 61.

17. Stafford and Peck were later promoted to brigadier general. Stafford was mortally wounded at the Wilderness, and Williams was killed at Gettysburg. Terry L. Jones, "Leroy Augustus Stafford," in Davis (ed.), *Confederate General*, V, 194–95; Lawrence L. Hewitt, "William Raine Peck," in Davis (ed.), *Confederate General*, V, 2–3; Jones (ed.), *Campbell Brown's Civil War*, 361.

18. Isaac G. Seymour to William J. Seymour, May 2, 1862, Seymour Papers, UM.

19. Ibid.; Gannon, *Irish Rebels*, 24.

20. Gannon, *Irish Rebels*, 2.

21. Ibid., 24–25.

22. Jones (ed.), *Campbell Brown's Civil War*, 80 (quotation); Bauer (ed.), *Soldier's Journey*, 4; Robert K. Krick, *Lee's Colonels: A Biographical Register of the Field Officers of the Army of Northern Virginia* (Dayton, 1992), 303; John W. Vollbrecht, "Hays' and Avery's Brigades: Biographical Sketches," *Battlefield Dispatch*, XVIII, No. 3 (March 2000), 6–9, in Box 6, Folder 1, Louisiana Brigades Boxes, GNMP.

23. Campbell Brown to mother, May 9, 1862, in Folder 9, Polk, Brown, and Ewell Family Collection, SHC (quotation). Stephens to parents, May 12, 1862, in Stephens Collection, NSU. Handerson, *Yankee in Gray*, 40–41. *OR*, Vol. XII, Pt. I, 458–60; Pt. XII, 882. William Allen, "History of the Campaign of Gen. T. J. (Stonewall) Jackson in the Shenandoah Valley of Virginia," *Southern Historical Society Papers*, n.s., V (1920), 199. Jones (ed.), *Campbell Brown's Civil War*, 80–81.

24. Parrish, *Richard Taylor*, 156–57; Pfanz, *Richard S. Ewell*, 178.

25. Taylor, *Destruction and Reconstruction*, 41.

26. Nisbet, *Four Years on the Firing Line*, 77–78 (first quotation); John H. Worsham, *One of Jackson's Foot Cavalry*, ed. James I. Robertson Jr. (1912; rpt. Jackson, Tenn., 1964), 41 (second quotation); Taylor, *Destruction and Reconstruction*, 41.

27. Taylor, *Destruction and Reconstruction*, 41 (first quotation); Stiles, *Four Years Under Marse Robert*, 172 (second and third quotations); Nisbet, *Four Years on the Firing Line*, 41; Worsham, *One of Jackson's Foot Cavalry*, 41; Clifford Dowdey, *The Land They Fought For: The Story of the South as the Confederacy, 1832–1865* (Garden City, N.Y., 1955), 176–77; John Overton Casler, *Four Years in the Stonewall Brigade* (1906; rpt. Marietta, Ga., 1951), 201.

28. Taylor, *Destruction and Reconstruction*, 42.

29. Ibid.; Burke Davis, *They Called Him Stonewall: A Life of Lt. General T. J. Jackson, C.S.A.* (New York, 1954), 27 (first quotation); Snakenberg, "Memoirs," 29, JPC (second quotation); Pfanz, *Richard S. Ewell,* 166–67.

30. Boyd, *Reminiscences of the War in Virginia,* 12 (first quotations); Taylor, *Destruction and Reconstruction,* 30 (last quotation).

31. James I. Robertson Jr., *Stonewall Jackson: The Man, the Soldier, the Legend* (New York, 1997), 373–92.

32. Parrish, *Richard Taylor,* 161–62.

33. Ibid., 166 (quotation); Taylor, *Destruction and Reconstruction,* 44.

34. Taylor, *Destruction and Reconstruction,* 45.

35. Jones (ed.), *Campbell Brown's Civil War,* 86.

36. Jones, *Tiger Rifles,* 121.

37. Parrish, *Richard Taylor,* 168; Robert G. Tanner, *Stonewall in the Valley: Thomas J. "Stonewall" Jackson's Shenandoah Valley Campaign, Spring 1862* (Mechanicsburg, Pa., 1996), 262.

38. Jones (ed.), *Campbell Brown's Civil War,* 86 (first quotation); Opelousas *Courier,* September 6, 1862, RNBP (second and third quotations).

39. Opelousas *Courier,* September 6, 1862, RNBP; Taylor, *Destruction and Reconstruction,* 46 (quotation).

40. Taylor, *Destruction and Reconstruction,* 47 (first quotation); Parrish, *Richard Taylor,* 170 (second quotation); Jones (ed.), *Campbell Brown's Civil War,* 366 (third, fourth, and fifth quotations); Opelousas *Courier,* September 6, 1862, RNBP; Jones, *Tiger Rifles,* 121.

41. Wren diary, May 30, 1862, in Wren Collection, EU; Cutrer and Parrish (eds.), *Brothers in Gray,* 93.

42. Jones, *Tiger Rifles,* 122.

43. Taylor, *Destruction and Reconstruction,* 47 (quotation); Parrish, *Richard Taylor,* 174; Dufour, *Gentle Tiger,* 176; *OR,* Vol. XII, Pt. I, 701–3, 778, 800–801; Oates, *15th Alabama,* 96–97; McHenry Howard, *Recollections of a Maryland Confederate Soldier and Staff Officer Under Johnston, Jackson and Lee* (1914; rpt. Dayton, Ohio, 1975), 106.

44. *OR,* Vol. XII, Pt. I, 703 (first quotation); Taylor, *Destruction and Reconstruction,* 47 (second quotation).

45. Henry Kyd Douglas, *I Rode with Stonewall* (Chapel Hill, 1940), 54 (first quotation); Schreckengost, *First Louisiana Special Battalion,* 109 (second quotation).

46. Taylor, *Destruction and Reconstruction,* 48 (quotation); *OR,* Vol. XII, Pt. I, 704–7, 726, 779, 800–801; Bound Volume 9 in Association of the Army of Northern Virginia, LHAC; Compiled Service Records, War Record Group 109, Microcopy 320, Roll 201, NA; Stephens to parents, June 14, 1862, in Stephens Collection, NSU; Freeman, *Lee's Lieutenants,* I, 387; Dufour, *Gentle Tiger,* 176–77; Davis, *They Called Him Stonewall,* 44–45; Robert L. Dabney, *Life and Campaigns of Lieut.-General Thomas J. Jackson* (New York, 1866), 371–72.

47. *OR,* Vol. XII, Pt. I, 726 (first quotation); Pt. III, 902 (second and third quotations). Freeman, *Lee's Lieutenants,* I, 390.

48. Handerson, *Yankee in Gray,* 42 (first quotation), 180–81; Parrish, *Richard Taylor,* 179 (second quotation); Taylor, *Destruction and Reconstruction,* 49 (third quotation); Opelousas *Courier,* September 6, 1862, RNBP.

49. Handerson, *Yankee in Gray*, 42 (first quotation); Parrish, *Richard Taylor*, 182 (second quotation); Taylor, *Destruction and Reconstruction*, 50 (third quotation).

50. James Huffman, *Ups and Downs of a Confederate Soldier* (New York, 1940), 47 (first quotation); Jones, *Tiger Rifles*, 129 (second quotation); Taylor, *Destruction and Reconstruction*, 51 (last quotations); Douglas, *I Rode with Stonewall*, 57.

51. Opelousas *Courier*, September 6, 1862, RNBP (first quotation); Parrish, *Richard Taylor*, 185 (second quotation).

52. Wren diary, May 31, 1862, in Wren Collection, EU (first quotation); Parrish, *Richard Taylor*, 186 (second quotation).

53. Parrish, *Richard Taylor*, 183–84 (first quotation), 186 (second quotation); Opelousas *Courier*, September 6, 1862, RNBP (third quotation); New Orleans *Times-Picayune*, February 15, 1932, in Melrose Scrapbook 228, NSU (fourth quotation); W. W. Goldsborough, *The Maryland Line in the Confederate Army, 1861–1865* (Baltimore, 1900), 45 (fifth quotation); Wren diary, May 31, 1862, in Wren Collection, EU.

54. Opelousas *Courier*, September 6, 1862, RNBP (first quotation); Douglas, *I Rode with Stonewall*, 58 (second quotation); Taylor, *Destruction and Reconstruction*, 51–52, 78; *OR*, Vol. XII, Pt. I, 404–7; Davis, *They Called Him Stonewall*, 52; Howard, *Recollections of a Maryland Confederate*, 111; Wren diary, May 31, 1862, in Wren Collection, EU; B. T. Johnson, "Memoir of the First Maryland Regiment," *Southern Historical Society Papers*, X (1882), 99 (third quotation); Worsham, *One of Jackson's Foot Cavalry*, 46 (fourth quotation); Goldsborough, *Maryland Line*, 45; Davis, *They Called Him Stonewall*, 53; Parrish, *Richard Taylor*, 187.

55. Wren diary, May 31, 1862, in Wren Collection, EU; Opelousas *Courier*, September 6, 1862, RNBP; Schreckengost, *First Louisiana Special Battalion*, 115.

56. Mrs. Cornelia McDonald, *A Diary with Reminiscences of the War and Refugee Life in the Shenandoah Valley, 1860–1865* (Nashville, 1934), 67–68.

57. Oates, *15th Alabama*, 98 (first quotation); Rev. Philip Slaughter, *A Sketch of the Life of Randolph Fairfax . . . Including a Brief Account of Jackson's Celebrated Valley Campaign* (Baltimore, 1878), 28–29 (second quotation); Taylor, *Destruction and Reconstruction*, 52 (third quotation); Opelousas *Courier*, September 6, 1862, RNBP (fourth quotation); see also Huffman, *Ups and Downs of a Confederate Soldier*, 47.

58. McDonald, *Diary*, 68 (first quotation); *Daily Dispatch* quoting a Baltimore paper, June 14, 1862, dlxs.richmond.edu (accessed October 29, 2015) (second and third quotations).

59. Taylor, *Destruction and Reconstruction*, 52 (first quotation); G. P. Ring to wife, June 14, 1862, typescript copy, in Army of Northern Virginia Papers, Part I, LHAC (second quotation); Parrish, *Richard Taylor*, 189.

60. McDonald, *Diary*, 68.

61. Ibid.; *OR*, Vol. XII, Pt. I, 780–81, 800–801.

62. *OR*, Vol. XII, Pt. III, 251 (first quotation); George M. Morgan to Joe, June 18, 1862, in Francis Warrington Dawson Letters, DU (second quotation).

63. Wren diary, May 25, 1862, in Wren Collection, EU.

64. Parrish, *Richard Taylor*, 190; Robertson, *Stonewall Jackson*, 412.

65. *OR*, Vol. XII, Pt. I, 682, 694–95, 707–9; Pt. III, 299. Jones (ed.), *Campbell Brown's Civil War*, 92. Taylor, *Destruction and Reconstruction*, 51–54.

66. Opelousas *Courier,* September 6, 1862, RNBP.

67. Eloise C. Strader (ed.), *The Civil War Journal of Mary Greenhow Lee (Mrs. Hugh Holmes Lee) of Winchester, Virginia* (Winchester, 2011), 80 (first and second quotations); Opelousas *Courier,* September 6, 1862, RNBP (third quotation).

68. *OR,* Series II, Vol. IV, 812; Francis R. T. Nicholls to Robert Carter, October 14, 1889, in Francis R. T. Nicholls Letters, LSU; Taylor, *Destruction and Reconstruction,* 54.

69. Ottawa *Free Trader,* March 20, 1869, *Chronicling America,* chroniclingamerica.loc.gov (accessed March 31, 2016).

70. Taylor, *Destruction and Reconstruction,* 53–54; Bauer (ed.), *Soldier's Journey,* 48.

71. Taylor, *Destruction and Reconstruction,* 57 (quotation); Bauer (ed.), *Soldier's Journey,* 48.

72. Taylor, *Destruction and Reconstruction,* 57 (first quotation); Parrish, *Richard Taylor,* 195 (second quotation).

73. Taylor, *Destruction and Reconstruction,* 55.

74. Ibid., 58; Pfanz, *Richard S. Ewell,* 201–2.

75. Taylor, *Destruction and Reconstruction,* 58–60.

76. Ibid., 60–61 (quotations); *OR,* Vol. XII, Pt. I, 730–31; Jones (ed.), *Campbell Brown's Civil War,* 93–94.

77. Bauer (ed.), *Soldier's Journey,* 49.

78. Ibid.

79. Ibid., 49–50; *OR,* Vol. XII, Pt. I, 711–12.

80. *OR,* Vol. XII, Pt. I, 781–84; Stephens to parents, June 14, 1862, in Stephens Collection, NSU; Taylor, *Destruction and Reconstruction,* 66–67.

81. Nisbet, *Four Years on the Firing Line,* 54.

82. Ibid., 53–54.

83. Parrish, *Richard Taylor,* 202.

84. Dabney, *Life and Campaigns of Jackson,* 419–20; Gannon, *Irish Rebels,* 49; Taylor, *Destruction and Reconstruction,* 67–68.

85. Nisbet, *Four Years on the Firing Line,* 67–69; *OR,* Vol. XII, Pt. I, 713–16, 741–42, 785–87; James I. Robertson Jr., *The Stonewall Brigade* (1963; rpt. Baton Rouge, 1977), 108–9; Howard, *Recollections of a Maryland Confederate,* 126; Dabney, *Life and Campaigns of Jackson,* 419–20; Parrish, *Richard Taylor,* 207–8; Henry B. Kelly, *Port Republic* (Philadelphia, 1886), 16.

86. George L. Wood, *The Seventh Regiment: A Record* (New York, 1865), 117.

87. Dufour, *Gentle Tiger,* 185 (first quotation); Huffman, *Ups and Downs of a Confederate Soldier,* 50 (second quotation); *OR,* Vol. XII, Pt. I, 713–16, 741–42, 750–53; Freeman, *Lee's Lieutenants,* I, 454–60; Robertson, *Stonewall Brigade,* 108–12; J. Hamp SeCheverell, *Journal History of the Twenty-Ninth Ohio Veteran Volunteers, 1861–1865, Its Victories and Its Reverses* (Cleveland, 1883), 46–47; Bauer (ed.), *Soldier's Journey,* 52.

88. Parrish, *Richard Taylor,* 209; Taylor, *Destruction and Reconstruction,* 68; Kelly, *Port Republic,* 16–18.

89. *Daily Picayune,* June 10, 1866.

90. Gannon, *Irish Rebels,* 54, 56 (first quotation); Woodsville (Ohio) *Spirit of Democracy,* July 9, 1862, *Chronicling America,* chroniclingamerica.loc.gov (accessed October 30, 2015) (second quotation); Schreckengost, *First Louisiana Special Battalion,* 134; Parrish, *Richard Taylor,* 210.

91. Kelly claimed that his regiment was the first to reach the battery, while other sources give that honor to Lt. Robert English, the Virginia guide, who was killed while far in advance of the attacking line. Kelly, *Port Republic*, 19; Washington, D.C., *National Tribune*, May 2, 1889, *Chronicling America*, chroniclingamerica.loc.gov (accessed October 30, 2015) (first quotation); Opelousas *Courier*, September 6, 1862, RNBP (second and third quotations).

92. Stephens to parents, June 14, 1862, in Stephens Collection, NSU (first quotation); Kelly, *Port Republic*, 20; Dufour, *Gentle Tiger*, 187 (other quotations).

93. Parrish, *Richard Taylor*, 210–11 (first and second quotations); Gannon, *Irish Rebels*, 57 (third quotation), 60 (fourth quotation).

94. Gannon, *Irish Rebels*, 58 (second quotation), 60 (first quotation).

95. Kelly, *Port Republic*, 20 (first quotation); Richmond (Va.) *Times*, June 14, 1902, *Chronicling America*, chroniclingamerica.loc.gov (accessed October 29, 2015) (other quotations); Gannon, *Irish Rebels*, 61; Taylor, *Destruction and Reconstruction*, 69; Pfanz, *Richard S. Ewell*, 217; Parrish, *Richard Taylor*, 212.

96. Parrish, *Richard Taylor*, 69 (quotation); Pfanz, *Richard S. Ewell*, 217; *OR*, Vol. XII, Pt. I, 693–97, 801–3; Wood, *Seventh Regiment*, 117–22: New Orleans *Daily Item*, August 25, 1896, in Scrapbook, Boyd Papers, LSU; John M. Paver, *What I Saw from 1861 to 1864* (1906; rpt. Ann Arbor, 1974), 81–82; John D. Imboden, "Stonewall Jackson in the Valley," in Johnson and Buel (eds.), *Battles and Leaders*, II, 295–96.

97. Taylor, *Destruction and Reconstruction*, 70 (first quotation); Jones, *Tiger Rifles*, 138 (second quotation); *National Tribune*, May 2, 1889 (third quotation).

98. For more casualty figures, see *Daily Advertiser & Register* (Mobile, Ala.), July 23, 1862, RNBP; Ring to wife, June 14, 1862, in Army of Northern Virginia Papers, Part I, LHAC (first quotation); Parrish, *Richard Taylor*, 227 (second and third quotations); Gannon, *Irish Rebels*, 63; Taylor, *Destruction and Reconstruction*, 70; *OR*, Vol. XII, Pt. I, 690, 787; Wood, *Seventh Regiment*, 117–27; Stephens to parents, June 14, 1862, in Stephens Collection, NSU; Bound Volume 8, in Association of the Army of Northern Virginia, LHAC.

99. Taylor, *Destruction and Reconstruction*, 69.

100. *OR*, Vol. XII, Pt. I, 786 (quotation).

101. Ring to wife, June 14, 1862, in Army of Northern Virginia Papers, Part I, LHAC (quotation); Bound Volume 6 in Association of the Army of Northern Virginia, LHAC; Gannon, *Irish Rebels*, 37.

102. Taylor, *Destruction and Reconstruction*, 71 (first quotation); Ring to wife, June 24, 1862, in Army of Northern Virginia Papers, Part I, LHAC (second quotation); Ben Hubert to Letitia, June 13, 1862, in Hubert Papers, DU; Opelousas *Courier*, September 6, 1862, RNBP.

103. T. J. Jackson to Gen. Samuel Cooper, June 10, 1862, in Compiled Service Records of Confederate General and Staff Officers, and Nonregimental Enlisted Men, War Record Group 109, Microcopy 331, Roll 243, NA (first quotation); Gannon, *Irish Rebels*, 64 (second quotation).

104. Boyd, *Reminiscences of the War in Virginia*, 18 (quotation); Bauer (ed.), *Soldier's Journey*, 53; Taylor, *Destruction and Reconstruction*, 71.

105. Boyd, *Reminiscences of the War in Virginia*, 15–16.

106. Ibid., 16 (quotations); Booth (comp.), *Louisiana Confederate Soldiers*, I, 197.

107. Jones was later promoted to brigadier general and was wounded twice before being

killed at the Battle of the Wilderness. Bauer (ed.), *Soldier's Journey,* 53 (first quotation); Handerson, *Yankee in Gray,* 43 (second quotation); Jones (ed.), *Campbell Brown's Civil War,* 103 (third quotation).

108. Wren diary, June 9, 1862, in Wren Collection, EU.

109. Murrel and Montgomery were later mortally wounded at Antietam and the Monocacy, respectively. Booth (comp.), *Louisiana Confederate Soldiers,* II, 1020, 1111; *National Republican,* June 16, 1862, *Chronicling America,* chroniclingamerica.loc.gov (accessed October 13, 2015).

110. Wren diary, June 14, 1862, in Wren Collection, EU.

111. Ibid., August 7, 1862.

112. Bauer (ed.), *Soldier's Journey,* 57; Handerson, *Yankee in Gray,* 43.

CHAPTER 5
"I HAVE GOT MY FILL OF FIGHTING"

1. Snakenberg, "Memoirs," 10 (first quotation), JPC; Charlton diary, n.d. (second quotation), JPC.

2. Sample, "Reminiscences," FSNMP.

3. Captain Coffey was wounded at Savage's Station a few weeks later, and the secretary of war dropped him from the rolls. Charlton diary, n.d., JPC (quotations); Booth (comp.), *Louisiana Confederate Soldiers,* I, 370.

4. *OR,* Vol. XI, Pt. I, 31, 651–54, 664–66 (quotation); Hudson (Wisc.) *North Star,* June 4, 1862, *Newspaper Archive,* newspaperarchive.com (accessed November 24, 2015); Point Pleasant (Va.) *Weekly Register,* May 29, 1862, *Chronicling America,* chroniclingamerica.loc.gov (accessed November 24, 2015).

5. Sears, *To the Gates of Richmond,* 117–18.

6. An English Combatant, *Battlefield of the South, from Bull Run to Fredericksburg, with Sketches of Confederate Commanders, and Gossip of the Camps* (New York, 1864), 253; J. W. Drane, "Louisiana Tigers at Fair Oaks, Va.," *Confederate Veteran,* XIV (1906), 521; Aurelia Austin, *Georgia Boys with "Stonewall" Jackson: James Thomas Thompson and the Walton Infantry* (Athens, 1967), 27; Mills Lane (ed.), *"Dear Mother: Don't Grieve About Me, If I Get Killed, I'll Only Be Dead": Letters from Georgia Soldiers in the Civil War* (Savannah, 1977), 130; *OR,* Vol. XI, Pt. I, 939–41.

7. *Daily Dispatch,* June 9, 1862, dlxs.richmond.edu (accessed November 24, 2015).

8. English Combatant, *Battlefields of the South,* 254; *OR,* Vol. XI, Pt. I, 982.

9. Unidentified newspaper clipping in New Orleans Civil War Scrapbook, Part I, TU; unidentified newspaper clipping in Army of Northern Virginia Papers, Part I, LHAC; Wallace, "Coppens' Louisiana Zouaves," 279; *OR,* Vol. XI, Pt. I, 939–41; see also David S. Moore, "A Letter from the Peninsula," *Military Images,* Vol. 20, No. 2 (September–October 1998), 23, and Laurence, "Letters from a North Louisiana Tiger," 139.

10. Moore, "Letter from the Peninsula," 23; Booth (comp.), *Louisiana Confederate Soldiers,* I, 65.

11. Moore, "Letter from the Peninsula," 23 (quotation); *Daily Dispatch,* June 13, 1862, dlxs. richmond.edu (accessed June 6, 2015).

12. Edmund Pendleton to daughter, June 18, 1862, in Elizabeth P. Coles Collection, SHC.

13. Charlton diary, n.d., JPC.

14. Sears, *To the Gates of Richmond*, 174–77.

15. *Daily Dispatch*, June 27, 1862, dlxs.richmond.edu (accessed June 13, 2016).

16. Shivers' wound was so severe that he was transferred back to Louisiana. The Pennsylvania-born Henderson was later captured at the Monocacy and survived seven months in Elmira prison camp. *Daily Dispatch*, June 27, 1862, dlxs.richmond.edu (accessed June 13, 2016) (quotation); Booth (comp.), *Louisiana Confederate Soldiers*, I, 263–64, and III, 553.

17. *OR*, Vol. XI, Pt. II, 787–91, 804–6, 807 (quotation); Bartlett, *Military Record of Louisiana*, 4; Bound Volume I in Association of the Army of Northern Virginia, LHAC; unidentified newspaper clipping in Army of Northern Virginia Papers, Part I, LHAC; Samuel Huey Walkup journal, June 25, 1862, in DU; Sears, *To the Gates of Richmond*, 186.

18. Sears, *To the Gates of Richmond*, 176.

19. *OR*, Vol. XI, Pt. II, 834–40, 877–81; Vol. LI, Pt. I, 117–18.

20. Robertson, *Stonewall Jackson*, 471–73.

21. Fogleman was later wounded at the Second Battle of Fredericksburg and captured at Rappahannock Station, but he survived to surrender at Appomattox. Isaiah Fogleman diary, typed copy, June 23, 1862, FSNMP (quotation); Bauer (ed.), *Soldier's Journey*, 59; Parrish, *Richard Taylor*, 227; Taylor, *Destruction and Reconstruction*, 76–77.

22. Bauer (ed.), *Soldier's Journey*, 59; Robertson, *Stonewall Jackson*, 473.

23. Handerson, *Yankee in Gray*, 44 (quotation); Taylor, *Destruction and Reconstruction*, 76–77; Jones (ed.), *Campbell Brown's Civil War*, 114; Fogleman diary, June 26, 1862, FSNMP.

24. Bauer (ed.), *Soldier's Journey*, 60.

25. Sears, *To the Gates of Richmond*, 229 (quotation); New Orleans *Daily Item*, August 25, 1896, in Scrapbook, Boyd Papers, LSU; Dufour, *Gentle Tiger*, 172, 190–93; Handerson, *Yankee in Gray*, 44–45; Oates, *15th Alabama*, 81–82; R. T. Walshe, "Recollections of Gaines' Mill," *Confederate Veteran*, VII (1899), 54–55; Wheat, "Memoir of Gen. C. R. Wheat," 57; Edgefield (S.C.) *Advertiser*, May 30, 1894, *Chronicling America*, chroniclingamerica.loc.gov (accessed February 14, 2016).

26. Snakenberg, "Memoirs," 12–13, JPC.

27. David Zable, "The Battle of Gaines' Mill," in Reminiscences, Executive and Army of Northern Virginia, LHAC.

28. *OR*, Vol. XI, Pt. II, 757.

29. New Orleans *Daily Item*, August 25, 1896, in Scrapbook, Boyd Papers, LSU (quotation); Dufour, *Gentle Tiger*, 193.

30. Parrish, *Richard Taylor*, 230 (first quotation); Handerson, *Yankee in Gray*, 45 (second and third quotations).

31. Parrish, *Richard Taylor*, 231 (quotation); Opelousas *Courier*, August 30, 1862, *Louisiana in the Civil War Message Board*, December 5, 2014, www.history-sites.com (accessed February 14, 2016); New Orleans *Commercial Bulletin*, July 30, 1862, in New Orleans Civil War Scrapbook, Part II, TU.

32. New Orleans *Daily Item*, August 25, 1896, in Scrapbook, Boyd Papers, LSU; Dufour, *Gentle Tiger*, 195 (quotations); Handerson, *Yankee in Gray*, 46; Douglas, *I Rode with Stonewall*, 102–3; Reid, *History of the Fourth S.C.*, 102; Edward Porter Alexander, *Military Memoirs of a Confederate* (New York, 1907), 34.

33. Handerson, *Yankee in Gray,* 46 (quotations); Gannon, *Irish Rebels,* 80; Jones (ed.), *Campbell Brown's Civil War,* 118; *OR,* Vol. XI, Pt. II, 552–59, 563, 605–7, 619–20; Walshe, "Recollections of Gaines' Mill," 54–55; Oates, *15th Alabama,* 116–21; New Orleans *Commercial Bulletin,* July 30, 1862, in New Orleans Civil War Scrapbook, Part II, TU.

34. Robertson, *Stonewall Jackson,* 478 (first quotation); Parrish, *Richard Taylor,* 231 (second quotation); Walshe, "Recollections of Gaines' Mill," 55 (third quotation).

35. Jones (ed.), *Campbell Brown's Civil War,* 118 (first and second quotations); Walshe, "Recollections of Gaines' Mill," 55 (third quotation).

36. Conner (ed.), "Letters of Lieutenant Robert H. Miller," 88.

37. Snakenberg claimed a soldier named Sprybery was the second color-bearer to be killed, but there is no record of him. Ulitius L. G. Sprabury did serve in the 14th Louisiana, but his service record indicates he was killed on November 27, 1863, at Payne's Farm. Snakenberg, "Memoirs," 12, JPC; *OR,* Vol. XI, Pt. II, 779–81, 973–84; Zable, "Battle of Gaines' Mill," in Reminiscences, Executive and Army of Northern Virginia, LHAC; Booth (comp.), *Louisiana Confederate Soldiers,* III, 665.

38. Conner (ed.), "Letters of Lieutenant Robert H. Miller," 88.

39. *OR,* Vol. XI, Pt. II, 609–10; Taylor, *Destruction and Reconstruction,* 78 (quotation).

40. Jones, *Tiger Rifles,* 147–48.

41. Cutrer and Parrish (eds.), *Brothers in Gray,* 101.

42. Singleton may have been William Singleton of Company D. He was later captured at the Monocacy and held at Point Lookout prison but survived the war. Bauer (ed.), *Soldier's Journey,* 61 (first quotation); Hancock, "William Singleton," *Confederate Veteran,* XIV (1906), 499 (second quotation); Booth (comp.), *Louisiana Confederate Soldiers,* III, 584.

43. Bauer (ed.), *Soldier's Journey,* 61; Jones (ed.), *Campbell Brown's Civil War,* 121 (quotation); Fogleman diary, June 29, 1862, FSNMP; Sears, *To the Gates of Richmond,* 267–69.

44. Charlton claimed it was Colonel Forno who questioned the Yankees in the dark. Charlton diary, June 29, 1862, JPC; *OR,* Vol. XI, Pt. II, 721 (quotation).

45. Charlton diary, June 29, 1862, JPC (quotation); *OR,* Vol. XI, Pt. II, 720–25; Benedict, *Vermont in the Civil War,* I, 140, 290–98.

46. Parrish, *Richard Taylor,* 235; Taylor, *Destruction and Reconstruction,* 83.

47. Bartlett, *Military Record of Louisiana,* 44 (quotation); John W. T. Leech, "The Battle of Frasier's Farm," *Southern Historical Society Papers,* XXI (1893), 163–64; Sears, *To the Gates of Richmond,* 302–3.

48. Snakenberg, "Memoirs," 12, JPC.

49. Buckley (ed.), *A Frenchman, a Chaplain, a Rebel,* 117–18.

50. "Battle Flag of the Third Georgia," *Southern Historical Society Papers,* XXXVIII (1910), 211.

51. Ibid.; *OR,* Vol. XI, Pt. II, 99, 266–67, 315, 329.

52. Washington, D.C., *Times,* April 26, 1897, *Chronicling America,* chroniclingamerica.loc.gov (accessed February 16, 2016); Brooks and Jones, *Lee's Foreign Legion,* 2–3.

53. Buckley (ed.), *A Frenchman, a Chaplain, a Rebel,* 121.

54. Brooks and Jones, *Lee's Foreign Legion,* 23; Booth (comp.), *Louisiana Confederate Soldiers,* III, 1095.

55. Edward Pinkowski, *Pills, Pen and Politics: The Story of General Leon Jastremski, 1843–1907* (Wilmington, Del., 1974), 40 (quotation).

56. After the battle, LeBleu deserted the regiment to join a cavalry unit. Pinkowski, *Pills, Pen and Politics*; Booth (comp.), *Louisiana Confederate Soldiers*, I, 698; Brooks and Jones, *Lee's Foreign Legion*, 22.

57. Anonymous address on the Battle of Malvern Hill in Reminiscences, Executive and Army of Northern Virginia, LHAC (first quotation). Brooks and Jones, *Lee's Foreign Legion*, 22. Buckley, *A Frenchman, a Chaplain, a Rebel*, 47, 121, 123. Pinkowski, *Pills, Pen and Politics*, 37–41. *OR*, Vol. XI, Pt. II, 720–25. Bartlett, *Military Record of Louisiana*, 13, 24–25, 29 (second quotation), 30. "Eugene Waggaman," *Southern Historical Society Papers*, XXV (1897), 183–84, 180–86; I (1876), 75. Eugene Waggaman to Louis Janin, July, 1862, in Box 56, Folder 9, Janin Family Papers, HL. *Times-Picayune*, May 16, 1862, in Melrose Scrapbook 230, NSU.

58. Sears, *To the Gates of Richmond*, 334.

59. New York *Tribune*, April 13, 1896, *Chronicling America*, chroniclingamerica.loc.gov (accessed June 14, 2016) (quotation); Brooks and Jones, *Lee's Foreign Legion*, 23; Edward Seton to Mother, July 27, 1862, in Seton Collection, MSU.

60. *Daily Dispatch*, July 12, 1862 (first quotation); Lichenstein memoir, USAERC (second and third quotations); Booth (comp.), *Louisiana Confederate Soldiers*, III, 1100.

61. Some historians have questioned whether the officer actually witnessed Jemison's death. *National Tribune*, April 19, 1906, typed copy, RNBP (quotations); Keith Bohannon, "Edwin Francis Jemison: A Private in the 2nd Louisiana Infantry," *Military Images*, Vol. 7, No. 5 (March–April 1986), 9.

62. Lichenstein memoir, USAERC; Booth (comp.), *Louisiana Confederate Soldiers*, II, 852.

63. Bauer (ed.), *Soldier's Journey*, 62–63 (first quotation); Handerson, *Yankee in Gray*, 48 (second quotation); see also Fogleman diary, July 1, 62, FSNMP.

64. Jones (ed.), *Campbell Brown's Civil War*, 128 (first three quotations); Handerson, *Yankee in Gray*, 50 (fourth quotation); *OR*, Vol. XI, Pt. II, 601, 609, 659–74, 748–50, 973–84; Taylor, *Destruction and Reconstruction*, 86; Johnson, "Memoir of the First Maryland," 217.

65. Bauer (ed.), *Soldier's Journey*, 63–64 (quotation); Edward Seton to Fanny, August 16, 1862, in Seton Collection, MSU.

66. Michael Cavanagh, *Memoirs of Gen. Thomas Francis Meagher . . . Including Personal Reminiscences* (Worcester, Mass., 1892), 450–51.

67. *OR*, Vol. XI, Pt. II, 601, 609, 659–74, 748–50, 973–84.

68. Buckley (ed.), *A Frenchman, a Chaplain, a Rebel*, 117 (first quotation); Sample reminiscences, FSNMP (second quotation).

69. Cutrer and Parrish (eds.), *Brothers in Gray*, 112.

70. Richardson was killed a year later at Gettysburg. *Mobile Daily Advertiser & Register*, July 23, 1862, photocopy, RNBP.

71. Cutrer and Parrish (eds.), *Brothers in Gray*, 112 (first quotation); Parrish, *Richard Taylor*, 241 (third quotation), 242 (second quotation); Douglas Southall Freeman, *Lee's Lieutenants*, I, 669 (fourth and fifth quotation); *OR*, Vol. XII, Pt. III, 917–18; Taylor, *Destruction and Reconstruction*, 93.

72. Parrish, *Richard Taylor*, 232 (quotation); *OR*, Vol. LI, Pt. II, 597; Schreckengost, *First Lou-*

isiana Special Battalion, 169; Jones (ed.), *Campbell Brown's Civil War*, 365; Fort Worth (Tex.) *Daily Gazette*, May 22, 1890, *Chronicling America*, chroniclingamerica.loc.gov (accessed July 27, 2016).

73. *OR*, Vol. XII, Pt. II I, 917–18; Vol. LI, Pt. 11, 597. Stephens to Tom Stephens, August 3, 1862, and Stephens to sister, August 15, 1862, in Stephens Collection, NSU. Terry L. Jones, "Harry Thompson Hays," in Davis (ed.), *Confederate General*, III, 78–81; Compiled Service Records, War Record Group 109, Microcopy 320, Roll 100. Handerson, *Yankee in Gray*, 99, 132. James McDowell Carrington to Eliza Henry Carrington, October 16, 1862, in Carrington Family Papers, VHS.

74. Eugene Janin to John McLean, August 18, 1862, in Folder 2, Janin Collection, SHC; *OR*, Vol. XI, Pt. II, 648–49, 656; Terry L. Jones, "William Edwin Starke," in Davis (ed.), *Confederate General*, VI, 199.

CHAPTER 6

DARK AND DISMAL FIELDS

1. "Researching Col. Henry Forno," *Louisiana in the Civil War Message Board*, April 12, 2004, and November 30, 2006, at www.history-sites.com (accessed January 13, 2016); Alison Moore, *The Louisiana Tigers; or, The Two Louisiana Brigades in the Army of Northern Virginia, 1861–1865* (Baton Rouge, 1961), 163; Buckley (ed.), *A Frenchman, a Chaplain, a Rebel*, 48, 57.

2. Fogleman diary, July 7, 1862, FSNMP (quotation); Bauer (ed.), *Soldier's Journey*, 68.

3. Conner (ed.), "Letters of Lieutenant Robert H. Miller," 89 (quotation); *OR*, Vol. XII, Pt. II, 224, 226–33; Jedediah Hotchkiss, *Make Me a Map of the Valley: The Civil War Journal of Stonewall Jackson's Topographer*, ed. Archie P. McDonald (Dallas, 1973), 126, 295.

4. Buckley (ed.), *A Frenchman, a Chaplain, a Rebel*, 132–33.

5. *National Tribune*, August 1, 1895, *Chronicling America*, chroniclingamerica.loc.gov (accessed August 2, 2016).

6. James W. Manney was later wounded and captured at Chancellorsville. Upon being exchanged, he was reported absent without leave and joined John Hunt Morgan's cavalry in the western theater. Booth (comp.), *Louisiana Confederate Soldiers*, II, 861; Lichenstein memoir, US-AERC (quotations); Snakenberg, "Memoirs," 13–14, JPC; Edward A. Seton to Fanny, August 16, 1862, in Seton Collection, MSU; John J. Hennessy, *Return to Bull Run: The Campaign and Battle of Second Manassas* (New York, 1993), 67–68; Emory M. Thomas, *Robert E. Lee: A Biography* (New York, 1995), 251–52.

7. Hewitt, "Confederate Foreign Legion," 129.

8. Durkin (ed.), *Confederate Chaplain*, 9; Compiled Service Records, War Record Group 109, Microcopy 320, Roll 148, NA; Jones (ed.), *Campbell Brown's Civil War*, 147–48; Jubal A. Early, "Jackson's Campaigns Against Pope in August, 1862," in Pamphlets, Part II, LHAC; Freeman, *Lee's Lieutenants*, II, 90–92; Oates, *15th Alabama*, 133–35; W. B. Taliaferro, "Jackson's Raid Around Pope," in Johnson and Buel (eds.), *Battles and Leaders*, II, 503; Dabney, *Life and Campaigns of Jackson*, 518.

9. Wren diary, August 27, 1862, in Wren Collection, EU (quotation).

10. Jones (ed.), *Campbell Brown's Civil War*, 148 (quotation); Hennessy, *Return to Bull Run*, 131–32; "8th La. Infantry," *Louisiana in the Civil War Message Board*, April 29, 2003, www.history-sites.com (accessed January 13, 2016); Fogleman diary, August 27, 1862, FSNMP.

11. *OR*, Vol. XII, Pt. II, 443–52, 455, 457, 461–62, 708–9, 716; Taliaferro, "Jackson's Raid," 506; Early, *War Memoirs*, 114–18; Frederick Phisterer (comp.), *New York in the War of the Rebellion, 1861 to 1865* (Albany, 1890), 376, 428–32; casualty list for the 5th and 8th Louisiana, September 1, 1862, MOC.

12. C. G. Chamberlayne (ed.), *Ham Chamberlayne—Virginian: Letters and Papers of an Artillery Officer in the War for Southern Independence, 1861–1865* (Richmond, 1932), 100 (first quotation); Edmond Stephens to parents, September 7, 1862, in Stephens Collection, NSU (second quotation); Brooks and Jones, *Lee's Foreign Legion*, 31; Snakenberg, "Memoirs," 16, JPC.

13. Durkin (ed.), *Confederate Chaplain*, 11–12.

14. Charlton diary, n.d., JPC.

15. Jones (ed.), *Campbell Brown's Civil War*, 150 (first quotation); Charlton diary, n.d., JPC.

16. *OR*, Vol. XII, Pt. II, 657 (quotation).

17. Ibid., 378, 554–58, 658, 668–69; Taliaferro. "Jackson's Raid," 510–11; John Pope, "The Second Battle of Bull Run," in Johnson and Buel (eds.), *Battles and Leaders*, II, 469; Rufus R. Dawes, *Service with the Sixth Wisconsin Volunteers*, ed. Alan T. Nolan (1890; rpt. Madison, 1962), 59–68; Early, *War Memoirs*, 119–21; Jones (ed.), *Campbell Brown's Civil War*, 155–56; Oates, *15th Alabama*, 137–38; Freeman, *Lee's Lieutenants*, II, 110, 138; Alexander, *Military Memoirs of a Confederate*, 199.

18. Robertson, *Stonewall Jackson*, 564; Hennessy, *Return to Bull Run*, 224.

19. Allan C. Redwood, "Jackson's 'Foot-Cavalry' at the Second Bull Run," in Johnson and Buel (eds.), *Battles and Leaders*, II, 535–36.

20. Lichenstein memoir, USAERC.

21. Charlton diary, n.d., JPC (first quotation); Snakenberg, "Memoirs," 17, JPC (second quotation).

22. Richard Wheeler, *Voices of the Civil War* (New York, 1976), 167 (quotation).

23. Ibid., 165–67; *OR*, Vol. XII, Pt. II, 445–46, 555–59, 645–47, 671–72, 710–14; Alexander, *Military Memoirs of a Confederate*, 204, 206; Pope, "Second Battle of Bull Run," 476–77; Freeman, *Lee's Lieutenants*, II, 116–18, 142; Early, "Jackson's Campaign," in Pamphlets, Part II, 36, 37, LHAC; anonymous account of Forno's brigade at the Second Battle of Bull Run, in Reminiscences, Executive and Army of Northern Virginia, LHAC; Wren diary, August 28, 1862, in Wren Collection, EU; Hennessy, *Return to Bull Run*, 283–84.

24. *OR*, Vol. XII, Pt. II, 671 (quotation), 812.

25. Bartlett, *Military Record of Louisiana*, 31.

26. Ibid., 4, 31; Hennessy, *Return to Bull Run*, 265, 266 (first and second quotations), 267–68; *OR*, Vol. XII, Pt. II, 664–68; Durkin (ed.), *Confederate Chaplain*, 15 (third quotation); Stephens to parents, September 7, 1862, in Stephens Collection, NSU.

27. Wren diary, August 29–30, 1862, in Wren Collection, EU.

28. Stephens to parents, September 7, 1862, in Stephens Collection, NSU (first quotation); Hennessy, *Return to Bull Run*, 340–41, 342 (second quotation), 343–48.

29. Hennessy, *Return to Bull Run*, 354.

30. Ibid., 341 (first quotation), 356 (second quotation); Lichenstein memoir (third quotation), USAERC.

31. Bartlett, *Military Record of Louisiana*, 31 (first quotation); Stephens to parents, September 7, 1862, in Stephens Collection, NSU (second quotation); Charlton diary, n.d., JPC (third and fourth quotations); Brooks and Jones, *Lee's Foreign Legion*, 3.

32. Oates, *15th Alabama*, 144–45 (first quotation); Hennessy, *Return to Bull Run*, 357 (second, third, and fourth quotations); see also Fogleman diary, August 30, 1862, FSNMP.

33. Robert M. Mayo, "The Second Battle of Manassas," *Southern Historical Society Papers*, VII (1879), 124.

34. Singleton was later captured at the Monocacy, and Lyon was captured in the Chancellorsville Campaign. Hancock, "William Singleton," 498 (quotation); Booth (comp.), *Louisiana Confederate Soldiers*, II, 822.

35. S. D. Lee, "The Second Battle of Manassas—A Reply to General Longstreet," *Southern Historical Society Papers*, VI (1878), 65–66 (first quotation); Charlton diary, n.d., JPC (second quotation).

36. Thomas Phifer to father, September 16, 1862 (first quotation), and Phifer to Sallie, September 1862 (second quotation), in 2nd Louisiana Folder, Louisiana Box, ANB; anonymous letter, November 26, 1862, in Folder 2, Janin Collection, SHC; *OR*, Vol. XII, Pt. II, 666–69, 812, 814; Handerson, *Yankee in Gray*, 98; Hancock, "William Singleton," 498; Chamberlayne (ed.), *Ham Chamberlayne*, 101; Durkin (ed.), *Confederate Chaplain*, 16; Freeman, *Lee's Lieutenants*, II, 142.

37. J. C. Goolsby, "Crenshaw Battery, Pegram's Battalion, Confederate States Artillery," *Southern Historical Society Papers*, XXVIII (1900), 345 (quotation); Hennessy, *Return to Bull Run*, 357; James Longstreet, "Our March Against Pope," in Johnson and Buel (eds.), *Battles and Leaders*, II, 520, 521; Douglas, *I Rode with Stonewall*, 139–41.

38. Durkin (ed.), *Confederate Chaplain*, 18–19 (quotation); see also Cutrer and Parrish (eds.), *Brothers in Gray*, 120.

39. Wren diary, August 31, 1862, in Wren Collection, EU (first quotation); Snakenberg, "Memoirs," 18–19, JPC (second quotation).

40. Gannon, *Irish Rebels*, 117.

41. Wren diary, September 1, 1862, in Wren Collection, EU (quotation); Hennessy, *Return to Bull Run*, 449–50.

42. Gannon, *Irish Rebels*, 120 (first quotation); Early, *War Memoirs*, 130 (second and fourth quotations); Jones (ed.), *Campbell Brown's Civil War*, 25 (third quotation); Durkin (ed.), *Confederate Chaplain*, 22–23 (fifth and sixth quotations); *OR*, Vol. XII, Pt. II, 555–59, 647, 714–15; Oates, *15th Alabama*, 150.

43. Hancock, "William Singleton," 498 (first and second quotations); Snakenberg, "Memoirs," 19, JPC (third quotation); Hennessy, *Return to Bull Run*, 450.

44. William Behan to father, October 14, 1862, in Behan Family Papers, TU; *OR*, Vol. XII, Pt. II, 717; see also the 7th Louisiana's casualty list, September 1, 1862, MOC; *OR*, Vol. XIX, Pt. I, 144–48; Compiled Service Records, War Record Croup 109, Microcopy 320, Roll 163, NA; Durkin (ed.), *Confederate Chaplain*, 23–24; Wren diary, September 4, 1862, in Wren Collection, EU; Gannon, *Irish Rebels*, 127.

45. Durkin (ed.), *Confederate Chaplain,* 25–26.

46. Wren diary, September 6, 1862, in Wren Collection, EU.

47. Snakenberg "Memoirs," 21, JPC; see also Fogleman diary, September 10, 1862, FSNMP.

48. Phifer to Sallie, September 1862, in 2nd Louisiana Folder, Louisiana Box, ANB.

49. Wren diary, September 7, 1862, in Wren Collection, EU (first quotation); Thomas Phifer to father, September 16, 1862, in La. Misc. File, Louisiana Box, ANB (second quotations).

50. Durkin (ed.), *Confederate Chaplain,* 27; Bartlett, *Military Record of Louisiana,* 31; Freeman, *Lee's Lieutenants,* II, 159; Pinkowski, *Pills, Pen and Politics,* 42.

51. Fogleman diary, September 12, 1862, FSNMP (first quotation); Wren diary, September 10, 1862, in Wren Collection, EU (second quotation); Phifer to father, September 16, 1862, in 2nd Louisiana Folder, Louisiana Box, ANB; Snakenberg, "Memoirs," 21, JPC.

52. Lichenstein memoir, USAERC (first quotation); G. P. Ring to wife, September 15, 1862, typescript copy, in Army of Northern Virginia Papers, Part I, LHAC (second quotation); Wren diary, September 15, 1862, in Wren Collection, EU (third quotation).

53. Phifer to father, September 16, 1862, in 2nd Louisiana Folder, Louisiana Box, ANB.

54. Isaiah Folgleman estimated the number of runaway slaves to be 3,500. Fogleman diary, September 15, 1862, FSNMP; Snakenberg, "Memoirs," 21, JPC; G. P. Ring to wife, September 15, 1862, typescript copy, in Army of Northern Virginia Papers, Part I, LHAC (quotation); Stephen W. Sears, *Landscape Turned Red: The Battle of Antietam* (New Haven, 1983), 150–54; *OR,* Vol. XIX, Pt. I, pp. 144–48, 952–55, 965, 1007, 1016.

55. Wren diary, September 15 (quotation) and 16, 1862, in Wren Collection, EU; Cutrer and Parrish (eds.), *Brothers in Gray,* 121–22; Snakenberg, "Memoirs," 22, JPC; Edmond Stephens to parents, September 21, 1862, in Stephens Collection, NSU; Early, *War Memoirs,* 139; *OR,* Vol. XIX, Pt. I, 967, 1007.

56. Snakenberg, "Memoirs," 22, JPC.

57. *OR,* XIX, Pt. I, 218 (quotation); Sears, *Landscape Turned Red,* 181–85; Alexander, *Military Memoirs of a Confederate,* 252.

58. G. P. Ring to wife, n.d., in Army of Northern Virginia Papers, Part I, LHAC (first quotation); Snakenberg, "Memoirs," 23, JPC (second quotation); Wren diary, September 17, 1862, in Wren Collection, EU (third quotation).

59. Jenkins died from his wounds. *Memphis Daily Appeal,* October 11, 1862, in *Camp Moore News,* Vol. 16, No. 2 (June 2014).

60. Introduction of Behan Family Papers, TU; Booth (comp.), *Louisiana Confederate Soldiers,* I, 155.

61. Wren diary, September 17, 1862, in Wren Collection, EU.

62. Sears, *Landscape Turned Red,* 189.

63. Wren diary, September 17, 1862, in Wren Collection, EU.

64. Michael Clark was later captured at both Rappahannock Station and Spotsylvania. Snakenberg, "Memoirs," 23, JPC (quotations); Booth (comp.), *Louisiana Confederate Soldiers,* I, 345.

65. G. P. Ring to wife, n.d., in Army of Northern Virginia Papers, Part I, LHAC; Gannon, *Irish Rebels,* 136; Sears, *Landscape Turned Red,* 188–90; *OR,* Vol. XIX, Pt. I, 923–28, 978–79; St. Joseph (La.) *Tensas Gazette,* October 24, 1935, in Melrose Scrapbook 231, NSU; William A. Frassanito, *Antietam: The Photographic Legacy of America's Bloodiest Day* (New York, 1978), 103,

112–15, 119–20; Early, *War Memoirs*, 150, 152; Alexander, *Military Memoirs of a Confederate*, 252, 254; John Bell Hood, *Advance and Retreat: Personal Experiences in the United States and Confederate States Armies*, ed. Richard N. Current (1880; rpt. Bloomington, 1959), 42–43; Milo M. Quaife (ed.), *From the Cannon's Mouth: The Civil War Letters of General Alpheus S. Williams* (Detroit, 1959), 130; Dawes, *Sixth Wisconsin*, 95; Vollbrecht, "Hays' and Avery's Brigades," 6; Memphis *Daily Appeal*, October 11, 1862, in *Camp Moore News*.

66. Fogleman diary, September 17, 1862, FSNMP.

67. Sears, *Landscape Turned Red*, 189.

68. Gannon, *Irish Rebels*, 139.

69. *OR*, Vol. XIX, Pt. I, 813; G. P. Ring to wife, n.d., in Army of Northern Virginia Papers, Part I, LHAC; Memphis *Daily Appeal*, October 11, 1862, in *Camp Moore News*; Zeller Letters, 6th Louisiana Folder, Louisiana Box, ANB; Ezra A. Carman, *The Maryland Campaign of September 1862*, ed. Thomas G. Clemens (El Dorado Hills, Calif., 2012), II, 270; Pryor, *Reminiscences of Peace and War*, 187.

70. Wren diary, September 17, 1862, in Wren Collection, EU.

71. Snakenberg, "Memoirs," 24, JPC.

72. Bradley P. Bengston, M.D., and Julian E. Kuz, M.D. (eds.), *Photographic Atlas of Civil War Injuries* (Kennesaw, Ga., 1996), 360.

73. *OR*, Vol. XIX, Pt. I, 1017; Welsh, *Medical Histories of Confederate Generals*, 204.

74. *OR*, Vol. XIX, Pt. I, 230, 233, 1008, 1012–13, 1016, 1017 (first quotation); Stephens to parents, September 21, 1862, in Stephens Collection, NSU (second quotation); Carman, *Maryland Campaign*, 78; Frassanito, *Antietam*, 126–29, 131–39; Dawes, *Sixth Wisconsin*, 87–92; Henry Kyd Douglas, "Stonewall Jackson in Maryland," in Johnson and Buel (eds.), *Battles and Leaders*, II, 628; C. A. Stevens, *Berdan's United States Sharpshooters in the Army of the Potomac, 1861–1865* (St. Paul, 1892), 202–3; Worsham, *One of Jackson's Foot Cavalry*, 87; Daugherty, "W. E. Moore in the Civil War," in Moore Papers, UT.

75. The Museum of the Confederacy holds a flag that may be the 1st Louisiana's colors. Sears, *Landscape Turned Red*, 194–95; Carman, *Maryland Campaign*, 79; Brooks and Jones, *Lee's Foreign Legion*, 34; see also Omaha *Daily Bee*, July 11, 1887, *Chronicling America*, chroniclingamerica.loc.gov (accessed February 26, 2016).

76. *OR*, Vol. XIX, Pt. I, 813, 1014–18; Stephens to parents, September 21, 1862, in Stephens Collection, NSU; Behan to father, October 14, 1862, in Behan Papers, TU; Carman, *Maryland Campaign*, 80; Brooks and Jones, *Lee's Foreign Legion*, 99; Edward Seton to mother, September 21, 1862, in Seton Collection, MSU.

77. Dawes, *Sixth Wisconsin*, 94 (quotations); Terry L. Jones, "The Dead of Antietam," New York *Times* "Disunion," September 24, 2012, opinionator.blogs.nytimes.com (accessed September 24, 2012); Fogleman diary, September 17, 1862, FSNMP; Cutrer and Parrish (eds.), *Brothers in Gray*, 12.

78. Wren diary, September 18, 1862, in Wren Collection, EU (first quotation); Gannon, *Irish Rebels*, 141 (second quotation).

79. *OR*, Vol. XIX, Pt. II, 669, 683–84; Wallace, "Coppens' Louisiana Zouaves," 280–82; Lathrop (ed.), "Autobiography of Francis T. Nicholls," 251; Mickey, "Coppens' Zouaves," 11.

80. Wren diary, October 10, 1862, in Wren Collection, EU; Booth (comp.), *Louisiana Confederate Soldiers*, I, 1165.

CHAPTER 7

FIGHTING THE GOOD FIGHT

1. Handerson, *Yankee in Gray,* 99 (first quotation); Gannon, *Irish Rebels,* 142 (second quotation); Bauer (ed.), *Soldier's Journey,* 75.

2. *National Tribune,* February 27, 1890, *Chronicling America,* chroniclingamerica.loc.gov (accessed February 27, 2016).

3. Trimonthly report of Ewell's division, in General Jubal A. Early Papers, 1861–1865, War Record Group 109, Entry 118, NA (quotation); Louisiana Troops, 7th Regiment Orderly Book, 1862–64, NYPL.

4. Durkin (ed.), *Confederate Chaplain,* 33–34; Muster Roll, Company H, 15th Louisiana, in Saucier Papers, LSU; "Report of Sick and Wounded" for 1st, 2nd, and 14th Louisiana, October 1862, MOC.

5. Edmond Stephens to brother, October 12, 1862 (first quotation), and Stephens to sister, November 27, 1862 (second quotation), in Stephens Collection, NSU; Clothing Account, 7th Regiment of Louisiana Volunteers, 1862, War Record Croup 109, Chap. V, Vol. 205, NA; see also Theodore A. Newell to uncle, December 7, 1862, in Box 1, Folder 2, Newell Papers, LSU; Durkin (ed.), *Confederate Chaplain,* 33–34; Handerson, *Yankee in Gray,* 99; Bartlett, *Military Record of Louisiana,* 44.

6. Cutrer and Parrish (eds.), *Brothers in Gray,* 130–31 (first quotation); James McDowell Carrington to Eliza Henry Carrington, October 16, 1862, in Carrington Family Papers, VHS (second and third quotations); Memorandum from Maj. W. F. Hawks to Maj. David F. Boyd, November 7, 1862, in Folder 1, David F. Boyd Selected Papers, LSU; Requisition Papers in Early Papers, War Record Group 109, Entry 118, NA.

7. Robert Grier Stephens Jr. (comp. and ed.), *Intrepid Warrior: Clement Anselm Evans, Confederate General from Georgia: Life, Letters, and Diaries of the War Years* (Dayton, 1992), 118–19.

8. Bauer (ed.), *Soldier's Journey,* 78; Robertson, *Stonewall Jackson,* 642–43.

9. Boyd, *Reminiscences of the War in Virginia,* 188–89.

10. Gruber was murdered in New Orleans the year after the war ended, and his funeral was one of the largest in the city's history. Boyd, *Reminiscences of the War in Virginia,* 31 (quotations); Booth (comp.), *Louisiana Confederate Soldiers,* I, 117.

11. Cutrer and Parrish (eds.), *Brothers in Gray,* 135 (first quotation), 138 (second quotation); see also Bauer (ed.), *Soldier's Journey,* 178.

12. Lichenstein memoir, USAERC (quotation); Robertson, *Stonewall Jackson,* 649–51.

13. Handerson, *Yankee in Gray,* 52 (quotations); *Bellville* (Tex.) *Countryman,* February 21, 1863, photocopy, FSNMP.

14. Emma Cassandra Riely Macon and Reuben Conway Macon, *Reminiscences of the Civil War* (n.p., 1911), 153.

15. Handerson, *Yankee in Gray,* 52 (quotations); Moore diary, December 14, 1862, TU.

16. *OR,* Vol. XXI, 561–62; Durkin (ed.), *Confederate Chaplain,* 36–37 (quotations); Booth (comp.), *Louisiana Confederate Soldiers,* III, 922.

17. Snakenberg, "Memoirs," 25, JPC; see also *Bellville Countryman,* February 21, 1863, photocopy, FSNMP.

18. Handerson, *Yankee in Gray,* 34; Durkin (ed.), *Confederate Chaplain,* 41; Charles Moore Jr., diary, March 9, 1863, in LHAC; Edward Seton to brother, December 29, 1862, and Edward Seton to John, January 25, 1863, in Seton Collection, MSU; Bauer (ed.), *Soldier's Journey,* 88.

19. Edmond Stephens to parents, March 17, 1863, in Stephens Collection, NSU.

20. Jones (ed.), *Civil War Memoirs of Capt. William J. Seymour,* 102–3.

21. Bound Volume 8, in Association of the Army of Northern Virginia, LHAC; Stephens to parents, February 25, 1863, in Stephens Collection, NSU; Cutrer and Parrish (eds.), *Brothers in Gray,* 139–40; Gannon, *Irish Rebels,* 149.

22. Cutrer and Parrish (eds.), *Brothers in Gray,* 135 (first quotation), 138 (second quotation); see also Edward Seton to Mother, February 24 and April 9, 1863, and Bauer (ed.), *Soldier's Journey,* 89–90.

23. Francis Rawle to Alex. Marks, December 10, 1862, in MC-3/MSS. 3, MOC.

24. Oliver Moss to Rose Marie Puro, January 31, 1863, in CSA Collection, MOC.

25. Ibid.; see also Brooks and Jones, *Lee's Foreign Legion,* 39.

26. Durkin (ed.), *Confederate Chaplain,* 37–38; Compiled Service Records, War Record Group 109, Microcopy 320, Roll 163, NA; Bound Volume 8 in Association of the Army of Northern Virginia, LHAC; Francis Rawle to Alex Marks, December 10, 1862, in MC-3/MSS. 3, MOC; Edmund Pendleton to unknown, December 9, 1862, in MC-3/MSS. 3, MOC; Pendleton to daughter, February 6, 1863, in Coles Collection, SHC; Jones (ed.), *Civil War Memoirs of Capt. William J. Seymour,* 101–3; Gannon, *Irish Rebels,* 149.

27. Nicholls' brigade Morning Report, January 26, 1863, in Taliaferro File, MOC.

28. Inspection report by John H. New, January 10, 1863, in Early Papers, War Record Group 109, Entry 118, NA.

29. *OR,* XXI, 1097–99.

30. Inspection reports by John H. New, January 17, 30, February 28, March 31, 1863, in Early Papers, War Record Group 109, Entry 118, NA; Hotchkiss, *Make Me a Map of the Valley,* 135.

31. Seton to John, January 25, 1863, in Seton Collection, MSU (first quotation); Newell to uncle, December 7, 1862, in Newell Papers, LSU (second quotation); see also Buckley (ed.), *A Frenchman, a Chaplain, a Rebel,* 57; Brooks and Jones, *Lee's Foreign Legion,* 49.

32. Baton Rouge *Louisiana Capitolian,* February 5, 1881, *Chronicling America,* chroniclingamerica.loc.gov (accessed October 12, 2015); Brooks and Jones, *Lee's Foreign Legion,* 244–45.

33. Seton to Mother, February 24, 1863, in Seton Collection, MSU (first quotation); Cutrer and Parrish (eds.), *Brothers in Gray,* 175 (second quotation); Charles Ward letters, photocopies, Box 119, Folder 23, file information, USAERC.

34. Order by Gen. Harry T. Hays, December 30, 1862, in Louisiana Troops, 7th Regiment Orderly Book, NYPL.

35. New Orleans *Times-Democrat,* in Reminiscences Division, n.d., Confederate Veteran Papers, DU.

36. Lichenstein memoir, USAERC.

37. Edmond Stephens to parents, March 17, 1863, in Stephens Collection, NSU (first and second quotations); Cutrer and Parrish (eds.), *Brothers in Gray,* 163 (third quotation); *OR,* XXI, 674–75, 686–88.

38. Cutrer and Parrish (eds.), *Brothers in Gray,* 164 (first quotation), 175 (second quotation).

39. Ibid., 178 (first quotation); Bauer (ed.), *Soldier's Journey,* 91 (second quotation).

40. Jones (ed.), *Civil War Memoirs of Capt. William J. Seymour,* 47.

41. Ibid., 48.

42. Bauer (ed.), *Soldier's Journey,* 97; Gannon, *Irish Rebels,* 154; Compiled Service Records, Microcopy 320, Roll 201, NA.

43. Jones (ed.), *Civil War Memoirs of Capt. William J. Seymour,* 47–48 (first quotation); Gannon, *Irish Rebels,* 155 (second quotation); Stephen W. Sears, *Chancellorsville* (Boston, 1996), 153–59.

44. Gannon, *Irish Rebels,* 155–56 (first quotation); Ernest B. Furgurson, *Chancellorsville 1863: The Souls of the Brave* (New York, 1992), 99 (second quotation).

45. Letter from anonymous Louisianian, n.d., published in unidentified Mobile newspaper, in Lawrence L. Hewitt Private Collection, Independence, La.

46. Jones (ed.), *Civil War Memoirs of Capt. William J. Seymour,* 49; Gannon, *Irish Rebels,* 156; Richmond *Sentinel,* April 29, May 14, 1863, photocopy, FSNMP; see also letter from 6th Louisiana soldier, probably Capt. G. P. Ring but signed "Chester," in Mobile *Advertiser & Register,* June 4, 1863, typed copy, FSNMP.

47. Fogleman diary, April 29, 63, FSNMP; Bauer (ed.), *Soldier's Journey,* 97; Jones (ed.), *Civil War Memoirs of Capt. William J. Seymour,* 49 (quotation).

48. Clegg's letter was written on captured Union stationary. William Clegg to cousin, May 9, 1863, typed copy, FSNMP (first quotation); Snakenberg, "Memoirs," 26, JPC (second quotation).

49. Clegg to cousin, May 9, 1863, FSNMP (quotation); Sears, *Chancellorsville,* 282–87.

50. Casler, *Four Years in the Stonewall Brigade,* 146–47.

51. Clegg to cousin, May 9, 63, FSNMP.

52. Lathrop (ed.), "Autobiography of Francis T. Nicholls," 252; Nichols, "Notes on Francis T. Nicholls," 308–9.

53. Paris (Ky.) *Bourbon News,* March 19, 1901, *Chronicling America,* chroniclingamerica.loc.gov (accessed July 11, 2016) (quotation); Lichenstein memoir, USAERC.

54. Clegg to cousin, May 9, 63, FSNMP (quotation); Furgurson, *Chancellorsville,* 234–39; Bound Volume 2, in Association of the Army of Northern Virginia, LHAC.

55. Gregg McIntosh, "The Chancellorsville Campaign," *Southern Historical Society Papers,* n.s., XL (1915), 89.

56. *OR,* Vol. XXV, Pt. I, 795–801, 943–44, 961–62, 986, 1003–6, 1007 (quotation), 1008–9, 1037–41; Battle reports of the 1st, 2nd, 10th, and 14th Louisiana, in Folder 2, Raleigh E. Colston Collection, SHC; anonymous obituary of Edmund Pendleton in Coles Collection, SHC; Bound Volume 2 in Association of the Army of Northern Virginia, LHAC; McIntosh, "Chancellorsville Campaign," 87; Laurence, "North Louisiana Tiger," 145; Brooks and Jones, *Lee's Foreign Legion,* 41; Buckley (ed.), *A Frenchman, a Chaplain, a Rebel,* 173–74.

57. Buckley (ed.), *A Frenchman, a Chaplain, a Rebel,* 173–74, 186; Brooks and Jones, *Lee's Foreign Legion,* 3, 41.

58. J. M. Batchelor to father, June 22, 1863, in Folder 6, Batchelor Papers, LSU (quotation); Glatthaar, *General Lee's Army,* 254.

59. Charles C. Davenport, "Life and Travels of Charles C. Davenport, Shot Blind at the

Battle of Chancellorsville, Virginia, in the Year 1863," in 7-LA2 2nd Louisiana Inf. Reg., Louisiana Brigades Boxes, GNMP.

60. Edward Seton to Emma, May 13, 1863, in Seton Collection, MSU.

61. Edward Seton to Mother, June 17, 1863, in Seton Collection, MSU; Brooks and Jones, *Lee's Foreign Legion*, 41.

62. Casler, *Four Years in the Stonewall Brigade*, 151.

63. Durkin (ed.), *Confederate Chaplain*, 43–44.

64. Jones (ed.), *Civil War Memoirs of Capt. William J. Seymour*, 51–52.

65. Ibid.; Gannon, *Irish Rebels*, 148, 159 (first quotation); Handerson, *Yankee in Gray*, 55 (second quotation); Bauer (ed.), *Soldier's Journey*, 99; Charles Moore Jr. diary, April 29–May 2, 1863, LHAC; *OR*, Vol. XXV, Pt. I, 1000–1002; Egidius Smulders to Henry B. Kelly, March 187[?], in Egidius Smulders Papers, Confederate Personnel, LHAC; Compiled Service Records, War Record Group 109, Microcopy 320, Roll 163, NA.

66. Joe M. Rice, "An Account of the Battle of Fredericksburg, 1863, Written by J. R. Williams," *Journal of the North Louisiana Historical Association* (Winter 1986), 39 (quotation), Jones (ed.), *Civil War Memoirs of Capt. William J. Seymour*, 53.

67. Mobile *Advertiser & Register*, June 4, 1863, FSNMP (quotation); Furgurson, *Chancellorsville*, 265.

68. Furgurson, *Chancellorsville*, 266–67; Sears, *Chancellorsville*, 373–36; Gannon, *Irish Rebels*, 162.

69. Compiled Service Records, War Record Group 109, Microcopy 320, Rolls 148, 187, NA; *OR*, Vol. XXV, Pt. I, 800–802, 839–41, 856, 1000–1002; Charles Moore Jr., diary, May 3, 1863, LHAC; Jones (ed.), *Civil War Memoirs of Capt. William J. Seymour*, 53; Bound Volume 8 in Association of the Army of Northern Virginia, LHAC; Early, *War Memoirs*, 204–11; Freeman, *Lee's Lieutenants*, II, 618; Alexander, *Military Memoirs of a Confederate*, 349–52; Rice, "Account of the Battle of Fredericksburg," 41 (quotation).

70. Mobile *Advertiser & Register*, June 4, 1863, FSNMP (first and third quotations); Rice, "Account of the Battle of Fredericksburg, 40 (second quotation).

71. Mobile *Advertiser & Register*, June 4, 1863, FSNMP (first and third quotations); Rice, "Account of the Battle of Fredericksburg," 40 (second quotation).

72. Handerson, *Yankee in Gray*, 57 (first and second quotations); Mobile *Advertiser & Register*, June 4, 1863, FSNMP (third quotation); Stephens to unknown, n.d., in Stephens Collection, NSU (fourth quotation).

73. Cutrer and Parrish (eds.), *Brothers in Gray*, 190.

74. Mobile *Advertiser & Register*, June 4, 1863, FSNP (first and fourth quotations); Handerson, *Yankee in Gray*, 57 (second and third quotations).

75. Mobile *Advertiser & Register*, June 4, 1863, FSNP.

76. Stephens to unknown, n.d., in Stephens Collection, NSU (first quotation); Richmond *Enquirer*, May 19, 1863, in Civil War Scrapbook, 1862–64, p. 193, TU (second quotation); Mobile *Advertiser & Register*, June 4, 1863, FSNP (third quotation); Cutrer and Parrish (eds.), *Brothers in Gray*, 190.

77. Stephens to unknown, n.d., in Stephens Collection, NSU.

78. Mobile *Advertiser & Register*, June 4, 1863, FSNP.

79. Furgurson, *Chancellorsville*, 298 (quotations); Irisburgh (Vt.) *Orleans Independent Stan-*

dard, May 22, 1863, *Chronicling America,* chroniclingamerica.loc.gov (accessed March 9, 2016); Gannon, *Irish Rebels,* 164.

80. Reed, *Private in Gray,* 30; *OR,* Vol. XXV, Pt. I, 600, 610, 614, 800–802, 1000–1002; Handerson, *Yankee in Gray,* 56–59, 101–3; Compiled Service Records, War Record Group 109, Microcopy 320, Roll 163, NA: Dr. G. M. G. Stafford, *General Leroy Augustus Stafford, His Forebears and Descendants* (New Orleans, 1943), 39; Benedict, *Vermont in the Civil War,* I, 143, 166, 367–72; Jones (ed.), *Civil War Memoirs of Capt. William J. Seymour,* 33–34.

81. New Orleans *Times-Democrat,* in Reminiscences Division, n.d., Confederate Veteran Papers, DU (first and second quotations); Rice, "Account of the Battle of Fredericksburg," 40 (third quotation); Fogleman diary, May 4, 1863, FSNMP.

82. Cutrer and Parrish (eds.), *Brothers in Gray,* 190.

83. A Mobile newspaper reported Hays' losses to be 73 dead, 296 wounded, and 293 missing, and a postwar account put Nicholls' total losses at 448. Unidentified newspaper clipping, in Bound Volume 51, Scrapbooks 1863–64, Association of the Army of Northern Virginia, LHAC; *OR,* Vol. XXV, Pt. I, 226, 809; Bartlett, *Military Record of Louisiana,* 3–11; Jones (ed.), *Civil War Memoirs of Capt. William J. Seymour,* 54–55; Battle report of the 1st Louisiana Volunteers in Colston Collection, SHC; *Richmond Enquirer,* May 19, 1863, in Civil War Scrapbook, 1862–64, p. 192, TU; Stephens to parents, June 1, 1863, in Stephens Collection, NSU; Clegg to cousin, May 9, 63, FSNMP; Brooks and Jones, *Lee's Foreign Legion,* 41; Gannon, *Irish Rebels,* 168; "15th Louisiana's Losses at Chancellorsville," *Louisiana in the Civil War,* December 29, 2011, www.louisianacivilwar.org (accessed March 11, 2016).

84. Richmond *Examiner,* May 21, 1863, in *Camp Moore News,* Vol. 15, No. 4 (December 2013).

85. Stephens to Mrs. T. E. and W. E. Paxton, May 18, 1863, in Stephens Collection, NSU (first quotation); Fogleman diary, May 29, 1863, FSNMP (second quotation).

86. *OR,* Vol. XXV, Pt. II, 810 (quotation); Buckley (ed.), *A Frenchman, a Chaplain, a Rebel,* 182.

87. The 8th Louisiana's Isaiah Fogleman reported that a Reverend Delaney also preached a funeral sermon for Jackson to the Louisiana Brigade that same day. W. B. Colbert to Mrs. C. M. and M. M. Potts, May 17, 1863, in Folder 59, North Louisiana Historical Association Archives, CC (first quotation); Stephens to Mrs. T. E. and W. E. Paxton, May 18, 1863, in Stephens Collection, NSU (second quotation); Cutrer and Parrish (eds.), *Brothers in Gray,* 198 (third quotation); Fogleman diary, May 17, 1863, FSNMP.

88. Rice, "Account of the Battle of Fredericksburg," 41; see also Seton to Emma, May 13, 1863, in Seton Collection, MSU.

89. J. H. Cosgrove, "Recollections and Reminiscences," *Cosgrove's Weekly,* August 26, 1911, in Melrose Scrapbook, 230, NSU.

CHAPTER 8

"GOING BACK INTO THE UNION AT LAST"

1. Because Union forces had seized most of the Mississippi River and cut east-west communications, Pierson's letter was delivered by a furloughed friend. Cutrer and Parrish (eds.), *Brothers in Gray,* 200 (quotation); Edmond Stephens to parents, June 20, 1863, in Stephens

Collection, NSU; *OR*, Vol. XXVII, Pt. II, 41–49, 313–15; Reed, *Private in Gray*, 35–36; Compiled Service Records, War Record Group 109, Microcopy 320, Roll 201, NA; Edward Seton to mother, June 17, 1863, in Seton Collection, MSU.

2. Scott L. Mingus Sr., *The Louisiana Tigers in the Gettysburg Campaign, June–July 1863* (Baton Rouge, 2009), 15–16.

3. Ibid., 16 (first quotation); Gannon, *Irish Rebels*, 170 (second quotation).

4. Edward A. Moore, *The Story of a Cannoneer under Stonewall Jackson* (New York, 1907), n.p., Project Gutenberg ebook, www.gutenberg.org (accessed July 21, 2016).

5. Reed, *Private in Gray*, 68.

6. I. G. Bradwell, "Capture of Winchester, Va., and Milroy's Army in June, 1863," *Confederate Veteran*, XXX (1922), 331 (quotation); Gannon, *Irish Rebels*, 170–71.

7. Reed, *Private in Gray*, 35 (quotation); Mingus, *Louisiana Tigers in the Gettysburg Campaign*, 28–30.

8. *OR*, Vol. XXVII, Pt. II, 459–64; Jones (ed.), *Civil War Memoirs of Capt. William J. Seymour*, 60–61; Mingus, *Louisiana Tigers in the Gettysburg Campaign*, 36.

9. Mingus, *Louisiana Tigers in the Gettysburg Campaign*, 36 (quotation); *OR*, XXVII, Pt. II, 462.

10. Opelousas *Courier*, October 2, 1880, *Chronicling America*, chroniclingamerica.loc.gov (accessed March 14, 2016) (first quotation); Samuel H. Chisholm, "Forward the Louisiana Brigade," *Confederate Veteran*, XXVII (1919), 449 (second quotation).

11. Mingus, *Louisiana Tigers in the Gettysburg Campaign*, 39 (first quotation); *OR*, Vol. XXVII, Pt. II, 477 (second quotation).

12. *OR*, Vol. XXVII, Pt. II, 439–42, 459–64, 476–78; Compiled Service Records, War Record Group 109, Microcopy 320, Roll 201, NA; Jones (ed.), *Civil War Memoirs of Capt. William J. Seymour*, 61–62.

13. Harry Gilmor, *Four Years in the Saddle* (London, 1866), 86–87 (first quotation); "Honor Medal to the 'Maid of Winchester,'" *Confederate Veteran*, VIII (1900), 540 (second quotation); Percy Gatling Hamlin, *"Old Bald Head" (General R. S. Ewell): The Portrait of a Soldier* (Strasburg, Va., 1940), 139; Bauer (ed.), *Soldier's Journey*, 106.

14. Mingus, *Louisiana Tigers in the Gettysburg Campaign*, 43 (first and third quotations); Reed, *Private in Gray*, 36–37 (second quotation).

15. Reed, *Private in Gray*, 37 (first quotation); Mingus, *Louisiana Tigers in the Gettysburg Campaign*, 45 (second quotation); J. Warren Jackson to brother, July 20, 1863, in Box 2, Folder 7, Boyd Civil War Papers, LSU (third quotation); Chisholm, "Forward the Louisiana Brigade," 449 (fourth quotation).

16. Reed, *Private in Gray*, 37 (quotation); Jones (ed.), *Civil War Memoirs of Capt. William J. Seymour*, 61–62; *OR*, Vol. XXVII, Pt. II, 451, 476–78; Bound Volume 5 in Association of the Army of Northern Virginia, LHAC; Gannon, *Irish Rebels*, 177.

17. *OR*, Vol. XXVII, Pt. II, 464 (first quotation); A. S. Hardy, "Terrific Fighting at Winchester," *Confederate Veteran*, IX (1901), 114 (second quotation).

18. Gilmor, *Four Years in the Saddle*, 87 (first quotation). Jones (ed.), *Civil War Memoirs of Capt. William J. Seymour*, 63 (second quotation). Hardy, "Terrific Fighting at Winchester," 114. Norfolk *Virginian*, May 17, 1896, *Chronicling America*, chroniclingamerica.loc.gov (accessed July 27, 2016); Roanoke *Daily Times*, July 5, 1896 (accessed July 27, 2016).

19. *OR*, Vol. XXVII, Pt. II, 62, 476; Bauer (ed.), *Soldier's Journey*, 109; Gannon, *Irish Rebels*, 179.

20. Bartlett, *Military Record of Louisiana*, 46.

21. Moreau was killed five months later at Payne's Farm. Brooks and Jones, *Lee's Foreign Legion*, 45; Bartlett, *Military Record of Louisiana*, 45–46; *OR*, Vol. XXVII, Pt. II, 313–15, 336, 439–42, 499–503, 512–14; "Reminiscences of R. C. Murphy as Told to His Daughter," in Folder 1, Murphy Sandlin Collection, NSU; W. G. Loyd, "Second Louisiana at Gettysburg," *Confederate Veteran*, VI (1898), 417.

22. Stephens to parents, June 20, 1863, in Stephens Collection, NSU (quotation); Jones (ed.), *Civil War Memoirs of Capt. William J. Seymour*, 63.

23. Jones (ed.), *Civil War Memoirs of Capt. William J. Seymour*, 64 (first and second quotations); Charles J. Batchelor to father, October 18, 1863, in Batchelor Papers, LSU (third quotation); untitled paper by David Zable, December 12, 1903, in Reminiscences, Executive and Army of Northern Virginia, LHAC (fourth quotation); Hancock, "William Singleton," 498–99.

24. Jackson to brother, July 20, 1863, in Boyd Civil War Papers, LSU.

25. Batchelor to father, October 18, 1863, in Batchelor Papers, LSU.

26. Loyd, "Second Louisiana," 117.

27. Taylor was later severely wounded in the chest and captured at the Monocacy. On his service record someone wrote, "Young, moral and modest, as gallant and brave as ever drew a breath. A general favorite of all." Booth (comp.), *Louisiana Confederate Soldiers*, III, 780; Richmond *Whig*, July 24, 1863 in 7-LA 8th Louisiana Inf. Reg., Louisiana Brigades Boxes, GNMP (second quotation); Mingus, *Louisiana Tigers in the Gettysburg Campaign*, 64 (first quotation).

28. Mingus, *Louisiana Tigers in the Gettysburg Campaign*, 65 (first quotation), 69 (second quotation).

29. Ibid., 68 (first quotation); Civil War Commission, *Fifteen Days Under the Confederate Flag* (Waynesboro, Pa., n.d.), in Louisiana Brigades Boxes, GNMP; "Louisiana Tigers Were Feared," 7-LA9 9th La. Inf Reg, in Louisiana Brigades Boxes, GNMP (second quotation).

30. Mingus, *Louisiana Tigers in the Gettysburg Campaign*, 69.

31. Jackson to brother, July 20, 1863, in Boyd Civil War Papers, LSU (first quotation); Richard S. Ewell to Lizzie Ewell, June 24, 1863, in Richard S. Ewell Papers, LC (second quotation); Jones (ed.), *Civil War Memoirs of Capt. William J. Seymour*, 66 (third quotation).

32. Stiles, *Four Years Under Marse Robert*, 200–201.

33. Jackson to brother, July 20, 1863, in Boyd Civil War Papers, LSU.

34. Batchelor to father, October 18, 1863, in Batchelor Papers, LSU (first quotation); Richmond *Whig*, July 24, 1863, in 7-LA 8th Louisiana Inf. Reg, Louisiana Brigades Boxes, GNMP (second quotation); E. A. Patterson, "Story of the War," FSNMP (third and fourth quotations).

35. Jones (ed.), *Civil War Memoirs of Capt. William J. Seymour*, 64–65.

36. Five days later, Fogleman was wounded in the shoulder not far from his campsite. Fogleman diary, June 26, 1863, FSNMP (first quotation); Mingus, *Louisiana Tigers in the Gettysburg Campaign*, 76 (second and third quotations); Reed, *Private in Gray*, 39 (fourth, fifth, and sixth quotations).

37. Booth (comp.), *Louisiana Confederate Soldiers*, II, 141–42 (quotation); Mingus, *Louisiana Tigers in the Gettysburg Campaign*, 99.

38. Jackson to brother, July 20, 1863, in Boyd Civil War Papers, LSU (first three quotations); Jones (ed.), *Civil War Memoirs of Capt. William J. Seymour*, 65–66 (fourth quotation).

39. Reed, *Private in Gray*, 40–41 (quotations); Jackson to brother, July, 20, 1863, in Boyd Civil War Papers, LSU.

40. Cutrer and Parrish (eds.), *Brothers in Gray*, 213.

41. Mingus, *Louisiana Tigers in the Gettysburg Campaign*, 90.

42. Ibid., 90–91.

43. Ibid., 93, 95.

44. Jones (ed.), *Civil War Memoirs of Capt. William J. Seymour*, 67.

45. *OR*, Vol. XXVII, Pt. 466.

46. Reed, *Private in Gray*, 41 (first quotation); Mingus, *Louisiana Tigers in the Gettysburg Campaign*, 93–94 (second and third quotations), 99.

47. Jones (ed.), *Civil War Memoirs of Capt. William J. Seymour*, 69.

48. S. Herman Dinkgrave to Maggie Lucas, June 28, 1863, in 7-LA2 2nd Louisiana Inf. Reg., Louisiana Brigades Box, GNMP.

49. Gannon, *Irish Rebels*, 181 (first quotation); Mingus, *Louisiana Tigers in the Gettysburg Campaign*, 97, 99 (second quotation); Newport News (Va.) *Daily Press*, May 17, 1906, *Chronicling America*, chroniclingamerica.loc.gov (accessed August 2, 2016).

50. Jones (ed.), *Civil War Memoirs of Capt. William J. Seymour*, 70 (quotation); Harry W. Pfanz, *Gettysburg—The First Day* (Chapel Hill, 2001), 22–23; Mingus, *Louisiana Tigers in the Gettysburg Campaign*, 101.

51. Jones (ed.), *Civil War Memoirs of Capt. William J. Seymour*, 70.

52. Opelousas *Courier*, October 2, 1880 (quotation); Mingus, *Louisiana Tigers in the Gettysburg Campaign*, 107; Jones (ed.), *Campbell Brown's Civil War*, 207–8.

53. Jones (ed.), *Civil War Memoir of Capt. William J. Seymour*, 71 (first quotation); Jackson to brother, July 20, 1863, in Boyd Civil War Papers, LSU (second quotation); Jones (ed.), *Campbell Brown's Civil War*, 209 (third quotation).

54. Reed, *Private in Gray*, 42.

55. Hancock, "William Singleton," 499.

56. Stiles, *Four Years Under Marse Robert*, 212–14.

57. Jackson to brother, July 20, 1863, in Boyd Civil War Papers, LSU (first quotation); Mingus, *Louisiana Tigers in the Gettysburg Campaign*, 116 (second and third quotations); Reed, *Private in Gray*, 42 (fourth quotation).

58. Another source puts Hays' casualties at one dead, forty-one wounded, and fifteen missing. Jones (ed.), *Civil War Memoirs of Capt. William J. Seymour*, 71 (quotation); Hays' brigade casualty list, in 7-LA-Brigades, Louisiana Brigades Boxes, GNMP; *OR*, Vol. XXVII, Pt. 11. 479–80; Mingus, *Louisiana Tigers in the Gettysburg Campaign*, 119.

59. Pfanz, *Richard S. Ewell*, 308–12; Jubal A. Early, "Causes of Lee's Defeat at Gettysburg," *Southern Historical Society Papers*, IV (1877), 296–97; Douglas Southall Freeman, *R. E. Lee: A Biography* (4 vols.; New York, 1935), III, 76–78; Early, *War Memoirs*, 266–71; *OR*, Vol. XXVII, Pt. II, 317–18, 444–46, 468–70; Jones (ed.), *Campbell Brown's Civil War*, 210–11.

60. Jones (ed.), *Civil War Memoirs of Capt. William J. Seymour*, 72 (quotation); Zable paper,

December 12, 1903, in Reminiscences, Executive and Army of Northern Virginia, LHAC; Pfanz, *Gettysburg—First Day*, 342–49.

61. Mingus, *Louisiana Tigers in the Gettysburg Campaign*, 126.

62. *National Tribune*, December 30, 1909, *Chronicling America*, chroniclingamerica.loc.gov (accessed March 17, 2016).

63. Glatthaar, *General Lee's Army*, 275 (first quotation); Mingus, *Louisiana Tigers in the Gettysburg Campaign*, 134 (second and third quotations).

64. *Salt Lake Herald*, October 9, 1898, *Chronicling America*, chroniclingamerica.loc.gov (accessed July 28, 2016).

65. Edward Marcus (ed.), *A New Canaan Private in the Civil War: Letters of Justus M. Silliman, 17th Connecticut Volunteers* (New Canaan, Conn., 1984), 41.

66. Ibid.

67. Zable paper, December 12, 1903, in Reminiscences, Executive and Army of Northern Virginia, LHAC (quotations); Batchelor to father October 18, 1863, in Batchelor Papers, LSU; Loyd, "Second Louisiana," 117; OR, Vol. XXVII, Pt. II, p. 503.

68. Mingus, *Louisiana Tigers in the Gettysburg Campaign*, 131.

69. Ibid.; Gannon, *Irish Rebels*, 189–90; Hancock, "William Singleton," 499.

CHAPTER 9

GETTYSBURG

1. Jones (ed.), *Civil War Memoirs of Capt. William J. Seymour*, 73 (first quotation); Mingus, *Louisiana Tigers in the Gettysburg Campaign*, 135, 142 (second quotation); Gannon, *Irish Rebels*, 191.

2. Jones (ed.), *Civil War Memoirs of Capt. William J. Seymour*, 73 (first quotation); Jackson to brother, July 20, 1863, in Boyd Civil War Papers, LSU (second and third quotations).

3. Mingus, *Louisiana Tigers in the Gettysburg Campaign*, 135.

4. Ibid.; Marcus (ed.), *New Canaan Private*, 42 (quotation).

5. Mingus, *Louisiana Tigers in the Gettysburg Campaign*, 141.

6. Jones (ed.), *Civil War Memoirs of Capt. William J. Seymour*, 74 (quotation): also see Moore diary, July 2, 1863, in Moore Papers, UT.

7. Zable paper, December 12, 1903, in Reminiscences, Executive and Army of Northern Virginia, LHAC.

8. *Daily Picayune*, n.d., in *Camp Moore News*, Vol. 13, No. 3 (September 2011).

9. Buckley (ed.), *A Frenchman, a Chaplain, a Rebel*, 193 (first quotation); Booth (comp.), *Louisiana Confederate Soldiers*, II, 1291 (second quotation); Brooks and Jones, *Lee's Foreign Legion*, 46.

10. Zable paper, December 12, 1903, in Reminiscences, Executive and Army of Northern Virginia, LHAC (quotation); "Reminiscences of R. C. Murphy," in Murphy Sandlin Collection, NSU.

11. Loyd was left behind in a barn and captured when Lee retreated from Gettysburg. Loyd, "Second Louisiana," 417; OR, Vol. XXVII, Pt. II, 503–5, 513, 532; Batchelor to father, October 18, 1863, in Batchelor Papers, LSU; Zable paper, December 12, 1903, in Reminiscences, Executive and Army of Northern Virginia, LHAC (quotation).

12. "Reminiscences of R. C. Murphy," in Sandlin Collection, NSU.

13. Batchelor to James Batchelor, August 12, 1863, and n.d., Batchelor Papers, LSU.

14. Clancy was captured again at Spotsylvania and escaped from Elmira prison on December 30, 1864. Memphis *Daily Appeal* (Atlanta, Ga.), August 8, 1863, *Louisiana in the Civil War*, www.louisianacivilwar.org (accessed March 2, 2010) (quotation); *National Republican*, September 6, 1875, *Chronicling America*, chroniclingamerica.loc.gov (accessed March 17, 2016); Booth (comp.), *Louisiana Confederate Soldiers*, II, 337; Lichenstein memoir, USAERC.

15. Zable paper, in Reminiscences, Executive and Army of Northern Virginia, LHAC (quotation); "Reminiscences of R. C. Murphy," in Sandlin Collection, NSU.

16. Jones (ed.), *Civil War Memoirs of Capt. William J. Seymour*, 73 (first quotation), 75 (second quotation); Mingus, *Louisiana Tigers in the Gettysburg Campaign*, 148 (third quotation); *OR*, Vol. XXVII, Pt. II, 470–71, 482–85.

17. Jones (ed.), *Civil War Memoirs of Capt. William J. Seymour*, 73.

18. Gilmor, *Four Years in the Saddle*, 97; Harry W. Pfanz, *Gettysburg: Culp's Hill and Cemetery Hill* (Chapel Hill, 1993), 240; Mingus, *Louisiana Tigers in the Gettysburg Campaign*, 148.

19. Jackson to brother, July 20, 1863, in Boyd Papers, LSU (first quotation); *Opelousas Courier*, October 2, 1880 (second quotation); Mingus, *Louisiana Tigers in the Gettysburg Campaign*, 147–48, 150 (third quotation); Gannon, *Irish Rebels*, 191.

20. Pfanz, *Gettysburg: Culp's Hill and Cemetery Hill*, 253.

21. Jackson to brother, July 20, 1863, in Boyd Civil War Papers, LSU (first quotation); *OR*, Vol. XXVII, Pt. II, 480 (second quotation); Jones (ed.), *Civil War Memoirs of Capt. William J. Seymour*, 73 (third quotation); William T. Parsons and Mary Shuler Heimburger (eds.), "Shuler Family Correspondence," *Pennsylvania Folklife*, XXIX (Spring 1980), 112 (fourth quotation); Mingus, *Louisiana Tigers in the Gettysburg Campaign*, 155 (fifth quotation); Brent Nosworthy, *The Bloody Crucible of Courage: Fighting Methods and Combat Experience of the Civil War* (New York, 2003), 442–43.

22. Mingus, *Louisiana Tigers in the Gettysburg Campaign*, 151.

23. Pfanz, *Gettysburg: Culp's Hill and Cemetery Hill*, 247–50, 258 (quotation).

24. Mingus, *Louisiana Tigers in the Gettysburg Campaign*, 146 (first quotation); David L. and Audrey J. Ladd (eds.), *The Bachelder Papers: Gettysburg in Their Own Words* (3 vols.; Dayton, 1994), I, 1119 (second quotation); Pfanz, *Gettysburg: Culp's Hill and Cemetery Hill*, 255 (third quotation).

25. Jacob Smith, *Camps and Campaigns of the 107th Ohio Volunteer Infantry* (n.p., n.d.), 226 (first quotation); Mingus, *Louisiana Tigers in the Gettysburg Campaign*, 162 (second quotation).

26. Mingus, *Louisiana Tigers in the Gettysburg Campaign*, 158–9 (first quotation); Pfanz, *Gettysburg: Culp's Hill and Cemetery Hill*, 256 (second quotation); Parsons and Heimburger (eds.), "Shuler Family Correspondence," 112 (third quotation); Gettysburg *Compiler*, November 20, 1894, in Louisiana Brigades Box, GNMP (fourth quotation).

27. Jackson to brother, July 20, 1863, in Boyd Civil War Papers, LSU (first quotation); Pfanz, *Gettysburg: Culp's Hill and Cemetery Hill*, 257 (second quotation).

28. Pfanz, *Gettysburg: Culp's Hill and Cemetery Hill*, 259.

29. Ibid., 260.

30. Ibid., 260, 267 (quotations); Terry L. Jones, *Cemetery Hill: Struggle for the High Ground, July 1–3, 1863* (Cambridge, Mass., 2003), 83.

31. Jones, *Cemetery Hill*, 83.

32. Gettysburg *Compiler*, November 20, 1894, in Louisiana Brigades Boxes, GNMP (first quotation); Nosworthy, *Bloody Crucible of Courage*, 443 (second quotation).

33. Oliver Otis Howard, *Autobiography of Oliver Otis Howard, Major General, United States Army* (New York, 1907), 429 (quotation); Perrysburg (Ohio) *Journal*, October 15, 1909, *Chronicling America*, chroniclingamerica.loc.gov (accessed March 31, 2016).

34. Jackson to brother, July 20, 1863, in Boyd Civil War Papers, LSU (quotation); Stafford, *General Leroy Augustus Stafford*, 40; Pfanz, *Gettysburg*, 169; Edwin B. Coddington, *Gettysburg Campaign: A Study in Command* (New York, 1968), 438–39.

35. Robert Hoffsommer (ed.), "The Rise and Survival of Private Mesnard," *Civil War Times Illustrated* (February 1986), 12.

36. Carl Schurz, *The Reminiscences of Carl Schurz* (3 vols., New York, 1907–8), III, 25 (first quotation); Coddington, *Gettysburg Campaign*, 438–39; Pfanz, *Gettysburg: Culp's Hill and Cemetery Hill*, 270 (second quotation).

37. *OR*, Vol. XXVII, Pt. II, 486 (quotation). Missoula (Mont.) *Daily Missoulian*, June 15, 1913, *Chronicling America*, chroniclingamerica.loc.gov (accessed March 31, 2016). Stafford, *General Leroy Augustus Stafford*, 40. Schurz, *Reminiscences*, III, 25. *National Tribune*, November 7, 1889; October 21, 1909, *Chronicling America*, chroniclingamerica.loc.gov (accessed March 31, 2016).

38. Schurz, *Reminiscences*, III, 25 (first and second quotations); Pfanz, *Gettysburg: Culp's Hill and Cemetery Hill*, 269 (third and fourth quotations); Mingus, *Louisiana Tigers in the Gettysburg Campaign*, 170.

39. Jackson to brother, July 20, 1863, in Boyd Civil War Papers, LSU (quotation); Mingus, *Louisiana Tigers in the Gettysburg Campaign*, 162.

40. Ladd and Ladd (eds.), *Bachelder Papers*, I, 310–12 (quotation); Opelousas *Courier*, August 7, 1909, *Chronicling America*, chroniclingamerica.loc.gov (accessed March 31, 2016).

41. Smith, *107th Volunteer Infantry*, 226; see also *National Tribune*, July 15, 1909, *Chronicling America*, chroniclingamerica.loc.gov (accessed March 31, 2016).

42. Gilmor, *Four Years in the Saddle*, 97.

43. Mingus, *Louisiana Tigers in the Gettysburg Campaign*, 176–77.

44. *OR*, Vol. XXVII, Pt. I, 234, 457, 705–6, 715–16, 720, 722, 894; Early, *War Memoirs*, 272–74; Early, "Causes of Lee's Defeat," 279; Patterson, "Story of the War," in Patterson Collection, FSNMP; Howard, *Autobiography*, 429.

45. Pfanz, *Gettysburg: Culp's Hill and Cemetery Hill*, 273 (first quotation), 274; *OR*, Vol. XXVII, Pt. I, 457 (second quotation); Hancock, "William Singleton," 499.

46. Pfanz, *Gettysburg: Culp's Hill and Cemetery Hill*, 274.

47. Austin C. Stearns, *Three Years with Company K*, ed. Arthur A. Kent (London, 1976), 192 (first quotation); Earl Schenck Miers and Richard A. Brown (eds.), *Gettysburg* (New Brunswick, N.J., 1948), 184 (second quotation); Mingus, *Louisiana Tigers in the Gettysburg Campaign*, 184 (third quotation); *National Tribune*, August 30, 1888.

48. *OR*, Vol. XXVII, Pt. II, 481.

49. Another casualty list shows Hays lost 29 dead, 159 wounded, and 28 missing. Mingus, *Louisiana Tigers in the Gettysburg Campaign*, 185–86 (quotations); casualty list for Hays' brigade,

in 70-LA-Brigades, Louisiana Brigades Box, GNMP; *OR*, Vol. XXVII, Pt. II, 330–31, 340, 506; inspection report of Hays' brigade, June 19 and July 8, 1863, in Early Papers, War Record Group 109, Entry 118, NA; Mingus, *Louisiana Tigers in the Gettysburg Campaign*, 180.

50. Booth (comp.), *Louisiana Confederate Soldiers*, II, 114 (first quotation); Opelousas (La.) *St. Landry Clarion*, August 16, 1913, *Chronicling America*, chroniclingamerica.loc.gov (accessed March 31, 2016) (second quotation).

51. Johns was captured again at Rappahannock Station but survived the war. Moore diary, July 2, 1863, in Moore Papers, UT; Booth (comp.), *Louisiana Confederate Soldiers*, III, 444.

52. Schurz, *Reminiscences*, III, 24 (first quotation); Freeman, *R. E. Lee*, III, 102 (second quotation).

53. *OR*, Vol. XXVII, Pt. II, 446–47; Early, *War Memoirs*, 272–74; Freeman, *R. E. Lee*, III, 134–35, 177.

54. Pfanz, *Gettysburg: Culp's Hill and Cemetery Hill*, 280–82; Coddington, *Gettysburg Campaign*, 439–40; Early, "Causes of Lee's Defeat at Gettysburg," 279–81.

55. Wilmington (N.C.) *Semi-Weekly Messenger*, July 2, 1897, *Chronicling America*, chroniclingamerica.loc.gov (accessed March 31, 2016) (quotations); Henderson (N.C.) *Gold Leaf Volume*, May 6, 1897 (accessed March 31, 2016); see also *National Tribune*, October 24, 1901 (accessed March 31, 2016).

56. Perrysburg *Journal*, October 15, 1909; *National Tribune*, October 21, 1909, and October 13, 1892, *Chronicling America*, chroniclingamerica.loc.gov (accessed March 31, 2016); *National Tribune*, June 10, 1909 (accessed March 31, 2016).

57. Richard C. S. Drummond to Sam Houston Jones, December 8, 1942, photocopy, JPC; see also Terry L. Jones, "Twice Lost: The 8th Louisiana Volunteers' Battle Flag at Gettysburg," *Civil War Regiments*, Vol. 6, No. 3 (1999).

58. Willis later lost his right arm at Rappahannock Station. "BG. Hay's LA Tiger, new found flag!" in the *Louisiana in the Civil War Message Board*, November 16, 2009, and other entries, www.history-sites.com (accessed March 31, 2016); Mingus, *Louisiana Tigers in the Gettysburg Campaign*, 189 (quotation); J. Arthur Taylor to father, July 9, 1863, in 7-LA8 8th Louisiana Inf. Reg., Louisiana Brigades Box, GNMP.

59. Pfanz, *Richard S. Ewell*, 319–20; Jones (ed.), *Civil War Memoirs of Capt. William J. Seymour*, 79.

60. Handerson, *Yankee in Gray*, 63–64.

61. Reed, *Private in Gray*, 43.

62. Mingus, *Louisiana Tigers in the Gettysburg Campaign*, 193–94.

63. Ibid., 195.

64. Zable paper, December 12, 1903, in Reminiscences, Executive and Army of Northern Virginia, LHAC.

65. Ibid.

66. Marcus (ed.), *New Canaan Private*, 44 (quotation); Sacramento (Calif.) *Record-Union*, March 12, 1896, *Chronicling America*, chroniclingamerica.loc.gov (accessed March 18, 2016).

67. Jones (ed.), *Campbell Brown's Civil War*, 225.

68. R. C. Hancock to Walter Stewart, April 19, 1908, in Folder 5, William and Walter Stewart Papers, Merritt M. Shilg Memorial Collection, LSU; John F. Gruber to David F. Boyd, August 25,

1863, in Boyd Civil War Papers, LSU; Wade G. Chick to "Miss Flora," March 2, 1864, photocopy, in Michael P. Musick Collection, USAERC; Gannon, *Irish Rebels*, 203.

69. "A Leaf from Memory," *Cosgrove's Weekly*, January 4, 1911, in Melrose Scrapbook 230, NSU (quotations); Murphy, "Reminiscences of R. C. Murphy," in Sandlin Collection, NSU.

70. Albert Batchelor to father, August 20, 1863, in Batchelor Papers, LSU (first and second quotations); Batchelor to father, October 18, 1863, in Batchelor Papers, LSU (third quotation).

71. "Auction of Civil War Soldier's Skull Found at Gettysburg Cancelled," Fox News, June 3, 2014, www.foxnews.com (accessed July 27, 2016).

72. *OR*, Vol. XXVII, Pt. II, 330–31, 340, 506; inspection report of Hays' brigade, June 19 and July 8, 1863, in Early Papers, War Record Group 109, Entry 118, NA; Louisiana casualties, in 7-LA Louisiana Troops General Information, Louisiana Brigades Boxes, GNMP; see also Cutrer and Parrish (eds.), *Brothers in Gray*, 204–6; Brooks and Jones, *Lee's Foreign Legion*, 46, 99; Loyd, "Second Louisiana," 417; Mingus, *Louisiana Tigers in the Gettysburg Campaign*, 204–5.

73. Delaware (Ohio) *Gazette*, August 21, 1863, *Chronicling America*, chroniclingamerica.loc.gov (accessed March 19, 2016) (first quotation); Clearfield (Pa.) *Raftsman's Journal*, August 5, 1863 (accessed March 19, 2016) (second quotation).

74. S. Herman Dinkgrave to Maggie Lucas, July 5, 1863, in 7-LA2 2nd Louisiana Inf. Reg., Louisiana Brigades Boxes, GNMP (first quotation); Zable paper, December 12, 1903, in Reminiscences, Executive and Army of Northern Virginia, LHAC (second quotation); Jones (ed.), *Campbell Brown's Civil War*, 225 (third quotation).

75. Durkin (ed.), *Confederate Chaplain*, 49–50 (first and second quotations); Reed, *Private in Gray*, 43 (second quotation).

76. Cutrer and Parrish (eds.), *Brothers in Gray*, 203.

77. Gruber to Boyd, August 25, 1863, in Boyd Civil War Papers. LSU.

78. *OR*, Vol. XXVII, Pt. II, 450 (first quotation); Gruber to Boyd, August 25, 1863, in Boyd Civil War Papers, LSU (other quotations).

79. Jones (ed.), *Civil War Memoirs of Capt. William J. Seymour*, 81.

80. *OR*, Vol. XXVII, Pt. III, 1013–14.

81. Terry L. Jones, "Leroy Augustus Stafford," in Davis (ed.), *Confederate General*, V, 194–95; Stafford, *General Leroy Augustus Stafford*, 30–34; Handerson, *Yankee in Gray*, 29 (first and second quotations); Vollbrecht, "Hays' and Avery's Brigades," 8, in Louisiana Brigades Boxes, GNMP (third and fourth quotations); *OR*, Vol. XXXVI, Pt. I, 1074.

82. Handerson, *Yankee in Gray*, 65–66.

83. Batchelor to father, October 18, 1863, in Batchelor Papers, LSU; see also Charles Batchelor to Cousin James, August 6, 1863, in Batchelor Papers, LSU.

CHAPTER 10

INTO THE WILDERNESS

1. Cutrer and Parrish (eds.), *Brothers in Gray*, 209.

2. William H. Oliver to Hiram Oliver, September 26, 1863, in Section 5, George Family

Papers, VHS (quotation); Jones (ed.), *Civil War Memoirs of Capt. William J. Seymour,* 83–83; Reed, *Private in Gray,* 49–50; Pas. R. Garcia to Marguerite E. Williams, October 1, 1863, in Folder 1, Marguerite E. Williams Collection, SHC; Compiled Service Records, War Record Group 109, Microcopy 320, Rolls 148 and 201, NA.

3. Gannon, *Irish Rebels,* 206 (first quotation); Fogleman diary, October 3, 1863, FSNMP (second quotation); Cutrer and Parrish (eds.), *Brothers in Gray,* 214; W. G. Ogden to father, October 21, 1863, in Ogden Papers, TU; Egidius Smulders to Henry B. Kelly, March 187[?], in Smulders Papers, Confederate Personnel, LHAC.

4. John Orr to J. M. Wilson, August 19, 1863, in Army of Northern Virginia Papers, Part I, LHAC; Gannon, *Irish Rebels,* 207 (quotation); James I. Robertson Jr., *General A. P. Hill: The Story of a Confederate Warrior* (New York, 1987), 233–39; Jones (ed.), *Civil War Memoirs of Capt. William J. Seymour,* 85–89.

5. Gannon, *Irish Rebels,* 208 (quotation); Fogleman diary, October 15, 1863, FSNMP; Freeman, *R. E. Lee,* III, 169–93; Jones (ed.), *Civil War Memoirs of Capt. William J. Seymour,* 90; W. G. Ogden to father, October 21, 1863, in Ogden Papers, TU; Reed, *Private in Gray,* 50–51; Compiled Service Records, War Record Group 109, Microcopy 320, Rolls 148, 163, 187, NA.

6. Antoine Gusman, who was educated in France, was serving as the regiment's acting major. When the war ended, he was one of only two prisoners at Fort Lafayette who refused to sign the oath of allegiance. As a result, he was not released until November 11, 1865, and was told to leave the country. Gusman lived in Mexico for a time but eventually resettled in Louisiana. "Major Antoine L. Gusman," *Louisiana in the Civil War Message Board,* February 9, 2003, www. history-sites.com (accessed March 20, 2016).

7. *OR,* Vol. XXIX, Pt. I, 619–20, 626–27; Early, *War Memoirs,* 307–9, 316; Gannon, *Irish Rebels,* 209.

8. *OR,* Vol. XXIX, Pt. I, 612–13, 618–29; Gannon, *Irish Rebels,* 210–11; Early, *War Memoirs,* 309–13; Jones (ed.), *Civil War Memoirs of Capt. William J. Seymour,* 92–93.

9. Jones (ed.), *Civil War Memoirs of Capt. William J. Seymour,* 92 (quotation).

10. Ibid., 91 (first quotation); Early, *War Memoirs,* 313 (second quotation).

11. Pierson escaped capture. Cutrer and Parrish (eds.), *Brothers in Gray,* 211 (quotation); *OR,* Vol. XXIX, Pt. I, 577, 85–90; 618–29; Early, *War Memoirs,* 313–15; Benedict, *Vermont in the Civil War,* 404–5.

12. Gannon, *Irish Rebels,* 213 (first and third quotations); Charles Batchelor to father, December 21, 1863, in Folder 6, Batchelor Papers, LSU (second quotation); Washington, D.C., *Evening Star,* September 20, 1892, *Chronicling America,* chroniclingamerica.loc.gov (accessed March 20, 2016).

13. Gannon, *Irish Rebels,* 213 (first quotation); *OR,* Vol. XXIX, Pt. I, 622 (second quotation); Patterson, "Story of the War," in Patterson Collection, FSNMP; Peter W. Hairston diary, November 7, 12, and 13, 1863, Vol. III, in Peter W. Hairston Collection, SHC; Jones (ed.), *Civil War Memoirs of Capt. William J. Seymour,* 92–94; M. McNamara, "Lieutenant Charlie Pierce's Daring Attempts to Escape from Johnson's Island," *Southern Historical Society Papers,* VIII (1880), 61–62; *OR,* Vol. XXIX, Pt. I, 591, 600.

14. After being exchanged, Penn was transferred west, only to be captured again at Athens, Georgia. Vollbrecht, "Hays' and Avery's Brigades," 8, in Louisiana Brigades Boxes, GNMP; An-

derson Court House (S.C.) *Intelligencer,* April 22, 1880, *Chronicling America,* chroniclingamerica. loc.gov (accessed March 20, 2016).

15. Edwards referred to the rebel officer as a colonel, but he was probably Capt. John G. Angeli, who temporarily commanded the 5th Louisiana. Lamoille (Hyde Park, Vt.) *News Dealer,* December 23, 1863, *Chronicling America,* chroniclingamerica.loc.gov (accessed March 20, 2016).

16. Anderson *Intelligencer,* April 22, 1880; Washington, D.C., *Herald,* November 7, 1913, *Chronicling America,* chroniclingamerica.loc.gov (accessed March 20, 2016).

17. Camille Baquet, *History of the First Brigade, New Jersey Volunteers from 1861 to 1865* (Trenton, 1910), 102 (first quotation); John McCormick to Williams, February 26, 1864, in Folder 1, Williams Collection, SHC (second quotation); Hairston to wife, November 10, 1863, in Folder 33, Hairston Collection, SHC (third quotation).

18. Gannon, *Irish Rebels,* 216 (first quotation); *OR,* Vol. XXIX, Pt. I, 590, 618–29; monthly returns for Hays' brigade, October 30 and November 10, 1863, in Early Papers, War Record Group 109, Entry 118, NA; Compiled Service Records, War Record Group 109, Microcopy 320, Roll 148, NA; Charles Cormier to unknown, November 15, 1863, in Army of Northern Virginia Papers, Part I, LHAC; Jno. S. Dea to Williams, January 29 and March 5, 1864, in Folder 1, Williams Collection, SHC (second quotation); Hairston diary, November 9, 10, 12, 1863, in Hairston Collection, SHC.

19. Richmond *Whig,* n.d., in Newsclippings and Miscellaneous Unidentified Material, LHAC.

20. "Rappahannock Humor," *Louisiana in the Civil War,* February 11, 2010, www.louisiana-civilwar.org (first quotation) (accessed March 22, 2016); "Uniforms and Such," *Louisiana in the Civil War Message Board,* September 21, 2006, www.history-sites.com (second quotation) (accessed March 22, 2016).

21. Charlton was later exchanged and rejoined his regiment at Spotsylvania in May 1864. The pistol remains in the family's possession. Charlton diary, November 8, 1863, JPC.

22. *Hornellsville* (N.Y.) *Tribune,* November 12, 1863, *Newspaper Archive,* newspaperarchive. com (accessed March 22, 2016).

23. Maddox was exchanged in March and survived the war. Cutrer and Parrish (eds.), *Brothers in Gray,* 220.

24. Hairston diary, November 12, 1863, in Hairston Collection, SHC (first and fourth quotations); *OR,* Vol. XXIX, Pt. I, 613 (second quotation); Cormier to unknown, November 15, 1863, in Army of Northern Virginia, Part I, LHAC (third quotation).

25. Thomas Gibbes Morgan Jr. to mother, December 9, 1863, in Thomas Gibbes Morgan Sr. and Jr. Papers, DU (first quotation); Hairston diary, November 12, 1863, in Hairston Collection, SHC (second quotation).

26. Jones (ed.), *Civil War Memoirs of Capt. William J. Seymour,* 95.

27. *OR,* Vol. XXIX, Pt. I, 825–27, 830–36, 838, 843.

28. Handerson, *Yankee in Gray,* 67 (first quotation); J. M. Batchelor to Albert Batchelor, n.d., in Batchelor Papers, LSU (second quotation).

29. "Capt. D. T. Merrick," *Confederate Veteran,* XV (1907), 325; *OR,* Vol. XXIX, Pt. I, 874.

30. Stafford, *General Leroy Augustus Stafford,* 42–43.

31. A detailed casualty list for Stafford's brigade can be found in an anonymous newspaper

clipping, in Batchelor Papers, LSU; Charles Batchelor to father, December 12, 1863, in Batchelor Papers, LSU; *OR*, Vol. XXIX, Pt. I, 846–49, 870–75; Bartlett, *Military Record of Louisiana,* 48.

32. Cutrer and Parrish (eds.), *Brothers in Gray,* 215.

33. Casler, *Four Years in the Stonewall Brigade,* 297.

34. Jones (ed.), *Civil War Memoirs of Capt. William J. Seymour,* 100–101 (quotations); Gannon, *Irish Rebels,* 217.

35. Cutrer and Parrish (eds.), *Brothers in Gray,* 220.

36. Edward Seton to Mama, February 4, 1864, in Seton Collection, MSU (first quotation); Opelousas *Courier,* November 26, 1864, *Chronicling America,* chroniclingamerica.loc.gov (accessed March 22, 2016) (second quotation).

37. Compiled Service Records, War Record Group 109, Microcopy 320, Roll 163, NA (first quotation); Jones (ed.), *Civil War Memoirs of Capt. William J. Seymour,* 101–2 (second quotation); Dea to Williams, March 5, 1864, and Garcia to Williams, January 5, 1864, in Folder 1, Williams Collection, SHC; 7th Louisiana Volunteers Quartermaster document, March 1864, in Compiled Service Records, War Record Group 109, Chap. V, Vol. 205, NASHC; Oliver to Oliver, September 26, 1863, in George Family Papers, VHS; Handerson, *Yankee in Gray,* 53; H. Evans to unknown, January 10, 1864, in H. Evans Letter, LSU; Batchelor to sister, April 3, 1864, in Batchelor Papers, LSU.

38. Gannon, *Irish Rebels,* 219.

39. Trahern, "Biography," RNBP, 24.

40. Stephens (ed.), *Intrepid Warrior,* 335.

41. Stephens to Mr. and Mrs. T. E. Paxton, January 14, 1864, in Stephens Collection, NSU (quotations); Compiled Service Records, War Record Group 109, Microcopy 320, Roll 163, NA; Richmond *Whig,* January 18, 1864, in *Camp Moore News,* Vol. 12, No. 4 (December 2010); Gannon, *Irish Rebels,* 220.

42. Edmond Stephens to parents, January 4, 1863[4], in Stephens Collection, NSU (first and second quotations); Cutrer and Parrish (eds.), *Brothers in Gray,* 219 (third quotation).

43. Evans to unknown, January 10, 1864, in Evans Letter, LSU (first quotation); Durkin (ed.), *Confederate Chaplain,* 73 (second quotation), 78 (third quotation).

44. *OR*, XXXIII, 1187 (first and third quotations); Robert E. Lee to Richard S. Ewell, February 18, 1864, typed copy, in Robert E. Lee Papers, WLU (second quotation).

45. Evans to unknown, January 10, 1864, in Evans Letter, LSU.

46. Garcia to Williams, March 22, 1864, in Folder 1, Williams Collection, SHC (quotation); Robertson, *Stonewall Brigade,* 216–17; Casler, *Four Years in the Stonewall Brigade,* 204.

47. "Hayes vs Stafford Brigade Baseball Game," *Louisiana in the Civil War Message Board,* June 13, 2007, history-sites.com (accessed March 22, 2016); see also Snakenberg, "Memoirs," 31, JPC.

48. Snakenberg, "Memoirs," 31, JPC.

49. Durkin (ed.), *Confederate Chaplain,* 78–79 (first and fourth quotations); *Daily Constitutionalist* (Augusta, Ga.), April 15, 1864, *Louisiana in the Civil War,* December 1, 2010, www.louisianacivilwar.org (accessed March 22, 2016) (second, sixth, and seventh quotations); Ben LaBree (ed.), *Camp Fires of the Confederacy* (Louisville, 1899), 57–58 (third and fifth quotations).

50. LaBree, *Camp Fires of the Confederacy,* 58 (first quotation); Casler, *Four Years in the Stonewall Brigade,* 202 (second quotation); Durkin (ed.), *Confederate Chaplain,* 79 (third quotation); Robert Harris Jr. to W. Crawford Harris, March 25, 1864, MSCA.

51. Mingus, *Louisiana Tigers in the Gettysburg Campaign*, 222.

52. Terry had been captured earlier at Second Fredericksburg, and Belcher was captured again at Spotsylvania. Booth's *Louisiana Confederate Soldiers* incorrectly gives Belcher's name as Beleher. Alexander Belcher, "A Pair of Mittens," *Southern Bivouac*, Vol. II, September 1883–August 1884 (Wilmington, N.C., 1992), 378; Booth (comp.), *Louisiana Confederate Soldiers*, I, 157, 793.

53. Garcia to Williams, March 22, 1864, in Williams Collection, SHC (first quotation); Dea to Williams, January 29, 1864, in Williams Collection, SHC (second quotation); Batchelor to sister, April 3, 1864, in Folder 7, Batchelor Papers, LSU (third and fourth quotations); see also Reuben Allen Pierson to sister, March 28, 1864, in Folder 17, Carver Collection, NSU; Charles S. Hollier, Company F, 8th Louisiana Volunteers, pension file, in LSA.

54. Durkin (ed.), *Confederate Chaplain*, 86 (quotation); Trahern, "Biography," 25, RNBP.

55. Durkin (ed.), *Confederate Chaplain*, 86–87; Freeman, *R. E. Lee*, III, 269–76; Gordon H. Rhea, *The Battle of the Wilderness, May 5–6, 1864* (Baton Rouge, 1994), 152–54; E. M. Law, "From the Wilderness to Cold Harbor," in Johnson and Buel (eds.), *Battles and Leaders*, IV, 121–28.

56. Durkin (ed.), *Confederate Chaplain*, 86–87; Rhea, *Battle of the Wilderness*, 147–52.

57. Handerson, *Yankee in Gray*, 70 (first quotation); Snakenberg, "Memoirs," 32, JPC (second quotation).

58. Handerson, *Yankee in Gray*, 70 (first quotation); Snakenberg, "Memoirs," 32, JPC (second quotation).

59. Snakenberg, "Memoirs," 33, JPC.

60. Bartlett, *Military Record of Louisiana*, 12, 49; Handerson, *Yankee in Gray*, 69–71; Stafford, *General Leroy Augustus Stafford*, 44–51; Richmond *Enquirer*, May 10, 1864; Robertson, *Stonewall Brigade*, 218–20; McHenry, *Recollections of a Maryland Confederate*, 274–75.

61. Stafford, *General Leroy Augustus Stafford*, 48 (quotations); Jones (ed.), *Civil War Memoirs of Capt. William J. Seymour*, 109.

62. Jones (ed.), *Civil War Memoirs of Capt. William J. Seymour*, 109–10.

63. Ibid., 110 (quotation); *OR*, Vol. XXXVI, Pt. I, 1071, 1077–78; Jubal A. Early, *A Memoir of the Last Year of the War for Independence . . . in the Year 1864 and 1865* (Lynchburg, 1867), 16–20: W. S. Dunlop, *Lee's Sharpshooters; or, The Forefront of Battle* (Little Rock, 1899), 390; G. P. Ring to wife, May 6, 1864, typescript copy, in Army of Northern Virginia, Part I, LHAC; Theodore H. Woodard Letters, typed copy, MOC.

64. Cutrer and Parrish (eds.), *Brothers in Gray*, 236 (first quotation); Trahern, "Biography," 25, MOC (second quotation); Ezra Denson to John F. Stephens, May 24, 1864, in Stephens Collection, NSU.

65. G. P. Ring to wife, May 6, 1864, typescript copy, in Army of Northern Virginia, Part I, LHAC (quotation); Rhea, *Battle of the Wilderness*, 357–72; Jones (ed.), *Civil War Memoirs of Capt. William J. Seymour*, 113.

66. Jones (ed.), *Civil War Memoirs of Capt. William J. Seymour*, 114–15; *OR*, Vol. XXXVI, Pt. I, 1071, 1077–78; Early, *Memoir of the Last Year of the War*, 16–20; Rhea, *Battle of the Wilderness*, 412–25; Freeman, *R. E. Lee*, III, 285–97.

67. Jones (ed.), *Civil War Memoirs of Capt. William J. Seymour*, 116 (first quotation); Egidius Smulders to Henry B. Kelly, March, 187[?], in Smulders Papers, Confederate Personnel, LHAC (second quotation).

68. Jones (ed.), *Civil War Memoirs of Capt. William J. Seymour,* 116–17.

69. Trahern, "Biography," 25, MOC.

70. Clifford Dowdey, *Lee's Last Campaign: The Story of Lee and His Men Against Grant—1864* (Boston, 1960), 194. Freeman, *R. E. Lee,* III, 304–5. Allen P. Tankersley, *John B. Gordon: A Study in Gallantry* (Atlanta, 1955), 146–47. Moore, *Louisiana Tigers,* 176. OR, Vol. XXXVI, Pt. II, 974; Vol. LI, Pt. II, 902.

71. Cutrer and Parrish (eds.), *Brothers in Gray,* 218 (first quotation); OR, Vol. XLIII, Pt. I, 610 (second and third quotations).

72. "A Private Letter of an Officer in Hays' La. Brigade, 6th Reg.," typed copy, *Daily Advertiser* (Mobile, Ala.), May 28, 1864, FSNMP.

73. Snakenberg, "Memoirs," 34, JPC.

74. Welsh, *Medical Histories of Confederate Generals,* 96; Jones (ed.), *Civil War Memoirs of Capt. William J. Seymour,* 120–21.

75. Jones (ed.), *Civil War Memoirs of Capt. William J. Seymour,* 122 (quotation); Booth (comp.), *Louisiana Confederate Soldiers,* II, 691; *Daily Advertiser,* May 28, 1864, FSNMP; Gordon C. Rhea, *The Battles for Spotsylvania Court House and the Road to Yellow Tavern, May 7–12, 1864* (Baton Rouge, 1997), 168–81.

76. Jones (ed.), *Civil War Memoirs of Capt. William J. Seymour,* 122; Rhea, *Spotsylvania Court House,* 215; Freeman, *R. E. Lee,* III, 306–26; OR, Vol. XXXVI, Pt. I, 1071, 1073, 1080; Dunlop, *Lee's Sharpshooters,* 456–66: Howard, *Recollections of a Maryland Confederate,* 292–94; Snakenberg, "Memoirs," 34, JPC.

77. R. D. Funkhauser, "Gen. Lee About to Enter Battle," *Confederate Veteran,* II (1894), 36.

78. Snakenberg, "Memoirs," 35, JPC.

79. Jones (ed.), *Civil War Memoirs of Capt. William J. Seymour,* 123 (first quotation); Reed, *Private in Gray,* 75 (second quotation); Snakenberg, "Memoirs," 36, JPC (third quotation).

80. Snakenberg, "Memoirs," 35, JPC.

81. Brooks and Jones, *Lee's Foreign Legion,* 63, 259; R. G. Cobb to Albert Batchelor, June 4, 1864, in Batchelor Papers, LSU; T. J. Stoern to J. A. Chalaron, June 9, 1864, in Flags, LHAC; Howard, *Recollections of a Maryland Confederate,* 295–98; Bartlett, *Military Record of Louisiana,* 49; Moore, *Louisiana Tigers,* 176; Worsham, *One of Jackson's Foot Cavalry,* 139–40.

82. This flag is currently in the collections of the Confederate Memorial Hall in New Orleans. Frederick Fisterer (comp.), *New York in the War of the Rebellion, 1861–1865,* 2nd ed. (Albany, 1890), 63, 141. *San Francisco Call,* April 7, 1901, *Chronicling America,* chroniclingamerica.loc.gov (accessed March 31, 2016); Washington, D.C., *Evening Star,* September 20, 1892 (accessed March 31, 2016).

83. "Medal of Honor recipients affiliated with New York: Civil War," *New York State Military Museum and Veterans Research Center,* dmna.ny.gov (accessed April 2, 2016); Houma (La.) *Courier,* July 17, 1897, *Chronicling America,* chroniclingamerica.loc.gov (accessed March 31, 2016).

84. Collins had been captured earlier at Rappahannock Station and was captured again at the Third Battle of Winchester, but he survived the war. Dunlop, *Lee's Sharpshooters,* 41 (first three quotations); Cutrer and Parrish (eds.), *Brothers in Gray,* 239 (fourth quotation); Booth (comp.), *Louisiana Confederate Soldiers,* I, 391; Gannon, *Irish Rebels,* 243–44; Jones (ed.), *Civil War Memoirs of Capt. William J. Seymour,* 123–25.

85. G. P. Ring to wife, May 15, 1864, typescript copy, in Army of Northern Virginia Papers, Part I, LHAC.

86. Jones (ed.), *Civil War Memoirs of Capt. William J. Seymour*, 127 (quotation); *OR*, Vol. XXXVI, Pt. I, 1072–73; unidentified newspaper clipping in Newsclippings and Miscellaneous Unidentified Material, LHAC; G. Norton Galloway, "Hand-to-Hand Fighting at Spotsylvania," in Johnson and Buel (eds.), *Battles and Leaders*, IV (1898), 177.

87. Durkin (ed.), *Confederate Chaplain*, 88–89 (quotation); Ring to wife, May 15, 1864, in Army of Northern Virginia Papers, Part I, LHAC; Casualty list of Company I, 9th Louisiana Volunteers, LHAC; Bartlett, *Military Record of Louisiana*, 12.

88. William W. Old, "Trees Whittled Down at Horseshoe," *Southern Historical Society Papers*, XXXIII (1905), 19; Snakenberg, "Memoirs," 36, JPC.

89. Ring to wife, May 15, 1864, in Army of Northern Virginia Papers, Part I, LHAC.

90. *OR*, Vol. XXXVI, Pt. I, 1073; unidentified newspaper clipping in Newsclippings and Miscellaneous Unidentified Material, LHAC.

91. Terry L. Jones, "Zebulon York," in Davis (ed.), *Confederate General*, VI, 166 (quotation), 167. Compiled Service Records of Confederate General and Staff Officers, War Record Group 109, Microcopy 331, Roll 122, NA. Conner (ed.), "Letters of Lieutenant Robert H. Miller," 88. *OR*, Vol. XXXVI, Pt. II, 974; III, 873–74; XLI, Pt. II, 1000; IV, 1073. Henry J. Egan to brother, June 21, 1864, in J. S. Egan Family Papers, LSU. Durkin (ed.), *Confederate Chaplain*, 65, 93, 97. Sigmund H. Uminski, "Poles and the Confederacy," *Polish American Studies*, XXII (1965), 102.

92. Booth (comp.), *Louisiana Confederate Soldiers*, III, 363.

93. From a paper read before the United Daughters of the Confederacy, n.d., in *Camp Moore News*, Vol. 15, No. 4 (December 2013).

94. Ring to wife, May 15, 1864, in Army of Northern Virginia Papers, Part I, LHAC; Egan to brother, June 21, 1864, in Egan Papers, LSU.

95. Gordon C. Rhea, *To the North Anna River: Grant and Lee, May 13–25, 1864* (Baton Rouge, 2000), 143 (first quotation); Egan to brother, June 21, 1864, in Egan Papers, LSU (second quotation); Charlton diary, May 18, 1864, JPC.

96. Cutrer and Parrish (eds.), *Brothers in Gray*, 239 (first quotation); Ring to wife, May 15, 1864, in Army of Northern Virginia Papers, Part I, LHAC (second quotation).

97. Cutrer and Parrish (eds.), *Brothers in Gray*, 240 (first quotation); Egan to brother, June 21, 1864, in Egan Papers, LSU (second quotation).

CHAPTER 11
ALL PLAYED OUT

1. Rhea, *To the North Anna River*, 177–80.

2. Charlton diary, May 27, 1864, JPC (quotation); Tull, "Tull's War Story," HLW.

3. Tull, "Tull's War Story," HLW.

4. Ibid.

5. Vollbrecht, "Hays' and Avery's Brigades," 6–9, in Louisiana Brigades Boxes, GNMP; D. T.

Merrick to E. D. Willett, December 9, 1863, in Reminiscences, Executive and Army of Northern Virginia, LHAC; Wallace H. McChesney, "Capt. Charles W. McLellan," *Confederate Veteran*, VI (1898), 506; Freeman, *R. E. Lee*, III, 334–71; Jones (ed.), *Civil War Memoirs of Capt. William J. Seymour*, 133; Bartlett, *Military Record of Louisiana*, 49–50; *OR*, Vol. XXXVI, Pt. I, 1073–74.

6. Reed, *Private in Gray*, 80–81 (quotation); Rhea, *Cold Harbor*, 368–76.

7. Brooks and Jones, *Lee's Foreign Legion*, 64; Jones (ed.), *Civil War Memoirs of Capt. William J. Seymour*, 133–34; Compiled Service Records of Confederate General and Staff Officers, War Record Group 109, Microcopy 331, Roll 275, NA; Freeman, *R. E. Lee*, III, 373–89; Bartlett, *Military Record of Louisiana*, 18; Bound Volume 8 in Association of the Army of Northern Virginia, LHAC; unidentified newspaper clipping in Box 1, Grace King Collection, SHC; unidentified newspaper clipping in Flags, SHC.

8. Tull, "Tull's War Story," HLW.

9. *OR*, Vol. LI, Pt. II, 1008.

10. Ibid., Vol. XXXVI, Pt. II, 971, 1071; XXXVII, Pt. I, 156, 346, 727, 756–60, 768. Frank E. Vandiver, *Jubal's Raid: General Early's Famous Attack on Washington in 1864* (New York, 1960), 6–7, 19, 35–37, 64. William W. Old diary, June 13–July 9, 1864, in Miscellaneous Manuscripts Collection, LC. Bound Volumes 5, 6, and 7 in Association of the Army of Northern Virginia, LHAC. Charles M. Blackford, "The Campaign and Battle of Lynchburg," *Southern Historical Society Papers*, XXX (1902) 279–332, 284, 288.

11. Tull, "Tull's War Story," HLW.

12. Ibid. (first quotation); Z. York, "Report of Brig. Gen. Zebulon York, July 22, 1864," *Historical Magazine*, IX (1871), 20, 19–21.

13. Tull, "Tull's War Story," HLW.

14. Ibid.

15. Two weeks later, Major Hodges was wounded and captured at the Monocacy. Tull, "Tull's War Story," HLW (quotations); Booth (comp.), *Louisiana Confederate Soldiers*, II, 323–24.

16. Bound Volume 8 (first quotation) and Volume 10 in Association of the Army of Northern Virginia, LHAC; York, "Report of Zebulon York," 19–20 (second and third quotations); Bartlett, *Military Record of Louisiana*, 51–52; Durkin (ed.), *Confederate Chaplain*, 94.

17. Gannon, *Irish Rebels*, 253.

18. York, "Report of Zebulon York," 19–20.

19. John B. Gordon, *Reminiscences of the Civil War* (New York, 1903), 311 (first quotation); York, "Report of Zebulon York," 19–20 (second and third quotation); Gannon, *Irish Rebels*, 256; Stephens (ed.), *Intrepid Warrior*, 424–26.

20. Zebulon York to B. B. Wellford, July 18, 1864, in Reel 1, White, Wellford, Taliaferro, and Marshall Collection, SHC (quotation); L. H. Stewart to J. F. Stephens, November 27, 1864, and Henry M. King to J. F. Stephens, August 15, 1864, in Stephens Collection, NSU; Old diary, July 9, 1864, in Miscellaneous Manuscripts Collection, LC; Vandiver, *Jubal's Raid*, 110–18; Robertson, *Stonewall Brigade*, 231; *OR*, Vol. XXXVII, Pt. I, 193, 200; Gordon, *Reminiscences of the Civil War*, 310–13.

21. York, "Report of Zebulon York," 20 (quotation); Gannon, *Irish Rebels*, 258.

22. Vollbrecht, "Hays' and Avery's Brigades," 6–9, in Louisiana Brigades Boxes, GNMP; York, "Report of Zebulon York," 20 (first quotation); Gannon, *Irish Rebels*, 258 (second quotation).

23. Jones (ed.), *Civil War Memoirs of Capt. William J. Seymour*, 137 (first quotation); OR, XXXVII, Pt. 1, 352 (second quotation); York, "Report of Zebulon York," 20 (third quotation); Durkin (ed.), *Confederate Chaplain*, 94 (fourth quotation).

24. York to Wellford, July 18, 1864, in White, Wellford, Taliaferro, and Marshall Collection, SHC.

25. Gannon, *Irish Rebels*, 259 (first quotation); York, "Report of Zebulon York," 20 (second quotation); OR, Vol. XXXVII, Pt. I, 348–49; Old diary, July 11, 1864, in Miscellaneous Manuscripts Collection, LC; Bartlett, *Military Record of Louisiana*, 51–52.

26. York, "Report of Zebulon York," 20.

27. Cutrer and Parrish (eds.), *Brothers in Gray*, 241–42.

28. Alexander Hart diary, *Jewish-American History Foundation*, www.jewish-history.com (accessed August 12, 2015).

29. Richard Colbert to Mrs. E. M. Potts, July 24, 1864, in Folder 57, North Louisiana Historical Association Archives, CC.

30. Tull, "Tull's War Story," HLW.

31. Ring to wife, July 24, 1864, in Army of Northern Virginia Papers, Part I, LHAC (quotation); Gannon, *Irish Rebels*, 262.

32. Ring to wife, July 24, 1864, in Army of Northern Virginia Papers, Part I, LHAC (quotation); Gannon, *Irish Rebels*, 263; Colbert to Potts, July 24, 1864, in North Louisiana Historical Association Archives, CC.

33. Ring to wife, July 24, 1864, in Army of Northern Virginia Papers, Part I, LHAC (quotation); Gannon, *Irish Rebels*, 263.

34. Colbert to Potts, July 24, 1864, in North Louisiana Historical Association Archives, CC (quotation); Ring to wife, July 24, 1864, in Army of Northern Virginia Papers, Part I, LHAC; Gannon, *Irish Rebels*, 263.

35. Ring to wife, July 24, 1864, in Army of Northern Virginia Papers, Part I, LHAC (quotation); Hart diary, July 24–26, 1864, *Jewish-American History Foundation*, www.jewish-history.com.

36. Hart diary, August 5–6, 25, 1864, *Jewish-American History Foundation*, www.jewish-history.com; Gannon, *Irish Rebels*, 267.

37. OR, Vol. XLIII, Pt. I, 609–10, 1002; Hart diary, August 29, 1864, *Jewish-American History Foundation*, www.jewish-history.com; Bartlett, *Military Record of Louisiana*, 52; Early, *Memoir of the Last Year of the War*, 74–75; Gannon, *Irish Rebels*, 270–71.

38. Ring to wife, September 21, 1864, in Army of Northern Virginia Papers, Part I, LHAC (first quotation); Jones (ed.), *Civil War Memoirs of Capt. William J. Seymour*, 140 (second quotation); Jeffry D. Wert, *From Winchester to Cedar Creek: The Shenandoah Campaign of 1864* (Carlisle, Pa., 1987), 52–54.

39. Ring to wife, September 21, 1864, in Army of Northern Virginia Papers, Part I, LHAC (quotations); Gannon, *Irish Rebels*, 273, 278; Jones (ed.), *Civil War Memoirs of Capt. William J. Seymour*, 140.

40. Ring to wife, September 21, 1864, in Army of Northern Virginia Papers, Part I, LHAC; Wert, *From Winchester to Cedar Creek*, 95–106; Bartlett, *Military Record of Louisiana*, 37–38; unidentified article on the 2nd Louisiana's flag in Flags, LHAC; Jones (ed.), *Civil War Memoirs of Capt. William J. Seymour*, 141–42.

41. Ring to wife, September 21, 1864, in Army of Northern Virginia Papers, Part I, LHAC.

42. Welsh, *Medical Histories of Confederate Generals,* 165, 241; Brooks and Jones, *Lee's Foreign Legion,* 68; Hart diary, *Jewish-American History Foundation,* www.jewish-history.com; Gannon, *Irish Rebels,* 288.

43. Ring to wife, September 21, 1864, in Army of Northern Virginia Papers, Part I, LHAC.

44. Ibid. (quotation); Wert, *From Winchester to Cedar Creek,* 106.

45. Jones (ed.), *Civil War Memoirs of Capt. William J. Seymour,* 144; Wert, *From Winchester to Cedar Creek,* 115–18.

46. Jones (ed.), *Civil War Memoirs of Capt. William J. Seymour,* 144 (first quotation); unidentified newspaper clipping in Newsclippings and Miscellaneous Unidentified Material, LHAC (second quotation); "NY Medal of Honor for Capturing Flags," *Civil War Flags Message Board,* May 1, 2016, www.history-sites.com (accessed June 21, 2016); Compiled Service Records, War Record Group 109, Microcopy 320, Rolls 148 and 163, NA; *OR,* Vol. XLIII, Pt. I, 556; Bartlett, *Military Record of Louisiana,* 52–53.

47. John H. Lane, "The Battle of Fisher's Hill," *Southern Historical Society Papers,* XVIII–XIX (1891), 294–95.

48. Charlton diary, October 4, 7, 1864, JPC.

49. Trahern, "Biography," 28, RNBP (quotations); Wert, *From Winchester to Cedar Creek,* 174–76.

50. Wert, *From Winchester to Cedar Creek,* 174–76; Trahern, "Biography," 29, RNBP (quotations).

51. Trahern, "Biography," 29, RNBP.

52. Captain Ring never returned to the 6th Louisiana. Gannon, *Irish Rebels,* 288, 294; Wert, *From Winchester to Cedar Creek,* 184–85.

53. Trahern, "Biography," RNBP, 30 (first quotation); Charlton diary, n.d., JPC; *OR,* Vol. XLIII, Pt. I, 561–64, 581; Bound Volume 6 in Association of the Army of Northern Virginia, LHAC; Bartlett, *Military Record of Louisiana,* 19, 53–54; "Fisher's Hill and 'Sheridan's Ride,'" *Confederate Veteran,* X (1902), 165.

54. Stephens (ed.), *Intrepid Warrior,* 497 (first quotation); Trahern, "Biography," 30, RNBP (second quotation).

55. *OR,* Vol. XLII, Pt. III, 912, 1195, 1365; Bartlett, *Military Record of Louisiana,* 54; monthly return for York's brigade, November 28, 1864, in Bound Volume 42, Association of the Army of Northern Virginia, LHAC; Lawrence L. Hewitt, "William Raine Peck," in Davis (ed.), *Confederate General,* V, 2–3; Jones (ed.), *Civil War Memoirs of Capt. William J. Seymour,* 142; Gannon, *Irish Rebels,* 296.

56. *OR,* Series IV, Vol. III, 824–25; Compiled Service Records of Confederate General and Staff Officers, War Record Group 109, Microcopy 331, Roll 275, NA; Woodard to father, January 18, 1864[5], MOC (quotation).

57. *OR,* Vol. XLVI, Pt. II, 1089.

58. Buckley (ed.), *A Frenchman, a Chaplain, a Rebel,* 227.

59. *OR,* Vol. XLVI, Pt. II, 1089–90.

60. Ibid., 1090.

61. Egidius Smulders to Henry B. Kelly, March, 187[?], in Smulders Papers, Confederate

Personnel, LHAC (quotation). Buckley (ed.), *A Frenchman, a Chaplain, a Rebel,* 227. Compiled Service Records of Confederate General and Staff Officers, War Record Group 109, Microcopy 331, Roll 275, NA. *OR,* Vol. XLVI, Pt. II, 1089–90; Series IV, Vol. III, 824–25, 1029.

62. J. H. Cosgrove, "Recollections and Reminiscences," *Cosgrove's Weekly,* August 26, 1911, in Melrose Scrapbook 230, NSU (first quotation); Charlton diary, February 6, 1865, JPC (second quotation).

63. Gannon, *Irish Rebels,* 300 (quotation); Woodard to father, January 18, 1864[5], MOC.

64. Gannon, *Irish Rebels,* 301–3 (first and third quotations); Charlton diary, February 8 and 9, 1865, JPC (second and fourth quotations).

65. *OR,* Vol. XLVI, Pt. I, 390–92; Booth (comp.), *Louisiana Confederate Soldiers,* I, 567; Marguerite Williams Collection, SHC; "8th Regiment Co. B—Louisiana Volunteers," *Louisiana in the Civil War Message Board,* July 4, 2003, www.history-sites.com (accessed March 5, 2015).

66. Gannon, *Irish Tigers,* 303.

67. Trahern, "Biography," 31, RNBP (first quotation); "Kindness of Yankees near Petersburg," *Confederate Veteran,* XVII (1909), 532 (second quotation).

68. "A Louisiana Hero—Col. David Zable," in *Camp Moore News,* Vol. 13, No. 3 (September 2011). *OR,* Vol. XLVI, Pt. I, 382; XLII, Pt. II, 956; XLII, Pt. III, 936; XLVI, Pt. I, 389; XLVI, Pt. II, 280, 287, 603; XLVI, Pt. III, 204, 373. Bound Volume 2 in Association of the Army of Northern Virginia, LHAC.

69. Gannon, *Irish Rebels,* i–ii (quotations), 304.

70. Ibid., 320.

71. A. Wilson Greene, *The Final Battles of the Petersburg Campaign: Breaking the Backbone of the Rebellion* (Knoxville, 2008), 112.

72. Stephens (ed.), *Intrepid Warrior,* 533–36; Noah Andre Trudeau, *The Last Citadel: Petersburg, Virginia, June 1864–April 1865* (Boston, 1991), 337–40.

73. One source claims the division's sharpshooters led the way, followed by Waggaman's brigade. Bartlett, *Military Record of Louisiana,* 39 (quotation); Stephens (ed.), *Intrepid Warrior,* 533–36; Trudeau, *Last Citadel,* 337–40; Gannon, *Irish Rebels,* 307–8.

74. Gordon, *Reminiscences of the Civil War,* 408–9.

75. Trudeau, *Last Citadel,* 337–38, 339 (quotation); Stephens (ed.), *Intrepid Warrior,* 533–36; Dunlop, *Lee's Sharpshooters,* 246; R. D. Funkerhauser, "Fort Stedman—So Near Yet So Far," *Confederate Veteran,* XIX (1911), 217.

76. Gannon, *Irish Rebels,* 307–8.

77. Trudeau, *Last Citadel,* 339 (first quotation); Bartlett, *Military Record of Louisiana,* 40 (second quotation); Gannon, *Irish Rebels,* 307–8.

78. Stephens (ed.), *Intrepid Warrior,* 535; Trudeau, *Last Citadel,* 339.

79. Stephens (ed.), *Intrepid Warrior,* 535 (first quotation); Bartlett, *Military Record of Louisiana,* 40 (second and third quotations); Gannon, *Irish Rebels,* 309; Greene, *Final Battles of the Petersburg Campaign,* 112–16; *OR,* Vol. XLVI, Pt. I, 173, 382–83; George L. Kilmer, "Gordon's Attack at Fort Stedman," in Johnson and Buel (eds.), *Battles and Leaders,* IV, 580; *OR,* Vol. XLVI, Pt. I, 173, 382–83; George L. Kilmer, "Gordon's Attack at Fort Stedman," in Johnson and Buel (eds.), *Battles and Leaders,* IV, 580.

80. Unidentified newspaper clipping in Newsclippings and Miscellaneous Unidentified Material, LHAC (quotation).

81. Stephens (ed.), *Intrepid Warrior*, 539–41.

82. Ibid., 541 (first quotation); Bartlett, *Military Record of Louisiana*, 55 (second quotation); E. G. Braswell, "Fort Steadman [*sic*] and Subsequent Events," *Confederate Veteran*, XXIII (1915), 21.

83. Stephens (ed.), *Intrepid Warrior*, 542; Bartlett, *Military Record of Louisiana*, 41–42, 55; Gordon, *Reminiscences of the Civil War*, 420–23; Freeman, *R. E. Lee*, IV, 229–40.

84. Stephens (ed.), *Intrepid Warrior*, 541–44, 545 (first quotation); Bartlett, *Military Record of Louisiana*, 55 (second quotation).

85. Bartlett, *Military Record of Louisiana*, 42–43.

86. Stephens (ed.), *Intrepid Warrior*, 547; Bartlett, *Military Record of Louisiana*, 55.

87. Edmund Pendleton to wife, April 6, 1865, in Coles Collection, SHC.

88. Stephens (ed.), *Intrepid Warrior*, 548; Bartlett, *Military Record of Louisiana*, 55.

89. Gordon, *Reminiscences of the Civil War*, 436–37 (quotation); William Marvel, *Lee's Last Retreat: The Flight to Appomattox* (Chapel Hill, 2002), 161–73; Stephens (ed.), *Intrepid Warrior*, 549–50.

90. Stephens (ed.), *Intrepid Warrior*, 550–51; Gordon, *Reminiscences of the Civil War*, 438 (quotation).

91. Stephens (ed.), *Intrepid Warrior*, 552–53; Gordon, *Reminiscences of the Civil War*, 423–24, 430, 436–38; Freeman, *R. E. Lee*, IV, 107–20; Bartlett, *Military Record of Louisiana*, 42, 55–56; William Kaigler, "Last Charge at Appomattox," *Confederate Veteran*, VII (1899), 357; *OR*, Vol. XLVI, Pt. I, 1303; *Times-Picayune*, February 15, 1931, in Melrose Scrapbook 228, NSU.

92. Stephens (ed.), *Intrepid Warrior*, 552.

CHAPTER 12

A LOUISIANA LEGACY

1. *National Tribune*, October 7, 1909, *Chronicling America*, chroniclingamerica.loc.gov (accessed April 2, 2016).

2. John Fitzpatrick to W. H. Lee, September 7, 1877, in John Fitzpatrick Letterbook, LSU; R. A. Brock, *The Appomattox Roster* (1887; rpt. New York, n.d.), 4, 6, 230–37. 456; Hewitt, "Confederate Foreign Legion," 137; Gannon, *Irish Rebels*, 312; Gordon Berl to author, email, August 5, 2016, JPC.

3. "Eugene Waggaman," *Southern Historical Society Papers*, XXV (1897), 185–86.

4. "Flags at Appomattox," *Louisiana in the Civil War Message Board*, August 20, 2013, history-sites.com (accessed April 10, 2016); Manning (S.C.) *Times*, May 17, 1899, *Chronicling America*, chroniclingamerica.loc.gov (accessed July 29, 2016).

5. "Distinguished Dead of Louisiana Division," *Southern Historical Society Papers*, XXVI (1898), 377–79; "Louisiana Troops in Virginia," n.p., in Melrose Scrapbook 228, NSU; "The DeSoto Blues," n.p., Melrose Scrapbook 235, NSU; John Dimitry, *Louisiana*, Vol. X of Clement Evans (ed.), *Confederate Military History* (10 vols.; Atlanta, 1899), 322–25; Consolidated report, Company G, 9th Louisiana Volunteers, January 16, 1865, in Bound Volume 42, Association of the Army of Northern Virginia, LHAC.

6. "Fontenots of the 8th Louisiana Infantry," *Louisiana in the Civil War*, www.louisianacivil-war.org (accessed September 10, 2015); Booth (comp.), *Louisiana Confederate Soldiers*, I, 884–86.

7. Brooks and Jones, *Lee's Foreign Legion*, 5, 258; Edward Seton to mother, June 17, 1863, in Seton Collection, MSU; Booth (comp.), *Louisiana Confederate Soldiers*, III, 373.

8. Brook and Jones, *Lee's Foreign Legion*, 259.

9. Ibid., 30, 233; Booth (comp.), *Louisiana Confederate Soldiers*, II, 432.

10. Vollbrecht, "Hays' and Avery's Brigades," 6–9, in Louisiana Brigades Box, GNMP; Gannon, *Irish Rebels*, 258.

11. C. A. Evans to Colonel Eugene Waggaman, April 11, 1865, in Box 1, Folder 3, Jastremski Papers, LSU.

12. John B. Gordon to Colonel Eugene Waggaman, April 12, 1865, in Box 1, Folder 3, Jastremski Papers, LSU.

13. "Louisiana Tigers Outdone?" *Louisiana in the Civil War*, July 13, 2010, www.louisianacivil-war.org (accessed April 10, 2016).

14. Jones, *Christ in the Camp*, 476 (quotation); Contributions for the Relief of the Fredericksburg Sufferers, Harry T. Hays Brigade, in Slaughter Papers, Part 1, FSNMP. For details of the Tigers' religious side, see Jones, *Christ in the Camp*; Durkin (ed.), *Confederate Chaplain*; and Buckley (ed.), *A Frenchman, a Chaplain, a Rebel*.

15. See appendix and Muster roll, 15th Louisiana Volunteers, May 1–August 31, 1862, in Gertrude B. Saucier Papers, LSU.

16. Booth (comp.), *Louisiana Confederate Soldiers*, II, 762 (quotation); T. W. Reynolds diary, in Army of Northern Virginia Papers, Part II, LHAC; Muster roll, Company B, 7th Louisiana Volunteers, n.d., in Saucier Papers, LSU.

17. Brooks and Jones, *Lee's Foreign Legion*, 53; "Galvanized Yankees from Louisiana," *Louisiana in the Civil War Message Board*, April 6, 7, and 9, 2013, history-sites.com (accessed April 2, 2016).

18. Pemberton's article states that the 104th Pennsylvania was stationed between the Appomattox and James rivers. The Tigers are only known to have served south of the Appomattox River, but records are scarce for their activities at this time, and they could have been moved around where needed. Booth (comp.), *Louisiana Confederate Soldiers*, I, 91–92; *National Tribune*, June 6, 1907, *Chronicling America*, chroniclingamerica.loc.gov (accessed April 2, 2016).

19. Reed, *Private in Gray*, 117–21; Krick, *Lee's Colonels*, 144; Gannon, *Irish Rebels*, 386; "A Leaf from Memory," *Cosgrove's Weekly*, January 4, 1911, in Melrose Scrapbook 230, NSU.

20. Grand Rapids (Mich.) *Morning Telegram*, June 18, 1885, *Chronicling America*, chroniclingamerica.loc.gov (accessed August 3, 2016); Opelousas (La.) *St. Landry Democrat*, June 27, 1885 (accessed August 3, 2016).

21. Hewitt, "William Raine Peck," 3; Jones, "Zebulon York," in Davis (ed.), *Confederate General*, VI, 167.

22. T. Michael Parrish, "Richard Taylor," in Davis (ed.), *Confederate General*, VI, 28–31. See this article for details of Taylor's postwar career.

23. Biographical sketch in Jastremski Papers, LSU; Brooks and Jones, *Lee's Foreign Legion*, 4–5, 76; Uminski, "Two Polish Confederates," 75–79; Pinkowski, *Pills, Pen and Politics*, 26–29.

24. Jones, "Harry T. Hays," in Davis (ed.), *Confederate General*, III, 80.

25. Washington, D.C., *Times*, April 26, 1897, *Chronicling America*, chroniclingamerica.loc.gov (accessed August 3, 2016); Brooks and Jones, *Lee's Foreign Legion*, 2–3, 247.

26. "George Lovich Pierce Wren," *Find a Grave*, www.findagrave.com (accessed August 4, 2016).

27. Henry E. Handerson, *Gilbertus Anglicus: Medicine of the Thirteenth Century* (Cleveland, 1918), Project Gutenberg ebook, www.gutenberg.org (accessed August 10, 2016), 9 (quotation), 10–15; Handerson, *Yankee in Gray*, 8–11.

28. Jones (ed.), *Civil War Memoirs of Capt. William J. Seymour*, 151–52.

29. Germaine M. Reed, *David French Boyd: Founder of Louisiana State University* (Baton Rouge, 1977), 6; biographical sketch in Boyd Scrapbook, LSU.

30. Terry L. Jones, "Francis Redding Tillou Nicholls," in Davis (ed.), *Confederate General*, IV, 196–200; Welsh, *Medical Histories of Confederate Generals*, 161; Krick, *Lee's Colonels*, 220; Smulders to Henry B. Kelly, March 187[?], Smulders Papers; see also Abbeville (La.) *Meridional*, July 30, 1892, *Chronicling America*, chroniclingamerica.loc.gov (accessed March 8, 2016).

31. Snakenberg Family Papers, JPC.

32. "William Bayliss Tull," *Find a Grave*, www.findagrave.com (accessed September 12, 2016).

33. Buckley (ed.), *A Frenchman, a Chaplain, a Rebel*, 233–34; Durkin (ed.), *Confederate Chaplain*, 163–64.

34. Jonesborough (Tenn.) *Union Flag*, November 2, 1866, *Chronicling America*, chroniclingamerica.loc.gov (accessed July 28, 2016) (first quotation); *Charlotte* (N.C.) *Democrat*, January 17, 1890 (accessed July 28, 2016) (second quotation); *Times Dispatch*, January 20, 1912 (accessed July 28, 2016) (third quotation).

35. Pittsburgh *Dispatch*, September 20, 1892, *Chronicling America*, chroniclingamerica.loc.gov (accessed July 28, 2016) (first quotation). Mingus, *Louisiana Tigers in the Gettysburg Campaign*, 225 (second quotation). Tensas *Gazette*, July 31, 1914, *Chronicling America*, chroniclingamerica.loc.gov (accessed July 28, 2016); Manning *Times*, October 3, 1888 (accessed July 28, 2016); *National Tribune*, May 13, 1897 (accessed July 28, 2016); *National Tribune*, August 25, 1887 (accessed July 28, 2016); *National Tribune*, April 8, 1886 (accessed July 28, 2016); Lexington (Va.) *Gazette*, March 16, 1898 (accessed July 27, 2016).

36. Ocala (Fla.) *Evening Star*, October 25, 1901, *Chronicling America*, chroniclingamerica.loc.gov (accessed July 29, 2016) (first quotation). New York *Times*, July 2, 1888, JPC (second quotation). Anderson *Intelligencer*, July 12, 1888, *Chronicling America*, chroniclingamerica.loc.gov (accessed July 27, 2016) (third quotation).

37. New York *Times*, July 2, 1888, JPC.

38. New York *Evening World*, July 2, 1888, *Chronicling America*, chroniclingamerica.loc.gov (accessed July 27, 2016).

39. New York *Times*, July 2, 1888, JPC (quotation); James D. Watkinson to author, email, July 3, 2013, in JPC.

40. New York *Times*, July 2, 1888, JPC.

41. Winston (N.C.) *Progressive Farmer*, August 7, 1888, *Chronicling America*, chroniclingamerica.loc.gov (accessed July 28, 2016).

42. *National Tribune*, February 7, 1889, *Chronicling America*, chroniclingamerica.loc.gov (accessed July 28, 2016).

43. Washington, D.C., *Times*, November 12, 1894, *Chronicling America*, chroniclingamerica. loc.gov (accessed July 27, 2016).

44. Gettysburg *Compiler*, November 20, 1804, *Newspaper Archive*, newspaperarchive.com (accessed August 2, 2016) (quotation); Opelousas *Courier*, December 1, 1894, *Chronicling America*, chroniclingamerica.loc.gov (accessed July 27, 2016).

45. Bayou Sara (La.) *True Democrat*, July 12, 1913, *Chronicling America*, chroniclingamerica. loc.gov (accessed July 27, 2016).

46. *St. Landry Clarion*, July 26, 1913, *Chronicling America*, chroniclingamerica.loc.gov (accessed July 27, 2016) (quotation); "Rev. Thomas Robinson 'T. R.' Carroll," *Find a Grave*, www. findagrave.com (accessed August 2, 2016).

47. Wichita (Kans.) *Daily Eagle*, June 7, 1898, *Chronicling America*, chroniclingamerica.loc.gov (accessed July 28, 2016).

48. *National Tribune*, September 2, 1882, *Chronicling America*, chroniclingamerica.loc.gov (accessed July 28, 2016) (first quotation); Napoleon (Ohio) *Democratic Northwest*, September 26, 1889 (accessed July 27, 2016) (second quotation).

49. *National Tribune*, July 4, 1895, *Chronicling America*, chroniclingamerica.loc.gov (accessed August 4, 2016) (quotation); Washington, D.C., *Evening Star*, June 6, 1917 (accessed July 28, 2016).

50. *National Tribune*, April 2, 1896, *Chronicling America*, chroniclingamerica.loc.gov (accessed July 27, 2016).

51. *National Tribune*, July 26, 1906, *Chronicling America*, chroniclingamerica.loc.gov (accessed July 27, 2016); see also *National Tribune*, April 4, 1907 (accessed July 27, 2016); *National Tribune*, January 31, 1907 (accessed July 28, 2016); Farmington (Mo.) *Times*, May 29, 1914 (accessed July 28, 2016); New York *Tribune*, July 2, 1922 (accessed July 27, 2016).

52. Baton Rouge *State-Times*, December 15, 1942, photocopy, JPC (quotation); Charles Hunter Coates Jr., *A Biography of Charles Hunter Coates: Soldier, Scholar, Athlete* (n.p., 2009); biographical information in Charles E. and Ollie Maurin Coates Family Papers, LSU.

53. See Minneapolis *Journal*, May 17, 1902, *Chronicling America*, chroniclingamerica.loc. gov (accessed July 28, 2016); Welsh (La.) *Rice Belt Journal*, September 24, 1921 (accessed July 28, 2016). Lubbock (Tex.) *Avalanche Journal*, December 9, 1935, *Newspaper Archive*, newspaperarchive.com (accessed August 4, 2016); Thomasville (Ga.) *Times Enterprise*, December 9, 1934 (accessed August 4, 2016); Amarillo *Globe*, December 26, 1946 (accessed August 4, 2016); Atlantic (Iowa) *News Telegraph*, October 9, 1948 (accessed August 4, 2016); Burlington (Iowa) *Hawk Eye Gazette* (September 9, 1959 (accessed August 4, 2016).

54. Newberry (S.C.) *Herald and News*, February 28, 1922, *Chronicling America*, chroniclingamerica.loc.gov (accessed July 28, 2016) (quotation); Covington (La.) *St. Tammany Farmer*, February 11, 1899 (accessed July 28, 2016).

55. "History of the 256th Infantry Brigade," *1st Cavalry Division Association*, www.1cda.org (accessed September 15, 2016); Terry L. Jones, "Brothers in Arms," New York *Times*, "Disunion," July 2, 2012, opinionator.blogs.nytimes.com (accessed June 2, 2016) (quotations).

56. *Irish America*, June–July 2006, irishamerica.com (accessed August 18, 2016); Terry L. Jones, "Brothers in Arms," New York *Times*, "Disunion," July 2, 2012, opinionator.blogs.nytimes. com (accessed June 2, 2016) (quotation).

APPENDIX: UNIT NUMBERS AND LOSSES

1. Unless otherwise stated, the sources used for the appendix are Bound Volumes 1–10 and 12, in Association of the Army of Northern Virginia, LHAC; *Adjutant General's Report, State of Louisiana* (New Orleans, 1890), 246–53; *Biennial Report of the Secretary of State of the State of Louisiana to His Excellency Samuel D. McEnery, Governor of Louisiana, 1886–1887* (Baton Rouge, 1888), 114–26; "Louisiana Troops. Infantry, Local Designations of Companies by Regiments and Battalions," in Bibliographical Material, LHAC; Compiled Service Records, War Record Group 109, Microcopy 320, NA; Louisiana Box, ANB; and Arthur W. Bergeron Jr., *Guide to Louisiana Confederate Military Units, 1861–1865* (Baton Rouge, 1989).

2. Powell A. Casey, "Confederate Units from North Louisiana," *Journal of the North Louisiana Historical Association,* VI (Spring, 1975), 105–15; *OR,* Vol. LI, Pt. II, 209.

3. Albert G. Blanchard, article on the Louisiana Guards in Reminiscences, Executive and Army of Northern Virginia, LHAC.

4. Gannon, *Irish Rebels,* xiii.

5. *OR,* Vol. LI, Pt. II, 209.

6. Ibid., 214.

7. A complete company roster can be found at "Company D, 2nd Louisiana," *DeSoto Parish, Louisiana,* www.countygenweb.com (accessed April 11, 2016); Natchitoches *Times,* April 12, 1929, in Melrose Scrapbook 1, NSU.

8. There is some duplication in these figures because some individuals were wounded, captured, and killed. A complete company roster can be found at "Regiment Roster," *Posey Civil War Letters,* freepages.military.rootsweb.ancestry.com (accessed April 10, 2016).

9. New Orleans *Delta Daily,* April 30, 1861.

10. Theodore Mandeville to Rebecca Mandeville, August 27, 1861, in Box 2, Folder 12, Mandeville Papers, LSU.

11. Lafayette McLaws to wife, July 30, 1861, in Folder 4, McLaws Collection, SHC.

12. Casey, "Confederate Units from North Louisiana," 105–15.

13. Dufour, *Gentle Tiger,* 120.

14. Compiled Service Records, War Record Group 109, Microcopy 320, Roll 148, NA.

15. Taylor, *Destruction and Reconstruction,* 39.

16. A complete regimental roster can be found in Gannon, *Irish Rebels,* and at "Roster of 6th Louisiana Infantry," docs.google.com (accessed April 10, 2016).

17. Gannon, *Irish Rebels,* iii, 250–51, 267, 328.

18. Ibid., xiv.

19. Ibid., 320.

20. "The Old Flag," Unidentified newspaper clipping, in CSA Collection, MOC.

21. Gannon, *Irish Rebels,* 319.

22. Ibid., xiv, 320; Lonn, *Foreigners in the Confederacy,* 108.

23. Lonn, *Foreigners in the Confederacy,* 108; Gannon, *Irish Rebels,* 318–19.

24. Gannon, *Irish Rebels,* xiv, 320.

25. Ibid.

26. Compiled Service Records, War Record Group 109, Microcopy 320, Roll 163, NA.

27. Taylor, *Destruction and Reconstruction,* 39.

28. William Harper Forman Jr., "William P. Harper in War and Reconstruction," *Louisiana History,* XIII (1972), 57.

29. "Lt. Louis Edmond LeBlanc, Co. C, 8th La. Inf.," *Louisiana in the Civil War Message Board,* March 26, 2004, www.history-sites.com (accessed March 5, 2015).

30. Taylor, *Destruction and Reconstruction,* 40 (quotation); W. R. Lyman, "Cross Keys and Port Republic," in Reminiscences, Executive and Army of Northern Virginia. LHAC.

31. A complete company roster can be found at "Company A, 8th Louisiana," files.usgwarchives.net (accessed April 11, 2016).

32. A complete company roster can be found at "Company B, 8th Louisiana," files.usgwarchives.net (accessed April 11, 2016).

33. A complete company roster can be found at "Company C, 8th Louisiana," files.usgwarchives.net (accessed April 11, 2016).

34. A complete company roster can be found at "Company D, 8th Louisiana," files.usgwarchives.net (accessed April 11, 2016).

35. A complete company roster can be found at "Company E, 8th Louisiana," files.usgwarchives.net (accessed April 11, 2016)

36. A complete company roster can be found at "Company F, 8th Louisiana," files.usgwarchives.net (accessed April 11, 2016).

37. A complete company roster can be found at "Company G, 8th Louisiana," files.usgwarchives.net (accessed April 10, 2016).

38. A complete company roster can be found at "Company H, 8th Louisiana," files.usgwarchives.net (accessed April 11, 2016).

39. A complete company roster can be found at "Company I, 8th Louisiana," files.usgwarchives.net (accessed April 11, 2016).

40. A complete company roster can be found at "Company K, 8th Louisiana," files.usgwarchives.net (accessed April 11, 2016).

41. A complete company roster can be found at "Company A, 9th Louisiana," files.usgwarchives.net (accessed April 10, 2016).

42. A complete company roster can be found at "Stafford Guards," files.usgwarchives.net (accessed April 10, 2016).

43. A complete company roster can be found at "Company C, 9th Louisiana," files.usgwarchives.net (accessed April 10, 2016).

44. A complete company roster of this can be found at "Company D, 9th Louisiana," files.usgwarchives.net (accessed April 10, 2016).

45. A complete company roster can be found at "Company F, 9th Louisiana," files.usgwarchives.net (accessed April 10, 2016).

46. A complete company roster can be found at "Company G, 9th Louisiana," files.usgwarchives.net (accessed April 10, 2016); M. H. Achord American Civil War Reminiscences Collection, Washington and Lee University.

47. A complete company roster can be found at "Company H, 9th Louisiana," files.usgwarchives.net (accessed April 10, 2016).

48. A complete company roster can be found at "Company I, 9th Louisiana," files.us-

gwarchives.net (accessed April 10, 2016); *Era Leader* (Franklinton, La.), October 13, 1910.

49. A complete company roster can be found at "Company K, 9th Louisiana." files.usgw-archives.net (accessed April 10, 2016).

50. A complete regimental roster can be found in Brooks and Jones, *Lee's Foreign Legion,* and at *Roster of 10th Louisiana Infantry,* docs.google.com (accessed April 11, 2016); Wiley, *Johnny Reb,* 323; *Times-Picayune,* May 16, 1926.

51. *Daily Picayune,* April 19, 1861.

52. Compiled Service Records, War Record Group 109, Microcopy 320, Roll 217, NA.

53. Hewitt, "Confederate Foreign Legion," 122 (quotation); Bartlett, *Military Record of Louisiana,* 44.

54. Bartlett, *Military Record of Louisiana,* 46; *OR,* Vol. LI, Pt. II, 214; Compiled Service Records, War Record Group 109, Microcopy 320, Roll 253, NA; Casey, "Confederate Units from North Louisiana," 105–15.

55. Hewitt, "Confederate Foreign Legion," 121, 138–39.

56. D. T. Merrick to E. D. Willett, December 9, 1893, in Reminiscences, Executive and Army of Northern Virginia, LHAC; Compiled Service Records, War Record Group 109, Microcopy 320, Roll 266, NA.

57. Taylor, *Destruction and Reconstruction,* 17.

58. New Orleans *Daily Item,* August 25, 1896, in Scrapbook, Boyd Papers, LSU.

59. New Orleans *Daily Crescent,* April 19, 1861.

60. Sample reminiscences, FSNMP (quotation); Bartlett, *Military Record of Louisiana,* 46.

61. Compiled Service Records, War Record Group 109, Microcopy 320, Roll 100, NA.

62. DeLeon, *Four Years in Rebel Capitals,* 66.

63. *OR,* Series IV, Vol. I, 747.

64. William E. Hughes to O. L. Putnam, July 20, 1899, in Flags, LHAC.

65. *OR,* Vol. LIII, 815–16.

66. "First Volunteers from Louisiana," 146.

67. Wallace, "Coppens' Louisiana Zouaves," 269; J. W. Minnich, article on Coppens' Zouaves, in Reminiscences, Executive and Army of Northern Virginia, LHAC; Lonn, *Foreigners in the Confederacy,* 102.

68. "1st Louisiana (Zouaves) Infantry Battalion," antietam.aotw.org (accessed April 12, 2016).

69. Wallace, "Coppens' Louisiana Zouaves," 269–82.

70. W. S. Michie, article on the 15th Louisiana Volunteers, in Reminiscences, Executive and Army of Northern Virginia, LHAC; List of Companies and Officers, St. Paul's Foot Rifles, Army of Northern Virginia Papers, Part I, LHAC.

71. Ibid.

72. Ibid.

73. *Daily Picayune,* April 18, 1861; *First Bull Run,* www.firstbullrun.co.uk (accessed July 7, 2016).

BIBLIOGRAPHY

PRIMARY SOURCES
Manuscript Collections

Antietam National Battlefield, Sharpsburg, Md.
    Louisiana Box.
        La. Misc. File.
        Phifer, Thomas H. Letters. 2nd Louisiana Folder.
        Zeller, George. Letters. 6th Louisiana Folder.

Centenary College, Shreveport, La.
    North Louisiana Historical Association Archives.

Duke University, Durham, N.C.
    Beauregard, Pierre Gustave Toutant. Papers.
    Browning, Amos G. Papers.
    Confederate States of America. Archives.
    Confederate Veteran. Papers.
    Dawson, Francis Warrington. Letters.
    Grand Military Ball Handbill.
    Hemphill Family. Papers.
    Hubert, Ben. Papers.
    Morgan, Thomas Gibbes, Sr. and Thomas Gibbes Morgan Jr. Papers.
    Solomons, M. J. Scrapbook.
    Stuart, James Ewell Brown. Papers.
    Walkup, Samuel Huey. Journal.

East Carolina University, Greenville, N.C.
     East Carolina Manuscript Collection.
     Young-Spicer Family Papers.

Emory University, Atlanta, Ga.
     Wren, G. L. P. Collection.

Fredericksburg and Spotsylvania National Military Park, Fredericksburg, Va.
     Clegg, William. Letters.
     Fogleman, Isaiah. Diary.
     Mobile *Advertiser & Register,* photocopy, June 4, 1863; May 28, 1864.
     Patterson, E. A. Collection.
     Sample, Hiram. Reminiscences.
     Slaughter Papers.

Gettysburg National Military Park, Gettysburg, Pa.
     Louisiana Brigades Boxes.

Handley Library, Winchester, Va.
     Tull, W. B. "W. B. Tull's War Story."

Historic New Orleans Collection, New Orleans, La.
     Walton-Glenny Family. Papers.

Huntington Library, San Marino, Calif.
     Janin Family. Papers.

Jones, Terry L. Private Collection. West Monroe, La.
     Berl, Gordon, to Terry L. Jones. Email. August 5, 2016.
     Charlton, John F. Diary.
     Duke, Benjamin Calvin, to Terry L. Jones. Email. February 27, 2013.
     New York *Times,* July 2, 1888.
     Snakenberg, William P. "Memoirs of W. P. Snakenberg."
     Snakenberg Family Papers.
     Watkinson, James D., to Terry L. Jones. Email. July 3, 2013.

Library of Congress, Washington, D.C.
     Ewell, Richard S. Papers.
     Miscellaneous Manuscripts Collection.

Louisiana State Archives, Baton Rouge, La.
  Hollier, Charles S. Pension File.

Louisiana State University at Shreveport, La.
  Beard, James H. Papers.
  Flournoy, Alfred, Jr. Papers.

Louisiana State University, Baton Rouge, La.
  Batchelor, Albert A., Papers.
  Boyd, David F. Civil War Papers.
  Boyd, David F. Papers.
  Boyd, David F. Selected Papers.
  Coates, Charles E. and Ollie Maurin. Family Papers.
  Egan, J. S. Family Papers.
  Evans, H. Letter.
  Fitzpatrick, John. Letterbook.
  Flournoy, Alfred. Papers.
  Jastremski, Leon. Family Papers.
  LaVillebeuvre, Jean Ursin. Family Papers.
  Liddell, Moses and St. John R. Family Papers.
  Mandeville, Henry D. Family Papers.
  Newell, Robert A. Papers.
  Nicholls, Francis R. T. Letter.
  Saucier, Gertrude B. Papers.
  Shilg, Merritt M. Memorial Collection.
  Smith, Benjamin. Letter.
  Stephens, John F. Correspondence.
  Stubbs, Jefferson W. Family Papers.
  Taylor, Miles. Family Papers.
  Washburne and Hesler Ledger.
  Wise, James Calvert. Papers.

Mansfield State Commemorative Area, Mansfield, La.
  Devine, John. Letters.
  Harris, Robert, Jr. Letter.
  Wharton, William H. Scrapbook.
  Williams, Boling. Diary.

McNeese State University, Lake Charles, La.
    Seton Collection.

Museum of the Confederacy, Eleanor S. Brockenbrough Library, Richmond, Va.
    Anderson File.
    CSA Collection.
    Logan, Sgt. Daniel D. Letters.
    MC-3/MSS. 3.
    9th Louisiana Order Book.
    Taliaferro File.
    Van Benthuysen, J. D. File.
    Woodard, Theodore H. Letters.

National Archives, Washington, D.C.
    Clothing Account. 7th Regiment of Louisiana Volunteers, 1862. War Record Group
109. Chapter V. Volume 205.
    Compiled Service Records of Confederate General and Staff Officers, and Nonreg-
imental Enlisted Men. War Record Group 109. Microcopy 331.
    Compiled Service Records of Confederate Soldiers Who Served in Organizations
from the State of Louisiana. War Record Group 109. Microcopy 320.
    Early, General Jubal A. Papers, 1861–65. War Record Group 109. Entry 118.
    Record Book of the Hospital of the 7th Regiment of Louisiana Volunteers. 1861.
War Record Group 109. Chapter VI. Volume 486.
    Register of Arrests, 1862–64. War Record Group 109. Chapter IX. Volume 244.
    7th Louisiana Volunteers Quartermaster Document, March, 1864. War Record
Group 109. Chapter V. Volume 205.

New York Public Library, Rare Books and Manuscripts Division, New York, N.Y.
    Louisiana Troops. 7th Regiment Orderly Book, 1862–64.

Northwestern State University, Natchitoches, La.
    Carver Collection.
    Mansfield Museum MSS.
    Melrose Scrapbooks.
    Sandlin, Murphy. Collection.
    Stephens, Judge Paul. Collection.
    Tooke, T. A. Letter.

Richmond National Battlefield Park, Richmond, Va.
    Mobile *Daily Advertiser & Register,* photocopy, July 23, 1862.

National Tribune, typed copy, April 19, 1906.

Opelousas (Louisiana) *Courier*, photocopy, September 6, 1862.

Trahern, William E. "A Biography of William E. Trahern, Written September 21, 1926."

Tulane University, Louisiana Historical Association Collection, New Orleans, La.

Army of Northern Virginia Papers.

Association of the Army of Northern Virginia.

Bibliographic Material.

Confederate Personnel.

Flags.

Moore, Charles, Jr. Diary, 1861–65.

Newsclippings and Miscellaneous Unidentified Material.

Pamphlets.

Reminiscences, Executive and Army of Northern Virginia.

Tulane University, New Orleans, La.

Behan Family Papers.

Civil War Manuscript Series.

Civil War Scrapbooks.

Herron Family Correspondence.

New Orleans Civil War Scrapbook.

Ogden Family Papers.

U.S. Army Education and Research Center, Carlisle, Pa.

Brake Collection.

Civil War Documents Collection.

Lichenstein, William. Memoir.

Robertson, Sidney Baxter. Memoir.

Ward, Charles. Letters.

University of Michigan, Ann Arbor, Mich.

Seymour, Isaac G. Papers.

Schoff Civil War Collection.

University of North Carolina at Chapel Hill, Southern Historical Collection, Chapel Hill, N.C.

Alexander, Edward Porter. Collection.

Coles, Elizabeth P. Collection.

Colston, Raleigh E. Collection.

Hairston, Peter W. Collection.
Janin, Eugene. Collection.
King, Grace. Collection.
McLaws, Lafayette. Collection.
Polk, Brown, and Ewell Collection.
Wheat, John T. Collection.
White, Wellford, Taliaferro, and Marshall Collection.
Williams, Marguerite E. Collection.

University of Texas, Austin, Tex.
Moore, William E. Papers.

Virginia Historical Society Library, Virginia Historical Society Collection, Richmond, Va.
Carrington Family Papers.
George Family Papers.

Virginia State Library, Richmond, Va.
Owen, Henry T. Papers.

Washington & Lee University, Lexington, Va.
M. H. Achord American Civil War Reminiscences Collection.
Lee, Robert E. Papers.

State and Federal Government Publications

Adjutant General's Report, State of Louisiana. New Orleans, 1890.
Biennial Report of the Secretary of State of the State of Louisiana to His Excellency Samuel D. McEnery, Governor of Louisiana, 1886–1887. Baton Rouge, 1888.
The War of the Rebellion: A Compilation of the Official Records of the Union and Confederate Armies. 130 vols. Washington, D.C., 1880–1901.

Memoirs and Reminiscences

Alexander, Edward Porter. *Military Memoirs of a Confederate.* New York, 1907.
Baquet, Camille. *History of the First Brigade, New Jersey Volunteers from 1861 to 1865.* Trenton, 1910.
Bartlett, Napier. *Military Record of Louisiana.* Baton Rouge, 1964.

Bauer, Keith G., ed. *A Soldier's Journey: The Civil War Diary of Henry C. Caldwell*. Baton Rouge, 2001.

Beers, Fannie A. *Memories: A Record of Personal Experience and Adventure During Four Years of War*. Philadelphia, 1889.

Benedict, G. G. *Vermont in the Civil War: A History of the Part Taken by the Vermont Soldiers and Sailors in the War for the Union, 1861–5*. 2 vols. Burlington, 1886.

Bengston, Bradley P., M.D., and Julian E. Kuz, M.D., eds. *Photographic Atlas of Civil War Injuries*. Kennesaw, Ga., 1996.

Blackford, Susan Leigh, comp., Charles M. Blackford and C. M. Blackford, eds. *Letters from Lee's Army; or, Memoirs of Life in and out of the Anny of Virginia During the War Between the States*. New York, 1947.

Booth, Andrew B., comp. *Records of Louisiana Confederate Soldiers and Louisiana Confederate Commands*. 3 vols. New Orleans, 1920.

Boyd, David French. *Reminiscences of the War in Virginia*. Ed. T. Michael Parrish. Baton Rouge, 1994.

Buckley, Cornelius M., trans. and ed. *A Frenchman, a Chaplain, a Rebel: The War Letters of Pere Louis-Hippolyte Gache, S.J.* Chicago, 1981.

Casler, John Overton. *Four Years in the Stonewall Brigade*. 1906. Rpt. Marietta, Ga., 1951.

Cavanagh, Michael. *Memoirs of Gen. Thomas Francis Meagher . . . Including Personal Reminiscences*. Worcester, Mass., 1892.

Chamberlayne, C. G., ed. *Ham Chamberlayne—Virginian: Letters and Papers of an Artillery Officer in the War for Southern Independence, 1861–1865*. Richmond, 1932.

Cutrer, Thomas W., and T. Michael Parrish, eds. *Brothers in Gray: The Civil War Letters of the Pierson Family*. Baton Rouge, 1997.

Dawes, Rufus R. *Service with the Sixth Wisconsin Volunteers*. Ed. Alan T. Nolan. 1890. Rpt. Madison, 1962.

DeLeon, Thomas Cooper. *Four Years in Rebel Capitals: An Inside View of Life in the Southern Confederacy, from Birth to Death*. Mobile, 1890.

Douglas, Henry Kyd. *I Rode with Stonewall*. Chapel Hill, 1940.

Dunlop, W. S. *Lee's Sharpshooters; or, The Forefront of Battle*. Little Rock, 1899.

Durkin, Rev. Joseph, ed. *Confederate Chaplain: A War Journal of Rev. James B. Sheeran . . . 14th Louisiana, C.S.A.* Milwaukee, 1960.

Early, Jubal Anderson. *A Memoir of the Last Year of the War for Independence . . . in the Year 1864 and 1865*. Lynchburg, 1867.

———. *War Memoirs: Autobiographical Sketch and Narrative of the War Between the States*. Ed. Frank E. Vandiver. 1912. Rpt. Bloomington, 1960.

An English Combatant [pseud.]. *Battlefields of the South, from Bull Run to Fredericksburg, with Sketches of Confederate Commanders, and Gossip of the Camps*. New York, 1864.

Fisterer, Frederick (comp.). *New York in the War of the Rebellion, 1861–1865.* 2nd ed. Albany, 1890.

Foster, John Y. *New Jersey and the Rebellion: A History of the Services of the Troops and People of New Jersey in Aid of the Union Cause.* Newark, 1868.

Gilmor, Harry. *Four Years in the Saddle.* London, 1866.

Goldsborough, W. W. *The Maryland Line in the Confederate Army, 1861–1865.* Baltimore, 1900.

Gordon, John B. *Reminiscences of the Civil War.* New York, 1903.

Handerson, Henry E. *Gilbertus Anglicus: Medicine of the Thirteenth Century.* Cleveland, 1918. Project Gutenberg ebook, www.gutenberg.org

———. *Yankee in Gray: The Civil War Memoirs of Henry E. Handerson, with a Selection of His Wartime Letters.* Cleveland, 1962.

Hewitt, Lawrence Lee. "A Confederate Foreign Legion: Louisiana 'Wildcats' in the Army of Northern Virginia." In *Louisianians in the Civil War.* Ed. Lawrence Lee Hewitt and Arthur W. Bergeron Jr. Columbia, Mo., 2002.

Hood, John Bell. *Advance and Retreat: Personal Experiences in the United States and Confederate States Armies.* Ed. Richard N. Current. 1880. Rpt. Bloomington, 1959.

Hotchkiss, Jedediah. *Make Me a Map of the Valley: The Civil War Journal of Stonewall Jackson's Topographer.* Ed. Archie P. McDonald. Dallas, 1973.

Howard, McHenry. *Recollections of a Maryland Confederate Soldier and Staff Officer Under Johnston, Jackson and Lee.* 1914. Rpt. Dayton, 1975.

Howard, Oliver Otis. *Autobiography of Oliver Otis Howard, Major General, United States Army.* New York, 1907.

Huffman, James. *Ups and Downs of a Confederate Soldier.* New York, 1940.

Johnson, R. V., and C. C. Buel, eds. *Battles and Leaders of the Civil War.* 4 vols. New York, 1884–88.

Jones, Rev. John William. *Christ in the Camp; or, Religion in Lee's Army.* Richmond, 1887.

Jones, Terry L., ed. *Campbell Brown's Civil War: With Ewell and the Army of Northern Virginia.* Baton Rouge, 2001.

———, ed. *The Civil War Memoirs of Capt. William J. Seymour: Reminiscences of a Louisiana Tiger.* Baton Rouge, 1991.

Kelly, Henry B. *Port Republic.* Philadelphia, 1886.

Ladd, David L. and Audrey J., eds. *The Bachelder Papers: Gettysburg in Their Own Words.* 3 vols. Dayton, 1994.

Lane, Mills, ed. *"Dear Mother: Don't Grieve About Me, If I Get Killed, I'll Only Be Dead": Letters from Georgia Soldiers in the Civil War.* Savannah, 1977.

Macon, Emma Cassandra Riely, and Reuben Conway Macon. *Reminiscences of the Civil War.* N.p., 1911.

Maguire, John Francis. *The Irish in America.* London, 1868.

Marcus, Edward, ed. *A New Canaan Private in the Civil War: Letters of Justus M. Silliman, 17th Connecticut Volunteers.* New Canaan, Conn., 1984.

McClellan, William Cowan. *Welcome the Hour of Conflict: William Cowan McClellan and the 9th Alabama.* Ed. John C. Carter. Tuscaloosa, 2007.

McDonald, Mrs. Cornelia. *A Diary with Reminiscences of the War and Refugee Life in the Shenandoah Valley, 1860–1865.* Nashville, 1934.

Moore, Edward A. *The Story of a Cannoneer under Stonewall Jackson.* New York, 1907. Project Gutenberg ebook, www.gutenberg.org

Myers, Frank M. *The Comanches: A History of White's Battalion, Virginia Cavalry, Laurel Brig., Hampton Div., A.N.V., C.S.A.* 1871. Rpt. Marietta, Ga., 1956.

Nisbet, James Cooper. *Four Years on the Firing Line.* Ed. Bell Irvin Wiley. 1914. Rpt. Jackson, Tenn., 1963.

Oates, William C. *The War Between the Union and Confederacy and Its Lost Opportunities with a History of the 15th Alabama Regiment and the Forty-eight Battles in Which It Was Engaged.* New York, 1905.

Paver, John M. *What I Saw from 1861 to 1864.* 1906. Rpt. Ann Arbor, 1974.

Pryor, Mrs. Roger A. *Reminiscences of Peace and War.* New York, 1905.

Putnam, Sallie A. *Richmond During the War: Four Years of Personal Observation.* New York, 1867.

Quaife, Milo M., ed. *From the Cannon's Mouth: The Civil War Letters of General Alpheus S. Williams.* Detroit, 1959.

Reed, Thomas Benton. *A Private in Gray.* Camden, Ark., 1905.

Reid, Jesse Walton. *History of the Fourth S.C. Volunteers, from the Commencement of the War Until Lee's Surrender.* 1892. Rpt. Dayton, Ohio, 1975.

Russell, Sir William Howard. *My Diary North and South.* Ed. Fletcher Pratt. 1863. Rpt. New York, 1954.

———. *Pictures of Southern Life, Social, Political and Military.* New York, 1861.

Schurz, Carl. *The Reminiscences of Carl Schurz.* 3 vols. New York, 1907–8.

SeCheverell, J. Hamp. *Journal History of the Twenty-Ninth Ohio Veteran Volunteers, 1861–1865, Its Victories and Its Reverses.* Cleveland, 1883.

Smith, Jacob. *Camps and Campaigns of the 107th Ohio Volunteer Infantry.* N.p., n.d.

Stearns, Austin C. *Three Years with Company K.* Ed. Arthur A. Kent. London, 1976.

Stephens, Robert Grier, Jr., comp. and ed. *Intrepid Warrior: Clement Anselm Evans, Confederate General from Georgia: Life, Letters, and Diaries of the War Years.* Dayton, 1992.

Stevens, C. A. *Berdan's United States Sharpshooters in the Army of the Potomac, 1861–1865.* St. Paul, 1892.

Stiles, Robert. *Four Years Under Marse Robert.* 4th ed. New York, 1910.

Strader, Eloise C., ed. *The Civil War Journal of Mary Greenhow Lee (Mrs. Hugh Holmes Lee) of Winchester, Virginia.* Winchester, 2011.

Taylor, Richard. *Destruction and Reconstruction: Personal Experiences of the Late War.* Ed. Charles P. Roland. 1879. Rpt. Xerox Corporation, Waltham, Mass., 1968.

Wilson, LeGrand James. *The Confederate Soldier.* Ed. James W. Silver. Memphis, 1973.

Wood, George L. *The Seventh Regiment: A Record.* New York, 1865.

Woodbury, Augustus. *The Second Rhode Island Regiment: A Narrative of Military Operations from the Beginning to the End of the War for the Union.* Providence, 1875.

Worsham, John H. *One of Jackson's Foot Cavalry.* Ed. James I. Robertson Jr. 1912. Rpt. Jackson, Tenn., 1964.

Articles

Allen, Columbus H. "About the Death of Col. C. D. Dreux." *Confederate Veteran,* XV (1907), 307.

"Battle Flag of the Third Georgia." *Southern Historical Society Papers,* XXXVIII (1910), 210–16.

Blackford, Charles M. "The Campaign and Battle of Lynchburg." *Southern Historical Society Papers,* XXX (1902), 279–332.

Bradwell, I. G. "Capture of Winchester, Va., and Milroy's Army in June, 1863." *Confederate Veteran,* XXX (1922), 330–32.

Braswell, E. G. "Fort Steadman [sic] and Subsequent Events." *Confederate Veteran,* XXIII (1915), 20–23.

"Capt. D. T. Merrick." *Confederate Veteran,* XV (1907), 325.

"Cheneyville (La.) Rifles' Flag Returned." *Confederate Veteran,* XIX (1911), 373–74.

Chisholm, Samuel H. "Forward the Louisiana Brigade." *Confederate Veteran,* XXVII (1919), 449.

Conner, Forrest P., ed. "Letters of Lieutenant Robert H. Miller to His Family, 1861–1862." *Virginia Magazine of History and Biography,* LXX (1962), 62–91.

Cox, William R. "Major General Stephen D. Ramseur: His Life and Character." *Southern Historical Society Papers,* XVIII (1890), 217–60.

Drane, J. W. "Louisiana Tigers at Fair Oaks, Va." *Confederate Veteran,* XIV (1906), 521.

Early, Jubal A. "Causes of Lee's Defeat at Gettysburg." *Southern Historical Society Papers,* IV (1877), 241–302.

"Eugene Waggaman." *Southern Historical Society Papers,* XXV (1897), 180–86.

"First Volunteers from Louisiana." *Confederate Veteran,* III (1895), 146.

"Fisher's Hill and 'Sheridan's Ride.'" *Confederate Veteran,* X (1902), 165–66.

Forman, William Harper, Jr. "William P. Harper in War and Reconstruction." *Louisiana History,* XIII (1972), 47–70.

Funkerhauser, R. D. "Fort Stedman—So Near Yet So Far." *Confederate Veteran,* XIX (1911), 217–18.

———. "Gen. Lee About to Enter Battle." *Confederate Veteran,* II (1894), 36.

Hancock, R. J. "William Singleton." *Confederate Veteran,* XIV (1906), 498–99.

Hardy, A. S. "Terrific Fighting at Winchester." *Confederate Veteran,* IX (1901), 114.

Hoffsommer, Robert, ed. "The Rise and Survival of Private Mesnard." *Civil War Times Illustrated* (February 1986), 10–17.

"Honor Medal to the 'Maid of Winchester.'" *Confederate Veteran,* VIII (1900), 540.

Johnson, General B. T. "Memoir of the First Maryland Regiment." *Southern Historical Society Papers,* X (1882), 46–223.

Kaigler, William. "Last Charge at Appomattox." *Confederate Veteran,* VII (1899), 357.

"Kindness of Yankees near Petersburg." *Confederate Veteran,* XVII (1909), 532.

Lane, John H. "The Battle of Fisher's Hill." *Southern Historical Society Papers,* XVIII–XIX (1891), 289–95.

Lathrop, Barnes F., ed. "An Autobiography of Francis T. Nicholls, 1834–1881." *Louisiana Historical Quarterly,* XVII (1934), 246–67.

Laurence, Debra Nance. "Dury Gibson: Letters from a North Louisiana Tiger." *Journal of the North Louisiana Historical Association,* X (Fall 1979), 130–47.

Lee, S. D. "The Second Battle of Manassas—A Reply to General Longstreet." *Southern Historical Society Papers,* VI (1878), 59–71.

Leech, John W. T. "The Battle of Frazier's Farm." *Southern Historical Society Papers,* XXI (1893), 160–65.

Lowe, Col. R. G. "The Dreux Battalion." *Confederate Veteran,* V (1897), 54–57.

———. "Magruder's Defense of the Peninsula." *Confederate Veteran,* VIII (1900), 105–8.

Loyd, W. G. "Second Louisiana at Gettysburg." *Confederate Veteran,* VI (1898), 417.

Mayo, Robert M. "The Second Battle of Manassas." *Southern Historical Society Papers,* VII (1879), 122–25.

McChesney, Wallace H. "Capt. Charles W. McLellan." *Confederate Veteran,* VI (1898), 506–7.

McGrath, John. "In a Louisiana Regiment." *Southern Historical Society Papers,* XXXVI (1908), 103 20.

McIntosh, Gregg. "The Chancellorsville Campaign." *Southern Historical Society Papers,* n.s., XL (1915), 44–100.

McNamara, M. "Lieutenant Charlie Pierce's Daring Attempts to Escape from Johnson's Island." *Southern Historical Society Papers,* VIII (1880), 61–67.

Old, William W. "Trees Whittled Down at Horseshoe." *Southern Historical Society Papers,* XXXIII (1905), 16–24.

Osborne, Fred D. "Dumfries on the Potomac—Spring of 1861." *Confederate Veteran,* XVII (1909), 557.

Parsons, William T., and Mary Shuler Heimburger, eds. "Shuler Family Correspondence." *Pennsylvania Folklife,* XXIX (Spring 1980), 98–113.

Rice, Joe M. "An Account of the Battle of Fredericksburg, 1863, Written by J. R. Williams." *Journal of the North Louisiana Historical Association* (Winter 1986), 39–42.

Turner, Charles W., ed. "Major Charles A. Davidson: Letters of a Virginia Soldier." *Civil War History*, XXII (1976), 16–40.

Vandiver, Frank E., ed. "A Collection of Louisiana Confederate Letters." *Louisiana Historical Quarterly*, XXVI (1943), 937–74.

Vollbrecht, John W. "Hays' and Avery's Brigades: Biographical Sketches." *Battlefield Dispatch*, XVIII, No. 3 (March 2000), 6–9.

Walshe, R. T. "Recollections of Gaines' Mill." *Confederate Veteran*, VII (1899), 54–55.

"What Confederate Flag Was It?" *Confederate Veteran*, X (1902), 389.

Wheat, Leo. "Memoir of Gen. C. R. Wheat." *Southern Historical Society Papers*, XVII (1889), 47–54.

York, Z. "Report of Brig. Gen. Zebulon York, July 22, 1864." *Historical Magazine*, IX (1871), 19–21.

Zettler, B. M. "Magruder's Peninsula Campaign." *Confederate Veteran*, VIII (1900), 197.

Newspapers and Newsletters

Abbeville, La. *The Meridional.*

Alexandria, Va. *Local News.*

Amarillo, Tex. Amarillo *Globe.*

Anderson Court House, S.C. Anderson *Intelligencer.*

Atlanta, Ga. Atlanta *Constitution.*

Atlantic, Iowa. Atlantic *News Telegraph.*

Baton Rouge, La. *Louisiana Capitolian.*

Bayou Sara, La. *True Democrat.*

Burlington, Iowa. *Hawk Eye Gazette.*

Charlotte, N.C. Charlotte *Democrat.*

Clearfield, Pa. *Raftsman's Journal.*

Cleveland, Ohio. Cleveland *Morning Leader.*

Columbus, Ohio. *Daily Ohio Statesman.*

Covington, La. *St. Tammany Farmer.*

Delaware, Ohio. *Delaware Gazette.*

Dubuque, Iowa. Dubuque *Herald.*

Ebensburg, Pa. *The Alleghanian.*

Edgefield, S.C. *Advertiser.*

Farmington, Mo. Farmington *Times.*

Fort Worth, Tex. Fort Worth *Daily Gazette.*

Franklinton, La. *Era Leader.*

Gallipolis, Ohio. Gallipolis *Journal.*
Gettysburg, Pa. Gettysburg *Compiler.*
Grand Rapids, Mich. *Morning Telegram.*
Harrisburg, Pa. *Star Independent.*
Henderson, N.C. *Gold Leaf Volume.*
Hillsborough, Ohio. *Highland Weekly News.*
Hornellsville, N.Y. Hornellsville *Tribune.*
Houma, La. Houma *Courier.*
Hudson, Wis. Hudson *North Star.*
Hyde Park, Vt. *Lamoille News Dealer.*
Iola, Iowa. Iola *Register.*
Irisburgh, Vt. *Orleans Independent Standard.*
Jonesborough, Tenn. *Union Flag.*
Kentwood, La. *Camp Moore News.*
Lexington, Va. Lexington *Gazette.*
Little Falls, Minn. Little Falls *Transcript.*
Lubbock, Tex. *Avalanche Journal.*
Manning, S.C. Manning *Times.*
Memphis, Tenn. Memphis *Daily Appeal.*
Minneapolis, Minn. *Minneapolis Journal.*
Missoula, Mont. *Daily Missoulian.*
Montpelier, Vt. *Daily Green Mountain Freeman.*
Napoleon, Ohio. *Democratic Northwest.*
Newberry, S.C. *Herald and News.*
New Orleans, La. *Daily Crescent.*
———. *Daily Delta.*
———. *Daily Picayune.*
———. *Times Picayune.*
New York City, N.Y. *Evening World.*
———. New York *Tribune.*
Newport News, V. *Daily Press.*
Newspaper Archive. newspaperarchive.com
Norfolk, Va. Norfolk *Virginian.*
Ocala, Fla. *Evening Star.*
Omaha, Neb. Omaha *Daily Bee.*
Opelousas, La. Opelousas *Courier.*
———. *St. Landry Clarion.*
———. *St. Landry Democrat.*
Ottawa, Canada. *Ottawa Free Trader.*

Paris, Ky. *Bourbon News.*

Perry, Iowa. Perry *Chief.*

Perrysburg, Ohio. Perrysburg *Journal.*

Phoenix, Ariz. *Arizona Republican.*

Pittsburgh, Pa. Pittsburgh *Dispatch.*

Plymouth, Ind. *Marshall County Republican.*

Point Pleasant, Va. *Weekly Register.*

Richmond, Va. *Daily Dispatch.* dlxs.richmond.edu

———. *Enquirer.*

———. *The Times.*

———. *Times Dispatch.*

Roanoke, Va. Roanoke *Daily Times.*

Sacramento, Calif. *Record-Union.*

Salt Lake City, Utah. Salt Lake *Herald.*

San Francisco, Calif. San Francisco *Call.*

St. Joseph, La. *Tensas Gazette.*

Stanford, Ky. *Semi-weekly Interior Journal.*

Staunton, Va. Staunton *Spectator.*

Thomasville, Ga. Thomasville *Times Enterprise.*

Washington, D.C. *Evening Star.*

———. *National Republican.*

———. *National Tribune.*

———. *Republican.*

———. *The Times.*

———. *Washington Herald.*

Washington, D.C. Library of Congress. *Chronicling America: Historic American Newspapers.* chroniclingamerica.loc.gov

Welsh, La. *Rice Belt Journal.*

Wichita, Kans. Wichita *Daily Eagle.*

Wilmington, N.C. *Semi-Weekly Messenger.*

Winchester, Tenn. *Home Journal.*

Winston, N.C. *Progressive Farmer.*

Woodsville, Ohio. *Spirit of Democracy.*

Web Sites

"1st Louisiana (Zouaves) Infantry Battalion." antietam.aotw.org

Grand Military Ball handbill. Duke University. www.archive.org

Hart, Alexander, diary. *Jewish-American History Foundation* Web site. www.jewish-history.com

Irish America. June/July 2006. irishamerica.com
Louisiana in the Civil War. www.louisianacivilwar.org
New York State Military Museum and Veterans Research Center. dmna.ny.gov
Posey Civil War Letters. freepages.military.rootsweb.ancestry.com
"A Remarkable Character." New York *Times*, January 18, 1886. query.nytimes.com

Secondary Sources
Books

Austin, Aurelia. *Georgia Boys with "Stonewall" Jackson: James Thomas Thompson and the Walton Infantry.* Athens, 1967.
Bean, W. G. *The Liberty Hall Volunteers: Stonewall's College Boys.* Charlottesville, 1964.
Bengston, Bradley P., M.D., and Julian E. Kuz, M.D., eds. *Photographic Atlas of Civil War Injuries.* Kennesaw, Ga., 1996.
Bergeron, Arthur W., Jr. *Guide to Louisiana Confederate Military Units, 1861–1865.* Baton Rouge, 1989.
Bill, Alfred Hoyt. *The Beleaguered City: Richmond, 1861–1865.* New York, 1946.
Brock, R. A. *The Appomattox Roster.* 1887. Rpt. New York, n.d.
Brooks, Thomas Walter, and Michael Dan Jones. *Lee's Foreign Legion: A History of the 10th Louisiana Infantry.* Gravenhurst, Ontario, 1995.
Carman, Ezra A. *The Maryland Campaign of September 1862.* Vol. II. Edited and annotated by Thomas G. Clemens. El Dorado Hills, Calif., 2012.
Coates, Charles Hunter, Jr. *A Biography of Charles Hunter Coates: Soldier, Scholar, Athlete.* N.p., 2009.
Coddington, Edwin B. *The Gettysburg Campaign: A Study in Command.* New York, 1968.
Dabney, Robert L. *Life and Campaigns of Lieut.-Gen. Thomas J. Jackson.* New York, 1866.
Davis, Burke. *They Called Him Stonewall: A Life of Lt. General T. J. Jackson, C.S.A.* New York, 1954.
Davis, William C., ed. *The Confederate General.* 6 vols. N.p., 1991.
Dimitry, John. *Louisiana.* Vol. X in Clement Evans, ed., *Confederate Military History.* Atlanta, 1899.
Dowdey, Clifford. *The Land They Fought For: The Story of the South as the Confederacy, 1832–1865.* Garden City, N.Y., 1955.
———. *Lee's Last Campaign: The Story of Lee and His Men Against Grant—1864.* Boston, 1960.
Dufour, Charles L. *Gentle Tiger: The Gallant Life of Roberdeau Wheat.* Baton Rouge, 1957.
Frassanito, William A. *Antietam: The Photographic Legacy of America's Bloodiest Day.* New York, 1978.
Freeman, Douglas Southall. *Lee's Lieutenants: A Study in Command.* 3 vols. New York, 1942, 1944.
———. *R. E. Lee: A Biography.* 4 vols. New York, 1935.

Furgurson, Ernest B. *Chancellorsville 1863: The Souls of the Brave.* New York, 1992.

Gannon, James G. *Irish Rebels, Confederate Tigers: A History of the 6th Louisiana Volunteers, 1861–1865.* Campbell, Calif., 1998.

Glatthaar, Joseph T. *General Lee's Army: From Victory to Collapse.* New York, 2008.

Greene, A. Wilson. *The Final Battles of the Petersburg Campaign: Breaking the Backbone of the Rebellion.* Knoxville, 2008.

Hamlin, Percy Gatling. *"Old Bald Head" (General R. S. Ewell): The Portrait of a Soldier.* Strasburg, Va., 1940.

Harper, Judith E. *Women During the Civil War: An Encyclopedia.* New York, 2004.

Hennessy, John J. *Return to Bull Run: The Campaign and Battle of Second Manassas.* New York, 1993.

Hess, Earl J. *Civil War Infantry Tactics: Training, Combat, and Small-Unit Effectiveness.* Baton Rouge, 2015.

Jones, Michael Dan. *The Tiger Rifles: The Making of a Louisiana Legend.* Lexington, Ky., 2011.

Jones, Terry L. *The American Civil War.* New York, 2010.

———. *Cemetery Hill: Struggle for the High Ground, July 1–3, 1863.* Cambridge, Mass., 2003.

Krick, Robert K. *Lee's Colonels: A Biographical Register of the Field Officers of the Army of Northern Virginia.* Dayton, 1992.

LaBree, Ben, ed. *Camp Fires of the Confederacy.* Louisville, 1899.

Lonn, Ella. *Foreigners in the Confederacy.* Chapel Hill, 1940.

Marvel, William. *Lee's Last Retreat: The Flight to Appomattox.* Chapel Hill, 2002.

Miers, Earl Schenck, and Richard A. Brown, eds. *Gettysburg.* New Brunswick, N.J., 1948.

Mingus, Scott L., Sr. *The Louisiana Tigers in the Gettysburg Campaign, June–July 1863.* Baton Rouge, 2009.

Moore, Alison. *He Died Furious.* Baton Rouge, 1983.

———. *The Louisiana Tigers; or, The Two Louisiana Brigades in the Army of Northern Virginia, 1861–1865.* Baton Rouge, 1961.

Nosworthy, Brent. *The Bloody Crucible of Courage: Fighting Methods and Combat Experience of the Civil War.* New York, 2003.

Parrish, T. Michael. *Richard Taylor: Soldier Prince of Dixie.* Chapel Hill, 1992.

Pfanz, Donald C. *Richard S. Ewell: A Soldier's Life.* Chapel Hill, 1998.

Pfanz, Harry W. *Gettysburg: Culp's Hill and Cemetery Hill.* Chapel Hill, 1993.

———. *Gettysburg—The First Day.* Chapel Hill, 2001.

Phisterer, Frederick, comp. *New York in the War of the Rebellion, 1861 to 1865.* Albany, 1890.

Pinkowski, Edward. *Pills, Pen and Politics: The Story of General Leon Jastremski, 1843–1907.* Wilmington, Del., 1974.

Reed, Germaine M. *David French Boyd: Founder of Louisiana State University.* Baton Rouge, 1977.

Rhea, Gordon C. *The Battle of the Wilderness, May 5–6, 1864.* Baton Rouge, 1994.

————. *The Battles for Spotsylvania Court House and the Road to Yellow Tavern, May 7–12, 1864.* Baton Rouge, 1997.

————. *Cold Harbor: Lee and Grant, May 13–25, 1864.* Baton Rouge, 2002.

————. *To the North Anna River: Grant and Lee, May 13–25, 1864.* Baton Rouge, 2000.

Robertson, James I., Jr. *General A. P. Hill: The Story of a Confederate Warrior.* New York, 1987.

————. *The Stonewall Brigade.* 1963. Rpt. Baton Rouge, 1977.

————. *Stonewall Jackson: The Man, the Soldier, the Legend.* New York, 1997.

Saxon, Lyle. *Fabulous New Orleans.* Gretna, La., 2004.

Schreckengost, Gary. *The First Louisiana Special Battalion: Wheat's Tigers in the Civil War.* Jefferson, N.C., 2008.

Sears, Stephen W. *Chancellorsville.* Boston, 1996.

————. *Landscape Turned Red: The Battle of Antietam.* New Haven, 1983.

————. *To the Gates of Richmond: The Peninsula Campaign.* New York, 1992.

Slaughter, Rev. Philip. *A Sketch of the Life of Randolph Fairfax . . . Including a Brief Account of Jackson's Celebrated Valley Campaign.* Baltimore, 1878.

Stafford, Dr. G. M. G. *General Leroy Augustus Stafford, His Forebears and Descendants.* New Orleans, 1943.

Tankersley, Allen P. *John B. Gordon: A Study in Gallantry.* Atlanta, 1955.

Tanner, Robert G. *Stonewall in the Valley: Thomas J. "Stonewall" Jackson's Shenandoah Valley Campaign, Spring 1862.* Mechanicsburg, Pa., 1996.

Thomas, Emory M. *Robert E. Lee: A Biography.* New York, 1995.

Trudeau, Noah Andre. *The Last Citadel: Petersburg, Virginia, June 1864–April 1865.* Boston, 1991.

Tucker, Glenn. *High Tide at Gettysburg: The Campaign in Pennsylvania.* Indianapolis, 1958.

Vandiver, Frank E. *Jubal's Raid: General Early's Famous Attack on Washington in 1864.* New York, 1960.

Warner, Ezra J. *Generals in Gray: Lives of the Confederate Commanders.* Baton Rouge, 1959.

Wellman, Manly Wade. *Rebel Boast: First at Bethel—Last at Appomattox.* New York, 1956.

Welsh, Jack D., M.D. *Medical Histories of Confederate Generals.* Kent, Ohio, 1995.

Wert, Jeffry D. *From Winchester to Cedar Creek: The Shenandoah Campaign of 1864.* Carlisle, Pa., 1987.

Wheeler, Richard. *Voices in the Civil War.* New York, 1976.

Wiley, Bell Irvin. *The Life of Johnny Reb: The Common Soldier of the Confederacy.* New York, 1962.

Winters, John D. *The Civil War in Louisiana.* Baton Rouge, 1963.

Articles

Allen, William. "History of the Campaign of Gen. T. J. (Stonewall) Jackson in the Shenandoah Valley of Virginia." *Southern Historical Society Papers,* n.s., V (1920), 111–295.

Bohannon, Keith. "Edwin Francis Jemison: A Private in the 2nd Louisiana Infantry." *Military Images*, Vol. 7, No. 5 (March–April 1986), 9.

Brooks, Ross. "Red Petticoats and Blue Jackets: 1st Confederate States Zouave Battalion, or Coppens' Louisiana Zouaves." *Military Collector & Historian*, Vol. 45, No. 4 (Winter 1993), 148–52.

Casey, Powell A. "Confederate Units from North Louisiana." *Journal of the North Louisiana Historical Association*, VI (Spring 1975), 105–15.

Coski, John M. "When Louisiana Came to Virginia." *From the Collections, Museum of the Confederacy*, Spring–Summer 2002, 10–12.

"Distinguished Dead of Louisiana Division." *Southern Historical Society Papers*, XXVI (1898), 377–79.

Forman, William Harper, Jr. "William P. Harper in War and Reconstruction." *Louisiana History*, XIII (1972), 45–70.

Jones, Michael D. "Jeff Davis' Pet Wolves." *Civil War Times Illustrated* (March 1989), 28–33.

Jones, Terry L. "Twice Lost: The 8th Louisiana Volunteers' Battle Flag at Gettysburg." *Civil War Regiments*, Vol. 6, No. 3 (1999), 89–105.

Kajencki, Francis C. "The Louisiana Tiger." *Louisiana History*, XV (1974), 49–59.

Mickey, Barry I. "Coppens' Zouaves: A Louisiana Battalion in Lee's Army." *Military Images*, Vol. 7, No. 2 (September–October 1985), 10–12.

Moore, David S. "A Letter from the Peninsula." *Military Images*, Vol. 20, No. 2 (September–October 1998), 23.

Nichols, C. Howard. "Some Notes on the Military Career of Francis T. Nicholls." *Louisiana History*, III (1962), 297–315.

Romero, Sidney J. "Louisiana Clergy and the Confederate Army." *Louisiana History*, II (1961), 277–97.

Thomas, Michael R. "Confederate Firing Squad at Centreville." *Northern Virginia Heritage*, June 1980, 3–6.

———. "Unearthing Two Tigers' Graves." *Northern Virginia Heritage*, June 1980, 7–8.

Uminski, Sigmund H. "Poles and the Confederacy." *Polish American Studies*, XXII (1965), 99–106.

———. "Two Polish Confederates." *Polish American Studies*, XXIII (1966), 65–81.

Wallace, Lee A., Jr. "Coppens' Louisiana Zouaves." *Civil War History*, VIII (1962), 269–82.

Theses

Leland, Edwin Albert. "Organization and Administration of the Louisiana Army During the Civil War." M.A. thesis, Louisiana State University, 1938.

Urquhart, Kenneth Trist. "General Richard Taylor and the War in Virginia, 1861–1862." M.A. thesis, Tulane University, 1958.

Web Sites

"Auction of Civil War Soldier's Skull Found at Gettysburg Cancelled." *Fox News*, June 3, 2014. www.foxnews.com

The Civil War Flags Message Board. www.history-sites.com

"Company A, 8th Louisiana." files.usgwarchives.net

"Company A, 9th Louisiana." files.usgwarchives.net

"Company B, 8th Louisiana." files.usgwarchives.net

"Company C, 8th Louisiana." files.usgwarchives.net

"Company C, 9th Louisiana." files.usgwarchives.net

"Company D, 8th Louisiana." files.usgwarchives.net

"Company D, 9th Louisiana." files.usgwarchives.net

"Company E, 8th Louisiana." files.usgwarchives.net

"Company F, 8th Louisiana." files.usgwarchives.net

"Company F, 9th Louisiana." files.usgwarchives.net

"Company G, 8th Louisiana." files.usgwarchives.net

"Company G, 9th Louisiana." files.usgwarchives.net

"Company H, 8th Louisiana." files.usgwarchives.net

"Company H, 9th Louisiana." files.usgwarchives.net

"Company I, 8th Louisiana." files.usgwarchives.net

"Company I, 9th Louisiana." files.usgwarchives.net

"Company K, 8th Louisiana." files.usgwarchives.net

"Company K, 9th Louisiana." files.usgwarchives.net

Desoto Parish, Louisiana. www.countygenweb.com

Find a Grave. www.findagrave.com

First Bull Run. www.firstbullrun.co.uk

The Louisiana in the Civil War Message Board. history-sites.com

New York *Times.* "Disunion." opinionator.blogs.nytimes.com

"Roster of 6th Louisiana Infantry." docs.google.com

"Roster of 10th Louisiana Infantry," docs.google.com

"Stafford Guards, 9th Louisiana." files.usgwarchives.net

INDEX